# Introductory
# Econometrics

# Introductory
# Econometrics

JAMES L. MURPHY
Professor of Economics
University of North Carolina

1973
RICHARD D. IRWIN, INC.  Homewood, Illinois  60430
IRWIN-DORSEY LIMITED  Georgetown, Ontario

11028

*First Printing, March 1973*

ISBN 0-256-01394-2
Library of Congress Catalog Card No. 72–86616
*Printed in the United States of America*

# Preface

This text is intended for use in a one-semester course for either advanced undergraduates or first-year graduate students. It has a dual objective in meeting the requirements of such students who need not necessarily be economics majors, as these same materials have been effective in teaching students majoring in geography, city and regional planning, sociology, psychology, and political science.

### Objectives of this text

First, the text is offered as a guide for noneconometric majors in understanding the goals and limitations of econometric methods while presenting the reader with a practical working knowledge of many of the most frequently used econometric concepts and to stimulate all readers to be unafraid of further study in applied mathematics and statistics. Second, this text is intended to serve as a worthwhile introduction for readers intending to be econometric majors and to whet their appetites for learning as much more about econometric topics as is dictated by their own choice or needs.

### Selection of topics

The selection of topics in the book is quite limited; the focus is on applied econometrics in estimating and testing linear models, proceeding from a simple regression model (Part II), to a multiple regression model with a general variance-covariance matrix of disturbances (Part III), to a simultaneous equations econometric model (Part IV). The topics included were selected by examining the type of empirical problems and research analysis encountered most frequently in modern journal articles in the areas of international economics, monetary economics, and human resources. Obviously, some important practical topics are omitted for brevity and simplicity, such as nonlinear estimation, problems of lagged endogenous variables, and restricted estimation. Also excluded is any "computerization" of the techniques. This latter popular digression is not included since I believe knowledge and use of the computer is important enough to warrant a separate course in which the student becomes fully acquainted with his *local* computer installation and the programs *available to him*. It is advisable for the use of this book (and completion of the exercises) that some Least Squares Regression program operating on some electronic calculator or computer system be available for student use.

## Other special features

It is important to call attention to some facets of the style and composition of this text which are included by design to help achieve the stated objectives. First, a rather loose, conversational rhetoric is often used to communicate directly with the reader, encouraging and advising him with the intention of teaching him rather than reciting for him the catalog of up-to-date achievements of econometricians. Especially for undergraduates, the literature of recent results will have to wait for further courses. Thus, excessive references to sources of more and more and more knowledge are not given since these often tend to discourage the beginning student.

Second, there is much repetition within the book. Experience in teaching mathematics and statistics tends to convince me that students often do not actually understand the definitions and interrelated concepts they have "learned" until the third or fourth pass. Consequently, I have deliberately built in overexposure of some important terms and concepts (such as best linear unbiased estimator, multicollinearity, autocorrelation, generalized least squares, or identification). These are often introduced in an informal way, with more rigorous definitions or technical explanations being given when the reader meets them for the second or third time.

Third, the chapters vary in length and in technical requirements, with an intermingling of mechanical, theoretical, practical, and discussion sections so that every student can have an occasional surprised sense of progress in finding something "easy" for him. Also, the example models used in the text are not always developed or defended in detail. The examples exist, after all, to help explain some econometric method, not to be an additional problem in economic theory. Also, experience indicates that fairly naïve models capture the attention of beginning students more readily and completely than carefully detailed models. In this sense, the author will not be upset with readers who attack his "stupid" example models and analyze their own *revised* models if this helps them to learn. Incidentally, references are usually given for the statistical data used in the examples in order to open horizons for the beginning student in recognizing available sources of data.

Fourth, several features of the format of the text should be noted. In a break with tradition, I recommend that all the sections be used although individuals may choose to omit certain ones. I do not identify sections as easy or optional (difficult) since I believe that such classification does a disfavor to many beginning students who precondition themselves to find all optional sections too difficult.

## Alternate semester outlines

In teaching these materials to undergraduates, it has been found that the details of some derivations and algebraic manipulations may be expanded from other sources or reduced in class presentation according to the interests and motivation of the students. For undergraduates who are not inclined toward mathematical presentations, the instructor might proceed more fruitfully through the text by *omitting* the following Sections:

5.2 and the review exercises following;

10.6 and maximum likelihood estimation in 10.5;

12.2, 12.4, and the Almon lag material in 12.6;

14.3, 14.4, 14.6, and 14.7 which more formally repeat some topics of Chapter 13;

15.3 and 15.5 on pooling time series and cross sectional data;

16.6 and the algebraic solution for bias in 16.4; and

18.4 on alternate estimators of parameters in a structural equation.

These are not necessarily the most difficult conceptual or analytical sections, but are a mixture of levels of difficulty. They are separately suggested for omission if one wishes to avoid some mathematical symbols and tedium in order to concentrate more on some other practical topics of the use of econometric methods.

For graduate student classes, the material in Chapters 1–7 should be considered primarily review, and consequently there should be sufficient time to cover all the Sections. If the reader does omit some Sections, he will discover later if some concept, topic, or formula in that omitted section was crucial, since extensive internal relating of items and back-references are provided throughout the book.

For tracing these internal references clearly, the sections of a chapter are numbered with a chapter prefix, such as Sections 6.1, 6.2, . . . , 6.6 in Chapter 6. Equations within a chapter are numbered consecutively with a chapter prefix but without regard to section, such as equations 9–1, 9–2, . . . , 9–12, in Chapter 9. Not all equations or expressions are burdened with numbers but only those which are important end results or which are needed for later reference in other sections or in exercises. When the same equation is repeated, it is given the same number as when it originally appeared. Also, when derivations are given, they are given completely step-by-step with explanations rather than with not-so-obvious "obvious" steps left for the reader to do. Tables and Figures within the text are ordered sequentially with a chapter prefix.

### Particular pedagogy

Finally, the format of each chapter is similar in including four special pedagogical characteristics. The first section of each chapter is a *Preview* section which informally specifies the new topics to be covered in that chapter. Often new terms and concepts are introduced with only an intuitive explanation.

Section two of each chapter (except the initial one) lists technical items of calculus, matrix algebra, or mathematical statistics which the reader should review or be ready to use before studying the remaining sections of the chapter. I believe this on-the-spot review is more fruitful for the student than a separate review chapter or appendix of quantitative topics, since it is more immediately relevant to his understanding of some particular topic in that chapter. Also, it enables the quantitatively weaker student to gradually build up his competence in a realistic fashion while enabling him to remain competitive throughout the course. These *Review* sections vary from a list of items to be reviewed to a more complete presentation sometimes followed by programmed exercises. Usually, it is presumed that the student has had some prior exposure. At least some acquaintance with the basic results and operations of calculus, matrix algebra, and statistics should precede the use of this text. The usual background might be one or two courses in probability and statistics and one or two courses in mathematics for economists (or other social scientists), including basic topics of calculus and matrix operations.

Each chapter ends with a *Summary* section or outline to aid the reader in recognizing where he has been and also where he is going next. New vocabulary concepts, and suggested references and exercises follow.

The fourth special pedagogical feature is the use of special *Notes* throughout the text as explained in Section 1.5. These serve as focal points within a discussion in anticipation of questions or points of confusion typically raised by beginning students.

In summary, this text is intended to be a learning device rather than an exposition of fancy results in econometrics. It emphasizes the commonly used practical tools for estimating and testing linear econometric models. While some of the topics included (such as distributed lags, pooling cross-sectional and time series data, seemingly unrelated regressions, two-stage least squares, etc.) are typically not introductory course material, the approach and presentation is not as rigorous as in advanced texts. The nature of the book may best be described as practical econometrics for the general social science researcher and, especially, for economics students.

## ACKNOWLEDGMENTS

I wish to acknowledge the Graduate School of Business Administration and the Department of Economics at the University of North Carolina, Chapel Hill, for providing an atmosphere and facilities encouraging to research and study, and to colleagues therein who read various parts of the manuscript and made suggestions on topics to be included in a beginning level text. Also, several reviewers were responsible for suggesting changes in the style and emphasis of several chapters. Many former students contributed both indirectly and directly to this volume: indirectly by serving as trial subjects for much of this material, and directly by permitting the inclusion of some of their assignments as examples in the text or as end-of-chapter exercises. Of course, I remain responsible for the final adaptations, inclusions, and exclusions of materials in the volume.

I am indebted to the Literary Executor of the late Sir Ronald A. Fisher, F.R.S., to Dr. Frank Yates, F.R.S., and to Oliver and Boyd, Edinburgh, for permission to reprint Table III and adapt Tables IV and V from their book *Statistical Tables for Biological, Agricultural and Medical Research.*

Mention is due to several typists and secretaries—Brenda Williams, Mrs. Pat Eichman, and Mrs. Cheryl Capps—for their cooperation in preparation of the manuscript; and to several friends and teachers who earlier contributed to my career choice, including Professors Sam Betty, John Powers, Rubin Saposnik, and Ron Stuckey. My interest in econometrics was stimulated by the fine texts on this subject by C. Christ, H. Theil, J. Johnston, A. S. Goldberger, and E. Malinvaud, and was encouraged significantly by Professors R. L. Basmann, Vernon L. Smith, and R. W. Pfouts. I hope that this text reflects some of the good efforts of all these and helps to interest and encourage more beginning students of econometrics to continue their study in this area.

Finally, I express my special gratitude to my parents for their encouragement and support throughout my education and to my family for their tolerance during this entire project.

*February 1973*                                        JAMES L. MURPHY

# Contents

**APPENDIXES OF TABLES**

# PART I

## The Study of Econometrics

*Chapter*
*1*

# INTRODUCTION

Econometrics is concerned with the analysis of measures of economic activity. Either the "economics" or the "metrics" view of analysis might be emphasized, but these cannot be entirely separated. Both a statistician and an economic theorist studying some economic problem could qualify as an econometrician, or conversely the best econometricians qualify for seats in either the ivory tower or the basement computer laboratory. In addition, any scholar in one of the specialized fields of economics or related subjects would often use some of the tools of the econometrician.

## 1.1 WHAT IT'S ALL ABOUT!

The need for this quantitatively oriented field in economics becomes emphasized as economists and others become more involved in practical economic issues, and as statisticians and others collect more data on all sectors of economies and develop more sophisticated and qualitatively better mathematical techniques for interpreting this data. The era of the computer has been an important factor in this development. More and more professional economists are getting involved with econometrics because this data cannot be ignored. It frequently relates to theoretical claims or counter claims and to policy questions. A theoretician, for example, must take into account the empirical evidence which supports or falsifies his propositions.

3

It may be important to recognize that changes have occurred in the price elasticity of demand for durable goods in the agricultural sector, or in the marginal propensity to save in less developed countries. Important policy questions may be partially answered by the empirical research of econometricians. Researchers may study the quantitative effect of rising interest rates on the construction industry, or the effect on textile production of reduced import controls, or the changes in the price of meat products due to increased personal income per capita in a given country.

Outside of economics proper, more and more other scholars in fields from statistics to social work, from engineering to public health, are getting involved with econometrics because the economic meaning of the data and the implied economic relations affect the purpose and interpretation of their own projects. For example, consider the questions of the economic benefits of a year of preschool training, or the economic cost of job discrimination within a society. Consider the role of population growth in economic growth or the economic externalities associated with a new immunization for rubella. Finally, consider the economic resources lost by pollution of the air and water, or the opportunity cost of resources utilized to counter such pollution.

Quite naturally, many others, including politicians, reporters, and businessmen are involved with econometrics in spite of themselves because of their interest in the relationships among economic variables, in the applicability of modern economics as a representation of observed rules of economic activity, and in the forecasts for future levels of economic magnitudes. The blending of all these characteristics results in economists engaged in the specialization termed econometrics.

## 1.2 THE SCOPE OF ECONOMETRICS AND OF THIS BOOK

Econometrics is constantly expanding into areas of application wider than statistics and economics themselves. Some econometric research involves psychological, social, religious, and political variables and relations, and may even be oriented toward historical or political objectives.

Econometrics also involves many levels of mathematical statistics. Some relatively simple concepts such as two-variable correlation and tests between means are fruitfully used by most econometricians. Some of these simple topics are reviewed and applied to problems of economic research in this book. They are referred to occasionally in intuitive explanations that are given to aid your understanding of analogous extensions.

At the other extreme, econometricians also use sophisticated mathematical techniques of advanced calculus, special functions, and statistical theory of probability distributions and sampling. Much research is done on this high-powered level to learn more about the properties of the distribution functions of estimators and of test statistics for finite samples. Some results of this research and some of these same methods are also included in this book. However, their treatment is not rigorous or impressive. Rather, the complexities are sifted out and the residue is interspersed with common language. Indeed, you may not realize how clever and knowledgeable these advanced econometricians must be unless you leave this book and study their original research papers.

## The linear explanatory economic model

In the large part, this book emphasizes the expansive middle ground of knowledge of econometric methods between these two extremes. Of principal concern is the linear explanatory economic model, or econometric model. This is the most widely used representation of economic relationships and has important uses for the economist regardless of his area of specialization.

For example, the simplest form of a linear explanatory economic model is $Y_t = \alpha_1 + \alpha_2 X_{t2} + \varepsilon_t$, where $Y_t$ and $X_{t2}$ represent economic variables measured at observation $t$, and $\varepsilon_t$ is an error or disturbance term. The parameters to be estimated, $\alpha_1$ and $\alpha_2$, represent the intercept and slope respectively for this linear equation. The term *economic model* refers to any specification relating economic variables. Implicitly, it is a representation of an economic theory; and explicitly, it is a supposition of the operative mechanism of an economic structure. The term *linear* refers to an expression or function in which no second or higher degree terms in the parameters occur. The term *explanatory* refers to the underlying meaning of the measures involved in the linear model. Commonly, the magnitude of the independent variable $X_{t2}$ is considered to be explaining the magnitude of the dependent variable $Y_t$.

The complete description and analysis of such a model with several extensions is the central theme of this book. Econometricians study the linear explanatory economic model in four phases. Recognition of these phases will aid in your attempts to foresee the purposes and intentions of the presentation to follow.

## 1.3 FOUR PHASES OF ECONOMETRIC ANALYSIS

### Specification

First in econometrics, the structural form of the model must be specified. It is an art to build models which are manageable, yet meaningful, both in terms of economic theory and economic reality (see Figure 1–1).

### Estimation

Second, econometrics is concerned with the estimation of parameters in such models. Much statistical research revolves about procedures to make the best guesses considering that the data may be scanty or erroneous in part, or considering that some estimators have more desirable statistical

FIGURE 1-1

**The four aspects of econometric model analysis**

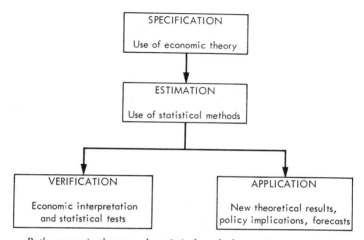

Econometric Model Analysis

*Both economic theory and statistical methods are important in econometric analysis. The verification of a model may vary depending on the purpose of its application, and its usefulness in various applications may vary depending on the results of the estimation and verification.*

characteristics than others, or considering that the computational effort and expense must be reasonable. Often, there is a tradeoff between the statistical qualities of the estimators and the cost in determining the estimates. In this book, primary consideration is placed on those methods and those estimators which are most commonly used and for which computer programs are most widely adapted. Certain estimators which are theoretically important in the development of econometric thought are utilized only to demonstrate comparisons. They are not developed in full.

## Verification

Third, the verification of such models is of great interest in econometrics. Decision rules must be established to test the success of the model. Criteria of success might be considered in terms of the model's accuracy in forecasting the levels of economic variables and/or its usefulness for clarifying and refining economic theory. Hopefully, these could be one and the same; however, it is too frequently evident that a model may give accurate forecasts even though its underlying economic meaning is not well understood.

For example, a model may be developed which accurately predicts state revenue in the next fiscal year. However, the reasons for the inclusion of certain variables and the exact interrelations among the variables may not even be explicitly considered in theory. Vice versa, a small model may clearly specify a testable economic relation even though it is not useful for making forecasts. Consider a simple consumption function which permits estimation of a marginal propensity to consume and determination of investment and government expenditure multipliers. The theory is explicit and clear, but forecasts of consumption based on the model may not be within $\pm 10$ percent of the true values in the future time period.

## Application

Fourth, econometrics involves the application of such models in one or a combination of the following four ways: (*a*) A successful model may be applied to establish numerical values for key parameters in economic theory. These might be values (usually for specific time periods in a specific location) of an income elasticity of demand, a marginal propensity to import, an elasticity of substitution among factor inputs, or a Gini coefficient of distribution of incomes. (*b*) The model may be usefully applied to test economic theorems such as the quantity theory of money, the Keynesian consumption function, liquidity preference function, or marginal efficiency of capital schedule. The test may be made simply by a comparison of the theorem with empirical evidence. Is there real evidence of money illusion, of a backward bending supply of labor curve, of a Phillips curve, or of the Hecksher–Olin theorem in international trade? (*c*) Often, the model provides evidence for or against certain policy actions. It may be designed to help assay the effect of a surtax on consumer credit purchases or of the effective lag in monetary policy. (*d*) A very common application of a model is to make forecasts of economic variables in regions or for time periods not considered within the scope of currently available data. Various motives and levels of sophistication may be envisioned in these forecasts of such variables as gross national product, population, school enrollment, or stock prices.

In this text, emphasis is placed on items two and three, estimation and verification. The latter is most often considered from the negative view of falsification rather than a positive verification due to the nature of statistical testing.

The fourth phase of application is included only insofar as it is a major factor in setting up rules for testing and in the presentation of examples and problems. The first phase of model building is difficult to explain, and it will be ignored except for these two hints. First, familiarize yourself with other models in your area of interest before constructing your own. Second, remember that your model should be designed so that it is testable in reference to the application you intend. Beyond these two hints, there is great freedom for expression of theory in models. Any abstract idea which tries to embody some important aspects of economic behavior while intentionally ignoring other less important regularities might be formulated into a model.

## 1.4 SPECIFYING AN ECONOMETRIC MODEL

There is no known correct set of economic definitions and postulates for all econometric models. There never will be. Great opportunities for research still exist in establishing manageable, meaningful, and useful models for all sectors and for all levels of aggregation of economic behavior. A description or historical summary of model specifications is not attempted in this text.

Most linear explanatory economic models have been constructed in order to estimate relationships between variables and to judge the validity of these relations. Sometimes, the purpose may be to construct a good forecasting model. Other times, it may be to test a specific hypothesis on an economic parameter or relation. Also, increasingly larger models are being built in attempts to describe the complete, complex dynamic interrelations among all the sectors of an economy. Of course, some models are built for combinations of these reasons. In the following discussions of estimation procedures and testing methods, these differing purposes will be kept in mind as some topics are more relevant to one set of purposes than to another.

## 1.5 A DIGRESSIVE NOTE ON SPECIAL NOTES IN THIS BOOK

It is occasionally possible to anticipate some questions or points of confusion which may arise among a wide range of readers of this book. A special format is used throughout the book to treat these special problems within the text itself instead of delegating them to footnotes or problem sections.

Implicit questions or points of confusion are given answers and further interpretation in *Notes* of four types. These are labeled and offset from the text discussion not so they can be skipped but so that special attention can be drawn to them. To make these *Notes* appear more formidable, they are given rather long names. An *Interpretive note* usually adds more explanation for some concept involved in the text discussion. An *Explicative Note* is also explanatory but is usually more concerned with the details of the analysis rather than a concept. A *Discursive Note* is more of a related digression from the immediate point in the text, thereby allowing more roving about and integration of related materials. The *Recursive Note* is a special type of digression in which the roving is always backward in thought to a preceding or simpler notion or notation in order to emphasize that the same concept or analysis is appearing again.

## 1.6 FORMAT OF THE BOOK

In the following chapters, the techniques of statistical estimation and testing of the parameters in linear explanatory economic models are emphasized. The next chapter completes the introduction with an examination of the components, notation, and applicability of the econometric model. Part II presents the analysis of the very simple two-variable single equation linear model. The presentation uses econometric terms rather than regression terminology wherever there is such overlap. Part II provides a common reference ground for further developments and is to be read not as a review but with an outlook toward extensions of the procedures, relaxation of the assumptions, and interpretation of the results for different economic specifications.

Part III extends the analysis to the multivariate single equation econometric model, including some discussion of special procedures for treating some common econometric problems. Part IV makes a final extension to the simultaneous equation econometric model. Within each of these parts are several chapters dealing with estimation methods, calculation examples, assumptions, problems, and use of test statistics.

The format within each chapter is similar and important for the reader to recognize. Each chapter begins with a nonrigorous, intuitive *Preview* in which no formal definitions are given. It is not expected that a reader can immediately understand fully all the topics included in this *Preview*. Indeed, the rest of the chapter is included to present the definitions, methods, and examples of the concepts mentioned in the preview. Thus, the first section of each chapter is merely a lead-in or a stage cue for the material that follows. It presents the concepts informally and gives some indications of the purposes and application of the subsequent materials.

In student's terminology, Section 2 of each chapter is a math-stat *Review* which lists terms and topics which should be studied to aid your understanding of the material in that chapter. Occasional examples and unworked exercises are provided as a further guide for review, and certain topics in mathematical statistics and matrix algebra are developed quite fully. However, these *Review* sections are not comprehensive enough to serve as a complete course in mathematics or statistics. They merely point to the particular concepts which are then applied to the following parts of the chapter.

|||||||||||||||||||||||||||||||||||||||||||||||||||||||||||||||||||||||||||||||||||||||||||||||||||||||||||||||||||||||||||||||

*Discursive note.*  These review topics do not necessarily become more difficult throughout the book. Very often, the new mathematical or statistical concept is a very simple one; nevertheless, these are also included in the *Review* so the reader can be on the lookout for its application in the econometric analysis.

|||||||||||||||||||||||||||||||||||||||||||||||||||||||||||||||||||||||||||||||||||||||||||||||||||||||||||||||||||||||||||||||

This systematic presentation should allow every student to discover what extra review is needed, if any. The text presumes some prior acquaintance with calculus, matrix algebra, and economic statistics.

Beginning in Section 3 of each chapter is the development of materials explaining the principles and important fundamental concepts of econometrics, often with some calculational example. Since the terms and ideas were met in the *Preview* and the mathematical definitions and operations were met in the *Review*, there will always be some repetition within the chapters.

Indeed, repetition is frequently by design in order to reduce the haunting surrealism often associated with econometrics. Theorems and other results of statistics are often employed without detailing the proof or derivation. Emphasis is placed on description of what methods econometricians use in economic research, why they use them, and how they use them, but not on how the computational formulas are derived nor on how the underlying theorems were proven. These latter topics become important as you continue into more advanced courses and desire to develop new methods rather than to become familiar with existing methods.

At the end of chapters, there is commonly a vocabulary list of important terms. Some of these terms may have formal definitions which the reader should know, but all of them should trigger some mental response of association between the terms and a basic concept or an important applied technique. There are also exercises and occasional references to help you further develop your knowledge, aptitude, and skills in econometrics.

In addition, remember that the four types of special *Notes* will be encountered throughout to emphasize particular conclusions or to relate similar developments. The following type note appears only once.

||||||||||||||||||||||||||||||||||||||||||||||||||||||||||||||||||||||||||||||||||||||||||||||||||||||||||||||||||||||||||||||||

*Ridiculous note.* After one learns all this, can he become a prestigious and highly paid econometrician?

||||||||||||||||||||||||||||||||||||||||||||||||||||||||||||||||||||||||||||||||||||||||||||||||||||||||||||||||||||||||||||||||

GOOD GRIEF!

## NEW VOCABULARY
Linear explanatory economic model
Parameters
Special *Notes*

## SUMMARY OUTLINE
I.  Four aspects of econometric analysis
   A.  Building the structural relations of the model
      1.  Manageable for understanding and computations
      2.  Meaningful in theory and in reality
   B.  Estimation of parameters in the model
      1.  Obtain " best " statistical properties of estimates
      2.  Find easy and cheap computational procedures
   C.  Verification of the model
      1.  Successful in depicting economic reality
      2.  Successful in expressing testable economic theory
   D.  Application of the model
      1.  To establish numerical values for parameters
      2.  To test economic relations
      3.  To provide guidelines for policy
      4.  To forecast levels of economic variables

II. Chapter format
   A. Preview in Section 1
      1. Informal, nonrigorous
      2. Sets the stage
   B. Review in Section 2
      1. Math-stat terms and topics
      2. Occasional exercises
   C. Presentation of material in Sections 3, 4, etc.
   D. Vocabulary list, summary, exercises, and/or references

## REFERENCES

For some discussion about econometric models and, perhaps, some stimulation to study econometrics, the reader may refer to:

Klein, L. *An Introduction to Econometrics.* Englewood Cliffs, N.J.: Prentice-Hall, Inc., 1962.

———. "The Use of Econometric Models as a Guide to Economic Policy." *Econometrica*, 1947.

Suits, D. B. "Forecasting and Analysis with an Econometric Model." *American Economic Review*, March 1962.

For a more historical perspective on the role of probability and statistics in econometrics, the reader may refer to:

Tinbergen, J. *Econometrics*, New York: The Blakiston Co., 1951.

Haavelmo, T. "The Probability Approach in Econometrics," chap. 1 and 2. *Econometrica*, Supplement to Vol. 12, 1944.

Marschak, J. "Statistical Inference in Economics: An Introduction," chap. 1. In *Statistical Inference in Dynamic Models*, edited by T. C. Koopmans, pp. 1–50. Cowles Commission Monograph 10, 1950.

| Chapter 2 | COMPOSITION, NOTATION, AND APPLICABILITY OF THE ECONOMETRIC MODEL |

## 2.1 PREVIEW

Imagine that it is a hot day and a small boy is about to eat a three-dip ice cream cone. Further, suppose that the cone itself now disappears leaving the boy with only the ice cream contents. An enjoyable and fairly simple action of eating an ice cream cone has become a grasping and messy, unsystematic, chore.

In a similar way, the task of relating and analyzing relations among economic variables can be a messy, grasping procedure without a model to contain and limit them. The model is to econometricians what the cone is to the small boy eating ice cream. Indeed, the model is almost a basic ingredient of econometrics. Particularly, in this book, the presentation builds on the statistical analysis of the econometric model. Consequently, in this chapter, a detailed summary of the composition of an econometric model is given. Also, the notation commonly used throughout the book is presented.

Finally, in response to a typical question, the extensions and generalizations of the econometric model are described to demonstrate its wide applicability.

## 2.2 REVIEW

This chapter is basically an introductory one, so no technical operations and results are described. However, to introduce the format of the *Review* sections of each chapter and to facilitate the presentation of the model notation in Sections 2.4 to 2.6, the following definitions are given.

### 1 Summation notation

A common symbol for "the summation of" is $\sum$. This symbol can be indexed to indicate which terms are to be summed. Thus $\sum_{t=2}^{4} X_t$ indicates addition of $X_2 + X_3 + X_4$ only. The indexing information is commonly omitted when no ambiguity arises. In such a case, the summation is taken over the entire subscript range, say $i$ from 1 to $G$, or $t$ from 1 to $T$ of the expressed subscript. Note, if the sum is taken of a constant with no subscript, this means to add the constant to itself the indicated number of times. Thus,

$$\sum_{t=1}^{T} \gamma_2 = T\gamma_2 .$$

### 2 Matrix

A matrix is a rectangular array of elements arranged in rows and columns often denoted by a capital letter, say $A$. The dimensions of the array are denoted in parentheses under the matrix symbol, such as $\underset{(T \times K)}{A}$, where $T$ indicates the number of rows and $K$ the number of columns in the matrix. Elements in a matrix are designated with two subscripts according to their position, say $A_{tk}$, representing the element in row $t$ and column $k$. In econometrics, these elements themselves are often sums of squares and cross products of sets of numbers.

### 3 Vector

In this text, a vector is a special size matrix with dimension $(T \times 1)$, a column vector. For example, the $K$ columns of a matrix $\underset{(T \times K)}{A}$ might be denoted as $A_1, A_2, \ldots, A_K$. Each of these $A_k$ is a vector of $T$ elements, a typical element being $A_{tk}$.

## 4 Matrix transpose.

A transpose of any matrix $\underset{(T \times K)}{A}$ with elements $A_{tk}$ is defined as the matrix $\underset{(K \times T)}{A'}$ with elements $A_{kt}$. That is, by interchanging the rows and columns of a matrix, a transpose matrix is obtained and denoted by a prime.

## 5 Inner product of vectors

Inner product is an operation defined for a vector and a transposed vector each with $K$ elements. The inner product is given by the sum of products of the corresponding $K$ elements of both vectors. Suppose $X$ is a vector of size $(K \times 1)$ with elements $X_1, X_2, \ldots, X_K$, and $C'$ is size $(1 \times K)$ with elements $C_1, C_2, \ldots, C_K$, then $C'K = \sum_{k=1}^{K} C_k X_k$.

## 2.3 THE COMPOSITION OF AN ECONOMETRIC MODEL

### Theoretical propositions

A linear explanatory economic model is not a simple structure but a conjunction of four types of statements. First, the specification of the model should include a mathematical formulation of the relations and a clear definition of the meaning of each of the variables. It may also include theoretical properties of the relation by postulates on the sign, size, or relative sizes of the parameters. The more precise these definitions and postulates are stated, the more sensitive the testing of the model becomes.

### Initial conditions

Second, the model combines two types of initial conditions. These include assertions that the exogenous variables assume certain measurable values at each observation point. It is important that the relation be clear between these statistical measures and the theoretical variables they intend to measure. One may want to include in the model a variable for the economic well-being of family units, but the measure of this theoretical concept may be an index involving family size, head of household income, and the amount of property tax paid by the family. The exact definitions of sources of data and methods of index construction are part of the initial conditions.

A second part of the initial conditions are assertions about other background conditions. These are given in terms of assumptions concerning the probability function of the disturbance term included in each equation of the econometric model. Usually, the general assertion is that the factors affecting the economy (whether internal or external to it, but excluded from the model) are controlled so that their effect remains approximately constant throughout the period or over the space of the sampling points. Besides this general statement, it is often very fruitful to specify particular aspects of constancy in the environment which are important for the validity and interpretation of the model. It may be essential within different models that "tax laws have not changed over the time period," or "tariffs and import controls on products A, B, and C have not changed," or "the ceiling on interest rates remains the same in all regions," or "the relative rate of growth of population between countries has not changed." Such assertions are part of the model since they affect the generality of the results derived from an analysis of the model.

## Technical rules

In conjunction with these first two types of statements are technical rules, both statistical and mathematical, that define the estimators of the parameters and appropriate test statistics. Two models with identical economic definitions and postulates and identical assertions of initial conditions would give different results and have varying degrees of success in different applications if they stated different technical rules.

## Predictive implications

Finally, a complete linear explanatory model ends with a set of predictive implications. These will be more or less extensive depending on the preciseness of the economic definitions and postulates. They will be more or less meaningful depending on the correctness of the initial conditions. They will be more or less useful depending on the thoroughness of the technical rules.

The predictive implications may be external statements of extrapolation or forecast of the future expected levels of endogenous variables included in the model. On the other hand, they may be internal statements of logical deductions concerning the acceptable levels of estimates and test statistics; that is, levels that are compatible with the economic postulates. Some of either or both of these type statements are essential in the completion of any econometric analysis .

## 2.4 EXTENSIONS OF THE SIMPLE LINEAR MODEL

The simple linear economic model is denoted as $Y_t = \alpha_1 + \alpha_2 X_{t2} + \varepsilon_t$. The presentation should include the meaning of $Y$ and $X_{t2}$, the sources of data, the assertions about $\varepsilon_t$ concerning the external environment, the purpose or intended application of this specification, and a description of the statistical procedure to be applied. Let us consider now only the form of the model itself. Can econometricians hope to describe meaningful economic relations and depict reality with formulations of such a simple type ?

||||||||||||||||||||||||||||||||||||||||||||||||||||||||||||||||||||||||||||||||||||||||||||||||||||||||||||||||||||||||||||||||||||||||||||||||||||||||||

*Interpretive note.* The simple linear model can appropriately describe more complex economic relations by extensions and transformations of variables. These changes help to make the econometrician's job of building and analyzing meaningful models an easier one. Some of these subtleties of the simple looking model are explored in this and the following sections.

||||||||||||||||||||||||||||||||||||||||||||||||||||||||||||||||||||||||||||||||||||||||||||||||||||||||||||||||||||||||||||||||||||||||||||||||||||||||||

## Single equation notation

Much econometric work entails discovery of first approximations to relations among economic variables. In such cases, when no theoretical relation is commonly acceptable and no one has previously investigated the same particular relations using the same measures of the variables, a linear relation is extremely useful. However, the two-variable simple model often needs to be extended. First, the dependent variable $Y_t$ can be explained in terms of many independent variables, $X_1, X_2, \ldots, X_K$. In such cases, it is convenient to fix $X_1$ at a value of one so that its coefficient $\alpha_1$ is the intercept value of the equation. Using shorthand notations of vectors the model is written $Y_t = X_t \Gamma + \varepsilon_t$ for $t = 1, 2, \ldots, T$, where $X_t \Gamma$ is the inner product of the two $K$-component vectors,

$$\Gamma = \begin{pmatrix} \gamma_1 \\ \gamma_2 \\ \vdots \\ \gamma_K \end{pmatrix}$$

and $X_t = (X_{t1}, X_{t2}, \ldots, X_{tK})$.

## Extension to two or more equations

Next, the single equation with one dependent variable can be extended to many equations equal to the number of dependent variables. For example, the model may have $G$ equations with $G$ jointly dependent variables, $Y_1, Y_2, \ldots, Y_G$ explained in terms of $K$ independent variables $X_1, X_2, \ldots, X_K$ and $G$ disturbance terms, one for each equation, $\varepsilon_1, \varepsilon_2, \ldots, \varepsilon_G$. The jointly dependent variables are called endogenous variables, and the independent variables are called exogenous variables. Furthermore, some equations may contain more than one of the endogenous variables.

||||||||||||||||||||||||||||||||||||||||||||||||||||||||||||||||||||||||||||||||||||||||||||||||||||||||||||||||||||||||||||||||||||||||||||||||||||||||||

*Explicative note.* It may seem confusing that each equation has an endogenous variable and some equations have more than one; however, in total, the number of endogenous variables is equal to the number of equations. All this really implies that some endogenous variables occur more than once in the system of linear equations that compose the model.

||||||||||||||||||||||||||||||||||||||||||||||||||||||||||||||||||||||||||||||||||||||||||||||||||||||||||||||||||||||||||||||||||||||||||||||||||||||||||

Indeed, this is usually the reason why a simultaneous model is required. Only in this way can the economic interrelations among the variables be expressed. An economic variable which is to be explained in one equation in terms of some explanatory variables may itself be an explanatory variable of another endogenous variable in another equation. Although its cause and effect role is different between the two equations, the variable is still considered to be endogenous due to its overall dependent role in the complete system of equations. A variable classified as exogenous must always assume an explanatory role in each equation in which it appears. A special type of explanatory variable can be specified in models whose economic variables are measured over time. The measure of an endogenous variable in a previous time period may be used strictly in an explanatory role in such a model. Such a lagged endogenous variable is then classified with the other explanatory exogenous variables in the broader class of predetermined variables.

||||||||||||||||||||||||||||||||||||||||||||||||||||||||||||||||||||||||||||||||||||||||||||||||||||||||||||||||||||||||||||||||||||||||||||||||||||

*Interpretive note.*   Several results are achieved by these extended specifications. Adding more variables allows recognition of other explanatory factors. The specification of the variables included and their characterization as endogenous or predetermined in each equation allows a particular hypothetical representation of the behavior of a segment of the economy. Adding more equations and jointly dependent variables to form a simultaneous equation model allows for complex interactions within the system conjoining these different segments. Using lagged endogenous variables allows for a dynamic representation of the equilibrium time path of the endogenous variables.

||||||||||||||||||||||||||||||||||||||||||||||||||||||||||||||||||||||||||||||||||||||||||||||||||||||||||||||||||||||||||||||||||||||||||||||||||||

By use of these extensions and different type variables, quite realistic and intricate specifications of economic theory or hypothetical economic relations can be constructed in the format of a linear explanatory economic model.

## 2.5 AN EXAMPLE MODEL WITH STANDARD NOTATION

A simple example of these types of variables is given in this national income model.

Consumption function:   $C_t = \beta_{13} Y_t + \gamma_{11} + \varepsilon_{t1}.$

Investment function:    $I_t = \beta_{23} Y_t + \gamma_{21} + \gamma_{22} I_{t-1} + \varepsilon_{t2}.$

Income identity:       $Y_t = C_t + I_t + Z_t.$

This linear explanatory economic model of three equations specifies three endogenous variables in time period $t$—consumption expenditure $C_t$, gross private investment $I_t$, and gross national product $Y_t$—to be jointly determined by two disturbance terms and three predetermined variables. One predetermined variable is $Z_t$, an exogenous variable in time period $t$ which might represent government expenditure and excess of exports over imports. Another is $I_{t-1}$, a lagged endogenous variable as indicated by its time subscript of the previous period. The third is an implied explanatory variable which could be denoted $X_{t1}$. It is conveniently set equal to one in all observations so that its coefficient in any equation is the intercept.

||||||||||||||||||||||||||||||||||||||||||||||||||||||||||||||||||||||||||||||||||||||||||||||||||||||||||||||||||||||||||||||||||||||||||||||||||||||||

*Explicative note.* A common and acceptable notation denotes the coefficients of endogenous variables by $\beta_{ig}$; the coefficients of predetermined variables by $\gamma_{ik}$. The subscripts are indexes: $i = 1, 2, \ldots, G$ for the number of the equation, $g = 1, 2, \ldots, G$ for the number of the endogenous variable, and $k = 1, 2, \ldots, K$ for the number of the predetermined variable. When the coefficient is equal to zero, the complete term in which it occurs is omitted.

||||||||||||||||||||||||||||||||||||||||||||||||||||||||||||||||||||||||||||||||||||||||||||||||||||||||||||||||||||||||||||||||||||||||||||||||||||||||

## The common matrix representation

These ordering procedures are clearly seen when the observed economic magnitudes for the endogenous variables, $C_t$, $I_t$, and $Y_t$, are labeled $Y_{1t}$, $Y_{2t}$, and $Y_{3t}$ respectively; and the observed economic magnitudes for the predetermined variables, $I_{t-1}$ and $Z_t$, are denoted $X_{2t}$ and $X_{3t}$ respectively. Using matrix and vector shorthand, the linear explanatory economic model can be written $B'Y' + \Gamma'X' = \varepsilon'$. The definition of these symbols is best presented by writing the corresponding matrices and vectors for this model in full detail. In this example $G = 3$ and $K = 3$, in the general form

$$\underset{(G \times G)(G \times T)}{B' \quad Y'} + \underset{(G \times K)(K \times T)}{\Gamma' \quad X'} = \underset{(G \times T)}{\varepsilon'} ,$$

which can be expanded by definition as follows:

$$\begin{pmatrix} 1 & 0 & -\beta_{13} \\ 0 & 1 & -\beta_{23} \\ -1 & -1 & 1 \end{pmatrix} \begin{pmatrix} Y_{11} & Y_{12} \cdots Y_{1T} \\ Y_{21} & Y_{22} \cdots Y_{2T} \\ Y_{31} & Y_{32} \cdots Y_{3T} \end{pmatrix}$$

$$+ \begin{pmatrix} -\gamma_{11} & 0 & 0 \\ -\gamma_{21} & -\gamma_{22} & 0 \\ 0 & 0 & 1 \end{pmatrix} \begin{pmatrix} X_{11} & X_{12} \cdots X_{1T} \\ X_{21} & X_{22} \cdots X_{2T} \\ X_{31} & X_{32} \cdots X_{3T} \end{pmatrix} = \begin{pmatrix} \varepsilon_{11} & \varepsilon_{12} \cdots \varepsilon_{1T} \\ \varepsilon_{21} & \varepsilon_{22} \cdots \varepsilon_{2T} \\ 0 & 0 \cdots 0 \end{pmatrix}$$

||||||||||||||||||||||||||||||||||||||||||||||||||||||||||||||||||||||||||||||||||||||||||||||||||||||||||||||||||||||||||||||||||||||||||||||||||||||||

*Explicative note.* The subscripts on the exogenous variables are reversed in the presentation of a simultaneous equation model compared to their use in the single equation model. This should create no difficulty since it is primarily to allow the matrix formulation to look more closely like the model being considered. That is, the formulation presents the equations of the model reading across the coefficient numbers from left to right. If the subscript notation were kept strictly the same, then the formulation would present the equations of the model reading down the coefficient matrices from top to bottom. Furthermore, this dichotomy in the use of subscripts between single equation and multiple equation models allows strikingly similar representations of the estimators and related statistics for both types of models. In all cases, the subscript "$t$" refers to the observation index and "$k$" refers to the exogenous variable index.

||||||||||||||||||||||||||||||||||||||||||||||||||||||||||||||||||||||||||||||||||||||||||||||||||||||||||||||||||||||||||||||||||||||||||||||||||||||||

In this formulation, $Y'$, $X'$, and $\varepsilon'$, are matrices of size $G \times T$, $K \times T$, and $G \times T$ respectively. The system of three equations is really repeated $T$ different times, once for each observation point. It is on the basis of these $T$ observations that the econometrician estimates, tests, and makes conclusions about the specification of the model.

## 2.6 NONLINEAR VARIATIONS OF THE SIMPLE LINEAR MODEL

The extensions of the simple model have allowed more complex representations, but they still appear to be linear.

However, Yankee ingenuity prevails. The variables $Y_g$ and $X_k$ which appear in the linear model may themselves be nonlinear functions of the underlying economic variables. For example, $X_k$ may be the reciprocal or the logarithm of an economic variable. Second and higher order relations, square roots, or exponential transformations may also be included. A few simple examples from economic research can be listed.

### Higher order transformations

The linear model can really represent a higher order relation. A common use of a higher order model is in determining trends or in finding the response surface for $Y$ with the best fit to a set of observations. Let $Y =$ employment $E$, and let $X_2 =$ output $Q$, and $X_3 =$ time period $t$, and $X_4 = t^2$. Then,

$$Y_t = \gamma_1 + \gamma_2 X_{t2} + \gamma_3 X_{t3} + \gamma_4 X_{t4} + \varepsilon_t$$

is a linear representation of an employment demand function with a quadratic trend; $E = \gamma_1 + \gamma_2 Q + \gamma_3 t + \gamma_4 t^2 + \varepsilon$ for each observation. A complete second order model with two independent variables, $Z$ and $W$, might be represented as

$$Y_t = \gamma_1 + \sum_{k=2}^{K} \gamma_k X_{tk} + \varepsilon_t$$

if we let $X_2 = Z$, $X_3 = Z^2$, $X_4 = W$, $X_5 = W^2$, and $X_6 = ZW$. Such a model allows for nonlinear, second degree curves (parabolic or hyperbolic response surfaces for example) to be fitted including an interaction term ($ZW = X_6$) between the two variables, yet the analysis involves only the linear model. Third, fourth, or higher order models can be developed similarly.

### Reciprocal transformations

A theoretical relation in economics may be nonlinear and have the built-in implication of an asymptotic level such as the Keynesian liquidity trap described by a relation $Y = \alpha_1 + \alpha_2/Z$ where $Y$ is investment and $Z$ is the interest rate. Figure 2-1 (*a*) depicts such a relation of a negative slope ($dY/dZ = -\alpha_2/Z^2$ for all $Z > 0$—see *Review* 3.2, item 1, for the rules of differentiation) which decreases in absolute value as $Z$ increases. Also, $Y$ approaches the asymptotic level $\alpha_1$. If $\alpha_2$ is negative, then $Y$ approaches the level $\alpha_1$ asymptotically from below with positive but decreasing slope as in Figure 2-1(*b*). A simple transformation of variable using the reciprocal

**FIGURE 2-1**

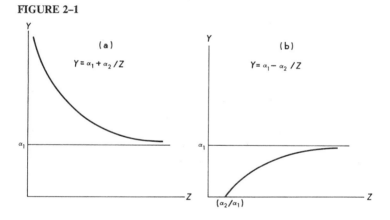

$X = 1/Z$ provides the linear model $Y = \alpha_1 + \alpha_2 X$ with constant slope $\alpha_2$ and intercept $\alpha_1$.

For example, consider the relation $Y = 5 + 40/Z$ where $Z$ is the interest rate in percent and $Y$ is investment. Using the following data, plots of this relation and the relation, $Y = 5 + 40(X)$, where $X = 1/Z$ are shown in Figure 2-2.

| $Y$ | $\infty$ | 45 | 25 | 15 | 13 | 10 | 9 | 7 | 6 | 5 |
|---|---|---|---|---|---|---|---|---|---|---|
| $Z$ | 0 | 1 | 2 | 4 | 5 | 8 | 10 | 20 | 40 | $\infty$ |
| $X$ | $\infty$ | 1 | 0.5 | 0.25 | 0.20 | 0.125 | 0.10 | 0.05 | 0.025 | 0 |

**FIGURE 2-2**

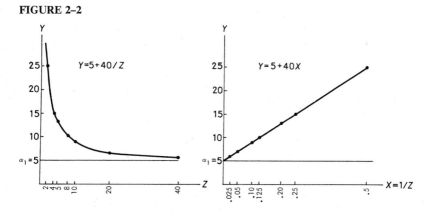

## Logarithmic transformations on $Y$ and $X$

Many theoretical relations in economics may be expressed in terms of multiplicative models rather than additive, such as the popular Cobb-Douglas production function, $Q = \gamma_1 L^{\gamma_2} K^{\gamma_3}$, where $Q$ measures output and $L$ and $K$ are labor and capital inputs respectively. Also, economists often use measures of elasticity in proffered economic laws. The linear model without variable transformation is not directly suitable for representing such statements.

In the model $Y = \alpha_1 + \alpha_2 X$, the elasticity of $Y$ with respect to $X$ is given as $\eta = (dY/dX)(X/Y)$, the percentage change in $Y$, $(dY/Y)$, relative to a percentage change in $X$, $(dX/X)$. The slope of the model is given by $(dY/dX) = \alpha_2$, which is constant. However, the elasticity changes along this straight line as the value of $(X/Y)$ changes. Since the line may be considered the line of average relationship between $Y$ and $X$, it is often common to use the average values of $Y$ and $X$ as the point at which the elasticity is measured; thus $\eta = \alpha_2(\overline{X}/\overline{Y})$.

If the theoretical relation suggests a constant rather than a changing elasticity, then a logarithmic transformation on both the endogenous and exogenous variables may be applied. The model obtained is linear in the logs,

$$(\ln Y) = \alpha_1 + \alpha_2(\ln X).$$

Such a specification really comes from an original multiplicative model, $Y = \delta X^{\alpha_2}$ where $\ln \delta = \alpha_1$. Also, since $dY/dX = \delta \alpha_2 X^{(\alpha_2 - 1)}$ for the original model, then the elasticity $\eta = (dY/dX)(X/Y)$ is given by

$$\eta = \delta \alpha_2 X^{(\alpha_2 - 1)} \left( \frac{X^1}{\delta X^{\alpha_2}} \right) = \alpha_2 \frac{(\delta X^{\alpha_2 - 1})}{(\delta X^{\alpha_2 - 1})} = \alpha_2.$$

The double log transformation corresponds to the economist's assumption of a constant elasticity of $Y$ with respect to $X$ that is given by the value of

**FIGURE 2–3**
**Double log transformation**
$$\ln Y = \alpha_1 + \alpha_2 \ln X$$

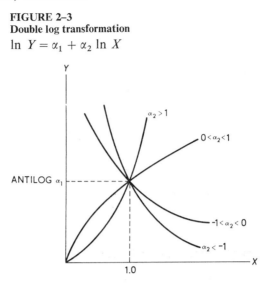

$\alpha_2$. Depending on this value, various nonlinear curves as illustrated in Figure 2–3 may be transformed into a linear model.

Returning to the Cobb-Douglas production function, it is obvious that if the double log transformation is used, $Q = \gamma_1 L^{\gamma_2} K^{\gamma_3}$ becomes $Y = \gamma_1{}^* + \gamma_2 X_2 + \gamma_3 X_3$ where $Y = \ln Q$, $X_2 = \ln L$, $X_3 = \ln K$, and $\gamma_1{}^* = \ln \gamma_1$.

## Logarithmic transformation on $X$ only

Some nonlinear economic relations may be represented in a linear model if only a semilog transformation is used. The model, $Y = \alpha_1 + \alpha_2 \ln X$, has a slope $(dY/dX) = \alpha_2/X$ which decreases as $X$ increases. The elasticity, $\eta = (dY/dX)(X/Y) = (\alpha_2/X)(X/Y) = \alpha_2/Y$, decreases as $Y$ increases. For some applications, such as the price elasticity of the supply of wheat produced, this may be a more appropriate form of the model. The nonlinear function to be represented by the semilog transformation is shown in Figure 2–4(a). If $Y =$ wheat output and $X =$ price, then no wheat is produced unless the price is at least $e^{-\alpha_1/\alpha_2}$, and the percentage increase in wheat production that is possible at very high output levels is limited by production constraints such as the amount of cultivated land.

The inverse of the function $Y = \alpha_1 + \alpha_2 \ln X$, given as $X = \delta_1 \delta_2{}^Y$ where $\delta_1 = e^{-\alpha_1/\alpha_2}$ and $\delta_2 = e^{1/\alpha_2}$ also has some interesting uses. One such use is the estimation of a rate of growth in a relation which is specified to have a constant rate of growth over time, $X = \delta_1 (1 + i)^t$. Let $X =$ population and $Y =$ time $= 0, 1, 2, \ldots, T$ periods of observation, and $\delta_2 = (1 + i)$ where

FIGURE 2–4(a)
Semilog transformation
$Y = \alpha_1 + \alpha_2 \ln X$

FIGURE 2–4(b)
Constant rate of growth function
$X = \delta_1 \delta_2{}^Y$

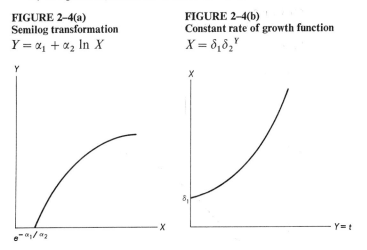

$i$ is the constant rate of growth to be estimated. Then, $X = \delta_1\delta_2{}^Y$ specifies a constant rate of growth in population over time as shown in Figure 2–4($b$). The estimate of $i$ is obtained from an estimate of $\delta_2$ by $i = \delta_2 - 1.0$. An estimate of $\delta_2$ is obtained from an estimate of $\alpha_2$ by $\delta_2 = e^{1/\alpha_2}$, where $\alpha_2$ is estimated in the linear model after making a semilog transformation of variable, $Y = \alpha_1 + \alpha_2 \ln X$, using $Y = t$ and $\ln X = \ln(\text{population})$.

## Logarithmic-inverse transformations

A model in which a combined transformation of variable is made to obtain $\ln Y = \alpha_1 - \alpha_2/X$ is known as a log-inverse model. It is useful when the theoretical specification has the form $Y = e^{(\alpha_1 - \alpha_2/X)}$, so that the underlying curve is assumed to have an inflection point at $X = \alpha_2/2$ where the rate of change in the positive slope reverses from positive to negative. Also, $Y$ is assumed to have an asymptote of $e^{\alpha_1}$ as $X$ increases (see Figure 2–5). Such curves may be useful in budget analysis of consumers where the marginal propensity to consume ($dY/dX$) varies and consumption capacity is limited, or as representations of functions in which the elasticity of $Y$ with respect to $X$ decreases as $X$ increases.

*Explicative note.* Since $dY/dX = e^{(\alpha_1 - \alpha_2/X)}(\alpha_2/X^2)$ for the function, $Y = e^{(\alpha_1 - \alpha_2/X)}$, then the elasticity

$$\eta = (dY/dX)(X/Y) = e^{(\alpha_1 - \alpha_2/X)}(\alpha_2/X^2)(X/e^{(\alpha_1 - \alpha_2/X)})$$

or $\eta = \alpha_2/X$.

**FIGURE 2–5**
**Log-inverse transformation**

$$\ln Y = \alpha_1 - \frac{\alpha_2}{X}$$

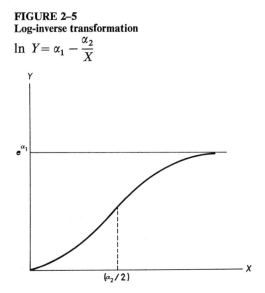

A particular example of such a theoretical parameter may be the income elasticity of food consumption. If food consumption $= Y$ and disposable income $= X$, then a model $Y = \alpha_1 + \alpha_2 X$ would seem inappropriate since the elasticity $\eta = \alpha_2(X/Y)$ would asymptotically approach 1.0 as $X$ increases given that $\alpha_2$ is the marginal propensity to consume food ($\alpha_2 = dY/dX$). However, (Ernst) Engel's law applied to food consumption would imply that the percentage increase in food consumption relative to a one percentage increase in income would decrease as income rises in absolute dollars. (See Figure 2–6.) That is, if two individuals Joe and Willy had incomes of $4,000 and $40,000 respectively, and each received a 1 percent increase in income ($40 and $400), Joe would make a larger percentage increase in food consumption than would Willy. The elasticity, $\eta = \alpha_2/X$, for the log-inverse model would give a result consistent with Engel's law.

||||||||||||||||||||||||||||||||||||||||||||||||||||||||||||||||||||||||||||||||||||||||||||||||||||||||||||||||||||||||||||||||

*Discursive note.* After making variable transformations, it is important to consider if the assertions about the external environment are satisfactorily represented in terms of the new transformed endogenous variable or the new disturbance term. In particular, the assumptions about the error term (given in Chapter 5 later) should hold for the new representation.

||||||||||||||||||||||||||||||||||||||||||||||||||||||||||||||||||||||||||||||||||||||||||||||||||||||||||||||||||||||||||||||||

It is fairly obvious that various combinations of these and other simple transformations allow for a wide variety of nonlinear representations within

**FIGURE 2–6**
**Engel's law**

$$\frac{d\eta}{d\,(\text{income})} < 0$$

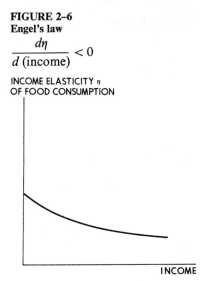

the context of the simple linear explanatory model. Often, only the cleverness of the model builder restrains him in formulating meaningful nonlinear economic relations in a linear representation. A few examples of such transformations from economic research articles are cited at the end of this chapter. Some others are included in the exercises.

### An example of combined transformations

One case of many in which a combination of several types of transformations occurs is reviewed here.[1] The original structural specification has actual output $Y$ given in terms of potential output $P$, and an exponential quadratic function of the unemployment rate, $w$. Also, potential output is given in a Cobb-Douglas function with arguments of effective capital stock $K$ and effective labor $L$. The specification is:

$$P_t = AK_t^{\gamma}L_t^{(1-\gamma)}e^{(\varepsilon_t)},$$
$$Y_t = P_t e^{(b+cw+dw^2)}.$$

It is desired to find estimates of $\gamma$, $c$, $d$, and the constant term in order to determine the extent of embodied technical change. The estimation is done on a linear model for $Y$ obtained by substitution of $P_t$ in the $Y_t$ equation and transformations. Begin with

$$Y_t = AK_t^{\gamma}L_t^{(1-\gamma)}e^{(b+cw+dw^2+\varepsilon_t)}.$$

---

[1] Michael D. Intriligator, "Embodied Technical Change and Productivity in the U.S., 1929–1958," *Review of Economics and Statistics*, Vol. 47 (1965), pp. 65–70.

Divide both sides by $L_t$ and simplify by using $L_t^{(1-\gamma)}/L_t = 1/L_t^{\gamma}$. Then, make the logarithmic transformation to get

$$\left(\ln \frac{Y_t}{L_t}\right) = (\ln A + b) + \gamma\left(\ln \frac{K_t}{L_t}\right) + cw + dw^2 + \varepsilon_t.$$

Clearly, this is the same form as

$$Y_t = \gamma_1 + \sum_{k=2}^{4} \gamma_k X_{tk} + \varepsilon_t.$$

Knowing how to estimate, test, analyze, and interpret this form of the econometric model is very important and is the central attention of this book. Further motivation to acquire such knowledge can be obtained individually by each student of economics by looking at the research papers in professional journals in his area of interest. Undoubtedly, the most commonly used statistical analysis in economic research is estimation of this form of model.

## Nonlinear relations

Equally clear is the limitation of this form of model. There are some relations which are intrinsically nonlinear and cannot be put into this form by any iterative transformations. Consider the specifications,

$$Y = \gamma_1 + \gamma_3 e^{(-\gamma_2 X_2)} + \varepsilon$$

or

$$Y = \gamma_1 + \gamma_2 X_2 + \gamma_3(\gamma_4)^{X_3} + \varepsilon.$$

These specifications are nonlinear in the parameters $\gamma_k$. Special methods for estimating some nonlinear functions are being developed by statisticians and econometricians in their research work. They involve iterative procedures which require more complex statistical and mathematical procedures than the linear case. These nonlinear techniques are not considered in this book.[2]

## NEW VOCABULARY

| | |
|---|---|
| Vector inner product | Exogenous variables |
| Logarithmic transformation | Predetermined variables |
| Subscript indexes $i$, $g$, $k$, and $t$ | Matrix transpose |
| Endogenous variables | Initial conditions |

---

[2] A discussion of nonlinear methods can be found in N. R. Draper, and H. Smith, *Applied Regression Analysis* (New York: John Wiley and Sons, Inc., 1966), chap. 10, which includes the method of nonlinear least squares estimation developed by D. W. Marquardt, "An Algorithm for Least Squares Estimation of Nonlinear Parameters," *Journal of Soc. Indust. Appl. Math.*, Vol. 11 (1963), pp. 431–41. Also see, H. Q. Hartley and A. Booker, "Nonlinear Least Squares Estimation," *Annals of Mathematical Statistics* 1965, pp. 638–50.

## SUMMARY OUTLINE

I. Composition of linear explanatory economic model
- A. Economic definitions and postulates; the theory
  1. Provide the specification of relations among the variables
  2. Give economic meaning to the formulation
- B. Initial conditions
  1. Assertions about values of the exogenous variables; the predetermined data
  2. Assertions about controls on the economic environment excluded from the model; the assumptions concerning the probability function of the disturbance terms
- C. Technical rules; the estimation and testing formulas and procedures
- D. Predictive implications
  1. External conclusions about expected levels of economic variables; forecasts
  2. Internal deductions about acceptable levels of estimates and test statistics; tests of hypotheses

II. Extensions of the simple model
- A. More variables and more relations
- B. Vector, matrix, and subscript notation

III. Transformation of variables
- A. Underlying theoretical relations are nonlinear
- B. Model remains linear in the parameters
- C. Types of transformations
  1. Higher orders in the variables
  2. Logarithmic and exponential
  3. Reciprocals and combinations

## REFERENCES

The example of a higher order theoretical relation for employment demand is developed in:

Brechling, F. P. R. "The Relationship between Output and Employment in British Manufacturing Industries." *Review of Economic Studies*, Vol. 32 (1965), pp. 187–216.

The common use of the logarithmic transformation in economic research is evident in the estimation of production functions and other multiplicative nonlinear theoretical specifications such as in:

Brittain, John A. "A Regression Model for Estimation of the Seasonal Component in Unemployment and Other Volatile Time Series." *Review of Economics and Statistics*, Vol. 44 (1962), pp. 24–36.

Komiya, Ryutara. "Technological Progress and the Production Function in the U.S. Steam Power Industry." *Review of Economics and Statistics*, Vol. 44 (1962), pp. 156–66.

Leontief, Wassily, "An International Comparison of Factor Costs and Factor Use." *American Economic Review*, Vol. 54 (1964), pp. 335–45.

Rapping, Leonard.  "Learning and World War II Production Functions." *Review of Economics and Statistics*, Vol. 47 (1965), pp. 81–86.

Walters, A. A.  "Production and Cost Functions: An Econometric Study." *Econometrica*, Vol. 31 (1963), pp. 1–66.

Williamson, Oliver E.  "Hierarchical Control and Optimum Firm Size." *The Journal of Political Economy*, Vol. 75 (1967), pp. 123–38. (See Appendix.)

## EXERCISES

1. Suppose it is posited that an individual's federal personal income tax liability $t$ is related to his adjusted gross income $y$ by the function,

$$t = ay^{b+1}e^{\varepsilon}.$$

Determine a representation of this theory which allows estimation of $a$ and $b$ as parameters in the simple linear model. Interpret the economic meaning of these parameters. (Taken from John O. Blackburn, "Implicit Tax Rate Reductions with Growth, Progressive Taxes, Constant Progressivity, and a Fixed Public Share." *American Economic Review*, Vol. 57 [1967], pp. 162–69.)

2. Suppose a variable $E$ representing hours of work per capita per week is determined in terms of a variable $Y$ representing per capita national income according to $E = aY^B\varepsilon$. Determine a representation of this theory which allows estimation of $a$ and $B$ as parameters in the simple linear model. Interpret the economic meaning of the parameters. (Taken from Gordon C. Winston, "An International Comparison of Income and Hours of Work," *Review of Economics and Statistics*, Vol. 48 [1966], pp. 136–48.)

3. Suppose a two-equation model is posited for determining the price $P$ and quantity $Q$ for a commodity in terms of disposable income $y_d$, total acreage allotments $A$, and disturbance terms $\varepsilon_1$ and $\varepsilon_2$.

$$P_t = \beta_{12}Q_t + \gamma_1 + \gamma_2(Y_d)_t + \varepsilon_{t1},$$
$$Q_t = \beta_{21}P_t + \gamma_3 + \gamma_4 A_t + \varepsilon_{t2}.$$

Rewrite this model in a detailed matrix specification using the notation as given in Section 2.5.

# PART II

# The Simple Econometric Model

In Chapters 3–7, material on the estimation and testing of the simple bivariate regression model is reviewed. Much attention is given to the intuitive understanding of the concepts and to practical use of the procedures. Although much of this material may be old hat to some readers, it still serves a useful purpose of presenting the terms, notation, and concepts which carry over into the extensions of the model in Parts III and IV. Furthermore, some topics of mathematics and statistics are introduced here which will be presumed in later chapters.

Chapters 3 and 4 present the basic mechanical procedures and formulas. Chapter 5 lists and discusses the important underlying assumptions. A more theoretical discussion of the properties of the estimators and their dependence on the assumptions is given in Chapter 6. The last chapter of Part II should be a useful reference for testing any simple model of your own and making inferences for economic theory or policy.

# LEAST SQUARES ESTIMATION METHOD

## 3.1 PREVIEW

"Least squares" is a method for finding the estimates $a_1$ and $a_2$ for the parameters $\alpha_1$ and $\alpha_2$ in a simple "bivariate" model, $Y_t = \alpha_1 + \alpha_2 X_{t2} + \varepsilon_t$. In principle, we wish to find estimates so that the difference is small between actual values of the variable $Y_t$ and estimated values of this variable based on the estimating equation $\hat{Y}_t = a_1 + a_2 X_{t2}$, where $a_1$ and $a_2$ are the estimates of $\alpha_1$ and $\alpha_2$. That is, the estimates should be determined so that the residual for any observation $t$, $e_t = Y_t - \hat{Y}_t$ is small. However, our criterion must be extended to apply to all residuals, or to the average residual for all observations. We might wish to use the principle that the sum of the residuals must be small. However, that principle is unworkable because some of the residuals are positive and some negative as we under- or overestimate. The sum of residuals could be zero simply by using a constant estimator equal to the mean of $Y$.

|||||||||||||||||||||||||||||||||||||||||||||||||||||||||||||||||||||||||||||||||||||||||||||||||||||||||||||||||||||||||||||||||||||||||||||||

***Interpretive note.*** The best criterion is to square the residuals and use the principle of minimizing the sum of the squares of the residuals. The method of *least squares* means to find the estimates $a_1$ and $a_2$ so that the sum of the *squares* of the residuals of the estimation will be the *least*.

|||||||||||||!!|||||||||||||||||||||||||||||||||||||||!|||||||||||||||||||||||||||||||||||||||||||||||||||||||||||||||||||||||||||||||||||||||||

In Chapter 6, a rationale of this principle of least squares is discussed from a more statistical point of view. In this chapter, we establish the mechanical procedures, derive the formulas for the estimators, and give an example calculation of ordinary least squares (OLS).

## 3.2 REVIEW

Topics in this chapter, as in most chapters and throughout econometrics, require some bits of knowledge from calculus, statistics, and matrix algebra. Briefly, some of the points to remember or learn are now given.

### 1 Rules of differentiation

Let $a$, $n$, be numbers; $x$, $y$, be variables; $u$, $v$, be functions of $x$; and $f$, a function of $u$.

Power rule:      If $y = ax^n$, $dy = nax^{n-1} dx$ .

Logarithm rule:    If $y = \ln_e x$, $dy = \dfrac{dx}{x}$.

Exponential rule:   If $y = e^x$, $dy = e^x dx$.

Product rule:     If $y = uv, \dfrac{dy}{dx} = u\dfrac{dv}{dx} + v\dfrac{du}{dx}$.

Quotient rule:    If $y = \dfrac{u}{v}, \dfrac{dy}{dx} = \dfrac{v\dfrac{du}{dx} - u\dfrac{dv}{dx}}{v^2}$.

Function of a
   function rule:   If $y = f(u), \dfrac{dy}{dx} = \dfrac{df}{du} \cdot \dfrac{du}{dx}$.

The notation $dy/dx$ is read as the derivative of $y$ with respect to $x$. If $y$ is a function of several variables such as $y = f(x, w, z)$, then the notion of a partial derivative applies. In symbols, $\partial y/\partial x$, represents the partial derivative of $y$ with respect to $x$, and $\partial y/\partial w$ or $\partial y/\partial z$ would be interpreted similarly. In the calculus of partial differentiation, the same rules as given above apply with the additional rule that variables other than the one under differentiation are treated as constants so that $\partial y/\partial x$ gives the rate of change of $y$ in the $x$ dimension holding $w$ and $z$ constant.

## 2 Maximum and minimum of a function of several variables

Necessary conditions for a point to be a maximum or minimum of a function are that the first order partial derivatives with respect to each variable be set equal to zero. We are excluding boundary solutions.

Sufficient conditions are stated in terms of second order partials. However, in cases such as minimizing the sum of squares of residuals, the possibility of a maximum is excluded by inspection. An estimating line which is not close to any observations would give larger squared residuals than one which is drawn through or among the cluster of observed points.

## 3 Statistical sample moment

The first moment of a variable is a measure of its central tendency, called a mean or an average, and designated by an upper bar, $\bar{Y} = \sum Y_t / T$.

The second moment is a measure of dispersion or variability. For any observation $Y_t$, the deviation of the observation from the average level of $Y_t$ can be calculated. Usually, a lowercase letter is the symbol of a deviation, say, $y_t = (Y_t - \bar{Y})$. The sum of all the deviations from the mean is necessarily zero since the mean is calculated as the average or balancing point of all the observations.

Often, a measure of all the deviations is desired as a guide to the degree of variability among the observations. Since $\sum y_t = 0$ always, it is not usable. Instead $\sum y_t^2 = \sum (Y_t - \bar{Y})^2$, the sum of the squares of the deviations is used and given the name, variation of the variable $Y_t$. If it is divided by $T$, it is the simple moment of $Y_t$, or second moment about the mean denoted $m_{yy}$.

It is easiest to calculate this simple moment in terms of the so-called raw moments, $(\sum Y_t / T)$ and $(\sum Y_t^2 / T)$, rather than in terms of the actual squared deviations. Also, the covariation between two variables is often desired and calculated in a similar way. Using $Y$ and $X$ to represent any two variables, the formulas are:

Variation:     $\sum y_t^2 = \sum (Y_t - \bar{Y})^2 = \sum Y^2 - T\bar{Y}^2$.

Covariation:   $\sum y_t x_t = \sum (Y_t - \bar{Y})(X_t - \bar{X}) = \sum (YX) - T\bar{X}\,\bar{Y}$.

## 4 Determinant

A determinant is a number associated with a square matrix (number of rows equal to the number of columns). For a $(2 \times 2)$ size matrix, say,

$$A = \begin{pmatrix} A_{11} & A_{12} \\ A_{21} & A_{22} \end{pmatrix},$$

the determinant is written,

$$\det A = \begin{vmatrix} A_{11} & A_{12} \\ A_{21} & A_{22} \end{vmatrix} = A_{11}A_{22} - A_{12}A_{21}.$$

For larger square matrices, the calculation is most easily done using expansion by cofactors.

A cofactor $C_{ij}$ of an element $A_{ij}$ in a square matrix is the determinant of the smaller square submatrix formed by deleting row $i$ and column $j$ from the original matrix; and, moreover, this determinant is multiplied by $(-1)$ if the sum of the position indexes $(i + j)$, is odd.

The calculation of a determinant of an $(n \times n)$ square matrix $A$ of elements $A_{ij}$ by expansion by cofactors is given by the rules:

$$A = \sum_{i=1}^{n} C_{ij}A_{ij} \qquad \text{for any column } j,$$

or

$$A = \sum_{j=1}^{n} C_{ij}A_{ij} \qquad \text{for any row } i.$$

That is, select any row or any column of the matrix and form the products of each element in the selected row (or column) with its corresponding co-factor. Then sum these $n$ products. Selection of a row or column with zero entries greatly reduces the work since no cofactor need be computed for that element. When $A_{ij} = 0$, then $C_{ij}A_{ij} = 0$ for any value of the cofactor $C_{ij}$.

## 5  Solution of simultaneous equations

Common algebraic solution methods for systems of equations are the methods of substitution and elimination. In the substitution method, we solve for one unknown in one of the equations in terms of the other unknowns. Then, the expression for this solution is substituted for the first unknown in all the other equations. Successive steps for the other unknowns eventually result in one remaining equation in only one unknown. The other unknowns can be found by iterative substitutions back into the previous expressions.

In the elimination method, multiples of one equation are added to another equation in order to get a zero coefficient for one of the unknowns in the summed equation. Successive steps of elimination again result in a final single equation in one unknown. A systematic procedure for this method is the Gaussian reduction of the coefficient matrix by applying elementary row transformations as used later in Chapter 12.

Another solution method for square systems of simultaneous equations is Cramer's method, using determinants. Suppose the equation system is written in vector form as $A_1Z_1 + A_2Z_2 + A_3Z_3 + \cdots + A_nZ_n = H$ where the $n$ unknowns are $Z_1, Z_2, \ldots, Z_n$; the coefficients of variable $Z_i$ in all $n$ equations are given by the column vector $A_i$; and the right-hand side of constants is given by the column vector $H$. Each column vector $A_1, A_2, \ldots, A_n$ and $H$ has $n$ components, one for each equation. The solution is given by:

$$Z_1 = \frac{|HA_2 A_3 \cdots A_n|}{|A_1 A_2 A_3 \cdots A_n|}\ ;\quad Z_2 = \frac{|A_1 H A_3 A_4 \cdots A_n|}{|A|}\ ;$$

$$\ldots ;\ Z_n = \frac{|A_1 A_2 \cdots A_{n-1} H|}{|A|}$$

The denominator is always the determinant of the matrix of coefficients, size $(n \times n)$. The numerator is similar, except the right-hand side vector of constants is always substituted for the column vector of coefficients $A_i$, of the respective unknown being determined, $Z_i$.

## 6   Random variable and probability density function

A random variable assumes at least two different values, each of which is associated with a positive real number between zero and one. This corresponding number is called the probability of the random variable taking on a certain value. For a continuous random variable the function which describes the levels of these probabilities over any interval is a probability density function. The integral of the function (sum of probabilities) over all values of the random variable must equal unity.

## 7   Estimators and estimates

It is common to distinguish between an estimator and an estimate. The estimator is the general term, estimate the specific term. An estimator is represented by a general formula; it is a function of sample observations; it is a random variable with a probability distribution. An estimate is the value of the estimator determined on the basis of a particular set of sample observations.

## REVIEW EXERCISES

R.1.   Find the partial derivatives: $f_x = \partial f/\partial x$ and $f_y = \partial f/\partial y$ for $f(x, y)$ given as

a)   $2xy + y^2$.      Ans.: $f_x = 2y$,   $f_y = 2(x + y)$.

b)   $1/x + 3x(x - y)^2$.      Ans.: $f_x = -1/x^2 + 3(x - y)^2 + 6x(x - y)$,
                 $f_y = 6xy - 6x^2$.

c)   $\dfrac{1}{x} e^{(-x+y)}$.      Ans.: $f_x = e^{-x+y}\left(-\dfrac{1}{x} - \dfrac{1}{x^2}\right)$,

                 $f_y = \dfrac{1}{x} e^{-x+y}$.

d)   $e^{\ln y - \sqrt{x}}$.      Ans.: $f_x = e^{(\ln y - \sqrt{x})}\left(\dfrac{-1}{2\sqrt{x}}\right)$,

                 $f_y = e^{(\ln y - \sqrt{x})}\left(\dfrac{1}{y}\right)$.

R.2.  Find all relative maxima or minima of the functions

a)  $f(x) = 2x^2 - 5x$     for  $-10 \le x \le 10$ .

b)  $f(V) = \dfrac{-T}{2} \ln V - \dfrac{1}{2V} K^2$ .

R.3.  Find the value of $V$ in terms of $n$ and $\sum X_t^2$ which maximizes

$$L(V) = -n \ln V - \frac{n}{2} \ln 2\pi - \left(\frac{1}{2V^2}\right)(\textstyle\sum X_t^2).$$

R.4.  Find the values of $x$ and $y$ which minimize

a)  $f(x, y) = 2xy + y^2 - 3x$ .       Ans.: $y = \dfrac{3}{2}, \ x = \dfrac{-3}{2}, \ f(x, y) = 2\frac{1}{4}$ .

b)  $f(x, y) = 3x^2 - xy + 4y$ .

R.5.  a)  Given the observations 45, 52, 58, 66, 71 on disposable income $(X)$, find the mean, the deviations, the variation, and second simple moment.

b)  Suppose corresponding values for consumption $(Y)$ are 46, 52, 56, 63, 67, find the variation of $Y$ and the covariation between $Y$ and $X$.

c)  Form a matrix

$$\begin{pmatrix} \sum y^2 & \sum yx \\ \sum xy & \sum x^2 \end{pmatrix}.$$

Note that this cross-product deviation matrix is symmetric. Find its determinant.

R.6.  Consider the equation system:

$$284 = 5a + 292b ,$$
$$16{,}937 = 292a + 17{,}490b .$$

Find the values for $a$ and $b$.

R.7.  a)  Use expansion by cofactors to find the determinant of

$$A = \begin{pmatrix} 2 & 1 & 3 \\ -1 & 0 & 4 \\ 0 & -2 & 3 \end{pmatrix}.$$

b)  Write in full detail the equation system represented by $Ax = b$ where

$$x = \begin{pmatrix} x_1 \\ x_2 \\ x_3 \end{pmatrix} \quad \text{and} \quad b = \begin{pmatrix} 7 \\ 1 \\ 7 \end{pmatrix}.$$

c)  Solve for $x_1$ using Cramer's method.

d)  Solve for $x_2$ and $x_3$ by algebraic elimination or substitution.

R.8.  Given    $3a_1 + 5a_2 - a_4 = 6$,          a)  Define the appropriate vectors
$2a_1 - 7a_3 - 3a_4 = 0$,               and matrices to rewrite this
$-4a_1 + 6a_3 \qquad = 3$.              linear equation system in matrix

b)  Solve the equation system                 and vector form, $Fa = b$.
using Cramer's rule.

R.9.  *a)*  Let $X$ be the random variable that describes the outcome of tossing a die. Graph the probability function of $X$.

*b)*  Let $Y$ be a random variable defined as:

$$Y = 2X \text{ when } X \text{ is odd,}$$

$$Y = X^2 \text{ when } X \text{ is even.}$$

List the values taken on by $Y$ and their associated probabilities.

R.10.  Let $X$ be a random variable with

$$f(x) = k(1 + x) \qquad \text{for} \qquad 0 \leq X \leq 2$$

$$= 0 \text{ elsewhere.}$$

Find the value of $K$ if $f(x)$ is a probability density function.

(*Hint:* $\displaystyle\int_{-\infty}^{\infty} f(x)\,dx = 1.0.$)

## 3.3 THE FOUR-VARIABLE "BIVARIATE" MODEL

The bivariate econometric model can be written in full as: $Y_t = a_1 X_{t1} + \alpha_2 X_{t2} + \varepsilon_t$. The endogenous random variable $Y_t$ is to be explained in terms of an intercept which is the coefficient of a fixed exogenous variable $X_{t1} = 1$, an exogenous random variable $X_{t2}$, and a random disturbance variable $\varepsilon_t$.

This model appears to have four variables, but only two of the variables, $Y_t$ and $X_{t2}$, will be observed in the sample data. The variable $X_{t1}$ is set equal to one for all observations. It is denoted as a variable for symmetry and ease of notation when the model is extended. The variable $\varepsilon_t$ is not observable. It represents the error remaining in the true linear relation between $Y_t$ and $X_{t2}$. Although the exact levels of these errors are unknown, the properties of the distribution of the errors are very important in the estimation and testing of an econometric model. A more detailed discussion of the disturbance variable, $\varepsilon_t$, is deferred until Chapter 5.

||||||||||||||||||||||||||||||||||||||||||||||||||||||||||||||||||||||||||||||||||||||||||||||||||||||||||||||||||||||||||||||||||||

*Explicative note.*  Throughout this book, the convention is followed that Greek symbols are used for population parameters and Roman letters are used for sample statistics as indicated in Figure 3–1. For example the true disturbance term in the population regression model is denoted by $\varepsilon$ (epsilon) whereas a calculated residual based on the sample regression is denoted by $e$.

||||||||||||||||||||||||||||||||||||||||||||||||||||||||||||||||||||||||||||||||||||||||||||||||||||||||||||||||||||||||||||||||||||

**FIGURE 3–1**
**Symbolic notation**

|  | Population parameter | | Sample statistics | |
|---|---|---|---|---|
| General: | Greek letters | | Roman letters | |
| Specific examples: | Coefficient | $\alpha$ | Estimator | $a$ |
|  | Variance | $\sigma^2$ | Variance | $s^2$ |
|  | Disturbance | $\varepsilon$ | Residual | $e$ |
|  | Correlation coefficient | $\rho$ | Correlation coefficient | $r$ |

## 3.4 LEAST SQUARES ESTIMATORS IN THE SIMPLE MODEL

For the model $Y_t = \alpha_1 + \alpha_2 X_{t2} + \varepsilon_t$, let the least squares estimators of $\alpha_1$ and $\alpha_2$ be $a_1$ and $a_2$ respectively, and let the residuals from the estimation be $e_t = Y_t - (a_1 + a_2 X_{t2})$. The residual is the difference between the actual value and the estimated value of $Y_t$.

### Geometric description

Observations of the exogenous variable $X_{t2}$ could be plotted against corresponding observations of the endogenous variable $Y_t$ to get a scattergram as in Figure 3–2. The method of least squares fits a line through the points

**FIGURE 3–2**
**Estimating line in scatter diagram**

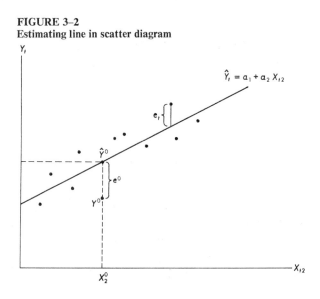

on the scattergram so as to minimize the sum of the squares of the residuals, $e_t$. Each residual, $e_t$, is measured vertically from the actual point value of $Y_t$ to the estimated value of $Y_t$ on the estimating line for each observed value of $X_{t2}$.

### Algebraic solution

From the algebraic representation, the sum of squares of the residuals can be written

$$\sum_{t=1}^{T} e_t^2 = \sum_{t=1}^{T} (Y_t - a_1 - a_2 X_{t2})^2.$$

The residuals are a function of the estimators of $\alpha_1$ and $\alpha_2$. By applying the calculus, the minimum of this function with respect to the unknowns, $a_1$ and $a_2$, can be determined.

||||||||||||||||||||||||||||||||||||||||||||||||||||||||||||||||||||||||||||||||||||||||||||||||||||||||||||||||||||||||||||||||||||||||||

*Explicative note.*  The same "least squares" techniques could be applied to more complex estimating functions merely by using the more complex corresponding representation for the residuals $e_t$ in the "least squares" function, $\sum_{t=1}^{T} e_t^2$.

||||||||||||||||||||||||||||||||||||||||||||||||||||||||||||||||||||||||||||||||||||||||||||||||||||||||||||||||||||||||||||||||||||||||||

*Step 1.*  Find the partial derivatives of $\sum e_t^2$ with respect to $a_1$ and $a_2$.

$$\frac{\partial(\sum e_t^2)}{\partial a_1} = 2 \sum_{t=1}^{T} (Y_t - a_1 - a_2 X_{t2})(-1) = -2(\sum Y_t - Ta_1 - a_2 \sum X_{t2}),$$

$$\frac{\partial(\sum e_t^2)}{\partial a_2} = 2 \sum_{t=1}^{T} (Y_t - a_1 - a_2 X_{t2})(-X_{t2})$$

$$= -2(\sum Y_t X_{t2} - a_1 \sum X_{t2} - a_2 \sum X_{t2}^2).$$

*Step 2.*  Set the partial derivatives equal to zero and solve for $a_1$ and $a_2$.

$$\sum Y_t = Ta_1 + a_2 \sum X_{t2},$$
$$\sum Y_t X_{t2} = \sum X_{t2} a_1 + \sum X_{t2}^2 a_2. \tag{3-1}$$

These are known as the normal equations. The solution can be found by the substitution method, elimination method, Cramer's method, Gaussian reduction method, or any other method of solving simultaneous equations.

||||||||||||||||||||||||||||||||||||||||||||||||||||||||||||||||||||||||||||||||||||||||||||||||||||||||||||||||||||||||||||||||||||||||||

*Explicative note.*  Throughout the following sections, all summations are over all $T$ observations. Thus, the summation index ($t$) will be dropped for simplicity of notation.

||||||||||||||||||||||||||||||||||||||||||||||||||||||||||||||||||||||||||||||||||||||||||||||||||||||||||||||||||||||||||||||||||||||||||

Using the substitution method, the first normal equation can be solved for

$$a_1 = \frac{\sum Y}{T} - \frac{\sum X_2}{T} a_2 = \bar{Y} - \bar{X}_2 a_2$$

where the upper bars represent the average of the variable.

This solution for $a_1$ is then substituted into the second normal equation to find $a_2$.

$$\sum YX_2 = \sum X_2 \left( \frac{\sum Y}{T} - \frac{\sum X_2}{T} a_2 \right) + \sum X_2^2 a_2,$$

$$\sum YX_2 = \sum X_2 \frac{\sum Y}{T} + \left[ \frac{-(\sum X_2)^2}{T} + \sum X_2^2 \right] a_2.$$

Using the definition for means, we obtain,

$$a_2 = \frac{\sum YX_2 - T\bar{Y}\bar{X}_2}{\sum X_2{}^2 - T\bar{X}_2{}^2}.$$

These expressions in the numerator and denominator are common in statistics and are frequently given a shorter representation in terms of the deviation of the variables from their respective means. That is, let

$$y_t = Y_t - \bar{Y} \quad \text{and} \quad x_{t2} = X_{t2} - \bar{X}_2.$$

Then

$$a_1 = \bar{Y} - a_2\bar{X}_2 \quad \text{and} \quad a_2 = \frac{\sum yx_2}{\sum x_2{}^2}. \tag{3-2}$$

❀

||||||||||||||||||||||||||||||||||||||||||||||||||||||||||||||||||||||||||||||||||||||||||||||||||||||||||||||||||||||||||||||||||||||||||||||||

**Recursive note.**    To make this substitution, refer to the definition in item 3 of *Review* 3.2.

||||||||||||||||||||||||||||||||||||||||||||||||||||||||||||||||||||||||||||||||||||||||||||||||||||||||||||||||||||||||||||||||||||||||||||||||

**Explicative note.**    This estimator for $a_2$ can be described in words as:

$$a_2 = \frac{\text{covariation between the endogenous and exogenous variable}}{\text{variation of the exogenous variable}}. \tag{3-2a}$$

||||||||||||||||||||||||||||||||||||||||||||||||||||||||||||||||||||||||||||||||||||||||||||||||||||||||||||||||||||||||||||||||||||||||||||||||

## 3.5 AN EXAMPLE OF LEAST SQUARES ESTIMATION

Let's consider some econometric model and apply this least squares principle to find estimates. Suppose a relation is postulated between the quantity of imported textiles as the endogenous variable and the average domestic retail price level of textiles as the exogenous variable.

Consider the data, Table 3–1, perhaps quarterly observations for country *A* in some appropriate units.

The model hypothesized is: imports = $\alpha_1 + \alpha_2$ (domestic price) + (unknown disturbances). Implicitly, the hypothesis claims that imports is dependent on domestic prices in a linear relation. Also, domestic prices are exogenous. They are fixed or determined by factors excluded from this model.

### Coding the data

It is generally wise to code the data by a multiple of 10 to transform the means of each variable into the same range between 1 and 10 approximately. This practice makes calculations to many digits unnecessary while avoiding

TABLE 3–1

**Example data**

| Quarterly observation | Textile imports | Domestic textile price level index |
|---|---|---|
| 1........ | 796 | 95 |
| 2........ | 779 | 97 |
| 3........ | 773 | 100 |
| 4........ | 833 | 100 |
| 5........ | 894 | 104 |
| 6........ | 896 | 105 |
| 7........ | 998 | 112 |
| 8........ | 1,016 | 120 |

Source: Class, 1969 (Worawan). (*Note:* Data used in some examples and exercises were collected in class projects by students who gave permission for use in this text.)

serious rounding errors. When using computer estimation techniques, it is advisable to have this coding included in the program for all intermediate calculations. Of course, any results in terms of the coded data should be decoded for a proper interpretation of the absolute magnitudes.

The coded data for the model $Y_t = \alpha_1 + \alpha_2 X_{t2} + \varepsilon_t$ is given in Table 3–2.

TABLE 3–2

**Coded example data**

| $t$ | $Y_t$ | $X_{t2}$ |
|---|---|---|
| 1............ | 7.96 | 9.5 |
| 2............ | 7.79 | 9.7 |
| 3............ | 7.73 | 10.0 |
| 4............ | 8.33 | 10.0 |
| 5............ | 8.94 | 10.4 |
| 6............ | 8.96 | 10.5 |
| 7............ | 9.98 | 11.2 |
| 8............ | 10.16 | 12.0 |

Where $Y_t =$ imports $\times 10^{-2}$,
$X_{t2} =$ price level $\times 10^{-1}$,
$T = 8$.

Following the method of least squares we derive the normal equations in terms of the estimators $a_1$ and $a_2$. These are:

$$\sum Y = Ta_1 + a_2 \sum X_2,$$
$$\sum YX_2 = \sum X_2 a_1 + \sum X_2{}^2 a_2,$$

(3–1)

and can be solved as before. We might use Cramer's method involving determinants to get the same answer. (See *Review* 3.2 item 5.)

$$a_1 = \frac{\begin{vmatrix} \sum Y & \sum X_2 \\ \sum YX_2 & \sum X_2^2 \end{vmatrix}}{\begin{vmatrix} T & \sum X_2 \\ \sum X_2 & \sum X_2^2 \end{vmatrix}} \quad \text{and} \quad a_2 = \frac{\begin{vmatrix} T & \sum Y \\ \sum X_2 & \sum YX_2 \end{vmatrix}}{\begin{vmatrix} T & \sum X_2 \\ \sum X_2 & \sum X_2^2 \end{vmatrix}}.$$

**The empirical results**

Values must be calculated from the data for $\sum Y$, $\sum X_2$, $\sum X_2^2$, and $\sum YX_2$ to find the solutions. It is wise to also find $\sum Y^2$ for later use. We obtain

$$\sum Y = 69.85, \quad \sum X_2 = 83.3, \quad \sum YX_2 = 732.535,$$
$$\sum Y^2 = 616.2187, \quad \sum X_2^2 = 872.19. \tag{3-3}$$

Therefore

$$a_1 = \frac{(69.85)(872.19) - (83.3)(732.535)}{8(872.19) - (83.3)^2} = \frac{-97.694}{38.63} = -2.529$$

and

$$a_2 = \frac{8(732.535) - (69.85)(83.3)}{38.63} = \frac{41.775}{38.63} = 1.0814.$$

The estimating equation depicted in Figure 3-3 is

$$\hat{Y}_t = -2.529 + 1.0814 X_{t2} \tag{3-4}$$

for the coded data. The same result is of course obtained by using the formula in terms of deviations. It is unnecessary to solve the normal equations for each problem. The general solution for the estimators is always the same; namely

$$a_1 = \overline{Y} - a_2 \overline{X}_2 \quad \text{and} \quad a_2 = \frac{\sum yx_2}{\sum x_2^2}. \tag{3-2}$$

The best method of performing the calculations, however, is still to find first the raw moments in terms of the coded data as given above in (3–3). Then, the covariations and variations are found from these according to the standard rules from *Review* 3.2, item 3.

$$\text{(variation of a variable } V) = \sum v^2 = \left[ \sum V^2 - T(\overline{V})^2 \right];$$

and

$$\text{(covariation of variables } V \text{ and } W) = \sum vw = \left[ \sum VW - T\overline{V}\overline{W} \right].$$

Using this procedure for our example, we obtain

$$\sum y^2 = 6.3409, \quad \sum x_2^2 = 4.8288, \quad \sum yx_2 = 5.2219,$$
$$\overline{Y} = 8.7312, \quad \overline{X}_2 = 10.4125. \tag{3-5}$$

**FIGURE 3–3**
**Plot of example regression**

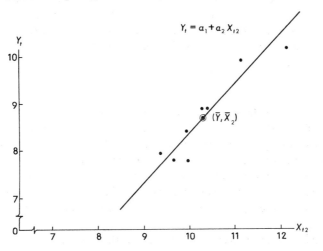

*This plot is obtained from the coded data of Table 3–2 and the least squares results given by equation (3–4). The regression line always passes through the point of means, in this case (8.73, 10.41). Its slope is given by $a_2 = 1.0814$.*

The estimates $a_1$ and $a_2$ are found to be:

$$a_2 = \frac{5.2219}{4.8288} = 1.0814,$$

$$a_1 = 8.7312 - (1.0814)(10.4125) = -2.529.$$

The estimating equation in terms of coded data is again

$$\hat{Y}_t = -2.529 + 1.0814X_{t2}. \tag{3-4}$$

This can be decoded to original magnitudes by dividing $a_1$ by $10^{-2}$ (the multiple of 10 used to code $Y_t$) and dividing $a_2$ by

$$10^{-1} = \left(\frac{\text{the multiple of 10 used to code } Y_t}{\text{the multiple of 10 used to code } X_{t2}}\right).$$

The resulting estimating equation in terms of the original data is

$$(\text{estimated imports}) = -252.9 + 10.814 \,(\text{domestic prices}). \tag{3-6}$$

For example the estimated value of imports for the fifth observation of the exogenous variable ($X_{52} = 104$), is

$$\hat{Y}_5 = -252.9 + 10.814(104) = 871.7.$$

The residual of the estimation for the fifth observation is

$$e_5 = Y_5 - \hat{Y}_5 = 894 - 871.7 = 22.3.$$

|||||||||||||||||||||||||||||||||||||||||||||||||||||||||||||||||||||||||||||||||||||||||||||||||||||||||||||||||||||||||||||||||||

*Interpretive note.* The estimate may not seem very close to the true value. The method of least squares does not guarantee that the estimates will be exact, or even close. This depends more on the appropriateness of the hypothesized model and on the representativeness of the sample.

|||||||||||||||||||||||||||||||||||||||||||||||||||||||||||||||||||||||||||||||||||||||||||||||||||||||||||||||||||||||||||||||||||

The method of least squares merely guarantees that the "most fitting" estimates for $a_1$, the intercept, and $a_2$, the slope, will be determined if we agree that "most fitting" means those estimates such that the sum of the squared residuals is the smallest. For these observations on the variables, we can be certain that if any other line is drawn through the scattergram or any other linear equation is written using any possible intercept or any possible slope, then the sum of the squared residuals will never be smaller than those obtained by using the equation (3-6).

All this is quite different from the claim that the residuals from the estimating equation will be small. This latter claim may or may not be true. The goodness of fit of the estimating equation or the smallness of the residuals from the estimating equation needs to be measured before this latter claim can be proven or disproven.

## 3.6 ECONOMIC INTERPRETATION OF THE EXAMPLE

Before going on to measures of fit of the estimating equation, consider the meaning of the results of the example. A linear regression between imports and domestic prices was made. The regression coefficients are estimated for the intercept and the slope of this linear equation.

|||||||||||||||||||||||||||||||||||||||||||||||||||||||||||||||||||||||||||||||||||||||||||||||||||||||||||||||||||||||||||||||||||

*Interpretive note.* The solution for the intercept, $a_1 = -252.9$, gives the mathematical value of imports when domestic prices are zero. ($\hat{Y} = -252.9 + a_2(0)$). The economic interpretation of such mathematical results must be made with care and good judgment.

|||||||||||||||||||||||||||||||||||||||||||||||||||||||||||||||||||||||||||||||||||||||||||||||||||||||||||||||||||||||||||||||||||

Here, the value of the intercept is not a realistic economic consideration. Prices will never be zero. Imports cannot be negative. It is simply an indication that if the relevant portion of the estimating line (the segment for domestic prices near the observed range of $X_2$ in the sample, say 90 to 125) were extended backward, the intersection of the line with the axis measuring imports would be at a negative level of imports.

More interesting is the estimate of the slope in the relevant price range. Since $a_2 = 10.814$, we might conclude that if the domestic price of textiles increases by one unit, then imports of textiles increases by 10.814 units, or

$$\frac{d(\text{imports})}{d(\text{domestic price})} = 10.814.$$

This might be an important consideration in industry pricing or in government tariff or quota policy.

### Estimating an elasticity

Another use of the slope would be to obtain an approximate measure of the domestic price elasticity of imports. This elasticity would be

$$\eta = \frac{d(\text{Im})}{d(P_d)} \cdot \frac{P_d}{\text{Im}}$$

for some level of imports and domestic prices. Most often, the level of means would be used; average imports = 873.12 and average domestic price index = 104.125 [from decoding the information in (3–5)]. The elasticity measured at this point is

$$\eta = 10.814 \left( \frac{104.125}{873.12} \right) = 1.29.$$

The econometrician might conclude that at the average levels of imports and domestic prices over the last eight quarters (two years), imports have been elastic with respect to domestic prices. That is, an increase in the domestic price of textiles is reflected in a greater percentage increase in imports of textiles. Further analysis would undoubtedly follow.

## 3.7 A LOG-LINEAR REVISION OF THE EXAMPLE MODEL

The measure of elasticity might have been obtained directly from the estimation by using a log-linear function in the specification of the linear explanatory economic model. Suppose $Y^* = \ln(\text{imports})$ and $X_2^* = \ln(\text{domestic prices})$ so the model is really nonlinear in the original variables, but linear in terms of the natural logarithm representation. (See Section 2.6.)

The specification is imports $= \alpha_1^*(\text{domestic price})^{\alpha_2^*}(e^\varepsilon)$ or $\ln(\text{imports}) = \ln \alpha_1^* + \alpha_2^* \ln(\text{domestic price}) + \varepsilon$. The estimating equation is

$$\hat{Y}_t^* = a_1^* + a_2^* X_{t2}^*$$

where $a_1^*$ and $a_2^*$ are the estimates of $\alpha_1^*$ and $\alpha_2^*$. The new model implies a constant elasticity of imports with respect to domestic price which can be estimated directly by $a_2$*. This result can be shown by differentiating both sides of the equation with respect to domestic price.

$$\frac{d(\ln \text{Im})}{dP_d} = \frac{d(\ln a_1{}^*)}{dP_d} + \frac{d[a_2{}^*(\ln P_d)]}{dP_d},$$

$$\frac{1}{\text{Im}} \frac{d(\text{Im})}{dP_d} = 0 + a_2{}^* \frac{1}{P_d}.$$

Solving for $a_2$*, we obtain

$$a_2{}^* = \frac{P_d}{\text{Im}} \frac{d(\text{Im})}{d(P_d)} = \text{price elasticity of textile imports.}$$

### Estimation and interpretation

The same formulas for the least squares estimates apply. Only the values used are changed. For this model, the data are coded into natural logarithms of the original data. The raw moments, means, variations, and covariations can then be determined in the same way as before.

The least squares estimates are given by the solution to the same normal equations, (3–1), except the variables $Y$ and $X_2$ have been transformed in the present case to $Y^* = \ln Y$ and $X_2{}^* = \ln X_2$. The results are:

$$\hat{Y}_t{}^* = -0.875 + 1.297 X_{t2}{}^*. \quad \text{(See Exercise 8.)}$$

The estimate of the constant price elasticity of imports is 1.297. In this example, the determination of an elasticity is the same by either method, direct estimation in a log-linear model, or calculation at the point of means in the original simple model. Usually a somewhat different result is obtained between the two different models. The proper choice of model is a theoretical issue in economics (see Section 2.6), not of statistics.

A more realistic model of the import price relation and the associated elasticities would include more variables. For example, the single equation model may be a logarithmic transformation of a relation determining imports in terms of the additional variables, exports, foreign price, and tariffs. Both price elasticity and tariff elasticity may be estimated.[1]

The original model used in this chapter will be extended later for a presentation of the methods of least squares estimation in a multiple regression.

### 3.8  A FINAL NOTE OF CAUTION

Remember these values of the estimates are calculated from a sample of all observations that might have been collected; and, furthermore, the events observed are only a sample of the events which might have occurred under the

---

[1] Lawrence B. Krause, "United States Imports, 1947–1958," *Econometrica*, Vol. 30 (1962), pp. 221–38.

same set of basic economic laws, or under the same well-ordered economic mechanism. Since it is only a sample and might have been affected by various other economic or noneconomic events, the sample and the estimates based on it might not be typical. Moreover, econometricians are not yet sure that there is a well-ordered economic mechanism out of which segments and individual relations can be meaningfully extracted.

Therefore, it is important to always remember that the estimates cannot be interpreted as exact values but rather more cautiously as guesses. The degree of their inexactness needs to be measured. The specified econometric model is not judged good or bad, right or wrong, based on a single fit of eight observations. Rather, each estimation of a model might be considered as an observation of attempts to represent a part of the economic system quantitatively. The value of the model must be judged in terms of its individual success in its contribution as an observation benefiting the collective efforts of econometricians to better portray and understand the operations of the economy and the underlying economic theory.

## NEW VOCABULARY

| | |
|---|---|
| Bivariate linear model | Covariation |
| Scattergram | Variation |
| Method of least squares | Coded data |
| Residuals | Deviations |
| Estimator | Random variable |
| Slope | Elasticity |

## SUMMARY OF LEAST SQUARES METHOD

| *General situation* | *Specific case* (*for simple model*) |
|---|---|
| 1. Find expressions for a residual, $$e_t = Y_t - \hat{Y}_t.$$ | $e_t = Y_t - a_1 - a_2 X_{t2}.$ |
| 2. Find function for sum of squares of residuals, $SS(e) = \sum e^2$. | $\sum e_t{}^2 = \sum (Y_t - a_1 - a_2 X_{t2})^2.$ |
| 3. Minimize $SS(e)$ with respect to the unknown parameters by setting partial derivatives equal to zero. Solve for the parameters. | Find $\dfrac{(\sum e_t{}^2)}{\partial a_1}$ and $\dfrac{(\sum e_t{}^2)}{\partial a_2}$, set equal to zero, and solve for $a_1$ and $a_2$. |
| 4. Simplify to obtain operational formulas for the estimators based on sample observations of the endogenous and exogenous variables. | $a_1 = \bar{Y} - a_2 \bar{X}_2,$ $a_2 = \dfrac{\sum xy}{\sum x^2}.$ |
| 5. Write the estimating equation. | $\hat{Y}_t = a_1 + a_2 X_{t2}.$ |

## EXERCISES

1.  Draw the scatter diagram for the coded data of Table 3–2 and include the estimating relation (3–4). Illustrate the residual for the fifth observation when $X_{52} = 104$.

2.  Use the data in *Review* Exercise 8, Section 3.2, to find the least squares estimating line for consumption on the exogenous variable, disposable income. Interpret the meaning of your estimate for the slope, $a_2$. Finally, compare the values of your estimates to the answers in *Review* Exercise 9, Section 3.2. (*Hint*: Compare the equation system in Exercise 9 to the normal equations (3–1), using the data from *Review* Exercise 8).

3.  Consider a model $Y_t = \alpha_1 + \alpha_2 X_{t2} + \varepsilon_t$ where $Y_t = $ long-term AAA corporate bond yield, $X_{t2} = $ (income velocity) $= \ln[\text{GNP}/(\text{money supply})]$. Using quarterly data from first quarter 1961 to third quarter 1967, we obtain:

$$T = 26 \qquad \sum Y = 118.27 \qquad \sum Y^2 = 541.77$$
$$\sum XY = 477.05 \qquad \sum X = 104.42 \qquad \sum X^2 = 420.72$$

   *a)* Find the least squares estimators for $\alpha_1$ and $\alpha_2$ based on these data. Interpret the meaning of your estimated model by considering the effect on the interest rate of a 0.2 unit decrease in income velocity due to an increased desire by people to hold cash. [Refer to H. Latane, "Income Velocity and Interest Rates, a Pragmatic Approach," *Review of Economics and Statistics*, Vol. 42 (November 1960).]

   *b)* If income velocity were 4.0, find the estimated value for $Y$. If the true interest rate at this level of income velocity were 4.29 percent, determine the residual $e$.

4.  Examine the relation between imports and national income for the U.S. experience during the peacetime period, 1955–65 using the data in the table below:

| Year | U.S. imports Y (billion dollars) | U.S. national income $X_2$ (billion dollars) |
|---|---|---|
| 1955 | 11.6 | 331 |
| 1956 | 12.9 | 351 |
| 1957 | 13.4 | 366 |
| 1958 | 13.4 | 368 |
| 1959 | 15.7 | 400 |
| 1960 | 15.1 | 414 |
| 1961 | 14.8 | 427 |
| 1962 | 16.5 | 458 |
| 1963 | 17.2 | 482 |
| 1964 | 18.8 | 517 |
| 1965 | 21.4 | 559 |

Source: *International Financial Statistics, Supplement,* 1966–67, pp. 272–74.

   *a)* By the least squares method estimate the model $Y_t = \alpha_1 + \alpha_2 X_{t2} + \varepsilon_t$.

*b)* Determine the value at the point of sample means for the income elasticity of U.S. imports.

5. The relation between consumption and national income in Thailand is represented in the model $C_t = \alpha_1 + \alpha_2(NI)_t = \varepsilon_t$. Based on the following sample data where $Y_t$ measures $C_t$ and $X_{t2}$ measures $(NI)_t$, find the least squares estimate for the marginal propensity to consume.

| Year | X (billion baht) | Y (billion baht) |
|------|------------------|------------------|
| 1957 | 45.2 | 34.9 |
| 1958 | 47.0 | 35.9 |
| 1959 | 50.3 | 37.9 |
| 1960 | 55.7 | 41.1 |
| 1961 | 59.9 | 43.5 |
| 1962 | 65.2 | 46.7 |
| 1963 | 68.9 | 48.9 |
| 1964 | 74.3 | 52.0 |
| 1965 | 81.2 | 56.1 |
| 1966 | 92.2 | 62.6 |

Discuss some problems in estimating this type consumption function. (See E. Malinvaud, *Statistical Methods of Econometrics* (Amsterdam: North Holland Pub. Co., 1970) chap. 4.)

6. Find $a$, the least squares estimator for $\alpha$, in the function $Y = \alpha X^3$ based on $T$ sample observations of $Y$ and $X$. Ans.: $a = \left( \sum X^3 Y / \sum X^6 \right)$.

7. Find the normal equations for determining the least squares estimators for $\alpha$ and $\beta$ in the relation $Y = 5\alpha X^2 + \frac{1}{3}\beta X$ based on $T$ sample observations of $Y$ and $X$.

8. Using a log-linear revision of the example model as discussed in Section 3.7 and using the natural logarithms of the data given in Table 3–2, one obtains:

| Variable | Mean | Variance | $\sum xy$ |
|----------|------|----------|-----------|
| $Y^* = \ln$ imports | 2.16 | 0.01150 | 0.0547 |
| $X^* = \ln$ prices | 2.34 | 0.006024 | |

Find the least squares estimators for $\alpha_1^*$ and $\alpha_2^*$ as given in Section 3.7.

9. A preliminary examination of the accelerator principle may be obtained by considering the model, $Y_t = \alpha_1 + \alpha_2 X_{t2} + \varepsilon_t$ where

$Y_t =$ annual capital expenditures,
$X_{t2} =$ ratio of current annual sales to previous year sales.

*a)* Explain how this relation might measure the accelerator effect and posit an acceptable range of values for $\alpha_2$ if one assumes a nonexplosive system. Also, suggest the inadequacy of this single equation as a representation of the relation between changes in income and changes in investment.

*b*)  Given the following data for a composite of 425 industrial corporations
from 73 separate industries:

| Year | $Y_t$ | $X_{t2}$ |
|------|------|----------|
| 1956. . . . . . . . . .4.14 | | 101.09 |
| 1957. . . . . . . . . .4.84 | | 101.97 |
| 1958. . . . . . . . . .3.58 | | 95.83 |
| 1959. . . . . . . . . .3.65 | | 108.13 |
| 1960. . . . . . . . . .4.23 | | 102.84 |
| 1961. . . . . . . . . .3.97 | | 100.07 |
| 1962. . . . . . . . . .4.41 | | 108.60 |
| 1963. . . . . . . . . .4.41 | | 105.99 |
| 1964. . . . . . . . . .5.71 | | 106.85 |
| 1965. . . . . . . . . .6.87 | | 110.25 |

Source: *Analysts Handbook* (New York:
Standard & Poors' Corporation).

Find estimates of $\alpha_1$ and $\alpha_2$ and give your best point forecast for $Y_t$ if
$X_{t2} = 104$. Explain if the value of $a_2$ seems acceptable to the theory of the
nonexplosive accelerator effect.

10.  Given the following data on annual disposable personal income and personal
consumption in the United States for years 1933 to 1943, find the linear regression of consumption $Y$ on disposable income $X_2$, by the method of least
squares. Interpret the meaning of your results. Then, using your estimated
relation, forecast the level of consumption in 1944 if disposable income is
$\$147 \times 10^9$. (The actual level of consumption for 1944 is $\$112 \times 10^9$.) Discuss
some problems in trying to make this type of forecast.

| ($ billion) $Y$ | 46 | 52 | 56 | 63 | 67 | 65 | 67 | 72 | 82 | 91 | 102 |
|-----------------|----|----|----|----|----|----|----|----|----|----|-----|
| ($ billion) $X_2$ | 45 | 52 | 58 | 66 | 71 | 66 | 70 | 76 | 92 | 117 | 132 |

11.  Given the following data for the decade 1951–60 in the United States where
$Y$ = beef consumption per capita, and $X$ = disposable personal income per
capita (DPI):

| Year | $X$ | $Y$ | Year | $Y$ | $X$ |
|------|-----|-----|------|-----|-----|
| 1951. . . . . .56.1 | | 1501 | 1956. . . . . .85.4 | | 1763 |
| 1952. . . . . .62.2 | | 1551 | 1957. . . . . .84.6 | | 1826 |
| 1953. . . . . .77.6 | | 1612 | 1958. . . . . .80.5 | | 1845 |
| 1954. . . . . .80.1 | | 1609 | 1959. . . . . .81.6 | | 1924 |
| 1955. . . . . .82.0 | | 1683 | 1960. . . . . .85.8 | | 1925 |

Source: *Statistical Abstract of the U.S.*, Agricultural Statistics.

a) Use a simple regression model to determine the amount of each extra dollar of $X$ which is spent on extra beef consumption.

b) Discuss why the variables (consumption/population) and (DPI/population) are used in the specification for the linear econometric model rather than simply the variables, consumption and DPI.

c) If $Y$ is considered to be the quantity of beef demanded, what is an estimate of the income elasticity of demand for beef based on these data?

12. An alternate specification for the accelerator analysis in Problem 9 above might express net investment as a linear function of the change in aggregate demand. Suppose we let $Y_t =$ net investment and $X_{t2} = NNP_t - NNP_{t-1}$.

| Year | Y | X | Year | Y | X |
|---|---|---|---|---|---|
| 1956......47.0 | | 45.9 | 1961......31.4 | | 18.0 |
| 1957......37.0 | | 37.8 | 1962......33.9 | | 33.9 |
| 1958......34.5 | | 27.5 | 1963......22.0 | | 4.4 |
| 1959......33.0 | | 35.5 | 1964......30.8 | | 18.8 |
| 1960......26.5 | | 14.6 | 1965......35.9 | | 18.7 |

Source: *Economic Report of the President*, 1966.

a) Find the least squares estimation $\hat{Y}_t = a_1 + a_2 X_{t2}$ and compare the interpretation and results with that of Problem 9.

b) In 1966, $X_0 = 54.8$ and $Y_0 = 53.9$. What is the estimated value of $Y$ in 1966 given $X_0 = 54.8$ and your estimating relation from part (a)? How large is the residual relative to the mean of $Y$? Would you consider this an accurate forecast? How could it be improved?

13. During the decade, 1951–60, there was some concern about the drain of productive resources and profits from Canada due to the operation of United States firms in Canada. An examination might be made to see if the earnings of such firms can be explained in a significant way on the basis of imports from Canada into the United States. As a first step, we wish to estimate the model

$$Y_t = \alpha_1 + \alpha_2 X_{t2} + \varepsilon_t$$

where

$Y_t =$ net income earned from direct foreign investment in Canada by U.S. firms ($\$10^7$), and

$X_{t2} =$ imports from Canada into the United States ($\$10^8$).

Find the least squares estimates and interpret their meaning based on the following data:

| Year | Y | $X_2$ | Year | Y | X |
|------|-----|-----|------|-----|-----|
| 1951......24 | | 28 | 1956......33 | | 38 |
| 1952......22 | | 30 | 1957......34 | | 39 |
| 1953......21 | | 32 | 1958......34 | | 38 |
| 1954......24 | | 31 | 1959......35 | | 41 |
| 1955......29 | | 37 | 1960......36 | | 40 |

Source: *The U.S. Balance of Payments* (International Economic Policy Association, 1966), Appendix E.

14. U.S. imports of goods and services nearly tripled in the decade after World War II. One obvious related factor is the increase in U.S. total product during these years as measured by the GNP.

a) Find the least squares estimation of the model $Y_t = \alpha_1 + \alpha_2 X_{t2} + \varepsilon_t$ using the data below.

b) Discuss what other measure than GNP might be better to use as an income proxy in this relation.

| Year | Imports ($ billion) | GNP ($ billion) | Year | Imports ($ billion) | GNP ($ billion) |
|------|-----|-----|------|-----|-----|
| 1946...... 7.2 | | 211 | 1952......15.8 | | 346 |
| 1947...... 8.2 | | 234 | 1953......16.6 | | 365 |
| 1948......10.3 | | 259 | 1954......16.1 | | 363 |
| 1949...... 9.7 | | 258 | 1955......17.9 | | 397 |
| 1950......12.1 | | 285 | 1956......19.8 | | 419 |
| 1951......15.1 | | 329 | 1957......20.7 | | 440 |

Source: *U.S. Income and Output*, 1958.

c) Discuss what additional variables might be used as explanatory variables in this relation.

15. A first formulation to examine the marginal profit rate in U.S. manufacturing industries might be $Y_t = \alpha_1 + \alpha_2 X_{t2} + \varepsilon_t$ where $Y_t$ = annual corporate profits (before taxes) for SIC groups 19–39 inclusive, and $X_{t2}$ = average monthly wholesale sales. The data is given below:

| Year | Y ($ billion) | X ($ billion) | Year | Y ($ billion) | X ($ billion) |
|------|-----|-----|------|-----|-----|
| 1948 ...... 16.8 | | 6.81 | 1956 ...... 23.5 | | 10.51 |
| 1949 ...... 15.3 | | 6.51 | 1957 ...... 22.9 | | 10.48 |
| 1950 ...... 20.4 | | 7.70 | 1958 ...... 18.3 | | 10.26 |
| 1951 ...... 24.4 | | 8.60 | 1959 ...... 25.4 | | 11.41 |
| 1952 ...... 21.1 | | 8.78 | 1960 ...... 23.0 | | 11.44 |
| 1953 ...... 21.4 | | 9.05 | 1961 ...... 21.7 | | 11.63 |
| 1954 ...... 18.4 | | 8.99 | 1962 ...... 24.7 | | 12.16 |
| 1955 ...... 25.0 | | 9.89 | 1963 ...... 26.7 | | 12.69 |

Source: *Supplement to Economic Indicators*, 1964, pp. 22, 73.

Since $Y$ is in annual terms and $X$ is in monthly terms, two approaches are possible.

a) Multiply each monthly rate of sales by 12 to get an average annual rate series for $X$. Then estimate the parameters using ordinary least squares.

b) Estimate the model using the given data and then scale the coefficient $a_2$ to an annual rate by multiplying by $1/12$. Use these methods to estimate the additional amount of annual profits related to an additional dollar of annual sales. Explain any discrepancy between the results of the two methods.

16. A significant change occurred in U.S. federal government expenditures on defense in the period 1940–48. Use the data below for $Y_t = $ GNP, and $X_{t2} = $ expenditures on national defense, both in billions of dollars.

| Year | 1940 | 1941 | 1942 | 1943 | 1944 | 1945 | 1946 | 1947 | 1948 |
|------|------|------|------|------|------|------|------|------|------|
| $Y_t$ | 99.7 | 124.5 | 157.9 | 191.6 | 210.1 | 211.9 | 208.5 | 231.3 | 257.6 |
| $X_{t2}$ | 1.5 | 6.1 | 24.0 | 63.2 | 76.8 | 81.3 | 43.2 | 14.4 | 11.8 |

a) Estimate the relation $Y_t = \alpha_1 + \alpha_2 X_{t2} + \varepsilon_t$ by the least squares method.

b) Interpret the meaning of the estimate of $\alpha_2$.

c) Determine the residuals for these eight observations.

d) By examining these results, discuss the adequacy of this linear least squares representation when enormous structural changes take place. Suggest a better specification of the relation between GNP and defense expenditures for the period 1940–48.

17. The following data measures $Y_t = $ current corporate investment, and $X_{t2} = $ retained earnings in the previous year. Formulate a model relating these two variables. Estimate and interpret the meaning of your specification and your results.

| $Y_t$ | $X_{t2}$ | $Y_t$ | $X_{t2}$ |
|-------|----------|-------|----------|
| 37.0 | 16.0 | 37.3 | 13.5 |
| 30.5 | 14.2 | 39.2 | 16.0 |
| 32.5 | 10.8 | 44.9 | 16.6 |
| 35.7 | 16.0 | 52.0 | 20.6 |
| 34.4 | 13.2 | 60.6 | 25.4 |

18. Suppose two labor groups are identified by their different education level attained and the number in each group is denoted by $L_1$ and $L_2$. The average wage levels of these labor groups are denoted by $W_1$ and $W_2$. Given data on these variables for $T$ regions, interpret the meaning of the parameters in a model,

$$\ln\left(\frac{W_1}{W_2}\right)_t = \alpha_1 + \alpha_2 \ln\left(\frac{L_1}{L_2}\right)_t + \varepsilon_t \quad \text{for} \quad t = 1, 2, \ldots, T.$$

(See S. Bowles, *Journal of Political Economy*, January–February 1970, pp. 68–76.)

Chapter
4

# MEASURES OF GOODNESS
# OF FIT

## 4.1 PREVIEW

The method of least squares gives us the "best" estimates according to its criterion of minimizing the sum of squared residuals. However, the "best" estimating equation may still not be very "good."

The situation is analogous to a mile race with many contestants. According to one criterion, the runner who finishes first is the "best." However, if his winning time is six minutes flat, this "best" miler is surely not classified as very "good."

Just as the group of contestants may all be slow or poorly conditioned, the econometricians bivariate model may be erroneous or poorly specified. Then, even the "best" estimates may not provide a "good" representation of the observed economic mechanism.

Since the major purpose of an econometrician's work is the discovery of quantitative expressions of the economic system that are suitable for testing theoretical propositions or for forecasting future economic conditions, it is important that the models used be "good." Thus, some other measures, comparable to the stopwatch which measures the performance of the runners, are needed to measure the "goodness of fit" of the least squares "best" estimates. Two types of measures are common: absolute and relative measures.

In the econometric model, it is the variation of the endogenous (dependent) variable which is being explained in terms of the variations in the exogenous (independent) variables. The important question of goodness of fit is concerned with the extent to which this variation in the endogenous variable is explained.

The absolute measure of goodness of fit, named the standard error of estimate, gives a measure of the typical size of the residuals from the estimation. It is measured in the same units as the endogenous variable. It is analogous to the stopwatch. When this measure is large, the performance of the estimation is poor; and vice versa, when this measure is small, it means the residuals are typically small so the estimated values correspond closely to the actual observations.

The relative measures of fit would be more analogous to a percentile ranking of these milers among all runners at any time and any place. The measures would range between 0 and 100 percentile. Not much consideration is given to any runner below 50 percentile, and the television sports announcer probably would not get interested in any competitor below 90 percentile, but would get very excited about someone ranked 99 percentile. Similarly, the relative measures named correlation coefficient and coefficient of determination are "like" percentile measures of goodness of fit. They provide information on the amount of variation in the endogenous variable which has been explained by the regression.

## 4.2 REVIEW

In studying econometrics it is necessary to continually refresh your knowledge of statistics. To build up confidence, this chapter includes few new terms, but one might profit from a review of the following topics.

### 1 Variance

Variance is a measure of dispersion, usually indicated by $V$(random variable). It is sort of the average variation. That is, for $T$ observations of a random variable $X$, the

$$V(X) = \frac{(\text{variation of } X)}{T-1} = \frac{\sum x^2}{T-1} = s_X^2,$$

the sample variance. This is used as an estimator of the variance of the entire population, $\sigma_X^2$.

### 2 Standard deviation

Another measure of dispersion of the distribution of a random variable is the standard deviation. For a sample, this standard deviation is denoted by $s_{(\text{random variable})}$; but for a population, the lower case sigma is used,

$\sigma_{\text{(random variable)}}$. Remember, the deviations are squared in computing both the variation and the variance. To obtain a standard measure of the deviations, the square root of the variance is used. That is,

$$s_X = \sqrt{\frac{\text{variation of } X}{T - 1}}$$

for $T$ sample observations of $X$ or $s_X = \sqrt{V(X)}$.

## 3 Degrees of freedom

In calculating sample statistics and in analyzing properties of their probability distributions, it is often important not to bias the answer. Statisticians have found that by correcting such calculations or analyses for degrees of freedom, the problem of bias is largely avoided. The number of degrees of freedom (d.f.) refers to the number of free or linearly independent sample observations used in the calculation of a sum of squares.

For example, consider eight observations, $X_1, X_2, \ldots, X_8$, of a random variable $X$. The sample mean is calculated on the basis of all eight observations. We calculate $\bar{X} = \sum X_t/T$.

Next the variance of $X$ is

$$V(X) = \frac{\sum (X_t - \bar{X})^2}{\text{d.f.}}.$$

In this calculation all eight observations and the sample mean are used. But if seven observations and the mean were known, then the eighth observation is determined. The eighth observation is not linearly independent of the other seven and the mean. The degrees of freedom are $T - 1$, or $8 - 1 = 7$.

Also, in calculating a residual, $e_t = Y_t - a_1 - a_2 X_{t2}$ from a regression equation, using eight observations, two linear restrictions on the observations are imposed in the solution for the estimates $a_1$ and $a_2$. Thus, the number of degrees of freedom remaining in the calculation of $\sum e_t^2$, is only $T - 2 = 6$.

## 4 Standardized variable

When the deviation of a variable from its mean is divided by the standard deviation of the variable, the transformed variable is standardized. In general,

$$\text{standardized variable} = \frac{\text{random variable} - \text{its mean}}{\text{its standard deviation}}$$

## 4.3 RELATIVE MEASURES OF GOODNESS OF FIT

The total variation of the endogenous variable, $\sum y_t^2 = \sum (Y_t - \bar{Y})^2$ can be split into two components—the variation in $Y$ that is explained by its specified relation to the variable $X$, and the variation remaining unexplained. This identity can be denoted,

$$\sum y_t^2 = \sum \hat{y}_t^2 + \sum e_t^2 \qquad (4\text{-}1)$$

where $\sum \hat{y}_t^2 = \sum (\hat{Y}_t - \overline{Y})^2$ and $\sum e_t^2 = \sum (Y_t - \hat{Y}_t)^2$ are the explained and unexplained portions of the total variation respectively.

## Coefficient of determination

The ratio $\sum \hat{y}_t^2 / \sum y_t^2$ is denoted by $r^2$ and called the coefficient of determination. It measures the proportion of the total variation that has been explained. In a perfect fitting relation, this proportion would be unity. Its lowest possible value would be zero if no variation in $Y$ were explained.

## Adjusted $r^2$

The coefficient of determination calculated by this ratio is biased too high. It should be corrected for this bias by adjusting for degrees of freedom. Otherwise, one could obtain a very misleading measure of goodness of fit when the number of observations is small.

The formula for $r^2$ can be written, $r^2 = 1 - \dfrac{\sum e_t^2}{\sum y_t^2}$ using the substitution

$$\sum \hat{y}^2 = \sum y^2 - \sum e^2. \qquad (4\text{-}1)$$

If both these sums of squares are divided by their respective degrees of freedom, then the adjusted $r^2$ is obtained.

$$r^2_{\text{adj.}} = 1 - \frac{\sum e^2/(T-2)}{\sum y^2/(T-1)} = 1 - \frac{s_e^2}{s_y^2}.$$

or since

$$\frac{\sum e^2}{\sum y^2} = 1 - r^2,$$

we can simplify the fraction term and write

$$r^2_{\text{adj.}} = 1 - (1 - r^2)\left(\frac{T-1}{T-2}\right). \qquad (4\text{-}2)$$

## Correlation coefficient

The square root of this ratio, denoted $r$, is the correlation coefficient. It has a range from $-1.0$ to $+1.0$ indicating perfect negative or perfect positive correlation, respectively. Values near zero indicate a very low level of association. The correlation coefficient can be calculated by many alternate and equivalent formulas, such as,

$$r = \frac{\sum xy}{\sqrt{\sum x^2 \sum y^2}} = \sqrt{r^2} = \sqrt{1 - \frac{\sum e^2}{\sum y^2}} = \sqrt{\frac{a_2^2 \sum x^2}{\sum y^2}} = \frac{a_2 s_x}{s_y}, \quad (4\text{-}3)$$

where $a_2$ is the least squares estimate, and $s_x$ and $s_y$ are the standard deviations of the variables $X$ and $Y$ respectively. All these forms are commonly used and can be obtained from each other by simple substitutions.

The first form can be interpreted as the ratio of covariation to the geometric mean of the variations of the individual variables. Thus, it is a standardized measure of the degree of association between the two variables.[1] That is, $r$ can be considered as the covariance between the two standardized variables, $x/s_x$ and $y/s_y$.

|||||||||||||||||||||||||||||||||||||||||||||||||||||||||||||||||||||||||||||||||||||||||||||||||||||||||||||||||||||||

*Explicative note.* The correlation coefficient is not affected by changes of scale in the data or by changes in the number of observations except to the extent that the different observations sets do, in fact, reflect different levels of association. For these reasons, it is better than the simple covariation as a measure of association between two variables.

|||||||||||||||||||||||||||||||||||||||||||||||||||||||||||||||||||||||||||||||||||||||||||||||||||||||||||||||||||||||

|||||||||||||||||||||||||||||||||||||||||||||||||||||||||||||||||||||||||||||||||||||||||||||||||||||||||||||||||||||||

*Interpretive note.* Comparisons of $r^2$ between models to determine which best fits the data are not useful if the models have different dependent variables, such as $Y$ and $\ln Y$. Also, a high level of $r^2$ does not imply causation in the model as it may just result from spurious correlation, such as if both $Y$ and $X$ have strong trend components. The theoretical role of the variables determines the direction of causality and should suggest removal of trends or seasonal variations when appropriate for the purpose of the analysis.

|||||||||||||||||||||||||||||||||||||||||||||||||||||||||||||||||||||||||||||||||||||||||||||||||||||||||||||||||||||||

## 4.4 AN ABSOLUTE MEASURE OF THE GOODNESS OF FIT

If the variations of equation (4–1) are divided by their degrees of freedom, then estimates of variance are obtained. (See *Review* 4.2, item 3.) They are absolute measures of the dispersion of the actual values, estimated values, and residuals respectively. They are used in statistics to make judgments on the reliability of the estimated equation.

---

[1] $r =$

$$\frac{\sum xy}{\sqrt{\sum x^2 \sum y^2}} = \frac{\sum xy}{(T-1)\sqrt{\dfrac{\sum x^2}{T-1} \dfrac{\sum y^2}{T-1}}} = \frac{\sum xy}{(T-1)s_x s_y} = \frac{\sum\left[\left(\dfrac{x}{s_x}\right)\left(\dfrac{y}{s_y}\right)\right]}{T-1} = Cov\left(\frac{x}{s_x} \frac{y}{s_y}\right).$$

In particular, the square root of the variance of the residuals is denoted

$$s_e = \sqrt{V(e)} = \sqrt{\frac{\sum e_t^2}{T-2}},$$

and is named the standard error of estimate of the equation. This is an absolute measure, in the same units as the endogenous variable $Y_t$, of the standard deviation of the distribution of residuals. This is, if all the residuals for $T$ observations are found and their standard deviation is calculated, $s_e$ gives a standard measure of the typical size of the error between the estimated and the observed values of the endogenous variable.

This standard error of estimate is important to the econometrician because it is used to determine the expected accuracy of forecasts or to make tests of hypothesis on the expected levels of the estimates, $a_1$ and $a_2$ (as in Chapter 7).

## 4.5 CALCULATION OF THE MEASURES OF GOODNESS OF FIT

Using the information from the example regression of Chapter 3, results (3–4) and (3–5), the measures of goodness of fit can be calculated. It is convenient to use the following sequence of formulas.

*a)*    Find the explained variation,[2]

$$\sum \hat{y}_t^2 = a_2 \sum x_{t2} y_t. \tag{4-4}$$

*b)*    Find the unexplained variation,

$$\sum e_t^2 = \sum y_t^2 - \sum \hat{y}_t^2. \tag{4-1}$$

*c)*    Calculate $r^2$ or $r$, and $s_e$.

$$\sum \hat{y}_t^2 = (1.0814)(5.2219) = 5.6470,$$

$$\sum e_t^2 = 6.3409 - 5.6470 = 0.694,$$

$$r^2 = \frac{\sum \hat{y}_t^2}{\sum y_t^2} = \frac{5.6470}{6.3409} = 0.8906, \qquad \text{(definition)}$$

$$r = \sqrt{0.891} \quad \text{or} \quad r = \frac{\sum x_{t2} y_t}{\sqrt{\sum x_{t2}^2 \sum y_t^2}} = 0.944, \qquad (4\text{-}3)$$

$$r^2_{\text{adj}} = 1 - (1 - 0.8906)\left(\frac{7}{6}\right) = 0.873, \qquad (4\text{-}2)$$

$$s_e = \sqrt{\frac{\sum e_t^2}{T-2}} = 0.340. \qquad \text{(definition)}$$

---

[2] $\dfrac{\sum \hat{y}^2}{\sum y^2} = r^2$ by definition, so

$$\sum \hat{y}^2 = (r^2) \sum y^2 = \left[\frac{(\sum xy)^2}{\sum x^2 \sum y^2}\right] \sum y^2,$$

$$\sum \hat{y}^2 = \left(\frac{\sum xy}{\sum x^2}\right) \sum xy = (a_2) \sum xy.$$

---

**Discursive note.** Both the relative and absolute measures of goodness of fit derive from the fundamental relation that total variation equals explained variation plus unexplained variation. Thus, it is possible to convert easily from the absolute to relative measures or vice versa. The proportion of variation explained is $r^2$; the proportion unexplained is then $(1 - r^2)$. Thus, $(1 - r^2) \sum y^2$ is the amount of variation in $Y$ left unexplained in the simple regression model. By definition, the unexplained variation is the quantity to be minimized by least squares and is represented by the sum of squares of residuals, $\sum e^2$, which is the numerator of the radical in determining $s_e$.

---

The standard error of estimate could also be determined from the relation between the absolute and relative measures of fit,

$$s_e = \sqrt{\frac{(1 - r^2) \sum y^2}{T - 2}} = \sqrt{\frac{0.1094 \times 6.3409}{6}} = 0.340.$$

## 4.6 INTERPRETATION OF THE RESULTS OF THE EXAMPLE

The bivariate model, $(\text{imports})_t = a_1 + a_2 (\text{domestic prices})_t + \varepsilon_t$ has been used to partially explain the fluctuations or changes in imports. In terms of our sample of eight observations, we find that 89.1 percent of these changes can be explained. There remains 10.9 percent of the variation in imports which is still unexplained.

Actually, some other variables also affect imports regularly and some disturbances may affect imports in an irregular manner. These other factors would account for the unexplained 10.9 percent if they could be identified and systematically included in the model.

---

**Discursive note.** It is also true that some of these other variables may be interrelated to both imports and to domestic prices. Thus, some of their effect is probably already included in the 89.1 percent that is explained. It is not unusual when these other variables are included in the model for the total percentage of explained variation to increase while the separate percentage of variation explained by previously included variables decreases.

---

Since the included exogenous variable may be a proxy for combined effects of this variable and other excluded exogenous variables, the econometrician must be careful not to interpret the 89.1 percent strictly as the single effect of one isolated variable. Also, the values of $r^2$ or the degree of correlation ($r = 0.944$ out of a possible perfect correlation of 1.00) must not be interpreted as a conclusion of cause and effect between domestic prices and imports. These are merely indexes of association. Any causal explanation is a theoretical implication from the specification of the model, not from these statistical measures.

The standard error of estimate for this estimated linear equation is 0.340 units in the same dimensions as $Y$. It is a typical size of error for the *coded* data estimation. If we desire the standard error of estimate for the equation in terms of original data, then $s_e$ must be decoded in the same way as $Y_t$ or $a_1$. In this case it must be multiplied by the factor $10^2$.

||||||||||||||||||||||||||||||||||||||||||||||||||||||||||||||||||||||||||||||||||||||||||||||||||||||||||||||||||||||||||||||||||||||||

*Interpretive note.*   The standard error of estimate for the original data is $s_e = 34.0$. Be careful, however, not to interpret this as an average residual for the estimation.

||||||||||||||||||||||||||||||||||||||||||||||||||||||||||||||||||||||||||||||||||||||||||||||||||||||||||||||||||||||||||||||||||||||||

The average residual, $\sum e_t/T$, will always be zero as the estimates are sometimes high, sometimes low, but on the average are in balance for the $T$ observations. $s_e$ is a measure of dispersion among all the residuals from their average of zero. All residuals of absolute value less than 34.0 are within one standard deviation measured from the average residual of zero; they are associated with corresponding observations of imports that are within one standard error of estimate measured vertically from the estimating line. Residuals larger than 34.0 are outside these same bounds.

||||||||||||||||||||||||||||||||||||||||||||||||||||||||||||||||||||||||||||||||||||||||||||||||||||||||||||||||||||||||||||||||||||||||

*Discursive note.*   The crucial question concerning the size of the residuals is *how many* of the residuals will be smaller and how many larger than 34.0, and *how much* smaller or larger is any particular residual likely to be. These are probabilistic questions about the distribution of the residuals: similar questions are to be raised about the probability distribution of the least squares estimators also.

||||||||||||||||||||||||||||||||||||||||||||||||||||||||||||||||||||||||||||||||||||||||||||||||||||||||||||||||||||||||||||||||||||||||

Do not forget that all these measures—$a_1$, $a_2$, $s_e$, $r$—are based on sample observations. They are sample statistics and are subject to sampling error. They are only guesses, respectively, of the true regression parameters, $\alpha_1$, and $\alpha_2$, of the true standard error of the equation, $\sigma_\varepsilon$, and of the true correlation coefficient $\rho$ for the entire population of all levels of imports and domestics prices which might have occurred. To continue the analysis and testing of the model, the econometrician must study the probability distributions of these sample statistics. This study is delayed until Chapter 6, however, because these distributions depend on the properties and distribution of $\varepsilon_t$, the disturbance term, also called the random, stochastic, or unknown term in the econometric model, which must be studied first.

## NEW VOCABULARY

| | |
|---|---|
| Unexplained variation | Standard error of estimate |
| Degrees of freedom | Coefficient of determination |

## SUMMARY OUTLINE

I.  Theoretical measures of goodness of fit
    A.  Relative measures
        1.  Correlation coefficient $r$
        2.  Coefficient of determination
            *a)*  $r^2$ and adjusted $r^2$
            *b)*  Proportion of variation in $Y$ explained by the linear relation of $Y$ with $X_2$
    B.  Absolute measure: Standard error of estimate
        1.  Standard deviation of the distribution of residuals, $s_e$
        2.  Used in tests of hypothesis on the parameters and in forecast intervals
II. Calculation formulas for the measures of goodness of fit

    A.  $r = \dfrac{\sum xy}{\sqrt{\sum x^2 \sum y^2}}.$

    B.  $r^2 = \dfrac{a_2 \sum xy}{\sum y^2}.$      $r^2_{\text{adj.}} = 1 - (1 - r^2)\left(\dfrac{T-1}{T-2}\right).$

    C.  $s_e = \sqrt{\dfrac{\sum e^2}{T-2}}$   where  $\sum e^2 = \sum y^2 - a_2 \sum xy.$

## EXERCISES

1.  Show all the steps in establishing the equivalence of

$$r = \frac{\sum xy}{\sqrt{\sum x^2 \sum y^2}} = \frac{a_2 s_x}{s_y}.$$

2.  Using the data from Problems 3, 4, and 5 in the exercises at the end of Chapter 3, find and interpret the meaning of $r$, $r^2$, and $s_e$.

3.  Given an estimating equation between variables $Y$ and $X$ based on 18 observations in which $\sum y^2 = 100$, $\sum x^2 = 40$, $\sum \hat{y}^2 = 80$. Find $s_e$, and find the slope of the estimating equation, $a_2$.

4.  It has often been stated that most short-term interest rates in the United States move together. Determine the value of the correlation coefficient between the two rates, $Y = $ stock exchange time loan rate and $X = $ prime commercial paper rate for each of the two periods 1911–17 and 1951–57. Compare and interpret the meaning of your answers.

| Year | Y | X | Year | Y | X |
|------|------|------|------|------|------|
| 1911......3.22 | | 4.75 | 1951......2.15 | | 2.16 |
| 1912......4.16 | | 5.41 | 1952......2.42 | | 2.33 |
| 1913......4.64 | | 6.20 | 1953......2.85 | | 2.52 |
| 1914......4.37 | | 5.47 | 1954......2.80 | | 1.58 |
| 1915......2.85 | | 4.01 | 1955......3.01 | | 2.18 |
| 1916......3.25 | | 3.84 | 1956......3.89 | | 3.31 |
| 1917......4.62 | | 5.07 | 1957......4.35 | | 3.81 |

Source: Class, 1970 (Lipscomb).

5. Find the correlation between the two variables, $Y =$ white unemployment rate in United States, and $X =$ nonwhite unemployment rate in United States for 17 months from March 1968 through July 1969.

| Y | 3.2 | 3.1 | 3.2 | 3.3 | 3.3 | 3.2 | 3.2 | 3.1 | 3.0 | 3.0 |
|---|-----|-----|-----|-----|-----|-----|-----|-----|-----|-----|
| X | 6.9 | 6.7 | 6.5 | 7.1 | 6.8 | 6.4 | 6.6 | 7.3 | 6.5 | 6.5 |

| Y | 3.0 | 2.9 | 3.1 | 3.1 | 3.1 | 3.0 | 3.2 |
|---|-----|-----|-----|-----|-----|-----|-----|
| X | 6.0 | 5.7 | 6.0 | 6.9 | 6.5 | 7.0 | 6.4 |

Source: Class, 1970 (Heaslet).

6–15. The data from Problems 8–17 at the end of Chapter 3 can be used to determine and interpret the meaning of $r^2$ and $s_e$ for each case.

# Chapter 5

# THE DISTURBANCE TERM IN THE ECONOMETRIC MODEL

## 5.1 PREVIEW

It is popular among econometricians to make the economic model stochastic. That is, they include in the model a *disturbance* term which is a random variable having an associated probability distribution. For statistical estimation and testing of the model, the properties of this probability distribution of the disturbance term are very important. For this reason, it is desirable to devote this preliminary chapter to a discussion of the disturbance term. The reader should seek to understand more fully why this disturbance term is included in the model, what assumptions about its properties are typically given, and what are the economic meaning of its inclusion and its assumed properties.

Since this term is an unknown, nonobservable variable, it is denoted by a Greek symbol, $\varepsilon_t$. The subscript designates the $t$th observation of this random term. Its associated probability density function (PDF) may be denoted, $p(\varepsilon_t)$[1]. By including $\varepsilon_t$ in the model, the researcher recognizes the imperfect nature of the specified model. Some of the many causes of such impreciseness are considered in Section 5.3 upcoming. In preparation, let it suffice to argue that it may be impossible, in a practical sense, to perfectly explain the changes in any economic variable in a quantifiable function with other theoretically related economic (or noneconomic) variables. It is presumed that the combined nature of all forgotten or excluded effects can be represented by a random variable $\varepsilon_t$. It is a "blotter" which soaks up the spillover of the intended theoretical specification.

Various assumptions about this random term can be stated mathematically, as in Section 5.4. For example, it may be assumed that the specified relation without a disturbance term would sometimes overestimate and sometimes underestimate the true (factual) values of the endogenous variable being estimated. Thus, the values of $\varepsilon_t$ may be positive or negative; but if the specified relation is true on the average, then the values of $\varepsilon_t$ should balance at the value zero.

This type assumption may be a result of theoretical judgment or intuitive appeal. Other assumptions about the probability density function, $p(\varepsilon_t)$, may result from considerations of mathematical simplicity. All the assumptions, however, are of crucial importance in determining the best way to estimate the unknown parameters both in the model, such as $\alpha_1$ and $\alpha_2$, and in the function $p(\varepsilon_t)$, such as $V(\varepsilon_t) = \sigma_\varepsilon^2$, the variance of the random variable $\varepsilon_t$. Also important, of course, is the validity of the one sample of economic data used in the measurement of the variables in the model.

Presuming that the sample is a valid descriptive representation of the entire population of all the events which might have occurred and be shaping the true relation among the economic variables, it is still necessary to closely examine the assumptions about $p(\varepsilon_t)$ in order to understand the meaning and judge the merit of the specified model.

Each assumption has some economic meaning relative to the particular model in which it appears. Thus, some of the assumptions which are made in order to simplify the statistical burden of calculating estimates and making tests of hypotheses can imply strict conditions on the economic and social environment in which the model is believed to be applicable. Economically, the properties of $p(\varepsilon_t)$ reflect the external or background conditions in which the model is intended to operate and is expected to represent a specific economic sector or economic law. These external conditions can and do involve variables, and relations among variables, other than those specifically included in the model.

---

[1] Where the meaning is not ambiguous, the same symbol will be used to denote the random variable, here $\varepsilon_t$, and to denote the set of any and all values of the random variable which appear as arguments in associated density functions, here $p(\varepsilon_t)$. At this level, it may be less confusing to reduce the number of symbols rather than to be mathematically unambiguous. A common mathematical notation is to use capital or lowercase letter distinctions such as a random variable $X$ with PDF $g(x)$. However, in this text we use this distinction in another common usage of econometrics to indicate original measures of a variable by $X$ and the deviation from its mean by $x = X - \overline{X}$.

Beginning in Section 5.4, a listing is given of the most frequently used assumptions in econometric models. To emphasize their importance, some interpretation is given of their meaning relative to these background conditions.

## 5.2 REVIEW

Quantitative topics to be reviewed for study of this chapter are elements of integral calculus and probability functions.

### 1 Discrete or continuous random variables

These are not variables which assume certain values at random. Rather they assume values according to a prescribed probability density function. They may be discrete or continuous depending on whether this probability function has a positive value at only a discrete set of values or over a continuum of values respectively.

A variable, say $\varepsilon_t$, which is normally distributed, is a continuous random variable. A variable, $X_t$, which assumes values 3, 473, and $-27$ with probabilities 3/8, 1/8, and 4/8 respectively, is a discrete random variable. The level of consumption expenditures which could occur in 1975 is assumed to be a continuous random variable with an unknown probability distribution. The observed value of consumption expenditures in 1975 is not a random variable. It is a sample value drawn from the distribution of all values which could have occurred.

### 2 Normal distribution

A random variable $X$ with mean $\mu$ and standard deviation $\sigma$ is normally distributed if its density function is specified as:

$$g(X) = \frac{1}{\sigma\sqrt{2\pi}} e^{-[(X-\mu)^2/2\sigma^2]}.$$

This distribution is the well-known, rounded, bell-shaped curve with these important characteristics. It is (a) symmetric, (b) unimodal, and (c) constructed so that the probability of randomly selecting specially large or small values becomes smaller and smaller the farther these values depart from the mean.

### 3 Integral calculus

The process of integration is conceptually the reverse of differentiation. Common terminology uses the expressions "taking" derivatives and "finding" integrals. If $dF(x)/dx = f(x)$, then $F$ is the indefinite integral of $f$.

That is,

$$\int f(x)\, dx = F(x) + C,$$

where $x$ is a variable and $C$ is a constant. If the integration is performed over a definite domain of values of the variable, the integral is called a definite integral. By the fundamental theorem of the calculus,

$$\int_a^b f(x)\, dx = F(b) - F(a).$$

**TABLE 5-1**

**Rules for integration**

1. $\displaystyle\int au(x)\, dx = a \int u(x)\, dx + C.$

2. $\displaystyle\int (u + v)\, dx = \int u\, dx + \int v\, dx + C.$

3. $\displaystyle\int u^n\, du = \begin{cases} \dfrac{u^{n+1}}{n+1} + C & \text{if } n \neq -1, \\[2mm] \ln u + C & \text{if } n = -1. \end{cases}$

4. $\displaystyle\int a^u\, du = \dfrac{a^u}{\ln a} + C \qquad \text{for } a > 0 \text{ but } a \neq 1.$

5. $\displaystyle\int e^u\, du = e^u + C.$

The symbols $u$ and $v$ represent functions of $x$; $a$, $n$, and $C$ are constants; and ln denotes a natural logarithm and $e$ denotes its base.

For example, consider $\int_a^b f(x)\, dx$ where $a = 2$, $b = 5$, $f(x) = 2x + 5$. Following the rules 1, 2, and 3 in Table 5–1,

$$\int_2^5 (2x + 5)\, dx = \left(\frac{2x^2}{2} + 5x\right)\Bigg|_2^5 ,$$

$$F(5) - F(2) = (25 + 25) - (4 + 10) = 36.$$

It is obvious that

$$\frac{dF(x)}{dx} = \frac{d(x^2 + 5x)}{dx} = 2x + 5 = f(x).$$

This example is shown graphically in Figure 5–1.

**FIGURE 5-1**

A graphic interpretation of the fundamental theorem of calculus

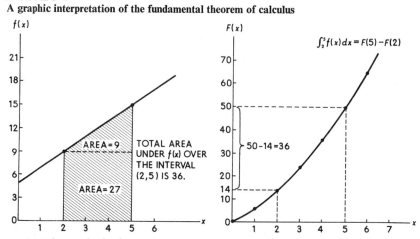

According to the fundamental theorem of calculus, the expression $\int_2^5 f(x)\,dx$ equals 36 as shown in the left-hand figure and is identical to the expression $F(5) - F(2)$ as shown in the right-hand figure. The data on which these figures are based is given below.

| $x$ | $f(x) = 2x + 5$ | $F(x) = x^2 + 5x$ |
|---|---|---|
| 0 | 5 | 0 |
| 1 | 7 | 6 |
| 2 | 9 | 14 |
| 3 | 11 | 24 |
| 4 | 13 | 36 |
| 5 | 15 | 50 |
| 6 | 17 | 66 |

## 4 Probability functions

Several types of probability functions for either discrete or continuous random variables are relevant. Probability density functions are used in stating properties of estimates, assumptions about the disturbance term, and assumptions about the distribution of exogenous random variables. Probability distribution functions are commonly found in statistical tables used to make tests of hypothesis and confidence statements.

Joint density and distribution functions of two or more combined random variables are natural extensions of these. For this case, marginal density functions and conditional probability density functions are used to define conditions of independence among the variables.

The measures of central tendency and of dispersion most commonly used for probability distributions are the expected value and the variance respectively. The symbols and definitions of all these concepts which you should review are summarized in Table 5–2 where $x$ and $y$ denote random variables, $x^o$ and $y^o$ denote values of these random variables, $h$ is a proxy variable in the same probability function where specified, $a$ and $b$ are constants, and $H$ is some region.

**TABLE 5–2**
**Probability functions**

|  | |
|---|---|
| *For discrete random variables* | *For continuous random variables* |

Probability density function used to find probability of an event:

$$g(x^o) = \Pr\{x = x^o\}$$                $$\int_a^b g(x^o)\, dx^o = \Pr\{a < x < b\}$$

Probability distribution function, a cumulative density function often used in tables:

$$G(x^o) = \Pr\{x \le x^o\}$$                Same

$$= \sum_{(h \le x^o)} g(h)$$                $$G(x^o) = \int_{-\infty}^{x^o} g(h)\, dh$$

Expected value of a random variable:

$$E(x) = \sum_{(\text{all } x^o)} x^o g(x^o)$$                $$E(x) = \int_{-\infty}^{\infty} x^o g(x^o)\, dx^o$$

Variance of a random variable:

$$V(x) = E[x^o - E(x)]^2$$                Same

$$= \sum_{(\text{all } x^o)} [x^o - E(x)]^2 g(x^o)$$                $$V(x) = \int_{-\infty}^{\infty} [x^o - E(x)]^2 g(x^o)\, dx^o$$

Standard deviation of a random variable

$$\sigma_x = \sqrt{V(x)}$$                Same

Joint probability density function for combined random variables

$$f(x^o, y^o) = \Pr\{x = x^o, y = y^o\}$$

Used to find probability of an event

$$\Pr\{(x, y) \text{ in } H\} = \sum_{(y^o \text{ in } H)} \sum_{(x^o \text{ in } H)} f(x^o, y^o)$$                $$\Pr\{(x, y) \text{ in } H\} = \iint_H f(x^o, y^o)\, dx^o\, dy^o$$

Marginal density functions for combined random variables:

$$g(x^o) = \Pr\{x = x^o\} = \sum_{(\text{all } y^o)} f(x^o, y^o)$$                $$g(x^o) = \int_{-\infty}^{\infty} f(x^o, y^o)\, dy^o$$

$$q(y^o) = \Pr\{y = y^o\} = \sum_{(\text{all } x^o)} f(x^o, y^o)$$                $$q(y^o) = \int_{-\infty}^{\infty} f(x^o, y^o)\, dx^o$$

Conditional probability density functions for combined random variables:

$$g(x^o | y^o) = \Pr\{x = x^o \text{ given } y = y^o\}$$                Same

$$= \frac{f(x^o, y^o)}{q(y^o)}$$

**TABLE 5-2**—(*Continued*)

| *For discrete random variables* | *For continous random variables* |
|---|---|
| $q(y^o \mid x^o) = \Pr\{y = y^o \text{ given } x = x^o\}$ | Same |
| $\qquad = \dfrac{f(x^o, y^o)}{g(x^o)}$ | |

Condition of independence for combined random variables $x$ and $y$:

| $\Pr\{x \text{ in } H_1, y \text{ in } H_2\}$ | Same |
|---|---|
| $\qquad = \Pr\{x \text{ in } H_1\} \cdot \Pr\{y \text{ in } H_2\}$ | |
| $f(x^o, y^o) = g(x^o) \cdot q(y^o)$ | |

or

| $g(x^o \mid y^o) = g(x^o)$ | Same |
|---|---|

and

$$q(y^o \mid x^o) = q(y^o)$$

The following programmed problems and exercises are given for review of these concepts and definitions. For learning what follows in this text, the mechanics of finding the solutions are not as important as an understanding of the meaning of these probability terms.

## REVIEW EXERCISES

Use Table 5–2 in working through these exercises.

R.1.  Given the probability function, $f(X^o)$ for a discrete random variable $X$ as follows: (See Figure 5–2.)

| $X^o$ | 1 | 2 | 3 | 4 | 5 | elsewhere |
|---|---|---|---|---|---|---|
| $f(X^o)$ | 0.2 | 0.3 | 0.05 | 0.4 | 0.05 | 0 |

**FIGURE 5–2**
$f(X^o)$ **for discrete random variable**

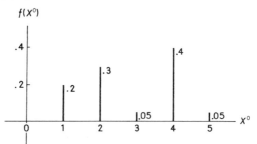

*a)*  The probability of a simple event is given by $f(X^o)$. For example,

$$\Pr\{X = 2\} = f(2) = 0.3.$$

The sum of the probabilities over all values of $X$ is unity.

b) A cumulative probability (frequently calculated and tabled for quick reference for many commonly used distributions) is found by summing.

$$\Pr\{\overset{\cdot}{X}\leq 3\} = F(3) = 0.2 + 0.3 + 0.05 = 0.55.$$

c) The probability of a combined event is also easily found. Show that

$$\Pr\{2 \leq X \leq 5\} = 0.8.$$

d) $E(X) = \sum X^\circ f(X^\circ) = $ _____ . Find this value and show it as the average value on a sketch of $f(X^\circ)$. Plot $f(X^\circ)$ on the vertical axis and the value of $X^\circ$ on the horizontal axis.

e) Define a function $g(X)$, say $g(X) = X^2$.

These function values are then also a random variable and follow the same probability function as $X$, namely $f(X^\circ)$.

The random variable $g(X)$ also has an expected value. Show that

$$E[g(X^\circ)] = \sum g(X^\circ)f(X^\circ) = 9.5.$$

f) This particular function $g(X) = X^2$ is used to determine the variance of $X$ as follows:

$$V(X) = \sigma_x{}^2 = E[X - E(X)]^2 = E(X^2) - [E(X)]^2.$$

Show that these two forms for $V(X)$ are equivalent by deriving the latter from expansion of the former. Then calculate $V(X)$ using the latter form and the answers from parts (d) and (e).

R.2. Consider the continuous random variable $Z$ with probability density function (PDF) given as

$$f(Z^\circ) = \begin{cases} Z/2 & \text{for } 0 \leq Z \leq 2 \\ 0 & \text{elsewhere} \end{cases} \quad \text{(See Figure 5–3.)}$$

**FIGURE 5–3**
$f(Z^\circ) = Z^\circ/2$ **for continuous random variable** $0 \leq Z \leq 2$.

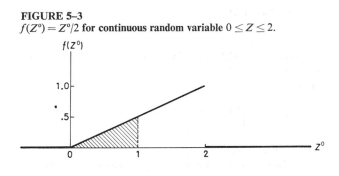

a) The probability of observing any particular value of $Z$ in a random draw from this distribution is zero.

For example, $\Pr\{Z = \tfrac{1}{2}\} = 1/\infty$ since there are an infinite number of points for which $f(Z^\circ)$ is defined. Thus, for a continuous random variable, the probability of a simple event must be considered as observing a value of $Z$ contained within some interval.

$$\Pr\{1 < Z < 2\} = \int_1^2 f(Z^\circ)\, dZ^\circ = \int_1^2 \frac{Z^\circ}{2}\, dZ^\circ = \frac{Z^2}{4}\bigg|_1^2 ,$$

$$\Pr\{1 < Z < 2\} = \tfrac{4}{4} - \tfrac{1}{4} = \tfrac{3}{4} .$$

If the end points are included in the interval, the answer remains the same since the probability of $Z$ being equal to either end point is zero.

b)  To show that $f(Z^\circ)$ is a PDF, its total probability measure must be unity. That is,

$$\int_{-\infty}^{\infty} f(Z^\circ)\, dZ^\circ = 1.0 .$$

Show this to be true by integrating $f(Z^\circ)$ over the relevant domain, $0 \le Z \le 2$. The other segments of the integral are zero as shown.

$$\int_{-\infty}^{0} (0)\, dZ^\circ = \int_2^{\infty} (0)\, dZ^\circ = 0 .$$

c)  The cumulative distribution function (CDF) is obtained by integrating the PDF over the specified interval. Show that

$$F(1) = \int_{-\infty}^{1} f(Z^\circ)\, dZ = 0.25 .$$

Shade in the relevant probability on a sketch of $f(Z^\circ)$. (See Figure 5–3.) Show geometrically that this is $\tfrac{1}{4}$ of the total area under $f(Z^\circ)$ over the interval, $0 \le Z \le 2$.

d)  Find $E(Z) = \int_0^2 Z^\circ f(Z^\circ)\, dZ^\circ = \tfrac{4}{3}$.

e)  Find $E[g(Z)]$ where $g(Z) = Z^2$.

f)  Show that $V(Z) = \tfrac{2}{9}$.

R.3.  An example of the definitions in Table 5–2 for continuous combined random variables $X$ and $Y$ follows.
  Given

$$f(X^\circ Y^\circ) = \begin{cases} K(2 - X^\circ - Y^\circ) & \text{for} \quad 0 \le X^\circ \le 2 - Y^\circ,\, 0 \le Y^\circ \le 2 \\ 0 & \text{elsewhere} \end{cases}$$

See Figure 5–4(a).

a)  To determine the value of $K$, remember that the total probability measure is unity. Thus,

$$K \int_0^2 \int_0^{2-Y^\circ} (2 - X^\circ - Y^\circ)\, dX^\circ\, dY^\circ = 1 .$$

Show that $K = \tfrac{3}{4}$.

b)  The probability over any region is also given by a double integral. See Figure 5–4(b).

**FIGURE 5–4**
**Illustrations for Exercise R.3**

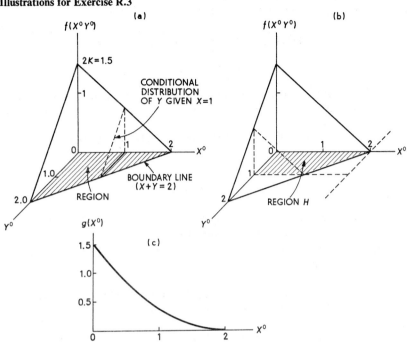

$$\Pr\{(X^\circ Y^\circ) \text{ in } H\}$$

$$= \Pr\{0 \le X^\circ \le 2, 0 \le Y^\circ \le 1\} = \frac{3}{4} \int_0^1 \int_0^{2-Y^\circ} (2 - X^\circ - Y^\circ)\, dX^\circ\, dY^\circ.$$

Show this probability to be $\frac{7}{8}$. Check the answer by scrutiny of Figure 5–4(*b*).

c) The marginal probability density function for $X$ is found by accumulating all the probability on the $X$ axis. Looking at Figure 5–4(*a*), imagine a bulldozer pushing the quarter pyramid of probability across all values of $Y$, thereby creating a pile of probability for each $X$ value. The end result is a mound of probability all piled up on the $X$-axis. The resulting distribution is the marginal PDF for $X$.

$$g(X^\circ) = \int_{-\infty}^{\infty} f(X^\circ Y^\circ)\, dY^\circ = \frac{3}{4} \int_0^{2-X^\circ} (2 - X^\circ - Y^\circ)\, dY^\circ = \tfrac{3}{8}(2 - X^\circ)^2.$$

This parabolic distribution is defined for $0 \le X^\circ \le 2$ and shown in Figure 5–4(*c*). Check to see that the sum of $g(X^\circ)$ over all values of $X$ is unity.

Suppose the bulldozer had worked from right to left piling up the probability on the $Y$-axis. Find the resulting $q(Y^\circ)$.

d) Now consider the conditional probability density function of $Y$ given $X$, namely

$$q(Y^\circ \mid X^\circ) = \frac{f(X^\circ Y^\circ)}{g(X^\circ)}.$$

Find $q(Y^\circ | X^\circ)$ for $X^\circ = 1$ and show this is a straight line. Compare your function to the Figure 5–4(a).

What should be the integral of $q(Y^\circ | 1)$ over all $Y^\circ$?

e)  Looking at the sketch for $g(X^\circ)$ in Figure 5.4(c), what do you think is the $E(X)$? Find

$$E(X) = \int_0^2 X^\circ [\tfrac{3}{8}(2 - X^\circ)^2]\, dX^\circ = \int_{-\infty}^{\infty} X^\circ f(X^\circ)\, dX^\circ.$$

f)  To check on the independence of $X$ and $Y$, determine if

$$f(X^\circ, Y^\circ) = g(X^\circ)q(Y^\circ).$$

$$\tfrac{3}{4}(2 - X^\circ - Y^\circ) \neq [\tfrac{3}{8}(2 - X^\circ)^2][\tfrac{3}{8}(2 - Y)^2].$$

$X$ and $Y$ are not independent.

R.4.  The PDF for a random variable $X$ is

$$\begin{aligned}
f(X^\circ) &= 1 - X^\circ &&\text{for}\quad 0 \le X^\circ \le 1 \\
&= X^\circ - 1 &&\text{for}\quad 1 \le X^\circ \le 2 \\
&= 0 &&\text{elsewhere.}
\end{aligned}$$

Sketch $f(X^\circ)$. Find $E(X)$, $V(X)$, and $\Pr\{0.8 \le X^\circ \le 1.1\}$. Ans.: $E(X) = 1.0$, $V(X) = \tfrac{1}{2}; 0.025$.

R.5.  The combined random variables $X_1$, $X_2$ have a joint probability function, $f(X_1^\circ, X_2^\circ)$, as given in the accompanying table. For other values of $X_1$ and $X_2$, $f(X_1^\circ, X_2^\circ) = 0$.

a)  Find the cumulative distribution function value, $F(2, 10)$.
b)  Find $E(X_1 + X_2)$ considering $(X_1 + X_2)$ as a function $g(X_1^\circ, X_2^\circ)$.
c)  Find $E(X_1) + E(X_2)$.
d)  Sketch the marginal probability functions, $f_1(X_1^\circ)$ and $f_2(X_2^\circ)$.
e)  Find $V(X_2)$ and $Cov(X_1, X_2)$ .
f)  Find the conditional values $f_1(2|5)$, $f_1(3|10)$, and $f_2(5|3)$ by using the definition of a conditional as a ratio of the joint over the marginal.
g)  Determine if $X_1$ and $X_2$ are independent.

| $X_1^\circ$ \ $X_2^\circ$ | 5 | 10 | 20 |
|---|---|---|---|
| 1 | 0.02 | 0.05 | 0.03 |
| 2 | 0.1 | 0.2 | 0.15 |
| 3 | 0.15 | 0.1 | 0.05 |
| 4 | 0.05 | 0.08 | 0.02 |

Answers: a)  0.37.
c)  $E(X_1) = 2.5$, $E(X_2) = 10.9$.
e)  $E(X_2^2) = 151$, $V(X_2) = 32.19$, $Cov(X_1 X_2) = -1.0$.

R.6.  A random variable $X$ takes on the value 5 if a fair die is tossed and has an odd number on top, and takes on values of the number on top if that number is even. Find:

a)  $E(X)$.        Ans.: 4.5.
b)  $\Pr X \ge 5$.    Ans.: $\tfrac{4}{6}$.
c)  $V(X)$.        Ans.: 1.583.

R.7.  Suppose a probability function for a random variable $y$ is given by $f(y^o) = \frac{3}{8}(2 - y^o)^2$ for $0 \le y^o \le 2$. Find the value of the cumulative distribution function for $y$ at $y = 0.5$. Ans.: 0.578.

R.8.  Suppose the joint probability function for discrete random variables $X$ and $Y$ is given by the following table:

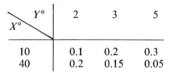

| $X^o$ \ $Y^o$ | 2 | 3 | 5 |
|---|---|---|---|
| 10 | 0.1 | 0.2 | 0.3 |
| 40 | 0.2 | 0.15 | 0.05 |

a)  What is the sum of all the probabilities in the table?

b)  The sum of probabilities across a row gives a value of the marginal probability function of _____.

c)  The value of the joint cumulative distribution for $F(X^o, Y^o) = F(40, 3)$ is

$$\sum_{(Y^o \le 3) X^o \le 40} \sum f(X^o Y^o) = 0.1 + \underline{\hspace{1cm}} + \underline{\hspace{1cm}} + \underline{\hspace{1cm}} = 0.65.$$

d)  Sketch the marginal probability function for $Y$, say $q(Y^o)$.

e)  The $E(Y)$ is the average of the values of $Y$ drawn in an infinite number of draws from the marginal probability function of $Y$.

$$E(Y) = \sum_{\text{all } Y^o} Y^o q(Y^o) = 2(0.3) + 3(\ \ ) + \underline{\hspace{1cm}} = 3.40.$$

f)  The variance of $Y$ is given by $V(Y) = E(Y^2) - [E(Y)]^2$. From part ($e$), $[E(Y)]^2 = (3.4)^2 = 11.56$. $E(Y^2)$ is the expected value of a function of $Y$.

$$E(Y^2) = \sum_{\text{all } Y^o} Y^{o\,2} q(Y^o) = 4(0.3) + 9(\ \ ) + \underline{\hspace{1cm}} = \underline{\hspace{1cm}}. \text{ Then,}$$

$$V(Y) = \underline{\hspace{1cm}} - 11.56 = 1.54.$$

g)  Show the values of $E(Y)$ and $\sqrt{V(Y)} = \sigma_y$ on your sketch in part ($d$).

h)  Sketch the conditional probability function $q(Y^o | X^o)$ for $X = 10$. There will be some positive probability for each of three values of $Y$. These are found as follows:

$$q(Y^o | 10) = \frac{f(10, Y^o)}{g(10)} \quad \text{for} \quad Y^o = 2, 3, \text{ and } 5.$$

That is,

$$q(2 | 10) = \frac{f(10, 2)}{g(10)} = \frac{0.1}{0.6} = \frac{1}{6}.$$

$$q(3 | 10) = \underline{\hspace{2cm}}, q(5 | 10) = \underline{\hspace{2cm}}.$$

i)  Suppose a function of $X$ and $Y$ is given by $g(X^o Y^o) = X^o + 2Y^o$. Find

$$E[g(X^o Y^o)] = \sum_{\text{all } X^o} \sum_{\text{all } Y^o} g(X^o Y^o) f(X^o Y^o)$$

$$= 14(0.1) + 44(0.2) + 16(\ \ )$$

$$+ \underline{\hspace{1cm}} + \underline{\hspace{1cm}} + \underline{\hspace{1cm}}$$

$$E[g(X^o Y^o)] = 28.8.$$

*j)* It may be of interest to know if $X$ and $Y$ are independent combined random variables. If $f(X^\circ Y^\circ) = f(X^\circ)q(Y^\circ)$ for *all* values of $X$ and $Y$, then they are independent. Consider

$$X^\circ = 10, \quad Y^\circ = 3,$$
$$f(10, 3) = 0.2,$$
$$f(10) = 0.6,$$
$$q(3) = 0.35.$$

A single contradiction demonstrates a lack of independence.

R.9. To demonstrate the meaning of these various density functions, consider a joint PDF (probability density function) for combined continuous random variables $X$ and $Y$ given as

$$f(X^\circ Y^\circ) = \begin{cases} \frac{1}{3}(2X^\circ + X^\circ Y^\circ) & \text{for} \quad 0 \le X^\circ \le 1 \\ & \qquad\qquad 0 \le Y^\circ \le 2 \\ \text{zero} & \text{elsewhere.} \end{cases}$$

*a)* For this to be a valid PDF, the values of $f(X^\circ Y^\circ)$ must be nonnegative at all values of $X$ and $Y$ and the total probability measure must be unity. Show that

$$\int_0^2 \int_0^1 \tfrac{1}{3}(2X^\circ + X^\circ Y^\circ)\, dX^\circ dY^\circ = 1.0.$$

*b)* Find the marginal PDF for $X$, say $g(X^\circ)$. This is found by accumulating all probabilities across $Y$ for each value of $X$.

$$g(X^\circ) = \int_0^2 \frac{1}{3}(2X^\circ + X^\circ Y^\circ)\, dY^\circ = \frac{1}{3}\left(2X^\circ Y^\circ + \frac{X^\circ Y^\circ}{2}\right)\Bigg]_0^2$$

$$= \tfrac{1}{3}6X^\circ = 2X^\circ.$$

Show that $g(X^\circ)$ is a valid PDF by integrating over the domain of $X^\circ$.

*c)* Find the conditional PDF for $Y$ given $X$, say $q(Y^\circ \mid X^\circ)$. This gives the probability distribution of $Y$ across a given value of $X$. If one imagines slicing the joint PDF surface along the value $X^\circ$, then $q(Y^\circ \mid X^\circ)$ is the profile of the surface facing open to such a cut.

$$q(Y^\circ \mid X^\circ) = \frac{f(X^\circ, Y^\circ)}{g(X^\circ)} = \frac{1}{3} + \frac{1}{6} Y^\circ.$$

Show that this is a valid PDF over the domain of $Y$.

*d)* Find the cumulative distribution function for $X$, say $G(X^\circ)$. This is the value of all probability measured by the marginal PDF for $X$, $g(X^\circ)$ for all values of $X$ not greater than $X^\circ$.

$$G(X^\circ) = \int_{-\infty}^{X^\circ} 2X\, dX = X^{\circ 2}.$$

In particular the cumulative probability $G(\tfrac{1}{2}) = (\tfrac{1}{2})^2 = 0.25$.

e) Sketch the surface $f(X^\circ Y^\circ)$, the marginal PDF $g(X^\circ)$, the conditional PDF $q(Y^\circ | X^\circ)$. Shade in the probability area representing $G(\frac{1}{2})$. Also, guess at the measure of $E(X^\circ)$ and $\sigma_x$ based on your sketch of $g(X^\circ)$.

f) $E(X)$ and $V(X)$ can be easily determined.

$$E(X) = \int_0^1 X^\circ g(X^\circ) \, dX^\circ = \int_0^1 X^\circ (2X^\circ) \, dX^\circ = \frac{2}{3},$$

$$V(X) = E(X^2) - [E(X)]^2,$$

$$= \int_0^1 X^{\circ 2} (2X^\circ) \, dX^\circ - (\frac{2}{3})^2 = \frac{1}{18}.$$

g) The probability of any event such as $\Pr\{0 < X < \frac{1}{5}, \, 0 \le Y \le \frac{4}{3}\}$ can also be determined from the joint PDF.

$$\Pr\{0 < X < \frac{1}{5}, 0 \le Y \le \frac{4}{3}\} = \int_0^{1/5} \int_0^{4/3} \frac{1}{3}(2X^\circ + X^\circ Y^\circ) \, dY^\circ \, dX^\circ$$
$$= 0.0237 = \frac{16}{675}.$$

h) Again, the question of independence of $X$ and $Y$ may be considered. We have $f(X^\circ, Y^\circ) = \frac{1}{3}(2X^\circ + X^\circ Y^\circ)$ and $g(X^\circ) = 2X^\circ$. Show that

$$q(Y^\circ) = \int_0^1 f(X^\circ Y^\circ) \, dX^\circ = \frac{1}{3} + \frac{1}{6} Y^\circ.$$

Then, it is apparent that $f(X^\circ, Y^\circ) = g(X^\circ)q(Y^\circ)$ or that $q(Y^\circ) = q(Y^\circ | X^\circ)$ so these variables are independent statistically even though they have a joint relationship. If random variables are statistically independent, then their covariance is zero.

|||||||||||||||||||||||||||||||||||||||||||||||||||||||||||||||||||||||||||||||||||||||||||||||||||||||||||||||||||||||||||||||||||

*Explicative note.* The opposite statement does not hold in all cases. However, if the combined random variables have a joint normal distribution, then zero covariance does imply independence. This result on covariances will be used frequently in econometrics.

|||||||||||||||||||||||||||||||||||||||||||||||||||||||||||||||||||||||||||||||||||||||||||||||||||||||||||||||||||||||||||||||||||

The covariance is found by $Cov(XY) = E(XY) - E(X)E(Y)$. In part (f), the $E(X)$ was found to be $\frac{2}{3}$.

The $E(Y)$ can be obtained as follows from $q(Y^\circ) = \frac{1}{3} + \frac{1}{6} Y^\circ$.

$$E(Y) = \int_0^2 Y^\circ q(Y^\circ) \, dY^\circ = 10/9.$$

Also,

$$E(XY) = \int_0^2 \int_0^1 X^\circ Y^\circ f(X^\circ Y^\circ) \, dX^\circ \, dY^\circ = \frac{20}{27}.$$

Thus,

$$Cov(XY) = \frac{20}{27} - (\frac{2}{3})(\frac{10}{9}) = 0.$$

R.10.   The joint probability function for the combined discrete random variables $X$ and $Y$ is given by the following table of $f(X^\circ Y^\circ)$:

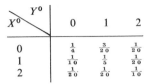

| $X^\circ$ \ $Y^\circ$ | 0 | 1 | 2 |
|---|---|---|---|
| 0 | $\frac{1}{4}$ | $\frac{3}{20}$ | $\frac{1}{20}$ |
| 1 | $\frac{1}{10}$ | $\frac{1}{5}$ | $\frac{1}{20}$ |
| 2 | $\frac{1}{20}$ | $\frac{1}{20}$ | $\frac{1}{10}$ |

a)   Find the marginal probability functions $g(X^\circ)$ and $q(Y^\circ)$.

b)   Find the conditional probability functions $f(X^\circ | Y^\circ = 0)$ and $f(X^\circ | Y^\circ = 1)$.

c)   Are $X$ and $Y$ independently distributed? Ans.: No. $Cov(X, Y) \neq 0$ since $E(XY) = 4/5$, $E(X) = 3/4$, and $E(Y) = 4/5$.

R.11.   Consider the joint PDF,

$$f(X^\circ Y^\circ) = \begin{cases} 4(1 - X^\circ - Y^\circ + X^\circ Y^\circ) \text{ for } 0 \leq X^\circ \leq 1, 0 \leq Y^\circ \leq 1 \\ 0 \text{ otherwise.} \end{cases}$$

a)   Does this function satisfy the requirements for a PDF?

b)   What is the $\Pr\{X^\circ < Y^\circ\}$? Ans.: $\frac{1}{2}$.

c)   Find the marginal PDF's for $X$ and $Y$. Ans.: $g(X^\circ) = 2 - 2X^\circ$.

d)   Find the conditional PDF for $Y$ given $X$. Ans.: Same form as (c).

e)   Are $X$ and $Y$ independent?

R.12.   Let the random variables $X$ and $Y$ have joint PDF $p(X^\circ Y^\circ) = (X^\circ + Y^\circ)/35$ for $0 \leq X^\circ \leq 2$, $0 \leq Y^\circ \leq 5$ and $p(X^\circ Y^\circ) = 0$ elsewhere.

a)   Find $E(Y | X^\circ)$ for $0 \leq X^\circ \leq 2$ and then find

$$E[E(Y|X)] = \int_{-\infty}^{\infty} E(Y | X^\circ)g(X^\circ) \, dX^\circ = 3.1.$$

b)   Find $q(Y^\circ)$ and $E(Y)$. Compare $E(Y)$ to $E[E(Y | X)]$ in part (a).

c)   Find $E[h(XY)]$ where $h(XY) = 2XY$. Ans.: $\frac{20}{3}$.

R.13.   An entrepreneur is faced with two investment opportunities that each require an initial outlay of $10,000. He estimates that the return on investment $X$ will be either $40,000, $20,000, or $0 with probabilities 0.25, 0.50, and 0.25 respectively. For investment $Y$ the returns should be $30,000, $20,000, or $10,000 with probabilities of one third in each case. Describe the returns from these investments in terms of random variables and compute the expected value and variance of each.

## 5.3  RATIONALE OF INCLUDING A DISTURBANCE TERM

The disturbance term is often included in the linear explanatory economic model when its specification is recognized as imperfect. If all the economic measurements were exact, if the economic theory were perfectly correct, and if the mathematical representation of this theory were exact, then $\varepsilon_t$ would not be necessary.

## Inexact measurement

Each of these three potential imperfections will now be considered in more detail. Consider first the problem of inexact measurement of the economic variables specified in the model. The major measurement errors are a result of either AGGREGATION OF DATA over dissimilar entities or the imperfect COLLECTION OF THE DATA BY SAMPLING. These difficulties may be either STATISTICAL or ECONOMIC considerations.

Concerning aggregation, statistical problems occur in forming indexes whereas one economic problem that makes aggregate data inappropriate for some purposes is changes in distribution. Concerning data collection, survey procedures to get data on economic variables are one type of statistical sampling that is inexact. Confidential information due to business competition (or collusion) represents one economic problem in attempts to acquire complete and exact data on certain economic variables.

Many other simple difficulties as well as many sophisticated problems could be added to this list. Some of these would be statistical considerations of sampling techniques, experimental design, and statistical inference. Others would be economic related problems, especially in attempts to combine or to jump from micro to macro level data.

## Incomplete specification

The second problem to be considered is the incompleteness of the economic theory expressed in the econometric model. Some additional relations between the variables included in the model may also exist besides the specified equation. Then, the model needs to include more equations which express these other relations.

There may also be interactions between the variables included in the model and other variables which are not included. Consequently, these other variables would need to be measured and their role in the model made explicit. There may be expressed leads and lags among the variables whose timing does not correspond exactly to all the important periodic cycles.

||||||||||||||||||||||||||||||||||||||||||||||||||||||||||||||||||||||||||||||||||||||||||||||||||||||||||||

*Discursive note.* Even if all the relevant economic variables, interaction effects, and leads and lags would be included in the model, the disturbance term would still be required. Unless the model also considers all relevant "noneconomic" variables of human behavior that directly or indirectly affect the economic environment and economic decision making, then there is still sufficient reason to include a disturbance term in the econometric model. It acts as a melting pot for all these excluded influences.

||||||||||||||||||||||||||||||||||||||||||||||||||||||||||||||||||||||||||||||||||||||||||||||||||||||||||||

## Inaccurate formulation

We now turn to the third problem. Even if the measurement of the variables is exact and if the theory is complete, the econometrician must also be convinced that the theory is formulated symbolically in a perfect representation of both the theory and the available data. Frequently, this is impossible. For example, the econometrician may theoretically desire an exact measure of standard of living in regions of developing countries, but the only measure available may be the number of indoor plumbing fixtures per 1,000 population.

In many instances, the exact theoretical specifications would require very specialized data or would demand very complex statistical procedures in order to estimate, test, and apply the model. Consequently, some nonlinear relationships are often linearized, perhaps improperly. The exact theoretical specification may be compromised by avoiding (or using) ratios of variables or changes in levels of variables. The disturbance term is used to represent the presumedly random nature of all these combined effects.

## 5.4 ASSUMPTIONS ABOUT THE DISTRIBUTION OF THE ERRORS AND EXOGENOUS VARIABLES

In the econometric model, $Y_t = \alpha_1 + \alpha_2 X_{t2} + \varepsilon_t$, the dependent variable is explained in terms of both variables, $X_{t2}$ and $\varepsilon_t$. Since $\varepsilon_t$ is a random variable always (and $X_{t2}$ may be), $Y_t$ is necessarily a random variable. It has a probability density function, say $q(Y_t)$, which depends at least partially on $p(\varepsilon_t)$, the PDF for $\varepsilon_t$.

The estimates to be calculated, most often by least squares, are $a_1$ and $a_2$ where $a_2 = \sum x_{t2} y_t / \sum x_{t2}^2$. This formula might be condensed to $a_2 = \sum h_t y_t$ where $h_t = x_{t2} / \sum x_{t2}^2$ is a constant given the $T$ observations of $X_{t2}$. Thus, $a_2$ can be written as a linear combination of the random variable $Y_t$: $a_2 = \sum h_t Y_t - \bar{Y} \sum h_t = \sum h_t Y_t$ since $\sum h_t = 0$ $\left(\text{recall } \sum x_t = 0\right)$. It follows that $a_2$ is a random variable with a probability density function that depends at least partially on $q(Y_t)$, and by transitivity, on $p(\varepsilon_t)$. The other estimate, $a_1$, is of course a linear function of $Y$ since $a_1 = \bar{Y} - a_2 \bar{X}_2$. It is likewise a random variable.

IIIIIIIIIIIIIIIIIIIIIIIIIIIIIIIIIIIIIIIIIIIIIIIIIIIIIIIIIIIIIIIIIIIIIIIIIIIIIIIIIIIIIIIIIIIIIIIIIIIIIIIIIIIIIIIIIIIIIIIIIIIII!!

*Explicative note.* All this demonstrates that the estimates $a_1$ and $a_2$, and any other subsequent statistics such as $\hat{Y}_t$, $e_t$, or test statistics involving $a_1$ or $a_2$, are all in some way dependent on $p(\varepsilon_t)$. Therefore, the assumptions or conditions prescribed for $p(\varepsilon_t)$ are specially important.

IIIIIIIIIIIIIIIIIIIIIIIIIIIIIIIIIIIIIIIIIIIIIIIIIIIIIIIIIIIIIIIIIIIIIIIIIIIIIIIIIIIIIIIIIIIIIIIIIIIIIIIIIIIIIIIIIIIIIIIIIIIII

In addition, the formula for $a_2$ involves the sample values of $X_{t2}$ as well as of $Y_t$. Thus, if $X_{t2}$ is a random variable with PDF $q(X_{t2})$, then any assumptions on this probability density function or any limitations on interactions between $\varepsilon_t$ and $X_{t2}$ will also affect all these same sample statistics. Therefore in studying the underlying assumptions for the econometric model, it is necessary to consider assumptions about the distributions of both the disturbance term and the exogenous variables.

## The common assumptions

Each assumption and its implications need to be studied. However, to get an overall view of the usual extent of the assumptions, read the following two statements carefully:

*a)*  The observations, $X_{12}$, $X_{22}$, ..., $X_{T2}$, on the exogenous variable are fixed and are independent of disturbance terms $\varepsilon_t$.

*b)*  The disturbances, $\varepsilon_1$, $\varepsilon_2$, ..., $\varepsilon_T$, are each normally, independently distributed random variables with a mean of zero and equal variances.

These assumptions involve several parts and have many implications which must be considered in more detail. Your understanding of some of the advanced research and methods in econometrics will be deeper and your applied skills in using these methods will be sharpened if you thoroughly understand the meaning of these assumptions from both the economics and statistics points of view. For this presentation, it is convenient to breakdown the overall statements into five separate assumptions. This listing is not unique and could be formulated in several other equally useful ways. With each assumption an informal discussion of its meaning is given.

ASSUMPTION 1  The exogenous variable $X_2$ is a fixed regressor that assumes different values as determined externally to the model.

This assumption that $X$ is not a *random* variable implies that the probability distribution of the endogenous variable can be determined by considering only the probability density function of the random variable $\varepsilon_t$ while handling the $X$ elements as if they were constants. It states that $X$ may be treated as a constant in the probability or expectation sense, but of course, $X$ is still a variable as it assumes different values for different observations.

$X$ may be considered as a random variable, but the complications which arise are not worth the extended generality at this level. The results in the following chapters would still hold if assumption one were revised to state that

*a)*  The combined random variables $X_{12}$, $X_{22}$, ..., $X_{T2}$ are identically and independently distributed;

*b)*  The conditional PDF's, $q(Y_t | X_{t2})$ are independent of each other for $t = 1, 2, ..., T$; and

c) The marginal density functions $g(X_{t2})$ are independent of the density function $p(\varepsilon_t)$ for any combinations of $t = 1, 2, \ldots, T$.

These assumptions are quite strong. The first implies that external factors are not changing the distribution of $X_2$ between different observations and that these different drawings of $X_{t2}$ do not affect the probability of the occurrence of each other.

The meaning of the second is more subtle and may be suggested by an example. With reference to the model discussed in Chapters 3 and 4, this assumption implies that the distribution of all possible values of imports in observation 3 say, given domestic price in period 3, is unaffected by the probabilities of drawing various values of imports in any other observation given the corresponding value for domestic price. This might not be true, for example, if imports in period 3 were all capital goods used to heighten levels of production, employment, and incomes substantially in period 4 and the new income level directly affected the level of imports in period 5 (in a significant way in addition to any related domestic price change).

One way of interpreting the third assumption is to recognize that the functions $g(X_{t2})$ must not involve the parameters $\alpha_1$, $\alpha_2$, and $V(\varepsilon_t)$. In an econometric model, this assumption implies, for example, that as the level of the variable $X_{t2}$ changes, there should be no correlated change in the size of the error $\varepsilon_t$. This assumption would not be true if the variable $X_2$ has a systematic measurement error of a set percentage, say 3% measurement error. The size of the error would then become larger or smaller as the size of $X_{t2}$ changes correspondingly. Rather, it is assumed that the specification must be equally exact or inexact for all levels of $X_2$.

The next group of assumptions concern the distribution, expected value, variance, and covariance among the errors $\varepsilon_t$ at different observations.

ASSUMPTION 2 The disturbance terms are normally distributed random variables.

The two essential properties implied in this function are symmetry and unimodality of the distribution. Assuming the exact shape of a normal distribution is rather strong and not essential but very common and convenient. If there is some reason to believe that the errors have some different distribution, then it should be used. Without any such knowledge, the normal assumption is the easiest to rationalize, if not justify.

If it can be argued that many (so many that the number approaches infinity) independent factors other than those specified in the model do, in fact, affect the endogenous variable $Y_t$, then by use of the Central Limit theorem of statistics, $\varepsilon_t$ is approximately normally distributed.

It has already been pointed out that many other factors are usually involved in explaining the dependent economic variable. However, for the Central Limit theorem to apply, these other factors must be independent. Thus the potential danger in this assumption lies in the complex interdependence of so many economic variables. Although there may be many other factors, $p(\varepsilon_t)$ cannot be considered even approximately normal if they are interdependent. Since the exact extent of such dependence or independence is often unknown, most econometricians assume there are more than just a few excluded, independent factors. They accept the result that the distribution of the errors is approximately normal.

ASSUMPTION 3. The expected value of the disturbances is zero;

$$E(\varepsilon_t) = 0 \quad \text{for} \quad t = 1, 2, \ldots, T.$$

In view of all possible occurrences, it seems reasonable that the errors should balance out, sometimes positive and sometimes negative. However, if the random endogenous variable $Y_t$ is an economic variable which is always measured at its optimum (perhaps by some submechanism), such as level of output given the most efficient combination and use of inputs, then this assumption may not be theoretically valid. The true distribution of the errors may not be symmetrical nor have a mean at zero. However in this case a transformation could be made to get a new model with a new disturbance $\varepsilon_t^*$ such that $E(\varepsilon_t^*) = 0$. For example, suppose $E(\varepsilon_t) = +5$. Then define $\varepsilon_t^* = \varepsilon_t - 5$ so $\varepsilon_t^* = Y - (\alpha_1 + 5) - \alpha_2 X_{t2} = Y - \alpha_1^* - \alpha_2 X_{t2}$. In the new model, $\alpha_1^* = \alpha_1 + 5$ and $E(\varepsilon_t^*) = E(\varepsilon_t) - 5 = 0$.

ASSUMPTION 4 The variance of the disturbance $\varepsilon_t$ is not infinite and is constant for all $t = 1, 2, \ldots, T$.

The variance for the nondegenerate normal distribution is always finite so this assumption overlaps with assumption 5. The assumption of constant variance is called homoscedasticity. When it is relaxed or not satisfied, the condition is called heteroscedasticity. This assumption implies that the probability of getting an error bigger than any specific value, $\varepsilon_t^\circ$, is the same each time an observation is drawn.

For the econometric model, this assumption means that the effects of the external causes underlying the error term (excluded variables, differences in human behavior, inexact measurements, imperfect specification) remain unchanged throughout the observations. No new causes of error are introduced after the first three measurements which change the dispersion of $\varepsilon_t$. The absolute influence of the 32nd cause is not substantially greater during observations 4–9 than it is during the other observations. The standard deviation of the disturbances remains unchanged, $\sigma_{\varepsilon_4} = \sigma_{\varepsilon_5} = \sigma_{\varepsilon_{32}}$. Also, the relative importance of causes number 3 and 4 does not change so severely that first one and then the other has the greater impact on the errors, thereby avoiding any change in variability among the errors.

These are strong conditions which are very difficult to prove. The variance may decrease after a certain number of observations because the method of measuring the data improved. It may increase during a period when the government is unstable. In our simple model relating imports with domestic prices, this assumption may not hold if there have been changes in tariffs or import quotas during the sample period.

Commonly, all a researcher can expect to do is indicate those changing causes which concern his model the most and present some plausible arguments for his courage in accepting the assumptions. Indeed, if a pattern of change is known, this could be included in the model, or it can be used to determine a more exact relation among the variances at different observations rather than setting them all equal. (See Chapters 13–15 for more on this procedure.)

||||||||||||||||||||||||||||||||||||||||||||||||||||||||||||||||||||||||||||||||||||||||||||||||||||||||||||||||||||||||||||||||||||

*Explicative note.* The assumption, $V(\varepsilon_t) = \sigma_\varepsilon^2$ for all $t$, permits a simple estimator; but if more complex relations are true, these should be used to obtain estimators with smaller variances.

||||||||||||||||||||||||||||||||||||||||||||||||||||||||||||||||||||||||||||||||||||||||||||||||||||||||||||||||||||||||||||||||||||

ASSUMPTION 5  The disturbance terms $\varepsilon_i$ and $\varepsilon_j$ are independent of each other for $i \neq j$ and both $i, j = 1, 2, \ldots, T$.

Since the error terms are normally distributed, the assumption of independence is equivalent to assuming zero covariance between any pair of disturbances. This means that the collection of underlying causes of the error term acts in the present observation independently of its own activity in previous or subsequent observations.

This assumption of nonautocorrelation is again a simplifying one which is often violated in econometric models. It is violated if any important underlying cause of $\varepsilon_t$ has a continuing effect on the error term over several observations. This is quite likely if weekly or daily time series data are being used. The same difficulty arises if the error term is largely influenced by some excluded variable which has a strong cyclical pattern throughout all or part of the observations. For example in our simple model relating imports to domestic prices, suppose that the foreign price fluctuates cyclically and independently of the domestic price, then this cyclical pattern becomes incorporated into the disturbance term (presuming that the foreign or imported price does affect the quantity of imports).

Any violation of this assumption is important to recognize because when the errors are autocorrelated, $Cov(\varepsilon_i, \varepsilon_j) \neq 0$ for $i \neq j$, the problem of making sensitive tests of the model or its parameters is more difficult. The common estimators of the unknown variances and covariances of the estimates $a_1$ and $a_2$ will not have the usually desirable properties. This concern will also be studied again in later chapters.

## 5.5 SUMMARY

These assumptions about the exogenous and disturbance variables are typical but not essential. They are useful in simplifying the statistical methods required for the analysis of the model and its parameters. Econometricians usually adopt all these assumptions to gain greater convenience in analysis and reduction in the cost of computation.

|||||||||||||||||||||||||||||||||||||||||||||||||||||||||||||||||||||||||||||||||||||||||||||||||||||||||||||||||||||||||||||||||||||||||||||

*Discursive note.* It may seem that the "metrics" part of econometrics is being favored over the "economics" part. On the other hand, it could be argued that concern for more testing and understanding of the economic relations by the economists has pushed the "metricians" to provide some first approximation techniques for analysis of the econometric model which are neither too cumbersome nor too difficult to learn.

|||||||||||||||||||||||||||||||||||||||||||||||||||||||||||||||||||||||||||||||||||||||||||||||||||||||||||||||||||||||||||||||||||||||||||||

The common adoption of these assumptions does not in itself make them any more or less valid for any particular model. The assumptions can always be questioned and frequently should be since they are an integral component of the specified model (recall the role of background and initial conditions in the composition of a model from Chapter 2).

## Testing the assumptions

Checking all the assumptions can be very difficult, however. All possible samples of $Y$ and $X_2$ cannot be taken and the true parameters $\alpha_1$ and $\alpha_2$ cannot be known. Obviously, then, the true errors $\varepsilon_t$ cannot be known, so they cannot be checked directly. Sometimes, their implication about the background conditions can be checked historically, but for any particular model, this may require a lifetime effort by 16 economic historians. Checking the assumptions by a thorough scrutiny of their meaning in each specific model is a long and difficult procedure. The implications of each assumption must be seriously challenged, accused, investigated, and acquitted. To do this, a thorough knowledge of the theory in the model and of the historical conditions is essential.

Neither can the econometrician usually observe any of the other values of $Y$ and $X_2$ which are not in the sample, nor can he know the true $\alpha_1$, $\alpha_2$, $\varepsilon_t$, $E(\varepsilon_t)$, or $Cov(\varepsilon_i, \varepsilon_j)$.

He usually assumes that there is some "world" in which his model, say $Y_t = \alpha_1 + \alpha_2 X_{t2} + \varepsilon_t$, exists with some true values of $\alpha_1, \alpha_2$, and $\varepsilon_t$. He makes assumptions 1 to 5, and he uses only one sample of $T$ observations to plug into some estimation rule and make guesses of $\alpha_1$ and $\alpha_2$. He can also find values of residuals $e_t$, of the mean of the residuals, and of the second moments of the residuals (variances and covariances). Some assumptions can be checked by analysis of these residuals and their sample distribution. Such tests are useful in indicating that certain assumptions may not be true; however, none of them can ever be conclusive in verifying the assumptions.

This lack of verification is unfortunate because these assumptions are of crucial importance in determining the proper or "best" estimators of the unknown parameters in the model. The necessity of these assumptions for obtaining estimators with desired properties and for testing the model and its parameters is seen in the next two chapters. Be on the alert for their use in theorems and derivations.

## NEW VOCABULARY

| | |
|---|---|
| Definite integral | Marginal PDF |
| Covariance | Conditional PDF |
| Independence | Normal distribution |
| Autocorrelation | Homoscedasticity |
| Disturbance term | Imperfect specification |

## SUMMARY OUTLINE

I. Reasons for including a disturbance term in a model
   A. Inexact measurement
      1. Aggregation problems
         a) Creating index numbers
         b) Changes in distribution
      2. Data collection
         a) Sample surveys
         b) Confidential or censored information
   B. Incomplete specification
      1. Other relations
      2. Other variables
      3. Leads and lags
   C. Improper formulation
      1. Compromise theory with available information
      2. Compromise nonlinearities for simplicity
II. Assumptions underlying the specified model
   A. Correct theoretical form and measures
   B. Statistical simplifications ($t = 1, 2, \ldots, T$)
      1. $X_{t2}$ are fixed and independent of $\varepsilon_t$
      2. $\varepsilon_t$ are normally distributed
      3. The expected value of each $\varepsilon_t$ is zero
      4. The variances of all $\varepsilon_t$ are equal
      5. $\varepsilon_t$ and $\varepsilon_{t-i}$ are independent, $i > 0$

## EXERCISES

1. Rewrite statements (*a*) and (*b*) at the beginning of Section 5.4 in mathematical formulation. Use joint and marginal PDF's when applicable.

2. Consider a model specifying aggregate consumption dependent on disposable personal income and a disturbance term, as in $C_t = \alpha_1 + \alpha_2 Y_t + \varepsilon_t$.

*a)* Give an economic interpretation of the restrictions imposed on the economic environment in which this model is presumed to operate as implied by each of the Assumptions 1–5.

*b)* Criticize one of the assumptions and suggest the economic reasons why it may impose an invalid background condition.

3. For each of the models specified in Exercises 3–4 and 11–17 at the end of Chapter 3 select one of the Assumptions 1–5 of this chapter, express its economic meaning in terms of the respective models, and suggest some economic " world " in which such an assumption would probably be violated.

4. Refer to Exercise 9 at the end of Chapter 3. Discuss which assumption(s) given in Section 5.4 might be violated in each of the following cases:

*a)* Businessmens' expectations of sales changes are a significant factor in determining investment.

*b)* A significant change in investment tax credit occurred in 1964.

*c)* A large number of the firms in the sample group are investment goods producers (i.e., their sales are capital expenditures for other firms).

*d)* Firms have greater difficulty in adjusting their investment to desired levels when changes in sales are greater.

*e)* The interest rate is rising during 1962–65 and having a significant damping effect on investment.

*f)* Sales in one year are dependent to a large extent on the sales in the previous year (but does this imply a dependence in the ratio $(S_t/S_{t-1})$?)

*g)* Profits are an important determinant of capital expenditures and profits are also highly correlated with changes in sales.

*h)* Larger values of $(S_t/S_{t-1})$ tend to stimulate institutional patterns of response and governmental actions that affect $\varepsilon_t$.

5. Consider which assumption(s) may be violated in each of the following cases for a simple model of the form $Y_t = \alpha_1 + \alpha_2 X_{t2} + \varepsilon_t$.

*a)* $Y_t$ and $X_{t2}$ are both growing over the observation period and the error in measurement of $X_{t2}$ is a constant 3 percent of the size of $X_{t2}$.

*b)* $Y$ measures wealth of an individual, $X_2$ measures his age, and $V(Y)$ probably increases with age.

*c)* $Y$ measures the change in average wages and $X_2$ measures unemployment for quarterly observations from 1960–70. During 1962–65, there are externally controlled wage and price guidelines so that the model consistently overpredicts wages during this period.

*d)* Observations on $Y$ and $X_2$ are daily stock price averages and volume of trading respectively.

*e)* The specified model is erroneous and the true form of the relation between $Y$ and $X_2$ is similar to the right half of a convex (with respect to $X$) parabola. (*Hint:* Draw a scatter diagram of such a parabolic relation and draw a straight line through it representing the best linear fit. Examine the signs of successive residuals.)

Chapter
6

# PROPERTIES OF THE LEAST
# SQUARES ESTIMATORS

## 6.1 PREVIEW

The properties of the least squares estimators in the simple model depend very closely on the assumptions or information on the distribution of the errors, $\varepsilon_t$. Thus, in discussing these properties, we need to bring together the estimators derived in Chapter 3 and the assumptions specified in Chapter 5 in order to determine the distributions of these estimators in Section 6.3.

Then, after defining two important properties, unbiasedness and efficiency, and examining their meaning in practice, some theoretical results of mathematical statistics are stated to obtain the properties of the least squares estimators. The discussion of the properties is in Section 6.4. The Gauss-Markov theorem and the principle of maximum likelihood estimation are the topics of Sections 5 and 6 respectively.

The importance and necessity of the assumptions for these theoretical results are summarized in the closing section. The following *Review* section presents some brief definitions, some new notions useful in the mechanics of maximum likelihood estimation, and concepts needed for continuing discussion related to the distribution and properties of the estimators.

## 6.2 REVIEW

### 1 Multiplication symbol

The symbol, capital pi, $\Pi$, is used for "the multiplication of" whatever follows it in a manner similar to the use of the summation sign. It is also indexed to indicate which terms are to be included in multiplication, such as

$$\prod_{i=2}^{4} A_i X_i = (A_2 X_2)(A_3 X_3)(A_4 X_4).$$

### 2 Logarithmic transformation

The natural logarithm of an expression can be taken symbolically just as the value of the logarithm for a number can be calculated. The rules for taking logarithms of an expression are the same as the rules for exponents in algebra, since the natural logarithm, $\ln_e A$, is simply the exponent to which the base $e$ must be raised to obtain the value $A$. For example, some common rules used in transforming the likelihood function to log form are:

$$\ln\left(\frac{AB}{C}\right) = \ln A + \ln B - \ln C,$$

$$\ln(A^B) = B \ln A,$$

$$\ln(e^A) = A.$$

### 3 Jacobian

A Jacobian of a transformation is the determinant of a matrix of the partial derivatives of each of the transformed variables with respect to each of the original variables.

Suppose a transformation is defined by $U = U(X, Y)$, $V = V(X, Y)$, then the Jacobian of the transformation is defined as

$$J\left(\frac{U, V}{X, Y}\right) = \begin{vmatrix} \dfrac{\partial U}{\partial X} & \dfrac{\partial U}{\partial Y} \\[2mm] \dfrac{\partial V}{\partial X} & \dfrac{\partial V}{\partial Y} \end{vmatrix},$$

the determinant of the matrix of partial derivatives.

Such a Jacobian is essential in finding the probability functions $q(Y_t)$ of random variables $Y_t$ from the known probability functions $p(\varepsilon_t)$ for random disturbances in an econometric model. The rule to follow is:

$$q(Y_t) = J\left(\frac{\varepsilon_t}{Y_t}\right)p(\varepsilon_t).$$

The Jacobian is also important in determining if a transformation from variables $X$ and $Y$ into $U$ and $V$ has an inverse. The transformation is called singular, and no inverse transformation from $U$ and $V$ into $X$ and $Y$ exists if $J(U, V/X, Y) = 0$ for all points in the domain of $X$ and $Y$. If this Jacobian is nonzero, then an inverse transformation does exist. Such analysis is particularly important in the discussion of the identifiability and testing of a simultaneous equation linear explanatory economic model discussed in Part IV of this book.

## 4 Algebra of expectations

Many derivations in econometrics make use of proven theorems concerning expected values and variances. Some of the basic and important results are listed in Table 6–1 for your convenience.

TABLE 6–1

**Rules of the algebra of expectations**

1.  If $a$ is a constant, then $E(a) = a$, $V(a) = 0$.
2.  For $X$ a random variable,

$$E(aX) = aE(X),$$
$$V(aX) = a^2V(X).$$

3.  For $X$ and $Y$ random variables:

$$E(a + X + Y) = a + E(X) + E(Y),$$
$$E(a - X - Y) = a - E(X) - E(Y),$$
$$V(a + X) = V(X).$$

4.  For $X$ and $Y$ *independent* random variables:

$$V(X + Y) = V(X) + V(Y),$$
$$V(X - Y) = V(X) + V(Y),$$
$$E(XY) = E(X)E(Y).$$

(Note: Always *add* variances.)

These rules are proven using the definitions of expected values and variances for discrete or continuous random variables as given in Table 5–2.[1]

---

[1] For example, consider rule 2 for a continuous random variable $X$.

$$E(aX) = \int_{-\infty}^{\infty} aXg(X)\,dX = a\int_{-\infty}^{\infty} Xg(X)\,dX = aE(X).$$

## 5  Bivariate normal distribution

Random variables $U$ and $V$ have a bivariate normal distribution if their joint probability function is given by[2]

$$f(U, V) = \frac{1}{2\pi\sigma_u\sigma_v\sqrt{1-\rho^2}} \exp\left\{-\frac{1}{2(1-\rho^2)}\left[\left(\frac{U-E(U)}{\sigma_u}\right)^2\right.\right.$$

$$\left.\left. - 2\rho\left(\frac{U-E(U)}{\sigma_u}\right)\left(\frac{V-E(V)}{\sigma_v}\right) + \left(\frac{V-E(V)}{\sigma_v}\right)^2\right]\right\},$$

where $E(U)$ and $E(V)$ are the expected values of $U$ and $V$, $\sigma_u$ and $\sigma_v$ are the standard deviations of $U$ and $V$, and $\rho$ is the correlation coefficient between $U$ and $V$.

The marginal density functions for $U$ and $V$, say $p(U)$ and $h(V)$, can be found by integration to be normal distributions. Note that if there is zero correlation, then the joint probability function is the product of the individual marginal density functions. That is, for $\rho = 0$,

$$f(U, V) = \frac{1}{\sqrt{2\pi\sigma_u^2}} e^{[-1/2(U-E(U)/\sigma_u)^2]} \frac{1}{\sqrt{2\pi\sigma_v^2}} e^{[-1/2(V-E(V)/\sigma_v)^2]},$$

$$f(U, V) = p(U)h(V).$$

Therefore, the condition of zero correlation between random variables with a joint bivariate normal distribution is equivalent to the condition of independence between these random variables.

When all this is extended to more than two variables, the joint density function would be a multivariate normal distribution if the individual marginal density functions are normal distributions. When the individual random variables are independent, all the covariation terms drop out and the joint density function is the product of the separate marginal density functions.

A final important result states that random variables which are linear combinations of independent normally distributed variables will have a multivariate normal distribution and each is normally distributed.[3]

This result is crucial for testing parameters in single equation econometric models on the basis of sample observations. The estimators of these parameters will be linear combinations of presumedly independent and normally distributed random variables, $Y_t$; and so, the estimators have a multivariate normal distribution.

---

[2] The form exp[...] indicates an exponent for the base of the natural logarithm. That is $3e^{2x}$ may be written $3 \exp(2X)$.

[3] See A. Wald, *Sequential Analysis* (New York: John Wiley & Sons, Inc., 1947), p. 70; or H. Cramér, *Mathematical Methods of Statistics* (Princeton, N.J.: Princeton University Press, 1946), p. 313; or R. V. Hogg and A. T. Craig, *Introduction to Mathematical Statistics* (2d ed.; New York: The Macmillan Co., 1965), p. 139. These sources, along with C. R. Rao, *Advanced Statistical Methods* (New York: John Wiley & Sons, Inc., 1952), can be consulted for details of other statistical theorems and proofs which are applied in this book.

## 6 The chi-square, $\chi_{v \text{ d.f.}}^2$, distribution

Many test statistics and expressions involving estimates of variance of random variables have an associated chi-square distribution. This is a positively skewed distribution characterized by the single parameter, degrees of freedom, designated by $v$.

Statisticians prove that certain random variables or functions of random variables have a $\chi_{v \text{ d.f.}}^2$ distribution by showing that they can be written as the sum of squares of $v$ independent normally distributed random variables which have mean zero and standard deviation one. This formal defining characteristic of the $\chi_{v \text{ d.f.}}^2$ distribution and such derivations are not necessary for our purposes. Rather, the results of such analysis will be used whenever a specified statistic is designated as a $\chi_{v \text{ d.f.}}^2$ distribution with $v$ degrees of freedom. It is important to know how to use a chi-square distribution table, as in Appendix A.

An important result in statistics that is seen often in the following chapters involves a chi-square distributed random variable. It is very useful to remember that if a random variable, say $V$, is defined as the ratio of an unbiased estimate of variance to the true variance, then $V$ times the proper degrees of freedom, $v$, is chi-square distributed with $v$ degrees of freedom.

The following problems are recommended for additional review practice.

## REVIEW EXERCISES

R.1.  Prove each of the following:
  a)  $V(aX) = a^2 V(X)$ for a random variable $X$.
  b)  $E(XY) = E(X)E(Y)$ for independent continuous combined random variables $X$ and $Y$.

R.2.  Define a transformation; $U = 2X - Y$, $V = X + Y/3$. Find the Jacobian $J$ for the transformation. If nonzero, find the inverse transformation, $X = X(U, V)$ and $Y = Y(U, V)$. Ans.: $J = 5/3$.

R.3.  For the transformation $U = X - 2Y$ and $V = 6Y - 3X$, show why no inverse transformation exists.

R.4.  Given the transformation $u = x + y$, $v = x/(x + y)$ for $x > 0$ and $y > 0$, find $J$ of this transformation. Find the inverse transformation, and $J$ of the inverse transformation, and show that

$$J\left(\frac{u, v}{x, y}\right) \cdot J\left(\frac{x, y}{u, v}\right) = 1.$$

  Ans.: $\left(\frac{-1}{x + y}\right) \cdot (-u) = \left(\frac{-1}{x + y}\right)(-x - y) = 1.$

R.5.  Follow the same instruction as in R.4 using the transformation $x = u$, $y = uv$ for $-\infty < u < \infty$, $-\infty < v < \infty$.

R.6.  The ratio of an unbiased estimate of variance times degrees of freedom to the true variance is a random variable with a chi-square distribution having the same degrees of freedom. For example

$$\frac{(n-1)s_x{}^2}{\sigma_x{}^2} \sim X^2_{(n-1)\text{d.f.}}$$

(Hogg and Craig, *Mathematical Statistics*, p. 145). Suppose in a sample of size 11, the sample variance is 48. What is the probability that the true variance is less than 30? Ans.: About $\frac{1}{10}$.

R.7.   It is hypothesized that the frequency of use of the university library reserve reading room is equal among all levels of students. Suppose, in a specific time period, each user is classified by his grade level, 1, 2, 3, 4, or graduate, and the frequencies observed are 16, 9, 10, 6, and 19 respectively. What is the approximate probability of this observed set of frequencies if the hypothesis of equal frequencies (number of users in each class $= \frac{1}{5}n = 12$) is true? *Hint*: The statistic

$$\frac{\sum (f_{obs} - f_{hyp})^2}{f_{hyp}}$$

is distributed as a chi-square random variable with $K-1$ degrees of freedom where $f_{obs}$ is observed frequency in any class, $f_{hyp}$ is hypothesized frequency for that class, and $K$ is the number of classifications. Ans.: $\Pr\{\chi^2_{4\,\text{d.f.}} \ge 9.5\} = 0.05$.

R.8.   Given the following joint probability function for combined discrete random variables $X$ and $Y$, work through the following rules for the algebra of expectations using the definitions of expected values and variances from *Review 5.2*.

| $X$ \ $Y$ | 6 | 8 | 4 |
|---|---|---|---|
| 5 | 1/6 | 1/12 | 1/12 |
| 7 | 1/6 | 1/12 | 1/12 |
| 3 | 1/6 | 1/12 | 1/12 |

a)   Find the marginal probability functions for $X$ and $Y$.
b)   Given four observations on a constant $k = 6$, show that $E(k) = k$ and $V(k) = 0$.
c)   Show that $E(3Y) = 3E(Y)$.
d)   Show that $V(3Y) = 9V(Y)$.
e)   Show that $V(Y) = E(Y^2) - [E(Y)]^2$.
f)   Find the conditional probability function for $(Y|X)$ for each value of $X$.
g)   Find $E(Y|X=5) = \sum [Y^\circ f(Y^\circ, 5)/f(5)]$.
h)   Find $E_x[E_Y(Y|X)] = \sum_x X^\circ f(X^\circ)\left[\sum_Y Y^\circ f(Y^\circ, X^\circ)/f(X^\circ)\right]$ and show this is equal to $E(Y)$.
i)   Let a function $h(X, Y) = 3X + XY + 2Y$. Find $E[h(X, Y)]$ directly and find $E_x\{E_Y[h(X, Y)/X]\}$. Show these to be equal. Ans.: 57.
j)   Show that $E(XY) = E(X)E(Y)$ by finding each. What does this suggest about the independence of $X$ and $Y$? Check this statistical independence formally.
k)   Show $V(X-Y) = V(X) + V(Y)$ by finding all three terms directly from the distributions of the random variables $X$, $Y$ and $(X-Y)$. You must compute the latter yourself.

## 6.3 THE DISTRIBUTIONS OF THE ESTIMATORS

The properties of estimators are often expressed in terms of the expected value and variance of the estimators. Thus, expressions for these measures of the distributions of the estimators must be determined.

### Normality

It has already been shown that the estimators $a_1$ and $a_2$ are linear functions of the variables $Y_t$. The variables $Y_t$ have a normal distribution since they are linear functions of the normally distributed independent random variables $\varepsilon_t$. Now, it is known from a theorem in statistics that random variables which are linear combinations of independent normally distributed variables will have a multivariate normal distribution and the marginal distribution of each is normal. (See *Review* 6.2, item 5.) Thus, $a_1$ and $a_2$ have a bivariate normal joint probability density function and normal marginal probability density functions which can be characterized by the expected values, variances, and covariance of $a_1$ and $a_2$. It is the purpose of this section to show how these moments can be determined.

### Means, variances and covariances

It is necessary to find $E(a_2)$, $E(a_1)$, $V(a_2)$, $V(a_1)$, and $Cov(a_1, a_2)$ to completely specify the distributions of $a_1$ and $a_2$ so that further analysis and testing of the model can be done.

||||||||||||||||||||||||||||||||||||||||||||||||||||||||||||||||||||||||||||||||||||||||||||||||||||||||||||||||||||||||||||||

*Interpretive note.* Obviously, a particular estimate, a single number, which we calculate cannot have an expected value and a variance. It is the expected value and variance of the estimator which is desired, not of the single estimate. If an infinite number of samples of $T$ observations could be drawn from all the values which might have occurred, then a mean and a variance of these estimates could be determined. In fact, only one of the estimates based on one set of $T$ observations is calculated, but the theoretical or general expression for the mean and variance of the distribution of all such estimates can often be found from a mathematical analysis of the general formula of the estimator.

||||||||||||||||||||||||||||||||||||||||||||||||||||||||||||||||||||||||||||||||||||||||||||||||||||||||||||||||||||||||||||||

We begin by finding the expected value of $a_2$. Since, by substitution $a_2 = \sum h_t \, Y_t$ where $h_t = x_{t2}/\sum x_{t2}$ and $Y_t = \alpha_1 + \alpha_2 X_{t2} + \varepsilon_t$, then

$$E(a_2) = E \sum_t [h_t(\alpha_1 + \alpha_2 X_{t2} + \varepsilon_t)]$$

$$= \sum_t h_t \alpha_1 + \sum_t h_t X_{t2} \alpha_2 + \sum_t E(\varepsilon_t) \quad \text{since } X_t \text{ is fixed,}$$

$$= 0 + 1\,(\alpha_2) + \sum (0) \qquad\qquad \text{since}$$

$$\sum x_{t2} = 0, \quad \sum h_t X_{t2} = \sum h_t x_t + \overline{X} \sum h_t = 1 + 0,$$

and by Assumption 3 that $E(\varepsilon_t) = 0$ for all $t$. Thus, the expected value of the estimator $a_2$ is the true value of the parameter, $\alpha_2$,

$$E(a_2) = \alpha_2 \tag{6-1}$$

**A typical derivation**

Not much would be lost if other results for $E(a_1)$, $V(a_1)$, etc., were merely accepted since these have been derived many times by skilled statisticians and students. However, to illustrate and emphasize the important use of the assumptions from Section 5.4, we shall proceed to derive $V(a_1)$ step by step. Working through one such derivation may also give some readers a sense of satisfaction for having done it themselves. At least, it provides a sample of the type of derivations required to analyze estimators and to determine their properties.

An expression for $a_1 - E(a_1)$ is needed. Remember $a_1$ can be written as a linear function of $Y_t$ by $a_1 = \sum (1/T - \overline{X}_2 h_t) Y_t$ where $h_t = x_{t2}/\sum x_{t2}^2$, and also, $Y_t = \alpha_1 + \alpha_2 X_{t2} + \varepsilon_t$. Combining these results, we can write

$$a_1 = \sum \left( \frac{1}{T} - \overline{X}_2 h_t \right)(\alpha_1 + \alpha_2 X_{t2} + \varepsilon_t)$$

$$= \left( \sum \frac{\alpha_1}{T} \right) - \left( \alpha_1 \overline{X}_2 \sum h_t \right) + \left( \frac{\alpha_2}{T} \sum X_{t2} \right) - \left( \alpha_2 \overline{X}_2 \sum h_t X_{t2} \right)$$

$$+ \left( \sum \left( \frac{1}{T} - \overline{X}_2 h_t \right)\varepsilon_t \right)$$

$$= \left( T\frac{\alpha_1}{T} \right) - \left( \alpha_1 \overline{X}_2 \frac{\sum x_{t2}}{\sum x_{t2}^2} \right) + (\alpha_2 \overline{X}_2) - \left( \alpha_2 \overline{X}_2 \frac{\sum x_{t2}}{\sum x_{t2}^2}(x_{t2} + \overline{X}_2) \right)$$

$$+ \sum \left( \frac{1}{T} - \overline{X}_2 h_t \right)\varepsilon_t .$$

Finally since the sum of deviations about the mean, $\sum x_{t2}$, always equals zero,

$$a_1 = \alpha_1 - 0 + \alpha_2 \overline{X}_2 - \alpha_2 \overline{X}_2(1) - \alpha_2 \overline{X}_2^2(0) + \sum \left( \frac{1}{T} - \overline{X}_2 h_t \right)\varepsilon_t .$$

Moving the term $\alpha_1$ to the left side, we write,

$$a_1 - \alpha_1 = \sum \left(\frac{1}{T} - \overline{X}_2 h_t\right)\varepsilon_t, \tag{6-2}$$

or if expectations of both sides are taken, we obtain

$$E(a_1) = E\left[\alpha_1 + \sum \left(\frac{1}{T} - \overline{X}_2 h_t\right)\varepsilon_t\right].$$

||||||||||||||||||||||||||||||||||||||||||||||||||||||||||||||||||||||||||||||||||||||||||||||||||||||||||||||||||||||||||||||||||||||||||

**Explicative note.** From this expression, the expected value of $a_1$ is easily found to be $\alpha_1$, since $E(\varepsilon_t) = 0$ by assumption.

||||||||||||||||||||||||||||||||||||||||||||||||||||||||||||||||||||||||||||||||||||||||||||||||||||||||||||||||||||||||||||||||||||||||||

In continuing to find $V(a_1)$, an expression for $a_1 - E(a_1)$ is now at hand. $E(a_1) = \alpha_1$, and by equation (6-2) above, $a_1 - \alpha_1$ is given. Thus

$$V(a_1) = E[a_1 - E(a_1)]^2 = E\left[\sum \left(\frac{1}{T} - \overline{X}_2 h_t\right)\varepsilon_t\right]^2.$$

Continuing with basic algebra and specifying the application of assumptions, the following sequence of steps is detailed:

1. Expand the sum (don't forget the cross-product terms)

$$V(a_1) = E\left[\sum_{t=1}^{T}\left(\frac{1}{T} - \overline{X}_2 h_t\right)^2 \varepsilon_t^2 + \sum_{i \neq j}\left(\frac{1}{T} - \overline{X}_2 h_i\right)\left(\frac{1}{T} - \overline{X}_2 h_j\right)(\varepsilon_i\varepsilon_j)\right].$$

2. Apply assumptions that $E(\varepsilon_i\varepsilon_j) = 0$ when $i \neq j$ and $V(\varepsilon_t) = \sigma_\varepsilon^2$ for any $t$; apply rule 3 from Table 6–1 that the expectation of a sum is the sum of the expectations; and consider $X_{t2}$ as fixed so $h_t$ is a constant with respect to the expectation. Then,

$$V(a_1) = \sum \left(\frac{1}{T} - \overline{X}_2 h_t\right)^2 \sigma_\varepsilon^2.$$

3. Expand the binomial, sum each term, and substitute for $h_t$.

$$V(a_1) = \left[T\left(\frac{1}{T^2}\right) - \frac{2\overline{X}_2}{T}\frac{\sum x_{t2}}{\sum x_{t2}^2} + \overline{X}_2^2\frac{\sum x_{t2}^2}{(\sum x_{t2}^2)^2}\right]\sigma_\varepsilon^2.$$

4. Simplify

$$V(a_1) = \left(\frac{1}{T} - 0 + \frac{\overline{X}_2^2}{\sum x_{t2}^2}\right)\sigma_\varepsilon^2.$$

5. Simplify over a common denominator and use in the numerator the substitution $\sum x^2 = \sum X^2 - T\overline{X}^2$,

$$V(a_1) = \sigma_\varepsilon^2\left(\frac{\sum x_{t2}^2 + T\overline{X}_2^2}{T\sum x_{t2}^2}\right) = \sigma_\varepsilon^2\left[\frac{\sum X_{t2}^2 - T\overline{X}_2^2 + T\overline{X}_2^2}{T\sum x_{t2}^2}\right].$$

Finally,

$$V(a_1) = \sigma_\varepsilon^2 \left( \frac{\sum X_{t2}^2}{T \sum x_{t2}^2} \right).$$

## The standard results

The other results needed are determined similarly. Collecting all these together, we have

$$E(a_1) = \alpha_1, \qquad V(a_1) = \sigma_\varepsilon^2 \frac{\sum X_{t2}^2}{T \sum x_{t2}^2},$$

$$E(a_2) = \alpha_2, \qquad V(a_2) = \sigma_\varepsilon^2 \frac{1}{\sum x_{t2}^2}, \qquad (6\text{-}3)$$

$$Cov(a_1, a_2) = \sigma_\varepsilon^2 \frac{-\overline{X}_2}{\sum x_{t2}^2}.$$

## 6.4 UNBIASEDNESS AND EFFICIENCY

Two important properties for an estimator are *unbiasedness* and *efficiency*. These and other properties of estimators only make sense in the abstract conceptual framework of all possible samples of events which could have happened. To examine these properties, it is necessary to consider the expected value and variance of the estimator, and comparisons of the latter to the variances of alternate estimators. Each of these properties is now considered in more detail.

### Unbiasedness

An estimator is unbiased if its expected value is equal to the true value of the parameter. This means that for all possible samples of size $T$, the average value of the estimates obtained would be equal to the true value. Even though an estimator is unbiased, an estimate from one set of observations will in general not be exactly true. It may be too high or too low. It may be different from another estimate from a sample of the same size drawn from the same distribution. However, the average of all such conceivable estimates would be the true value.

### Efficiency

An estimator is efficient if it has the minimum variance among all estimators in its class. Again, if all possible estimates from all possible samples could be obtained, the variance of the estimator is a measure of the dispersion of the distribution of these many estimates. A minimum variance is desired because it indicates that the different estimates will be clustered together rather than widely scattered. Hopefully, then, an estimate obtained from the one sample actually observed would generally be close to an estimate obtained from any other sample which could have occurred.

In practice, it is not possible to know the exact variance of the least squares estimator $a_2$ since all possible samples are not available. Instead, another estimator, [Est. $V(a_2)$], is obtained to give an estimate of the variance of the first estimator. Remember, all the problems of getting the primary estimate apply to this secondary estimate also. It should likewise be a value of an estimator which is unbiased and of minimum variance. Even so, it need not be the true value.

Fortunately, the probability is low that misleading estimates will be obtained for the parameters and for the variance of these estimates when proper estimators are used. To examine the property of minimum variance, the variance of the estimator must be found and compared to the variance of any arbitrary estimator of the same general class.

Figure 6–1 illustrates the properties of unbiasedness and efficiency for arbitrary estimators $\hat{\Theta}_i$ with probability functions $p_i(\hat{\Theta}_i)$.

**FIGURE 6–1**
**Unbiasedness and efficiency**

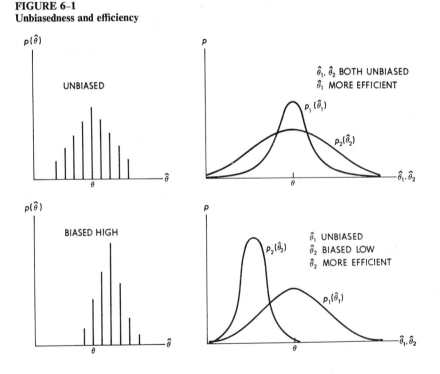

## Formal definitions

Unbiasedness of an estimator $\hat{\Theta}$ for a parameter $\Theta$ is defined as the property, $E(\hat{\Theta}) = \Theta$. Efficiency of the estimator $\hat{\Theta}$ is the same as the statistical quality of reliability. It is defined as the condition that $E[\hat{\Theta} - E(\Theta)]^2$ is a minimum. Sometimes an argument can be made for preferring an estimator with the minimum variance even if it is biased (providing that the bias is known).

Among a set of unbiased estimators, the property of efficiency is useful in selecting the "best" one. In this case, efficiency is the same as the statistical quality of accuracy given by the statement that the mean square deviation of the estimator about the true parameter is a minimum, $E(\hat{\Theta} - \Theta)^2$ is a minimum.

## 6.5 THE GAUSS-MARKOV THEOREM

It is now appropriate to put together the assumptions of Chapter 5, the least squares estimators of Chapter 3, and the properties of estimators in this chapter. The result obtained is known as the Gauss-Markov theorem which is examined further in the general case of an extended model in Chapter 14.

THEOREM Given Assumptions 1, 3, 4, and 5, from Section 5.4 and the least squares estimators $a_1$ and $a_2$ from formula (3–2), these estimators are BLUE (*best linear unbiased estimators*).[4]

Several important realizations are contained within this theorem. First Assumption 2 of normality is not necessary for the least squares estimators to be BLUE. Second, the term "best," meaning minimum variance, is a relative concept. It means best in comparison to any other estimator of the same general class. In this case, the general class is all other linear unbiased estimators.

It is Assumptions 1 and 3 which specify $X$ to be fixed and $E(\varepsilon_t) = 0$ that are necessary for the least squares estimators to be unbiased. The formulation of $a_2 = \sum h_t \, Y_t$ expresses the condition of linearity. The theorem states that among all arbitrary linear estimators which are unbiased, the particular least squares estimators with variances as given in (6–3) have the smallest variance. This result may be proven by solving a constrained minimization problem of minimizing the variance of an arbitrary estimator subject to the conditions for linearity and unbiasedness and finding that the solution is identical with the least squares estimator. The Lagrangian multiplier technique is used. Alternatively, the result may be demonstrated by solving for the variance of such an arbitrary estimator and showing that it can never be smaller than the variance of the least squares estimator. (See Exercise 10 for a detailed format of this method and work Exercise 11 to demonstrate the Gauss-Markov theorem for the estimator of the slope, $a_2$.)

---

[4] F. N. David and J. Neyman, "Extension of the Markov Theorem on Least Squares," *Statistical Research Mems.*, 1938, pp. 105–16.

It is Assumptions 4 and 5 of constant variance (homoscedasticity) of $\varepsilon_t$ and zero covariances among the disturbances (nonautocorrelation) that permit the derivation of these variances and the resulting "best" property of efficiency for the least squares estimators.

## 6.6 MAXIMUM LIKELIHOOD ESTIMATORS OF $a_1$ AND $a_2$

One further concept of estimation helps to explain the widespread use of least squares estimation and of the assumptions in Section 5.4. That is the principle of maximum likelihood estimation, a very rigorous statistical method of estimation that is also very appealing intuitively. It enables us to obtain estimates of parameters which are the most likely to be true given the sample that has been observed.

||||||||||||||||||||||||||||||||||||||||||||||||||||||||||||||||||||||||||||||||||||||||||||||||||||||||||||||||||

*Interpretive note.*  The notion of the likelihood of a parameter given a sample is the analog to the notion of the probability of a sample value given the defining PDF of the population. We refer to the "probability" of a sample statistic and to the "likelihood" of a population parameter.

||||||||||||||||||||||||||||||||||||||||||||||||||||||||||||||||||||||||||||||||||||||||||||||||||||||||||||||||||

A simple example can be used to illustrate the concept of maximum likelihood estimation as the opposite analysis from a question of probability of a sample statistic.

Suppose we have a large gas-filled balloon which is released to float freely for one hour after which its location is reported. The experiment may be done many times, say $n$ times, and each trial provides one sample value on the air current velocity and direction.

If it were known that the prevailing winds at the release point were always from west to east and that the wind velocity was a normally distributed random variable with expected value, $E(w) = 7$ miles per hour, and known variance, then a typical question in probability may be phrased, "What is the *probability* that for $n$ independent trials, the average distance to the east that the balloon travels from the release point in one hour is greater than 10 miles?"

The reverse type question is the important one for purposes of statistical inference. Suppose it is again known that the prevailing winds are always west to east so that only the wind velocity need be estimated. Further, suppose it is assumed that this velocity is a normally distributed random variable with a known variance. Then consider the question, "If 15 independent trials are made and the average distance to the east that the balloon travels from the release point in one hour is 5.6 miles, what is the *likelihood* that the true expected value of the wind velocity is at least 7 miles per hour?"

Obviously, the answer to either the probability question or the likelihood question involves some of the same statistical concepts and makes use of the PDF of the random variable. It is clear that the likelihood of the true parameter being 7 or more is greater than the likelihood of it being 9 or more given that the sample mean is 5.6. In maximum likelihood estimation, one wishes to determine the point value for the true parameter that is *most likely*. Which value of $E(w)$ has the *maximum likelihood* of being true?

The procedure for determining maximum likelihood estimators is simply stated but not so simply performed. The steps are:

1. Determine the likelihood function for the unknown parameter, say $L(\Theta)$ as the joint PDF of the $n$ sample random variables $X_1, X_2, \ldots, X_n$, where each marginal PDF involves the unknown parameter $\Theta$.
2. Maximize the likelihood functions with respect to $\Theta$, often by maximizing the logarithm of $L(\Theta)$ for simplicity.

Some examples of this procedure are presented in the exercises at the end of the chapter. In particular, Exercise 15 presents the MLE for the unknown parameters, $\alpha_1$, $\alpha_2$, and $\sigma_\varepsilon^2$, in the simple model.

||||||||||||||||||||||||||||||||||||||||||||||||||||||||||||||||||||||||||||||||||||||||||||||||||||||||||||||||||||||||||||||||

***Explicative note.*** The resulting MLE of $\alpha_1$ and of $\alpha_2$ are shown to be identical to the least squares estimators of (3–2). The use of the normality assumption, number 2 in Section 5.4, is essential in obtaining this result.

||||||||||||||||||||||||||||||||||||||||||||||||||||||||||||||||||||||||||||||||||||||||||||||||||||||||||||||||||||||||||||||||

## 6.7 SUMMARY

The least squares estimators of $\alpha_1$ and $\alpha_2$ in the simple model are the most frequently used type estimator in econometrics. The reasons for this popularity should now be understandable. First, the estimators and their variances and covariances are quite easily computed by the formulas (3–2) and (6–3). These formulas, using the substitution of $s_e^2$ as an unbiased estimator of $\sigma_\varepsilon^2$, are presented together here as the most important formulas to remember for use in the next chapter.

$$a_1 = \overline{Y} - a_2 \overline{X}_2 \qquad\qquad a_2 = \frac{\sum x_{t2} y_t}{\sum x_{t2}^2}$$

$$E(a_1) = \alpha_1 \qquad\qquad E(a_2) = \alpha_2$$

$$[\text{Est. } V(a_1)] = \frac{\sum X_{t2}^2}{T \sum x_{t2}^2} s_e^2 \qquad\qquad [\text{Est. } V(a_2)] = \frac{1}{\sum x_{t2}^2} s_e^2 \qquad (6\text{–}4)$$

$$[\text{Est. } Cov(a_1, a_2)] = \frac{-\overline{X}_2}{\sum x_{t2}^2} s_e^2 \qquad [\text{Est. } (\sigma_\varepsilon^2)] = s_e^2 = \frac{\sum e_t^2}{T-2}$$

where Est. stands for "the estimate of."

Second, the least squares estimators (LSE) have the desirable properties of unbiasedness and efficiency. This is summarized in the Gauss-Markov result by stating that the LSE are BLUE.

Third, the LSE are identical to maximum likelihood estimators of $\alpha_1$ and $\alpha_2$. (Again, see Exercise 15 at the end of this chapter.)

||||||||||||||||||||||||||||||||||||||||||||||||||||||||||||||||||||||||||||||||||||||||||||||||||||||||||||||||||||||||||

*Recursive note.* This result, that the least squares estimators are BLUE and MLE, depends on the assumptions for the model as given in Section 5.4. In particular the necessity of the assumptions for these special properties may be outlined as follows:

| Property | Assumptions | |
|----------|--------|------|
|  | Number | Name |
| Unbiasedness | 1 | $X$ fixed and independent of $\varepsilon$ |
|  | and 3 | $E(\varepsilon_t) = 0$ |
| Efficiency | 4 | Homoscedasticity |
|  | and 5 | No autocorrelation |
| MLE | 2 | Normality |

||||||||||||||||||||||||||||||||||||||||||||||||||||||||||||||||||||||||||||||||||||||||||||||||||||||||||||||||||||||||||

The role of the assumptions continues to be important for the statistical testing of the model and its parameters in the next chapter. The reader can be assured that this is not the last time he will be confronted with issues and answers concerning properties of estimators. Much current econometric research centers on discovering and comparing various estimators for specific models and for specific exceptions to some of our underlying assumptions. In this text, some of these concerns are investigated more generally in Chapters 13–15.

## NEW VOCABULARY

Maximum likelihood estimator (MLE)
BLUE
Estimate of the variance of an estimator
Unbiased estimator

Efficient estimator (minimum variance)
Jacobian
Chi-square distribution
Likelihood function

## EXERCISES

1. Consider a simple model $Y_t = \alpha_1 + \alpha_2 X_{t2} + \varepsilon_t$ where $V(\varepsilon_t)$ is unknown. Suppose an estimate of $V(\varepsilon_t)$ with $(T - 2)$ degrees of freedom is obtained by using the standard error of estimate $s_e^2$. Based on 22 sample values, suppose $s_e^2 = 25.128$. What is the probability that $V(\varepsilon_t)$ is as small as 16? *Hint*: Use $(T - 2)s_e^2/V(\varepsilon_t) \sim \chi^2_{(T-2)\text{d.f.}}$. Ans.: 0.05.

2. A random sample of size $N$ is taken from a normal population for the random variable $X$ with mean $\mu$ and standard deviation 1. Complete the steps in determining the maximum likelihood estimator of $\mu$.

   a) Write the PDF for a single $X_i$.

   $$f(X_i) = \frac{1}{\sqrt{2\pi\sigma^2}} \exp\left[-\frac{1}{2\sigma^2}(X_i - \mu)^2\right]$$

   and substitute $\sigma = 1$.

   b) Using the property of independence due to random sampling and the identical PDF for each $X_i$ since they are drawn from the same population, write the likelihood function which is the joint PDF for all $X_i$, $i = 1, 2, \ldots, N$.

   $$L(\mu) = f(X_1, X_2, \ldots, X_n; \mu, 1) = \prod_{i=1}^{n} f(X_i) = \underline{\hspace{3cm}}$$

   c) Simplify and take the natural logarithm of the likelihood function

   $$\ln L(\mu) = -\frac{n}{2}\ln 2\pi - \frac{1}{2}\sum_{i}^{n}(X_i - \mu)^2.$$

   d) Find $d \ln L(\mu)/d\mu$ and set it equal to zero. Solve for the MLE of $\mu = \sum X_i/n = \bar{X}$.

3. Suppose the time interval $X$ between successive peaks of production for a certain agriculture product is a random variable with PDF

   $$f(X) = \theta \exp[-\theta X] \text{ for } X > 0 \text{ and}$$

   $$f(X) = 0 \text{ otherwise.}$$

   Observations are made on $N$ time intervals $X_1, X_2, \ldots, X_N$. Show that the MLE of $\theta$ is $(1/\bar{X})$.

4. What are the general conditions for which least squares and maximum likelihood estimators of coefficients in a single equation linear model, $Y_t = \alpha_1 + \alpha_2 X_{t2} + \varepsilon_t$, will be identical?

5. Discuss whether unbiasedness or efficiency is the more desirable property of an estimator to be used to estimate the student enrollment in each public school in a given state for purposes of budget allocations to the schools on a per student basis.

   a) Suppose you are a legislator and need a correct total allocation.

   b) Suppose you are a local school administrator and want more than your fair share.

6. Discuss whether unbiasedness or efficiency is the more desirable property of an estimator to be used to estimate the annual exports of each product of a developing country.

   a) Suppose you wish to establish a long-run average annual growth rate for total exports.

   b) Suppose you wish to establish import controls for a given year based on the amount of foreign exchange available from exports.

7. Explain what is meant by—
   a) The variance of an estimator.
   b) An efficient linear unbiased estimate.
   c) The standard error of estimate $s_e$.
   d) Degrees of freedom.

8. Let $X$ be a random variable associated with a binomial probability situation where $X$ measures the number of successes in $N$ independent trials with $p$ equal to the probability of success in a single trial. Let $X = \sum Y$ where $Y = 1$ if a success occurs, and $Y = 0$ if a failure occurs. If $f(Y_i; p) = p^{Y_i}(1 - p)^{(1 - Y_i)}$, set up the likelihood function for $p$ and find the MLE for $p$. Ans.: $X/n$.

9. Derive

$$V(a_2) = \sigma_\varepsilon^2 \, \frac{1}{\sum x_{t2}^2}$$

using a procedure similar to that shown in Section 6.3 for $V(a_1)$.

10. The LSE of $\alpha_1$, the intercept in the simple model has been shown to be a linear estimator,

$$a_1 = \sum_t \left( \frac{1}{T} - \bar{X}h_t \right) Y_t$$

where $h_t = x_t / \sum X_t^2$, and an unbiased estimator, $E(a_1) = \alpha_1$. It is also often referred to as the "best" linear unbiased estimator where best means efficient. Complete the following steps to show this result.

a) Consider any other arbitrary linear estimator of $\alpha_1$, say $a^*$,

$$a^* = \sum_t \left[ \frac{1}{T} - \bar{X}(h_t + k_t) \right] Y_t$$

where $k_t$ are some fixed constants in this arbitrary linear combination. Substitute in this expression for $Y_t = (\alpha_1 + \alpha_2 X_t + \varepsilon_t)$.

b) Expand the product to obtain

$$a^* = \alpha_1 - \alpha_1 \bar{X} \sum (h_t + k_t) + \frac{\alpha_2}{T} \sum X_t - \alpha_2 \bar{X} \sum X_t(h_t + k_t)$$

$$+ \sum \left[ \frac{1}{T} - \bar{X}(h_t + k_t) \right] \varepsilon_t.$$

c) Take the $E(a^*)$ by summing the expected value of each term and assume $E(\varepsilon_t) = 0$ and consider $X_t$, $h_t$, and $k_t$ as fixed.

d) Show that for $a^*$ to be unbiased, that is, $E(a^*) = \alpha_1$, then two conditions must hold, namely, (i) $\sum(h_t + k_t) = 0$ which implies $\sum k_t = 0$ since $\sum h_t = \sum x_t / \sum x_t^2 = 0$, and (ii) $\sum(h_t + k_t)X_t = 1$ which implies $\sum k_t X_t = 0$ if you show that $\sum h_t X_t = 1$.

e) Now write $V(a^*) = E[a^* - E(a^*)]^2 = E[a^* - \alpha_1]^2$ since $a^*$ should be unbiased. A simplified expression for $(a^* - \alpha_1)$ is obtained from step (b) by applying necessary conditions (i and ii) for unbiasedness given in step (d). We obtain

$$V(a^*) = E\left\{ \sum \left[ \frac{1}{T} - \bar{X}(h_t + k_t) \right] \varepsilon_t \right\}^2 = \sigma_\varepsilon^2 \sum \left[ \frac{1}{T} - \bar{X}(h_t + k_t) \right]^2.$$

*f)* Expand the square and collect terms with foresight to get

$$V(a^*) = \sigma_\varepsilon^2 \left[ \frac{1}{T^2} - \frac{2\bar{X}}{T} \sum h_t + \bar{X}^2 \sum h_t^2 \right]$$

$$+ \sigma_\varepsilon^2 \left[ 2\bar{X}^2 \sum h_t k_t - 2\frac{\bar{X}}{T} \sum k_t + \bar{X}^2 \sum k_t^2 \right].$$

Consider the terms in the latter bracket. We know $\sum k_t = 0$ and $\sum k_t X_t = 0$ from step *(d)*. Since

$$\sum h_t k_t = \frac{\sum x_t k_t}{\sum x_t^2} = \frac{\sum X_t k_t - \bar{X} \sum k_t}{\sum x_t^2},$$

it also is zero. The first bracket encloses a perfect square, $(1/T - \bar{X}\sum h_t)^2$. From Section 6.3, step (2) of the derivation of $V(a_1)$, we obtain $V(a_1) = \sigma_\varepsilon^2(1/T - \bar{X}\sum h_t)^2$. Substituting all this information into $V(a^*)$ above, we obtain $V(a^*) = V(a_1) + \sigma_\varepsilon^2(0 - 0 + \bar{X}^2 \sum k_t^2)$.

*g)* Since $\sigma_\varepsilon^2 \bar{X}^2 \sum k_t^2$ involves all squared terms, it cannot be negative; and so, $V(a^*) \geq V(a_1)$. The equality would hold only if all $k_t = 0$ since $\sigma_\varepsilon^2$ and $\bar{X}^2$ cannot be assured to be zero. But if all $k_t = 0$, then from the initial step, $a^* = \sum [1/T - \bar{X}(h_t + 0)] Y_t = a_1$. The only way that the arbitrary linear unbiased estimator $a^*$ could have a variance as small as the variance for the LSE $a_1$ is if $a^*$ is, in fact, identical to $a_1$. Otherwise, the variance of $a^*$ is always larger. That is, $a_1$ is the minimum variance estimator in its class.

11. Use the pattern of Exercise 10 above to show that $a_2$ is the minimum variance linear unbiased estimator of $\alpha_2$. Begin with an arbitrary estimator $\tilde{a} = \sum_t (h_t + k_t) Y_t$ where $h_t = x_t/\sum x_t^2$.

12. Suppose a random variable $X$ has probability function $f(x) = 2KX^k$. A sample of size $n$ is taken. Find the MLE for $k$. Ans.: $k = -n/\sum \ln X$.

13. Considering the simple model $Y_t = \alpha_1 + \alpha_2 X_{t2} + \varepsilon_t$, let the $\varepsilon_t$ be distributed as $N(kX_t, \sigma_\varepsilon^2)$ and let $T$ observations on $Y_t$ and $X_{t2}$ be available where $X_{t2}$ is a fixed (nonrandom) variable. Find the maximum likelihood estimators for $\alpha_1$ and $\alpha_2$. Ans.: $\tilde{a}_1 = \bar{Y} - (\tilde{a}_2 + k)\bar{X}$, $\tilde{a}_2 = (\sum xy - k\sum X^2)/\sum x^2$.

14. A random sample, $X_1, X_2, \ldots, X_T$, is drawn from a normal population with mean 3 and standard deviation $\sigma$. Find the MLE of $\sigma$. (Refer to Exercise 2 above.)

15. To find the MLE of $\alpha_1$, $\alpha_2$, and $\sigma_\varepsilon^2$, we need to determine the joint PDF of the combined random variables $Y_1, Y_2, \ldots, Y_T$ for given fixed values of $X_{12}, X_{22}, \ldots, X_{T2}$.

The distribution of $Y_t$ can be obtained from the assumed distribution of $\varepsilon_t$ by using the Jacobian of this transformation. Thus,

$$q(Y_1, Y_2, \ldots, Y_t) = J\left( \frac{\varepsilon_1, \varepsilon_2, \ldots, \varepsilon_T}{Y_1, Y_2, \ldots, Y_t} \right) p(\varepsilon_1, \varepsilon_2, \ldots, \varepsilon_T),$$

where the Jacobian equals one for this transformation since

$$\frac{\partial \varepsilon_i}{\partial Y_j} = \begin{cases} 1 & \text{for } i = j \\ 0 & \text{for } i \neq j \end{cases}.$$

Therefore, $q(Y_t) = p(\varepsilon_t)$; and it is then known that the probability density function of $Y_t$ is normal by Assumption 2 and contains the unknown parameters, $\alpha_1$, $\alpha_2$, and $\sigma_\varepsilon^2$. Since $E(\varepsilon_t) = 0$ by Assumption 3, then

$$E(Y_t) = E(\alpha_1 + \alpha_2 X_{t2} + \varepsilon_t) = \alpha_1 + \alpha_2 X_{t2}.$$

Also, from Assumptions 4 and 5, $V(Y_t) = V(\varepsilon_t) = \sigma_\varepsilon^2$ and $Cov(Y_i, Y_j) = Cov(\varepsilon_i \varepsilon_j) = 0$ for $i \neq j$ and fixed values of $X_{t2}$ by Assumption 1. Thus,

$$q(Y_t^\circ) = \frac{1}{\sqrt{2\pi\sigma_\varepsilon^2}} \exp[-(Y_t^\circ - \alpha_1 - \alpha_2 X_{t2}^\circ)^2/2\sigma_\varepsilon^2].$$

The likelihood function can be written,

$$L(\alpha_1, \alpha_2, \sigma_\varepsilon^2) = f(Y_1^\circ, Y_2^\circ, \ldots, Y_T^\circ; \alpha_1, \alpha_2, \sigma_\varepsilon^2 \mid X_{12}^\circ, X_{22}^\circ, \ldots, X_{T2}^\circ).$$

Using the normal distribution for $q(Y_t^\circ)$ given above and the condition of independence for the $Y_t$'s so that the joint PDF equals the product of the marginal PDF's, this becomes

$$L(\alpha_1, \alpha_2, \sigma_\varepsilon^2) = \prod_{t=1}^{T} \frac{1}{\sqrt{2\pi\sigma_\varepsilon^2}} \exp[-(Y_t^\circ - \alpha_1 - \alpha_2 X_{t2}^\circ)^2/2\sigma_\varepsilon^2]$$

$$= 2\pi^{-T/2}(\sigma_\varepsilon^2)^{-T/2} \exp\left[-\frac{1}{2\sigma_\varepsilon^2} \sum_{t=1}^{T}(Y_t^\circ - \alpha_1 - \alpha_2 X_{t2}^\circ)^2\right].$$

This likelihood function can be maximized with respect to $\alpha_1$, $\alpha_2$, $\sigma_\varepsilon^2$ by maximizing the natural logarithm of the function, $\ln L(\alpha_1, \alpha_2, \sigma_\varepsilon^2)$, with respect to these unknown parameters. The maximum value of either function, given the values $Y_t^\circ$ and $X_{t2}^\circ$, will occur at the same values of the parameters. Using this procedure, we get

$$\ln L(\alpha_1, \alpha_2, \sigma_\varepsilon^2) = -\left(\frac{T}{2}\right)\ln 2\pi - \left(\frac{T}{2}\right)\ln \sigma_\varepsilon^2 - \frac{1}{2\sigma_\varepsilon^2}\sum_{t=1}^{T}(Y_t^\circ - \alpha_1 - \alpha_2 X_{t2}^\circ)^2.$$

This function is continuous with respect to $\alpha_1$, $\alpha_2$, and $\sigma_\varepsilon^2$ and exists everywhere except $\sigma_\varepsilon^2 = 0$ which can be ignored since $\varepsilon_t$ is a random variable with $V(\varepsilon_t) = \sigma_\varepsilon^2 \neq 0$.

Now, proceed with the maximization by differentiating $L(\alpha_1, \alpha_2, \sigma_\varepsilon^2)$ partially with respect to $\alpha_1$, $\alpha_2$, and $\sigma_\varepsilon^2$ and by setting the partial derivatives all equal to zero.

$$\frac{\partial(\ln L)}{\partial\alpha_1} = \frac{1}{\sigma_\varepsilon^2}\sum_t (Y_t^\circ - \alpha_1 - \alpha_2 X_{t2}^\circ),$$

$$\frac{\partial(\ln L)}{\partial\alpha_2} = \frac{1}{\sigma_\varepsilon^2}\sum_t X_{t2}^\circ(Y_t^\circ - \alpha_1 - \alpha_2 X_{t2}^\circ),$$

and

$$\frac{\partial(\ln L)}{\partial(\sigma_\varepsilon^2)} = -\frac{T}{2}\frac{1}{\sigma_\varepsilon^2} + \frac{1}{2}\sum_t (Y_t^\circ - \alpha_1 - \alpha_2 X_{t2}^\circ)^2 \frac{1}{(\sigma_\varepsilon^2)^2}.$$

||||||||||||||||||||||||||||||||||||||||||||||||||||||||||||||||||||||||||||||||||||||||||||||||||||||||||||||||||||||||||||||||||||||||||||||

***Explicative note.*** The last differentiation is with respect to $(\sigma_\varepsilon^2)$, not $\sigma_\varepsilon$. Thus, the two relevant terms follow the rules

$$\frac{d\,(K\,\ln z)}{dz} = K\left(\frac{1}{z}\right)$$

and

$$\frac{d}{dz}\left(K\frac{1}{z}\right) = K\left(\frac{-1}{z^2}\right),$$

where $z$ represents $\sigma_\varepsilon^2$, and $K$ is the proper constant.

||||||||||||||||||||||||||||||||||||||||||||||||||||||||||||||||||||||||||||||||||||||||||||||||||||||||||||||||||||||||||||||||||||||||||||||

Setting the first two partials above equal to zero and solving for $\alpha_1$ and $\alpha_2$ gives the familiar least squares estimators,

$$\tilde{\alpha}_1 = \overline{Y} - \tilde{\alpha}_2\,\overline{X}_2$$

and

$$\tilde{\alpha}_2 = \frac{\sum y_t x_{t2}}{\sum x_{t2}^2}.$$

Setting the third partial equal to zero gives an estimate of the important variance of the disturbance.

$$[\text{Est. } V(\varepsilon_t)] = \sum_t \frac{(Y_t - a_1 - a_2 X_{t2})^2}{T} = \frac{1}{T}\sum e_t^2.$$

As examined in *Review* 4.2, this estimate would be biased. The bias is easily corrected by dividing the sum of squares by degrees of freedom rather than by $T$. For the simple model with two coefficients being estimated, the unbiased estimate of $V(\varepsilon_t)$ becomes $s_e^2 = \sum e^2/(T-2)$.

# Chapter 7

# TESTS FOR THE SIMPLE MODEL

## 7.1 PREVIEW

An econometrician and his model are similar to a football coach and his team. The football coach would get little satisfaction from recruiting players for a football team and having them practice everyday if the team did not ever enter into competition nor play any games. The coach may brag about how fast and strong and coordinated the players are and how balanced and powerful the team is, but no one is going to be convinced until they prove themselves in a game. Thus, the coach desires some competitive testing of his team, not on the practice field but in the stadium.

If the team plays only one game and loses, its ranking in the eye of the public is quite low. Its claim to fame has been falsified. The coach would like to have another chance to win in another game. On the other hand, if the team wins its one game, the public keeps it in consideration but will not believe it has earned top honors until it shows its ability to win again and again. Each time the team wins, its popularity and ranking may increase. However, even after a long winning streak, it is likely that some people will still doubt that the team is the best. Indeed, this absolute verification of its superiority is likely to be impossible to attain as other teams and the game conditions keep changing.

A linear explanatory economic model specified by a researcher meets a similar fate. Regardless how much care is taken in its construction, the selection of its variables, and their specified relations, the model needs to be tested, not in the mind of the econometrician but in terms of economic experience as revealed by the economic data.

Usually the data for the model are gathered, the model is fit, and the parameters are estimated only once. The econometrician only gets one chance to establish his case. If the performance of the model is not good, it gets discarded or revamped. If the model performs well, it is often put into the literature for consideration, but it is certainly not accepted by everyone as the best possible explanatory model for the specific economic mechanism it describes. Econometricians continue to construct other models. New data become available, so the testing of the models needs to be repeated.

There is not really one special test of the model which is authoritative or which is definitive for all applications of the econometric model. It is not necessarily true that a model which fits the data well is also suitable for testing economic postulates. And vice versa, a model may consistently result in estimates within 95 percent confidence limits of an hypothesized true value for the parameter but never generate forecasts within 2 percent of the actual future value of the endogenous variable.

The most frequently used tests of a model involve the measures of goodness of fit as presented in Chapter 4. These are used to determine if the specified linear relation is significant. However, since the model does represent economic theory, it is likely that the econometrician wishes to specify and test more than merely the existence of a linear relation among the variables. He may postulate certain values, or range of values, or comparisons between values, for the parameters of the model which reflect various elasticities or marginals in economic theory. These additional specifications are sometimes testable using statistical notions of testing of hypothesis and confidence intervals.

Also, the econometrician often discusses the forecasting accuracy of his model. Unfortunately, there is no reason why a specific point estimate which generates a point forecast should be correct. Thus, testing of forecasts of the mean value or of a particular value of the endogenous variable given values of the exogenous variables is best done in terms of forecast intervals which are analogous to confidence intervals.

Some common methods of making such tests using statistics with $t$, $\chi^2$, and $F$ distributions are presented in this chapter.

## 7.2 REVIEW

Again, mathematical statistics provides the quantitative concepts underlying topics of this chapter. Some of the relevant definitions, procedures, and theorems are presented in this section as a guide for review.

### 1 Quadratic forms and their distributions

A quadratic form in $n$ variables is a homogeneous second degree polynomial in those variables. For example, $\sum a_i{}^2 X_i{}^2 + \sum a_i a_j X_i X_j = Q$ is a quadratic form in $n$ variables. The form does not contain a constant term.

Another particular illustration of a quadratic form is the one associated with combined random variables with a multivariate normal distribution. Let $Y_t, t = 1, 2, \ldots, T$, denote independent random variables which are normally distributed with expected value $\mu_t$ and variance $\sigma_t{}^2$, $t = 1, 2, \ldots, T$. The exponent in the joint PDF of $Y_1, Y_2, \ldots, Y_T$ is $-\frac{1}{2} \sum (Y_t - \mu_t)^2 / \sigma_t{}^2$. The reader can refer to *Review* 6.2, item 5, for the case of $T = 2$. Associated with this joint normal PDF is $Q = \sum (Y_t - \mu_t)^2$, a quadratic form in the variables $(Y_t - \mu_t)$ obtained from the numerator of the exponent by dropping the coefficient $(-\frac{1}{2})$. If the variables were not mutually independent, then the form $Q$ would also include cross-product terms in which the correlation coefficients between $Y_i$ and $Y_j$ would occur.

Many testing procedures in econometrics make use of the distribution of such quadratic forms. An important theorem of statistics will be used several times in establishing such tests.

THEOREM. If $Q, Q_1, Q_2, \ldots, Q_k$ are $k + 1$ random variables that are real quadratic forms in $n$ mutually independent normally distributed random variables with means $\mu_1, \mu_2, \ldots, \mu_n$ and the same variance $\sigma^2$ such that $Q = Q_1 + Q_2 + \cdots + Q_k$, and $Q_k$ is nonnegative, and such that $Q/\sigma^2$, $Q_1/\sigma^2$, $\ldots$, $Q_{k-1}/\sigma^2$ have chi-square distributions with degrees of freedom $V, v_1, v_2, \ldots, v_{k-1}$ respectively, then (i) $Q_1, Q_2, \ldots, Q_k$ are mutually independent; (ii) $Q_k/\sigma^2$ is also chi-square distributed with $v_k = V - (v_1 + v_2 + \cdots + v_{k-1})$ degrees of freedom.[1]

---

[1] R. V. Hogg and A. T. Craig, *Introduction to Mathematical Statistics* (2d ed.; New York: The MacMillan Co., 1965), sec. 13.2, pp. 348–58, especially Theorem 3, p. 355. Extensions of the theorem involving quadratic forms in random variables that have a joint multivariate normal distribution with a positive definite covariance matrix are also applied in some later cases to get the same conclusions.

The importance and wide use of this theorem will become apparent as we do in fact use it. It provides one way of being sure when two $\chi^2$ random variables are independent. It will often help provide information on the distribution of a quadratic form in an additive collection of such forms. This is particularly relevant when we also remember the following result in statistics.[2] If a random sample, $Y_1, Y_2, \ldots, Y_T$ is drawn from a normal distribution with mean $\mu$ and variance $\sigma^2$, then the random variable, $\sum (Y_t - \mu)^2/\sigma^2 = vs^2/\sigma^2$ is chi-square distributed with $v$ degrees of freedom where $s^2$ is an unbiased sample estimate of $\sigma^2$. This result has already been suggested in previous chapters and continues to be used in this chapter and again in Chapter 11.

## 2 The $t$-distributed statistic

A theorem that is often used to advantage states that a random variable has a $t$-distribution if it is distributed as the ratio $\dfrac{z\sqrt{v}}{\sqrt{\chi^2_{v\,\text{d.f.}}}}$ where $z$ is a random variable having a standardized normal distribution and is independent of the chi-square distributed variable $\chi^2$ which has $v$ degrees of freedom.[3] Several of these type statistics will be formed. The $t$-distribution is symmetric about mean zero and approaches the standardized normal as its one parameter, degrees of freedom, approaches infinity. (See Appendix C.)

## 3 The $F$-distributed statistic

A random variable has an $F$-distribution if it is the ratio of two independently distributed chi-square variables, say $\chi_1{}^2$ and $\chi_2{}^2$, each divided by their degrees of freedom, $v_1$ and $v_2$ respectively.[4] This distribution depends on two parameters, the degrees of freedom in the numerator and denominator. That is, the random variable

$$F_{(v_1, v_2)\,\text{d.f.}} = \frac{\chi_1{}^2/v_1}{\chi_2{}^2/v_2}$$

has an $F$-distribution with degrees of freedom $v_1$ and $v_2$. The $F$-distribution is positively skewed. (See Appendix D.)

## 4 Confidence intervals

A confidence interval is a form of a probability statement of the event "a parameter is contained within an interval to be determined in a specific way on the basis of sample observations," or the event "a test statistic to be

[2] Ibid., pp. 139–45.
[3] Ibid., p. 126.
[4] Ibid., p. 127.

determined is contained within a specified interval." The former type event is derivable from the latter since the test statistic will involve the true parameter.

In general denote the true parameter by $\Theta$, and denote by $P$ the test statistic which has a known probability distribution that includes $\Theta$. Then a $(1 - \alpha)$ 100 percent confidence interval on the test statistic is designated as the interval between $P_{(1-\alpha/2)}$ and $P_{(\alpha/2)}$. See Figure 7–1 and continue on for the meaning of these symbols.

**FIGURE 7–1**
**Illustration of a confidence interval with interpretation for two-sided test of hypothesis**

PDF FOR P

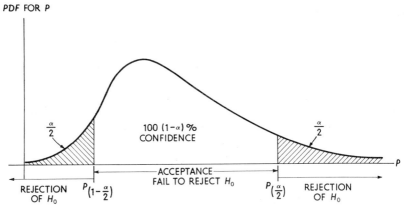

The symbol $\alpha$ denotes the level of significance which is the risk in probability terms that the test statistic may not be within this interval because an improbable sample was drawn. Thus $(1 - \alpha)$ is the confidence level or the probability that the test statistic will be within this interval. These levels are usually multiplied by 100 and expressed in percentages. A commonly used confidence level would be 95 percent with an $\alpha$ risk of 0.05.

The symbol $P_{(1-\alpha/2)}$ denotes that value of the test statistic such that the probability is $(1 - \alpha/2)$ of drawing at random from its distribution and observing a value larger than it. Similarly, the symbol $P_{(\alpha/2)}$ denotes that value of $P$ such that the probability is $\alpha/2$ of observing a larger value. A precise probability statement which includes all the meaning of a confidence interval is

$$\Pr\{P_{(1-\alpha/2)} < P < P_{(\alpha/2)}\} = 1 - \alpha.$$

Solutions of the inequalities for the true parameter $\Theta$ provide a similar probability statement about its value based on the sample to be drawn. In particular, confidence intervals can be established for the parameters $\alpha_1$, $\alpha_2$, and $\sigma_\varepsilon^2$ or for the expected value of a forecast and an individual forecast itself.

## 5 Test of hypothesis

All tests of hypothesis on a parameter $\Theta$ follow the same basic steps. These are listed with some explanatory comments.

a)  State the null hypothesis, usually an equality statement such as $H_0: \alpha_1 = 3$.

b)  State the alternate hypothesis. This is a statement of the proposition to be accepted if the null hypothesis is rejected. It can be either a *greater than, less than,* or *not equal to* type statement such as $H_a: \alpha_1 > 3$; $H_a: \alpha_1 < 3$; or $H_a: \alpha_1 \neq 3$ respectively. If the alternate hypothesis is the first form, an upper one-tailed test is desired. For the second form, a lower one-tailed test is desired. If it is the third type, then a two-tailed test is needed. The null and alternate hypothesis should be formulated so that the alternate statement best expresses the result we hope to obtain in making the test.

c)  Select a significance level, $\alpha$. This is the risk of rejecting the null hypothesis when it is true, commonly set at 0.05 or 0.01.

d)  Determine an appropriate test statistic $P$ and its probability distribution when the null hypothesis is true. Commonly $P$ will have a normal, $t$, $\chi^2$, or $F$-distribution.

e)  Determine the so-called critical region or rejection region. This is the range of values of $P$ such that the null hypothesis will be rejected. These values are determined from a table of the probability distribution of $P$ and depend on the level of risk $\alpha$ and the degrees of freedom of $P$ for the particular sample being used in the test. For an upper one-tailed test the rejection region is all values of $P$ larger than $P_\alpha$. For a lower one-tailed test, it is all values of $P$ smaller than $P_{(1-\alpha)}$. For a two-tailed test (which is in principle identical to a confidence interval), the rejection region is split into two parts. It is all values of $P$ either larger than $P_{\alpha/2}$ or smaller than $P_{(1-\alpha/2)}$. (See Figure 7–1.)

f)  Calculate $P$, the test statistic, from the sample observations.

g)  Make a decision. If the calculated test statistic lies in the rejection region, then reject the null hypothesis with a known chance of error of $\alpha$ in this decision. The probability of obtaining a value of $P$ in the rejection region is so small (less than $\alpha$) under the assumption that the null hypothesis is true that one must decide to reject that assumption.

If the calculated test statistic is not in the rejection region, then the null hypothesis is not rejected. It is, say, accepted, subject to an undetermined risk that it may be accepted, although it is false. The larger the sample the smaller this risk, other things being unchanged.

The null hypothesis can never be verified, however, just as a confidence level of 100 percent can never be established since observation of the whole population would be required. For testing parameters in an econometric model, this requirement is impossible since it implies that all conceivable samples can be observed.

To help redevelop a skill in setting confidence limits and making tests of hypothesis, the following problems are suggested. Working them will also help improve your facility in using $t$ and $F$ distributions for specified degrees of freedom and significance levels.

## REVIEW EXERCISES

R.1.  For a test statistic $P$ with a $t$-distribution, what is the value of $P_{(\alpha)}$ if:

a)  $\alpha = 0.05$ and $v = 3$.     d)  $\alpha = 0.01$ and $v = 3$.
b)  $\alpha = 0.05$ and $v = 10$.     e)  $\alpha = 0.01$ and $v = 10$.
c)  $\alpha = 0.05$ and $v = 20$.     f)  $\alpha = 0.01$ and $v = 20$.

R.2.  For a test statistic $P$ with a $t$-distribution, what are the values of $P_{(\alpha/2)}$ and $P_{(1-\alpha/2)}$ in the same situations (a) to (f) of Exercise R.1.

R.3.  For a test statistic $P$ with an $F$-distribution, what is the value of $P_{(\alpha)}$ if $\alpha = 0.05$ and

a)  $v_1 = 2$, $v_2 = 2$.     d)  $v_1 = 5$, $v_2 = 2$.
b)  $v_1 = 2$, $v_2 = 10$.     e)  $v_1 = 10$, $v_2 = 2$.
c)  $v_1 = 2$, $v_2 = 20$.     f)  $v_1 = 10$, $v_2 = 10$.

R.4.  Let $P = z/\sqrt{\chi^2/v}$ where the stochastically independent variables $z$ and $\chi^2$ are standardized normal and chi-square with $v$ degrees of freedom respectively. Form $P^2$ and show that it has an $F$-distribution with one and $v$ degrees of freedom. (*Hint*: Remember the definition of a chi-square from *Review* 6.2, item 6, and apply it to the numerator of $P^2$.)

R.5.  The test statistic $P = (\bar{X} - \mu)/s_{\bar{X}}$ has a $t$-distribution with $n - 1$ degrees of freedom where $\bar{X}$ is a sample mean and $s_{\bar{X}}$ a sample standard error of the mean based on $n$ observations, and $\mu$ is the (hypothesized) population mean.

a)  Find a 95 percent confidence interval for $P$ if $n = 18$. (*Hint*: $\alpha = 1 - 0.95 = 0.05$.)

b)  From part (a) solve for a 95 percent confidence interval on $\mu$ if $\bar{X} = 35$ and $s_{\bar{X}} = 6$.

R.6.  A sample of 25 observations has mean $\bar{X} = 12$ and standard deviation $s = 1.5$. Test the null hypothesis, $H_0$: $\mu = 11$, against the alternate, $H_a$: $\mu > 11$ using $\alpha = 0.01$. (*Hint*: $s_{\bar{X}} = s/\sqrt{n}$. Use the statistic from Exercise R.5.)

R.7.  The distribution of incomes by households is claimed to be different between two regions $A$ and $B$. In particular, region $A$ is claimed to have a larger variance. Samples are taken from each region and the sample variances (in $000) are $W_A = 810$ and $W_B = 650$, corrected for degrees of freedom 50 and 25 respectively. Given that $W_A/W_B$ is distributed as $F$ with 50 and 25 degrees of freedom, determine if this sample statistic exceeds $F_{(\alpha)}$ where $\alpha = 0.05$. If so, you would reject the hypothesis of equal variance in these distributions between regions $A$ and $B$.

R.8.  Ten households in a certain county are selected at random and their expenditure on food per quarter is measured. The average food expenditure is $620 with a standard deviation of $200. Test if the true average for this county is less than $725 per month using a significance level of 0.05. (*Hint*: Refer to Exercises R.5 and R.6.)

## 7.3 TESTS RELATED TO MEASURES OF GOODNESS OF FIT

Statistical tests can be made involving either the absolute or relative measures of goodness of fit for the estimation of the econometric model. In Chapter 4, the only criteria presented to evaluate these measures are that the standard error of estimate should be "small," and the correlation coefficient should be "close" to unity, either positive or negative. Let us first consider the absolute measure of goodness of fit, the standard error of estimate. This is the standard deviation of the distribution of residuals from the least squares estimation corrected for degrees of freedom. Its square can be used as an estimate of the parameter $\sigma_\varepsilon^2$, the unknown variance of the disturbance term $\varepsilon$. It also appears in every test statistic concerning the parameters of the model. In particular, the test statistic which is essential for many different tests is the random variable $(T - 2)s_e^2/\sigma_\varepsilon^2$. The square of the standard error of estimate, $s_e^2 = \sum e^2/(T - 2)$, is an unbiased estimate of $\sigma_\varepsilon^2$, and $(T - 2)s_e^2/\sigma_\varepsilon^2 = \sum e^2/\sigma_\varepsilon^2$ where $\sum e^2$ is a quadratic form in the normally distributed random variable $e_t = Y_t - a_1 - a_2 X_{t2}$ with mean zero and variance $\sigma_\varepsilon^2$. Consequently, referring back to *Review* 7.2, item 1, the statistic $(T - 2)s_e^2/\sigma_\varepsilon^2$ is chi-square distributed with $(T - 2)$ degrees of freedom. Thus, it can be used directly to make tests or to set confidence limits on $\sigma_\varepsilon^2$.

### Confidence statements on $V(\varepsilon)$

The null hypothesis $H_0: \sigma_\varepsilon^2 = N_0$, where $N_0$ is any real positive number, can be tested using the statistic

$$\chi^2_{(T-2)\text{ d.f.}} = \frac{(T - 2)s_e^2}{N_0}. \tag{7-1}$$

The hypothesis would be rejected at a significance level $\alpha$, in, say, an upper one-tailed test if this calculated $\chi^2$ were larger than the value $\chi_\alpha^2$, determined from a table for the corresponding number of degrees of freedom.

Confidence intervals for $\sigma_\varepsilon^2$ can be found from the probability statement,

$$\Pr\left\{\chi^2_{(1-\alpha/2)} < \frac{(T - 2)s_e^2}{\sigma_\varepsilon^2} < \chi^2_{\alpha/2}\right\} = (1 - \alpha).$$

Solving for $\sigma_\varepsilon^2$, one obtains the $(1 - \alpha)$ 100 percent confidence interval,

$$\left(\frac{(T - 2)s_e^2}{\chi^2_{\alpha/2}} < \sigma_\varepsilon^2 < \frac{(T - 2)s_e^2}{\chi^2_{(1-\alpha/2)}}\right) \tag{7-2}$$

### Test on the correlation coefficient

It is also common to test the significance of the relative measure of the goodness of fit, the correlation coefficient. The null hypothesis on the population correlation coefficient is $\rho = 0$ and the alternate may be $\rho \neq 0$ or one-sided if the direction of correlation in the population is known a priori. The correlation coefficient will be significantly different from zero only if $\rho^2$, the coefficient of determination is also significantly greater than zero. This occurs when the proportion of variation explained is significant. (Refer to Section 4.3 for the interpretive definition of the sample measures $r$ and $r^2$.)

### The theory underlying the test

Recalling that total variation equals the sum of variation explained and unexplained, we write

$$\sum y^2 = \sum \hat{y}^2 + \sum e^2 \qquad (4\text{-}1)$$

Now $y_t = \alpha_2 x_{t2} + \varepsilon_t$ so $\sum y^2$ can be written as a quadratic form in the random variable $\varepsilon_t$, $t = 1, 2, \ldots, T$, which is assumed to have a normal distribution with mean zero and variance $\sigma_\varepsilon^2$. Also, $\hat{y}_t = a_2 x_{t2}$ and $a_2$ is a linear function of $y$. Thus $\hat{y}_t$ is also a function of $\varepsilon_t$, and $\sum \hat{y}_t^2$ can be expressed as a quadratic form in $\varepsilon_t$. Obviously, $e = y - \hat{y}$ so $\sum e^2$ is another quadratic form in $\varepsilon_t$. Consequently, we could characterize the algebraic identity, $\sum y^2 = \sum \hat{y}^2 + \sum e^2$ by $Q = Q_1 + Q_2$ where these are quadratic forms satisfying the conditions of the theorem in *Review* 7.2, item 1. We can apply this theorem to determine that $Q_1/\sigma_\varepsilon^2$ is independent of $Q_2/\sigma_\varepsilon^2$. Moreover, each of these is a chi-square distributed random variable whose degrees of freedom can be determined by the additivity property of degrees of freedom for sums of chi-square distributed random variables.

---

***Discursive note.*** Total variation, $\sum y^2 = Q$ has $T - 1$ degrees of freedom since variation is measured about the mean $\bar{Y}$, whose calculation imposes one linear restriction on the sample data, namely $\bar{Y} = \sum Y/T$. The unexplained variation, $\sum e^2 = Q_2$, has $T - K$ degrees of freedom (as discussed in *Review* 4.2, item 3). Thus, the degrees of freedom of explained variation, $\sum \hat{y}^2 = Q_1 = (Q - Q_2)$ is $(T - 1) - (T - K) = (K - 1)$.

---

### The test statistic

Armed with all this information, we return to the problem of testing the significance of $\rho$ using the sample correlation coefficient $r$. If the correlation is very high, then the variation explained would exceed the variation unexplained. Their ratio is a measure of their comparative sizes. Moreover, the ratio,

$$\frac{\sum \hat{y}^2/(K-1)}{\sum e^2/(T-K)},$$

has a well-defined probability distribution known as the $F$-distribution. (See *Review* 7.2, item 3.)

From the above discussion, $\sum \hat{y}^2/(K-1) = Q_1/(K-1)$ and $\sum e^2/(T-K) = Q_2/(T-K)$ and $Q_1$ and $Q_2$ are independent. Also, $Q_1/\sigma_\varepsilon^2$ and $Q_2/\sigma_\varepsilon^2$ are chi-square distributed.

Thus,

$$\frac{Q_1/\sigma_\varepsilon^2}{Q_2/\sigma_\varepsilon^2}$$

is the ratio of independently distributed chi-square random variables. From this, we obtain

$$\frac{Q_1/(K-1)}{Q_2/(T-K)}$$

which is an $F$-distributed random variable with $(K-1)$ and $(T-K)$ degrees of freedom.

For our test on the significance of the correlation coefficient, we have $K = 2$ in the simple model, $Q_2/(T-2) = \sum e^2/(T-2) = s_e^2$, and

$$Q_1 = \sum \hat{y}^2 = a_2 \sum yx_2. \tag{4-4}$$

Thus,

$$F_{(1, T-2)\,\text{d.f.}} = \frac{a_2 \sum yx_2}{s_e^2}. \tag{7-3}$$

If the correlation is significant, then the explained variation is "large," the calculated test statistic has a numerator that exceeds the denominator, and $F > F_\alpha$. Thus, the null hypothesis of zero correlation is rejected.[5] The opposite situation of low correlation results in a larger denominator and a smaller numerator so the $F$ value is small. The null hypothesis of no correlation is not rejected.

---

[5] An equivalent test on the same null hypothesis, $\rho = 0$, can be made using a $t$-distributed random variable with $(T-2)$ degrees of freedom. The test statistic is

$$t_{(T-2)\,\text{d.f.}} = r\sqrt{\frac{T-2}{1-r^2}}.$$

If the calculated $t$ exceeds $t_\alpha$, then the null hypothesis of no correlation is rejected.

||||||||||||||||||||||||||||||||||||||||||||||||||||||||||||||||||||||||||||||||||||||||||||||||||||||||||||||||||||||||||||||||||||||||||||||||||||||||

*Interpretive note.*   A high correlation corresponds to a large proportion of variation *explained* by the relation. A low correlation corresponds to a large proportion of variation left *unexplained* by the relation. Consequently, for the simple model, this test of significance of $\rho$ is also a test of the significance of the hypothesized linear model.

||||||||||||||||||||||||||||||||||||||||||||||||||||||||||||||||||||||||||||||||||||||||||||||||||||||||||||||||||||||||||||||||||||||||||||||||||||||||

*Discursive note.*   This same formal procedure of examining quadratic forms to get independent chi-square distributed random variables whose ratio is the basis of an *F*-distributed random variable occurs frequently in developing econometric tests. It is the theory underlying analysis of variance tests and others to be presented in the following sections and in Chapter 11.

||||||||||||||||||||||||||||||||||||||||||||||||||||||||||||||||||||||||||||||||||||||||||||||||||||||||||||||||||||||||||||||||||||||||||||||||||||||||

## 7.4 TESTS ON THE COEFFICIENTS IN THE MODEL

Another common technique for formulating a test statistic must be presented now for developing tests on the coefficients in the econometric model. The input information comes from the results of Chapter 6 in which the estimates of the coefficients of the model $Y_t = \alpha_1 + \alpha_2 X_{t2} + \varepsilon_t$ were found to be $a_1 = \overline{Y} - a_2 \overline{X}_2$ which is distributed as[6]

$$N\left(\alpha_1, \frac{\sum X_2{}^2}{T \sum x_2{}^2} \sigma_\varepsilon{}^2\right)$$

and $a_2 = \sum yx_2 / \sum x_2{}^2$ which is distributed as

$$N\left(\alpha_2, \frac{1}{\sum x_2{}^2} \sigma_\varepsilon{}^2\right).$$

However, tests cannot be made on $\alpha_1$ and $\alpha_2$ directly using the standardized normal variable

$$z = \frac{\text{estimate—its mean}}{\text{its standard deviation}}.$$

If this statistic is derived, one obtains

$$z_1 = \frac{a_1 - \alpha_1}{\sqrt{\sigma_\varepsilon{}^2 \dfrac{\sum X_2{}^2}{T \sum x_2{}^2}}} = \frac{(a_1 - \alpha_1)\sqrt{T \sum x_{t2}{}^2}}{\sigma_\varepsilon \sqrt{\sum X_{t2}{}^2}}$$

---

[6] The notation, $N(E, V)$ indicates that the distribution is normal with expected value $E$ and variance $V$.

and

$$z_2 = \frac{a_2 - \alpha_2}{\sqrt{\dfrac{\sigma_\varepsilon^2}{\sum x_2^2}}} = \frac{(a_2 - \alpha_2)\sqrt{\sum x_2^2}}{\sigma_\varepsilon}.$$

Both of these include the unknown value $\sigma_\varepsilon$ so the analysis is stymied.

## A useful transformation

However, each of these statistics is distributed independently of the

$$\chi^2_{(T-2)\text{d.f.}} = \frac{(T-2)s_e^2}{\sigma_\varepsilon^2};$$

and so, a fruitful change to a $t$-distributed statistic can be made.[7]
The statistic,

$$\frac{z\sqrt{v}}{\sqrt{\chi^2_{v\,\text{d.f.}}}},$$

has a $t$-distribution where $z$ is a normally distributed standardized variable and $v$ is the degrees of freedom of an independently distributed $\chi^2$ variable. Forming the appropriate $t$-distribution statistics, one obtains,

$$t_{(T-2)\text{d.f.}} = \frac{(a_1 - \alpha_1)\sqrt{T\sum x_2^2}\sqrt{T-2}}{\sigma_\varepsilon\sqrt{\sum X_2^2}} \bigg/ \frac{s_e\sqrt{T-2}}{\sigma_\varepsilon} = \frac{(a_1 - \alpha_1)\sqrt{T\sum x_2^2}}{s_e\sqrt{\sum X_2^2}}$$

and

$$t_{(T-2)\text{d.f.}} = \frac{(a_2 - \alpha_2)\sqrt{\sum x_2^2}\sqrt{T-2}}{\sigma_\varepsilon} \bigg/ \frac{s_e\sqrt{T-2}}{\sigma_\varepsilon} = \frac{(a_2 - \alpha_2)\sqrt{\sum x_2^2}}{s_e}.$$

||||||||||||||||||||||||||||||||||||||||||||||||||||||||||||||||||||||||||||||||||||||||||||||||||||||||||||||||||||||||

***Explicative note.*** These statistics involve only the known sample observations, as the unknown term $\sigma_\varepsilon^2$ has canceled out. The formal switch from the normal to the $t$ appears to involve only a change from the variance $\sigma_\varepsilon^2$ to its sample estimate $s_e^2$.

||||||||||||||||||||||||||||||||||||||||||||||||||||||||||||||||||||||||||||||||||||||||||||||||||||||||||||||||||||||||

## Statistical inferences on individual coefficients

Tests on a hypothesis of the type $H_0: \alpha_1 = N_1$ or $H_0: \alpha_2 = N_2$ where $N_1$ and $N_2$ are any real numbers, can be performed using these $t$-distributed statistics,

$$t_{(T-2)\text{d.f.}} = \frac{(a_1 - N_1)\sqrt{T\sum x_2^2}}{s_e\sqrt{\sum X_2^2}} \tag{7-4}$$

---

[7] See Hogg and Craig, *Mathematical Statistics*, pp. 232–34, 310, 334 for the basic statistical theorems and proof of this independence. We continue to make use of this result.

and

$$t_{(T-2) \text{ d.f.}} = \frac{(a_2 - N_2)\sqrt{\sum x_2{}^2}}{s_e} \tag{7-5}$$

Confidence intervals on $\alpha_1$ and $\alpha_2$ may be derived from the probability statements,

$$\Pr\left\{t_{(1-\alpha/2)} < \frac{(a_1 - \alpha_1)\sqrt{T\sum x_2{}^2}}{s_e \sqrt{\sum X_2{}^2}} < t_{\alpha/2}\right\}$$

and

$$\Pr\left\{t_{(1-\alpha/2)} < \frac{(a_2 - \alpha_2)\sqrt{\sum x_2{}^2}}{s_e} < t_{\alpha/2}\right\}$$

respectively. Solving for the $(1 - \alpha)$ 100 percent confidence limits on $\alpha_1$ and $\alpha_2$ and substituting $(-t_{\alpha/2})$ for $t_{(1-\alpha/2)}$ since the $t$-distribution is symmetrical, one obtains

$$\left(a_1 - t_{\alpha/2} \frac{s_e\sqrt{\sum X_2{}^2}}{\sqrt{T\sum x_2{}^2}} < \alpha_1 < a_1 + t_{\alpha/2} \frac{s_e\sqrt{\sum X_2{}^2}}{\sqrt{T\sum x_2{}^2}}\right) \tag{7-6}$$

and

$$\left(a_2 - t_{\alpha/2} \frac{s_e}{\sqrt{\sum x_2{}^2}} < \alpha_2 < a_2 + t_{\alpha/2} \frac{s_e}{\sqrt{\sum x_2{}^2}}\right). \tag{7-7}$$

## 7.5 DIGRESSION ON A TEST WITH OVERLAPPING MEANINGS

A test of significance of the coefficient $\alpha_2$ is obtained from the $t$-distributed statistic of (7-5) by setting $N_2 = 0$. This gives a test of the significance of the correspondence between $Y_t$ and $X_{t2}$ according to the linear relation. Since $X_{t2}$ is the only explanatory variable in this relation, such a test carries the same meaning as the test on the significance of the correlation coefficient given in Section 7.3.

If the standardized normal variable

$$z_2 = \frac{(a_2 - \alpha_2)\sqrt{\sum x_2{}^2}}{\sigma_\varepsilon}$$

is squared, then $z_2{}^2$ could be considered as the sum of the square of one standardized normal variable. Therefore, by definition, the distribution of

$$z_2{}^2 = \frac{(a_2 - \alpha_2)^2 \sum x_2{}^2}{\sigma_\varepsilon{}^2}$$

is $\chi^2$ with one degree of freedom. Again, this statistic involving $a_2$ is independent of the $\chi^2_{(T-2)\,\text{d.f.}}$ distributed statistic involving $s_e$, $(T-2)s_e^2/\sigma_\varepsilon^2$, given our assumptions. Thus their ratio has an $F$-distribution with one and $T - 2$ degrees of freedom.

Forming this statistic and substituting $\alpha_2 = N_2 = 0$ for the test of significance, we have

$$
F_{(1,\,T-2)\,\text{d.f.}} = \frac{\left[\dfrac{(a_2 - 0)^2 \sum x_2^2}{\sigma_\varepsilon^2}\bigg/1\right]}{\left[\dfrac{(T-2)s_e^2}{\sigma_\varepsilon^2}\bigg/(T-2)\right]} = \frac{a_2^2 \sum x_2^2}{s_e^2} = \frac{a_2^2 \left(\dfrac{\sum yx_2}{a_2}\right)}{s_e^2} = \frac{a_2 \sum yx_2}{s_e^2}
$$

since the estimate

$$
a_2 = \left(\frac{\sum yx_2}{\sum x_2^2}\right).
$$

||||||||||||||||||||||||||||||||||||||||||||||||||||||||||||||||||||||||||||||||||||||||||||||||||||||||||||||||||||||||||||||||||||||||||||

***Recursive note.*** This statistic is identical to the test statistic (7–3) for testing the significance of the correlation coefficient when $K - 1 = 1$. Also, it is the square of the $t$-statistic of (7–5) when $N_2 = 0$, since an $F$-statistic with one and $v$ degrees of freedom is the same as the square of a $t$-statistic with $v$ degrees of freedom.

||||||||||||||||||||||||||||||||||||||||||||||||||||||||||||||||||||||||||||||||||||||||||||||||||||||||||||||||||||||||||||||||||||||||||||

A similar result is true in the case of several explanatory variables. The simultaneous test of significance for all their coefficients is equivalent to a test of significance of the linear relation.

## 7.6 TEST ON LINEAR COMBINATIONS OF COEFFICIENTS

Linear combinations of coefficients from an econometric model are frequently of theoretical interest. In general, such a linear combination can be written $\sum_{i=1}^{K} m_i \alpha_i = N$ where the $m_i$ and $N$ are numbers. The expression may concern combinations of marginals, or sums of elasticities, or the relative importance of one exogenous variable to another.

The econometrician may suppose that $\alpha_1 > \alpha_2$, or that $\alpha_1 + 3\alpha_2 > 5$, in some given model. These type of suppositions are part of his specification of the econometric model and need to be tested. If tests could be made on linear combinations, then these suppositions are testable as alternate hypothesis to the proper null hypothesis. For example, the rejection of the null hypothesis $H_0: (1)\alpha_1 + (-1)\alpha_2 = 0$ in favor of the alternate hypothesis $H_a: (1)\alpha_1 + (-1)\alpha_2 > 0$ gives an acceptance of the supposition $\alpha_1 > \alpha_2$.

||||||||||||||||||||||||||||||||||||||||||||||||||||||||||||||||||||||||||||||||||||||||||||||||||||||||||||||||||||||||||||||||||||||||||||||||||||||||||||||||||||||

*Interpretive note.* A hypothesis suitable for testing the other example of a linear combination above is obtained by letting $m_1 = 1$, $m_2 = 3$, and $N = 5$ to form the null hypothesis, $(1)\alpha_1 + 3\alpha_2 = 5$.

||||||||||||||||||||||||||||||||||||||||||||||||||||||||||||||||||||||||||||||||||||||||||||||||||||||||||||||||||||||||||||||||||||||||||||||||||||||||||||||||||||||

For the simple model, tests of such expressions derived from theory are not too common because one parameter is the intercept. This type of test is very useful in testing economic theory built into more complex models. However, it is easier to develop the test now in simple terms and expand it later. Also, this same type of formulation is applicable to the forecasting test in the next section.

The expression $m_1\alpha_1 + m_2\alpha_2$ is a linear combination of the coefficients $\alpha_1$ and $\alpha_2$. We desire to form an estimate of this expression which is unbiased and has minimum variance, called the "best linear unbiased estimate," or BLUE. The term "linear" refers, as before, to linear in the endogenous variables $Y_t$, whose probability density functions are known by assumptions about the probability distribution of the variables $\varepsilon_t$.

## Deriving the test statistic

To find BLUE for this linear combination of coefficients, it is proper to use the same linear combination of BLUE for the coefficients. That is, the best estimate of $m_1\alpha_1 + m_2\alpha_2$ is $m_1a_1 + m_2a_2$ where $a_1$ and $a_2$ are the least squares estimates.

As a first step toward deriving the test statistic, the expected value and variance of the combined random variable, $m_1a_1 + m_2a_2$, need to be derived. Easily, $E(m_1a_1 + m_2a_2) = m_1E(a_1) + m_2E(a_2) = m_1\alpha_1 + m_2\alpha_2$ since the estimates are unbiased. Also,

$$V(m_1a_1 + m_2a_2) = E\{[(m_1a_1 + m_2a_2) - (m_1\alpha_1 + m_2\alpha_2)]^2\}$$

by definition.

We obtain the following sequence of expressions for the right-hand side:

*a)* By rearrangement

$$= E\{[m_1(a_1 - \alpha_1) + m_2(a_2 - \alpha_2)]^2\}.$$

*b)* By expansion

$$= E[m_1^2(a_1 - \alpha_1)^2] + E[m_2^2(a_2 - \alpha_2)^2] + E[2m_1m_2(a_1 - \alpha_1)(a_2 - \alpha_2)].$$

*c)* By definitions

$$= m_1^2 V(a_1) + m_2^2 V(a_2) + 2m_1m_2 \, Cov(a_1a_2).$$

*d)* By substitution from (6–3)

$$= \sigma_\varepsilon^2 \left[ m_1^2 \frac{\sum X_2^2}{T\sum x_2^2} + m_2^2 \frac{1}{\sum x_2^2} + 2m_1m_2 \frac{-\overline{X}_2}{\sum x_2^2} \right].$$

e)   By using $X_2 = x_2 + \overline{X}_2$ and $\sum \overline{X}_2{}^2 = T\overline{X}_2{}^2$,

$$= \sigma_\varepsilon{}^2 \left[ \frac{m_1{}^2}{T} \left( \frac{\sum x_2{}^2 + 2\overline{X}_2 \sum x_2{}^2}{\sum x_2{}^2} \right) + \frac{m_1{}^2}{T} \frac{T\overline{X}_2{}^2}{\sum x_2{}^2} + \frac{m_2{}^2}{\sum x_2{}^2} - \frac{2m_1 m_2 \overline{X}_2}{\sum x_2{}^2} \right].$$

f)   By using $\sum x_2 = 0$ and simplifying the last three terms,

$$V(m_1 a_1 + m_2 a_2) = \sigma_\varepsilon{}^2 \left[ \frac{m_1{}^2}{T} + \frac{(m_2 - m_1 \overline{X}_2)^2}{\sum x_2{}^2} \right]. \tag{7-8}$$

Now $a_1$ and $a_2$ have a bivariate normal distribution so $(m_1 a_1 + m_2 a_2)$ is distributed as normal with mean $(m_1 \alpha_1 + m_2 \alpha_2)$ and variance given in (7-8). However, testing in terms of this normal distribution is impossible because the variance involves the unknown $\sigma_\varepsilon{}^2$.

Once again, a shift to the $t$-distribution is fruitful using the independent chi-square distributed statistic, $(T - 2)s_e{}^2/\sigma_\varepsilon{}^2$. Forming the appropriate ratio of the standardized normal to the square root of the $\chi^2$, one obtains,

$$t_{(T-2)\,\mathrm{d.f.}} = \frac{[(m_1 a_1 + m_2 a_2) - (m_1 \alpha_1 + m_2 \alpha_2)]\sqrt{T - 2}}{\sigma_\varepsilon \sqrt{\dfrac{m_1{}^2}{T} + \dfrac{(m_2 - m_1 \overline{X}_2)^2}{\sum x_2{}^2}}} \left/ \frac{s_e \sqrt{T - 2}}{\sigma_\varepsilon} \right. .$$

Thus, to test the hypothesis $H_0 : m_1 \alpha_1 + m_2 \alpha_2 = N$, the test statistic is

$$t_{(T-2)\,\mathrm{d.f.}} = \frac{m_1 a_1 + m_2 a_2 - N}{s_e \sqrt{\dfrac{m_1{}^2}{T} + \dfrac{(m_2 - m_1 \overline{X}_2)^2}{\sum x_2{}^2}}}. \tag{7-9}$$

Confidence limits on the expression $m_1 a_1 + m_2 a_2$ can be found for the $(1 - \alpha)$ 100 percent level of confidence to be

$$\left[ m_1 a_1 + m_2 a_2 \pm t_{\alpha/2}\, s_e \sqrt{\frac{m_1{}^2}{T} + \frac{(m_2 - m_1 \overline{X}_2)^2}{\sum x_2{}^2}} \right]. \tag{7-10}$$

## 7.7 TEST ON A FORECAST

Often, a researcher uses the econometric model to make forecasts. Estimates of $\alpha_1$, $\alpha_2$, and $\sigma_\varepsilon{}^2$ are found on the basis of observations of past behavior. Then, a new observation of $X_2$, say $X_{j2}$ is observed or estimated independently of the model. Using the estimates, $a_1$, $a_2$, and $s_e{}^2$, and the new value $X_{j2}$, tests and confidence intervals can be developed for the forecast value $Y_j$. A similar application arises when a complete, additional observation $(Y_j, X_{j2})$ becomes available, perhaps of another firm or another bank, from a delinquent survey report, from another region, or from a more recent quarterly or annual report. The econometrician wishes to check if the new observation fits the model as developed on the basis of the past or previously available data.

That is, can the relation, $Y_t = \alpha_1 + \alpha_2 X_{t2} + \varepsilon_t$, be used to represent the new observation with the same estimates as before so that $\hat{Y}_j = a_1 + a_2 X_{j2}$ gives an estimated value close to the true value $Y_j$.

## Notation for this test

Given a value $X_{j2}$, the forecast $\hat{Y}_j = a_1 + a_2 X_{j2}$ is a random variable since it is a linear combination of the random variables $a_1$ and $a_2$. Given $n$ repeated observations of the same value $X_{j2}$, one would draw repeated forecasts from the distribution of this random variable. The average of these forecasts could be called the mean forecast, denoted $f_n$. This mean forecast is also a random variable since repeated sets of $n$ forecasts would give different values of $f_n$. If all conceivable forecasts given the value $X_{j2}$ could be considered then this mean forecast would be an estimate of expected forecast, using expected in the probability sense of expected value. That is, $f_\infty = [\text{Est. } E(Y_j | X_{j2})]$, and we shall denote this estimated expected forecast by $\bar{f}$.

## A special case of the previous derivation

To develop the test statistic for a forecast $Y_j$, the distribution, mean, and variance of this random variable are required. As a preliminary, the mean and variance of $\bar{f}$ are found.

Given $X_{j2}$, the true expected value of $Y_j$ is $E(Y_j | X_{j2}) = \alpha_1 + \alpha_2 X_{j2}$ using the assumption, $E(\varepsilon_j) = 0$. The BLUE for this linear combination is $\bar{f} = a_1 + a_2 X_{j2}$ where both $a_1$ and $a_2$ are subject to error since they are sample estimates. The expected value of $\bar{f}$ is $E(\bar{f} | X_{j2}) = E(a_1 + a_2 X_{j2}) = \alpha_1 + \alpha_2 X_{j2}$. The variance of $\bar{f}$ is $V(\bar{f} | X_{j2}) = E[\bar{f} - E(\bar{f})]^2$ which can be determined in the same way as for any linear combination of $a_1$ and $a_2$. In the preceding section,

$$V(m_1 a_1 + m_2 a_2) = \sigma_\varepsilon^2 \left[ \frac{m_1^2}{T} + \frac{(m_2 - m_1 \bar{X}_2)^2}{\sum x_2^2} \right]. \tag{7-8}$$

In this case, let $m_1 = 1$ and $m_2 = X_{j2}$, then the variance of $\bar{f}$ is

$$V[(1)a_1 + X_{j2} a_2] = \sigma_\varepsilon^2 \left[ \frac{1}{T} + \frac{(X_{j2} - \bar{X}_2)^2}{\sum x_2^2} \right]. \tag{7-11}$$

The situation can be explained with the aid of Figure 7.2. The estimated relation is shown by the line, $a_1 + a_2 X_2$. For a particular value of $X_2$, say $X_{j2}$, a distribution of forecasts could occur. The distribution of these estimates is normal since $\bar{f}$ is a linear combination of normally distributed estimators $a_1$ and $a_2$. The best estimate of the expected forecast is given by the point, $E(\bar{f} | X_{j2})$, on the estimated relation. The standard deviation of the distribution is given by the standard error of $(\bar{f} | X_{j2})$ shown as $\sqrt{V(\bar{f} | X_{j2})}$.

**FIGURE 7–2**
Normally distributed forecasts and a confidence band for single forecasts, $(\hat{Y}_j | X_{j2})$, and expected forecasts $(\bar{f} | X_{j2})$

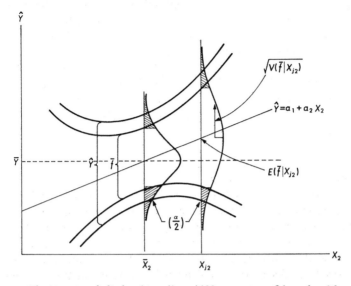

The inner parabolic band is a $(1 - \alpha)100$ percent confidence band for expected forecasts $(\bar{f} | X_{j2})$ which tend to be normally distributed with mean $\bar{Y}$ and variance given by (7–11). The outer band is a $(1 - \alpha)100$ percent confidence band for individual forcasts $(\hat{Y}_j | X_{j2})$ which tend to be normally distributed with the same mean (given by the point on the estimated relation) and variance given by (7–12). The outer band is wider due to the extra variation about the mean (dependent on $\sigma_\varepsilon^2$) which is implicit in an individual forecast. Both bands are narrowest at the mean value, $\bar{X}_2$.

|||||||||||||||||||||||||||||||||||||||||||||||||||||||||||||||||||||||||||||||||||||||||||||||||||||||||||||||||||||||||||

*Interpretive note.* This standard error varies depending on the distance between the new observation $X_{j2}$ and the mean $\bar{X}_2$ of the observations used in estimating the specified relation. The further $X_{j2}$ lies from $\bar{X}_2$, the larger the square in the second term of (7–11). Thus, a confidence band for $\bar{f}$ at different values of $X_{j2}$ is parabolic on each side of the line of best estimates.

|||||||||||||||||||||||||||||||||||||||||||||||||||||||||||||||||||||||||||||||||||||||||||||||||||||||||||||||||||||||||||

### The distribution of an individual forecast

Using these results for $\bar{f}$, similar results can be obtained easily for an individual forecast $\hat{Y}_j$ given a single observation of the value $X_{j2}$. The true value for $Y_j$ given $X_{j2}$ is $(Y_j | X_{j2}) = \alpha_1 + \alpha_2 X_{j2} + \varepsilon_j$. In this case, the unknown disturbance $\varepsilon_j$ must be included since we are not averaging over all possible forecasts. The BLUE for this linear combination is again $\hat{Y}_j = a_1 + a_2 X_{j2}$.

||||||||||||||||||||||||||||||||||||||||||||||||||||||||||||||||||||||||||||||||||||||||||||||||||||||||||||||||||

***Interpretive note.*** The estimator, $(a_1 + a_2 X_{j2})$, is BLUE for both $(Y_j | X_{j2})$ and $E(Y_j | X_{j2})$. Intuitively this seems correct. Suppose $Y$ denotes incomes of U.S. farmers (owning their own farm), and $X_2$ denotes number of acres of the farm. Further, suppose the conditional PDF of income given farm size has mean, $g(X_2)$, some function of the given farm size. Now, draw a sample of, say, 200 farmers with the same size farm, $X_{j2}$. The best guess of the average income of these 200 farmers would be $(\bar{f}_{200}) = g(X_{j2})$. Also, select only one farmer whose farm size is $X_{j2}$. The best guess of his income is likewise $\hat{Y}_j = g(X_{j2})$.

||||||||||||||||||||||||||||||||||||||||||||||||||||||||||||||||||||||||||||||||||||||||||||||||||||||||||||||||||

Following the same pattern as before in Section 7.6 to obtain (7–8) and hence, the variance of $\bar{f}$, (7–11), the derivation of the variance of $\hat{Y}_j$ results. It includes the same terms as in (7–11) plus extra terms involving the variance $\sigma_\varepsilon^2$ and the covariances between $\varepsilon_j$ and $a_1$ and between $\varepsilon_j$ and $a_2$. Now, these covariances are zero because of the independence between the disturbance term $\varepsilon_j$ associated with the new observation, $(Y_j, X_{j2})$, and the estimates $a_1$ and $a_2$ based on observations and disturbance terms in the previous independently drawn sample. The relevant assumptions are fixed regressors $X_{t2}$ and zero autocorrelation, $E(\varepsilon_j, \varepsilon_t) = 0$, $t = 1, 2, \ldots, T$ (Assumptions 1 and 5 from Section 5.4). Consequently, the only new term in the variance of $Y_j$ which does not occur in the variance of $\bar{f}$, (7–11), is an additional variance of the disturbance term, $\sigma_\varepsilon^2$.

||||||||||||||||||||||||||||||||||||||||||||||||||||||||||||||||||||||||||||||||||||||||||||||||||||||||||||||||||

***Explicative note.*** The variance of $\bar{f}$ refers to the expected forecast, and on the average, $\varepsilon_t = 0$. A single forecast $\hat{Y}_j$, however, varies about the true mean forecast with variance $V(\varepsilon_j)$ independent of the variance of $\bar{f}$. See Figure 7–2 again.

||||||||||||||||||||||||||||||||||||||||||||||||||||||||||||||||||||||||||||||||||||||||||||||||||||||||||||||||||

Thus, $V(\hat{Y}_j | X_{j2}) = V(\bar{f} | X_{j2}) + V(\varepsilon_j)$, and using the previous result for $V(\bar{f})$ in (7–11), and the assumption of constant variance (from Assumption 4 in Section 5.4) so that $V(\varepsilon_j) = \sigma_\varepsilon^2$,

$$V(\hat{Y}_j | X_{j2}) = \sigma_\varepsilon^2 \left[ 1 + \frac{1}{T} + \frac{(X_{j2} - \bar{X}_2)^2}{\sum x_2^2} \right]. \tag{7–12}$$

||||||||||||||||||||||||||||||||||||||||||||||||||||||||||||||||||||||||||||||||||||||||||||||||||||||||||||||||||

***Discursive note.*** The first term within brackets in (7–12) might be generalized to $1/n$ where $n$ is the number of repeated observations at the value $X_{j2}$ for which an average forecast is required. In the case of a single observation, $n = 1$, and we obtain (7–12). In the case of an expected forecast over all conceivable observations drawn at the value $X_{j2}$, we have $n = \infty$ and $1/\infty = 0$. Thus, the term drops out and we obtain (7-11).

|||||||||||||||||||||||||||||||||||||||||||||||||||||||||||||||||||||||||||||||||||||||||||||||||||||||||||||||||||||||||||||||||||||||||||||||||||||||||||||||||||||||||||||||||||||||||

## Constructing the test statistics

Remember that our objective is to formulate a test statistic for forecasts based on the regression model. Now the forecasts are normally distributed with known mean and variance which, unfortunately, involves the unknown $\sigma_\varepsilon^2$ again. But such a situation has been encountered before, and fortunately, the solution is similar. The forecast $\hat{Y}_j$ is a linear function of the estimators $a_1$ and $a_2$ which are independent of $s_e^2$. Thus, the intuitively obvious procedure turns out to be valid. The chi-square distributed random variable, $(T-2)s_e^2/\sigma_\varepsilon^2$, is independently distributed of the normally distributed random variable $\hat{Y}_j$. By forming the ratio of the standardized normal and the square root of the chi-square random variables, the appropriate $t$-distributed test statistic with $(T-2)$ degrees of freedom is easily derived to be:

$$t_{(T-2)\text{d.f.}} = \left[ \frac{(\hat{Y}_j - Y_j)\sqrt{T-2}}{\sigma_\varepsilon \sqrt{\left(\frac{1}{T} + \frac{(X_{j2} - \bar{X}_2)^2}{\sum x_{t2}^2} + 1\right)}} \right] \bigg/ \left( \frac{s_e \sqrt{T-2}}{\sigma_\varepsilon} \right).$$

For making tests of hypothesis on an individual forecast, such as $H_0: (Y_j | X_{j2}) = N$, one obtains

$$t_{(T-2)\text{d.f.}} = (\hat{Y}_j - N) \bigg/ s_e \sqrt{\left(\frac{1}{T} + \frac{(X_{j2} - \bar{X}_2)^2}{\sum x_{t2}^2} + 1\right)} \tag{7-13}$$

where $N$ is a real number.

Also, the $(1 - \alpha)100$ percent confidence limits for this individual forecast $Y_j$ are given by

$$\left\{ \hat{Y}_j \pm t_{\alpha/2} s_e \sqrt{\left(\frac{1}{T} + \frac{(X_{j2} - \bar{X}_2)^2}{\sum x_{t2}^2} + 1\right)} \right\}. \tag{7-14}$$

## 7.8 EXAMPLE CALCULATION OF ALL THESE TESTS

Some additional comments about these tests are best incorporated into an example. For this illustration, the data given in Chapter 3 is used along with the estimation results of Sections 3.5 and 4.5.

The results previously obtained are summarized below, all for the coded data.

| For variable | $Y_t$ | $X_{t2}$ |
|---|---|---|
| Sum of observations | 69.85 | 83.3 |
| Sum of squares of observations | 616.219 | 872.19 |
| Mean of observations | 8.7312 | 10.4125 |
| Sum of squares of deviations | 6.3409 | 4.8288 |

*Other results*

Sum of cross products of observations $\sum Y_t X_{t2} = 732.535$
Sum of cross products of deviations $\quad \sum y_t x_{t2} = 5.2219$

Explained variation of $Y_t$, $\qquad \sum \hat{y}_t^2 = 5.6470$
Unexplained variation of $Y_t$, $\qquad \sum e_t^2 = 0.6939$

Estimate of $\alpha_1$, $\qquad\qquad\qquad a_1 = -2.529$
Estimate of $\alpha_2$, $\qquad\qquad\qquad a_2 = 1.0814$

Correlation coefficient $\qquad\qquad r = 0.944$

Standard error of estimate squared $\quad V(e_t) = [\text{Est. } V(\varepsilon_t)] = s_e^2 = 0.1156$
Standard error of estimate $\qquad [\text{Est. } \sigma_\varepsilon] = s_e = 0.340$

*a)* Test if the correlation is significant and positive, say at 0.01 level of significance.

The null hypothesis and alternate hypothesis may be stated as

$$H_0: \rho = 0$$

$$H_a: \rho > 0.$$

A one-sided alternate is specified because we desire the test to be specially sensitive to a positive correlation, since the estimate $a_2$ is positive. An appropriate test statistic is given by (7–3) and has an $F$-distribution with one and $T - 2$ degrees of freedom. In this case, the number of observations on each variable was 8, so $T - 2 = 6$. See Figure 7–3. Using an $F$-distribution table, we find $\underset{\substack{(1,6)\,\text{d.f.}\\ \alpha=0.01}}{F} = 13.74$ which is the critical value for the test. The test statistic is calculated by substituting the values determined on the basis of the observations.

$$F = \frac{\sum \hat{y}_t^2 / 1}{\sum e_t^2 / 6} = \frac{5.6470}{0.1156} = 48.83.$$

Thus, the calculated $F$ exceeds the critical value. It lies in the rejection region for the test. We conclude that the null hypothesis, $\rho = 0$, is rejected, and there is a significant positive correlation.

**FIGURE 7–3**
Acceptance and rejection regions for the $F$-statistic to test the significance of the correlation coefficient

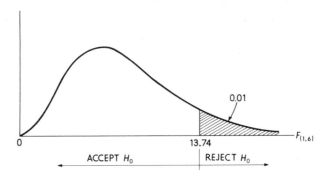

b)  Find a 90 percent confidence interval for the variance of the unknown disturbances.

The result (7–2) can be applied. Using a $\chi^2$ distribution table, one obtains $\chi^2_{6\ \text{d.f.}\ (0.05)} = 12.592$ and $\chi^2_{6\ \text{d.f.}\ (0.95)} = 1.635$ since $T - 2 = 6$, $\alpha/2 = 0.05$, and $(1 - \alpha/2) = 0.95$. Making the substitutions, the 90 percent confidence statement is

$$\text{Pr}\left\{ \frac{(T - 2)s_e^{\ 2}}{\chi^2_{\alpha/2}} < \sigma_\varepsilon^{\ 2} < \frac{(T - 2)s_e^{\ 2}}{\chi^2_{(1-\alpha/2)}} \right\} = 1 - \alpha,$$

$$\text{Pr}\left\{ \frac{6(0.1156)}{12.592} < \sigma_\varepsilon^{\ 2} < \frac{6(0.1156)}{1.635} \right\} = \text{Pr}\{0.055 < \sigma_\varepsilon^{\ 2} < 0.424\} = 0.90.$$

**FIGURE 7–4**
**Confidence region using a chi-square statistic**

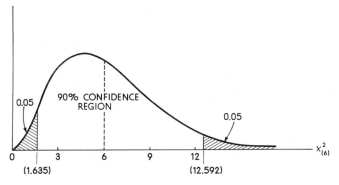

*Interpretive note.*   The best estimate of $\sigma_\varepsilon^{\ 2}$ is $s_\varepsilon^{\ 2} = 0.1156$ which is not in the numerical center of this interval. It is in the probabilistic center of this range of values for $\sigma_\varepsilon^{\ 2}$, however, because the $\chi^2$ distribution is positively skewed.

c)  Test if the slope of the linear estimation is greater than one with a significance level of 0.05.

This is a test of the null hypothesis

$$H_0\!: \alpha_2 = \frac{d(\text{imports})}{d(\text{domestic price})} = 1$$

against the one-sided alternate $H_a\!: \alpha_2 > 1$ using the $t$-distributed test statistic of (7–5).

There is no need to test the significance of the coefficient $\alpha_2$, since the result would be the same as part (a). If we consider $\alpha = 0.01$ and consult a $t$-distribution table, we find $t_{6 \text{ d.f.} \atop \alpha/2 = 0.005} = 3.707$ and the square $t^2 = (3.707)^2 = 13.74$ is the same as the $F_{(1, 6)\text{d.f.}}$ of part ($a$). It has already been shown in Section 7.5 that the test statistic would be the same also. Using $\alpha = 0.05$, then $t_{6 \text{ d.f.} \atop \alpha = 0.05} = 1.943$ is the critical value for this test. The test statistic from (7–5) can be rewritten as

$$t = \frac{(a_2 - 1)\sqrt{\sum x_{t2}^2}}{s_e} = \frac{(a_2 - 1)}{s_{a_2}},$$

if we recall that

$$[\text{Est. } V(a_2)] = s_e^2 \frac{1}{\sum x_{t2}^2}$$

and define the estimate of the standard deviation of the estimate as $s_{a_2} = \sqrt{[\text{Est. } V(a_2)]}$, analogously to $s_e = \sqrt{[\text{Est. } V(\varepsilon_t)]}$. It is common to calculate $s_{a_2}$ for the hint which it provides of the dispersion of all possible values of $a_2$ which might have occurred. See Figure 7–5.

Thus,

$$t = \frac{(1.0814 - 1)\sqrt{4.8288}}{0.340} = \frac{0.0814}{0.155} = 0.525 \quad \text{and} \quad s_{a_2} = 0.155.$$

The value of the test statistic is less than $t_\alpha$ so the null hypothesis cannot be rejected. Based on the sample evidence, we cannot be 95 percent sure that $\alpha_2 > 1$.

**FIGURE 7–5**
**Test of hypothesis on the slope**

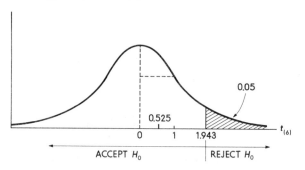

*Since the calculated t-value of 0.525 is within the acceptance region (the estimated slope is within 0.525 standard deviations of the hypothesized value of 1.0), the null hypothesis fails to be rejected.*

*d*) Find an 80 percent confidence interval for $\alpha_1$.

Again, a *t*-distributed statistic is used according to the derived interval of (7–6). This expression also includes the estimate of the standard deviation of the estimate $a_1$. Denote $\sqrt{[\text{Est. } V(a_1)]}$ by $s_{a_1}$ and recall that

$$[\text{Est. } V(a_1)] = s_e^2 \left( \frac{\sum X_{t2}^2}{T \sum x_{t2}^2} \right).$$

$$\Pr\left\{ a_1 - t_{\alpha/2} \frac{s_e \sqrt{\sum X_{t2}^2}}{\sqrt{T \sum x_{t2}^2}} < \alpha_1 < a_1 + t_{\alpha/2} \frac{s_e \sqrt{\sum X_{t2}^2}}{\sqrt{T \sum x_{t2}^2}} \right\} = 1 - \alpha.$$

From a *t*-distribution table, $t_{\substack{6 \text{ d.f.} \\ \alpha/2 = 0.10}} = 1.440$. Making all the necessary substitutions, the confidence limits are

$$-2.529 \pm 1.440 \frac{(0.340)\sqrt{872.19}}{\sqrt{8(4.8288)}} = -2.529 \pm 1.440(1.616),$$

where $1.616 = s_{a_1}$. The confidence statement is

$$\Pr\{-4.856 < \alpha_1 < -0.202\} = 0.80.$$

See Figure 7–6.

**FIGURE 7–6**
**80 percent confidence interval on the intercept**

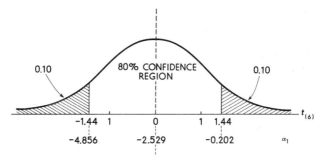

*The end points of the interval are obtained for the t-scale from Appendix C and are converted into the corresponding end points on the scale for the intercept.*

*e*) Suppose $X_{j2} = 124$, or in terms of coded data, $X_{j2} = 12.4$, is an additional observation for domestic prices. What is the 95 percent confidence interval for the expected value of the estimate of imports given this information?

The estimate is calculated first to be

$$\bar{J} = a_1 + a_2 X_{j2} = -2.529 + 1.0814(12.4)$$
$$= 10.88.$$

The formula to be applied for the confidence interval is based on (7–11) and involves a $t$-distributed test statistic.

From the $t$-distribution tables,

$$t_{\substack{6\,\text{d.f.}\\ \alpha/2=0.025}} = 2.447.$$

The solution obtained for the confidence limits is

$$\bar{f} \pm t_{\alpha/2}\, s_e \sqrt{\frac{1}{T} + \frac{(X_{j2} - \bar{X}_2)^2}{\sum x_{t2}{}^2}},$$

where the entire factor multiplied by $t_{\alpha/2}$ is the estimate of the standard deviation of the estimate of the expected forecast. Making the numerical substitutions, one obtains,

$$10.88 \pm 2.447(0.340)\sqrt{\frac{1}{8} + \frac{(12.4 - 10.4125)^2}{4.8288}} = 10.88 \pm 2.447(0.330)$$

$$= 10.88 \pm 0.808$$

The confidence statement in terms of coded data is

$$\Pr\{10.07 < E(Y_j \mid 12.4) < 11.69\} = 0.95.$$

Decoding, and for averaging over many drawings of domestic prices at 124 so that the disturbances cancel each other out, the expected forecast of imports is between 1,007 and 1,169.

||||||||||||||||||||||||||||||||||||||||||||||||||||||||||||||||||||||||||||||||||||||||||||||||||||||||||||||||||

*Interpretive note.*  This is a rather wide interval for any precise policy judgements related to these imports. Suppose the units are $10^4$ dollars in value of textiles and the country is concerned about a balance of payments deficit. For planning purposes of export equalization, international loans, or domestic monetary policy, there would be 1.62 million dollars difference in value between 1,007 and 1,169 units. More importantly, a precise plan based on the point estimate of 1,088 may be very competent and well executed, and yet be more than a half million dollar disaster if the actual amount of imports is near the extreme of the interval. And this calculation has been for an *average* estimate. All this could not be seen if only point estimates and the correlation coefficient were considered.

||||||||||||||||||||||||||||||||||||||||||||||||||||||||||||||||||||||||||||||||||||||||||||||||||||||||||||||||||

The use of the estimates of variance and of the probability distributions is extremely important in determining the true reliability and accuracy of the fit of the model to the observed data. In this example, it seems clear that the model is not well enough specified for the purpose of forecasting. Perhaps some other explanatory variables need to be added.

*f)*  Find a 95 percent confidence interval for an individual forecast given the same situation as in (*e*).

For comparison, we now use the expression derived in (7–14) which includes the estimate of the standard deviation of the estimate of an individual forecast. See Figure 7–7.

**FIGURE 7–7**
Comparative 95 percent confidence regions for an expected forecast and an individual forecast using the $t$-statistic with 6 d.f.

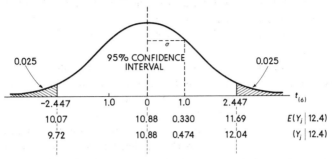

The same $t$-statistic value,

$$t_{\substack{6\,\text{d.f.} \\ \alpha/2=0.025}} = 2.447,$$

and the same estimate, $\hat{Y}_j = 10.88$, are used. The confidence limits are:

$$\hat{Y}_j \pm t_{\alpha/2} s_e \sqrt{\left(\frac{1}{T} + \frac{(X_{j2} - \overline{X}_2)^2}{\sum x_{t2}^2} + 1\right)}$$

$$= 10.88 \pm 2.447(0.340) \sqrt{\left(\frac{1}{8} + \frac{(12.4 - 10.4125)^2}{4.8288} + 1\right)}$$

$$= 10.88 \pm 2.447(0.474) = 10.88 \pm 1.16.$$

The confidence statement is

$$\Pr\{9.72 < (Y_j \mid 124) < 12.04\} = 0.95.$$

Imports on a single shot trial might be between 972 and 1204 units in terms of decoded data. The remarks of part ($e$) are even more pertinent now.

‖‖‖‖‖‖‖‖‖‖‖‖‖‖‖‖‖‖‖‖‖‖‖‖‖‖‖‖‖‖‖‖‖‖‖‖‖‖‖‖‖‖‖‖‖‖‖‖‖‖‖‖‖‖‖‖‖‖‖‖‖‖‖‖‖‖‖‖‖‖‖‖‖‖‖‖‖‖‖‖‖‖‖‖‖‖‖‖‖‖‖‖

*Explicative note.* The size of the estimates of the standard deviation for the statistics changed between parts ($e$) and ($f$) from 0.330 to 0.474. The change is due to the extra consideration of the disturbance term which can affect the individual forecast, but which is averaged over many different forecasts when the expected forecast is obtained. Also, the point forecast of 1088 lies midway between the interval limits in both ($e$) and ($f$) since the $t$-distribution being applied is symmetrical.

‖‖‖‖‖‖‖‖‖‖‖‖‖‖‖‖‖‖‖‖‖‖‖‖‖‖‖‖‖‖‖‖‖‖‖‖‖‖‖‖‖‖‖‖‖‖‖‖‖‖‖‖‖‖‖‖‖‖‖‖‖‖‖‖‖‖‖‖‖‖‖‖‖‖‖‖‖‖‖‖‖‖‖‖‖‖‖‖‖‖‖‖‖

## 7.9 ADDITIONAL REMARKS ON TESTING

The particular tests most suited to any particular model depend on the original purpose of constructing the model. Three separate, but not necessarily distinct purposes were suggested in Chapter 1. First, the model may be specified in order to get a quantitative expression of some hypothesized economic mechanism. In this case, the researcher wants a good fitting model and numerical interval estimates for the parameters. He might test the significance of the correlation coefficient using the $F$-statistic from (7–3). He might also find confidence limits for $\sigma_{\varepsilon}^2$, $\alpha_1$, and $\alpha_2$, using (7–2), (7–6), and (7–7) respectively.

Second, the econometrician may have specified the model to get a testable hypothesis on some special economic parameter, such as the marginal propensity to save or the price elasticity of demand for imports. When such theoretical propositions are made explicit in an appropriate mathematical form, they may be tested in terms of the sample data by making tests of hypothesis on the coefficients in the model, singly, or jointly, or perhaps, in some linear combination. Test statistics as given by (7–1), (7–4), (7–5), and (7–9) might be used.

Third, a model may be specified solely for the purpose of generating accurate and useful forecasts. In this case, the econometrician would want to check that $s_e$ was small relative to the mean of $Y$, and that $r^2$ was large so that the model fits the past observations closely. However, in making the forecast, he should determine the forecast interval (using 7–14) at a selected confidence level, $(1 - \alpha)100$ percent. The width of such an interval provides an important insight for the accuracy of the point forecast.

### Some problems in the forecast test

Since the width of the forecast interval depends on the square of the distance of the new observation from the mean of the previously available (and used) observations, $(X_{j2} - \bar{X}_2)^2$, the forecast interval increases in width as the value $X_{j2}$ becomes outside the scope of the original data. This problem decreases the accuracy of the common forecast test applied to economic data which has a time trend.

In the forecast test, the statistic from (7–13) is used where the actual new observation for $Y_j$ is used as the hypothesized value $N$. In this way, the significance of the difference between an estimated forecast and the actual value can be tested. However, if the variable $X_2$ has a time trend, then the new value in time period $j = T + 1$ may be larger than any of the previous $X_{t2}$, $t = 1$, $2$, $\ldots$, $T$, and different from the sample mean $\bar{X}_2$ by a large amount. To counteract this problem, the econometrician who is concerned primarily with the forecast test will transform his original data to remove a trend. Also, a transformation such as using first differences (define a new $X_{t2}^* = X_{t2} - X_{t-1,2}$ for $t = 2$, $3$, $\ldots$, $T$) or a logarithmic transformation (define a new $X_t^* = \ln(X_{t2}/X_{t-1,2})$ helps to insure that extra sample experience will result in new observations that are within the range of the previously observed sample.[8] In this way, the forecasting test is made more useful as a guide to the accuracy of the specified model to represent, characterize, and simulate the particular economic mechanism under investigation.

### Interpreting the forecast test results

Nevertheless, the researcher must be careful to limit his conclusions based on forecast tests. A successful forecast does not imply a "good" model in all respects (particularly not for purpose two above of testing theoretical propositions). There is no available test statistic which allows one to determine the probability of $n$ consecutive acceptable forecasts if the theoretical propositions about the coefficient in the model are true. Indeed, rather than testing the economic theory in the model, forecasting more nearly provides a suitable test of the stability of the background conditions to determine if the observations are consistently drawn from the same environment and can be reflected by the same economic relation. However, in an indirect sense, if the forecasts are usually accurate, it indicates that the model is conformable to reality since it continues to characterize the observed values of the economic variables.

This result is a long-run conclusion though. A single good or bad forecast is not at all conclusive evidence about the theory in the model since it depends on the coincidence of similar observations.

Also, models in which the estimates of coefficients are tested to be significant and within acceptable confidence limits of theoretical values may or may not be models which will give accurate forecasts. Conversely, for a model which permits accurate forecasts, the null hypothesis concerning the coefficients may or may not be acceptable.

However, these remarks concern a single test and single forecasts based on a single set of observations. Econometricians believe that the probability is very small that this divergence between the two types of test results could occur consistently over repeated sets of observations. Thus, it seems that repeated tests of a model can add significantly, in the long run, to the improvement in the specification of a model and to the total knowledge about the economic system gained through proper analysis of the model.

### 7.10 SUMMARY

In this chapter, several test statistics have been presented. In 7.3, these apply to the measures of goodness of fit of the estimation. They help to determine if the specified model can be used as an accurate representation of the economic observations.

---

[8] In the case of several independent variables, $X_2, X_3, \ldots, X_K$ in the model, this type transformation on all time-series observations also helps to eliminate multicollinearity (the linear dependencies among the exogenous variables when $K > 2$).

This problem is considered in more detail in Chapter 15.

The tests concerning the estimates of the coefficients of the model are in 7.4–7.6. They are used to make tests of theoretical propositions about the sizes or signs of the coefficients and their relative magnitudes. The results of such tests depend on the particular sample observations drawn, and they are only true if the assumptions of the model which lead to the known probability distributions of the test statistics are true. Thus, in a strict sense, these tests of hypothesis can only test the theory if the historical background conditions and measures of the variables conform to the assumptions in Chapter 5.

This limitation is one reason for the interest of econometricians in economic history. If econometric tests of theoretical propositions specified as part of the model do depend on historical assumptions and accurate measurements of data for their validity, then interchange and overlapping skills between econometricians and economic historians is quite natural and necessary.

The testing of forecasts in 7.7 will also give different results depending on which observations happen to be drawn. The forecasts will be within the forecast interval if the new observations reflect the same relation as does the original observation set which was used as a basis for calculating the least squares estimate.

The basic test statistics to remember in this chapter are those designated as 7–1, 7–2, 7–3, 7–4, 7–5, and 7–13. Each can be used to form confidence intervals on the important parameters and forecasts.

## NEW VOCABULARY

| | |
|---|---|
| $t$ distribution | BLUE |
| $F$ distribution | Forecast |
| Confidence limits | Level of significance |
| Tests of hypothesis | Estimated expected forecast |
| Rejection region | Alpha error |

## EXERCISES

1. Try to develop a formal argument for the independence of estimators $a_2$ and $s_e$.

2. *a)* Find a 95 percent confidence interval for a population mean based on a sample of size 25 with sample mean of 40 and sample variance of 100.

   *b)* Let $Y_t = \alpha_1 + \alpha_2 X_t + \varepsilon_t$. Test the significance (0.05 level) of a population parameter $\alpha_2$ based on a sample of size 25 with least squares estimator $a_2 = 40$, and standard error of the coefficient, $s_{a_2} = 2$.

   *c)* Use an $F$ statistic to test the significance (0.05 level) of a linear relation $Y_t = \alpha_1 + \alpha_2 X_t + \varepsilon_t$ based on 25 sample observations with $\sum y^2 = 6769$, $\sum e^2 = 368$, and $\sum x^2 = 4$.

   *d)* Explain the reasons for the similarity among parts *(a)–(c)* of this question.

3. Based on the behavior of major trading countries from 1950 through 1957, it has been suggested (R. Triffin, *Gold and the Dollar Crisis*) that a country is critically illiquid when its reserves are less than 30 percent of its imports.

Based on the following random sample of size 10 selected from the 8 years after 1957 from 23 trading nations, does it appear that these trading nations have, on the average, been liquid? Test if the population mean exceeds 0.30 at the 0.005 significance level. How would the conclusion be affected if the test statistic is adjusted for the finite population size $N$ by multiplying by the factor $\sqrt{(N-1)/(N-10)}$? Ans.: $t = 5.38$. Conclusion that $\mu > 0.30$ is strengthened if finite multiplier is applied.

| Selected country and year | Ratio of reserves to imports |
|---|---|
| New Zealand, 1964 | 0.172 |
| Greece, 1964 | 0.318 |
| Sweden, 1963 | 0.224 |
| Australia, 1958 | 0.697 |
| Finland, 1960 | 0.263 |
| Italy, 1962 | 0.624 |
| South Africa, 1962 | 0.459 |
| United Kingdom, 1958 | 0.289 |
| Austria, 1959 | 0.610 |
| France, 1959 | 0.340 |

Source: *International Financial Statistics Supplement* to 1966/67 issues.

4. Find the size of a sample necessary for 90 percent confidence that the sample mean will be within 5 units of the true mean of a normally distributed random variable with population standard deviation of 40.

5. From a linear regression of $Y$ on $X$, one obtains $\sum e_t^2 = 130$ with a sample size of 15 where $e_t$ is the residual for observation $t$. Establish 95 percent confidence limits on $\sigma_\varepsilon^2$, the variance of the disturbance term.

6. You are interested in the relationship between value of output of a firm and the number of employees of the firm. You plan to select at random five firms each with a monthly output of 100 ($000), to determine the number of employees of each, and to compute the average number of employees for this size firm. You plan to repeat this procedure using firms with monthly output valued at multiples of 10 ($000) from 100 to 200 ($000) inclusive, thus using 11 sizes of firms and 55 firms. Let $Y_i$ denote the average number of employees of the 5 firms with monthly output of $X_i = 100 + 10(i-1)$ thousands of dollars, $i = 1, 2, \ldots, 11$. You wish to set up a model such that the mean number of employees is a linear function of the size of the firm as measured by monthly output value.

a) State the assumptions you require to set up this model and to find estimates for the parameters.

b) Suppose on making the observations you find

$$1/11 \sum_{i=1}^{11} X_i Y_i = 15{,}300$$

$$\overline{Y} = 100$$

$$s_y = 10$$

Find 95 percent confidence limits for the parameters $\alpha_1$ and $\alpha_2$.

    *c*)  Test at the 4 percent significance level the hypothesis that $\sigma_i = 6$ against the alternative $\sigma_i \neq 6$ where $\sigma_i$ is the standard deviation of the number of employees in an *individual* firm.

7.  Using the data and model from Exercise 9 of Chapter 3,

    *a*)  Find 90 percent confidence limits for $\sigma_\varepsilon^2$. Ans.: $0.39 < \sigma_\varepsilon^2 < 2.2$.

    *b*)  Test the significance of $\rho$ at the 0.001 level.

    *c*)  Test if $\alpha_2$ is significantly smaller than 0.3 at the 0.05 level of significance. Ans.: $t = -2.654$.

    *d*)  Find 95 percent confidence limits for the expected level of capital expenditures given that the sales ratio is 112. Ans.: $4.3 < E(Y/112) < 6.9$.

8.  Given the data and model from Exercise 10 of Chapter 3,

    *a*)  Test if the MPC is significantly greater than 0.55 at the 0.01 significance level.

    *b*)  Find 95 percent confidence limits for the intercept of the consumption function. Interpret the economic meaning and validity of this confidence interval.

    *c*)  Find a 90 percent confidence interval for the variance of the disturbance term.

    *d*)  Test the significance of the correlation coefficient.

    *e*)  Find 95 percent confidence limits on the forecast value for 1944 if disposable income is given as $\$(147 \times 10^9)$. Comment on the validity of the model (and on the validity of such a test for examining the validity of the model) given that actual consumption in 1944 was $\$(112 \times 10^9)$.

||||||||||||||||||||||||||||||||||||||||||||||||||||||||||||||||||||||||||||||||||||||||||||||||||||||||||||||||

*Discursive note.* Your instructor may elect to expand on the data and models of other exercises in Chapter 3 to provide more problems on testing as he finds useful. Some suggested parts of such problems follow in Exercises 9–18.

||||||||||||||||||||||||||||||||||||||||||||||||||||||||||||||||||||||||||||||||||||||||||||||||||||||||||||||||

9.  See Exercise 5, Chapter 3. Find a confidence interval on the multiplier, $1/(1 - \text{MPC})$ by first finding the confidence interval on $\alpha_2 = \text{MPC}$.

10.  See Exercise 4, Chapter 3.

    *a*)  Test the significance of $\rho$ at the 0.01 level.

    *b*)  Test at the 0.01 level if the marginal propensity to import, MPI, satisfies $(0.02 < \text{MPI} < 0.05)$ by making a one-sided test on each end point of the interval. (Be sure to set up the tests so that your conclusion has a known probability of error.)

    *c*)  Test if $(\alpha_1/\alpha_2) < -20$ at the 0.05 level. (Set up as a linear combination, $1\alpha_1 + 20\alpha_2 = 0$.)

    *d*)  Given that national income is 280 for 1951, test if a level of imports of 10.5 for this year is consistent with the 1955–65 experience. Use the 0.05 level of significance.

11.  See Exercise 11, Chapter 3. Find the standard errors of both coefficient estimators.

12.  See Exercise 12, Chapter 3. Is the data point $(Y_j, X_j) = (53.9, 54.8)$ for 1966 consistent with the period 1956–65 as determined by the regression equation and a forecast $(\hat{Y}_j \mid X_j)$.

13.  See Exercise 13, Chapter 3. Make and interpret a test of hypothesis, $H_0: \alpha_2 = 1.0$, $H_0: \alpha_2 > 1.0$, at the 0.025 level of significance.

14.  Test the significance (at 0.001 level) of the linear estimation of Exercise 14, Chapter 3.

15.  For the data and model of Exercise 15, Chapter 3, find a 90 percent confidence interval on $\sigma_\varepsilon^2$.

16.  Find the U.S. expenditure on defense and GNP for the current year $j$. Using the relation estimated in Exercise 16, Chapter 3, find the residual $e_j = Y_j - \hat{Y}_j$.

17.  See Exercise 17, Chapter 3. Test the hypothesis $H_0: \alpha_2 = 2$ at the 0.10 significance level.

18.  See Exercise 3, Chapter 3. Find 95 percent confidence intervals for $\alpha_1$ and for $\alpha_2$.

19.  For the log-linear model of the text example (Section 3.7) based on 8 observations of the log-transformed data, one obtains $a_2 = 1.2977$ with a standard error for this coefficient of 0.1936. Test if the price elasticity of imports is greater than 1.0 at the 0.05 significance level. Make a test of the same hypothesis using the data and results of the text model in this chapter. (*Hint:* Find the value for the slope at the point of means such that the elasticity equals unity.)

20.  Test the significance of the correlation coefficient from Exercises 4 and 5 in Chapter 4 using $\alpha = 0.01$.

21.  Given the following regression results using 17 observations,

$$Y_t = 0.509 + 0.387 X_t \quad \text{with} \quad r = 0.512 \quad \text{and} \quad s_e = 0.0352.$$
$$(0.168)$$

  *a*)  Test the significance of the slope coefficient at the 0.05 level. (The standard error for the coefficient is customarily given below the coefficient in parentheses.)

  *b*)  Test the significance of the correlation coefficient at the 0.05 level.

  *c*)  Compare and explain the similarity between the results for parts (*a*) and (*b*), both numerically and interpretively.

  *d*)  By shuffling various formula, try to determine the standard error of the estimate of the intercept based on the given information.

22.  Given the following data for a given commodity on price and quantity demanded, estimate a demand function of the form, $Q_t = \alpha_1 + \alpha_2 P_t + \varepsilon_t$. Do a complete analysis of your results including their economic interpretation and some test of hypothesis that you think would be particularly relevant.

| Q | P | Q | P |
|---|---|---|---|
| 8 | 59 | 18 | 43 |
| 6 | 58 | 24 | 42 |
| 11 | 56 | 19 | 39 |
| 22 | 53 | 23 | 38 |
| 14 | 50 | 26 | 30 |
| 17 | 45 | 40 | 27 |

23. Let $Y =$ rate of increase in money wages and $X_2 =$ percent of civilian work force unemployed. The concept of a Phillips curve implies that as the percentage unemployed drops, the rate of increase in money wages rises. Test this hypothesis using the following data:

| Year | Y | $X_2$ | Year | Y | $X_2$ |
|---|---|---|---|---|---|
| 1956......4.84 | | 4.2 | 1961......2.65 | | 6.7 |
| 1957......5.13 | | 4.3 | 1962......3.02 | | 5.6 |
| 1958......2.93 | | 6.8 | 1963......2.93 | | 5.7 |
| 1959......3.79 | | 5.5 | 1964......2.85 | | 5.2 |
| 1960......3.10 | | 5.6 | 1965......3.16 | | 4.6 |

Source: Class, 1969 (Hale).

# PART III

# Multivariate Single Equation Econometric Model

Few economists tend to construct models and represent economic theories with only two variables. Indeed, there is usually a long list of potential explanatory variables. Thus, econometricians try to select the best of these to include in a model. Each variable that is added tends to make the calculations longer but does not add much additional complexity to the analysis. Consequently, it is practical, using computers for the calculations, to construct models with 10 or more explanatory variables rather than merely 1. Therefore, it is useful to understand the concepts of estimation and testing of such models, and to be able to perform the required calculations in a systematic way. It then becomes easier to understand the computer program for these procedures and to read the computer output intelligently.

For many purposes, though, a model with the two or three best explanatory variables suffices. Besides, it is very difficult to find 10 economic variables which are independent of each other, and yet, which serve together as a representation of the joint economic mechanism determining one other endogenous variable.

The seven chapters of Part III do not involve computerization techniques. The emphasis remains on the meaning of the fundamental concepts including examples of the routine calculations for the analysis of the multivariate single equation linear explanatory economic model.

## The general model

The form of the model to be considered can be written symbolically by

$$Y_t = \gamma_1 + \gamma_2 X_{t2} + \gamma_3 X_{t3} + \cdots + \gamma_K X_{tK} + \varepsilon_t.$$

141

Many of the expressions throughout the analysis can be shortened and made clearer by using vector and matrix notation. Thus, the model can also be written

$$
Y_t = (X_{t1}, X_{t2}, \ldots, X_{tK}) \begin{pmatrix} \gamma_1 \\ \gamma_2 \\ \vdots \\ \gamma_K \end{pmatrix} + \varepsilon_t \quad \text{or} \quad Y = X\Gamma + \varepsilon.
$$

Many of the procedures of estimation and testing for this model are simply extensions of those processes presented in Part II which really serves as the review portion of this book. Building on this foundation, much of the explanation offered now is intuitive and informal using comparisons with the analogous results for the simple model. A more advanced or formal presentation with its extensive derivations is intentionally avoided.

## The order of discussion

Chapter 8 presents the new interpretations and formulas for the partial regression coefficients and partial correlation coefficients of the multivariate model. Chapters 9 and 12 present some solution methods and example calculations for obtaining these statistics.

The assumptions commonly associated with the analysis of the multivariate model, the application of the Gauss-Markov theorem, and the properties of the estimators are considered in Chapter 10. The extension of the test statistics for the multivariate model and some example calculations of the various tests are in Chapter 11. Some other useful topics for model building are considered in Chapter 12, namely the use of dummy variables and distributed lags.

Finally, we must focus our attention on some of the common problems of all this analysis on the single equation model. These difficulties arise when the sample observations of economic variables provide implicit evidence that one or more of our basic assumptions may be violated. Methods of analyzing residuals to detect such violations are the topic of Chapter 13. The effect of such violations on the ordinary least squares estimators, as considered in Chapter 14, leads to the revised solution of classical linear estimation for the more general case (with less restrictive assumptions). Chapter 15 ends Part III on the single equation model with further discussion of two frequently met econometric problems. Some corrective procedures are suggested when the researcher is faced with a problem of pooling cross-sectional and time-series data or with multicollinearity.

Chapter
8

# NEW CONCEPTS IN THE
# EXTENDED MODEL

## 8.1 PREVIEW

The extension of the bivariate single equation econometric model to the multivariate single equation econometric model is rather simple. The general model is also a mathematical representation of the explanation of one endogenous variable. The only change in structure and meaning is the inclusion of more than one explanatory variable. In the general model, several explanatory factors combine with each other to allow more realistic representations of an economic sector or economic law. The model builder is not limited to a single explanatory variable.

Each independent explanatory factor may help to explain the changes in the endogenous variable. The scattergram of observed points is now a multidimensional figure. Many regressions and simple correlations are implicit in the analysis of this general model. The procedures used in this analysis are merely extensions of those applied to the simple model. However, the multidimensional combinations of factors and the separating of their individual effects involves some new terminology, some new meanings, and a few new mathematical expressions.

143

All these new concepts can be presented in reference to an extended model which has only one extra explanatory variable beyond our simple model. With reference to the previous example model, an additional variable, $X_{t3}$, might be per capita income in the importing country. In subsequent chapters, the analysis is extended further to a general model with even more variables without any change in concepts, only a change in form to vector and matrix notation.

## 8.2 REVIEW

As an inducement to continue on to the following chapters, no specially new mathematical or statistical concepts are used in this chapter. Rather, six results from the analysis of the simple model are extended. It might be useful to list these concepts.

a)  Total variation equals the sum of explained and unexplained variation.

$$\sum y_t^2 = \sum \hat{y}_t^2 + \sum e_t^2. \qquad (4\text{–}1)$$

If all these terms are divided by total variation, the result is:

$$1 = r_{Y2}^2 + \frac{\sum e_t^2}{\sum y_t^2}$$

where $r_{Y2}$ is the correlation coefficient between variables $Y$ and $X_2$. Solving for this value,

b)  $r_{Y2} = \sqrt{1 - \dfrac{\sum e_t^2}{\sum y_t^2}}$, or rewriting again solving for $\sum e_t^2$,

c)  $\sum e^2 = (1 - r_{Y2}^2) \sum y_t^2.$

The estimator for $\alpha_2$ was found to be $a_2 = \dfrac{\sum y_t x_{t2}}{\sum x_{t2}^2}$ from the normal equations

$$\begin{pmatrix} T & \sum X_{t2} \\ \sum X_{t2} & \sum X_{t2}^2 \end{pmatrix} \begin{pmatrix} a_1 \\ a_2 \end{pmatrix} = \begin{pmatrix} \sum Y_t \\ \sum Y_t X_{t2} \end{pmatrix}. \qquad (3\text{–}1)$$

This expression can also be rewritten by multiplying both numerator and denominator by $\sqrt{\sum y_t^2/(T-1)}$. This gives

$$a_2 = \left( \frac{\sum y_t x_{t2}}{\sqrt{\sum x_{t2}^2 \sum y_t^2}} \right) \frac{\sqrt{\sum y_t^2/(T-1)}}{\sqrt{\sum x_{t2}^2/(T-1)}} \ ;$$

or defining $s_Y$ and $s_{X_2}$ as the standard deviations of the variables $Y$ and $X_2$, the result is,

d)  $a_2 = r_{Y2} \dfrac{s_Y}{s_{X_2}}.$

Finally, the explained variation can be calculated by the formula,

e)   $\sum \hat{y}_t^2 = a_2 \sum y_t x_{t2}$, and the coefficient of determination has the meaning,

f)   $r_{Y2}^2 = \dfrac{\text{variation of } Y \text{ explained by } X_2}{\text{total variation of } Y}$.

## 8.3 THE EXTENSION OF THE SIMPLE MODEL

The extended model may be written $Y_t = \gamma_1 + \gamma_2 X_{t2} + \gamma_3 X_{t3} + \varepsilon_t$. It includes three coefficients to be estimated rather than two. Also, three simple correlations are involved rather than one, namely of $Y$ and $X_2$, of $Y$ and $X_3$, and of $X_2$ and $X_3$. Finally, a multiple correlation of $Y$ and the combined factors $X_2$ and $X_3$ is involved. However, all these are similar to the same concepts in the simple model.

### Similarities with the simple model

The values of estimates $C_1$, $C_2$, and $C_3$ for the coefficients can be obtained using the principle of least squares or the principle of maximum likelihood. In either case, the same sum of squares of residuals is involved and the same normal equations are obtained, if the same type assumptions as in 5.4 are maintained.[1]

*Explicative note.*   In the extended model, the true coefficients are designated by $\gamma_i$ rather than $\alpha_i$ since they have a new meaning to be explained in the next section. The estimator of the coefficient $\gamma_i$ is denoted by the corresponding $C_i$ based on the set of sample observations.

The normal equations for the extended model are:

$$C_1 T + C_2 \sum X_{t2} + C_3 \sum X_{t3} = \sum Y_t,$$
$$C_1 \sum X_{t2} + C_2 \sum X_{t2}^2 + C_3 \sum X_{t2} X_{t3} = \sum Y_t X_{t2}, \qquad (8\text{-}1)$$
$$C_1 \sum X_{t3} + C_2 \sum X_{t2} X_{t3} + C_3 \sum X_{t3}^2 = \sum Y_t X_{t3}.$$

If all terms involving $X_{t3}$ and $C_3$ are omitted, the two remaining equations are identical to the normal equations for the simple model (3–1). These three equations can be solved for the estimates $C_1$, $C_2$, and $C_3$ by substitution, by Cramer's method, or by using matrix methods presented in the next chapter and Chapter 12.

---

[1] See Chapter 10 for a reconsideration of these assumptions in the multivariate model.

||||||||||||||||||||||||||||||||||||||||||||||||||||||||||||||||||||||||||||||||||||||||||||||||||||||||||||||||||||||||||||

*Discursive note.* Once you have mastered a solution to the normal equations and have performed the matrix calculations, it is probably not desirable to do it again. The general process should be remembered conceptually, but some computer or programmable electronic calculator system should be used for repeated computations. If you are not already familiar with such a system and program for doing a multiple regressions analysis, you should now seek out and acquire this familiarity.

||||||||||||||||||||||||||||||||||||||||||||||||||||||||||||||||||||||||||||||||||||||||||||||||||||||||||||||||||||||||||||

There is no change in the calculation or the interpretation of the simple correlation coefficients $r_{Y2}$, $r_{Y3}$, and $r_{23}$. They measure the degree of association between the three pairs of variables $(Y, X_2)$, $(Y, X_3)$, and $(X_2, X_3)$. In the simple model, there was only one of these simple correlation coefficients which measured the correlation between the single pair of variables $Y$ and $X_2$.

## The multiple correlation coefficient

$r_{Y2}$ also represented the total measure of association between the endogenous variable and all the independent variables in the relation. For the extended model, an additional statistic is needed for this latter measure since there is more than one exogenous variable. The multiple correlation coefficient is denoted $R_{Y.23}$ and defined just as in (*b*) of the *Review* section,

$$R_{Y.23} = \sqrt{1 - \sum e_t^2 / \sum y_t^2}.$$

Its square, $R_{Y.23}^2$ is again a measure of the proportion of the variation in $Y$ which has been explained. The residual in the extended model is measured about the regression plane in three dimensions rather than about the regression line in two dimensions. It is $e_t = Y_t - C_1 - C_2 X_{t2} - C_3 X_{t3}$, so we can write the meaning of $R_{Y.23}^2$ similarly to (*f*) in the *Review* section as:

$$R_{Y.23}^2 = \frac{\text{variation of } Y \text{ explained by } X_2 \text{ and } X_3}{\text{total variation of } Y}.$$

Using substitutions similar to (*e*) in the *Review* section for explained variation, a formula for calculations can be found,

$$R_{Y.23}^2 = \frac{C_2 \sum y_t x_{t2} + C_3 \sum y_t x_{t3}}{\sum y_t^2}. \tag{8-2}$$

## 8.4 NEW INTERPRETATIONS FOR THE EXTENDED MODEL

A new concept in the extended model is the partial correlation coefficient, which is a first order correlation coefficient compared to the zero order simple correlation coefficients and the second order multiple correlation coefficient.

|||||||||||||||||||||||||||||||||||||||||||||||||||||||||||||||||||||||||||||||||||||||||||||||||||||||||||||||||||||||||||||||||||||||||||||||||||||||||

*Interpretive note.* Order refers, in some sense, to a degree of complexity. There is a hierarchy among correlation coefficients in the sense that one of a given order can always be expressed in terms of those of the next lower order and eventually in terms of zero order coefficients. For example $R_{Y \cdot 23}$ can be obtained from,

$$R_{Y \cdot 23}{}^2 = \frac{r_{Y2}{}^2 + r_{Y3}{}^2 - 2r_{Y2}r_{Y3}r_{23}}{1 - r_{23}{}^2}. \tag{8–3}$$

Such reductions are often useful for substitutions and for simplifying complex expressions, but memorizing them or deriving them has dubious long-run benefits.

|||||||||||||||||||||||||||||||||||||||||||||||||||||||||||||||||||||||||||||||||||||||||||||||||||||||||||||||||||||||||||||||||||||||||||||||||||||||||

## Partial correlation coefficients

The first order correlation coefficients for the extended model are denoted $r_{Y2 \cdot 3}$, $r_{Y3 \cdot 2}$, and $r_{23 \cdot Y}$. In each case these are correlations between the first two subscripted variables while holding the effect of the third variable constant. Such coefficients sometimes are of particular interest to the econometrician because they reflect the frequent economic assumption of holding other things constant.

To determine a partial correlation coefficient, the linear effect of the third variable is removed from each of the first two. Then, the simple correlation is found between the residual parts of the first two variables. Consider $r_{Y \cdot 32}$; the linear effect of $X_2$ on both $Y$ and $X_3$ must be removed so that the remaining parts of $Y$ and $X_3$ are separated from $X_2$. As far as these leftover parts are concerned, $X_2$ is a constant.

This can be illustrated further if some additional notation is defined. First, regress $Y$ on $X_2$, say $Y_t = \alpha_{Y1} + \alpha_{Y2} X_{t2} + \omega_t$. Then regress $X_3$ on $X_2$, say $X_{t3} = \alpha_{31} + \alpha_{32} X_{t2} + v_t$. Let the estimates of each $\alpha$ be denoted by $a$ and the residuals be denoted by $W$ and $V$ respectively. Then, $W_t = y_t - a_{Y2} x_{t2}$ and $V_t = x_{t3} - a_{32} x_{t2}$, using the deviation form of the estimating lines.

The partial correlation coefficient $r_{Y3 \cdot 2}$ is defined to be equal to the simple correlation coefficient $r_{WV}$. That is,

$$r_{Y3 \cdot 2} = \frac{\sum WV}{\sqrt{\sum W^2 \sum V^2}} = r_{WV}.$$

Using a substitution for the residual sum of squares analogous to (c) in *Review* 8.2, we obtain

$$r_{Y3 \cdot 2} = \frac{\sum (y_t - a_{Y2} x_{t2})(x_{t3} - a_{32} x_{t2})}{\sqrt{\sum y_t{}^2(1 - r_{Y2}{}^2)} \sqrt{\sum x_{t3}{}^2(1 - r_{23}{}^2)}}. \tag{8–4a}$$

||||||||||||||||||||||||||||||||||||||||||||||||||||||||||||||||||||||||||||||||||||||||||||||||||||||||||||||||||||||||||||||||||||||||||||||||||

**Explicative note.** If either of the sample correlations in the denominator are perfect, equal to one, then both the numerator and the denominator are zero. In this case the partial correlation coefficient is not defined. That is, if either the residual $W_t$ or $V_t$ is equal to zero, then there is no leftover part in either $Y_t$ or $X_{t3}$ respectively after the linear effect of $X_2$ is removed.

||||||||||||||||||||||||||||||||||||||||||||||||||||||||||||||||||||||||||||||||||||||||||||||||||||||||||||||||||||||||||||||||||||||||||||||||||

Any other partial correlation coefficient can be defined similarly. Expansion of the numerator above and substitution for the least squares estimators $a_{Y2}$ and $a_{32}$ provides another calculational formula,

$$r_{Y3 \cdot 2} = \frac{r_{Y3} - r_{Y2} r_{32}}{(1 - r_{Y2}{}^2)(1 - r_{23}{}^2)}. \qquad (8\text{-}4b)$$

## Partial regression coefficients

A second new interpretation in the extended model, $Y_t = \gamma_1 + \gamma_2 X_{t2} + \gamma_3 X_{t3} + \varepsilon_t$, concerns the coefficients $\gamma_2$ and $\gamma_3$. These are no longer the simple slopes in bivariate linear relations between the endogenous variable and each corresponding exogenous variable. In the simpler model, $Y_t = \alpha_1 + \alpha_2 X_{t2} + \varepsilon_t$, the regression coefficient $\alpha_2$ was a simple slope, a derivative of $Y$ with respect to $X_2$. The parameter $\gamma_2$ represents the slope in the relation between $Y$ and $X_2$ holding $X_3$ constant. It is a partial derivative of $Y$ with respect to $X_2$ holding $X_3$ constant. Because of this interpretation, the multiple regression technique is widely used to examine the distinct and separate contributions of several exogenous variables in explaining variation in a single endogenous variable.

The so-called partial regression coefficients for the extended model can be written in terms of the partial correlation coefficients by formulas similar to (d) in *Review* 8.2. Thus,

$$C_2 = r_{Y2 \cdot 3} \frac{s_{Y \cdot 3}}{s_{2 \cdot 3}} \qquad \text{and} \qquad C_3 = r_{Y3 \cdot 2} \frac{s_{Y \cdot 2}}{s_{3 \cdot 2}}$$

where $s_{Y \cdot 2}$ and $s_{3 \cdot 2}$ are standard deviations of the leftover parts of $Y$ and $X_3$ after removing $X_2$. In the above notation, they are the standard deviations of the residuals $W_t$ and $V_t$ respectively. Similarly, the expressions for $r_{Y2 \cdot 3}$, $s_{Y \cdot 3}$, and $s_{2 \cdot 3}$ are obtained for the case holding $X_3$ constant.

The partial regression coefficients, $C_2$ and $C_3$, can also be written in terms of the zero order expressions as

$$C_2 = \frac{r_{Y2} - r_{Y3} r_{23}}{1 - r_{23}{}^2} \frac{s_Y}{s_2} \qquad \text{and} \qquad C_3 = \frac{r_{Y3} - r_{Y2} r_{23}}{1 - r_{23}{}^2} \frac{s_Y}{s_3}. \qquad (8\text{-}5)$$

where $s_2$ and $s_3$ are the standard deviations of the sample observations on $X_2$ and $X_3$ respectively.[2]

||||||||||||||||||||||||||||||||||||||||||||||||||||||||||||||||||||||||||||||||||||||||||||||||||||||||||||||||||||||||||||||||

*Recursive note.* Again, it is clear that if $r_{23} = 1$, then neither $C_2$ nor $C_3$ would be defined. If the exogenous variables are not really independent but are perfectly linearly dependent, then the estimation of the coefficients breaks down. It is impossible to separate the distinct effects of variables $X_2$ and $X_3$ in the regression model.

||||||||||||||||||||||||||||||||||||||||||||||||||||||||||||||||||||||||||||||||||||||||||||||||||||||||||||||||||||||||||||||||

It is obvious from these expressions (8–5) that the determination of each coefficient in the extended model takes into account the degree of association among all pairs of variables in the model.

## An alternate description

One final way of describing the partial regression coefficients returns to the residual notation used earlier. Again, let $W$ denote the residual from the regression of $Y$ on $X_2$ and $V$ denote the residual from the regression of $X_3$ on $X_2$. That is,

$$W_t = y_t - a_{Y2} x_{t2} \quad \text{and} \quad V_t = x_{t3} - a_{32} x_{t2}.$$

Then $C_3$, the estimate of

$$\gamma_3 = \left( \frac{\partial Y}{\partial X_3} \right)_{x_2 \text{ constant}}$$

in the model $Y_t = \gamma_1 + \gamma_2 X_{t2} + \gamma_3 X_{t3} + \varepsilon_t$, can be expressed as the simple regression coefficient for the regression of $W$ on $V$.[3] This expresses the partial relation between the variables $Y$ and $X_3$ after the linear effect of the variable $X_2$ has been removed from each. Thus, it must be recognized that regression coefficients have different interpretations depending on which other variables are considered to be held constant within the regression model. To generalize, each least squares estimate of a coefficient in a multiple regression is a simple regression coefficient between a *pair of residuals* obtained

---

[2] These type formulas should always be looked up before using them. Their derivation is outlined in Exercise 5 at the end of the chapter.

[3] It could be computed as

$$C_3 = \begin{vmatrix} 1 & a_{32} \\ a_{Y3} & a_{Y2} \end{vmatrix} \Big/ \begin{vmatrix} 1 & a_{32} \\ a_{23} & 1 \end{vmatrix}$$

where $a_{Y3}$ and $a_{23}$ are defined as simple regression coefficients in the regressions of $Y$ and $X_2$ respectively on $X_3$. The expression can be generalized to any order. See D. J. Cowden, "A Procedure for Computing Regression Coefficients," *Journal of American Statistical Association*, Vol. 53 (1958), pp. 144–50.

by removing the linear influence of all other variables in the model from both the endogenous variable and the exogenous variable whose coefficient is being estimated.

‖‖‖‖‖‖‖‖‖‖‖‖‖‖‖‖‖‖‖‖‖‖‖‖‖‖‖‖‖‖‖‖‖‖‖‖‖‖‖‖‖‖‖‖‖‖‖‖‖‖‖‖‖‖‖‖‖‖‖‖‖‖‖‖‖‖‖‖‖‖‖‖‖‖‖‖‖‖‖‖‖‖‖‖‖‖‖‖‖‖‖‖

*Discursive note.* If this linear influence removed from the exogenous variable is perfectly complete, then no residual remains and the partial regression coefficient would not be defined. Even if this linear dependency among the exogenous variables is not perfect but very strong, the residuals left will be small and estimates of variance based on these residuals, in particular, [Est. $V(C_i)$], will be overstated. In this situation, called multicollinearity, the results must be interpreted cautiously since the available knowledge about the true parameters $\gamma_i$ is imprecise.

‖‖‖‖‖‖‖‖‖‖‖‖‖‖‖‖‖‖‖‖‖‖‖‖‖‖‖‖‖‖‖‖‖‖‖‖‖‖‖‖‖‖‖‖‖‖‖‖‖‖‖‖‖‖‖‖‖‖‖‖‖‖‖‖‖‖‖‖‖‖‖‖‖‖‖‖‖‖‖‖‖‖‖‖‖‖‖‖‖‖‖‖

All this discussion concerning the independence of the exogenous variables $X_2$ and $X_3$ has an implication for a later assumption commonly used in the analysis of the general model (see Chapter 10) and for some tests concerning multicollinearity (see Chapter 15).

## 8.5 PROPORTIONAL MEASURES OF VARIATION EXPLAINED

In the extended model, two variables are used to explain part of the variation in $Y$. The total variation of $Y$ can be written similarly to result (a) of *Review* 8.2 if the disturbance is assumed to be independent of both $X_2$ and $X_3$. The total variation in $Y$ is composed of the variation in $Y$ explained by $X_2$ and $X_3$, and the variation in $Y$ left unexplained. The square of the multiple correlation coefficient, $R_{Y2.3}{}^2$, describes the proportion of the variation in $Y$ which is explained by both $X_2$ and $X_3$ [recall (8–2)]. In addition, a new concept of the individual or partial contributions of each variable is provided by the square of the partial correlation coefficient.

### The partial coefficient of determination

The coefficient, $r_{Y3.2}{}^2$, is also a proportional measure of variation explained but relative to a different base from the multiple or simple coefficients of determination. The base for this partial coefficient concerns the variation in $Y$ which has not been explained by $X_2$. Then, the extra variation explained by $X_3$ is compared to this base of residual variation to obtain the proportion $r_{Y3.2}{}^2$. Thus,

$$r_{Y3.2}{}^2 = \left( \frac{\text{extra variation in } Y \text{ explained by } X_3 \text{ beyond that amount already explained by } X_2}{\text{residual variation in } Y \text{ not already explained by } X_2} \right).$$

**FIGURE 8–1**
Components of variation in an endogenous variable with
two exogenous variables

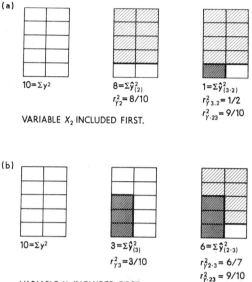

(a)

$10 = \Sigma y^2$

$8 = \Sigma \hat{y}_{(2)}^2$
$r_{Y2}^2 = 8/10$

VARIABLE $X_2$ INCLUDED FIRST.

$1 = \Sigma \hat{y}_{(3 \cdot 2)}^2$
$r_{Y3 \cdot 2}^2 = 1/2$
$r_{Y \cdot 23}^2 = 9/10$

(b)

$10 = \Sigma y^2$

$3 = \Sigma \hat{y}_{(3)}^2$
$r_{Y3}^2 = 3/10$

VARIABLE $X_3$ INCLUDED FIRST.

$6 = \Sigma \hat{y}_{(2 \cdot 3)}^2$
$r_{Y2 \cdot 3}^2 = 6/7$
$r_{Y \cdot 23}^2 = 9/10$

For example [see Figure 8–1(a)], the total variation of $Y$ may be $\sum y^2 = 10$ units. The variation explained by a regression of $Y$ on $X_2$ may be $\sum \hat{y}_{(2)}^2 = 8$ units with 2 units left unexplained. Thus, using a zero order coefficient, $r_{Y2}^2 = \frac{8}{10} = 0.80$. The additional variation explained by $X_3$ after removing the effect of $X_2$ on $X_3$ may be $\sum \hat{y}_{(3 \cdot 2)}^2 = 1$ unit. The first order coefficient is $r_{Y3 \cdot 2}^2 = \frac{1}{2}$, not $\frac{1}{10}$.

‖‖‖‖‖‖‖‖‖‖‖‖‖‖‖‖‖‖‖‖‖‖‖‖‖‖‖‖‖‖‖‖‖‖‖‖‖‖‖‖‖‖‖‖‖‖‖‖‖‖‖‖‖‖‖‖‖‖‖‖‖‖‖‖‖‖‖‖‖‖‖‖‖‖‖‖‖‖‖‖‖‖‖‖‖‖

***Explicative note.*** In this case, the multiple coefficient of determination would be $R_{Y \cdot 23}^2 = \frac{9}{10}$, since the combined explanation is
9 units out of 10.

‖‖‖‖‖‖‖‖‖‖‖‖‖‖‖‖‖‖‖‖‖‖‖‖‖‖‖‖‖‖‖‖‖‖‖‖‖‖‖‖‖‖‖‖‖‖‖‖‖‖‖‖‖‖‖‖‖‖‖‖‖‖‖‖‖‖‖‖‖‖‖‖‖‖‖‖‖‖‖‖‖‖‖‖‖‖

Another form for the partial coefficient of determination which corresponds
most closely in meaning to the written description above would be

$$r_{Y3 \cdot 2}^2 = \frac{R_{Y \cdot 23}^2 - r_{Y2}^2}{1 - r_{Y2}^2}, \qquad (8\text{--}6)$$

giving

$$r_{Y3 \cdot 2}^2 = \frac{\frac{9}{10} - \frac{8}{10}}{1 - \frac{8}{10}} = \frac{1}{2}.$$

In this same example [see Figure 8–1($b$)] the variation in $Y$ explained by a regression on $X_3$ need not be one unit. When none of the variation in $Y$ has been accounted for by $X_2$, then $X_3$ may explain more than only one unit of variation, perhaps $\sum \hat{y}_{(3)}^2 = 3$ units. Thus $r_{Y3}^2 = \frac{3}{10}$, leaving 7 units unexplained. Then, the additional variation explained by considering $X_2$ would be $\sum \hat{y}_{(2 \cdot 3)}^2 = 6$ units, so that the total amount explained, $\sum \hat{y}^2 = 9$ units and $R_{Y \cdot 23}^2 = \frac{9}{10}$, regardless which variable, $X_2$ or $X_3$, is considered first. The partial correlation coefficient, $r_{Y2 \cdot 3}^2 = \frac{6}{7}$, not 6/10 if the definition is applied correctly.

Finally, in this example, $X_2$ and $X_3$ must be correlated since they overlap as explanatory factors for $Y$. Separately, they explain 8/10 and 3/10 of the variation in $Y$ respectively, but together they explain only 9/10. Since they each explain some of the same part of the variation in $Y$, then they must also explain some of the variation in each other. Indeed $r_{23}^2$ would be about $\frac{2}{3}$ as determined by substitution into (8–3) of the appropriate values from this example, assuming all simple correlations are positive.

### Multiple-partial coefficients

In a more general case, a model may have $(K - 1)$ exogenous variables. Suppose these are separated into one group of variables $A$ and the remaining group of variables $B$. A coefficient denoted $r_{YA \cdot B}^2$, sometimes termed a multiple-partial coefficient, can be described as the following ratio,

$$r_{YA \cdot B}^2 = \left( \frac{\text{extra variation in } Y \text{ explained by the variables } A, \text{ beyond that amount already explained by the variables } B}{\text{residual variation in } Y \text{ not explained by the variables in group } B} \right).$$

||||||||||||||||||||||||||||||||||||||||||||||||||||||||||||||||||||||||||||||||||||||||||||||||||||||||||||||||||||||||

***Recursive note.*** It is important that in any partial correlation coefficient the base for comparison used in the denominator is not the total variation of $Y$ but a residual variation in $Y$ after removing the linear influence of one or a group of variables.

||||||||||||||||||||||||||||||||||||||||||||||||||||||||||||||||||||||||||||||||||||||||||||||||||||||||||||||||||||||||

### 8.6 USEFULNESS OF THESE NEW CONCEPTS

The multiple and partial correlation coefficients can provide useful information to the econometrician for guidance in building his model and for revising the model if the tests show some deficiencies. These statistical measures of correspondence can provide information on redundant variables or can be used to select variables which will provide a good fit. However, they do not in themselves serve as a test of the model nor imply any causal structure among the variables.

## For model specification

The econometrician may use these concepts of variation explained and unexplained to construct models which explain the most variance of $Y_t$. This criterion may allow him to save time in arriving at an acceptable forecasting model. Nevertheless, one must be careful to avoid judging a model on the basis of the same observations and the same criterion which are used to select the variables for inclusion in the model. It would be nonscientific to use a sample observation set $A$ to select exogenous variables for the model which explain the most variation in the endogenous variable; and then to judge the acceptability of the model based on these proportional measures of variation explained or on the accuracy of forecasts which are also computed from the observations in sample set $A$.

## For model verification

The econometrician will also use the measures of variation explained in setting up $F$-distributed test statistics for analysis of variance and for tests of hypothesis about the parameters. In so doing, the measures emphasized are those which help provide estimates of variance. For making judgements on the significance of the parameters, the various correlation coefficients are not as important as the standard errors of the estimates. Indeed, such tests, and even confidence intervals for forecasts, can be established without any direct use of these correlation coefficients at all.

On the other hand, they are often used as summary statistics representing the goodness of fit among selected variables. For this reason, it is important to recognize their meaning and interpretation, and also their limitation. A complete analysis of an econometric model involves much more than merely the considerations of these correlation measures.

## NEW VOCABULARY

Multiple correlation coefficient
Partial correlation coefficient
Partial regression coefficient

## EXERCISES

1. Using the least squares principle, derive the normal equations of (8–1) for the extended model, $Y_t = \gamma_1 + \gamma_2 X_{t2} + \gamma_3 X_{t3} + \varepsilon_t$.
2. Interpret the meaning of the conditions under which the partial correlation coefficient, $r_{Y3 \cdot 2}$, would equal the simple correlation coefficient, $r_{Y3}$. [Refer to (8–4b).]
3. Show all the steps in the algebra and the substitutions used to reduce (8–4a) to (8–4b).
4. Show that the right-hand sides of (8–2) and (8–3) are equal.

5.  Perform the derivation of (8–5) following these steps:
    a)  Write the last two normal equations in (8–1) in deviation form.
    b)  Solve the resulting equations for $C_2$ and $C_3$ by Cramer's method.
    c)  Divide both numerator and denominator of the expressions for $C_2$ and $C_3$ by $(\sum x_3{}^2)(\sum y^2)(\sum x_2{}^2)$ and form the proper terms to write as correlation coefficients.
    d)  Simplify, multiply, and divide by $\sqrt{T-1}$, and substitute for the standard deviations as needed.
6.  a)  Write a defining formula for $r_{Y2 \cdot 3}{}^2$ similar to (8–6) and substitute in the values from the example (Figure 8–1) to obtain $r_{Y2 \cdot 3}{}^2 = 6/7$.
    b)  Using the same example data (Figure 8–1) plus $r_{23}{}^2 = 2/3$, write an equation for $r_{Y2 \cdot 3}$ similar to (8–4b) and show that $r_{Y2 \cdot 3} = \sqrt{6/7} = 0.9258$.
7.  Refer to the data (Table 3–2) and the results of the text example in Chapters 3, 4, and 7. Suppose another variable $X_{t3}$ is added to the model where $X_{t3}$ is per capita income in the importing country. Its values are given below:

| Observation | 1 | 2 | 3 | 4 | 5 | 6 | 7 | 8 |
|---|---|---|---|---|---|---|---|---|
| $X_{t3}$ | 2.19 | 2.20 | 2.25 | 2.39 | 2.49 | 2.58 | 2.77 | 2.82 |

    a)  Find the simple correlation coefficients, $r_{Y2}$, $r_{Y3}$, and $r_{23}$. Using (8–4b) find $r_{Y3 \cdot 2}$.
    b)  Find the estimating line $\hat{X}_{t3} = a_{31} + a_{32} X_{t2}$ using ordinary least squares. Ans.: $\hat{X}_{t3} = -0.50 + 0.284 X_{t2}$.
    c)  Using the result from (b) and from the text (3–4), find the residuals $W_t$ and $V_t$ as defined in Section 8.4. Find the simple correlation of the residuals $r_{WV}$ and compare it to your answer in part (a) for $r_{Y3 \cdot 2}$.
    d)  Find the partial regression coefficient $C_3$ using (8–5).
    e)  Using least squares, find the estimating line, $W_t = b_1 + b_2 V_t$, and compare the value of $b_2$ to your answer in part (d).
    f)  Show that $\sum x_{t2} W_t = \sum x_{t2} V_t = 0$. Explain why.
    g)  Determine if $\sum y_t V_t = \sum x_{t3} W_t = \sum W_t V_t$ and explain your result intuitively and algebraically.

**Chapter 9**

# MATRIX SOLUTION FOR LEAST SQUARES ESTIMATION OF THE GENERAL MODEL

## 9.1 REVIEW

The general model is an extension of the extended model of Chapter 8. This extension is one of size only, not of concept. The general model allows for any number of exogenous variables, $X_1, X_2, \ldots, X_K$. The model is written $Y_t = \gamma_1 + \gamma_2 X_{t2} + \gamma_3 X_{t3} + \cdots \gamma_K X_{tK} + \varepsilon_t$. The first variable $X_{t1}$ is understood to be equal to one for all observations.

All the same concepts as in the extended model and all the same types of calculations as in the simple model can be applied to this general model. However, writing all the expressions in detail becomes so cumbersome that it is much better to adopt matrix and vector notation from this point on throughout the book. The concepts and operations of matrix analysis are introduced in section two of each chapter where they are first used. These are not absolutely necessary, but they are a common shorthand to simplify all the presentation and make the results clearer. In any case, if one intends to read some econometric literature, it is essential to become familiar with the matrix algebra formulations.

In this chapter, the matrix notation for the general model is introduced and used in finding the least squares estimates and measures of goodness of fit for this model. Additional practical comments are included with the example calculation.

## 9.2 REVIEW TOPICS

For materials in this chapter, a familiarity and facility with basic vector and matrix operations is required. Some important concepts are listed for your review.

### 1 Size and types of matrices

The matrix $A$ can be characterized by its size, usually given as $(m \times n)$ where the numbers $m$ and $n$ refer to the number of rows and columns in the matrix respectively. The elements of $A$ are denoted $a_{ij}$ where the subscripts $i$ and $j$ refer to the particular row and column position of this element in the matrix. The principal or main diagonal of a matrix consists of the elements where $i = j$. Some matrices are given special names.

*a)*  An $(m \times 1)$ matrix is called a column vector; a $(1 \times n)$ matrix is a row vector; and a $(1 \times 1)$ matrix is a scalar.

*b)*  A matrix in which $m = n$ is called a square matrix of size $(n \times n)$.

*c)*  A square matrix whose determinant (see *Review* 3.2) is nonzero is a nonsingular matrix.

*d)*  A square matrix with zeros in all positions except on the main diagonal is a diagonal matrix.

*e)*  A diagonal matrix with equal diagonal elements is a scalar matrix.

*f)*  A scalar matrix whose diagonal elements are all one is an identity matrix, denoted $\underset{(n \times n)}{I}$. For example

$$\underset{(3 \times 3)}{I} = \begin{pmatrix} 1 & 0 & 0 \\ 0 & 1 & 0 \\ 0 & 0 & 1 \end{pmatrix}.$$

### 2 Matrix operations

Several simple operations can be performed on matrices to obtain a new matrix. Their description involves the concept of matrix equality. The equality statement, $A = B$ for matrices, means all the corresponding elements of the matrices are the same. The matrices must be the same size. Now some operations are listed.

*a)*  Two matrices can be added or subtracted if they are the same size by adding or subtracting their corresponding elements, position by position. The resulting matrix is the same size as each of the original matrices. The associative and commutative laws apply. That is,

$$\underset{(2 \times 3)}{A} + \underset{(2 \times 3)}{B} - \underset{(2 \times 3)}{C} = \underset{(2 \times 3)}{(B} + \underset{(2 \times 3)}{A)} - \underset{(2 \times 3)}{C}$$

or

$$= \underset{(2 \times 3)}{A} + \underset{(2 \times 3)}{(B} - \underset{(2 \times 3)}{C)}$$

$$= \underset{(2 \times 3)}{D}.$$

b)   Any size matrix can be multiplied by a scalar by multiplying each element of the matrix by the scalar.

$$3\begin{pmatrix} a_{11} & a_{12} \\ a_{21} & a_{22} \end{pmatrix} = \begin{pmatrix} 3a_{11} & 3a_{12} \\ 3a_{21} & 3a_{22} \end{pmatrix}.$$

The distributive law holds, namely $3(A + B) = (3A + 3B)$ when the sum is defined.

c)   Any size matrix can be transposed by interchanging its rows and columns. That is, replace the element $a_{ij}$ with the element $a_{ji}$. The operation is indicated by a prime on the matrix.

$$\text{Suppose } A = \begin{pmatrix} 2 & 1 & 4 \\ 5 & 6 & 7 \end{pmatrix}; \text{ then}$$

$$A' = \begin{pmatrix} 2 & 1 & 4 \\ 5 & 6 & 7 \end{pmatrix}' = \begin{pmatrix} 2 & 5 \\ 1 & 6 \\ 4 & 7 \end{pmatrix}.$$

Also, the transpose of the transpose of any matrix is the original matrix back again.

$$(A')' = \begin{pmatrix} 2 & 5 \\ 1 & 6 \\ 4 & 7 \end{pmatrix}' = \begin{pmatrix} 2 & 1 & 4 \\ 5 & 6 & 7 \end{pmatrix} = A.$$

The size of the transpose of an $(m \times n)$ matrix is necessarily $(n \times m)$; the indicators are merely reversed. Note that the transpose of a column vector with any number of elements, $h$, is always a row vector with the same $h$ elements in the same order. In this book all vectors are column vectors unless otherwise designated by a prime.

If the transpose of a matrix is equal to the matrix itself, then it is called a symmetric matrix. $A$ is symmetric if $A = A'$.

d)   Two vectors can be multiplied together to obtain their inner product if the first is a row vector and the second a column vector, both with the same number of elements. The inner product is a scalar defined to be the sum of the products of the corresponding elements in the two vectors.

$$\text{If } C = \begin{pmatrix} C_1 \\ C_2 \\ C_3 \end{pmatrix} \quad \text{and} \quad X = \begin{pmatrix} X_1 \\ X_2 \\ X_3 \end{pmatrix}, \quad \text{then}$$

$$C'X = (C_1 \; C_2 \; C_3)\begin{pmatrix} X_1 \\ X_2 \\ X_3 \end{pmatrix} = \sum_{i=1}^{3} (C_i X_i).$$

In general, if $C'$ is of size $(1 \times K)$, then $X$ must be size $(K \times 1)$ in order for the inner product $C'X$ to be defined. The answer is size $(1 \times 1)$, a scalar.

The inner product of any vector with itself gives the sum of squares of its elements.

$$\text{Suppose } e = \begin{pmatrix} e_1 \\ e_2 \\ e_3 \\ e_4 \end{pmatrix}, \quad \text{then} \quad e'e = \sum_{i=1}^{4} e_i^2.$$

e)   Two matrices can be multiplied if the number of columns in the first equals the number of rows in the second. The product matrix has the same number of rows as the first and the same number of columns as the second. This is much simpler put in symbols.

$$\underset{(m \times h)}{A} \cdot \underset{(h \times n)}{B} = \underset{(m \times n)}{C} .$$

Using the size indicators, the product is defined only if the inner indicators, $(m \times \underbrace{h) (h}_{\text{inner}} \times n)$, are equal. The size of the product matrix is given by the outer indicators, $(\underbrace{m \times h) (h \times n}_{\text{outer}})$, to be $(m \times n)$.

|||||||||||||||||||||||||||||||||||||||||||||||||||||||||||||||||||||||||||||||||||||||||||||||||||||||||||||||||||||||||||||||||

***Recursive note.*** The vector inner product above is only a special case of the matrix product. For two vectors $\underset{(8 \times 1)}{C}$ and $\underset{(8 \times 1)}{X}$, then $C'X$ can be visualized by using the size indicators $(1 \times 8) (8 \times 1)$. The product is defined since the number of elements in each vector is equal, $8 = 8$; and the product is size $(1 \times 1)$, a scalar. If we multiply $CX'$, we get a different case of $(8 \times 1) (1 \times 8)$. The product is defined, but the answer is an $(8 \times 8)$ matrix of all 64 possible products of pairs of elements, one from $C$ and one from $X$.

|||||||||||||||||||||||||||||||||||||||||||||||||||||||||||||||||||||||||||||||||||||||||||||||||||||||||||||||||||||||||||||||||

The elements in the product matrix are always an inner product of two vectors, a row vector from the first matrix with a column vector from the second matrix. Calculation of the entire product matrix involves all possible inner products of row vectors of the first matrix with column vectors of the second matrix.

If $AB = C$, then the element $c_{ij}$ of the product matrix is the inner product of row $i$ of $A$ and column $j$ of $B$; or in symbols, if $A$ is $(m \times h)$ and $B$ is $(h \times n)$, then

$$c_{ij} = \sum_{k=1}^{h} a_{ik} b_{kj} .$$

Suppose

$$A = \begin{pmatrix} 1 & 2 & 3 \\ 4 & 5 & 6 \end{pmatrix}, \qquad B = \begin{pmatrix} 7 & p \\ 8 & s \\ 9 & d \end{pmatrix},$$

then the product $C = AB$ is defined and has size $(2 \times 3)(3 \times 2)$ or $(2 \times 2)$. The element $c_{11} = (1 \cdot 7) + (2 \cdot 8) + (3 \cdot 9) = 50$. The element $c_{22} = 4p + 5s + 6d$. The product $D = BA$ is also defined but $D$ is size $(3 \times 3)$, and $D \neq C$. The commutative law does not necessarily hold for matrix multiplication.

A specially easy matrix multiplication involves the identity matrix. The product of any matrix $A$ multiplied by an identity matrix of appropriate size (so the inner size indicators are equal) is always the same matrix $A$. This operation is analogous to multiplication of any number $N$ by the number 1. The answer is always $N$. Furthermore, the operation is often implicit as the factor 1 is commonly omitted. Similarly the matrix $\underset{(n \times n)}{I}$ can commonly be omitted or inserted as desired without changing the resulting product matrix.

The associative law holds for matrix multiplication, $(AB)C = A(BC)$ if all the multiplications are defined.

*f)* *Matrix inverse.* The inverse matrix exists only for a nonsingular matrix and is unique for that matrix. The inverse matrix of a matrix $A$ is denoted by $A^{-1}$ to indicate the analogy to a reciprocal in real numbers. Just as multiplication of a number $a$ by its reciprocal always equals one, $aa^{-1} = a(1/a) = 1$, so also, the multiplication of a matrix by its inverse matrix always gives the identity matrix as the product,

$$\underset{(n \times n)}{A} \underset{(n \times n)}{A^{-1}} = \underset{(n \times n)}{A^{-1}} \underset{(n \times n)}{A} = \underset{(n = n)}{I}.$$

The inverse matrix is defined as $A^{-1} = (1/\det A)(\text{Adjoint } A)$ where (Adjoint $A$) is the transpose of the matrix of cofactors (see *Review* 3.2, item 4) of all the corresponding elements of $A$.

For a $(2 \times 2)$ nonsingular matrix, the calculation of the inverse is very easy. Consider $A = \begin{pmatrix} a & b \\ c & d \end{pmatrix}$; then $\det A = ad - bc$. Also the cofactor of element $a$ is $d$, of element $d$ is $a$, of element $c$ is $(-b)$, and of element $b$ is $(-c)$. Therefore, the cofactor matrix is $\begin{pmatrix} d & -c \\ -b & a \end{pmatrix}$ and the adjoint matrix is

$$(\text{Adjoint } A) = \begin{pmatrix} d & -c \\ -b & a \end{pmatrix}' = \begin{pmatrix} d & -b \\ -c & a \end{pmatrix}.$$

A short cut for finding the adjoint matrix of a $(2 \times 2)$ matrix is the following: (i) interchange the elements on the main diagonal; and (ii) change the sign of the off-diagonal elements.

For example, if $A = \begin{pmatrix} 2 & 6 \\ 1 & 5 \end{pmatrix}$, then $A^{-1} = 1/(10 - 6) \begin{pmatrix} 5 & -6 \\ -1 & 2 \end{pmatrix}$

$= \begin{pmatrix} 1.25 & -1.5 \\ -0.25 & 0.5 \end{pmatrix}$.

The calculation can be checked by matrix multiplication,

$$AA^{-1} = \begin{pmatrix} 2 & 6 \\ 1 & 5 \end{pmatrix} \begin{pmatrix} 1.25 & -1.2 \\ -0.25 & 0.5 \end{pmatrix} = \begin{pmatrix} 2.5 - 1.5 & -3.0 + 3.0 \\ 1.25 - 1.25 & -1.5 + 2.5 \end{pmatrix}$$

$$= \begin{pmatrix} 1 & 0 \\ 0 & 1 \end{pmatrix} = \underset{(2 \times 2)}{I} .$$

For larger size matrices, the calculation of the cofactors, and hence of the adjoint matrix and of the inverse, would be more tedious. However, such calculations are commonly done by a computer within a multiple regression program. A partitioning method can also be used (see Exercise R.6 at the end of this section).

*g)* Transpose and inverse of a product and of each other.

Some simple theorems are exceedingly useful and frequently applied.[1]

(i)   The transpose of a defined product of matrices is the product of the transpose matrices in reverse order

$$\underset{(m \times h)}{(A} \underset{(h \times n)}{B)'} = \underset{(n \times h)}{B'} \underset{(h \times m)}{A'}$$

(ii)  The inverse of a product of nonsingular matrices of the same size $(n \times n)$ is the product of the inverse matrices in reverse order.

$$(ABC)^{-1} = (C^{-1}B^{-1}A^{-1}).$$

(iii) The transpose of an inverse matrix is the inverse of the transpose matrix.

$$(A')^{-1} = (A^{-1})'.$$

As an example of the first of these rules, find the transpose of a matrix product, $X'X$, where $X$ is size $(m \times n)$. First, $X'X$ is size $(n \times m)(m \times n)$. Applying rule (i), $(X'X)' = X'(X')' = X'X$. The matrix $(X'X)$ is symmetric. (See an application of this situation in step *(b)* of Section 9.6.)

---

[1] For these results and further discussion on all these topics, see G. Hadley, *Linear Algebra* (Reading, Mass.: Addison-Wesley Publishing Co., Inc.), chap. 3.

## 3 Vector and matrix differentiation

Using the rules of calculus, it is easy to find partial derivatives of the linear expression, $f = 3C_1 - 5C_2 + 8C_3$, with respect to the unknowns $C_1$, $C_2$, and $C_3$. We can write

$$\frac{\partial f}{\partial C_1} = 3; \quad \frac{\partial f}{\partial C_2} = -5; \quad \text{and} \quad \frac{\partial f}{\partial C_3} = 8.$$

Suppose we write $f$ in vector form as $C'X$ where $C' = (C_1\ C_2\ C_3)$ and $X = \begin{pmatrix} 3 \\ -5 \\ 8 \end{pmatrix}$. By vector differentiation, we mean a shorthand expression for these partial derivatives, where $\partial(C'X)/\partial C = X$, defined as the vector

$$\begin{pmatrix} \dfrac{\partial f}{\partial C_1} \\[2mm] \dfrac{\partial f}{\partial C_2} \\[2mm] \dfrac{\partial f}{\partial C_3} \end{pmatrix} = \begin{pmatrix} 3 \\ -5 \\ 8 \end{pmatrix}.$$

Similarly, the partial derivatives of more complex vector and matrix terms can be written using this shorthand. Suppose

$$f = C'ZC = (C_1\ C_2\ C_3) \begin{pmatrix} 1 & 4 & 5 \\ 4 & 2 & 6 \\ 5 & 6 & 3 \end{pmatrix} \begin{pmatrix} C_1 \\ C_2 \\ C_3 \end{pmatrix},$$

$$f = C_1{}^2 + 2C_2{}^2 + 3C_3{}^2 + 4C_1 C_2 + 5C_1 C_3 + 6C_2 C_3 + 4C_2 C_1 + 5C_3 C_1 + 6C_3 C_2.$$

Note that the matrix $Z$ is symmetric. This is a matrix expression for a quadratic form in the variables $C_1$, $C_2$, and $C_3$ (see *Review* 7.2, item 1).

The partial derivatives can be written

$$\frac{\partial f}{\partial C_1} = 2(C_1) + 2(4C_2) + 2(5C_3) = 2(C_1 + 4C_2 + 5C_3),$$

$$\frac{\partial f}{\partial C_2} = 2(2C_2) + 2(4C_1) + 2(6C_3) = 2(4C_1 + 2C_2 + 6C_3),$$

$$\frac{\partial f}{\partial C_3} = 2(3C_3) + 2(5C_1) + 2(6C_2) = 2(5C_1 + 6C_2 + 3C_3).$$

These expressions are simply the inner products of vector $C'$ with each of the columns of $A$ or the inner product of each of the rows of $A$ with the vector $C$ (multiplied in each case by the factor 2). These inner products are merely numbers, the components of a row vector $2C'Z$ or of a column vector $2ZC$. Thus, we may represent the partial derivative of $f$ as $\partial(C'ZC)/\partial C = 2C'Z$ or $2ZC$ depending on our choice for a row or column vector. Visually, the result is very similar to $d(zc^2)/dc = 2zc$, and this sort of comparison almost always indicates the correct result.

## REVIEW EXERCISES

R.1.  *a)*  Define the appropriate vectors and matrices to rewrite this linear equation system in matrix and vector form:

$$3X_1 + 5X_2 - X_4 = 6,$$
$$2X_1 - 7X_3 - 3X_4 = 0,$$
$$-4X_1 + 6X_3 = 3.$$

*b)*  Write out the following matrix and vector representation in detail:

$$\begin{pmatrix} 2 & -4 & 1 & 0 \\ 1 & 2 & 0 & -2 \\ 0 & 3 & -3 & 0 \end{pmatrix} \begin{pmatrix} X_1 \\ X_2 \\ X_3 \\ X_4 \end{pmatrix} = \begin{pmatrix} 4 \\ -1 \\ 3 \end{pmatrix}.$$

R.2.  Given the following matrices:

$$A = \begin{pmatrix} 2 & 7 & 3 \\ 5 & 4 & 8 \\ 1 & 9 & 0 \end{pmatrix}, \quad B = \begin{pmatrix} 8 & 1 & 6 \\ 2 & -3 & 4 \end{pmatrix}, \quad C = \begin{pmatrix} 3 & 2 & 1 & 4 \\ 6 & 2 & 1 & 8 \end{pmatrix},$$

$$D' = (1 \quad 2 \quad 0 \quad -3), \quad E = (8 \quad 6 \quad 4 \quad 2), \quad Z = \begin{pmatrix} 1 & 0 \\ -1 & 2 \\ 2 & 3 \end{pmatrix},$$

$$G = \begin{pmatrix} -3 \\ -1 \end{pmatrix}, \quad X' = (X_1 \quad X_2 \quad X_3).$$

Find if defined (if not, say why)

*a)*  $A - B$
*b)*  $3A'$
*c)*  $E' - D$
*d)*  $C'D$
*e)*  $G'Z' + X'$
*f)*  $BIZG$
*g)*  $IA$
*h)*  $(DE)'$
*i)*  $E'E$
*j)*  $X'AX$
*k)*  A symmetric matrix $F$ such that the quadratic forms $X'AX$ and $X'FX$ are equal. [*Hint:* Let the elements of $F$ be $f_{ij} = \frac{1}{2}(a_{ij} + a_{ji})$.]
*l)*  $\partial(X'FX)/\partial X$.

R.3.  For the matrix $A$ of Exercise R.2, find
*a)*  Adjoint $A$.
*b)*  Inverse of $A = A^{-1}$.
*c)*  $(A')^{-1}$.
*d)*  The solution vector $X$ in $AX = (-1 \quad 2 \quad -3)'$. [Make use of $A^{-1}$ from part (*b*).]

R.4.   For the matrix $Z$ of Exercise R.2, find $(Z'Z)^{-1}$.

R.5.   Given the following matrices:

$$A = \begin{pmatrix} 1 & 3 & 4 \\ 2 & 0 & 7 \\ 5 & 6 & 9 \end{pmatrix}, \quad B = \begin{pmatrix} 0 & 3 & 7 \\ 1 & 8 & 9 \end{pmatrix}, \quad C = \begin{pmatrix} 1 & 2 & 4 & 5 \\ 3 & 1 & 0 & 2 \end{pmatrix},$$

$$D = (1 \ 0 \ 7 \ 8)', \quad E = (2 \ 4 \ 9 \ 6), \quad G = \begin{pmatrix} 2 \\ 3 \end{pmatrix},$$

$$F = \begin{pmatrix} 3 & 7 & 1 \\ 2 & 6 & 1 \\ 1 & 4 & 0 \end{pmatrix}, \quad X = \begin{pmatrix} X_1 \\ X_2 \\ X_3 \end{pmatrix}.$$

Find if defined (if not, say why)

a)  $F + A$

b)  $-2C$

c)  $C - GE$

d)  $CD + 4G$

e)  $BA$

f)  $G'BA$

g)  $FI$

h)  $D'D$

i)  $(B'G)'$

j)  $AF$ (does this equal $FA$?)

k)  $|A|$

l)  $B^{-1}$

m)  $\dfrac{\partial(BX)}{\partial X}$

n)  $X'FX$.

R.6.   Any square matrix $A$ of dimension $n = h + m$ can be partitioned into sub-matrices as shown

$$\underset{(n \times n)}{A} = \begin{pmatrix} \underset{(h \times h)}{A_{11}} & \underset{(h + m)}{A_{12}} \\ \underset{(m \times h)}{A_{21}} & \underset{(m \times m)}{A_{22}} \end{pmatrix}.$$

Define a matrix

$$\underset{(m \times m)}{P} = A_{22} - A_{21}A_{11}^{-1}A_{12},$$

then

$$A^{-1} = \begin{pmatrix} A_{11}^{-1} + A_{11}^{-1}A_{12}P^{-1}A_{21}A_{11}^{-1} & -A_{11}^{-1}A_{12}P^{-1} \\ -P^{-1}A_{21}A_{11}^{-1} & P^{-1} \end{pmatrix}.$$

This permits the calculation of $A^{-1}$ from simpler matrix operations on inverses of submatrices of smaller dimensions.

    Consider

$$\underset{(3 \times 3)}{A} = \begin{pmatrix} 2 & 1 & 2 \\ 2 & 3 & 1 \\ 3 & 2 & 2 \end{pmatrix}.$$

a)  Partition $A$ so that $A_{22}$ has dimension $(2 \times 2)$.

b)  Form $P$.   Ans.: $P = \begin{pmatrix} 3 & 1 \\ 2 & 2 \end{pmatrix} - \begin{pmatrix} 2 \\ 3 \end{pmatrix}(0.5)(1 \ 2) = \begin{pmatrix} 2 & -1 \\ 0.5 & -1 \end{pmatrix}.$

c)  Find $P^{-1}$.

d)  Find $A^{-1}$.   Ans.: $A^{-1} = \begin{pmatrix} -4/3 & -2/3 & 5/3 \\ 1/3 & 2/3 & -2/3 \\ 5/3 & 1/3 & -4/3 \end{pmatrix}.$

R.7.  Using matrices $A$ and $F$ from Exercises R.5, find

a) $A^{-1}$

b) The solution for $AX = (6 \quad 2 \quad 1)'$ by Cramer's Rule (*Review* 3.2, item 5).
   Ans.: $X' = 1/57 (-237 \quad 81 \quad 84)'$.

c) The solution in part (*b*) using $X = A^{-1}(6 \quad 2 \quad 1)'$.

d) $F^{-1}$

e) $(F^{-1})'$

f) $(F')^{-1}$

g) $(AF)^{-1}$

## 9.3  MATRIX PRESENTATION OF THE GENERAL MODEL

Much effort and space can be saved if matrix notation is adopted for the writing and analysis of the general model. Also, the calculations for the general model are most easily done in terms of deviations of coded data rather than in terms of original data. It is important to understand at the beginning the exact meaning of the symbols to be used.

### Notation

Denote the general model in deviation form by $Y = X\Gamma + \varepsilon$. $Y$ is a $(T \times 1)$ column vector of deviations,

$$Y = \begin{pmatrix} y_1 \\ y_2 \\ \vdots \\ y_T \end{pmatrix}$$

of the endogenous variable. $X$ is a $[T \times (K - 1)]$ matrix of deviations of the exogenous variables $X_{t2}, \dots, X_{tk}$,

$$X = \begin{pmatrix} x_{12} & x_{13} & \cdots & x_{1K} \\ x_{22} & x_{23} & \cdots & x_{2K} \\ \vdots & \vdots & & \vdots \\ x_{T2} & x_{T3} & \cdots & x_{TK} \end{pmatrix}$$

$\varepsilon$ is a $(T \times 1)$ column vector of disturbances,

$$\varepsilon = \begin{pmatrix} \varepsilon_1 \\ \varepsilon_2 \\ \vdots \\ \varepsilon_T \end{pmatrix}$$

$\Gamma$ is a $[(K - 1) \times 1]$ column vector of coefficients,

$$\Gamma = \begin{pmatrix} \gamma_2 \\ \gamma_3 \\ \vdots \\ \gamma_K \end{pmatrix}.$$

The intercept $\gamma_1$ for the linear equation can easily be calculated separately given these coefficients. The first indexed variable $X_{t1}$ assumes the value one for all observations.

Writing the model algebraically for any observation $t$, the equation to be estimated is $y_t = \gamma_2 x_{t2} + \gamma_3 x_{t3} + \cdots + \gamma_K x_{tK} + \varepsilon_t$. The equation could be repeated $T$ times, once for each observation. We try to find the coefficients $\gamma_k$, $k = 2, 3, \ldots, K$, which make the right side of the equation, excluding $\varepsilon_t$, most closely equal to the left side on the average for all $T$ repeated observations.

**The least squares representation**

The special criterion used might be the principle of least squares. Denote the least squares estimates by $C$, a $[(K-1) \times 1]$ column vector of elements $(C_2, C_3, \ldots, C_K)'$ corresponding to the parameters $\gamma_k$. Then, the residuals from the estimation are denoted by the $(T \times 1)$ column vector $e = (e_1, e_2, \ldots, e_T)'$ determined by $e = Y - XC$. Least squares requires that $\sum e_t^2$ be minimized.

That is, minimize $e'e = (Y - XC)'(Y - XC)$. The size of these vectors are $(1 \times T)$ and $(T \times 1)$ so the product is simply a $(1 \times 1)$ scalar, the unexplained variation. By expansion of this product, remembering the rule for transpose of a product matrix, $e'e = Y'Y - Y'XC - C'X'Y + C'X'XC$.

The size of the term, $Y'XC$, is $(1 \times T)[T \times (K-1)][(K-1) \times 1]$ or $(1 \times 1)$. Since a scalar matrix is necessarily symmetric (the same and only element of the matrix is in the $a_{11}$ position for both the matrix and its transpose), then $Y'XC = (Y'XC)' = C'X'Y$, and the two middle terms in the expression for $e'e$ can be combined. The resulting expression for the sum of squares of residuals to be minimized is

$$e'e = Y'Y - 2C'X'Y + C'X'XC. \tag{9-1}$$

**9.4 SOLUTION FOR THE LEAST SQUARES ESTIMATES**

Continuing with the principle of least squares, the partial derivatives of $\sum e_t^2$ with respect to each $C_k$, $k = 2, 3, \ldots, K$, must be determined and set equal to zero. This can be accomplished in shorter form by vector differentiation. We obtain

$$\frac{\partial(e'e)}{\partial C} = \frac{\partial(Y'Y - 2C'X'Y + C'X'XC)}{\partial C} = -2X'Y + 2X'XC,$$

where the differentiation is analogous to

$$\frac{\partial(2Cxy + xxC^2)}{\partial C} = 2xy + 2xxC$$

if $C$, $x$, and $y$ represented ordinary variables.

Since the term $X'Y$ has size $[(K - 1) \times T](T \times 1)$ and the term $X'XC$ has size $[(K - 1) \times T][T \times (K - 1)][(K - 1) \times 1]$, the solution represents a $[(K - 1) \times 1]$ column vector where each element is a partial derivative of $\sum e_t^2$ with respect to the corresponding $C_k$.

Setting this vector of partial derivatives equal to zero and solving includes these steps,

$$X'XC = \tfrac{2}{2}X'Y \tag{9-2}$$

$$(X'X)^{-1}(X'X)C = (X'X)^{-1}(X'Y)$$

$$C = (X'X)^{-1}(X'Y) \tag{9-3}$$

where the right-hand side has size

$$[(K - 1) \times T][T \times (K - 1)][(K - 1) \times T](T \times 1),$$

or

$$[(K - 1) \times (K - 1)][(K - 1) \times 1],$$

or $[(K - 1) \times 1]$ which is the correct size for the vector of estimates $C = (C_2, C_3, \ldots, C_K)'$.

||||||||||||||||||||||||||||||||||||||||||||||||||||||||||||||||||||||||||||||||||||||||||||||||||||||||||||||||||||||||||||||||||||||||

***Recursive note.***    The solution is analogous to the estimate of $a_2$ in the simple model,

$$a_2 = \frac{\sum x_{t2} y_t}{\sum x_{t2}^2} = \frac{X_2'Y}{(X_2'X_2)} = (X_2'X_2)^{-1}(X_2'Y),$$

where $X_2$ and $Y$ are size $(T \times 1)$ for the $T$ observations of the variable $X_2$ and $Y$ respectively; and $a_2$ has size $[(1 \times T)(T \times 1)][(1 \times T)(T \times 1)$ or $(1 \times 1)$.

||||||||||||||||||||||||||||||||||||||||||||||||||||||||||||||||||||||||||||||||||||||||||||||||||||||||||||||||||||||||||||||||||||||||

***Explicative note.***    A particular estimate, say $C_5$, for the fifth of eight coefficients in the model $Y_t = \gamma_1 + \gamma_2 X_{t2} + \cdots + \gamma_5 X_{t5} + \cdots + \gamma_8 X_{t8} + \varepsilon_t$, would be calculated as the fourth of seven components in the vector $C = (X'X)^{-1}X'Y$. It is obtained by taking the inner product of the fourth row of the $(7 \times 7)$ inverse matrix $(X'X)^{-1}$ with the $(7 \times 1)$ column vector $X'Y$.

||||||||||||||||||||||||||||||||||||||||||||||||||||||||||||||||||||||||||||||||||||||||||||||||||||||||||||||||||||||||||||||||||||||||

The calculation for each estimate involves the observations on all the variables included in the model. No information from the sample is wasted.

||||||||||||||||||||||||||||||||||||||||||||||||||||||||||||||||||||||||||||||||||||||||||||||||||||||||||||||||||||||||||||||||

*Interpretive note.* The elements of the matrix $X'X$ are variations and covariations among all exogenous variables, and the elements of the vector $X'Y$ are covariations between the endogenous variable and each exogenous variable. The regression coefficients are always some measure of the covariation between endogenous and exogenous variables relative to the variation of the exogenous variable itself (see 3–2a).

||||||||||||||||||||||||||||||||||||||||||||||||||||||||||||||||||||||||||||||||||||||||||||||||||||||||||||||||||||||||||||||||

*Recursive note.* The solution for the estimates was obtained from $X'XC = (2/2)X'Y$, in the matrix equation (9–2). Eliminating the unit element (2/2), these are the $(K - 1)$ normal equations. If $K = 2$ this is the same as the second normal equation for the simple model given in (3–1). If $K = 3$, they are the same as the final two normal equations for the extended model given in (8–1).

||||||||||||||||||||||||||||||||||||||||||||||||||||||||||||||||||||||||||||||||||||||||||||||||||||||||||||||||||||||||||||||||

The coefficient $C_1$ can be determined according to the formula

$$C_1 = \overline{Y} - C_2 \overline{X}_2 - C_3 \overline{X}_3 - \ldots - C_K X_K = \overline{Y} - C'\overline{X}. \qquad (9\text{–}4)$$

This is known because the estimating $(K - 1)$ dimension hyperplane in the $K$-dimensional sample space (analogous to the estimating line in two-dimension space for the simple model or the estimating plane in three-dimension space for the extended model) must pass through the point of means for all the variables. We design it specially so that this is true. We determine it so that on the average for all observations, it is the best possible estimating hyperplane.

## 9.5 THE RELATIVE MEASURES OF GOODNESS OF FIT

The simple correlation coefficients among all pairs of variables in the model are determined exactly the same way as before. For the column vectors of $T$ deviations from the mean for any pair of variables $W$ and $Z$,

$$r_{WZ} = \frac{W'Z}{\sqrt{W'W}\sqrt{Z'Z}} = \frac{\sum w_t z_t}{\sqrt{\sum w_t^2 \sum z_t^2}}.$$

The partial correlation coefficients can be calculated if desired from these simple correlation coefficients.

The multiple correlation coefficient is best determined as the square root of

$$R_{Y \cdot 234 \cdots K}^2 = \frac{\text{explained variation}}{\text{total variation}} = \frac{\sum y_t^2 - \sum e_t^2}{\sum y_t^2}.$$

In vector form, $\sum y_t^2 = Y'Y$ and $\sum e_t^2 = e'e$. Thus, the explained variation can be written $Y'Y - e'e$. This can be rewritten by substituting for $e'e$ from (9-1) and then for $C$ from (9-3).

The sequence of manipulations is:

$$Y'Y - e'e = Y'Y - [Y'Y - 2C'X'Y + C'X'XC]$$
$$= (Y'Y - Y'Y) + 2C'X'Y - C'(X'X)[(X'X)^{-1}X'Y]$$
$$= 0 + 2[C'X'Y] + (-1)[C'(I)X'Y],$$
$$Y'Y - e'e = (+1)C'X'Y. \tag{9-5}$$

Therefore, the explained variation for the general model is $C'X'Y$, a $(1 \times 1)$ scalar, perfectly analogous to the explained variation in the simple model of $a_2 \sum x_{t2} y_t$ [see (4-4)]. The relative measure of goodness of fit for the general model is then,

$$R_{Y \cdot 234 \cdots K}^2 = \frac{C'X'Y}{Y'Y}. \tag{9-6}$$

## Adjusted $R^2$

Some analysts prefer to compute the adjusted $R^2$ rather than the preceding multiple coefficient of determination. The adjusted $R^2$, denoted by $\bar{R}^2$, is adjusted for the degrees of freedom in the estimating equation to avoid the upward bias in the unadjusted $R^2$ when the sample size is small relative to the number of explanatory variables in the model. The calculation of the adjusted $R^2$ is similar to that for the simple $r^2$ in (4-2),

$$\bar{R}^2 = 1 - (1 - R^2)\frac{T-1}{T-K}. \tag{9-6a}$$

Without such an adjustment, the goodness of fit measure can be made arbitrarily close to unity, indicating a perfect fit, simply by approaching equality between the number of coefficients to be estimated and the number of observations.

Just as two observation points can be fit perfectly by a straight line with two coefficients (a slope and an intercept), so also can $T$ observation points be fit perfectly by a $T - 1$ dimension hyperplane with $T$ coefficients (such as if $K = T$ so the model has an intercept and $T - 1$ explanatory variables). Each separate variable added can contribute to the amount of variation in $Y$ explained by the regression equation, thereby increasing the numerator of (9-6) and increasing $R^2$. The adjusted value, $\bar{R}^2$, offsets the extra variation explained with the loss of one extra degree of freedom.

‖‖‖‖‖‖‖‖‖‖‖‖‖‖‖‖‖‖‖‖‖‖‖‖‖‖‖‖‖‖‖‖‖‖‖‖‖‖‖‖‖‖‖‖‖‖‖‖‖‖‖‖‖‖‖‖‖‖‖‖‖‖‖‖‖‖‖‖‖‖‖‖‖‖‖‖‖‖‖‖‖‖‖

*Explicative note.* For a numerical comparison, suppose two equations each based on 30 observations have standard $R^2 = 0.64$. However, case A has 2 explanatory variables and an intercept while case B has 10 explanatory variables and an intercept. The adjusted values for $\bar{R}^2$ would reflect this difference. For case A, $\bar{R}^2 = 1 - (1 - 0.64)\frac{29}{27} = 0.613$, and for case B, $\bar{R}^2 = 1 - (1 - 0.64)\frac{29}{19} = 0.450$. The equation in case A has the relatively better fit considering the number of variables included.

‖‖‖‖‖‖‖‖‖‖‖‖‖‖‖‖‖‖‖‖‖‖‖‖‖‖‖‖‖‖‖‖‖‖‖‖‖‖‖‖‖‖‖‖‖‖‖‖‖‖‖‖‖‖‖‖‖‖‖‖‖‖‖‖‖‖‖‖‖‖‖‖‖‖‖‖‖‖‖‖‖‖‖

## 9.6 EXAMPLE CALCULATION

Consider the model, imports $= \gamma_1 + \gamma_2$(domestic prices) $+ \gamma_3$(domestic per capita national income) $+ \varepsilon_t$, and denote the statistics representing the variables as $Y_t$, $X_{t2}$, and $X_{t3}$. Using the same data as before for $Y$ and $X_2$, and adding eight observations of $X_3$, gives the information in the left half of Table 9–1.

**TABLE 9–1**

Example problem data

| Observation | Original data | | | Coded data | | |
| --- | --- | --- | --- | --- | --- | --- |
| | $Y$ | $X_2$ | $X_3$ | $Y$ | $X_2$ | $X_3$ |
| 1........... | 796 | 95 | 2,190 | 7.96 | 9.5 | 2.19 |
| 2........... | 779 | 97 | 2,200 | 7.79 | 9.7 | 2.20 |
| 3........... | 773 | 100 | 2,250 | 7.73 | 10.0 | 2.25 |
| 4........... | 833 | 100 | 2,390 | 8.33 | 10.0 | 2.39 |
| 5........... | 894 | 104 | 2,490 | 8.94 | 10.4 | 2.49 |
| 6........... | 896 | 105 | 2,580 | 8.96 | 10.5 | 2.58 |
| 7........... | 998 | 112 | 2,770 | 9.98 | 11.2 | 2.77 |
| 8...........| 1,016 | 120 | 2,820 | 10.16 | 12.0 | 2.82 |

Again, the data can be coded to reduce rounding errors. The appropriate factors to be multiplied by the observations on $Y$, $X_2$, and $X_3$ are $10^{-2}$, $10^{-1}$, and $10^{-3}$ respectively. From this point on, the coded data on the right side of Table 9–1 is to be used. The following sequence of steps gives some order to the analysis:

*a)* Find the sums, means, and raw moments for the coded data.
*b)* Determine the dispersion matrix of variations and covariations among the variables, $X'X$, often called the cross-product deviation matrix.

*c)*  Find the inverse of the matrix $(X'X)$.
*d)*  Calculate the least squares estimates.
*e)*  Write the estimating equation.
*f)*  Calculate the explained variation.
*g)*  Find the square of the multiple correlation coefficient.
*h)*  Find any simple or partial correlation coefficients of interest.

All these steps or their equivalents are commonly done in any least squares regression program for a computer. For this small problem, they can be done easily using a desk calculator.

## Step (a)

The sums, means, and raw moments which do not involve $X_3$ have been calculated previously. The new calculations are done in the same way to find $\sum X_{t3}$, $\overline{X}_3$, $\sum X_{t3}^2$, $\sum X_{t2} X_{t3}$, and $\sum Y_t X_{t3}$. All the results are summarized again from (3–3).

**TABLE 9–2**

**Summary measures of example problem data**

| Variable | $Y$ | $X_2$ | $X_3$ | $Y$ |
|---|---|---|---|---|
| Sum . . . . . . . . . . . . . . . | 69.85 | 83.3 | 19.69 | |
| Mean . . . . . . . . . . . . . | 8.7312 | 10.4125 | 2.46125 | |
| Sum of squares . . . . . . | 616.2183 | 872.19 | 48.8925 | |
| Sum of cross products | →732.535← | →206.395← | →173.544← | |

Source: Table 9–1.

## Step (b)

The variations and covariations are all calculated the same way using the information from step (*a*). Using *Review* 3.2, item 3, we obtain for any variable $Z$,

$$\sum z^2 = \sum Z^2 - (\sum Z)^2/T;$$

and for any pair of variables $Z$ and $W$,

$$\sum zw = \sum ZW - (\sum Z)(\sum W)/T.$$

Arranging the results of this calculation into matrix form, we have the dispersion matrix,

$$\begin{pmatrix} Y'Y & Y'X \\ X'Y & X'X \end{pmatrix} = \begin{pmatrix} (\sum yy) & (\sum yx_2 & \sum yx_3) \\ \begin{pmatrix} \sum x_2 y \\ \sum x_3 y \end{pmatrix} & \begin{pmatrix} \sum x_2 x_2 & \sum x_2 x_3 \\ \sum x_3 x_2 & \sum x_3 x_3 \end{pmatrix} \end{pmatrix}$$

$$= \begin{pmatrix} 6.3409 & 5.2219 & 1.6266 \\ 5.2219 & 4.8289 & 1.3730 \\ 1.6266 & 1.3730 & 0.4305 \end{pmatrix}. \tag{9-7}$$

||||||||||||||||||||||||||||||||||||||||||||||||||||||||||||||||||||||||||||||||||||||||||||||||||||||||||||||||||||||||||||||||||||

*Explicative note.* The covariations are the same regardless of the ordering of the two variables involved, $\sum yx_2 = \sum x_2 y$, and so on. Thus, this matrix is always symmetric and only the upper triangular elements of the matrix (elements on or above and to the right of the principal diagonal) need be calculated. Then, the lower elements below and to the left of the diagonal may be filled in by copying, using the symmetric property.

||||||||||||||||||||||||||||||||||||||||||||||||||||||||||||||||||||||||||||||||||||||||||||||||||||||||||||||||||||||||||||||||||||

*Discursive note.* It is sometimes worthwhile to rescale or to code the data again using the matrix of part (*c*) as a guide. If the elements of any column or row are much different in scale from the remaining elements, they can be multiplied by some factor to rescale them. Such an operation helps to keep the subsequent calculations accurate without carrying an excessive number of decimals. However, in the final result, this rescaling must also be decoded to get back to the scale of the original economic variables.

||||||||||||||||||||||||||||||||||||||||||||||||||||||||||||||||||||||||||||||||||||||||||||||||||||||||||||||||||||||||||||||||||||

## Step (c)

The crucial step where scaling pays off in avoiding rounding errors and excessive decimals is in the calculation of the inverse of the matrix $(X'X)$. Recall that the normal equations are of the form $(X'X)C = X'Y$. To solve for $C$, the left side must be cleared of the term $(X'X)$ by multiplying by its inverse on both sides of the equation (analogous to multiplying both sides of $3C = 12$ by the reciprocal of 3 to solve for $C = \frac{1}{3} \cdot 12$).

$X'X$ is size $[(K - 1) \times T][T \times (K - 1)]$ so it is always a square matrix. In our example $K = 3$, so $X'X$ is $(2 \times 2)$ in size and the inverse is very simple to find.

||||||||||||||||||||||||||||||||||||||||||||||||||||||||||||||||||||||||||||||||||||||||||||||||||||||||||||||||||||||||||||||||||||

*Discursive note.* If there were 50 observations rather than $T = 8$, then $X'X$ would still be size $(2 \times 2)$. If we had included variables $X_2$, $X_3, \ldots, X_8$, in addition to the intercept variable $X_1 = 1$, to explain the changes in the endogenous variable, then $X'X$ would be size $(7 \times 7)$, and the calculation of the inverse would be best done using a computer. Or, in such a situation, the methods of Chapter 12 are useful. (Also see Exercise R.6 at the end of *Review* 9.2.)

||||||||||||||||||||||||||||||||||||||||||||||||||||||||||||||||||||||||||||||||||||||||||||||||||||||||||||||||||||||||||||||||||||

The inverse of $(X'X)$ is given by $(X'X)^{-1} = [1/\det(X'X)]$ Adjoint $(X'X)$. Thus,

$$(X'X)^{-1} = \frac{1}{0.1937}\begin{pmatrix} 0.4305 & -1.3730 \\ -1.3730 & 4.8289 \end{pmatrix} = \begin{pmatrix} 2.2225 & -7.0882 \\ 7.0882 & 24.9298 \end{pmatrix}. \quad (9\text{--}8)$$

‖‖‖‖‖‖‖‖‖‖‖‖‖‖‖‖‖‖‖‖‖‖‖‖‖‖‖‖‖‖‖‖‖‖‖‖‖‖‖‖‖‖‖‖‖‖‖‖‖‖‖‖‖‖‖‖‖‖‖‖‖‖‖‖‖‖‖‖‖‖‖‖‖‖‖‖‖‖‖‖‖‖‖‖‖‖‖‖

*Explicative note.* The inverse matrix is also size $(K-1) \times (K-1)$ or $(2 \times 2)$ in this case, and is also symmetric.

‖‖‖‖‖‖‖‖‖‖‖‖‖‖‖‖‖‖‖‖‖‖‖‖‖‖‖‖‖‖‖‖‖‖‖‖‖‖‖‖‖‖‖‖‖‖‖‖‖‖‖‖‖‖‖‖‖‖‖‖‖‖‖‖‖‖‖‖‖‖‖‖‖‖‖‖‖‖‖‖‖‖‖‖‖‖‖‖

It is common to check the accuracy of the inverse by multiplication with the matrix $(X'X)$. The check calculation shows

$$(X'X)(X'X)^{-1} = \begin{pmatrix} 1.00002 & -0.00001 \\ -0.00001 & 1.00007 \end{pmatrix}$$

rather than a perfect $(2 \times 2)$ identity matrix. By counting decimals before the imperfection, a measure of the accuracy of the subsequent calculations is obtained. In this case, the following calculation of the least squares estimates will be quite accurate to four significant digits. If the matrix product above had been

$$\begin{pmatrix} 1.03 & -0.06 \\ +0.04 & 0.95 \end{pmatrix},$$

then the inverse is not accurate enough and the estimates will only be accurate to one significant digit. In such a case, the coding of the data or of the matrix in step (b) needs to be improved or more decimal places must be used in the calculations of the means and the dispersion matrix.

‖‖‖‖‖‖‖‖‖‖‖‖‖‖‖‖‖‖‖‖‖‖‖‖‖‖‖‖‖‖‖‖‖‖‖‖‖‖‖‖‖‖‖‖‖‖‖‖‖‖‖‖‖‖‖‖‖‖‖‖‖‖‖‖‖‖‖‖‖‖‖‖‖‖‖‖‖‖‖‖‖‖‖‖‖‖‖‖

*Interpretive note.* The above discussion concerns purely arithmetic accuracy, not the validity of these decimal place values. Throughout the example, it is presumed that the data are correct— a set of exact numbers. Since the data may be exact to only two digits in fact, then it is dangerous to believe in the results of the calculations beyond two digits. It is still advisable to carry the calculations to as many decimals as in the means of the data before rounding to the final answer.

‖‖‖‖‖‖‖‖‖‖‖‖‖‖‖‖‖‖‖‖‖‖‖‖‖‖‖‖‖‖‖‖‖‖‖‖‖‖‖‖‖‖‖‖‖‖‖‖‖‖‖‖‖‖‖‖‖‖‖‖‖‖‖‖‖‖‖‖‖‖‖‖‖‖‖‖‖‖‖‖‖‖‖‖‖‖‖‖

These statements concerning accuracy of the estimates refer only to calculational accuracy, not to statistical accuracy. It is not true that the estimates calculated in our example must be equal to the true value of the parameter up to four significant digits. Even the first digit may be wrong if the unknown sampling error is high.

## Step (d)

The least squares estimates are $C = (X'X)^{-1} X'Y$ or

$$\begin{pmatrix} C_2 \\ C_3 \end{pmatrix} = \begin{pmatrix} 2.2225 & -7.0882 \\ -7.0882 & 24.9298 \end{pmatrix} \begin{pmatrix} 5.2219 \\ 1.6266 \end{pmatrix}$$

using the portion of the matrix in step $(b)$ labeled $X'Y$. Thus,

$$\begin{pmatrix} C_2 \\ C_3 \end{pmatrix} = \begin{pmatrix} 0.076 \\ 3.54 \end{pmatrix}. \tag{9-9}$$

The estimate of the intercept $\gamma_1$ can be found by:

$$C_1 = \bar{Y} - C_2\bar{X}_2 - C_3\bar{X}_3 = 8.73125 - 0.076(10.4125) - 3.54(2.46125),$$
$$C_1 = -0.733. \tag{9-10}$$

## Step (e)

The estimating equation is then

$$\hat{Y}_t = -0.773 + 0.076X_{t2} + 3.54X_{t3} \tag{9-11}$$

in terms of coded data. In terms of original data[2], the estimating equation is

$$\hat{Y}_t = -77.3 + 0.76X_{t2} + 0.354X_{t3}. \tag{9-12}$$

It is interesting to compare this equation with the estimating equation for the simple model involving only $Y$ and $X_2$. From (3–6), we repeat, $\hat{Y}_t = -252.9 + 10.814X_{t2}$. Both equations are illustrated in Figure 9–1.

Based on the data in Table 9–1, it has been determined that a unit increase in domestic prices (holding constant the linear effect of domestic national income per capita) is reflected by an increase of 0.76 units of imports. Price changes do not carry as great an impact as in the simple model for which $d$ (imports)$/d$(domestic prices) $= 10.8$ units.

A calculation at the point of means of the price elasticity of imports (holding constant the linear effect due to changes in national income per capita) based on the coefficient $C_2$ gives.

$$\eta_{(X_3\text{ constant})} = 0.76 \frac{104.125}{873.125} = 0.09.$$

This result indicates a very inelastic relation between imports and domestic prices, whereas the result of the simple model indicated an elastic relation ($\eta = 1.29$ from Sections 3.6 and 3.7).

The use of the particular value of the coefficient of $X_2$ or of this elasticity for theoretical analysis or for policy implications is somewhat dangerous. The specification of the model, and especially a precise knowledge of which variables are being held constant, is crucial in the interpretation and use

---

[2] The coefficient of $X_3$ is decoded by dividing the estimated coefficient based on the coded data by the ratio,

$$\left( \frac{\text{the factor multiplied times } Y \text{ in coding}}{\text{the factor multiplied times } X_3 \text{ in coding}} \right) = \frac{10^{-2}}{10^{-3}} = 10,$$

because the coefficient reflects $(\partial Y/\partial X_3)$.

FIGURE 9–1
Plane described by the general model (9–12) and the line described by the simple
model (3–6)

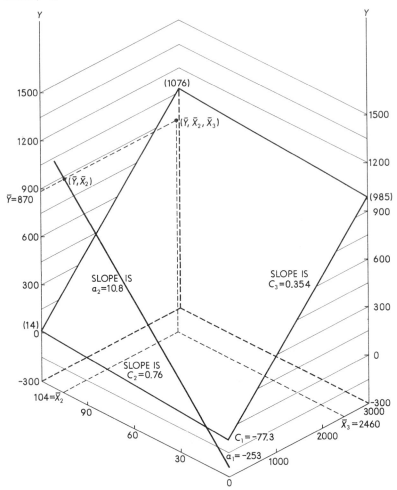

of the estimated relation. When the variable $X_3$ is added, the intercept decreases and the coefficient of the second variable drops considerably. It
appears that much of the burden of the explanation has been shifted to the
new variable, $X_3$, per capita domestic income.[3]

Also, for comparison, the estimating equation for the simple model gives

---

[3] This is a common occurrence and must be interpreted carefully. For example, compare
the results of Models I, II, III, and IV, and critically examine the interpretation given by
W. L. Hansen, B. A. Weisbrod, and W. J. Scanlon, "Schooling and Earnings of Low-
Achievers," *American Economic Review*, June 1970, pp. 409–18.

an estimate of imports for the fifth observation of 871.7. The residual between this estimate and the observed value of 894 was $e_5 = 22.3$ units. Using the new estimating equation (9–12) for the fifth observation on $X_2$ and $X_3$, we obtain, (Est. imports) $= -77.3 + 0.76(104) + 0.354(2,490) = 883.2$; which gives a residual $e_5 = 10.8$.

The fact that this single residual has decreased does not imply that the new estimating equation will have smaller residuals for every observation. To determine how the explanatory role of the variables has shifted away from $X_2$ and how the combined residuals from all observations have changed, the proportional measures of variation explained can be used.

## Step (f)

The explained variation is

$$C'X'Y = (0.076 \quad 3.54)\binom{5.2219}{1.6266} = 6.1387.$$

This compares to an explained variation in the simple model of 5.6470 units (see Section 4.5).

Thus, the variation explained has been increased by the combination of explanatory factors, $X_2$ and $X_3$, but the portion explained by $X_2$ alone has decreased.

Since the total variation in imports is still the same, 6.3409, then the amount of variation left unexplained, a measure of the combined size of the residuals, has decreased from $(6.3409-5.6470) = 0.6939$ to $(6.3409-6.1387) = 0.2022$, a decrease of almost 71 percent.

## Step (g)

The multiple coefficient of determination is the ratio of explained variation in $Y$ to the total variation. Using (9–6), we obtain

$$R_{Y \cdot 23}{}^2 = \frac{6.1387}{6.3409} = 0.968 .$$

This is higher than the similar coefficient of 0.8906 for the simple model (see Section 4.5). Invariably, when an extra explanatory variable is added to the model, this $R^2$ statistic will increase, but sometimes by a very small and insignificant amount.

## Step (h)

Any simple correlation coefficients can be found very easily from the matrix in step (b). The off-diagonal terms are covariations while the main diagonal terms are variations. Thus, if each element, $m_{ij}$, of this matrix is divided by the square root of the diagonal elements in the same row $i$ and column $j$, the result is a correlation matrix.

The matrix will be symmetric with diagonal elements equal to one by definition since

$$\frac{m_{ii}}{\sqrt{m_{ii}}\sqrt{m_{ii}}} = 1.0.$$

Only the upper triangular elements above and to the right of the diagonal need be computed. The lower left elements can be copied due to symmetry. For our example, the correlation matrix is

$$\begin{pmatrix} 1 & r_{Y2} & r_{Y3} \\ r_{2Y} & 1 & r_{23} \\ r_{3Y} & r_{32} & 1 \end{pmatrix} = \begin{pmatrix} 1.0 & 0.9437 & 0.9845 \\ 0.9437 & 1.0 & 0.9523 \\ 0.9845 & 0.9523 & 1.0 \end{pmatrix}.$$

Of course, the simple correlation between variables $Y$ and $X_2$ is the same as in (4–3) of Section 4.5, namely $r_{Y2} = 0.944$. Also, it is interesting to observe the high correlation between $X_2$ and $X_3$, $r_{23} = 0.95$; thus permitting much of the explanatory power to shift from $X_2$ to $X_3$. However, this high multicollinearity can affect the preciseness of our estimates (see Chapter 15).

From these simple correlations, any first order partial correlation coefficients can be calculated.[4] For example using (8–4b)

$$r_{Y3\cdot2} = \frac{r_{Y3} - r_{Y2}r_{23}}{\sqrt{1 - r_{Y2}^2}\sqrt{1 - r_{23}^2}} = 0.849 \quad \text{and} \quad r_{Y3\cdot2}^2 = 0.71.$$

The addition of $X_3$ explains 71 percent of the residual variation in $Y$ after removing the influence of $X_2$. As noted in step $(f)$, the unexplained variation decreases by 71 percent when $X_3$ is added.

The conclusion from all these measures in steps $f$, $g$, and $h$ must be that the inclusion of per capita income in the model is worthwhile; it does help to explain the variation in imports.

However, the level of significance of this inclusion, its effect on the significance of the variable, domestic prices, on confidence intervals for the estimates, and on forecast intervals must also be determined in order to learn more about the appropriateness and usefulness of the model. This analysis will involve test statistics for the general model which are analogous to those developed in Chapter 7 for the simple model. Before itemizing such tests in Chapter 11, the assumptions underlying the least squares principle and the properties of these least squares estimators should be reviewed.

---

[4] Refer back to Exercise 7 at the end of Chapter 8. One might also use the formula (8–6) to obtain,

$$r_{Y3\cdot2}^2 = \frac{R_{Y\cdot23}^2 - r_{Y2}^2}{1 - r_{Y2}^2} = \frac{0.968 - (0.944)^2}{1 - (0.944)^2} = 0.71.$$

## SUMMARY

Comparison table of least squares estimators and some related statistics in the simple and general model

| *General model* | *Simple model* |

1. Using deviation form:

$Y = X\Gamma + \varepsilon$ $\qquad\qquad y_t = \alpha_2 x_{t2} + \varepsilon_t$

2. Sum of squares of residuals
   (unexplained variation being minimized):

$e'e = (Y - XC)'(Y - XC)$ (9-1) $\qquad \Sigma\, e_t^2 = \Sigma\, (y_t - a_2 x_{t2})^2$

3. Estimators for coefficients:

$C = (X'X)^{-1} X'Y$ (9-3) $\qquad a_2 = (\Sigma\, x^2)^{-1} \Sigma\, xy$ (3-2)

4. Estimator for intercept:

$C_1 = \bar{Y} - C'\bar{X}$ (9-4) $\qquad a_1 = \bar{Y} - a_2 \bar{X}_2$ (3-2)

5. Variation explained by the regression:

$\hat{Y}'\hat{Y} = Y'Y - e'e$
$\quad\ = C'X'Y$ (9-5) $\qquad \begin{aligned}\Sigma\, \hat{y}^2 &= \Sigma\, y^2 - \Sigma\, e^2 \\ &= a_2 \Sigma\, xy\end{aligned}$ (4-4)

6. Interpretation of coefficient:

$C_2 = (\partial Y/\partial X_2)_{X_3 = \text{constant}}$ $\qquad a_2 = (dY/dX_2)$

## NEW VOCABULARY

Vector differentiation   Symmetric matrix
Estimating hyperplane   Matrix inverse
Matrix multiplication   Adjoint matrix
Adjusted multiple coefficient of determination, $\bar{R}^2$

## EXERCISES

1. For a model $Y_t = \gamma_1 + \gamma_2 X_{t2} + \gamma_3 X_{t3} + \varepsilon_t$ we have the following sample information:

$$\begin{pmatrix} T & \Sigma\, Y & \Sigma\, X_2 & \Sigma\, X_3 \\ & \Sigma\, y^2 & \Sigma\, yx_2 & \Sigma\, yx_3 \\ & & \Sigma\, x_2^2 & \Sigma\, x_2 x_3 \\ \text{(symmetric)} & & & \Sigma\, x_3^2 \end{pmatrix} = \begin{pmatrix} 21 & 22.8 & 18.6 & 20 \\ & 4.2457 & 3.5657 & 3.3057 \\ & & 4.2057 & 2.4757 \\ & & & 5.0324 \end{pmatrix}$$

In terms of the matrix notation for deviations in this chapter.
a) What is $(X'X)$, and find $(X'X)^{-1}$.
b) Find $C = (C_2\ C_3)'$, the estimate of $\Gamma = (\gamma_2\ \gamma_3)'$. Ans.: $C = (0.6491, 0.3375)'$.
c) Find $(e'e)$ and $R^2$. Explain their meaning. Ans.: $e'e = 0.815$, $R^2 = 0.808$.
d) Find $r_{Y2 \cdot 3}$ and explain its meaning.
e) Write the complete estimating equation for $\hat{Y}_t$.

2. One of the problems in textile manufacturing is breakage of the feed-in material to the loom from the spindle, a condition known as "ends down." The frequency of the "ends down" condition depends, of course, on the type of material being used. However, there is also a variation of ends down conditions within

the same material. Some of this may be explainable by changing climatic conditions within the factory.

Consider the model $Y_t = \gamma_1 + \gamma_2 X_{t2} + \gamma_3 X_{t3} + \varepsilon_t$, where $Y =$ number of ends down per thousand spindle hours, $X_2 =$ relative humidity, $X_3 =$ temperature, degrees fahrenheit.

Based on 93 randomly selected operating days, the following cross-product deviation matrix is obtained:

$$
\begin{array}{c} y \\ x_2 \\ x_3 \end{array}
\begin{pmatrix}
\begin{array}{ccc} y & x_2 & x_3 \end{array} \\
\begin{array}{ccc} 14{,}656.336 & 21.344 & -30.084 \\ & 1{,}324.708 & -136.896 \\ \text{(symmetric)} & & 1{,}299.224 \end{array}
\end{pmatrix}
$$

with means $\bar{Y} = 48.129$, $\bar{X}_2 = 45.053$, $\bar{X}_3 = 83.172$.

a)  Find $(X'X)^{-1}$ and use it to find the least squares regression coefficients.
b)  Find the multiple coefficient of determination, $R_{Y.23}{}^2$.
c)  Comment on your results.

3.  It may be interesting to examine the linear relation between rates of change in national accounting deflators in the post–World War II period. Using the U.S. data from second quarter, 1947, through fourth quarter, 1951, the following model can be estimated:

$$ Y_t = \gamma_1 + \gamma_2 X_{t2} + \gamma_3 X_{t3} + \varepsilon_t $$

where

$Y =$ quarterly percentage change in GNP deflator,
$X_2 =$ quarterly percentage change in personal consumption deflator,
$X_3 =$ quarterly percentage change in investment deflator.

The changes in the deflator from one quarter to the next are used instead of the actual levels because of the high degree of colinear movement among such time series.

For 19 observations, the following cross-product deviation matrix is obtained.

$$
\begin{array}{c} y \\ x_2 \\ x_3 \end{array}
\begin{pmatrix}
\begin{array}{ccc} y & x_2 & x_3 \end{array} \\
\begin{array}{ccc} 14.944 & & \text{symmetric} \\ 14.333 & 17.238 & \\ 14.545 & 17.184 & 23.392 \end{array}
\end{pmatrix}
$$

as well as the sums: $\sum Y = 12.1$, $\sum X_2 = 13.5$, $\sum X_3 = 20.5$.

(Source: Class, 1969, McIntyre.)

a)  Find the estimating equation. Ans.: $Y_t = 0.031 + 0.79 X_{t2} + 0.04 X_{t3}$.
b)  Find $r_{Y2.3}{}^2$ and explain its meaning. Ans.: 0.059.

4.  For a recent year, data are obtained for 50 states on income per capita, $X_2$ and general revenue per capita $Y$. Summary measures of the data are given:

$$
\begin{pmatrix}
T & \sum Y & \sum X_2 \\
& \sum Y^2 & \sum YX_2 \\
& & \sum X_2{}^2
\end{pmatrix}
=
\begin{pmatrix}
50 & 21{,}869.36 & 129{,}027 \\
& 10{,}061{,}395 & 57{,}569{,}360 \\
& & 343{,}372{,}800
\end{pmatrix}.
$$

a)  Find the simple regression $Y_t = \alpha_1 + \alpha_2 X_{t2} + \varepsilon_t$ using the procedure of Chapter 3. Ans.: $a_2 = \sum yx / \sum x^2 = 0.109$, $a_1 = 156.2$.

*b)* Define $X_{t1} = 1$ for all $t = 1, 2, \ldots, 50$, and define $(X'X)$ as the $(2 \times 2)$ cross-product sum matrix in original measure, not in deviations. Find the regression using the matrix form,

$$\binom{a_1}{a_2} = (X'X)^{-1} X'Y$$

where $Y$ is defined as the vector of original observations $(Y_1, Y_2, \ldots, Y_{50})'$. Compare the answer to part *(a)*.

5.  Cross-sectional data from the 50 states provides information on the following:

$Y = $ income per capita (dollars),
$X_2 = $ percent mineral production within the United States,
$X_3 = $ manufacturing output (dollars).

The means for these variables are

$$\bar{Y} = \$2,967.70, \quad \bar{X}_2 = 2, \quad \text{and} \quad \bar{X}_3 = \$5,026,636.72.$$

Before any further computation, it is wise to code the data so that all the means are within a factor of 10 of each other (to reduce rounding errors and/or the need for carrying an excessive number of digits).
Let the coded data be given as:

$$Y_c = Y \times 10^{-3}, \quad X_2 = X_2, \quad \text{and} \quad X_4 = X_3 \times 10^{-6}.$$

*a)* Using the following cross-product deviation matrix for the coded data, find the least squares regression equation, $Y_c = C_1 + C_2 X_2 + C_3 X_4$. Ans.: $Y_c = 2.8311 + 0.2929 X_2 + 0.03883 X_4$.
*b)* Decode this result to obtain an equation representing the original model. $Y_t = \gamma_1 + \gamma_2 X_{t2} + \gamma_3 X_{t3} + \varepsilon_t$.

$$
\begin{array}{c}
\begin{array}{ccc} \quad\quad y_c \quad\quad & \quad x_2 \quad & \quad x_4 \quad \end{array} \\
\begin{array}{c} y_c \\ x_2 \\ x_4 \end{array}
\begin{pmatrix} 12.4175 & -12.8601 & 71.2302 \\ & 771.0713 & 250.4036 \\ \text{symmetric} & & 2023.4587 \end{pmatrix}.
\end{array}
$$

(Source: Class, 1970, Smith.)

6.  Using data from 60 counties of Kentucky, a partial analysis of voter profiles can be obtained for the 1960 presidential election. Define the following variables:

$Y = $ percent vote to Republican in county,
$X_2 = $ median family income in thousands of dollars,
$X_3 = $ median number of school years completed by voters.

In terms of original data, these results are given:

$\sum X_2 = 187.8$        $\sum X_2{}^2 = 653$        $\sum X_2 Y = 9835.42$
$\sum X_3 = 484.9$        $\sum X_3{}^2 = 4,038.89$        $\sum X_3 Y = 26,242.93$
$\sum Y = 3,266.3$        $\sum Y^2 = 191,766.56$        $\sum X_2 X_3 = 1,517.17$

(Source: Class, 1970, Mabry.)

*a)* Solve for the estimate of the model $Y = \gamma_1 + \gamma_2 X_2 + \gamma_3 X_3 + \varepsilon_t$ using the matrix inverse method. Ans.: $Y = 83.714 - 5.965 X_2 - 1.312 X_3$.

*b*)   In your best role as political analyst, describe and interpret the results.

7.  For each of the following problems, determine the adjusted measure of fit, $\bar{R}^2$, and comment on its interpretation:

*a*)   The example problem in the text, see step (*g*) of Section 9.6;

*b*)   Exercise 1 above, see item (*c*);

*c*)   Exercise 2 above, see item (*b*).

Chapter
10

# ASSUMPTIONS FOR THE
# GENERAL MODEL AND THE
# PROPERTIES OF THE OLS
# ESTIMATORS

## 10.1 PREVIEW

In the previous chapter the mechanics were given for computing least squares estimates for the coefficients in the general model. Before continuing to further tests and analysis of such least squares regression results in Chapter 11, it is imperative to review again the underlying assumptions. Also, the properties of the resulting estimators and their sampling moments must be clarified in order to derive and to prevent misuse of the following tests. Perhaps the need for this discussion can be elucidated by comparing the use of the least squares formulas to the use of a common toaster.

181

It is relatively simple to connect an electric toaster into a receptacle and toast slices of bread. However, to make different types of toast requires some additional knowledge of the properties of the toaster. Fortunately, these are often embodied in the toaster by a thermostat for the temperature and an automatic timing device. Without these, it would be necessary for the operator to understand more about the underlying theory in order to make toasting adjustments.

Finally, all this assumes a proper voltage and current feeding to the toaster. If this assumption is violated, other corrections in the electrical circuits or modifications in the use of the toaster will be necessary.

It is also relatively easy to plug the values of sample moments into the least squares technique of Chapter 9. However, to make the proper interpretation and use of the results, the properties of the least squares estimators must be known. Fortunately, the derivation of these properties has already been done by skilled mathematical statisticians using a basic set of underlying assumptions and the special tools of their trade.

Without this previous work, it would be necessary for the beginning econometrician to understand more statistical theory in order to develop the derivations himself. Finally, if one or more of the basic assumptions is violated, some modifications in the estimating procedure and/or in the tests are necessary. These are to be discussed in Chapters 13, 14, and 15.

In examining the properties of the least squares estimators in the general model we follow the pattern used in Chapter 6 for BLUE in the simple model and some theorems concerning maximum likelihood estimators.

The least squares estimators given in Chapter 3 were followed in Chapter 5 by a discussion of the assumptions and in Chapter 6 by a discussion of their properties. Then, the commonly derived tests relating to the simple model were given in Chapter 7. Now for the general model, the least squares estimators were given in Chapter 9. In this chapter, the assumptions and properties of these estimators are presented. In the next chapter, the commonly used tests are presented.

## 10.2  REVIEW

In this chapter, the presentation makes use of some fundamental definitions of terms from statistics and from linear algebra. The reader should supplement this *Review* section as needed to understand these topics.[1] The following list serves more as a guide for study than as a complete presentation.

### 1  Positive definite quadratic form

The quadratic form $u'Au$ is said to be positive definite if $u'Au > 0$ for all $u$ except $u = 0$.

For example, if $A$ is diagonal, then $u'Au = \sum a_{ii} u_i^2$. The form is a weighted sum of squares in the components of the vector $u$. If the diagonal elements of

---

[1] The reader is advised to use his favorite and most familiar introductory texts in mathematical statistics and matrix and linear algebra.

$A$ are all positive, this form would obviously be positive definite. Such a case could occur if $A$ were a variance-covariance matrix of independent normal random variates. Then all the diagonal terms would be variances and necessarily positive, and all the off-diagonal terms would be zero covariances indicating the independence condition.

## 2 Sample moment matrix

A sample moment refers to the second moment in this case and is defined as the average variation of a set of sample observations on a single variable or as the average covariation of the paired sample observations on two variables. (See *Review* 3.2, item 3.) The second moments are sample estimates of variance and covariance. If $Y$ and $Z$ are each vectors of $T$ sample observations, then $m_{YY} = (1/T) \sum y^2$, $m_{ZZ} = (1/T) \sum z^2$, and $m_{ZY} = m_{YZ} = (1/T) \sum yz$ where the lowercase symbols indicate deviations from the respective sample means.

The sample moment matrix $M$ is defined as the array with the average variations on the diagonal and the average covariations in corresponding off-diagonal positions. It is always a symmetric matrix. For the vectors $Y$ and $Z$, as denoted above, the sample moment matrix would be

$$M = \begin{pmatrix} m_{YY} & m_{YZ} \\ m_{ZY} & m_{ZZ} \end{pmatrix}.$$

For a set of $T$-component observation vectors on predetermined variables in an econometric model, $(X_{t2}, X_{t3}, \ldots, X_{tK})$, the sample moment matrix of size $[(K - 1) \times (K - 1)]$ is $m_{XX} = (1/T)X'X$, where $X'X$ is the cross-product deviation matrix.

## 3 Orthogonal matrix

A square matrix $Q$ is said to be orthogonal if its inverse is the same as its transpose, that is, if $Q'Q = Q^{-1}Q = QQ' = I$. This condition is satisfied when the $n$-component columns of the matrix $Q$, given by $q_1, q_2, \ldots, q_n$, are an orthonormal set of vectors.

Orthonormal implies that the vectors are orthogonal and of unit length. Such vectors lie at right angles to one another so the cosine of the angle between each pair of vectors is zero. Algebraically, this means that their inner product is zero.

Also, the lengths of the orthogonal vectors $q_i$ are normalized to unity so that $q_i'q_i = 1.0$ for each $i = 1, 2, \ldots, n$.

An example of an orthogonal matrix is

$$Q = (q_1, q_2) = \begin{pmatrix} \dfrac{1}{\sqrt{2}} & \dfrac{+1}{\sqrt{2}} \\ \dfrac{+1}{\sqrt{2}} & \dfrac{-1}{\sqrt{2}} \end{pmatrix}.$$

Its column vectors are normalized and orthogonal;

$$q_1'q_1 = q_2'q_2 = 1/2 + 1/2 = 1.0, \text{ and } q_1'q_2 = 1/2 - 1/2 = 0.$$

||||||||||||||||||||||||||||||||||||||||||||||||||||||||||||||||||||||||||||||||||||||||||||||||||||||||||||||||||||||||||||||||||||||||||||||

*Discursive note.* This result is commonly written in terms of the *Kronecker delta* as

$$q_i'q_j = \delta_{ij} = \begin{cases} 1 & \text{if } i = j \\ 0 & \text{if } i \neq j. \end{cases}$$

||||||||||||||||||||||||||||||||||||||||||||||||||||||||||||||||||||||||||||||||||||||||||||||||||||||||||||||||||||||||||||||||||||||||||||||

Thus,

$$Q'Q = \begin{pmatrix} 1 & 0 \\ 0 & 1 \end{pmatrix} = I.$$

Frequently, an orthogonal matrix is used as a transformation matrix for simplification purposes. For example, suppose $Y = QX$ defines a transformation from $X$ into $Y$. This specifies a rigid rotation of the coordinate axes about their origin without changing the relative distances of $X$. If $Y = QX$, then $Q^{-1}Y = Q^{-1}QX$. If $Q$ is orthogonal $Q^{-1} = Q'$ so $Q'Y = X$. The length of $X$ is then $X'X = Y'QQ'Y = Y'IY$ which is the length of $Y$.

## 4 Linear independence and rank of a matrix

A set of vectors $V_1, V_2, \ldots, V_n$ are linearly independent if and only if the only linear combination of them which gives a null vector $O$ is the trival one with all coefficients of the combination equal to zero. Symbolically, a linear combination of vectors is given by $\sum_{i=1}^{n} h_i V_i$ where the $h_i$ are scalars. The set of vectors is linearly independent if $\sum h_i V_i = O$ only if each $h_i = 0$. It is not possible to express any one vector in the set as a linear combination or multiple of any subgroup of the other vectors. Repeating the condition again a third way, no linear dependencies exist among the set of vectors.

If the set of vectors represents the column vectors of an $(n \times n)$ matrix, then the rank of the matrix is defined as the greatest number of linearly independent column vectors. The rank can be any integer from zero for a null matrix to $n$ for a matrix of full rank.

One common method used for determining the rank of a matrix $A$ involves the calculation of determinants of square submatrices within $A$. If the largest such submatrix with nonzero determinant is size $(r \times r)$, then the rank of $A = r$. The number of linearly independent columns must be $r$ since anytime a matrix has dependent columns, its determinant is zero.

Some other useful properties concerning rank are that the rank of $A'$ is always the same as the rank of $A$ and the rank of $A'A =$ rank of $AA' =$ rank of $A$. Finally, the rank of $AQ$ is equal to the rank of $A$ if $Q$ is a matrix of full rank (det $Q \neq 0$).

## REVIEW EXERCISES

R.1. Given three observations on each of two variables by the observation matrix

$$X = \begin{pmatrix} 1 & 2 \\ 2 & 3 \\ 1 & 1 \end{pmatrix},$$

*a)* Find the sample moment matrix $M$.

*b)* Find the quadratic form $u'Mu$ where $u' = (u_1, u_2)$ and show that it is positive definite.

R.2. Given a matrix

$$Z = \begin{pmatrix} 1 & 0 \\ -1 & 2 \\ 2 & 3 \end{pmatrix},$$

*a)* Find $A = I_3 - Z(Z'Z)^{-1}Z'$.

*b)* Show that $A$ has rank 1.

*c)* Show that the rank of $A = $ (rank of $I_3$) $-$ rank $[Z(Z'Z)^{-1}Z']$.

R.3. Use the matrix $X$ in Exercise R.1, denote $X = Z$, and do the same steps as in Exercise R.2.

R.4. *a)* Find the rank (number of linearly independent columns) in each of the following matrices:

$$A = \begin{pmatrix} 1 & 2 & 1 & 4 \\ 2 & 3 & 0 & 2 \end{pmatrix}, \quad B = \begin{pmatrix} 1 & 2 \\ 2 & -1 \end{pmatrix}, \quad C = \begin{pmatrix} 1 & -2 & 4 \\ 3 & -6 & 12 \end{pmatrix},$$

$$D = \begin{pmatrix} 1 & 3 & -5 \\ 0 & -2 & 4 \\ 3 & 0 & 3 \end{pmatrix}, \quad E = \begin{pmatrix} 2 & -4 \\ -1 & 1 \end{pmatrix}.$$

*b)* Show that the rank $C = $ rank $C'$.

*c)* Show that the rank $DD' = $ rank $D$.

R.5. Consider a single equation model $\underset{(T \times 1)}{Y} = \underset{(T \times K)}{X} \underset{(K \times 1)}{\Gamma} + \underset{(T \times 1)}{\varepsilon}$ where each $\varepsilon_t$ has a normal distribution with mean zero and the variance matrix of $\varepsilon$ is

$$V\text{-}Cov(\varepsilon) = \sigma_\varepsilon^2 I_T = \begin{pmatrix} \sigma_\varepsilon^2 & 0 & 0 \\ 0 & \sigma_\varepsilon^2 & 0 \\ 0 & 0 & \sigma_\varepsilon^2 \end{pmatrix}.$$

Suppose the sum of squares of residuals $e'e$ can be written as a quadratic form in $\varepsilon$ as $e'e = \varepsilon'A\varepsilon$ where $A$ is symmetric, $AA = A$, and $A$ has rank $(T - K)$. Further, suppose $Q$ is an orthogonal matrix associated with $A$.

*a)* Define a transformation $\varepsilon = Qv$ and find an expression for $e'e$ in terms of the new variables.

*b)* Explain why each $v_t$ is normally distributed. [*Hint*: A linear transformation is used.]

*c)* Show that $E(v_t) = 0$ for any $t$.

*d)* Show that $E(v_i v_j) = 0$ for $i \neq j$.

*e)* Show that $E(v_t^2) = \sigma_\varepsilon^2$ for any $t$.

*f)* Explain why $e'e/\sigma_\varepsilon^2$ has a chi-square distribution with $(T - K)$ degrees of freedom. (*Hint*: Refer to *Review* 6.2, item 6.)

## 10.3 ASSUMPTIONS FOR THE GENERAL MODEL

In order for the simple least squares technique to be the most desirable in obtaining estimates of the general model, seven underlying assumptions may be specified. These represent an "ideal" or "perfect" set of background conditions for the operation of the economic relations being specified in the model. The first five are repetitions or extensions of Assumptions 1 to 5 from Section 5.4 for the simple model. Assumptions 6 and 7 are completely new and are required in order for the mathematical technique of Chapter 9 to have a nontrivial solution for the least squares estimates.

Since the meaning of the assumptions were explained previously in the case of a single exogenous variable, no extensive discussion of the generalized assumptions for the case of $K$ exogenous variables is presented. Rather, the reintroduction of the assumption set emphasizes the matrix-vector notation as commonly presented in research publications. In order to read current economic literature, it is useful at some point to learn the "matrix language" and to be able to relate the symbols to the complete concept they represent— in this case, the underlying assumption. Also, reviewing the assumptions will help remind us of their prominent role in the theory of estimation and testing.

ASSUMPTION 1 The exogenous variables are fixed rather than random so that $(X'X)$ is a matrix of real numbers, and the vector of values for any $X_k$, $k = 2, 3, \ldots, K$ is independent of the disturbance term.

The effects of this assumption are several. First, any $X_k$ or function of $X_k$ or combination of several different $X_i$, $X_j$, and $X_k$ may be treated as a constant with respect to any mathematical expectation. Second, any covariance terms between any $X_k$ and the disturbance are zero. Third, and these are all related to each other, the value is zero for any partial derivatives of functions of the $X_k$ with respect to any of the parameters, $\gamma_k$ or $\sigma_\varepsilon$, whose distributions depend on the PDF of $\varepsilon$.

The next four assumptions repeat those in Section 5.4 which directly concern the distribution of the random variables $\varepsilon_t$, $t = 1, 2, \ldots, T$, representing the disturbance term in the model.

ASSUMPTION 2 For $t = 1, 2, \ldots, T$, $\varepsilon_t$ is a normally distributed random variable.

ASSUMPTION 3 For $t = 1, 2, \ldots, T$, the expectation of $\varepsilon_t$ is zero.

ASSUMPTION 4 For $t = 1, 2, \ldots, T$, $\varepsilon_t$ has a finite variance $\sigma_\varepsilon^2$.

ASSUMPTION 5 Noncontemporaneous disturbances are independently distributed. For any $t \neq s$, both $t, s, = 1, 2, \ldots, T$, $E(\varepsilon_t \varepsilon_s) = 0$.

Assumptions 2–4 are often combined in the notational statement, $\varepsilon_t \sim N(0, \sigma_\varepsilon^2)$ for all $t$. On the other hand, it is also common to combine assumptions 4 and 5 into a single matrix statement that the variance-covariance matrix of disturbances is $V\text{-}Cov(\varepsilon) = I\sigma_\varepsilon^2$ where $I$ is the identity matrix of dimension $(T \times T)$.

||||||||||||||||||||||||||||||||||||||||||||||||||||||||||||||||||||||||||||||||||||||||||||||||||||||||||||||||||||||||||||||||||||||

*Discursive note.*    Assumption 2 of normality is crucial for obtaining the maximum likelihood estimators of $\Gamma$ which are identical to the least squares estimates $C$. The other assumptions are used for mathematical simplicity in obtaining the OLS estimators which are BLUE, best due to Assumptions 4 and 5 and unbiased due to Assumptions 1 and 3.

||||||||||||||||||||||||||||||||||||||||||||||||||||||||||||||||||||||||||||||||||||||||||||||||||||||||||||||||||||||||||||||||||||||

The meaning and interpretation of these assumptions remains the same as presented in Chapter 5. However, their validity must be questioned anew relevant to each model that is specified. Assumptions 4 and 5 are frequently singled out for careful consideration since the reliability of the ordinary least squares estimators depends on these assumptions about the variance-covariance matrix of disturbances. In general this matrix may be designated $V\text{-}Cov(\varepsilon) = \Omega\sigma_\varepsilon^2$ where $\sigma_\varepsilon^2$ is a scalar and $\Omega$ is a $(T \times T)$ matrix.

$$\Omega\sigma_\varepsilon^2 = \begin{pmatrix} V(\varepsilon_1) & Cov(\varepsilon_1\varepsilon_2) & Cov(\varepsilon_1\varepsilon_3) & \dots & Cov(\varepsilon_1\varepsilon_T) \\ Cov(\varepsilon_2\varepsilon_1) & V(\varepsilon_2) & Cov(\varepsilon_2\varepsilon_3) & \dots & Cov(\varepsilon_2\varepsilon_T) \\ \vdots & & & & \vdots \\ Cov(\varepsilon_T\varepsilon_1) & Cov(\varepsilon_T\varepsilon_2) & Cov(\varepsilon_T\varepsilon_3) & \dots & V(\varepsilon_T) \end{pmatrix} \quad (10\text{--}1)$$

If all the variances on the matrix diagonal are equal, then Assumption 4, the condition of homoscedasticity, holds. If all the off-diagonal covariance terms are zero, then Assumption 5 of nonautocorrelation holds. Under these conditions, the common variance on the diagonal may be factored out as a scalar, call it $\sigma_\varepsilon^2$, multiplying the identity matrix $I$ of the proper size. Thus, under these assumptions,

$$\Omega\sigma_\varepsilon^2 = I\sigma_\varepsilon^2 = V\text{-}Cov(\varepsilon).$$

Two additional assumptions are now included to insure the existence of a nontrivial solution for the least squares estimators.

ASSUMPTION 6. The number of observations exceeds the number of coefficients to be estimated: $T > K$.

The force and meaning of this assumption is nearly self-evident. It is a minimal condition for having a positive number of degrees of freedom for statistical inference based on the sample observations and the regression model.

||||||||||||||||||||||||||||||||||||||||||||||||||||||||||||||||||||||||||||||||||||||||||||||||||||||||||||||||||||||||||||||||||||||

*Explicative note.*    If the number of independent variables is equal to the number of observed sample points, then the hyperplane defined by the model has sufficient dimensions to pass perfectly through all the sample points. If $T < K$, then there are an infinite number of such hyperplanes that each make $\sum e^2 = 0$. The situation becomes equivalent to finding the " best " line to pass through a single point.

||||||||||||||||||||||||||||||||||||||||||||||||||||||||||||||||||||||||||||||||||||||||||||||||||||||||||||||||||||||||||||||||||||||

ASSUMPTION 7 The set of predetermined variables, $X_2, X_3, \ldots, X_K$ are linearly independent so that $(X'X)^{-1}$ exists.

This assumption specifies the general independence condition among the "independent" variables in the model. It is often stated in the following equivalent way; the rank of $(X'X)$ is $(K - 1)$; or, the $\det(X'X)$ is nonzero.

||||||||||||||||||||||||||||||||||||||||||||||||||||||||||||||||||||||||||||||||||||||||||||||||||||||||||||||||||||||||

*Explicative note.* When $K > 3$, this condition is stronger than merely requiring pairwise mutual independence among the set $X_2$, $X_3, \ldots, X_K$. Students are warned against interpreting this condition as a requirement that the simple correlation coefficients between these variables cannot be very close to one. It is true that if any two of the variables are perfectly correlated, then the set is linearly dependent and $(X'X)^{-1}$ does not exist. However, it is also possible that each simple correlation coefficient $r_{ij}$ (for variables $X_i$ and $X_j$, $i \neq j$ and both $i, j, = 2, 3, \ldots, K$) may be small and yet some linear combination of a subset of the variables may be equivalent to another of the variables. Then, the set is also linearly dependent and $(X'X)^{-1}$ would not exist.

||||||||||||||||||||||||||||||||||||||||||||||||||||||||||||||||||||||||||||||||||||||||||||||||||||||||||||||||||||||||

Although Assumption 7 is sufficient to guarantee a solution for the least squares estimates $C = (X'X)^{-1}(X'Y)$, (9–3), it does not guarantee the accuracy of those estimates. Often, the independent variables will satisfy Assumption 7, although a high level, but not perfect, dependency does exist among them. This condition is known as multicollinearity and is considered in more detail in Chapter 15.

## 10.4 FURTHER PROPERTIES OF ESTIMATORS

In Chapter 6, the properties of unbiasedness and efficiency (minimum variance among the class of linear, unbiased estimators) were presented. These properties apply to any finite sample size $T$. Econometricians also often refer to asymptotic or large sample properties that characterize different estimators. Theoretically, these properties refer to sample sizes approaching infinity and are presented most conveniently in terms of limits.

||||||||||||||||||||||||||||||||||||||||||||||||||||||||||||||||||||||||||||||||||||||||||||||||||||||||||||||||||||||||

*Interpretive note.* The econometrician never actually observes an infinite size sample, but these theoretical properties apply to large size samples in an approximate sense. Moreover, the definition of "large" in practice may be "more than 30 observations," or "about 100 observations." Such conclusions appear in research studies on specific asymptotic properties related to specific estimators in specific models. No generalized rules are applicable.

Even if "large" meant near-infinite, a theoretical knowledge of such asymptotic properties is still worthwhile for comparing different estimators and for selecting estimators such that the results obtained for similar studies under different sampling by different researchers have the highest probability of being comparable. If every research study on consumption functions used different estimators with different properties, then the collective results of all such studies would have little more value than any single one of the studies.

||||||||||||||||||||||||||||||||||||||||||||||||||||||||||||||||||||||||||||||||||||||||||||||||||||||||||||||||||||||||||||||||||||||

## Consistency

Probably the most important and certainly most often considered asymptotic property is *consistency*. For an estimator $\hat{\Theta}$ which depends on the sample size $T$, consistency requires that the PDF of $\hat{\Theta}(T)$ converge to the true parameter value $\Theta$ as the sample size approaches infinity. Figure 10–1 illustrates such a convergence by picturing a probability density function for $\hat{\Theta}(3)$, $\hat{\Theta}(30)$, and $\hat{\Theta}(\infty)$. Two sufficient conditions for consistency are evident.

*a)* The mean error of the estimator approaches zero as the sample size approaches infinity, or $\lim_{T \to \infty} \hat{\Theta}(T) = \Theta$.

||||||||||||||||||||||||||||||||||||||||||||||||||||||||||||||||||||||||||||||||||||||||||||||||||||||||||||||||||||||||||||||||||||||

*Recursive note.* Condition (*a*) above is called asymptotic unbiasedness. If the mean error, $E(\hat{\Theta}) - \Theta$, is zero for any size sample, the estimator $\hat{\Theta}$ is unbiased. An unbiased estimator is necessarily also asymptotically unbiased.

||||||||||||||||||||||||||||||||||||||||||||||||||||||||||||||||||||||||||||||||||||||||||||||||||||||||||||||||||||||||||||||||||||||

*b)* The variance of the distribution of the estimator decreases toward zero as the sample size approaches infinity, or $\lim_{T \to \infty} V(\hat{\Theta}) = 0$.

The joint effect of these two conditions is that as $T \to \infty$, the PDF of $\hat{\Theta}$ degenerates toward a single spike at the value of the true parameter $\Theta$.

||||||||||||||||||||||||||||||||||||||||||||||||||||||||||||||||||||||||||||||||||||||||||||||||||||||||||||||||||||||||||||||||||||||

*Explicative note.* Consistency does not imply that the distribution of $\hat{\Theta}$ gets closer and more pinched about the true value $\Theta$ for each single step increase in sample size. It does not mean that an estimate you calculate using a consistent estimator will be better if you use a sample of size 10 rather than a sample of size 9. The condition holds at the limit.

||||||||||||||||||||||||||||||||||||||||||||||||||||||||||||||||||||||||||||||||||||||||||||||||||||||||||||||||||||||||||||||||||||||

**FIGURE 10–1**
The property of consistency for Θ̂

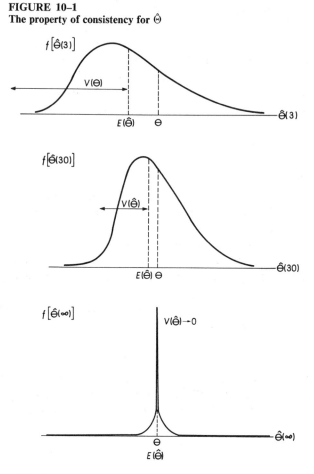

## Asymptotic efficiency

A second commonly cited asymptotic property for the special class of estimators which are asymptotically normal and consistent is asymptotic efficiency. This property is similar to efficiency in both its meaning and usefulness. Examination of estimators in this class to find the one which is asymptotically efficient helps to select the "best" estimator for use in a practical situation in which the sample size may be moderately large, say 50 to 100, but is certainly not infinite.

Consider two *consistent* estimators Θ̂ and Θ̃, let the PDF of each of them approach a normal density (finite mean and variance) as the sample size approaches infinity. At some arbitrarily large finite sample size, say $T = T_o$, both estimators have some positive variance. If $V[\hat{\Theta}(T_o)] < V[\tilde{\Theta}(T_o)]$, then Θ̂ is the more efficient estimator. Although both estimators have variance approaching zero in the limit, the one whose approach path results in the lower

**FIGURE 10–2**
The property of asymptotic efficiency for $\hat{\Theta}$

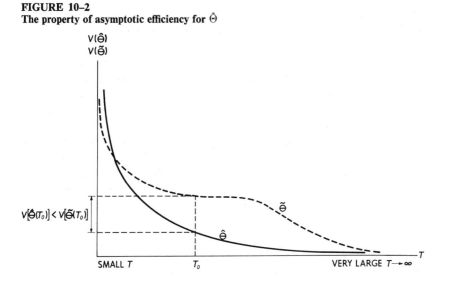

variance for $T = T_o < \infty$ is the one with the property of asymptotic efficiency. Figure 10–2 illustrates this comparison.

Before proceeding to the application of these results, some attention should be given to the derivation or discovery of such properties of estimators. The derivation of the asymptotic properties from given axioms and assumptions on the underlying PDF's is an often complex exercise in mathematical statistics and probability theory. Anyone intending to study further the tools and analysis of econometrics needs to become well grounded in these areas.

## Use of Monte Carlo methods

The consideration of the applicability of these properties to estimators calculated on the basis of finite-sized samples also requires a strong foundation in mathematical analysis and special function theory. Even then, the mathematical derivation of definitive results may not be easy. In such cases, the so-called Monte Carlo method is often tried to approximate the unknown distribution of a specific estimator for finite-sized samples and then to examine its properties.

The method derives its name from the replicative nature of the experiment, much in tone with the repeated trials of a gambler at the gaming tables of Monte Carlo. In this method, the researcher using a computer may simulate thousands of different samples drawn from a known population and calculate several different estimators, $\hat{\Theta}_i, \tilde{\Theta}_i, \Theta_i^+, \ldots, \Theta_i^*$ based on each sample. The individual probability distributions of each estimator can be determined approximately from thousands of different values calculated. The properties of an estimator can be determined by comparing its approximate distribution to those of the other estimators and to the true value for the parameter derived from knowledge of the population from which the samples were simulated.

This Monte Carlo technique is being used more frequently, even in conjunction with problems in which an exact mathematical derivation is possible, as computer technology advances and makes more and more such studies feasible. The reader need not be presently concerned, however, since neither advanced mathematical derivations nor simulation studies of the properties of estimators are included within the purpose of this book. Many interesting Monte Carlo studies are reported in the econometric literature. One which is related to the topics forthcoming in Chapters 13–15 is H. Thornber, " Finite Sample Monte Carlo Studies: An Autoregressive Illustration," *Journal of the American Statistical Association* (1967), pp. 801–18.

## 10.5 PROPERTIES AND MOMENTS OF THE OLS ESTIMATORS

In this section, a return is made to less philosophical and more nitty-gritty matters, the recognition of the properties of the least squares estimators. The results can be stated quickly. Then the actual determination of the expected values and variances of these estimators follows in a more lengthy manner.

### Properties of the estimators

Given the Assumptions 1–7, the results of Chapter 6 apply equally well in the general case giving the following conclusions. First, the OLS estimates of the coefficients $\Gamma$ are BLUE.[2] That is, each $C_k$, determined from $C = (X'X)^{-1}X'Y$ is:

*a)*    *B*est in the sense of efficiency,
*b)*    a *L*inear function of the sample observations of $Y$, and
*c)*    an *U*nbiased *E*stimator.

*Second*, given the Assumptions 1–7, especially the normality Assumption 2, these least squares estimators are identical to maximum likelihood estimators of the unknown coefficients. In the general case, the likelihood function formed from the joint PDF for the random variables involves a multivariate normal so that the solution is analogous to that described for the simple model in Chapter 6, Exercise 15. Again, maximization of the likelihood function with respect to $\Gamma$ involves only the maximization of its negative exponent, a quadratic form in $(Y - X\Gamma)$. This is equivalent to minimizing the positive exponent,

$$\text{Min}\left(\frac{1}{\sigma_\varepsilon^2}\right)(Y - X\Gamma)'\Omega^{-1}(Y - X\Gamma). \tag{10-2}$$

---

[2] This result is known as the Gauss-Markov theorem of least squares estimation.

‖‖‖‖‖‖‖‖‖‖‖‖‖‖‖‖‖‖‖‖‖‖‖‖‖‖‖‖‖‖‖‖‖‖‖‖‖‖‖‖‖‖‖‖‖‖‖‖‖‖‖‖‖‖‖‖‖‖‖‖‖‖‖‖‖‖‖‖‖‖‖‖‖‖‖‖‖‖‖‖‖‖‖‖‖‖‖‖‖‖

*Explicative note.* If we recognize that $(Y - X\Gamma)$ is a matrix expression for the vector of disturbances $\varepsilon$, then if the estimate $C$ replaces $\Gamma$, we obtain $(Y - XC) = e$, the vector of residuals. Also, if Assumptions 4 and 5 of Section 10.3 hold, then $\Omega = I$ and $\Omega^{-1} = I^{-1} = I$. The constant term $(1/\sigma_\varepsilon^2)$ does not affect the minimization values for $C$.

‖‖‖‖‖‖‖‖‖‖‖‖‖‖‖‖‖‖‖‖‖‖‖‖‖‖‖‖‖‖‖‖‖‖‖‖‖‖‖‖‖‖‖‖‖‖‖‖‖‖‖‖‖‖‖‖‖‖‖‖‖‖‖‖‖‖‖‖‖‖‖‖‖‖‖‖‖‖‖‖‖‖‖‖‖‖‖‖‖‖

Letting the MLE for $\Gamma$ be denoted by $C$, and assuming that $\Omega = I$, the minimization condition (10–2) reduces to $\text{Min}(e'Ie) = \text{Min}(e'e)$ which is identical to the least squares criterion for finding the best estimates.[3] The same solution is inevitable so that the MLE of $\Gamma$ is given by

$$C = (X'X)^{-1}X'Y. \tag{9-3}$$

The MLE for $\sigma_\varepsilon^2$ could also be found (see Exercise 4) as

$$\tilde{\sigma}_\varepsilon^2 = \frac{1}{T}(Y - X\Gamma)'\Omega^{-1}(Y - X\Gamma).$$

Again if $\Omega^{-1} = I$ and $(Y - X\Gamma)$ is estimated by $(Y - XC) = e$, then $\tilde{\sigma}_\varepsilon^2 = (1/T)e'e$. The result is identical to that for the simple model.

Third, the MLE (and also the identical least squares estimators) of $\Gamma$ in the general model, $Y = X\Gamma + \varepsilon$, are:

*d*)  consistent,
*e*)  normally distributed, and
*f*)  asymptotically efficient.

Also, the MLE estimator for $\sigma_\varepsilon^2 = (1/T)e'e$ is a consistent estimator even though it is biased low.[4]

‖‖‖‖‖‖‖‖‖‖‖‖‖‖‖‖‖‖‖‖‖‖‖‖‖‖‖‖‖‖‖‖‖‖‖‖‖‖‖‖‖‖‖‖‖‖‖‖‖‖‖‖‖‖‖‖‖‖‖‖‖‖‖‖‖‖‖‖‖‖‖‖‖‖‖‖‖‖‖‖‖‖‖‖‖‖‖‖‖‖

*Recursive note.* The unbiased estimator for $\sigma_\varepsilon^2$ is obtained as $(1/v)e'e$ where $v$ is the proper degrees of freedom. (See *Review* 4.2.) In the general model, the correct $v$ for this estimator is $v = T - K$. Now since the MLE, $(1/T)e'e$, is consistent and both $(1/T)e'e$ and $[1/(T - k)]e'e$ converge to the same limit as $T \to \infty$, then the unbiased estimator, $[1/(T - K)]e'e = s_e^2$ is also consistent.

‖‖‖‖‖‖‖‖‖‖‖‖‖‖‖‖‖‖‖‖‖‖‖‖‖‖‖‖‖‖‖‖‖‖‖‖‖‖‖‖‖‖‖‖‖‖‖‖‖‖‖‖‖‖‖‖‖‖‖‖‖‖‖‖‖‖‖‖‖‖‖‖‖‖‖‖‖‖‖‖‖‖‖‖‖‖‖

---

[3] The quadratic form in (10–2) is a sum of squares so it is a positive definite quadratic form. Such forms are a strictly convex function with a unique absolute minimum. The solution for the minimum involves the same normal equations as the least squares solution which minimizes the same sum of squares. See Exercise 3 at the end of this chapter.

[4] These results are commonly demonstrated in many texts, such as Wm. C. Hood and T. C. Koopmans, *Studies in Econometric Method* (New York: John Wiley & Sons, Inc., 1953), sec. 3, chap. VI. This book is an essential part of any study of MLE in simultaneous equation econometric models.

The two primary motives for calculating estimators by the method of least squares are now obvious. First, they are relatively simple to compute, and second, they have the above listed desirable properties.

## Determining the moments of the estimators

We now turn to the hard labor of determining the variance of any $C_k$ and the covariances between any two coefficient estimators, $C_k$ and $C_j$. We begin with the definition of the variance-covariance matrix, $V\text{-}Cov(C) = E[(C - E(C))(C - E(C))']$.

||||||||||||||||||||||||||||||||||||||||||||||||||||||||||||||||||||||||||||||||||||||||||||||||||||||||||||||||||||||||||||||||||||||||||||||||||

*Explicative note.*    In the deviation form of the model, the vector $C$ has $K - 1$ components so this matrix has size $[(K - 1) \times (K - 1)]$.

||||||||||||||||||||||||||||||||||||||||||||||||||||||||||||||||||||||||||||||||||||||||||||||||||||||||||||||||||||||||||||||||||||||||||||||||||

Using the property of unbiasedness, it is known that $E(C) = \Gamma$. Thus, to apply the definition, an expression is needed for $(C - \Gamma)$. By substituting in the OLS estimator, $C = (X'X)^{-1}X'Y$, from the model specification, $Y = X\Gamma + \varepsilon$, we obtain

$$C = (X'X)^{-1}X'(X\Gamma + \varepsilon) = I\Gamma + (X'X)^{-1}X'\varepsilon.$$

By subtracting $\Gamma$ from both sides, we obtain,

$$C - \Gamma = (X'X)^{-1}X'\varepsilon. \tag{10--3}$$

||||||||||||||||||||||||||||||||||||||||||||||||||||||||||||||||||||||||||||||||||||||||||||||||||||||||||||||||||||||||||||||||||||||||||||||||||

*Recursive note.*    Taking the expected value of both sides of (10–3), one obtains $E(C) - \Gamma = O$ since $E[(X'X)^{-1}X'\varepsilon] = E(\varepsilon) = O$ by Assumptions 1 and 3 of Section 10.3. This demonstrates the property of unbiasedness of the vector estimator $C$.

||||||||||||||||||||||||||||||||||||||||||||||||||||||||||||||||||||||||||||||||||||||||||||||||||||||||||||||||||||||||||||||||||||||||||||||||||

Expression (10–3) can be substituted into the definition of $V\text{-}Cov(C)$ to obtain in three steps:

1. $V\text{-}Cov(C) = E[(X'X)^{-1}X'\varepsilon][\varepsilon'X(X'X)^{-1}]$ since $[(X'X)^{-1}]' = (X'X)^{-1}$.
2. $V\text{-}Cov(C) = (X'X)^{-1}X' \, (\Omega\sigma_\varepsilon^2)X(X'X)^{-1}$ by taking the expected value of $(\varepsilon\varepsilon')$ independent of $X$.
3. $V\text{-}Cov(C) = \sigma_\varepsilon^2(X'X)^{-1}X'IX(X'X)^{-1}$ by Assumptions 7 and 8 that $\Omega = I$. Then, by matrix multiplication, the result obtained is

$$V\text{-}Cov(C) = \sigma_\varepsilon^2(X'X)^{-1}. \tag{10--4}$$

The main diagonal elements of $\sigma_\varepsilon^2(X'X)^{-1}$ are the $(K-1)$ variances of the estimates $C_2$, $C_3$, ..., $C_K$, and the off-diagonal elements are the covariances between pairs of these estimates. The square roots of the diagonal elements are the standard errors of the corresponding coefficient estimates. All these elements are crucial in testing hypothesis or setting confidence intervals on the parameters of the model.

|||||||||||||||||||||||||||||||||||||||||||||||||||||||||||||||||||||||||||||||||||||||||||||||||||||||||||||||||||||||||||||||||

***Discursive note.*** If the matrix $X$ is defined as the $(T \times K)$ matrix of original observations rather than the $[T \times (K-1)]$ matrix of deviations, then the matrix $(X'X)$ is size $(K \times K)$ and must have rank $K$ to satisfy assumption 7 of Section 10.3. The $(K \times 1)$ estimator vector $C$ is then $C = (X'X)^{-1}X'Y$, and the first element of $C$ is the estimate $C_1$ of the intercept. Also, the variance-covariance matrix $V\text{-}Cov(C) = \sigma_\varepsilon^2(X'X)^{-1}$ is then size $(K \times K)$ and the first diagonal element is the variance of the estimate $C_1$ of the intercept. This variance is important if a hypothesis or confidence interval is desired concerning $\gamma_1$, the true intercept.

|||||||||||||||||||||||||||||||||||||||||||||||||||||||||||||||||||||||||||||||||||||||||||||||||||||||||||||||||||||||||||||||||

## Moments concerning the estimator of the intercept

When the deviation form of the model and deviation matrix

$$\underset{[T \times (K-1)]}{X}$$

is used, the estimate $C_1$ and its variance are not directly determined by these formulas. The estimate $C_1$ can be calculated given the vector

$$\underset{[(K-1) \times 1]}{C}$$

from the condition that the regression hyperplane must pass through the point of means. That is,

$$C_1 = \overline{Y} - C_2\overline{X}_2 - C_3\overline{X}_3 - \cdots - C_K\overline{X}_K. \tag{9-4}$$

The variance of $C_1$ can be determined in a way similar to (10–4) for the variance of the other coefficient estimates.[5] If a vector of means of the exogenous variables is defined as $\overline{X}' = (\overline{X}_2, \overline{X}_3, \ldots, \overline{X}_K)$, then

$$V(C_1) = \sigma_\varepsilon^2\left(\frac{1}{T} + \overline{X}'(X'X)^{-1}\overline{X}\right). \tag{10-5}$$

---

[5] If the covariances are desired between the estimate of the intercept $C_1$ and any of the slope estimates $C_k$, $k = 2, 3, \ldots, K$, they can be determined from $Cov(C_1 C) = -\sigma_\varepsilon^2(X'X)^{-1}\overline{X}$. See E. Malinvaud, *Statistical Methods of Econometrics* (Chicago: Rand McNally, 1966), chap. 6, sec. 5.

|||||||||||||||||||||||||||||||||||||||||||||||||||||||||||||||||||||||||||||||||||||||||||||||||||||||||||||||||||||||||||||||||||||||||||||||||||||||||||||||

*Discursive note.*  All this demonstrates that the same results can be obtained when the computations are done in terms of the original observations where $(X'X)$ is size $(K \times K)$ or in terms of the deviations from the means where $(X'X)$ is size $[(K - 1) \times (K - 1)]$. For noncomputer calculations as presented in this book, the latter method is somewhat better since it deals with one less dimension and smaller size values.

|||||||||||||||||||||||||||||||||||||||||||||||||||||||||||||||||||||||||||||||||||||||||||||||||||||||||||||||||||||||||||||||||||||||||||||||||||||||||||||||

## Estimates of these moments of the estimators

The practical use of these formulas in testing the model is deferred to the next chapter where some example calculations are given. However, it is evident that in order to evaluate any of the variance or covariance elements, some number must be used for the term $\sigma_\varepsilon^2$ which is a factor in each element. This variance of the disturbance term $\varepsilon$ is unknown; and so, the best estimate for it is used, namely, $s_e^2$.

## 10.6 TWO NOTATIONAL AND INTERPRETIVE DIGRESSIONS

Under the assumption, $\Omega = I$, an alternate notation for the quadratic form $\varepsilon'\varepsilon$ is often used in econometric literature. Familiarity with it is not essential for this development but should be useful to the reader in other contexts. If $(Y - X\Gamma)'\ (Y - X\Gamma)$ is expanded, one obtains $Y'Y - Y'X\Gamma - \Gamma'X'Y + \Gamma'X'X\Gamma$. If a matrix $M$ of sample moments of the variables is defined by,

$$
\underset{(k \times k)}{M} = \frac{1}{T}\left( \begin{pmatrix} (\sum y^2) & (\sum yx_2) & \cdots & \sum yx_K) \\ \begin{pmatrix} \sum x_2\, y \\ \vdots \\ \sum x_K\, y \end{pmatrix} & \begin{pmatrix} \sum x_2{}^2 & \cdots & \sum x_2 x_K \\ \vdots & & \vdots \\ \sum x_K x_2 & \cdots & \sum x_K{}^2 \end{pmatrix} \end{pmatrix} \right) = \frac{1}{T}\begin{pmatrix} Y'Y & Y'X \\ X'Y & X'X \end{pmatrix} \tag{10-6}
$$

then the quadratic form can be rewritten

$$(Y - X\Gamma)'(Y - X\Gamma) =$$

$$
\underset{(1 \times K)}{T(1 \quad -\Gamma')} \ \underset{(K \times K)}{M} \ \underset{(K \times 1)}{(1 \quad -\Gamma')'} = (1 \quad -\Gamma') \begin{pmatrix} Y'Y & Y'X \\ X'Y & X'X \end{pmatrix} \begin{pmatrix} 1 \\ -\Gamma \end{pmatrix}
$$

By matrix multiplication, it is easily shown that this representation gives the same result as the other.

$$(Y - X\Gamma)'(Y - X\Gamma) = (Y'Y - \Gamma'X'Y \quad Y'X - \Gamma'X'X)\begin{pmatrix} 1 \\ -\Gamma \end{pmatrix}$$

$$= Y'Y - \Gamma'X'Y - Y'X\Gamma + \Gamma'X'X\Gamma.$$

||||||||||||||||||||||||||||||||||||||||||||||||||||||||||||||||||||||||||||||||||||||||||||||||||||||||||||||||||

***Recursive note.*** This result gives another common way of expressing $e'e$. If the estimate of $\Gamma$ is denoted by $C$, then the above equation becomes equivalent to the least squares expression for $e'e$ in (9–1).

||||||||||||||||||||||||||||||||||||||||||||||||||||||||||||||||||||||||||||||||||||||||||||||||||||||||||||||||||

This new expression,

$$e'e = T(1 \; - \; C')M(1 \; - \; C')' \qquad (10\text{–}7)$$

gives the sum of squares of residuals from a least squares regression of $Y$ on the variables $X$ in terms of submatrices of the sample moment matrix $M$. This result is shown by two algebraic steps:

1. Substitute $C = (X'X)^{-1}X'Y$ and $C' = Y'X(X'X)^{-1}$ into (10–7).
2. Collect terms and simplify.

One obtains $e'e = Y'Y - 2Y'X(X'X)^{-1}(X'Y) + Y'X(X'X)^{-1}X'Y$,

$$e'e = Y'Y - Y'X(X'X)^{-1}(X'Y), \qquad (10\text{–}8)$$

$$= Y'Y - Y'XC, \qquad (9\text{–}5)$$

or, unexplained variation equals total variation minus explained variation (4–1).

## A general form for residual sum of squares

To generalize this result, suppose the matrix $M$ in (10–6) is always partitioned such that

$$M = \begin{pmatrix} M_1 & M_c \\ M_c' & M_2 \end{pmatrix}$$

where $M_1$ is the sample moment matrix of the endogenous variable(s), $M_2$ is the sample moment matrix of the predetermined variables, and $M_c$ is the matrix of sample cross-moments between the two sets of variables. Referring to (10–6), the previous result in (10–8) becomes

$$e'e = T(M_1 - M_c M_2^{-1} M_c'). \qquad (10\text{–}9)$$

This result, (10–9), gives the sum of squares of residuals [and sums of cross products of residuals if the dimension of $M_1$ exceeds $(1 \times 1)$] of least squares regressions of each endogenous variable in the first subset on all the predetermined variables in the second subset.

||||||||||||||||||||||||||||||||||||||||||||||||||||||||||||||||||||||||||||||||||||||||||||||||||||||||||||||||||

***Discursive note.*** While this result may not have extreme importance in itself, it is a most common substitution employed in econometric literature, especially in that concerning estimators in simultaneous equation econometric models. Reference to it will appear later in Part IV.

||||||||||||||||||||||||||||||||||||||||||||||||||||||||||||||||||||||||||||||||||||||||||||||||||||||||||||||||||

## A starting point for principal components analysis

A special point for digression concerns other interpretations of the quadratic form (10–2) itself. A result of primary usefulness applies to any quadratic form which occurs as the exponent of a nonsingular $T$-dimensional multinormal density function. Such a quadratic form is always distributed as a chi-square with $T$ degrees of freedom. In particular, replacing $\Gamma$ by its estimate $C$ in this quadratic form and assuming that $\Omega = I$ under Assumptions 4 and 5, we obtain the result that

$$(1/\sigma_\varepsilon^2)(Y - XC)'\Omega^{-1}(Y - XC) = (1/\sigma_\varepsilon^2)(e'Ie) = (e'e)/\sigma_\varepsilon^2$$

is chi-square with $T$ degrees of freedom. This is the familiar result used previously to form many test statistics in Chapter 7.

Finally, if this type of quadratic form (10–2) is set equal to some constant $N_0$, then the equation $(Y - X\Gamma)'\,(\Omega\sigma^2)^{-1}(Y - X\Gamma) = N_0$ has a geometrical representation as an ellipsoid in $T$-dimensional space. This result along with the previous knowledge of the chi-square distribution of this quadratic form is useful in establishing elliptical shaped confidence regions for the parameters of the quadratic form.

The axes and center of the ellipsoid associated with (10–2) can be determined.[6] The principal axis is the line passing through the ellipsoids greatest dimension. Knowledge of these axes, their translation and rotation, is important in principal components analysis.

## Uses of principal components

These methods are useful for analyzing the correlations and dependencies among multinormal populations in which there is no causal relation or endogenous-exogenous relation specified. Since the results of a regression analysis depend on the choice of a variable as endogenous and on the specification of the included predetermined variables, it is not a suitable technique for efficiently examining the dependencies among observation sets. Principal components analysis was developed by H. Hotelling (1933) as a means of grouping the factors underlying the variation into a smaller number of independent groups. One obvious use of the technique is to help econometricians identify dependency structures and specify the most ideal regression model. Ideal in this case might mean the model for which the important Assumptions 1–7 are best satisfied among those alternate models which still express the intended economic theory.

---

[6] The axes are given by the orthonormal characteristic vectors associated with the characteristic roots of $(\Omega\sigma^2)$. The center of the ellipsoid is at $(X\Gamma)$. See Donald F. Morrison, *Multivariate Statistical Methods* (New York: McGraw-Hill Book Co., 1967), pp. 82–85, and Chapter 7.

## 10.7 A MORE GENERAL STATEMENT OF THE PREVIOUS RESULT

In Section 10.5, the distribution, mean, and variance of the vector estimator $C$ were presented. These results are a specific case of a more widely used theorem. The statement of the theorem is not difficult, and its application is likely to be seen again as the reader continues his study (see Sections 11.6 and 11.8 for example). After giving the theorem, the previous results will be seen as a special case.

THEOREM. If $Z$ is a $T$-dimensional random vector whose components have a multivariate normal density function with mean vector $\mu$ and nonsingular variance-covariance matrix $V$, and if $H$ is any matrix of size $n \times T$ with rank $n \leq T$, then the random vector $\theta = HZ$ has $n$ components which are multivariate normal with mean vector, $E(\theta) = H\mu$ and variance-covariance matrix $V\text{-}Cov(\theta) = (HVH')$.

‖‖‖‖‖‖:‖‖‖‖‖‖‖‖‖‖‖‖‖‖‖‖‖‖‖‖‖‖‖‖‖‖‖‖‖‖‖‖‖‖‖‖‖‖‖‖‖‖‖‖‖‖‖‖‖‖‖‖‖‖‖‖‖‖‖‖‖‖‖‖‖‖‖‖‖‖‖‖‖

*Interpretive note.* By the phrase, random vector whose components are multivariate normal, several statements are summarized. This means that each component of the vector is a random variable with a univariate normal marginal probability density function. Also, the joint PDF of any set of components of the vector is a multivariate normal distribution.

‖‖‖‖‖‖‖‖‖‖‖‖‖‖‖‖‖‖‖‖‖‖‖‖‖‖‖‖‖‖‖‖‖‖‖‖‖‖‖‖‖‖‖‖‖‖‖‖‖‖‖‖‖‖‖‖‖‖‖‖‖‖‖‖‖‖‖‖‖‖‖‖‖‖‖‖‖‖‖

*Recursive note.* As a corollary of this theorem, the exponent of the multivariate normal distribution of $\theta$ is a quadratic form, $[\theta - E(\theta)]' (HVH')^{-1}[\theta - E(\theta)]$. Setting this form equal to a constant gives the equation of an ellipsoid. The form itself has a chi-square distribution with $n$ degrees of freedom. (Refer back to Section 10.6.)

‖‖‖‖‖‖‖‖‖‖‖‖‖‖‖‖‖‖‖‖‖‖‖‖‖‖‖‖‖‖‖‖‖‖‖‖‖‖‖‖‖‖‖‖‖‖‖‖‖‖‖‖‖‖‖‖‖‖‖‖‖‖‖‖‖‖‖‖‖‖‖‖‖‖‖‖‖‖‖

### Application of the theorem in least squares estimation

As an example of the theorem, consider $Z = Y$, the $T$-component vector of observations on an endogenous variable defined by the model $Y = X\Gamma + \varepsilon$. Under the assumptions of Section 10.3, $Y$ is multivariate normal with mean vector, $X\Gamma$, and variance-covariance matrix, $V\text{-}Cov(Y) = \Omega\sigma_\varepsilon^2 = I\sigma_\varepsilon^2$. Now, the maximum likelihood or least squares estimates of $\Gamma$ are given (under the assumptions of Section 10.3) by $C = HY$ where $n = K - 1$ and $H = (X'X)^{-1}X'$ which has size $[(K-1) \times T]$ and rank $[K-1]$. The conditions of the theorem are satisfied, and the result is that the $K - 1$ element vector $C$ of estimates is multivariate normal with mean vector $E(C) = H(X\Gamma) = (X'X)^{-1}X'X\Gamma = I\Gamma = \Gamma$ and variance-covariance matrix

$V\text{-}Cov(C) = (H\Omega\sigma_\varepsilon^2 H') = (X'X)^{-1}X'IX(X'X)^{-1}\sigma_\varepsilon^2 = (X'X)^{-1}\sigma_\varepsilon^2$. The results are identical to (10–3) and (10–4) in Section 10.5. The estimators $C$ are normal and unbiased with $V\text{-}Cov(C) = (X'X)^{-1}\sigma_\varepsilon^2$.

### Derivation of a widely-used quadratic form

The exponent of this joint PDF is a quadratic form in $(C - \Gamma)$. In particular, it is $(C - \Gamma)'(H\Omega\sigma_\varepsilon^2 H')^{-1}(C - \Gamma) = 1/\sigma_\varepsilon^2 (C - \Gamma)'(HIH')^{-1}(C - \Gamma)$. Since $H = (X'X)^{-1}X'$, then $HH' = (X'X)^{-1}X'X(X'X)^{-1} = (X'X)^{-1}$, and $(HH')^{-1} = [(X'X)^{-1}]^{-1} = (X'X)$. The quadratic form,

$$(1/\sigma_\varepsilon^2)(C - \Gamma)'(X'X)(C - \Gamma), \qquad (10\text{–}10)$$

has a chi-square distribution and therefore it can be used for joint testing and setting joint confidence regions on the parameters $\Gamma$ based on the sample observations which determine $C$ and $(X'X)$. This result will be used in the next chapter.

### 10.8 SUMMARY

This chapter is primarily a theoretical break between two computational chapters, 9 and 11. In it, the common assumptions underlying the least squares estimation are itemized. The properties of these estimates are also presented, based on the Gauss-Markov theorem and maximum likelihood estimators. The entire discussion concerns the "ideal" case for a regression model when all these assumptions are satisfied. In this sense, this chapter is the foundation for the study of "nonideal" situations taken up in Chapters 13, 14, and 15. When one or more assumptions are violated, some improvisation from the ordinary least squares estimation is required; some of the nice properties of the least squares estimators no longer hold true.

This chapter also presents the formulas for the moments of the estimators and some statistical generalizations that bear fruit in the practical tests of the next chapter. In particular, the reader will find equations (10–4), (10–5), (10–8), and (10–10), commonly used in establishing efficient computational procedures for various terms in common test statistics. The other formulas are frequently encountered in statements of definitions and in theoretical derivations.

Finally, two digressions within the chapter serve notice of the importance and usefulness in econometrics of the Monte Carlo and principal components techniques of statistics. These are each more specialized topics that the reader might pursue in an individual study program or term paper.

### NEW VOCABULARY

| | |
|---|---|
| Rank of a matrix | Asymptotic unbiasedness |
| Linear independence | Asymptotic efficiency |
| Principal components | Monte Carlo method |
| Consistency | |

# EXERCISES

1. Determine the simple moment matrix based on the data of Exercise 1, Chapter 9. Determine $e'e$ using formula (10–9) and compare to the answer of part (c) of that exercise.

2. Using the data and results of Exercise 2, Chapter 9,
   a) Find $e'e$ using formula (10–9).
   b) Find $s_e^2$.
   c) Using $s_e^2$ as an estimate of $\sigma_\varepsilon^2$, find a consistent estimate of the $V\text{-}Cov(C)$. [*Hint*: Use (10–4).]
   d) Using formula (10–5), find $V(C_1)$.

3. Beginning with the likelihood function,

$$L(\Gamma, \sigma_\varepsilon^2) = (2\pi)^{-T/2}(\sigma_\varepsilon^2)^{-T/2}(\det \Omega)^{-1/2} \exp\left[\frac{-1}{2\sigma_\varepsilon^2}(Y - X\Gamma)'\Omega^{-1}(Y - X\Gamma)\right],$$

   and using the Assumptions 1–7, derive the MLE for $\Gamma$.

4. Using the same likelihood function as in Exercise 3, show that the MLE for $\sigma_\varepsilon^2 = (1/T)(Y - X\Gamma)'(Y - X\Gamma)$.

5. Explain how you would design a Monte Carlo experiment to determine:
   a) If an estimator $\theta = f(T, X_t)$ is consistent;
   b) Which of two consistent estimators is asymptotically efficient if both are asymptotically normally distributed.

6. Using the data and results of Exercise 6, Chapter 9, find:
   a) $e'e$ and $s_e^2$;
   b) A consistent estimator of $V\text{-}Cov(C)$ by substituting $s_e^2$ for $\sigma_\varepsilon^2$ in (10–4);
   c) The standard errors of the coefficients $C_2$ and $C_3$, and reinterpret the results of the regression equation specifying which exogenous variable seems more important; and
   d) $V(C_1)$ using (10–5).
   e) Using $s_e^2$ for $\sigma_\varepsilon^2$, set the quadratic form (10–10) equal to 5 and graph the resulting equation using $\gamma_2$ and $\gamma_3$ on the rectangular coordinate axes with origin at $(0, 0)$.

Chapter
11

# TESTING THE GENERAL
# MODEL

## 11.1  PREVIEW

For many beginning students of econometrics, the review of statistical
topics and the theoretical discussions of estimators in the previous chapters
are viewed similarly to reruns and panel discussions while the topics of this
chapter are elevated to the status of a Super Bowl or first-run feature. In some
respects, this perspective may be warranted since the tests and interpretation
of results of the econometric model are certainly of crucial importance.

Indeed, most readers will probably refer back to this chapter more than any other in this book as they proceed in their studies, readings, and research in their specialized areas.

Nevertheless, it can also be argued with persuasion that this chapter is merely a listing of procedures whose development and validity are based on the topics of the previous chapters which are of primary importance. Then again, since both the previous topics and the testing procedures of this chapter are included, some readers may share the author's view that these go together like a ball-point pen and its ink filler cartridge. Trying to write with only one of these is unsatisfactory.

### Purpose of this chapter

This chapter is intended as a recipe book for making various types of tests related to the general single equation econometric model. These include tests on the measures of goodness of fit, on the coefficients, on forecasts, and on the differences between a restricted and unrestricted model estimated with the same data and between the results using two data sets on the same model.

### Some tests not included

The list of tests is not comprehensive. There are other tests which are also used for making comparable judgments and for doing further or different analysis. The reader should never feel limited in the tests he can make by the relatively small number considered here. In fact, when faced with the need to analyze an econometric model for a specific purpose, none of these tests may be the exact best one to use. However, the tests described are quite commonly used; and if the reader can master these, he should be confident of his ability to seek out and learn any other specific test when the need arises.

### Format for presenting the tests

Since a mere listing of the recipes for the tests would be rather dull, each is presented in the context of some cooked-up problem situation. At the risk of being accused of using a case approach, the author believes this format will aid the beginning practitioner. Therefore, for each section, 11.3 to 11.11, a situation is developed where some analysis of results of the estimation of a general model is necessary. Please keep in mind that these models are serving as an instructive device and are not claimed to be the best conceivable models by the author or by econometricians in general. They are kept simple, perhaps naive, so the reader can appreciate the testing methods and not be boggled by extensive model specifications.

After the need for analysis is suggested, the theory and development of the test statistic and its distribution is presented, sometimes by analogy to the simple tests in Chapter 7, and often with reference to some statistical results presented previously. Then, the application of the test is presented with a final interpretation of the results in terms of the problem situation. The summary gives a broad perspective on the place of these tests in the overall study of the general econometric model.

## 11.2 REVIEW

In the *Review* Section 2 of each chapter, essential new topics in mathematics and statistics are presented. Would the reader believe that all the necessary tools and theorems for the topics of Chapter 11 have already been introduced? This is indeed the case, although the reader who does not need to look back occasionally, when studying this chapter, is certainly smarter than he realizes. For the rest of us, references to previous *Review* items or formulas are given throughout the chapter.

We can now pass by additional *Review* topics and proceed directly to Sections 11.3–11.11. Within these sections the reader can deepen his understanding if he avoids temptations to memorize the test statistics and concentrates on learning the patterns of formulation for the tests and on discovering where and how previous information and assumptions are used in developing and interpreting the tests.

## 11.3 TEST ON THE SIGNIFICANCE OF THE LINEAR GENERAL MODEL

When a model, $Y = X\Gamma + \varepsilon$, has been specified and estimated on the basis of sample observations, the most immediate questions are usually, "How well does the model fit?" and "Are the coefficients significant?" To answer these questions the econometrician commonly uses three test statistics: (*a*) one concerning the relative measure of goodness of fit, the multiple correlation coefficient; (*b*) one concerning the absolute measure of the goodness of fit, the standard error of estimate; and (*c*) one concerning each partial regression coefficient. These three common test statistics are given in Sections 11.3, 11.4, and 11.5. All will be considered in terms of the same model since the analyses of these three tests are complementary.

### The problem situation

In the late 1960s U.S. banks were quite active in the Euro-dollar market. In this period of restrictive Federal Reserve policy, the demand for Euro-dollars increased as U.S. banks may have been seeking to escape the impact of the tight monetary policy. If this were the case, then the Euro-dollar market presents an obstacle to effective monetary policy since banks can use this market to offset decreasing levels of excess reserves.[1]

---

[1] The subsequent imposition on member banks of reserve requirements on Euro-dollar deposits indicates a recognition and partial remedy for the problem. A Euro-dollar is a deposit liability which is denominated in dollars and held in a foreign bank, usually European. The bank uses them to make short-term loans to customers needing to make dollar transactions.

Even more important is the effect of Euro-dollar rates on international capital flows and the monetary policies of foreign nations. If the Euro-dollar market is capable of transmitting U.S. monetary conditions to foreign countries, there are important questions of international monetary policy yet to be answered. Some means must be found to prevent the U.S. banking system from transforming its demand for reserves into a drain on foreign reserves, which may conflict with foreign monetary policies.

## Formulating the example model

An economist interested in monetary theory and international finance might try to develop an explanatory model for analysis of the Euro-dollar interest rate. He may hypothesize that the Euro-dollar market provides a source of reserves over which the Federal Reserve has relatively little control. A tight monetary policy, and the consequent reductions in the reserve base, may stimulate banks to bid up the rate of Euro-dollar deposits. This occurs for as long as the banks can profitably borrow Euro-dollars to lend in the domestic market. Excess reserves are assumed to be a reliable indicator of the member banks' reserve positions and are posited to be inversely related to Euro-dollar rates.

The level of 90-day certificate of deposit rates is assumed to be another factor operating in the Euro-dollar market. In a tight money situation banks may increase the certificate of deposit rates to attract new reserves. However, Euro-dollars pay rates higher than certificate of deposit rates and are highly liquid. They do not entail the risk of a capital loss as a certificate of deposit does in the event it must be cashed in prior to maturity. Thus, a short-term investor may still prefer to buy Euro-dollars (ED), and the level of certificate of deposit (CD) rates must be increased further. A positive relation develops between CD rates and ED rates. A model is hypothesized as $Y_t = \gamma_1 + \gamma_2 X_{t2} + \gamma_3 X_{t3} + \varepsilon_t$ where $Y =$ Euro-dollar rates (EDR), $X_2 =$ excess reserve (ER), and $X_3 =$ certificate of deposit rates (CDR).

## Statement of the testable hypotheses

If the model is a useful and close-fitting relation in terms of the experience evidenced by the sample data, then the multiple correlation coefficient $R$ should be greater than zero, and $s_e$, the standard error of estimate, should be acceptably small. If the posited relations are supported, then $\gamma_2$ should be negative and $\gamma_3$ positive.

## The sample data

To estimate the relation and make such tests, 34 monthly observations are made covering the period from January 1967 to October 1969. The data are obtained from three sources. Euro-dollar deposits are obtained from weekly issues of *The Economist*. The rate used is that for the third week of each month. The quotation date for the third week rate fell between the 13th and the 20th of each month. These were the rates prevailing in the London Euro-dollar market on the quotation date.

Rates on 90-day certificates of deposit are obtained from weekly issues of *Barron's*. The quotation dates for these third week rates are the same as those for Euro-dollar rates.

The monthly data on the excess reserves of all member banks are obtained from monthly issues of the *Federal Reserve Bulletin*. The reserve data are expressed in terms of billions of dollars.

### Exploring the theory underlying the test

The first hypothesis to be tested is whether or not this model is useful in representing the observed data. The specified linear model is intended to explain the variation in EDR by relating this variable to the independent variables ER and CDR. This total variation in the endogenous variable about its mean can be broken down into two components giving,

$$\frac{\text{variation in } Y}{\text{about } \overline{Y}} = \frac{\text{variation in } \hat{Y}}{\text{about } \overline{Y}} + \frac{\text{variation in } Y}{\text{about } \hat{Y}}.$$

This can be written in terms of sum of squares (*SS*) as,

$$\text{total } SS = \text{explained } SS + \text{residual } SS$$

or

$$\sum (Y - \overline{Y})^2 = \sum (\hat{Y} - \overline{Y})^2 + \sum (Y - \hat{Y})^2$$

or

$$\sum y^2 = \sum \hat{y}^2 + \sum e^2. \tag{4-1}$$

If the regression equation fits the data closely, then a large portion of the total variation will be explained by the regression and only a small portion will be left unexplained. Consequently, the test for significance of the fitted linear relation can be expressed in terms of the relative size of $(\sum \hat{y}^2 / \sum y^2) = R_{Y \cdot 23}^2$ (see Section 8.3), or the relative size of $(\sum \hat{y}^2 / \sum e^2)$ corrected for degrees of freedom.

### Deriving the test statistic

The test derivation follows the same pattern as in Section 7.3. Each of the sum of square terms in (4-1) can be written as a quadratic form in the random variable $\varepsilon_t$ giving $Q = Q_1 + Q_2$ satisfying the theorem in *Review* 7.2, item 1. Therefore $Q_1/\sigma_\varepsilon^2$ and $Q_2/\sigma_\varepsilon^2$ are independent and have chi-square distributions with $(K - 1)$ and $(T - K)$ degrees of freedom respectively. The ratio,

$$\frac{Q_1/\sigma_\varepsilon^2 (K - 1)}{Q_2/\sigma_\varepsilon^2 (T - K)}$$

has the *F*-distribution with $(K - 1)$ and $(T - K)$ degrees of freedom. The test associated with the situation is termed analysis of variance, or ANOVA.

A systematic presentation of this information is provided by the analysis of variance table, Table 11-1.

**TABLE 11-1**

**ANOVA for the complete regression**

| (1) | (2) | (3) | (4) [=(3)/(2)] |
|---|---|---|---|
| *Source of variation* | *d.f.* | *Calculated SS* | *Mean square* |
| Total | $T - 1$ | $Y'Y$ | — |
| Explained by all $X$ | $K - 1$ | $C'X'Y$ | $C'X'Y/(K - 1)$ |
| Unexplained residual | $T - K$ | $e'e$ (by subtraction) | $s_e^2$ |

In the first column of an ANOVA table, the source of variation is described. The corresponding degrees of freedom are listed in column 2. The calculated sum of squares giving the value of the sample variation described is shown in column 3. Finally the mean-square in column 4 is obtained by dividing the sum of squares by its respective degrees of freedom. The test statistic is then written,

$$\underset{(K-1,\, T-K)}{F} = \frac{\text{mean square explained}}{\text{mean square residual}}. \tag{11-1}$$

The total variation is given in the table for reference and calculational purposes only. It is not directly used in the test.

||||||||||||||||||||||||||||||||||||||||||||||||||||||||||||||||||||||||||||||||||||||||||||||||||||||||||||||||||||||||||||||||

***Discursive note.*** It has already been shown that $E(s_e^2) = \sigma_\varepsilon^2$. It can also be shown that $E[C'X'Y/(K - 1)] = \sigma_\varepsilon^2 + \Gamma'X'X\Gamma$. If the linear relation is not significant on the basis of the data, then all the coefficients differ from zero only by chance and the true $\Gamma = O$. If $\Gamma = O$, then $E[C'X'Y/(K - 1)] = \sigma_\varepsilon^2$. The ratio of these mean squares is then expected to be $(\sigma_\varepsilon^2/\sigma_\varepsilon^2) = 1.0$, and the $F$-value would not be significant. On the other hand, if the calculated $F$-value exceeds the critical $F$-value, then it is probable that $\Gamma$ is not a null vector and the linear relation is significant.

||||||||||||||||||||||||||||||||||||||||||||||||||||||||||||||||||||||||||||||||||||||||||||||||||||||||||||||||||||||||||||||||

## Restating the hypothesis

For the application of this test to the above situation, several statements representing the null and alternate hypothesis could be used.

$H_0$: $\Gamma = O$, both coefficients $\gamma_2$ and $\gamma_3$ are not different from zero so neither $ER$ nor $CDR$ are useful in explaining the variation in $EDR$; or

$R^2 = 0$, the model does not explain a significant amount of the variation in the endogenous variable, EDR; or the specified econometric model is not useful in representing the economic experience under consideration.

$H_a$: $\Gamma \neq O$, at least one of the coefficients, $\gamma_2$ or $\gamma_3$, or both, are different from zero indicating that the corresponding variable, ER or CDR, or both, are useful in partially explaining the variation in EDR; or

$R^2 \neq 0$, the specified model is somewhat useful in representing the variation in levels of EDR.

## The empirical results

Based on the data, the results in Table 11–2 are obtained using a least squares regression program.[2]

**TABLE 11–2**

**Results: Euro-dollar model**

Dependent variable EDR    90-day Euro-dollar rates

*Variables in the equation*

| Variable | B | Std. error B | F |
|---|---|---|---|
| CDR | 1.40283 | 0.08495 | 272.70554 |
| ER | −1.92455 | 1.29289 | 2.21581 |
| (Constant) | −0.95636 | | |

*Analysis of variance*

| Variance | d.f. | Sum of squares | Mean square | F |
|---|---|---|---|---|
| Regression | 2 | 124.39400 | 62.19700 | 243.09617 |
| Residual | 31 | 7.93146 | 0.25585 | |

Multiple $R$ square    0.94006
Standard error    0.50582

Source: Class, 1969 (Picou).

||||||||||||||||||||||||||||||||||||||||||||||||||||||||||||||||||||||||||||||||||||||||||||||||||||||||||||||||||||||||||||||||||||||||||||||||||

*Discursive note.*  More results are given in Table 11–2 than are needed to carry out this test of hypothesis. Moreover, the format and labeling may not be exactly as we would desire it. However, it is often more efficient and practical to use such a "canned" program and reinterpret the results in your own terminology rather than to write your own program in your own terms.

||||||||||||||||||||||||||||||||||||||||||||||||||||||||||||||||||||||||||||||||||||||||||||||||||||||||||||||||||||||||||||||||||||||||||||||||||

---

[2] The output shown is an excerpt of the SPSS *regression* procedure. SPSS is a widely adopted set of routines for data description and analysis, the Statistical Package for the Social Sciences.

In Table 11–2, the least squares estimation is given for the specified model, $EDR = \gamma_1 + \gamma_2 ER + \gamma_3 CDR + \varepsilon_t$, along with measures of goodness of fit, the estimated standard errors of the coefficient estimates, and $F$-values associated with each coefficient (see Section 11.7) and an ANOVA table. This latter item is used in the present test. The test of hypothesis is presented in detail following the standard pattern of *Review* 7.2, item 5.

a)  $H_0$: the entire linear relation is not significant and $R = 0$.
b)  $H_a$: the entire linear relation is significant and $R > 0$.
c)  Select $\alpha = 0.01$, the probability that we will conclude the relation is significant when it is not.
d)  Use the statistic in (11–1) which has an $F$-distribution with 2 and 31 degrees of freedom.
e)  From the $F$-distribution table, $F(0.01; 2, 31) = 5.36$. Therefore, the null hypothesis will be rejected if the calculated value of the test exceeds 5.36.

‖‖‖‖‖‖‖‖‖‖‖‖‖‖‖‖‖‖‖‖‖‖‖‖‖‖‖‖‖‖‖‖‖‖‖‖‖‖‖‖‖‖‖‖‖‖‖‖‖‖‖‖‖‖‖‖‖‖‖‖‖‖‖‖‖‖‖‖‖‖‖‖‖‖‖‖‖‖‖‖‖‖‖‖‖‖‖‖‖‖‖‖‖‖

*Recursive note.* The number of observations is $T = 34$ so total $SS$ degrees of freedom are $T - 1 = 33$. The number of coefficients estimated are $K = 3$ so residual $SS$ degrees of freedom are $T - K = 31$. This gives the regression or explained $SS$ degrees of freedom as $K - 1 = 2$.

‖‖‖‖‖‖‖‖‖‖‖‖‖‖‖‖‖‖‖‖‖‖‖‖‖‖‖‖‖‖‖‖‖‖‖‖‖‖‖‖‖‖‖‖‖‖‖‖‖‖‖‖‖‖‖‖‖‖‖‖‖‖‖‖‖‖‖‖‖‖‖‖‖‖‖‖‖‖‖‖‖‖‖‖‖‖‖‖‖‖‖‖‖‖

f)  The ratio of the explained mean square to the residual mean square is given in Table 11–2 as $F = 62.197/0.256 = 243.096$.
g)  This result is certainly significant. The null hypothesis is rejected in favor of the alternate hypothesis that the specified model is useful in the sense that it does fit the data measuring the historical experience under consideration.

‖‖‖‖‖‖‖‖‖‖‖‖‖‖‖‖‖‖‖‖‖‖‖‖‖‖‖‖‖‖‖‖‖‖‖‖‖‖‖‖‖‖‖‖‖‖‖‖‖‖‖‖‖‖‖‖‖‖‖‖‖‖‖‖‖‖‖‖‖‖‖‖‖‖‖‖‖‖‖‖‖‖‖‖‖‖‖‖‖‖‖‖‖‖

*Explanatory note.* This result does not in itself imply that the theory underlying the specification of the model is good or bad, correct or wrong. The econometrician must continue to make further tests of this estimation and then further estimations on other data sets if possible.

Also, this result in no way guarantees that the model would fit well with data measuring the same economic variables in the future or any other time period. Of course, the above result does not deny this possibility. The econometrician must consider the accuracy of forecasts based on this model in terms of statistical confidence intervals (see Section 11.8).

‖‖‖‖‖‖‖‖‖‖‖‖‖‖‖‖‖‖‖‖‖‖‖‖‖‖‖‖‖‖‖‖‖‖‖‖‖‖‖‖‖‖‖‖‖‖‖‖‖‖‖‖‖‖‖‖‖‖‖‖‖‖‖‖‖‖‖‖‖‖‖‖‖‖‖‖‖‖‖‖‖‖‖‖‖‖‖‖‖‖‖‖‖‖

## Interpretation of the test conclusion

The model seems to be an appropriate representation of Euro-dollar rates in terms of related economic variables. Indeed, the computed value of $R^2 = 0.94$ implies that 94 percent of the total variation in the sample data for EDR has been statistically explained by this linear relation. While this is good supporting evidence, it is not the same as stating that the economic variables, excess reserves, and certificate of deposit rates theoretically explain 94 percent of the changes in Euro-dollar rates.

|||||||||||||||||||||||||||||||||||||||||||||||||||||||||||||||||||||||||||||||||||||||||||||||||||||||||||||||||||||||||||||||||||||||||

*Explicative note.* The point to remember is that statistical results based on a sample do not extend directly to economic interpretation for the population.

|||||||||||||||||||||||||||||||||||||||||||||||||||||||||||||||||||||||||||||||||||||||||||||||||||||||||||||||||||||||||||||||||||||||||

## 11.4 CONFIDENCE INTERVAL ON $\sigma_\varepsilon$

Consider the same specification as in the previous section. If the estimated model fits well, the specified model tends to be supported. If not, then interest in the specified model may not be very widespread. Another way to examine this closeness of fit besides the ANOVA test of Section 11.3 is to set confidence limits on the size of the standard error of estimate.

### Examining the size of the standard error of estimate

If the model fits well, the variance of the errors about the regression hyperplane should be relatively small compared to the variance of the endogenous variable being explained. That is, the static and random noise in the econometric model due to the disturbance term, $\varepsilon_t$, should be drowned out by the clear channel representation of the endogenous variable in terms of the true predetermined variables.

|||||||||||||||||||||||||||||||||||||||||||||||||||||||||||||||||||||||||||||||||||||||||||||||||||||||||||||||||||||||||||||||||||||||||

*Recursive note.* Remember that any mismeasurement of the true variables is represented as a component of the noise. See Section 5.3.

|||||||||||||||||||||||||||||||||||||||||||||||||||||||||||||||||||||||||||||||||||||||||||||||||||||||||||||||||||||||||||||||||||||||||

### Formulating the confidence statement

The best estimate of the variance of the disturbance term, $\sigma_\varepsilon{}^2$, is given by $s_e{}^2$. Moreover, the distribution of a test statistic involving these terms is known for the general model in the same way as for the simple model described in Section 7.3. We obtain,

$$\chi^2 = (T - K)s_e^2/\sigma_\varepsilon^2 \qquad (11\text{-}2)$$

with $T - K$ degrees of freedom.

This statistic can be used to test hypotheses about particular values of the unknown disturbance variance, or it can be used to frame a $(1 - \alpha)$ 100 percent confidence interval on $\sigma_\varepsilon^2$ according to [see (7–2)]

$$(T - K)s_e^2/\chi^2_{\alpha/2} \quad < \quad \sigma_\varepsilon^2 \quad < \quad (T - K)s_e^2/\chi^2_{(1 - \alpha/2)}.$$

### Using the empirical results

Returning to Table 11–2 for the results of the estimation, it is found that $T - K = 31$ and $s_e^2 = (0.50582)^2 = 0.25585 = $ mean square residual. From a chi-square distribution table with $\alpha = 0.10$, d.f. $= 31$, we find $\chi^2_{(0.05;31)} \doteq 44$ and $\chi^2_{(0.95;31)} \doteq 19$. Thus the 90 percent confidence interval on $\sigma_\varepsilon^2$ is given by:

$$\frac{31(0.25585)}{44} < \sigma_\varepsilon^2 < \frac{31(0.25585)}{19}, \qquad \text{or} \qquad (0.1803 < \sigma_\varepsilon^2 < 0.4318),$$

$$\text{or} \qquad (0.43 < \sigma_\varepsilon < 0.66).$$

### Interpretation of the result

This is an absolute measure in the same units (percentages) as the endogenous variable, Euro-dollar rates. From the original 34 observations (not given here) the mean and standard deviation for EDR are 7.053 percent and 2.00 percent respectively. Thus, the standard deviation of the disturbance term is approximately one fourteenth the size of the mean and one fourth the size of the standard deviation of EDR. The amount of noise is not excessive, but it is not so small as to be disregarded either. It indicates that it would be very probable (probability of about 0.68 given that $\varepsilon_t$ is normally distributed) under this model to get random variations (not otherwise included in the specification) of perhaps 0.6 percent in Euro-dollar rates for any given period. In the real world of 90-day investments and international finance, a six tenths of 1 percent interest rate differential could be very important. This result should create some caution in any practical or policy-oriented use of the model.

### 11.5 TEST ON AN INDIVIDUAL COEFFICIENT

The final test to be considered of the model presented in Section 11.3 is a test for hypothesized claims on the signs or values of a single regression coefficient. As the following sections will show, this is not the last possible test that might be made but it is the last to be considered in answering the common and basic questions presented before. In particular, repeating the question again, are the coefficients significant and of the theoretically hypothesized "correct" sign. These hypotheses, $\gamma_2 < 0$ and $\gamma_3 > 0$, can be examined as alternate hypothesis of individual tests using a test statistic based on the BLU estimate $C_2$ or $C_3$ if its distribution can be determined.

### Exploring the theory underlying the test

From the discussion of Section 10.5 and formulas (10–3) and (10–4), it is known that $C \sim N[\Gamma, \sigma_\varepsilon^2 (X'X)^{-1}]$. If the diagonal elements of the inverse matrix of the cross-product deviation matrix $(X'X)^{-1}$ are denoted by $x^{kk}$, $k = 1, 2, \ldots, K$, then an individual estimator $C_k$ has a univariate normal distribution with mean $\gamma_k$ and variance $\sigma_\varepsilon^2 x^{kk}$.

### Deriving the test statistic

Just as before in Section 7.4, some transformation must be made to eliminate the unknown term $\sigma_\varepsilon^2$ from the standardized normal statistic $z = (C_k - \gamma_k)/\sigma_\varepsilon^2 \sqrt{x^{kk}}$.

Recall that $(T - K)s_e^2/\sigma_\varepsilon^2$ has a chi-square distribution with $T - K$ d.f. and that this $\chi^2$ is independent of the above $z$ statistic due to the assumed independence between exogenous variables and the disturbance term which makes $C$ and $e$ independent.[3] Therefore, the ratio, $z\sqrt{T - K}/\sqrt{\chi^2}$ is a $t$-distributed random variable with $T - K$ d.f. The test statistic is obtained as,

$$t = \frac{(C_k - \gamma_k)\sqrt{T - K}}{\sigma_\varepsilon^2 \sqrt{x^{kk}}} \left/ \frac{s_e\sqrt{T - K}}{\sigma_\varepsilon^2} \right. ,$$

or by simplifying,

$$t = (C_k - \gamma_k)/s_e\sqrt{x^{kk}} \qquad (11\text{–}3)$$

with $(T - K)$ degrees of freedom.

### The empirical test

An example of the use of this test statistic is made on the hypothesis that a negative relation exists between Euro-dollar rates (EDR) and excess reserves (ER) of U.S. member banks.

a)  $H_0$: $\gamma_2 = 0$. ER is not a useful explanatory variable; its coefficient differs from zero only due to chance.

b)  $H_0$; $\gamma_2 < 0$. There is a systematic linear relation between ER and EDR; in particular when ER decreases, EDR increases.

---

[3] R. V. Hogg and A. T. Craig, *Introduction to Mathematical Statistics* (New York: The Macmillan Co., 1966), pp. 232–34, 310, 334.

c)   Select $\alpha = 0.05$, the probability that $\gamma_2$ will be accepted as negative when in fact it does not differ from zero.

d)   The test statistic (11–3) can be used with $T - K = 31$ degrees of freedom.

e)   The null hypothesis will be rejected if the calculated $t$-value is smaller than the critical $t$-value of $t_{(0.05;\,31)} = -1.695$. This will be construed as probabilistic evidence that $\gamma_2$ is less than zero.

f)   Referring to Table 11–2, the output for the regression gives $C_2 = -1.92455$ with standard error of 1.29289. This standard error is calculated from the standard error of estimate $s_e$ and the inverse matrix $(X'X)^{-1}$. Frequently, this inverse matrix is not printed out in "canned" regression programs but only used internally in the intermediate steps of calculation. The interpretation of the output presented in Table 11–2 is that the reported standard error $= 1.29289 = s_e\sqrt{x^{kk}}$.

## The test result and interpretation

The $t$-statistic is $t = (-1.92455 - 0)/1.29289 = -1.4886$. This value is not smaller than the critical value.

||||||||||||||||||||||||||||||||||||||||||||||||||||||||||||||||||||||||||||||||||||||||||||||||||||||||||||||||||||||||||||||||||||||||||||

*Discursive note.* This $t$-value is the square root of the $F$-value, 2.21581 in Table 11–2 associated with the coefficient for ER. This $t$-test is equivalent to an ANOVA test for the significance of a single additional variable in the general model (see Section 11.7). Theoretically, $t$ with $v$ d.f. is equal to $F$ with 1 and $v$ d.f. in this situation.

||||||||||||||||||||||||||||||||||||||||||||||||||||||||||||||||||||||||||||||||||||||||||||||||||||||||||||||||||||||||||||||||||||||||||||

We conclude that although the coefficient $\gamma_2$ appears to be negative as hypothesized, it may differ from zero only due to chance. Its corresponding variable, $X_2 = \text{ER}$, does not play a significant role in explaining EDR in this particular model specification based on this particular set of sample observations.

## Some further analysis of the example model

An identical test can be applied to the other coefficient, $\gamma_3$, associated with the variable CDR. The result is $t = (1.40283 - 0)/0.08495 = 16.514$ where the degrees of freedom are again $T - K = 31$. The coefficient $\gamma_3$ does seem to be significant and of positive sign. The variable CDR is useful in partially explaining the variation of the endogenous variable EDR.

## Some "philosophical" comments about these tests

The hypothesis that these two interest rates tend to move together is confirmed. This result does not necessarily confirm the particular theoretical mechanism or causal supposition that was advanced to explain this relation. The proposed explanation may even be irrelevant with some other causal explanation being far more accurate. The statistical results provide information on the extent of the relation but not directly on the theory underlying the relation. If there are alternate explanations in theory for this co-movement between CDR and EDR, this single result neither confirms nor falsifies one theory relative to the other. It is the role of the econometrician to derive some empirically testable theoretical implications of each theory which are mutually contradictory.

The present test has only separated between theories which imply a positive relation and those which imply a negative relation. Some further tests of hypothesis would need to be designed to distinguish among those theories which imply such a positive relation.

The overall analysis of this model, explaining the level of Euro-dollar rates, $EDR = \gamma_1 + \gamma_2 ER + \gamma_3 CDB + \varepsilon_t$, has utilized the assumptions of Section 10.3, especially the normality assumptions, to obtain the estimates and to form the test statistics. The overall result indicates that the model is somewhat useful in explaining the variation of EDR, but not good enough to make high-precision estimates ($s_e$ is too large). One problem is the insignificant role of the variable, excess reserves. Perhaps some other formulations should be considered including,

a) The measure of free reserves rather than excess reserves as a truer indicator of tightness for member banks; or

b) Lag values of one month for the independent variables to allow a reaction time between recognition by banks of the squeeze on reserves and their action in the Euro-dollar market.

## The special usefulness of this *t*-test

The test statistic, $t = (C_k - \gamma_k)/s_e\sqrt{x^{kk}}$, (11–3), has been used in this example merely to test significance of the coefficient. There are also other tests which can serve this purpose (see Section 11.7). The *t*-statistic, however, is singularly applicable for testing a hypothesis on a particular nonzero value for a coefficient, or to determine a confidence interval for an individual coefficient.

Using the same results in Table 11–2, these two uses can be illustrated. Suppose one wishes to make the following test, $H_0: \gamma_3 = 1$ against the alternate, $H_a: \gamma_3 > 1$. Using $\alpha = 0.05$ and 31 degrees of freedom, the null hypothesis is to be rejected if the calculated *t*-value exceeds 1.695. We obtain,

$t = (C_k - \gamma_k)/s_e\sqrt{x^{kk}}$, and by substitution of values, $t = (1.40283 - 1.0)/$ $0.08495 = 4.74$. We conclude that the coefficient $\gamma_3$ is significantly greater than one.

Second, one may desire to establish a confidence interval on a parameter, say in this case, a 90 percent confidence interval on $\gamma_3$. Using the $t$-statistic (11–3) and the $t$-values $\pm 1.695$, the confidence limits on $\gamma_3$ are found to be: $C_3 \pm t_{0.05}(s_e\sqrt{x^{33}})$, or $1.40283 \pm 1.695(0.08495)$, or $1.2588$ and $1.5468$.

Using samples of size 31 and computing a least squares estimate $C_3$ and its standard error, and forming such confidence limits, we expect the true parameter $\gamma_3$ to lie within such limits 90 out of 100 times on the average. In terms of the example model of Section 11.3, this indicates that if the linear effect of changes in excess reserves is held constant, then a one percentage point change in the certificate of deposit rate indicates a change in the Euro-dollar rate of approximately 1.26 to 1.55 percentage points in the same direction.

Making an interval estimate for certain parameters in an econometric model is often of primary importance to the researcher interested in empirical tests of theoretical propositions. Such confidence intervals on coefficients are less important for the researcher interested in developing a good forecasting model. He is likely to make use of the single point estimates for the coefficients in an estimated model with a very high degree of closeness of fit as measured by $R^2$ and $s_e$.

## 11.6 JOINT TEST ON THE COEFFICIENTS IN THE GENERAL MODEL

The $t$-distributed statistic (11–3) in the previous section is used for making tests and setting confidence intervals on an individual coefficient in the general model, $Y = X\Gamma + \varepsilon$. A more elaborate test is needed if two or more coefficients are jointly included in a test of hypothesis.

### Another suggested model and data

An economist interested in urban problems may consider a model, $Y_t = \gamma_1 + \gamma_2 X_{t2} + \gamma_3 X_{t3} + \varepsilon_t$, which purports to help explain domestic net migration of whites in urban areas in the United States over a 10-year period between two recent census years. The variables in the model are:

$Y =$ net changes in SMSA population due to white migration,

$X_2 =$ average population size in SMSA during the period,

$X_3 =$ change in civilian, nonagricultural employment.

The measures of the variables are determined from public documents for 24 urban regions (selected SMSA's) making proper adjustments for changes which occurred in the definition of these regions during the decade.[4] Particular data sources are the *Census of Population*, the *Census of Housing*, and annual issues of *Vital Statistics*.

### Preliminary hypotheses

Suppose we posit that the effect on the endogenous variable $Y$ due to $X_2$ is negative since white migration has a relatively smaller effect on urban population growth the greater the absolute size of the urban area. Also, a positive relation is hypothesized between variables $X_3$ and $Y$ as urban areas with greater increases in employment (reflecting new job opportunities) will attract more migrating persons.

A joint null hypothesis might be $H_0: \gamma_2 = 0$ *and* $\gamma_3 = 0$. This would be a joint test of significance on the two coefficients and could be done by the usual analysis of variance test (Sections 11.7 and 11.3). However, suppose that the null hypothesis specifies some nonzero level of the parameters.

### Determining the appropriate test statistic

A different form of test is needed if we change the null hypothesis to be $H_0: \gamma_2 = -0.5$ *and* $\gamma_3 = 0.2$ against the alternate $H_a: \gamma_2 < -0.5$ *and* $\gamma_3 > 0.2$.

|||||||||||||||||||||||||||||||||||||||||||||||||||||||||||||||||||||||||||||||||||||||||||||||||||||||||||||||||||||||||||||||||||||||||||||

*Explanatory note.* Such hypothesized nonzero values may come from some theoretical suppositions of the researcher or others, from results of a previously done related research study, or from some public statements of "politico-practical" men—government agencies, population experts, field representatives in social work, chamber of commerces, etc. If an important economic issue is at stake, such latter statements must not remain unchallenged by the facts.

|||||||||||||||||||||||||||||||||||||||||||||||||||||||||||||||||||||||||||||||||||||||||||||||||||||||||||||||||||||||||||||||||||||||||||||

From (10–10), the quadratic form, $Q_4/\sigma_\varepsilon^2 = (C - \Gamma)'(X'X)(C - \Gamma)/\sigma_\varepsilon^2$, is chi-square distributed with $(K - 1)$ degrees of freedom. From *Review* 7.2, item 1, the quadratic form $Q_2/\sigma_\varepsilon^2 = e'e/\sigma_\varepsilon^2$ is also chi-square distributed with $T - K$ degrees of freedom. Again, based on the independence assumptions of Section 10.3, these two chi-square random variables are independent due to the independence between the parameters and the disturbances in the

---

[4] SMSA stands for the Census Bureau demographic classifications of cities and their economic and business related suburbs or counties as *Standard Metropolitan Statistical Areas*.

regression model. The ratio of these quadratic forms divided by their respective degrees of freedom is an $F$ distributed statistic (*Review* 7.2, item 4) with $K - 1$ and $T - K$ degrees of freedom,

$$F_{(K-1,\,T-K)} = \frac{Q_4/\sigma_\varepsilon^2(K-1)}{Q_2/\sigma_\varepsilon^2(T-K)} = \frac{(C-\Gamma)'(X'X)(C-\Gamma)/(K-1)}{e'e/(T-K)}. \quad (11\text{-}4)$$

The unknown term, $\sigma_\varepsilon^2$, cancels out leaving only sample statistics and hypothesized values in the $F$-statistic.

‖‖‖‖‖‖‖‖‖‖‖‖‖‖‖‖‖‖‖‖‖‖‖‖‖‖‖‖‖‖‖‖‖‖‖‖‖‖‖‖‖‖‖‖‖‖‖‖‖‖‖‖‖‖‖‖‖‖‖‖‖‖‖‖‖‖‖‖‖‖‖‖‖‖‖‖‖‖‖‖‖‖‖‖‖‖‖‖‖‖‖‖‖‖‖‖‖‖‖‖‖‖‖‖‖‖‖‖‖‖‖‖

*Recursive note.* If the joint test is one of significance using the null hypothesis, $\Gamma = O$, then this statistic (11–4) reduces to the statistic (11–1). The numerator of (11–4) becomes $(C - O)'(X'X)(C - O)/(K - 1) = C'X'XC/(K - 1) = C'X'X(X'X)^{-1}X'Y/(K - 1) = C'X'Y/(K - 1)$ which is the mean square explained by the regression. The denominator of (11–4) is identically the mean square residual. A test on the significance of all the coefficients is identically a test of significance on the complete linear relation.

‖‖‖‖‖‖‖‖‖‖‖‖‖‖‖‖‖‖‖‖‖‖‖‖‖‖‖‖‖‖‖‖‖‖‖‖‖‖‖‖‖‖‖‖‖‖‖‖‖‖‖‖‖‖‖‖‖‖‖‖‖‖‖‖‖‖‖‖‖‖‖‖‖‖‖‖‖‖‖‖‖‖‖‖‖‖‖‖‖‖‖‖‖‖‖‖‖‖‖‖‖‖‖‖‖‖‖‖‖‖‖‖

## The empirical results and statistical test

Table 11–3 provides computer output for the analysis of the model posed at the beginning of this section.[5] To perform the test, the computer output must be interpreted and used correctly. The excerpt of the output given in Table 11–3 gives the relative and absolute measures of goodness of fit, $R_{Y \cdot 23}$ and $s_e$, the mean, standard deviation and sample covariance matrix of the variables, the estimates of the coefficients and their standard error and an analysis of variance table. The information is sufficient to do any of the tests described in Sections 11.3, 11.4, and 11.5. Also, it can be used to compute the test statistic (11–4) and perform the following test.[6]

*a)*  $H_0$: $\gamma_2 = -0.5$ *and* $\gamma_3 = 0.2$.
*b)*  $H_a$: $\gamma_2 \neq -0.5$ *and* $\gamma_3 \neq 0.2$.
*c)*  Select $\alpha = 0.05$.
*d)*  The $F$-distributed statistic in (11–4) is used with 2 and 21 degrees of freedom ($T = 24$, $K = 3$).
*e)*  Reject the null hypothesis if the calculated $F$-value exceeds $F_{(0.05;\,2,\,21)} = 3.47$.

---

[5] Another commonly available regression package was used for this problem, the BMDO2R originally developed by Health Sciences Computing Facility, UCLA.

[6] The test could be done in terms of a linear restriction as in Section 11.9 which results in somewhat easier hand calculation. That test involves running two separate regressions with and without the hypothesized restriction.

**TABLE 11–3**

**Results, migration model**

|                    |        | Variable | Mean    | Std. dev. |
|--------------------|--------|----------|---------|-----------|
| Dependent variable | Y      | Y        | 1.19105 | 6.87431   |
| Multiple $R$       | 0.8095 | $X_2$    | 9.33911 | 14.30110  |
| Std. error of est. | 4.2235 | $X_3$    | 5.25841 | 6.95656   |

*Variables in equation*

| Variable   | Coefficient | Std. error | F       |
|------------|-------------|------------|---------|
| (constant) | 2.58239     |            |         |
| $X_2$      | −1.00494    | 0.18917    | 28.2227 |
| $X_3$      | 1.52021     | 0.38888    | 15.2819 |

*Analysis of variance*

|            | d.f. | Sum of squares | Mean square | F      |
|------------|------|----------------|-------------|--------|
| Regression | 2    | 712.296        | 356.148     | 19.966 |
| Residual   | 21   | 374.595        | 17.838      |        |

*Covariance matrix*

|       | Y      | $X_2$    | $X_3$    |
|-------|--------|----------|----------|
| Y     | 47.256 | −62.529  | −20.963  |
| $X_2$ |        | 204.521  | 94.067   |
| $X_3$ |        |          | 48.394   |

Source: Class, 1969 (Kraft).

*f*) The denominator of the $F$ statistic is $Q_2/(T - K) = e'e/(T - K) = s_e^2$ and is easily obtained by squaring the reported value for the standard error of estimate, $(4.2235)^2 = 17.83795$. The same value is obtained even more directly from the analysis of variance table as the mean square residual, $e'e/(T - K) = 17.838$.

In calculating the numerator of the $F$-statistic, $(C - \Gamma)'(X'X)(C - \Gamma)$, let us first find the vector $(C - \Gamma)' = (C_2 - \gamma_2, C_3 - \gamma_3)'$. The estimates $C_2$ and $C_3$ are reported to be −1.00494 and 1.52021 respectively. Substituting the values for $\gamma_2$ and $\gamma_3$ from the null hypothesis, we obtain $(C - \Gamma)' = (-0.50494, 1.32021)'$.

The sample cross-product deviation matrix $(X'X)$ is not directly given in the output, but the sample covariance matrix is given. Its elements are simply the variation-covariations divided by degrees of freedom, $(T - 1)$ (*Review* 4.2). The lower right $(2 \times 2)$ submatrix of this covariance matrix (remember it is a symmetric matrix and only the upper triangular section is printed out) involves only the exogenous variables and can be denoted by

$$(X'X)/(T - 1) = \begin{pmatrix} 204.521 & 94.067 \\ 94.067 & 48.394 \end{pmatrix}.$$

The matrix $(X'X)$ is obtained by simply multiplying this submatrix by $(T - 1) = 23$.

The quadratic form $Q_4$ is then,

$$Q_4 = (-0.50494, 1.32021)\begin{pmatrix} 204.521 & 94.067 \\ 94.067 & 48.394 \end{pmatrix}(23)\begin{pmatrix} -0.50494 \\ 1.32021 \end{pmatrix} = 254.7972.$$

The numerator of the $F$-statistic (11–4) is then $Q_4/2 = 127.3986$. The resulting $F$-value is

$$F_{(2, 21)} = \frac{(C - \Gamma)'(X'X)(C - \Gamma)/2}{s_e^2} = \frac{127.3986}{17.838} = 7.142.$$

### Interpretation of the test result

This result is significant so the null hypothesis is rejected in favor of the alternate that $\partial Y/\partial X_2 \neq -0.5$ *and* $\partial Y/\partial X_3 \neq 0.2$. These partial derivatives can be interpreted in terms of the model and the meanings of the variables $Y$, $X_2$, and $X_3$, by the reader. The direction of the difference from the hypothesized values is obvious from the values of the estimates.

### Formulating a joint confidence statement

In many instances, a joint confidence interval on the parameters may be desired. This same test statistic can be used so that a joint $(1 - \alpha)$ 100 percent confidence region is obtained as the surface and interior of the $(K - 1)$ dimensional ellipsoid in the parameters, $\gamma_2, \gamma_3, \ldots, \gamma_K$,

$$Q_4/Q_2 = (C - \Gamma)'(X'X)(C - \Gamma)/e'e \leq \frac{(K - 1)}{(T - K)} F_{(\alpha; K-1, T-K)}. \quad (11\text{–}5)$$

‖‖‖‖‖‖‖‖‖‖‖‖‖‖‖‖‖‖‖‖‖‖‖‖‖‖‖‖‖‖‖‖‖‖‖‖‖‖‖‖‖‖‖‖‖‖‖‖‖‖‖‖‖‖‖‖‖‖‖‖‖‖‖‖‖‖‖‖‖‖‖‖‖‖‖‖‖‖‖‖‖‖‖‖‖‖‖‖‖‖‖‖‖‖‖

*Explicative note.* For this example with $K - 1 = 2$, the joint confidence region is not the rectangle formed by the same level confidence limits on the individual coefficients but an ellipse which lies entirely within such a rectangle. See Figure 11–1.

‖‖‖‖‖‖‖‖‖‖‖‖‖‖‖‖‖‖‖‖‖‖‖‖‖‖‖‖‖‖‖‖‖‖‖‖‖‖‖‖‖‖‖‖‖‖‖‖‖‖‖‖‖‖‖‖‖‖‖‖‖‖‖‖‖‖‖‖‖‖‖‖‖‖‖‖‖‖‖‖‖‖‖‖‖‖‖‖‖‖‖‖‖‖‖

### The calculated joint confidence region

For the example problem and results of Table 11–3, the 90 percent confidence regions on the individual parameters $\gamma_2$ and $\gamma_3$ would be determined as intervals according to the methods of Section 11.5. Using $T - K = 21$ degrees of freedom and the $t$-value of 1.721 for $\alpha = 0.10$, these confidence intervals are [estimate $\pm$ ($t$-value)(standard error of the coefficient estimate)] giving $[-1.00494 \pm 1.721(0.18917)]$ as the limits on $\gamma_2$ and $[1.52021 \pm 1.721(0.38888)]$ as the limits on $\gamma_3$. The two intervals are found to be $(-1.3305, -0.6794)$ for $\gamma_2$ and $(0.8509, 2.1895)$ for $\gamma_3$.

**FIGURE 11–1**
Individual and joint confidence regions on regression coefficients

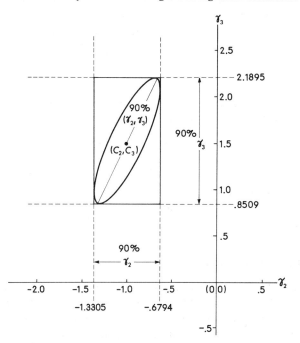

*The 90 percent joint confidence region on $\gamma_2$ and $\gamma_3$ is not the rectangle formed by the extension and intersection of the individual 90 percent confidence intervals on $\gamma_2$ and $\gamma_3$ but it is an ellipse within the rectangle with center $(C_2, C_3)$.*

The joint 90 percent confidence interval on $\gamma_2$ *and* $\gamma_3$ is not the solid line rectangle in Figure 11–1 formed by the extension of these interval limits. This area is larger than the true 90 percent probability region in the two-dimensional probability space for $\gamma_2$ *and* $\gamma_3$. The correct 90 percent confidence region is defined by the quadratic form in (11–5) using the results from Table 11–3 and an $F$-value for 2 and 21 degrees of freedom. It is illustrated by the ellipse in Figure 11–1.

|||||||||||||||||||||||||||||||||||||||||||||||||||||||||||||||||||||||||||||||||||||||||||||||||||||||||||||||||||||||||||||||||||||||||||||||

***Recursive note.*** It is obvious why the joint hypothesis, $\gamma_2 = -0.5$ *and* $\gamma_3 = 0.2$, was rejected since these values lie outside the joint elliptical confidence region and even outside the rectangle. The reader may wish to test the joint hypothesis, $\gamma_2 = -0.7$ *and* $\gamma_3 = 1.0$. Although each of these values lies within the 90 percent confidence limits for $\gamma_2$ and $\gamma_3$ respectively (inside the rectangle), the vector $(-0.7, 1.0)$ lies outside the joint 90 percent confidence region for $\gamma_2$ *and* $\gamma_3$ (outside the ellipse).

|||||||||||||||||||||||||||||||||||||||||||||||||||||||||||||||||||||||||||||||||||||||||||||||||||||||||||||||||||||||||||||||||||||||||||||||

The center of the ellipse is at the point of the best estimates, $(C_2, C_3)$. The confidence region formed by the ellipse degenerates toward the principal axis (straight line) when the two estimates, $C_2$ and $C_3$, have a large covariance relative to the product of their individual standard errors. On the other hand, as the covariance between $C_2$ and $C_3$ nears zero, then the ellipse broadens out and approaches the entire rectangle.

## 11.7 JOINT SIGNIFICANCE TEST ON A SUBGROUP OF REGRESSION COEFFICIENTS

Suppose a researcher wishes to include some independent variables, $X_j$, $j = 2, 3, \ldots, K^*$, in his model because these are theoretically and empirically known to have an important relation with the endogenous variable $Y$. In addition, some other variables, $X_i$, $i = K^* + 1, K^* + 2, \ldots, K$, may be considered. The question of their additional importance given the already included set of $K^*$ variables is a common problem.

### A description of the test

The solution involves an analysis of variance type test using an $F$-distributed statistic. The rationale and derivation of the statistic follows closely that already presented in Section 11.3. Rather than repeat this mathematical logic, attention is now focused on constructing an appropriate ANOVA table for the present test (see Table 11–4).

### Notation and setup for the test

Again, the starting point is the total variation in $Y$, $(\sum y^2 = Y'Y)$, which can be decomposed into the part explained by $X_j$ (the vector of variables with index 2 to $K^*$), the additional part explained by variables $X_i$ (the vector of variables with index $K^* + 1$ to $K$), and the part remaining as residual variation, $(\sum e^2 = e'e)$.

The computation involves consideration of two models, one including all variables $X = (X_j, X_i) = (X_2, X_3, \ldots, X_K)$, and the other including only the variables $X_j$. The models are:

$$a) \quad Y_t = \gamma_1 + \sum_{k=2}^{K} \gamma_k X_{tk} + \varepsilon_t, \quad \text{or} \quad Y = X\Gamma + \varepsilon = (X_j, X_i)\binom{\Gamma_j}{\Gamma_i} + \varepsilon,$$

and

$$b) \quad Y_t = \delta_1 + \sum_{j=2}^{K^*} \delta_j X_{tj} + v_t, \quad \text{or} \quad Y = X_j \Delta + v.$$

Model (*a*) is the complete model with all independent variables included. Model (*b*) is the restricted model using only those independent variables in which the researcher has prior confidence or whose effect is to be included and held constant in testing the significance of the other variables indexed $K^* + 1, K^* + 2, \ldots, K$. Estimating both models $(a)$ and $(b)$ is necessary to obtain the results needed to complete the ANOVA Table 11–4 and to perform the desired test.

## The construction of Table 11–4

From model $(a)$, we find the residual variation in $Y$ after removing the effect of all variables, $X_2, X_3, \ldots, X_K$. Subtracting this from the total variation gives the variation explained by all variables. The results of model $(b)$ give the variation explained by the included variables $X_2, X_3, \ldots, X_{K^*}$. The difference between the explained variation in models $(a)$ and $(b)$ is due to the addition of the other $K - K^*$ variables. The mean square due to the addition of these $K - K^*$ variables is denoted by " MS added " in Table 11–4.

TABLE 11–4

ANOVA for a subgroup of coefficients

| (1)<br>Source of variation | (2)<br>d.f. | (3)<br>Calculated SS | (4) = (3)/(2)<br>Mean square |
|---|---|---|---|
| Total | $T - 1$ | $Y'Y$ | |
| Less residual in model $(a)$ | $T - K$ | $e'e$ | $s_e^2$ |
| Explained by all variables<br>$X_k, k = 2, 3, \ldots, K$ | $K - 1$ | $C'X'Y$ | |
| Less explained by model $(b)$<br>variables $X_j, j = 2, 3, \ldots,$<br>$K^*$ | $K^* - 1$ | $D'X^{*'}Y$ | |
| Explained by addition of<br>variables $X_i, i = K^* + 1,$<br>$K^* + 2, \ldots, K.$ | $K - K^*$ | (by subtraction) | MS added |

||||||||||||||||||||||||||||||||||||||||||||||||||||||||||||||||||||||||||||||||||||||||||||||||||||||||||||||||

*Explicative note.* Although this seems to be a roundabout procedure, it would be inappropriate to calculate the variation explained by the additional $K - K^*$ variables directly. A model such as $Y = X_i \Theta + \eta$ would provide the amount of variation explained directly by the variables $X_i$, but this is not the desired quantity. It is the extra variation explained by these variables $X_i$ in addition to that explained by variables $X_j$ which is important. The above model does not consider that the effect of the variables $X_j$ is being included and held constant. It does not allow for any interaction or overlapping effects between any of the added $K - K^*$ variables with the already included variables, $X_j$.

||||||||||||||||||||||||||||||||||||||||||||||||||||||||||||||||||||||||||||||||||||||||||||||||||||||||||||||||

To make a test of the null hypothesis $[H_0: \Gamma_i = O]$ against the alternate $[H_a:$ at least one of these $K - K^*$ coefficients is nonzero], an $F$-distributed statistic is used.

|||||||||||||||||||||||||||||||||||||||||||||||||||||||||||||||||||||||||||||||||||||||||||||||||||||||||||||||||||||||||||||||||

***Recursive note.*** To review again, a mean square explained is independent of the mean square residual and their ratio is equivalent to the ratio of two independent chi-square distributed random variables. By definition, an $F$-distributed random variable results.

|||||||||||||||||||||||||||||||||||||||||||||||||||||||||||||||||||||||||||||||||||||||||||||||||||||||||||||||||||||||||||||||||

**Deriving the test statistic**

The formation of the $F$-statistic uses previous results and can be outlined in the following steps:

1. A ratio of the form (mean square)(d.f.)$/\sigma_\varepsilon^2$ has a chi-square distribution. Thus, from rows 2 and 5 of Table 11–4,

2. $\dfrac{s_e^2(T - K)}{\sigma_\varepsilon^2} \sim \chi^2_{(T-K)}$ and $\dfrac{(\text{MS added})(K - K^*)}{\sigma_\varepsilon^2} \sim \chi^2_{(K-K^*)}$

3. These two chi-square random variables are independent. Their ratio gives,

4. $\dfrac{\chi^2_{(K-K^*)}/(K - K^*)}{\chi^2_{(T-K)}/(T - K)} \sim F_{[(K-K^*),(T-K)]}$

5. By substitution and simplification,

$$\frac{(\text{MS added})}{s_e^2} = F_{(K-K^*,\,T-K)} \tag{11–6}$$

The null hypothesis is rejected if this calculated $F$-value using (11–6) exceeds the tabled $F$-value for the selected significance level.

|||||||||||||||||||||||||||||||||||||||||||||||||||||||||||||||||||||||||||||||||||||||||||||||||||||||||||||||||||||||||||||||||

***Explicative note.*** This test is appropriate for any size subgroup of variables such that $1 \leq K - K^* \leq K - 1$. If $K - K^* = 1$, then this test is equivalent to the test of significance on a single coefficient given in Section 11.5 and provides the meaning for the $F$-value shown in Table 11–2. Each of these is for a test of the significance of the additional influence of that single variable in the econometric model.

In using this test, the reader should recognize that regardless of the size of $K - K^*$, it is essential that the MS added by the $K - K^*$ variables be compared relative to the mean square residual in the model (*a*) including all variables $X_2, X_3, \ldots, X_K$, and not to the mean square residual from model (*b*). The denominator in the *F*-statistic (11–6) is unchanged for any given econometric model whether the significance of a subgroup of two, three, or $K - 1$ coefficients within that model are being tested.

||||||||||||||||||||||||||||||||||||||||||||||||||||||||||||||||||||||||||||||||||||||||||||||||||||||||||||||||||||||||||||||||||||||||||||

## A problem situation for applying this test

For an example of this test, consider a model for explaining the variation in percentage of federal defense payroll expenditures spent in each state in a recent year. One related variable is the population of the state relative to U.S. population. A political scientist wishes to test whether the participation by state senators and representatives on important congressional committees also influences this level of expenditures within the corresponding states.

## Definition of the variables

The variables are all defined in a ratio unit of measurement with each unit being 1 percent as follows:

$Y =$ the percentage of total civil and military payrolls spent by the Department of Defense in each state in 1969. Source of data is U.S. Bureau of the Census, *Statistical Abstract of the United States, 1970*

$X_2 =$ state's percentage of total U.S. population in 1970 according to U.S. Bureau of the Census, *1970 Census of Population*.

$X_3, X_4, X_5,$ and $X_6$ are additional variables which reflect the power or influence of the state's congressmen in directly controlling $Y$. Each is measured as a percentage of total committee seats held by each state's congressmen during the decade preceding the measurement of $Y$ as obtained from the *Congressional Directory*. The particular committees believed to be most influential are:

$X_3 =$ House Armed Services Committee,
$X_4 =$ House Appropriations Subcommittee for Defense,
$X_5 =$ Senate Armed Services Committee, and
$X_6 =$ Senate Appropriations Subcommittee for Defense.

## The hypothesis to be tested

The hypothesis to be tested is whether the variables $X_3$ to $X_6$ are jointly significant in explaining the variation in $Y$ beyond the amount accounted for by variable $X_2$. The two models which must be considered are (the observation subscript $t$ is dropped for simplicity of notation):

$$a) \quad Y = \gamma_1 + \gamma_2 X_2 + \cdots + \gamma_6 X_6 + \varepsilon_t,$$

and

$$b) \quad Y = \delta_1 + \delta_2 X_2 + v.$$

The hypothesis to be tested using the 0.01 level of significance is $[H_0: \gamma_3 = \gamma_4 = \gamma_5 = \gamma_6 = 0]$ against $[H_a:$ at least one of $\gamma_3$ to $\gamma_6$ is nonzero]. The appropriate test follows the ANOVA Table 11–4 and uses the $F$-statistic (11–6).

## The empirical results

Using a computer regression program on each model (a) and (b), the results in Table 11–5 are obtained. From this table, it is obvious that the complete model (a) fits the data better than the restricted model (b). Based on observations for 50 states, it gives a higher $R^2$ and lower $s_e$. The question, however, is whether the extra variables $X_3$ to $X_6$ jointly make a significant improvement in the model.

Using the analysis of variance output for each model the ANOVA table for testing the significance of a subgroup of coefficients can be determined.

Table 11–6 is filled in by using the residual variation and explained variation from the complete model. Summing these gives the total variation in row one (although it is not necessary to find this). The sum of squares in row 4 is that explained by the restricted model (b). By subtraction of

**TABLE 11–5**

**Results, defense expenditures model**

| Dependent variable | Payroll share, $Y$ |
|---|---|
| Variables in the equation | Percent of total population, $X_2$ |
| | House Armed Services Committee, $X_3$ |
| | House Appropriations DOD, $X_4$ |
| | Senate Armed Services Committee, $X_5$ |
| | Senate Appropriations DOD, $X_6$ |

$R^2 = 0.59519$      $s_e = 1.74951$

| Analysis of variance | d.f. | Sum of squares | Mean square | F |
|---|---|---|---|---|
| Regression | 5 | 198.01348 | 39.6027 | 12.939 |
| Residual | 44 | 134.67526 | 3.0608 | |

| Dependent variable | Payroll share, $Y$ |
|---|---|
| Variables in the equation | Percent of total population, $X_2$ |

$R^2 = 0.47541$      $s_e = 1.90682$

| Analysis of variance | d.f. | Sum of squares | Mean square | F |
|---|---|---|---|---|
| Regression | 1 | 158.16193 | 158.16193 | 43.499 |
| Residual | 48 | 174.52681 | 3.63598 | |

Source: Class, 1970, (Grizzle).

TABLE 11-6

Results, ANOVA for subgroup of coefficients

| Source of variation | d.f. | Calculated SS | Mean square |
|---|---|---|---|
| Total | 49 | 332.68874 | |
| Less residual in complete model | 44 | 134.67526 | 3.0608 |
| Explained by all variables $X_2$ to $X_6$ | 5 | 198.01348 | |
| Less explained in restricted model by $X_2$ | 1 | 158.16193 | |
| Explained by addition of variables $X_3$ to $X_6$ | 4 | 39.85155 | 9.963 |

values in row 4 from those in row 3, the degrees of freedom and sum of squares for the additional variation explained by the political variables $X_3, X_4, X_5$, and $X_6$ is obtained. The mean square residual and mean square added are calculated by single divisions.

### The test conclusion

Returning to the test, the null hypothesis is to be rejected if the calculated $F$-value exceeds $F_{(0.01; 4, 44)} = 3.78$. Using (11–6), we obtain $F = $ (MS added)/ $s_e^2 = 9.963/3.0608 = 3.255$. Therefore, we fail to reject the null hypothesis at the 0.01 level of significance (it would be rejected at the 0.05 level since $F_{(0.05; 4, 44)} = 2.58$). The coefficients $\gamma_3$ to $\gamma_6$ in the specified model may differ from zero only due to chance. The joint addition of variables $X_3$ to $X_6$ in the model is not a significant improvement.

||||||||||||||||||||||||||||||||||||||||||||||||||||||||||||||||||||||||||||||||||||||||||||||||||||||||||||||||||||||||||||||||||||||||

*Interpretive note.* The political scientist may wish to consider some other subgroup of variables to include in the model. Perhaps you could suggest some other economic or demographic variables which you think should be included.

||||||||||||||||||||||||||||||||||||||||||||||||||||||||||||||||||||||||||||||||||||||||||||||||||||||||||||||||||||||||||||||||||||||||

### 11.8 TEST ON A LINEAR COMBINATION OF REGRESSION COEFFICIENTS

A commonly used test concerns any linear combination of the regression coefficients. It is appropriate if a researcher wishes to test if one coefficient is greater than another. Often, a testable hypothesis based on the underlying economic theory may be in the form of a linear combination. For example, the parameters in a consumption function may represent current and lagged marginal propensities to consume. A test on the value of the *long-run* marginal propensity to consume involves a simple linear combination of the short run MPC coefficients.[7] Probably the most frequent use of the test on a linear combination, $H'\Gamma = \sum_{k=2}^{K} h_k \gamma_k$, is the test on an expected forecast using the regression equation and some newly obtained extra sample observations on the variables. A forecast is merely a special case of the linear combination where the vector $H' = (x_{j2}, x_{j3}, \ldots, x_{jK})$ is the vector of deviations of the new observation values from their respective sample means based on the original $T$ observations. The test in the general model is an extension of the similar tests in the simple model as given in Sections 7.6 and 7.7.

### Formulating the test statistic

The hypothesis to be tested is, $H_0: H'\Gamma = N_0$ against either a one- or two-sided alternate where $N_0$ is a real number. The appropriate test statistic is derived using the theorem of Section 10.7. The estimator vector $C$ has been shown (Section 10.5) to have a multivariate normal distribution with $E(C) = \Gamma$ and $V\text{-}Cov(C) = \sigma_\varepsilon^2 (X'X)^{-1}$ (10–4). If $H$ is a transformation vector of size $[(K-1) \times 1]$, then the theorem states that $H'C$ is normally distributed with $E(H'C) = H'E(C) = H'\Gamma$ and $V\text{-}Cov(H'C) = H'\sigma_\varepsilon^2 (X'X)^{-1}H$.

‖‖‖‖‖‖‖‖‖‖‖‖‖‖‖‖‖‖‖‖‖‖‖‖‖‖‖‖‖‖‖‖‖‖‖‖‖‖‖‖‖‖‖‖‖‖‖‖‖‖‖‖‖‖‖‖‖‖‖‖‖‖‖‖‖‖‖‖‖‖‖‖‖‖‖‖‖‖‖‖‖‖‖‖‖‖‖‖‖‖‖‖‖‖‖‖‖‖‖‖‖‖‖‖‖‖‖‖‖‖‖‖‖‖‖‖‖‖‖‖‖‖‖‖

***Explicative note.*** $V\text{-}Cov(H'C)$ in this case is simply a scalar, size $(1 \times 1)$, giving the variance of the random variable $H'C$.

‖‖‖‖‖‖‖‖‖‖‖‖‖‖‖‖‖‖‖‖‖‖‖‖‖‖‖‖‖‖‖‖‖‖‖‖‖‖‖‖‖‖‖‖‖‖‖‖‖‖‖‖‖‖‖‖‖‖‖‖‖‖‖‖‖‖‖‖‖‖‖‖‖‖‖‖‖‖‖‖‖‖‖‖‖‖‖‖‖‖‖‖‖‖‖‖‖‖‖‖‖‖‖‖‖‖‖‖‖‖‖‖‖‖‖‖‖‖‖‖‖‖‖

Consequently, a standardized normal variable can be formed as

$$z = \frac{H'C - E(H'C)}{\sqrt{V(H'C)}} \quad \text{or} \quad z = \frac{H'C - H'\Gamma}{\sigma_\varepsilon \sqrt{H'(X'X)^{-1}H}}.$$

Again, this is distributed independently of the chi-square statistic $\chi^2_{(T-K)} = s_e^2(T-K)/\sigma_\varepsilon^2$. Therefore, a $t$-distributed statistic can be formed as $t = z\sqrt{T-K}/\sqrt{\chi^2}$, or

$$t_{(T-K)} = \frac{(H'C - H'\Gamma)\sqrt{T-K}\,\sigma_\varepsilon}{s_e\,\sigma_\varepsilon \sqrt{H'(X'X)^{-1}H}\sqrt{T-K}} = \frac{H'C - H'\Gamma}{s_e\sqrt{H'(X'X)^{-1}H}}. \quad (11\text{--}7)$$

---

[7] See E. Malinvaud, *Statistical Methods of Econometrics* (Chicago: Rand McNally, 1966), pp. 111–17.

In the special case of a forecast, then $H' = X_j' = (x_{j2}, x_{j3}, \ldots, x_{jK})$ and $H'\Gamma = E(y_j|X_j)$, where $X_j$ is a vector of deviations as defined above and $y_j$ is the deviation of the forecast from the mean of the original $T$ sample values of the endogenous variable.

The $t$-statistic (11–7) can also be used to establish confidence intervals on the value of the linear combination or on the expected forecast.

## Another problem description

Consider a consumption function given by the model $Y = \gamma_1 + \gamma_2 X_2 + \gamma_3 X_3 + \gamma_4 X_4 + \varepsilon$ where the measures of the variables are taken from *U.S. Business Statistics*, and are defined as

$Y =$ annual per capita personal consumption expenditures in the United States in constant 1947–49 dollars,

$X_2 =$ annual per capita personal disposable income in the United States in constant 1947–49 dollars,

$X_3 =$ lagged annual per capita personal disposable income in constant 1947–49 dollars, and

$X_4 =$ 100 times the reciprocal of the annual interest rate on U.S. government five-year issue securities taken from daily averages.

The specification of the model (and remember these example models are not claimed to be the best possible forms) follows the Keynesian notion that consumption per capita depends mainly on disposable income. Keynes also suggests that a higher degree of wealth will cause a higher consumption out of a given income and that an increased interest rate will increase savings, thereby decreasing consumption expenditure. These notions are represented by the inclusion of a lagged income variable to express wealth and by the inverse interest rate variable. All coefficients should be positive. The analysis of the model might be based on 21 annual observations.

## Statement of the test hypothesis

The particular hypothesis to be tested is whether current income has a larger effect on consumption than that of lagged income. The null hypothesis could be written $\gamma_2 = \gamma_3$ and the alternate written $\gamma_2 > \gamma_3$. In terms of the test on a linear combination, let $H' = (1, -1, 0)$ and let the hypothesized value of $H'\Gamma$ be zero. That is, the null hypothesis can be rewritten as $H_0 : H'\Gamma = (1)\gamma_2 + (-1)\gamma_3 + (0)\gamma_4 = 0$. The alternate hypothesis is one sided, $H_a : H'\Gamma > 0$. The $t$-statistic of (11–7) can be used and the null hypothesis will be rejected based on the 21 observations if the calculated $t$-value exceeds $t_{(0.05;\,T-K)} = t_{(0.05;\,17)} = 1.74$.

## The empirical results

The results of a least squares regression are given by the computer output adapted for Table 11–7. The output gives summary statistics of the goodness of fit, the estimates of the regression coefficients and the estimates of the standard errors of these estimates, and the inverse of the sample cross-product deviation matrix used in computing these estimates according to formulas (9–3) and (10–4).

TABLE 11–7

**Results, consumption model**

Dependent variable    Consumption $Y$, $\bar{Y} = 1420.72583$

| Variable in the equation | Mean | Coefficient | Std. error |
|---|---|---|---|
| (constant) | | 130.297 | |
| Income $X_2$ | 1539.39917 | 0.80382 | 0.07224 |
| Lagged income $X_3$ | 1507.80786 | 0.04244 | 0.08024 |
| Interest rate reciprocal $X_4$ | 3625.70825 | −0.00302 | 0.00401 |

$R^2 = 0.9968$      $s_e = 16.038$

$$(X'X)^{-1} = \begin{pmatrix} 20.2865 \times 10^{-6} & -20.5238 \times 10^{-6} & -16.4046 \times 10^{-6} \\ & 25.0315 \times 10^{-6} & -25.7339 \times 10^{-6} \\ \text{(symmetric)} & & 62.3793 \times 10^{-6} \end{pmatrix}$$

Source: Class 1970 (Gustafson).

||||||||||||||||||||||||||||||||||||||||||||||||||||||||||||||||||||||||||||||||||||||||||||||||||||||||||||||||||||||||||||||||||||||||||||||||

*Discursive note.* Some computer programs do not provide $(X'X)^{-1}$ in the output. They may give $(X'X)$ or the covariance matrix $= (X'X)/(T-1)$ from which the researcher must determine the inverse. Most computer centers have a packaged routine for finding the inverse of a matrix.

Still other standard regression programs may give the correlation matrix $R = D(X'X)D$ where $D$ is a diagonal matrix with $K - 1$ rows and columns whose diagonal elements are $d_{kk} = 1/\sqrt{x_{kk}}$ where $x_{kk}$ is the $k$th diagonal element of $(X'X)$. Since $\sqrt{x_{kk}/(T-1)}$ is the sample standard deviation of the variable $X_k$, $k = 2, 3, \ldots, K$, and standard deviations of the variables are usually available in the computer output, then $d_{kk}$ can be found by $d_{kk} = 1/s_{X_k}\sqrt{T-1}$. Thus, $(X'X)^{-1}$ can be found by $(X'X)^{-1} = DR^{-1}D$ when the correlation matrix $R$ (or the inverse of the correlation matrix, $R^{-1}$) as well as the standard deviations of all the predetermined variables are given.

||||||||||||||||||||||||||||||||||||||||||||||||||||||||||||||||||||||||||||||||||||||||||||||||||||||||||||||||||||||||||||||||||||||||||||||||

By substituting the results from Table 11–7 into the $t$-statistic (11–7), one obtains

$$t_{(17)} = (H'C - 0)/s_e\sqrt{H'(X'X)^{-1}H},$$

or

$$t_{(17)} = (0.80382 - 0.04244 + 0)/16.038\left[(1, -1, 0)(X'X)^{-1}\begin{pmatrix} 1 \\ -1 \\ 0 \end{pmatrix}\right]^{1/2}.$$

Making the final substitution for $(X'X)^{-1}$ and simplifying by matrix multiplication, one obtains $t_{(17)} = 0.76138/16.038(86.366 \times 10^{-6})^{1/2} = 5.108$.

## The test conclusion

Since $5.108 > 1.74$, the test indicates that the null hypothesis is rejected and $H'\Gamma > 0$. In terms of the model, this indicates that the effect of the current year income is significantly greater than the effect of the lagged income variable. Indeed, a test on the significance of the coefficient $\gamma_3$ would indicate that the individual effect of the lagged income variable is insignificant.

||||||||||||||||||||||||||||||||||||||||||||||||||||||||||||||||||||||||||||||||||||||||||||||||||||||||||||||||||||||||||||||||||||||||||||||||||||||||

*Interpretive note.* This result does not imply directly that the wealth effect is not important but only that this specification of the wealth effect, based on this data, is not worthwhile. The reader may suggest some other specification.

||||||||||||||||||||||||||||||||||||||||||||||||||||||||||||||||||||||||||||||||||||||||||||||||||||||||||||||||||||||||||||||||||||||||||||||||||||||||

## Determining a forecast interval

Since the specified consumption function has only one significant variable, the researcher would ordinarily revise the model before using it for forecasting. However, to provide an example of setting a forecast interval without introducing a new model and new results, we can courageously use the results of Table 11–7.

Suppose new observations of the predetermined variables are given as $X_{j2} = 1900$, $X_{j3} = 1850$, and the interest rate is 5.75 percent. We find $X_{j4} = (100)1/0.0575 = 1,739.13044$. The vector of deviations from the previously computed means is used as the transformation vector,

$$H = X_j = \begin{pmatrix} X_{j2} - \bar{X}_2 \\ X_{j3} - \bar{X}_3 \\ X_{j4} - \bar{X}_4 \end{pmatrix} = \begin{pmatrix} 360.60083 \\ 342.19214 \\ -1886.57781 \end{pmatrix}.$$

The 90 percent confidence limits on the deviation from $\bar{Y}$ of the expected forecast are obtained from (11–7) by solving for $E(y_j | X_j) = H'\Gamma$. The resulting limits are

$$H'C \pm t_{(\alpha/2; T-K)} s_e\sqrt{H'(X'X)^{-1}H}. \tag{11–8}$$

In this example $H'C = 310.078$, $t_{(0.05;17)} = 1.74$, $s_e = 16.038$, and the term under the radical is 177.1042. By substitution, this gives the 90 percent confidence limits on $E(y_j | X_j)$ as $310.078 \pm 1.74(16.038)(13.308)$, or $-61.296$ and $+681.45$. Since $y_j = Y_j - \bar{Y}$, the 90 percent confidence limits on the expected forecast are obtained by adding the sample mean of $Y$, $\bar{Y} = 1420.72583$, to these limits. One obtains, \$1,359.43 < (expected forecast of consumption per capita) < \$2,102.18.

|||||||||||||||||||||||||||||||||||||||||||||||||||||||||||||||||||||||||||||||||||||||||||||||||||||||||||||||||||||||||||||||

*Interpretive note.* Obviously, the forecast interval is too wide to be useful for any planning or policy purposes. This wide interval is a result of the use of insignificant variables in the model whose coefficients are too small relative to the size of their standard errors. Better forecasts require good fitting models to past data (so that $s_e$ is small) and significant coefficients for all the variables in the model. Discovering such models is an art in itself.

|||||||||||||||||||||||||||||||||||||||||||||||||||||||||||||||||||||||||||||||||||||||||||||||||||||||||||||||||||||||||||||||

## 11.9 TEST ON LINEAR RESTRICTIONS ON THE COEFFICIENTS

A variation in the previous test occurs when $H$ is a transformation matrix of size $[m \times (K - 1)]$ such that $H'\Gamma = O$ represents a set of $m < K$ homogeneous linear restrictions on the coefficients of the model. In this case, the researcher really has two specifications of the model, one unrestricted with $(K - 1)$ predetermined variables and the other a restricted model with $(K - 1 - m_1)$ predetermined variables. The symbol $m_1$ denotes the rank of the matrix $H$; it is the number of linearly independent restrictions in the set of $m$ restrictions. These are usually the same $(m = m_1)$, but if many restrictions are imposed, some redundancies may exist within the set and not be apparent to the researcher.

### The problem situation

Consider the problem of an economist interested in security analysis who tries to specify a model which reliably predicts corporate earnings for a company in the next period.[8] Define the variables in the model, $Y = X\Gamma + \varepsilon$, as:

$Y_t = E_{t+1}$, cash earnings (after tax before depreciation) in the next period;
$X_2 = E_t$, cash earnings in this period;

---

[8] H. A. Latane′, D. L. Tuttle, *Security Analysis and Portfolio Management* (New York: The Ronald Press Co., 1970), is a comprehensive text including many such related models with a discussion of results.

$X_3 =$ inflationary effect on earnings depending on $E_t$ and on the inflation rate in year $t$;

$X_4 =$ marginal earnings from reinvested cash income $= M = \text{ROI}(E_t - D_t)$, where ROI $=$ return on investment and $D_t =$ dividends in period $t$;

$X_5 =$ growth rate in sales $= S_t/S_{t-1}$; and

$X_6 =$ decreased earnings due to maturing investments $= \text{ROI}(DE)_t NP_t/S_t$ where $DE_t$ is the depreciation rate in percent in period $t$, $NP_t$ is the value of the net plant in period $t$, and $S_t$ are the common shares outstanding in period $t$ (an average).

In a market where constancy of price and quantity in product and factor markets exists, a firm (in the simplest case) can earn in period $t + 1$ an amount equal to $E_t + \text{ROI}(E_t - D_t)$ given no other externalities. Since the market is uncertain and $E_{t+1}$ reflects such things as inflation, sales growth, investments maturing, etc., these must also be included in the model. For this example, cash earnings are used for simplicity since maturing investments may not bring the same rate of return as present investments due to changing costs.

## The hypothesis to be tested

One problem in this specification is the inclusion in $X_2$, $X_3$, and $X_4$ of the component $E_t =$ current earnings. This may result in multicollinearity among this group of predetermined variables. Consequently, a revised and simpler model may be formulated under the restriction that $\gamma_2 = -\gamma_3 = \gamma_4$. That is, variables $X_2$, $X_3$, and $X_4$ are combined into a single earnings variable defined by $Z_2 = X_2 - X_3 + X_4$.

The question for the researcher to test is whether there is a significant difference between the unrestricted and the restricted models. If not, then the restricted model may be appropriate.

## Exploring the theory underlying the test

The development of the test statistic is similar to the analysis of variance and involves the use of independent chi-square distributed quadratic forms in the same underlying normally distributed error variable. In this latter sense, the theorem of *Review* 7.2, item 1, is again applicable. Let the unrestricted model in the original variables including the intercept be, $Y = \underset{(T \times K)(K \times 1)}{X \quad \Gamma} + \varepsilon$ and let the restricted model be $Y = \underset{[T \times (K - m_1)][(K - m_1) \times 1]}{Z \quad \Delta} + \varepsilon$. Then, the sum of squares of residuals in the unrestricted model is a quadratic form $Q_1 = e'e = Y'Y - C'X'Y$ where $C$ is the vector of least squares estimates of $\Gamma$. Similarly, the sum of squares of residuals in the restricted model may be denoted by a quadratic form $Q = Y'Y - D'Z'Y$ where $D$ is the vector of least squares estimates of $\Delta$. $Q_1$ has degrees of freedom $T - K$, and $Q$ has degrees of freedom $T - (K - m_1) = T - K + m_1$.

‖‖‖‖‖‖‖‖‖‖‖‖‖‖‖‖‖‖‖‖‖‖‖‖‖‖‖‖‖‖‖‖‖‖‖‖‖‖‖‖‖‖‖‖‖‖‖‖‖‖‖‖‖‖‖‖‖‖‖‖‖‖‖‖‖‖‖‖‖‖‖‖‖‖‖‖‖‖‖‖‖‖‖‖‖‖‖‖‖‖‖‖‖‖

*Interpretive note.* The amount of variation explained by the un-restricted model is necessarily at least as large as that explained by the restricted model. The unrestricted model includes more variables with freely estimated coefficients. A better fit to the observation set can be obtained by a $K$ dimensional hyperplane than by a $(K - m_1) < K$ di-mensional hyperplane. Hence, the residual sum of squares $Q_1$ is smaller than the residual sum of squares $Q$.

‖‖‖‖‖‖‖‖‖‖‖‖‖‖‖‖‖‖‖‖‖‖‖‖‖‖‖‖‖‖‖‖‖‖‖‖‖‖‖‖‖‖‖‖‖‖‖‖‖‖‖‖‖‖‖‖‖‖‖‖‖‖‖‖‖‖‖‖‖‖‖‖‖‖‖‖‖‖‖‖‖‖‖‖‖‖‖‖‖‖‖‖‖‖

The ratios $Q_1/\sigma_\varepsilon^2$ and $Q/\sigma_\varepsilon^2$ are each chi-square distributed with $T - K$ and $T - K + m_1$ degrees of freedom respectively. Using the theorem from *Review* 7.2, the difference between the two sums of squares is $Q_2 = Q - Q_1$, and $Q_2/\sigma_\varepsilon^2$ is also chi-square distributed with $[T - K + m_1 - (T - K)] = m_1$ degrees of freedom and is independent of the ratio $Q_1/\sigma_\varepsilon^2$.

## The test statistic

An *F*-distributed random variable can be formed in the usual way.

$$F_{(m_1, T-K)} = \frac{(Q - Q_1)/m_1}{Q_1/(T - K)}. \tag{11-9}$$

Under the assumption that the errors $\varepsilon_t$ are normally and independently distributed, this distribution is exact.

‖‖‖‖‖‖‖‖‖‖‖‖‖‖‖‖‖‖‖‖‖‖‖‖‖‖‖‖‖‖‖‖‖‖‖‖‖‖‖‖‖‖‖‖‖‖‖‖‖‖‖‖‖‖‖‖‖‖‖‖‖‖‖‖‖‖‖‖‖‖‖‖‖‖‖‖‖‖‖‖‖‖‖‖‖‖‖‖‖‖‖‖‖‖

*Interpretive note.* The difference $Q_2 = Q - Q_1$ is the change in the sum of squares due to the restrictions, $H'\Gamma = O$. If the restricted model is a true representation on the basis of the sample data, then $Q_2$ would be small and the restrictions acceptable. If the restrictions are inappropriate, then the unrestricted model would show a sig-nificantly higher degree of fit on the basis of the sample data. The calculated value of the *F*-statistic (11–9) would exceed the critical *F*-value for the test.

‖‖‖‖‖‖‖‖‖‖‖‖‖‖‖‖‖‖‖‖‖‖‖‖‖‖‖‖‖‖‖‖‖‖‖‖‖‖‖‖‖‖‖‖‖‖‖‖‖‖‖‖‖‖‖‖‖‖‖‖‖‖‖‖‖‖‖‖‖‖‖‖‖‖‖‖‖‖‖‖‖‖‖‖‖‖‖‖‖‖‖‖‖‖

## Setting up the test

The hypothesis to be tested is, $H_0: H'\Gamma = O$ against the alternate, $H_a: H'\Gamma \neq O$. For the example concerning corporate earnings, the restriction, $\gamma_2 = -\gamma_3 = \gamma_4$ can be separated into three restrictions, $\gamma_2 + \gamma_3 = 0, \gamma_2 - \gamma_4 = 0$, and $\gamma_3 + \gamma_4 = 0$. These are represented by

$$H'\Gamma = \begin{pmatrix} 0 & 1 & 1 & 0 & 0 & 0 \\ 0 & 1 & 0 & -1 & 0 & 0 \\ 0 & 0 & 1 & 1 & 0 & 0 \end{pmatrix} \begin{pmatrix} \gamma_1 \\ \gamma_2 \\ \vdots \\ \gamma_6 \end{pmatrix} = O.$$

The number of restrictions is $m = 3$, but the number of independent restrictions is obviously $m_1 = 2$.

‖‖‖‖‖‖‖‖‖‖‖‖‖‖‖‖‖‖‖‖‖‖‖‖‖‖‖‖‖‖‖‖‖‖‖‖‖‖‖‖‖‖‖‖‖‖‖‖‖‖‖‖‖‖‖‖‖‖‖‖‖‖‖‖‖‖‖‖‖‖‖‖‖‖‖‖‖‖‖‖‖‖‖‖‖‖‖‖‖‖‖‖‖‖‖‖‖

*Explicative note.* If $\gamma_2 = -\gamma_3$ and $\gamma_2 = \gamma_4$, then $-\gamma_3 = \gamma_4$ necessarily. In the matrix $H'$, row 1 minus row 2 gives row 3. The (rank of $H$) $= 2$.

‖‖‖‖‖‖‖‖‖‖‖‖‖‖‖‖‖‖‖‖‖‖‖‖‖‖‖‖‖‖‖‖‖‖‖‖‖‖‖‖‖‖‖‖‖‖‖‖‖‖‖‖‖‖‖‖‖‖‖‖‖‖‖‖‖‖‖‖‖‖‖‖‖‖‖‖‖‖‖‖‖‖‖‖‖‖‖‖‖‖‖‖‖‖‖‖‖

The unrestricted model is $Y = X\Gamma + \varepsilon$ as defined earlier. To find the restricted model, we use the restrictions, $H'\Gamma = O$, and solve for $m_1$ of the coefficients in terms of the other $K - 1 - m_1$. Substituting these solutions back into the original model gives the restricted model,

$$Y = \delta_1 + \delta_2 Z_2 + \cdots + \delta_{(K-m_1)} Z_{(K-m_1)} + \varepsilon.$$

In this example

$$(K - m_1) = (6 - 2) = 4, \quad \text{and} \quad Z_2 = X_2 - X_3 + X_4,$$

$$Z_3 = X_5, \quad \text{and} \quad Z_4 = X_6.$$

## The data and empirical results

To make the test, data are collected on 25 corporations from the source, *Value Line Investment Survey*. All variables are measured in dollars per share except $X_5$, the product demand adjustment ratio, which has no dimensions. The computation of the $F$-statistic (11–9) is best organized in a table similar to an analysis of variance table (see Table 11–9). The null hypothesis is rejected at the 0.05 level of significance if the calculated $F$-value exceeds $F_{(0.05; m_1, T-K)} = F_{(0.05; 2, 19)} = 3.52$.

To obtain the necessary results for this test, two regressions are calculated; one for the unrestricted model and the other for the restricted model. Part of the computer output for these two least squares regressions is given in Table 11–8.[9]

As often occurs, the output from a prepackaged regression program may not give the exact statistics desired. For our test, the sum of squares of residuals in each model is needed. The relevant values from the output of Table 11–8 are the number of observations, the number of variables included in the models, and the mean square residual, and/or the multiple correlation coefficient and the variance of the endogenous variable. In general, the re-

---

[9] These calculations were done on a Call-A-Computer system using the common typewriter-paper tape console and a packaged BASIC II language program. Exceptionally sophisticated computers or programs are not necessary to perform these seemingly complex tests.

**TABLE 11–8**

**Results, corporate earnings models**

**Unrestricted model**

Dependent variable $Y$, cash earnings per share, $\overline{Y} = 2.4344$, $V(Y) = 1.96804$
Twenty-five observations

| Variable | Mean | Coefficient | Std. error | |
|---|---|---|---|---|
| $X_2$ | 2.2712 | 1.376 | 0.560 | |
| $X_3$ | 0.0572 | −15.668 | 21.418 | |
| $X_4$ | 0.1388 | 1.875 | 1.129 | Mean square residual 0.135415 |
| $X_5$ | 1.076 | 1.058 | 1.069 | $R = 0.972382$ |
| $X_6$ | 0.0664 | − 1.419 | 1.335 | |
| (Constant) | | − 1.098 | 1.210 | |

**Restricted model**

Dependent variable $Y$, cash earnings per share, $\overline{Y} = 2.4344$, $V(Y) = 1.96804$
Twenty-five observations

| Variable | Mean | Coefficient | Std. error | |
|---|---|---|---|---|
| $Z_2$ | 2.3532 | 1.045 | 0.070 | Mean square residual 0.128145 |
| $Z_3$ | 1.076 | 1.178 | 0.920 | $R = 0.971095$ |
| $Z_4$ | 0.0664 | −0.988 | 1.240 | |
| (Constant) | | −1.228 | 1.045 | |

Source: Class, 1970 (Meyer).

searcher needs to determine the values in the last two rows of Table 11–9. The complete table is given as a convenient summary of the relevant information. Each row is now explained in detail.

**TABLE 11–9**

**Results, example test on linear restrictions**

| Variation due to | d.f. | Sum of squares | Mean square | F |
|---|---|---|---|---|
| Total | 24 | 47.239296 | | |
| Less explained by restricted model | 3 | 44.547837 | | |
| Residual in restricted model | 21 | $Q = 2.691459$ | | |
| Less residual in unrestricted model | 19 | $Q_1 = 2.572921$ | 0.135415 | |
| Difference between restricted and un-restricted models | 2 | $Q_2 = 0.118538$ | 0.059269 | 0.438 |

## Calculation of the test statistic

The degrees of freedom for the total variation are $T - 1 = 24$. The total sum of squares is found from the variance, $V(Y) = Y'Y/(T - 1)$. Thus $Y'Y = 1.96804(24) = 47.239296$. The proportion of variation explained in the restricted model is determined by $R^2 = (0.971095)^2$. The amount of variation explained is then $D'Z'Y = R^2(Y'Y) = 44.547837$. The degrees of freedom are determined by counting the number of exogenous variables (excluding the intercept) in the equation. The residual sum of squares in the restricted model is then found by subtraction $Q = Y'Y - D'Z'Y = 2.691459$, with degrees of freedom $T - K + m_1 = 25 - 6 + 2 = 21$. Alternately, $Q$ could be found from the mean square residual as $Q/d.f. = $ mean square residual. This latter method might be employed to find the residual sum of squares in the unrestricted model, $Q_1 = (T - K)(\text{mean square residual}) = 19(0.135415) = 2.572921$. The degrees of freedom and sum of squares in the final row are obtained by subtraction. Finally, the $F$-value corresponding to (11–9) is the ratio of the mean square of the difference to the mean square residual in the unrestricted model, $F = 0.059269/0.135415 = 0.438$.

## The test conclusion

This value is not significant and the null hypothesis, $H'\Gamma = O$, is not rejected. In this example, there is no significant difference between the restricted and unrestricted models. Therefore, the model under the restrictions $H'\Gamma = O$ is deemed to be just as appropriate as the original one.

||||||||||||||||||||||||||||||||||||||||||||||||||||||||||||||||||||||||||||||||||||||||||||||||||||||||||||||||||||||||||||||||||||||||||||

*Discursive note.* The multiple correlation coefficient is larger and the residual sum of squares is smaller in the unrestricted model than in the restricted models as is always true. These statistics have not been adjusted for degrees of freedom. However, the adjusted multiple $R^2$ $\bar{R}^2 = 1 - (s_e^2/s_Y^2)$ (refer to Sections 4.3 and 9.5) would be smaller and the mean square residual larger in the unrestricted model. This result only occurs when the additional variation explained by the unrestricted variables is not sufficient to offset the loss of the additional degree of freedom. That is, $Q \geq Q_1$ always, but $Q/(T - K + m_1)$ may be larger or smaller than $Q_1/(T - K)$.

||||||||||||||||||||||||||||||||||||||||||||||||||||||||||||||||||||||||||||||||||||||||||||||||||||||||||||||||||||||||||||||||||||||||||||

## 11.10 TEST ON COEFFICIENTS IN DIFFERENT ESTIMATIONS OF THE SAME MODEL

The final test considered in this chapter is a test of equality between coefficients in two identical models based on two different data sets. It is commonly known as the Chow test and has frequent application.[10]

---

[10] Gregory C. Chow, "Tests of Equality between Sets of Coefficients in Two Linear Regressions," *Econometrica*, Vol. 28 (July 1960), pp. 591–605. A more readable exposition of the test is found in F. M. Fisher, "Tests of Equality between Sets of Coefficients in Two Linear Regressions: An Expository Note," *Econometrica* (March 1970), pp. 361–66.

An econometrician may have a model which adequately describes some economic relations for data from region A. Then, he acquires new data on region B and wishes to test if the same regression model is satisfactory. For another example, he may have a model describing some aspect of banking behavior for large city banks and desires to emphasize the difference between the coefficients in this model and those which would be most appropriate for the same model based on observations of small rural banks. Again, a researcher may have an established relation based on historical data and then new observations become available with the passage of time. He might test to see if the same model fits the new data.

### Notation and formulation for the Chow test

The development of the test statistic is similar to the tests of the previous two sections. The pattern includes the determination of independent quadratic forms calculated from residual sums of squares in least squares regressions, their degrees of freedom, and an $F$-statistic formed by the proper ratio.

Some new notation is convenient to designate the two datasets, say subscript roman numerals I and II. The models under consideration may be written, $Y_I = X_I \Gamma_I + \varepsilon_I$ and $Y_{II} = X_{II} \Gamma_{II} + \varepsilon_{II}$ where the number of observations in the two datasets are $T_I$ and $T_{II}$ respectively, both larger than $K$.[11] The usual assumptions (see Section 10.3) are made for both $\varepsilon_I$ and $\varepsilon_{II}$.

The null hypothesis to be tested is $H_0: \Gamma_I = \Gamma_{II}$ against the alternate, $H_a: \Gamma_I \neq \Gamma_{II}$. If there is no difference between the coefficients in the two models, then the two datasets could be pooled with no loss in explanatory power in the model. If all $T_I + T_{II}$ observations are pooled and the $K$ coefficients estimated by $C$ in the model

$$\begin{pmatrix} Y_I \\ Y_{II} \end{pmatrix} = \begin{pmatrix} X_I \\ X_{II} \end{pmatrix} \Gamma + \begin{pmatrix} \varepsilon_I \\ \varepsilon_{II} \end{pmatrix},$$

then the sum of squares of residuals in the "pooled" model is a quadratic form

$$Q = (Y_I \ Y_{II}) \begin{pmatrix} Y_I \\ Y_{II} \end{pmatrix} - C'(X_I \ X_{II}) \begin{pmatrix} Y_I \\ Y_{II} \end{pmatrix}.$$

||||||||||||||||||||||||||||||||||||||||||||||||||||||||||||||||||||||||||||||||||||||||||||||||||||||||||

*Recursive note.* This is simply the usual expression for residual sum of squares, $e'e = Y'Y - C'X'Y$ (9–5). In this case, the observation matrices $Y$ and $X$ are partitioned into two components.

||||||||||||||||||||||||||||||||||||||||||||||||||||||||||||||||||||||||||||||||||||||||||||||||||||||||||

The associated degrees of freedom for $Q$ are $T_I + T_{II} - K$.

Instead of pooling the data, which would be inappropriate if the co-

---

[11] If dataset II has $T_{II} \leq K$, a slightly different test is appropriate. See the article by Chow, "Tests of Equality."

efficients $\Gamma_I$ and $\Gamma_{II}$ are different, each of the models could be estimated independently. The combined sum of squares from these two regressions would also be a quadratic form, $Q_1 = (Y_I'Y_I - C'X_I'Y_I) + (Y_{II}'Y_{II} - C_{II}'X_{II}'Y_{II})$ where these combined terms have degrees of freedom $T_I - K$ and $T_{II} - K$ respectively. Hence, $Q_1$ has degrees of freedom $T_I + T_{II} - 2K$.

||||||||||||||||||||||||||||||||||||||||||||||||||||||||||||||||||||||||||||||||||||||||||||||||||||||||||||||||||||||||||||||||||||||

*Interpretive note.* The amount of variation explained by the pooled data model is smaller than the combined amount from the two separate estimations. One can always get at least as good and usually a better fit when dealing with more homogeneous subgroups of data rather than with the relatively heterogenous pooled dataset. Consequently, the residual sum of squares $Q_1$ is smaller than the residual sum of squares $Q$.

||||||||||||||||||||||||||||||||||||||||||||||||||||||||||||||||||||||||||||||||||||||||||||||||||||||||||||||||||||||||||||||||||||||

## The test statistic

Since both these quadratic forms are reducible to expressions in terms of identically and normally distributed disturbance variables, the theorem from *Review* 7.2 again applies. The ratios $Q/\sigma_\varepsilon^2$ and $Q_1/\sigma_\varepsilon^2$ are each chi-square distributed with $(T_I + T_{II} - K)$ and $(T_I + T_{II} - 2K)$ degrees of freedom respectively. The difference between the two quadratic forms is $Q_2 = Q - Q_1$, and $Q_2/\sigma_\varepsilon^2$ is also chi-square distributed with $[(T_I + T_{II} - K) - (T_I + T_{II} - 2K)] = K$ degrees of freedom and is independent of the ratio $Q_1/\sigma_\varepsilon^2$. An $F$-distributed random variable is again formed as

$$F_{(K, T_I+T_{II}-2K)} = \frac{(Q - Q_1)/K}{Q_1/(T_I + T_{II} - 2K)}. \tag{11-10}$$

||||||||||||||||||||||||||||||||||||||||||||||||||||||||||||||||||||||||||||||||||||||||||||||||||||||||||||||||||||||||||||||||||||||

*Interpretive note.* The difference $Q_2$ represents the residual sum of squares due to changes between the two datasets. If the pooled data all fits the same model, then $Q_2$ is small and the restriction that $\Gamma_I = \Gamma_{II}$ is acceptable. If these coefficients differ, then $Q_2$ is relatively large and the calculated value of the $F$-statistic (11–10) would exceed the critical $F$-value for the test.

||||||||||||||||||||||||||||||||||||||||||||||||||||||||||||||||||||||||||||||||||||||||||||||||||||||||||||||||||||||||||||||||||||||

## A problem situation

For an illustration of this test, suppose an economist interested in corporate investment specifies a model for explaining the annual level of capital spending by a single firm over time.[12] The model might be, $Y = X\Gamma + \varepsilon$ with

---

[12] See James L. Murphy, "An Appraisal of Repeated Predictive Tests on an Econometric Model," *Southern Economic Journal*, Vol. 35 (April 1969), pp. 293–307, for results which indicate that such a model should be a simultaneous equations model.

$K = 5$ where

$Y_t$ = gross capital expenditures in year $t$,
$X_{t2}$ = company net profits after taxes in year $t - 2$,
$X_{t3}$ = change in company net sales between years $t - 2$ and $t - 3$,
$X_{t4}$ = company depreciation in year $t$, and
$X_{t5}$ = the reciprocal of short-term interest rate in year $t - 1$.

Underlying this specification are the hypotheses that sales changes and profits are proxy variables for expectations and should be significant factors. Depreciation shows the replacement need for capital spending, and the interest rate shows the opportunity cost involved. All of the variables except depreciation are lagged as decisions to invest are made one or two periods prior to the actual spending. The model is presumed to be relevant for a wide variety of firms and is estimated and compared for two particular firms of different size in the same industry.

Data from both companies is in current dollars and is taken from annual reports. The period covered uses capital spending from 1955 to 1968, a total of 14 observations. Sales changes, profits, capital expenditures, and depreciation are all in thousands of dollars. The short-term interest rate used is the market yield on 30-day Treasury Bills as reported in the *Federal Reserve Bulletin*.

## The hypothesis to be tested

The model was estimated on the basis of dataset I for company I. The results indicated that variables $X_2$ and $X_3$ were most important with the additional variables $X_4$ and $X_5$ increasing $R^2$ by only 0.0021. (See Problem 8 at the end of the chapter.) Consequently, the reduced model $Y_t = \gamma_1 + \gamma_2 X_{t2} + \gamma_3 X_{t3} + \varepsilon_t$ is maintained as the best representation considered.

For company I, the estimating equation is

$$Y = 0.80304 + 0.42619X_2 + 0.16313X_3 \qquad \text{with } R = 0.8234.$$
$$\phantom{Y = 0.80304 + }(0.20440) \qquad (0.06544)$$

||||||||||||||||||||||||||||||||||||||||||||||||||||||||||||||||||||||||||||||||||||||||||||||||||||||||||||||||||||||||||||||||||||||||

*Recursive note.* The estimates of the standard errors of the estimates of the coefficients are commonly given in parentheses under the corresponding coefficient. These are the square roots of the diagonal elements of Est. $[V\text{-}Cov(C)] = s_e(X'X)^{-1}$ from (10–4).

||||||||||||||||||||||||||||||||||||||||||||||||||||||||||||||||||||||||||||||||||||||||||||||||||||||||||||||||||||||||||||||||||||||||

The same model estimated on the basis of dataset II for company II gives,

$$Y = 12.93414 + 1.2613X_2 + 0.1347X_3 \qquad \text{with } R = 0.6470.$$
$$\phantom{Y = 12.93414 + }(0.45149) \qquad (0.15790)$$

We desire to test if the coefficients of these two relations are equal or not based on this sample evidence. To perform the test, one more regression equation must be estimated using the pooled dataset I and II, and the sum of squares of residuals must be calculated for each of the three estimations. Using a significance level of 0.01 and the test statistic from (11–10), the null hypothesis, $H_0$: $\Gamma_I = \Gamma_{II}$ is rejected if the calculated $F$-value exceeds

$$F_{(0.01; K, T_I + T_{II} - 2K)} = F_{(0.01; 3, 22)} = 4.82.$$

## The empirical results and calculation of the test statistic

The relevant results are excerpted from a computer output and given in Table 11–10.

### TABLE 11–10

Results, corporate investment model

**Dataset I**

Dependent variable $Y$, investment, $\bar{Y} = 4.74378$, $s_Y = 1.8279$

| Analysis of variance | d.f. | Sum of squares | Mean square | F |
|---|---|---|---|---|
| Regression | 2 | 29.452 | 14.726 | 11.584 |
| Residual | 11 | 13.984 | 1.271 | |

**Dataset II**

Dependent variable $Y$, investment, $\bar{Y} = 27.17657$, $s_Y = 7.83903$

| Analysis of variance | d.f. | Sum of squares | Mean square | F |
|---|---|---|---|---|
| Regression | 2 | 334.448 | 167.224 | 3.961 |
| Residual | 11 | 464.408 | 42.219 | |

**Pooled data**

Dependent variable $Y$, investment, $\bar{Y} = 15.96011$, $s_Y = 12.71464$

| Analysis of variance | d.f. | Sum of squares | Mean square | F |
|---|---|---|---|---|
| Regression | 2 | 3094.289 | 1547.144 | 30.442 |
| Residual | 25 | 1270.583 | 50.823 | |

Source: Class, 1970 (Harman).

The details of the calculation of the test statistic are easily organized in Table 11–11. The residual sum of squares $Q$ for the " pooled" regression has $T_I + T_{II} - K = 14 + 14 - 3 = 25$ degrees of freedom and is obtained directly from the analysis of variance table for this regression. The combined sum of squares $Q_1$ from the separate regressions is obtained directly from the corresponding analysis of variance tables by summation. The value is 13.984 + 464.408 = 478.392, and its degrees of freedom are $T_I + T_{II} - 2K = 14 + 14 - 6 = 22$. The final row in Table 11–11 is obtained by subtraction, and the $F$-value from (11–10) is calculated to be 12.144. This is greater than the critical value of 4.82; and so, we conclude that the coefficients of the models for companies I and II are different. The effects of sale changes and profits on gross investment is different for these two different firms.

**TABLE 11–11**

**Results, example of Chow test**

| Variation due to | d.f. | Sum of squares | Mean square | F |
|---|---|---|---|---|
| Total in pooled data | 27 | 4364.872 | | |
| Less explained by pooled data model | 2 | 3094.289 | | |
| Residual in pooled data model | 25 | $Q = 1270.583$ | | |
| Less residuals using dataset I and dataset II separately | $(11 + 11)$ | $Q_1 = \begin{matrix} 13.984 \\ +464.408 \end{matrix}$ | 21.745 | |
| | | | | 12.144 |
| Difference between coefficients based on datasets I and II | 3 | $Q_2 = 792.191$ | 264.064 | |

## A similar test on subgroups of coefficients

A slight variation of the above test is often useful to know and is quite easily understood as a special situation. This extra test concerns the equality of a subset of coefficients in two linear regressions. It is also formulated in the paper by Chow. The steps in making the test are summarized without another accompanying numerical example.

## A description of the test

Suppose the regression model contains $K - 1$ predetermined variables (plus an intercept) and is hypothesized to apply to two different datasets, I and II with $T_I$ and $T_{II}$ observations respectively. Moreover, the coefficients on $m < K$ of the variables are hypothesized to be equal in both regressions. For convenience, consider the first $m$ variables, $X_1, X_2, \ldots, X_m$ to be those whose coefficients, $\gamma_1, \gamma_2, \ldots, \gamma_m$, are hypothesized to be equal. Denote the remaining predetermined variables by $Z_1, Z_2, \ldots, Z_{K-m}$ with coefficients, $\delta_1, \delta_2, \ldots, \delta_{K-m}$. For a given observation set, the model is written

$$Y = X\Gamma^* + Z\Delta + \varepsilon = \gamma_1 X_1 + \cdots + \gamma_m X_m + \delta_1 Z_1 + \cdots + \delta_{K-m} Z_{K-m} + \varepsilon.$$

Using the subscripts I and II to denote the dataset on which the observation matrices and the coefficients are based, the hypothesis to be tested is $H_0: \Gamma_I^* = \Gamma_{II}^*$ against the alternate, $\Gamma_I^* \neq \Gamma_{II}^*$.

## Forming the test statistic

Three regression equations can be estimated and the corresponding sum of squares of residuals calculated. A four-step process is suggested:

1. Consider $H_0$ true, combine the data, and estimate coefficients $\Gamma^*$, $\Delta_I$, and $\Delta_{II}$ by the regression

$$\begin{pmatrix} Y_I \\ Y_{II} \end{pmatrix} = \Gamma^*\begin{pmatrix} X_I \\ X_{II} \end{pmatrix} + \Delta_I\begin{pmatrix} Z_I \\ O_{II} \end{pmatrix} + \Delta_{II}\begin{pmatrix} O_I \\ Z_{II} \end{pmatrix} + \begin{pmatrix} \varepsilon_I \\ \varepsilon_{II} \end{pmatrix},$$

where $O_I$ and $O_{II}$ are null matrices of sizes $[T_I \times (K - m)]$ and $[T_{II} \times (K - m)]$ respectively. Calculate the residual sum of squares, $Q^*$ with $T_I + T_{II} - m - 2(K - m) = (T_I + T_{II} - 2K + m)$ degrees of freedom.

||||||||||||||||||||||||||||||||||||||||||||||||||||||||||||||||||||||||||||||||||||||||||||||||||||||||||||||||||||||||||||||||||||||||||

*Explicative note.* The number of observations in the pooled dataset is $T_I + T_{II}$. The number of coefficients being estimated is $m$ applying over both datasets, ($\Gamma^*$), plus $K - m$ for dataset I, ($\Delta_I$), plus another $K - m$ for dataset II, ($\Delta_{II}$). This allows the coefficients of the variables $Z$ to be different for the two datasets while restricting the coefficients of the variables $X$ to be equal.

||||||||||||||||||||||||||||||||||||||||||||||||||||||||||||||||||||||||||||||||||||||||||||||||||||||||||||||||||||||||||||||||||||||||||

2. Consider $\Gamma_I^* \neq \Gamma_{II}^*$, do two regressions based on datasets I and II separately, and then add together the two resulting sum of squares of residuals to obtain $Q_1^*$ with $T_I + T_{II} - 2K$ degrees of freedom.

||||||||||||||||||||||||||||||||||||||||||||||||||||||||||||||||||||||||||||||||||||||||||||||||||||||||||||||||||||||||||||||||||||||||||

*Discursive note.* Alternately, one regression equation may be computed for the model,

$$\begin{pmatrix} Y_I \\ Y_{II} \end{pmatrix} = \Gamma_I^*\begin{pmatrix} X_I \\ O_{II}^* \end{pmatrix} + \Gamma_{II}^*\begin{pmatrix} O_I^* \\ X_{II} \end{pmatrix} + \Delta_I\begin{pmatrix} Z_I \\ O_{II} \end{pmatrix} + \Delta_{II}\begin{pmatrix} O_I \\ Z_{II} \end{pmatrix} + \begin{pmatrix} \varepsilon_I \\ \varepsilon_{II} \end{pmatrix}$$

whose residual sum of squares gives $Q_1^*$ directly.

The null matrices $O_I^*$ and $O_{II}^*$ have dimension $(T_I \times m)$ and $(T_{II} \times m)$ respectively. The number of coefficients estimated is $m$, ($\Gamma_I^*$), plus $m$, ($\Gamma_{II}^*$), plus $K - m$, ($\Delta_I$), plus $K - m$, ($\Delta_{II}$), which totals $2K$.

||||||||||||||||||||||||||||||||||||||||||||||||||||||||||||||||||||||||||||||||||||||||||||||||||||||||||||||||||||||||||||||||||||||||||

3. Find the quadratic form $Q_2^* = Q^* - Q_1^*$ which represents the sum of squares due to the difference between the coefficients $\Gamma_I^*$ and $\Gamma_{II}^*$. $Q_2^*$ has degrees of freedom $(T_I + T_{II} - 2K + m) - (T_I + T_{II} - 2K) = m$.

4. Form an $F$-distributed statistic as the ratio

$$F_{(m,\, T_I + T_{II} - 2K)} = \frac{Q_2^*/m}{Q_1^*/(T_I + T_{II} - 2K)}. \tag{11-11}$$

If the calculated $F$-value exceeds the critical value for the test, then one concludes that the coefficients for the subset of $m < K$ variables are not equal in the two regressions of the same model based on the two different sample datasets.

## 11.11  SUMMARY

The analysis and testing of a specified econometric model often involves more than merely recognizing which coefficients are largest and whether the multiple coefficient of correlation is sufficiently large. In this chapter, some of the frequently useable testing procedures are formalized and applied to example situations. The headings of the sections indicate the nature of the test discussed within each section. The formulas (11–1) to (11–11) present the basic test statistics. The broad applicability of analysis of variance tests and similarly developed $F$ ratios is emphasized.

It is not unlikely that the reader may sometime find a need to develop or to search for some other closely related statistic to test some theoretical hypothesis. It is hoped that the information in this chapter can serve as a framework so that the reader will recognize the type of test he needs and the basic pattern which may underlie its derivation.

The examples in the chapter and the following exercises provide many ideas of the types and purposes of models that could be developed. It is hoped that further consideration and analysis of them by the reader may encourage him to search recent economic literature to learn more about the type of econometric model most interesting to him. Indeed, it is certainly not inappropriate to try and formulate your own explanatory economic linear model, to collect some data, and to test your theoretical suppositions about the model.

The next chapter presents a statistical method frequently used (and misused) to aid researchers in selecting the proper predetermined variables to include in a model. However, the basic ingredient for specifying one's own model is a theoretical motivation. A deeper understanding of the theoretical relations also is most useful in interpreting the results and in considering the validity of the assumptions underlying the least squares estimation procedure and these testing procedures. The last three chapters on the general single equation model (Chapters 13, 14, and 15) highlight this latter consideration.


## NEW VOCABULARY

Joint elliptical confidence region
Restricted model
Mean square added
Chow test


## EXERCISES

The results for the examples within this chapter and other excerpts of computer output for models described in the following problems could be used for many different tests. Although only one or two tests may be suggested in the problem, the reader may wish to use the numerical results to practice some of the other tests also.

1. Do an ANOVA test using $\alpha = 0.05$ on the significance of the explanatory role of variable $X_2 = ER$ for the model and data of Section 11.3. Compare the result to a one-sided $t$-test using $\alpha = 0.025$ on the coefficient $\gamma_2$ as in Section 11.5. Explain any relation between the tests, their critical regions, and the calculated values of the test statistics.

2. Test the significance of each coefficient and of the linear relation posed in Section 11.6 using the results in Table 11–3.

3. Using Table 11–3, test at the 0.10 level the joint hypothesis, $\gamma_2 = -0.7$ *and* $\gamma_3 = 1.0$. Explain how your result is consistent with the fact that each of these hypothesized values lies within a 90 percent confidence interval for the corresponding parameter based on these same results in Table 11–3.

4. Trace the role of the assumption of normality (Assumption 2, Section 10.3) for the disturbance term, $\varepsilon_t$, in developing the test statistics in Sections 11.5 to 11.10.

5. Specify the role, if any, of the assumption of independence between $X$ and $\varepsilon$ (Assumption 1, Section 10.3) in the development and validity of use of the tests described in Sections 11.3 to 11.7.

6. Test the significance of the individual coefficients and of the linear model given in Section 11.8 using the results in Table 11–7.

7. Using formula (11–8) and the results of Table 11–7 in Section 11.8, find the 95 percent confidence interval on the expected forecast of consumption per capita based on the new observation vector, $(X_{j2}, X_{j3}, X_{j4}) = (1500, 1400, 2000)$.

8. Test the significance of each of the coefficients in the model of Section 11.10, $Y = X\Gamma + \varepsilon$ with $K = 5$. Use the 0.05 level of significance and the following results. Suggest a new formulation by dropping out the two most insignificant variables. Test the joint significance in the original model of the variables which you find should be dropped. (Use the results for dataset I in Table 11–10 as necessary.)

**Results of complete corporate investment model dataset I**

Dependent variable $Y$      Investment      $\bar{Y} = 4.74378$
Multiple $R$      0.8247      $s_Y = 1.8279$
Std. error of est.   1.2424

| Analysis of variance | d.f. | Sum of squares | Mean square |
|---|---|---|---|
| Regression | 4 | 29.544 | 7.386 |
| Residual | 9 | 13.892 | 1.544 |

| Variable | | Coefficient | Std. error | F |
|---|---|---|---|---|
| | | *Variables in equation* | | |
| (Constant) | | 0.07822 | | |
| Profit | $X2$ | 0.50816 | 0.43637 | 1.3561 |
| Sales | $X3$ | 0.15669 | 0.07763 | 4.0737 |
| Deprec | $X4$ | -0.03256 | 0.43836 | 0.0055 |
| $I$-rate | $X5$ | 0.08544 | 0.44647 | 0.0366 |

9. For the following results:
   a) What are the values of $K$ and $T$ for this model estimation? Ans.: $K = 3$, $T = 14$ from the degrees of freedom.
   b) What is the value and meaning of $R^2$ and $\bar{R}^2$? Ans.: $R^2 = 0.4186$,
   $$\bar{R}^2 = 1 - \frac{s_e^2}{s_Y^2} = 1 - \frac{42.219}{61.450} = 0.313 \text{ or } \bar{R}^2 = 1 - (1 - R^2)\tfrac{13}{11} = 0.313.$$
   c) Test at $\alpha = 0.05$, the significance of $R$.
   d) Set a 95 percent confidence interval on $\sigma_\varepsilon^2 = V(\varepsilon)$.

| Multiple $R$ | 0.6470 |
|---|---|
| Std. error of estimate | 6.4976 |

| Analysis of variance | d.f. | SS | Mean square |
|---|---|---|---|
| Regression | 2 | 334.448 | 167.224 |
| Residual | 11 | 464.408 | 42.219 |

10. Do an analysis of the following results for the unrestricted corporate earnings model of Section 11.9 based on nine observations for American Chain Co. Explain what tests you are using and their purpose, and give an interpretation of the test results.

| Variable | Mean | Standard deviation |
|---|---|---|
| $Y1$ | 4.0389 | 1.1385 |
| $X2$ | 3.7811 | 1.1436 |
| $X3$ | 0.1144 | 0.0646 |
| $X4$ | 0.2344 | 0.1591 |
| $X5$ | 1.0556 | 0.1048 |
| $X6$ | 0.0478 | 0.0211 |

| | |
|---|---|
| Multiple $R$ | 0.93390 |
| $R$ square | 0.87217 |
| Standard error | 0.66470 |

*Variables in the equation*

| Variable | C | Standard error |
|---|---|---|
| $X6$ | −106.71239 | 129.46936 |
| $X2$ | 5.43353 | 2.98723 |
| $X3$ | − 12.39312 | 27.20047 |
| $X4$ | − 13.61637 | 19.19730 |
| $X5$ | − 0.81814 | 3.82301 |
| (Constant) | − 5.93320 | |

| Analysis of variance | d.f. | Sum of squares | Mean square |
|---|---|---|---|
| Regression | 5 | 9.04400 | 1.80880 |
| Residual | 3 | 1.32549 | 0.44183 |

11. An economist interested in human resources and public finance may formulate a model relating $Y$, per capita expenditures by state and local governments on education, as a function of $X_2$ and $X_3$, per capita annual income in the state and the state's population density in persons per square mile, respectively.

Income, in this case, reflects ability to pay for education; and population density reflects tastes to some extent. Data are obtained from the *Statistical Abstract of the United States*. Results are given below:

| Multiple $R$ | 0.70287 |
|---|---|
| $R$ square | 0.49403 |
| Standard error | 27.37663 |

*Variables in the equation*

| Variable | | $C$ | Standard error $C$ |
|---|---|---|---|
| Avinc | $X2$ | 0.05263 | 0.00821 |
| Popden | $X3$ | −0.10437 | 0.02087 |
| (Constant) | | −0.82996 | |

| Variable | | Mean | Standard deviation |
|---|---|---|---|
| Edexp | $Y$ | 152.7118 | 37.6935 |
| Popden | $X3$ | 141.1260 | 213.5147 |
| Avinc | $X2$ | 3197.3400 | 542.5552 |

*Simple correlation matrix*

| | Edexp | Avinc | Popden |
|---|---|---|---|
| Edexp | 1.00 | 0.47414 | −0.22810 |
| Avinc | | 1.00 | 0.47933 |
| Popden | | | 1.00 |

Source: Class, 1970 (Kushman).

*a)* Interpret the meaning of $\gamma_2$ and $\gamma_3$ in the model $Y = X\Gamma + \varepsilon$ and postulate an economic argument for your hypothesized signs of $\gamma_2$ and $\gamma_3$.

*b)* Find a 90 percent confidence interval on $V(\varepsilon)$.

*c)* Test the significance of the linear model at $\alpha = 0.05$ by using an ANOVA table.

*d)* Test the hypothesized significance and sign of the individual coefficients $\gamma_2$ and $\gamma_3$ using $\alpha = 0.025$.

*e)* Suppose a simple regression of $Y$ on only $X_2$ gives $R = 0.47414$. Set up an ANOVA test as in Section 11.7 to test the significance of the effect of the variable $X_3$ in the model. Use $\alpha = 0.05$ and compare your results to that of part (*c*).

*f)* Find $(X'X)$ and $(X'X)^{-1}$.

*g)* Test the joint hypothesis, $\gamma_2 > 0.02$ *and* $\gamma_3 < 0.05$.

*h)* Set a 95 percent confidence interval on the value of the intercept. [Refer to formula (10–5) and substitute the best estimate of $\sigma_\varepsilon^2$.]

*i)* Suppose values for the exogenous variable can be estimated for a state in the following year. The new values are $(X_{J2}, X_{J3}) = (3400, 130)$. Find a 90 percent confidence interval on the expected forecast of $Y_J$.

12. Consider a model as in Section 11.6 to explain net migration; however, suppose a more thorough model is specified using six predetermined variables. This expanded model is used on two sets of data, one for white migration and the other on nonwhite migration for 25 SMSA's. Test if there is a significant difference in the coefficients between the white and nonwhite migration models based on the following results. Use the 0.01 significance level.

| Dataset | Analysis of variance | d.f. | Sum of squares |
|---|---|---|---|
| White migration data | Regression | 6 | 847.043 |
| | Residual | 17 | 239.848 |
| Nonwhite migration data | Regression | 6 | 11,157.773 |
| | Residual | 17 | 1,252.435 |
| Pooled data | Regression | 6 | 4,570.312 |
| | Residual | 41 | 10,266.379 |

13. Another model relating economic variables is estimated for two time periods, the first using 19 quarterly observations from the second quarter 1947, through the fourth quarter 1951, and the other using 21 quarterly observations from the first quarter 1965 through the first quarter 1970. Test if the coefficients in the model are similar based on the data for the two different periods. Use $\alpha = 0.05$ and the results below.

| Dataset | Analysis of variance | d.f. | Sum of squares |
|---|---|---|---|
| 2, 1947 − 4, 1951 | Regression | 2 | 17.15234 |
| | Residual | 16 | 6.23926 |
| 1, 1965 − 1, 1970 | Regression | 2 | 3.43043 |
| | Residual | 18 | 0.81530 |
| Pooled data | Regression | 2 | 16.07889 |
| | Residual | 37 | 5.12085 |

14. A model is specified as $Y = \gamma_1 + \gamma_2 X_2 + \gamma_3 X_3 + \varepsilon$ and estimated for 40 observations to test the following propositions:

   a)  The linear fit is significant at the 0.05 level;
   b)  Each coefficient is significant and positive at the 0.10 level;
   c)  $0 < \gamma_1 < 1$ with at least 95 percent confidence; and
   d)  $\gamma_2 < \gamma_3$ with 90 percent confidence.

   Set up the appropriate null and alternate hypothesis and make tests for each of the above propositions using the following results:

$$(X'X) = \begin{pmatrix} 21.19974 & 18.68280 \\ 18.68280 & 21.74985 \end{pmatrix} \quad \begin{aligned} Y'Y &= 28.58392 \\ R^2 &= 0.6101 \\ s_e &= 0.5488 \end{aligned}$$

| Variable | Mean | Std. deviation | C |
|---|---|---|---|
| Y | 1.0125 | 0.85611 | |
| $X_2$ | 0.8725 | 0.73728 | 0.11377 |
| $X_3$ | 0.8025 | 0.74679 | 0.79601 |

Ans.: (a) $F = 28.9522$; (b) $t(\gamma_2) = 0.47054$, $t(\gamma_3) = 3.3451$.

15. For the model and results in Exercise 1, Chapter 9, test the null hypothesis, $H_0: \gamma_2 + \gamma_3 < 1.0$ using $\alpha = 0.10$.

16. For the model and results in Exercise 2, Chapter 9, find the standard errors of the estimates and test the significance of each coefficient.

17. Make a thorough analysis of the model and results of Exercise 5, Chapter 9. Specify the hypothesis being tested and interpret your test results.

18. Return to Exercise 6, Chapter 9, and expand on your answer there to part (b) in light of confidence intervals for the coefficients and for $\sigma_\varepsilon^2$.

19. Consider a model relating price of pork chops, $Y$ to pounds consumed per capita of various meat substitutes, namely $X_2$ for beef and veal, $X_3$ for all pork excluding lard, $X_4$ for lamb and mutton, and $X_5$ for chicken and turkey (ready to cook). Data are obtained from *Historical Statistics of the U.S., Colonial Times to 1957*, pp. 128, 186, 187, for years 1909 to 1957.

Two models are specified as follows:

Model I,    $Y = X\Gamma + \varepsilon$ with $K = 5$ as described above.
Model II,    Like Model I but $\gamma_2$ and $\gamma_3$ restricted to be zero.

The following results are obtained:

**Model I**

| Multiple $R$ | 0.94993 |
|---|---|
| $R$ square | 0.90236 |
| Standard error | 6.99813 |

*Variables in the equation*

| Variable | | $C$ | Std. error $C$ |
|---|---|---|---|
| Beef | $X_2$ | $-0.11471$ | 0.13875 |
| Q pork | $X_3$ | $-0.68940$ | 0.19313 |
| Lamb | $X_4$ | $-9.37097$ | 1.05305 |
| Chicken | $X_5$ | 2.83124 | 0.26557 |
| (Constant) | | 99.22665 | |

**Model II**

| Multiple $R$ | 0.93455 |
|---|---|
| $R$ square | 0.87339 |
| Standard error | 7.79379 |

*Variables in the equation*

| Variable | | $C$ | Std. error $C$ |
|---|---|---|---|
| Lamb | $X_4$ | $-9.31193$ | 1.14371 |
| Chicken | $X_5$ | 2.54510 | 0.24163 |
| (Constant) | | 50.22894 | |

| Analysis of variance | d.f. | Sum of squares |
|---|---|---|
| Regression | 2 | 19,275.46458 |
| Residual | 46 | 2,794.18282 |

Source: Class, 1971 (Gottfried).

a) Compare the adjusted $\bar{R}^2$ for the two models.

b) Test the joint significance of all coefficients in Model I, and similarly, in Model II.

c) Test the added significance of including variables $X_2$ and $X_3$ in Model I with nonzero coefficients.

d) Give a general interpretation of your results to suggest which model you prefer and why.

e) Suggest a better model for describing the changes in annual average pork chop prices from 1909–57. (Consider changes in income, tastes, and supply conditions.)

20. A monetary economist is interested in a model for the demand for cash balances by the manufacturing sector in order to test conflicting contentions about the sales and interest elasticity of this function.

The model to be estimated on the basis of quarterly data from 1955 second quarter, to 1969 second quarter, is derived from an inventory model and expressed as $Y = \gamma_1 X_2{}^{\gamma_2} X_3{}^{\gamma_3} \varepsilon$ where ln $\varepsilon$ satisfies the assumptions related to the disturbance term given in Section 10.3, and

$Y = $ cash holdings at the end of period $t$,
$X_2 = $ sales during period $t$, and
$X_3 = $ the 90-day government bill rate in period $t - 1$.

Although this model may not be as precise as desired, it has possibilities of importance if some empirical light can be shed on the conflict between economists such as Baumol, on the one hand, and Brunner and Meltzer, on the other hand, over the existence of large economies of scale in the holding of cash balances. For example, Baumol argues that firms' elasticity of demand for cash balances with respect to sales will be approximately one half—large economies of scale will exist. Brunner and Meltzer, however, argue that the elasticity with respect to sales will be approximately unity—no economies of scale will exist. Using data from the *Federal Reserve Bulletin* and the *FTC-SEC Quarterly Financial Report* and linearizing the model by the transformations $Y^* = \ln Y$, $X_2{}^* = \ln X_2$, and $X_3{}^* = \ln X_3$ to get $Y^* = \ln \gamma_1 + \gamma_2 X_2{}^* + \gamma_3 X_3{}^* + \ln \varepsilon$, these contentions might be tested.

In this model $\gamma_2$ represents a constant sales elasticity of cash balances and $\gamma_3$ represents a constant interest elasticity of cash balances. Theory suggests that $\gamma_2 > 0$ and $\gamma_3 < 0$. The two conflicting views above are represented by the hypotheses $\gamma_2 = 1/2$ or $\gamma_2 = 1$. Make the appropriate analysis of the following results to judge the usefulness of the model and to test these hypotheses.

Multiple $R = 0.93580$
$s_e \qquad = 0.06234$

| Variable | C | Std. error C |
|---|---|---|
| ln $X_2$ | 0.66678 | 0.05048 |
| ln $X_3$ | −0.05451 | 0.03476 |
| (Constant) | 1.35499 | |

| Analysis of variance | d.f. | Sum of squares |
|---|---|---|
| Regression | 2 | 1.47882 |
| Residual | 54 | 0.20987 |

21. As an individual or group project, readers might formulate, estimate, and test a model of their own choosing. The following steps may serve as a guideline:

    a) Specify some interesting economic relation in terms of the single equation econometric model,

    b) Discuss the economic meaning of the coefficients and postulate some theoretical hypotheses to be tested,

    c) Gather some relevant data and use OLS to estimate the model,

    d) Make the appropriate tests to examine the fit of your model and to test your hypotheses set out in part (b) above on the basis of your sample data.

# STEPWISE REGRESSION, DUMMY VARIABLES, AND DISTRIBUTED LAGS

## 12.1 PREVIEW

An obvious dilemma for any econometrician wishing to make tests on economic propositions using sample observations is to specify the best model which embodies those economic propositions. Since the pure theoretical variables may not have exact corresponding measures in terms of the data, there is often some inevitable and arbitrary picking and choosing from among available and related predetermined variables.

When the variables are not presumed to be quantitative and continuous but are qualitative or classified into discrete categories, then they may be represented in the model by so-called *dummy variables*. These may be used in the formulation of the model to distinguish between different time intervals, different regions, different age cohorts, or different sexes to list a few of the many possibilities. Such distinctions help the model builder to break down heterogeneous datasets into more homogeneous subgroupings. It enables him to specify a better model for the distinct classifications and to estimate the marginal differences among the classes with respect to their effect on the endogenous variables.

When the model builder has alternative measures available which may serve as proxies for a particular theoretical variable or when he has many theoretically feasible variables which could be used as predetermined variables, he may use stepwise regression methods to detect which subgroup of variables is most significant. This procedure is sometimes used to reduce the time and expense of considering all possible models involving various combinations of the feasible predetermined variable set. The best way of reducing the alternatives to a meaningful model is by wise theoretical judgment. However, in many exploratory studies and in research on new economic problems where the theory is not too fully developed, the researcher, after first attempting to formulate the theory, may use this statistical method of stepwise regression to refine his model and to suggest revisions of the theoretical relations.

Finally, in models oased on time-series observations, the econometrician sometimes desires to let the value of an exogenous variable affect not only the contemporaneous value of the endogenous variable but also have a continuing (perhaps declining) effect on future period values of the endogenous variable. This concept is equivalent to specifying a current endogenous variable as a function of current and past (or lagged) values of the exogenous variable. Since an infinite number of such functions are possible, using different finite lagged periods and different weighting schemes for their partial effects, some common practices are presented as another hint for building models.

Thus, in this chapter, we examine three separate topics. Their only connection is that each may sometimes be useful to know in helping the reader to formulate his own model or to be critical in examining the models and presentations of others. The exercises at the end of the chapter suggest that the reader critically examine the application of these methods to various example models used here and in earlier chapters.

## 12.2 REVIEW

Another method of solving systems of equations is the Gaussian reduction procedure using elementary row transformations to reduce the coefficient matrix to an identity matrix. An explanation of these terms and the procedure follows.

### 1 Elementary row transformations

Three types of elementary row transformations are defined.

*a)*    Two rows of a matrix can be interchanged. The transformation is denoted by $(R_{ij})$ where rows $i$ and $j$ are interchanged.

*b)*    One row of the matrix can be multiplied by a scalar. The transformation is denoted by $(kR_i)$ where row $i$ is multiplied by the scalar $k$.

*c)*    A scalar multiple of one row may be added to another row. The transformation is denoted by $(kR_{i,j})$ where row $i$ is multiplied by $k$ and added to row $j$. In this transformation, row $j$ is changed while row $i$ remains the same.

### 2 Equivalent systems of equations

Two systems of equations are equivalent if any solution of one system is also a solution of the other. An important result of linear algebra is the statement that two matrices are equivalent if one is obtained from the other using elementary row transformations.

Suppose two systems of equations are written $AW = P$ and $BZ = Q$ where $A$ and $B$ are coefficient matrices of size $(m \times n)$, $P$ and $Q$ are $(m \times 1)$ vectors of real numbers, and $W$ and $Z$ are $(n \times 1)$ vectors of unknowns. Specify the augmented matrix for the system of equations as the matrix of size $[m \times (n + 1)]$ obtained by writing the right-hand vector as an extra column of the coefficient matrix. Thus $(A \quad P)$ and $(B \quad Q)$ are augmented matrices, not matrix products.

A further result of linear algebra reveals that equation systems are equivalent if their augmented matrices are equivalent. That is, if $(B \quad Q)$ can be obtained from $(A \quad P)$ by applying row transformations, then any solution $W^*$ for $AW^* = P$, is also a solution for $BW^* = Q$.[1]

Consequently, it often becomes advantageous to transform the augmented matrix of a system of equations into another augmented matrix for an

---

[1] See a linear algebra text, for example, Robert R. Stall, *Linear Algebra and Matrix Theory* (New York: McGraw-Hill Book Co., 1952), chap. 1.

equivalent system of equations. Any one or more or combinations of elementary row transformations can be used. This process is advantageous if the solution for the transformed system of equations is obvious, or at least much easier to determine, than the solution for the original system.

## 3 Premultiplication by elementary matrices

Applying a row transformation to a matrix gives the same result as premultiplying the matrix by an appropriate transformation matrix. For example, suppose the matrix $\begin{pmatrix} a & b \\ c & d \end{pmatrix}$ is transformed by interchanging the first and second rows to obtain $\begin{pmatrix} c & d \\ a & b \end{pmatrix}$. The same result occurs as the product matrix of $\begin{pmatrix} 0 & 1 \\ 1 & 0 \end{pmatrix}\begin{pmatrix} a & b \\ c & d \end{pmatrix} = \begin{pmatrix} c & d \\ a & b \end{pmatrix}$. Or suppose, the matrix $\begin{pmatrix} a & b \\ c & d \end{pmatrix}$ is transformed by adding three times the first row to the second to obtain $\begin{pmatrix} a & b \\ c + 3a & d + 3b \end{pmatrix}$. The same result occurs as the product matrix of

$$\begin{pmatrix} 1 & 0 \\ 3 & 1 \end{pmatrix}\begin{pmatrix} a & b \\ c & d \end{pmatrix} = \begin{pmatrix} a & b \\ 3a + c & 3b + d \end{pmatrix}.$$

||!|||||||||||||||||||||||||||||||||||||||||||||||||||||||||||||||||||||||||||||||||||||||||||||||||||||||||||||||||||||||||||||||||||||||||||||||||

*Explicative note.* The appropriate premultiplier matrix is called an elementary matrix, $E$, and is obtained by applying the desired row transformation to the identity matrix. Thus, to interchange rows 1 and 2, you use the matrix obtained by interchanging rows 1 and 2 of the identity matrix, $\begin{pmatrix} 1 & 0 \\ 0 & 1 \end{pmatrix} \xrightarrow{R_{12}} \begin{pmatrix} 0 & 1 \\ 1 & 0 \end{pmatrix}$. Or, in the second case above, the matrix $\begin{pmatrix} 1 & 0 \\ 3 & 1 \end{pmatrix}$ is obtained from $\begin{pmatrix} 1 & 0 \\ 0 & 1 \end{pmatrix}$ by adding three times the first row to the second.

|||||||||||||||||||||||||||||||||||||||||||||||||||||||||||||||||||||||||||||||||||||||||||||||||||||||||||||||||||||||||||||||||||||||||||||||||||

Successive elementary row transformations can also be represented by successive premultiplications by elementary matrices, $E_s, \ldots, E_3, E_2, E_1$, obtained by applying each of the desired row transformations to the identity matrix.

A specially useful succession of such transformations for a square matrix are those which transform the original matrix into an identity matrix. The result is the same as if the original matrix were premultiplied by its inverse matrix. That is, transforming a matrix $\underset{(n \times n)}{A}$ into a matrix $\underset{(n \times n)}{I}$ can be done using row transformations or by a sequence of premultiplications by $(n \times n)$ elementary matrices which is the same as premultiplying $A$ by its inverse.

$$(E_s \cdot E_{s-1} \cdot \ldots \cdot E_3 \cdot E_2 \cdot E_1)A = A^{-1}A = \underset{(n \times n)}{I}.$$

Applying these same transformations to any other vector or any other matrix is the same as premultiplying that vector or matrix by the inverse of $A$ also. In particular, if the same transformations are applied to an identity matrix, the result is the inverse matrix, $A^{-1}$.

## 4 The Gaussian reduction method

This concept can now be applied to obtain a solution to a system of equations,

$$\underset{(n \times n)}{A} \quad \underset{(n \times 1)}{X} = \underset{(n \times 1)}{P} .$$

A solution for $X$, denoted by $X^*$, is obtained by forming the augmented matrix $(A \quad P)$ and applying row transformations which reduce the leftmost $(n \times n)$ section of the matrix to the identity matrix $I$. At the same time, these transformations are applied to the rightmost column $P$ since the row transformation is performed on all $n + 1$ elements in the row. The result of the transformation $(A \quad P) \to (I \quad X^*)$ is the same as premultiplying $P$ by the inverse $A^{-1}$ to obtain $A^{-1}P = X^*$.

As an example, let's apply this procedure of Gaussian reduction to the normal equations for the simple model as given in (3–1). The equation system has two equations and two unknowns.

$$\begin{pmatrix} T & \sum X_{t2} \\ \sum X_{t2} & \sum X_{t2}^2 \end{pmatrix} \begin{pmatrix} a_1 \\ a_2 \end{pmatrix} = \begin{pmatrix} \sum Y_t \\ \sum X_{t2} Y_t \end{pmatrix} .$$

The augmented matrix is

$$\begin{pmatrix} T & \sum X_{t2} & \sum Y_t \\ \sum X_{t2} & \sum X_{t2}^2 & \sum X_{t2} Y_t \end{pmatrix} .$$

We desire to reduce the two left columns to a $(2 \times 2)$ identity matrix by application of row transformations. A systematic reduction procedure is to transform the element in position $(1, 1)$ to unity and then clear other elements in column one to zero. Then, transform the element in the next main diagonal position, $(2, 2)$, to unity and clear all other elements in column 2 to zero. Next, the process would continue for element in position $(3, 3)$ and other elements in column 3, and so on, until finally, the element in position $(n, n)$ is changed to unity and all other elements in column $n$ are changed to zero. In this example, $n = 2$, so the procedure is repeated only twice.

The transformations and results at each step are given in the following tableau form:

**TABLEAU 12-1**

**Solution of the two normal equations by Gaussian reduction**

$$\begin{pmatrix} T & \sum X_{t2} & \sum Y_t \\ \sum X_{t2} & \sum X_{t2}^2 & \sum X_{t2} Y_t \end{pmatrix}$$

*Step 1:* $\dfrac{1}{T} R_1$ $\quad\Big|\quad$ $\left(\text{multiply row one by the scalar } \dfrac{1}{T}\right)$

$$\begin{pmatrix} 1 & \sum X_{t2}/T & \sum Y_t/T \\ \sum X_{t2} & \sum X_{t2}^2 & \sum X_{t2} Y_t \end{pmatrix}$$

*Step 2:* $\left(\sum X_{t2}\right) R_{1,2}$ (add to row 2, a scalar multiple of row one
$\quad\quad$ using the scalar $\left(-\sum X_{t2}\right)$

$$\begin{pmatrix} 1 & \sum X_{t2}/T & \sum Y_t/T \\ 0 & \sum X_{t2}^2 - \dfrac{(\sum X)^2}{T} & \sum X_{t2}Y - \dfrac{\sum X_{t2} \sum Y_t}{T} \end{pmatrix}$$

*Step 3:* $\left(\dfrac{1}{\sum x_{t2}^2}\right) R_2$ (multiply row two by the scalar $\left(\dfrac{1}{\sum x_{t2}^2}\right)$,
$\quad\quad$ and simplify the expressions by using the
$\quad\quad$ notation for means and simple moments.

$$\begin{pmatrix} 1 & \bar{X}_2 & \bar{Y} \\ 0 & 1 & \sum x_{t2} y_t / \sum x_{t2}^2 \end{pmatrix}$$

*Step 4:* $\left(-\bar{X}_2\right) R_{2,1}$ (add to row one, a scalar multiple of row two
$\quad\quad$ using the scalar, $-\bar{X}_2$)

$$\begin{pmatrix} 1 & 0 & \bar{Y} - \left(\sum x_{t2} y_t / \sum x_{t2}^2\right)\bar{X}_2 \\ 0 & 1 & \sum x_{t2} y_t / \sum x_{t2}^2 \end{pmatrix}.$$

The process is completed, and the result is the same as if we had used a matrix inverse for premultiplication. The original normal equations have been transformed into an equivalent system given as,

$$\begin{pmatrix} 1 & 0 \\ 0 & 1 \end{pmatrix}\begin{pmatrix} a_1 \\ a_2 \end{pmatrix} = \begin{pmatrix} \bar{Y} - a_2 \bar{X} \\ \dfrac{\sum x_{t2} y_t}{\sum x_{t2}^2}, \end{pmatrix}$$

in which the solution is obvious and identical to that obtained for the least squares estimates using a matrix inverse procedure. [See (3–2) and Exercise 4, Chapter 9.]

## REVIEW EXERCISES

R.1.  Do the Gaussian reduction on the normal equations for the extended model as given in (8–1).

R.2.  Use row transformations to reduce the matrix

$$A = \begin{pmatrix} 1 & 2 & 4 \\ 2 & 3 & 2 \\ 1 & 5 & 2 \end{pmatrix} \text{ to an identity matrix, } \underset{(3 \times 3)}{I}.$$

R.3.  Apply the same sequence of row transformations as used in R.2 above this time beginning with the identity matrix, $\underset{(3 \times 3)}{I}$ . Show that the resulting matrix is $A^{-1}$ (referring to $A$ in R.2).

R.4.  Find the set of elementary matrices which correspond to the sequence of row transformations used in R.2 and R.3. Use these as premultipliers of the matrix $\underset{(3 \times 6)}{(A \quad I)}$ to transform it into $(I \quad A^{-1})$.

R.5.  Try to use row transformations to reduce the matrix

$$B = \begin{pmatrix} 2 & 4 & 0 \\ 3 & -1 & 7 \\ 0 & 1 & -1 \end{pmatrix} \text{ to an identity matrix, } \underset{(3 \times 3)}{I}.$$

Explain the problem which results. (*Hint*: Consider the rank of the matrix $B$.)

## 12.3 STEPWISE REGRESSION

Given the model $Y = X\Gamma + \varepsilon$ to be estimated on the basis of sample observations, we have discussed the multiple calculation procedure in Chapter 9. This method includes all predetermined variables into the model as specified in a single step and uses the matrix inverse solution for the coefficient vector,

$$C = (X'X)^{-1}X'Y. \tag{9-3}$$

Stepwise regression differs in that it includes only one (or a subgroup of) predetermined variable(s) into the estimation at the first step. The selection of the first variable (or first subgroup of variables) to be included may be specified by the model builder. Theory or previous empirical research or both may require that this variable(s) be included in the specification. Alternately, the selection of the first entry may be made by the computer based on significance levels of the variables being considered. We return to this point shortly.

After the first step, another variable (or a subgroup of variables) may be included into the estimation in a second step. Following this is a third, fourth, fifth step, and so on as necessary until the procedure is stopped. The stopping point may be when all predetermined variables have been included or when all statistically *significant* predetermined variables have been included, or when a prescribed number of steps have been completed. Actual procedures of this type can and do vary, and the user of a stepwise regression program performed by a computer should be certain to read the respective program documentation to understand exactly how it operates and how the results may be interpreted.

## The forward stepwise method

Consider a specified model, $Y = \gamma_1 + \gamma_2 X_2 + \cdots + \gamma_K X_K + \varepsilon$ to be estimated in stepwise fashion presuming that no specific order of entry of the predetermined variables is dictated by the user. The forward procedure is computationally efficient in examining no more variables than necessary while providing that the fit of the model to the data, as measured by $R^2$, is improved at each step.[2]

|||||||||||||||||||||||||||||||||||||||||||||||||||||||||||||||||||||||||||||||||||||||||||||||||||||||||||||||||||||||||||||||||||||||||||||||||||||||||

*Recursive note.*   In later steps of such a process, it is often true that $\bar{R}^2$, the adjusted multiple coefficient of determination, does not increase but decreases.

|||||||||||||||||||||||||||||||||||||||||||||||||||||||||||||||||||||||||||||||||||||||||||||||||||||||||||||||||||||||||||||||||||||||||||||||||||||||||

The procedure for selection among the set, $X_2, X_3, \ldots, X_K$, can be outlined as follows:

*a*) From the simple correlations, $r_{Yk}$, $k = 2, 3, \ldots, K$, select the exogenous variable with the highest $r_{Yk}^2$. Without loss of generality, call it variable $X_K$.

*b*) Include $X_K$ as exogenous in a simple model and test its coefficient for significance using the $t$-test of Section 11.5. If significant, continue; if not, stop.

$a_2$) From the first order (partial) correlations, $r_{Yj \cdot K}$, $j = 2, 3, \ldots, K - 1$, select the variable with the highest correlation with $Y$ after accounting for the effect of the previously included variable, $X_K$. Call this variable $X_J = X_{K-1}$ without any loss of generality, just the proper reordering of the predetermined variables.

$b_2$) Include $X_J$ as exogenous in an extended model and test its explanatory contribution using the $t$-test of Section 11.5 on its coefficient or the $F$-test of Section 11.7 applied to a single added variable. If significant, continue; if not, stop.

$a_3$) From the second order (partial) correlations, $r_{Yi \cdot JK}$, $i = 2, 3, \ldots, K - 2$, select the variable with the highest correlation to $Y$ after accounting for the effect of the previously included variables, $X_K$ and $X_J, \ldots$, and continue on to step $(b_3)$, and on and on with steps $(a_4), (b_4), \ldots$. Stop when all $K - 1$ variables are included or there is no further significant variable to be added.

---

[2] The SPSS (Statistical Package for the Social Sciences) stepwise option in the *regression* program is an example of a forward procedure.

III

*Discursive note.*   As each variable is added, all the estimates of the coefficients will change, unless the variable has zero correlation with the variable(s) already included. In that case, there would be no interaction between these variables; and so, the previous coefficient estimate corresponding to that variable(s) would not change. This interpretation is directly related to the notion of misspecification bias to be discussed in the next topic.

IIIIIIIIIIIIIIIIIIIIIIIIIIIIIIIIIIIIIIIIIIIIIIIIIIIIIIIIIIIIIIIIIIIIIIIIIIIIIIIIIIIIIIIIIIIIIIIIIIIIIIIIIIIIIIIIIIIIIIIIIIIIIIIIIIIIIIIIIIIIIIIIIIIIIIIII

The major difficulty with the forward procedure is that it does not allow for the possibility of dropping out a previously included variable in a later step as its effect may become insignificant in the presence of the combination of the new variables included.

## The in-and-out stepwise method

This procedure does look at the individual significance of all included variables at each step, not just the significance of the most recently added variable. Moreover, any insignificant variable may be dropped out of the specification. This procedure is more efficient in finding the best-fitting combination of variables.[3]

Briefly, the procedure may be sketched in these steps:

*a)*   Select the variable with the highest $r_{Yk}^2$, and enter and test as in the forward procedure.

*b)*   Select the variable with the highest $r_{Yj \cdot K}^2$, and enter and test as in the forward procedure.

*c)*   Also test the significance of the inclusion of variable $X_K$ if it had entered after variable $X_J$. Allow it to drop if it is insignificant in this sense. It remains eligible to be included again at a later step in a different combination of predetermined variables.

*d)*   Select the next variable to enter as in the forward procedure. Test it and test each of the previously included variables as if each were the last to enter into this current combination. Among any insignificant ones, drop the one whose added contribution is the smallest. Continue on until a stopping rule applies.

## Some dangers in stepwise regressions

In either of these stepwise procedures, only one variable is added (or dropped) in a single step. Consequently, if the list of variables is long, the computation may be excessively lengthy and costly.

Also, the tests of significance used apply only to a single coefficient and its corresponding variable. The significance levels used are not joint significance levels. Furthermore, it may be argued that each step and corre-

---

[3] The stepwise regression program BMD03R (UCLA Biomedical Programs) is an example of this method.

sponding test uses a degree of freedom so that the resulting degrees of freedom for analysis of the final model are unclear.

## Beware of improper reasoning

Although these internal dangers of use of the stepwise method are important, a greater danger lies hidden in the interpretation and conclusions based on stepwise regressions. The first of these is the problem of letting the tail wag the dog. Since stepwise methods are useful in helping to select a " good " set of predetermined variables for a model, the danger is the problem of letting the statistical method substitute for sound theoretical reasoning. The user of such methods should remember that the results are based on a particular set of sample data which may reflect some strange and purely coincidental (spurious) correlations. One must not let his imagination take over to invent theory solely for the sake of being in agreement with these sample results.

Secondly, there is a real danger in considering many possible predetermined variables and arriving at the best-fitting combination of them to explain the endogenous variable. By trying to fit a given dataset too closely, variables may be included which coincidently help to explain an extra 0.5 percent of variation in $Y$ for that particular sample. However, their inclusion may increase multicollinearity in the model and reduce the accuracy of all the estimates. (See Chapter 15.)

## Specification errors

Also, abandoning theory may create a misspecification bias in the least squares estimators of the coefficients.[4] This bias is not a result of including variables in the model which really do not belong, but rather of excluding variables which should be retained in the model. Consider a simpler case of the two alternate models,

$$Y = \gamma_1 + \sum_{j=2}^{K-1} \gamma_j X_j + \varepsilon \quad \text{and} \quad Y = \gamma_1 + \sum_{k=2}^{K} \gamma_k X_k + \varepsilon.$$

The second model includes one more variable, $X_K$, in addition to an intercept and $K - 2$ other variables which are the same in both models. Suppose the second model is the true model but that the first model is specified and estimated. The least squares estimates $C_j$ of $\gamma_j$, $j = 2, 3, \ldots, K - 1$, reflect not only the explanatory effect of the respective variable $X_j$ on $Y$ but also they give $X_j$ some credit for the influence of $X_K$ on $Y$ (which should be included in the model and estimated by $C_K$). The extent to which a variable

---

[4] See A. S. Goldberger, "Stepwise Least Squares; Residual Analysis and Specification," *JASA*, Vol. 56 (1961), pp. 998–1000; and H. Theil, "Specification Errors and the Estimation of Economic Relationships," *Review of the International Institute of Statistics*, Vol. 25 (1957), pp. 41–51. The former really discusses stagewise regression where the residual of the first step is regressed on the second step variable(s). The bias effect of misspecification of included variables is still relevant. The latter considers misspecification of the form of the relation as well.

$X_j$ assumes this extra explanatory role depends on the strength of the correlation between $X_j$ and $X_K$.

The result is clear. The estimates $C_j$ are biased due to the misspecification of not including $X_K$ in the model, assuming that it is a relevant and significant variable. The opposite situation of the inclusion of more variables than should be specified in the true relation does not result in biased estimators. However, obtaining too good a fit to a socioeconomic relation based on one particular sample (region, time period, etc.) may result in a severe loss of applicability and clouding of the important basic relations across various other samples. One must be careful in social science research not to infer theoretical relations from coincidental fitting of part of the random noise or disturbance.

### Improper use of the data

Finally, the econometrician must always be careful not to base test conclusions on the same data that were used in a stepwise procedure to find the best-fitting model. Such reasoning would be obviously circular and is most easily explained by citing what *NOT TO DO*.

It would be *improper* to use a set of data and the stepwise procedure to "discover" a good fitting model with a high $R^2$ and significant coefficients for the variables, and then to use that same data to make tests of the model as in Chapter 11. It would be redundant to do an $F$-test on the significance of the relation or $t$-tests on the coefficients. It would also be circular to show that the model gives forecasts for $\hat{Y}$ close to the actual $Y$ observed since these were the same values used in determining the best associated or predicting variables.

If the researcher realizes that only one set of data is available, he must be honest in splitting it into at least two subsets (say by random selection of cases, or by excluding every third observation, or by separation into the first half and second half, etc.). These subsets must be clearly defined and not intentionally biased toward any particular hypothesis to be tested. Then, he may use one subset of data to develop his model and the other subset of data to test the model. In practice, a large subset is often used to develop a model while a few observations are held out to check its forecasting accuracy.

### 12.4 FINDING LEAST SQUARES ESTIMATES BY STEPWISE GAUSSIAN REDUCTION

One process of computing the least squares estimates in the general model was given in Chapter 9. It necessitated finding the inverse matrix of $(X'X)$ by finding the determinant and adjoint matrix of $(X'X)$. For models with many exogenous variables, this procedure is quite tedious and must be done on a computer.

However, an alternate approach exists which can be applied using only a desk calculator. It finds the inverse of $(X'X)$ by the Gaussian reduction method applying row transformations. The major reason for presenting this method is to obtain new insights about multiple regression results and to illustrate a stepwise method. The first step of the procedure gives the least squares estimates and the unexplained variation for the regression of the endogenous variable on only one exogenous variable (as in a simple bivariate model). Successive steps give the results for a model using two exogenous variables (as in the extended model), then three exogenous variables, and so on up to $K - 1$ exogenous variables. The final result is the same as the one jump procedure of Chapter 9.

The stepwise method also provides information at each step on the co-efficients in a regression of *each* variable not yet included at that step on *all* the other variables already included at that step. Such information can be very useful to the econometrician if he tries to revise and improve his model. It gives him some knowledge about which variables are most independent of each other and about which combinations of variables decrease the unexplained variation the most.

### The Gaussian transformation to find $C$

Consider a general linear model,

$$Y_t = \gamma_1 + \gamma_2 X_{t2} + \gamma_3 X_{t3} + \cdots + \gamma_K X_{tK} + \varepsilon_t.$$

The $(K - 1)$ normal equations for determining the estimates, $C_2, C_3, \ldots, C_K$ of the $K - 1$ coefficients of the exogenous variables are given as: $(X'X)C = X'Y$, where the matrix $X$ and vector $Y$ are the same as those defined in Section 9.3. They are in terms of deviations $x_{tk}$ and $y_t$.

Referring to the Review 12.2, the augmented matrix for this system of equations is $(X'X \quad X'Y)$ of size $[(K - 1) \times (K - 1 + 1)]$ or $[(K - 1) \times K]$. The leftmost $(K - 1)$ columns can be transformed into a $[(K - 1) \times (K - 1)]$ identity matrix by applying the appropriate sequence of row transformations. This is equivalent to premultiplying $(X'X)$ by its inverse $(X'X)^{-1}$ to obtain $(X'X)^{-1}(X'X) = I$. These same transformations can be applied simultaneously on the column $X'Y$ to give $(X'X)^{-1}(X'Y)$ which is the vector of least squares estimates $C$. Thus, the transformation is $(X'X \quad X'Y) \to (I \quad C)$.

Such a procedure is quite practical for finding the least squares estimates $C_2, \ldots, C_K$. However, with some small additions, even more satisfactory output can be obtained.

### Finding the residual sum of squares by Gaussian reduction

Suppose the matrix $(X'X \quad X'Y)$ is appended in two ways. First, add an extra row of the dispersions involving the endogenous variable in the model. The complete, symmetrical dispersion matrix for $Y$ and $X_2, X_3, \ldots, X_K$ is obtained; namely,

$$\begin{pmatrix} \underset{(K-1)\times(K-1)}{X'X} & \underset{[(K-1)\times 1]}{X'Y} \\ \underset{[1\times(K-1)]}{Y'X} & \underset{(1\times 1)}{Y'Y} \end{pmatrix}$$

which is size $(K \times K)$.

Suppose we also use row transformations of the third type (*Review* 12.2, item 1*c*) to add linear combinations of the first $(K - 1)$ rows to the bottom row in order to transform the row vector $Y'X$ into a zero vector. An equivalent representation of this transformation is obtained by multiplying the upper $(K - 1)$ rows by the $[1 \times (K - 1)]$ size matrix $[- Y'X(X'X)^{-1}]$ and adding the product matrix to the bottom row. The result of the transformation is

$$\begin{pmatrix} X'X & X'Y \\ Y'X & Y'Y \end{pmatrix} \xrightarrow{[- Y'X(X'X)^{-1}]R_{(1, 2, \ldots, K-1), K}}$$

$$\begin{pmatrix} X'X & X'Y \\ Y'X - Y'X(X'X)^{-1}X'X & Y'Y - Y'X(X'X)^{-1}X'Y \end{pmatrix}.$$

In the transformed matrix, the elements of the bottom row can be simplified. The first $(K - 1)$ elements are

$$Y' - X Y'X(X'X)^{-1}(X'X) = Y'X - Y'X(I) = O.$$

The final element is $Y'Y - Y'X[(X'X)^{-1}X'Y] = Y'Y - Y'XC = e'e.$   (9-5)

||||||||||||||||||||||||||||||||||||||||||||||||||||||||||||||||||||||||||||||||||||||||||||||||||||||||||||||||||||||||||

*Recursive note.* The least squares estimates $C$ are precisely $(X'X)^{-1}(X'Y)$, and the term $Y'XC$ is a $(1 \times 1)$ scalar, equal to its transpose $C'X'Y$, which gives the amount of variation in $Y$ that is explained by the variables $X_2, X_3, \ldots, X_K$. Therefore, the bottom right element in the transformed matrix is $Y'Y - Y'XC$, total variation less explained variation, which is equal to $e'e$, the unexplained variation.

||||||||||||||||||||||||||||||||||||||||||||||||||||||||||||||||||||||||||||||||||||||||||||||||||||||||||||||||||||||||||

The total transformation can be visualized as reducing $Y'X$ to $O$ by adding to it the proper linear combinations of the rows of $X'X$, and also reducing $X'X$ to $I$. Since these transformations are applied across the entire row, the total result is:

$$\begin{pmatrix} X'X & X'Y \\ Y'X & Y'Y \end{pmatrix} \rightarrow \begin{pmatrix} I & C \\ O & e'e \end{pmatrix}.$$

It is well worth the marginal effort to clear out one extra row to zero elements in order to obtain directly the amount of unexplained variation.

### Finding the intercept by Gaussian reduction

A second addition to the matrix which in no way changes any of the above results is the inclusion of an extra vector of the means of each variable. This new row vector is

$$(1, \bar{X}', \bar{Y}) = (1, \bar{X}_2, \bar{X}_3, \ldots, \bar{X}_K, \bar{Y}).$$

If this vector is added to the matrix as its first row and the unit vector of size $(K \times 1)$ is added as its first column, $(1, 0, 0, \ldots, 0)'$, then the starting matrix is size $[(K + 1) \times (K + 1)]$. The same interpretation for the transformations applies and now the overall matrix includes all variables $X_1, X_2, \ldots, X_K$, and $Y$, and the resulting vector of least squares estimates includes $C_1$ as well as $C_2, C_3, \ldots, C_K$.

The transformation is,

$$
\begin{pmatrix} 1 & \overline{X}' & \overline{Y} \\ O & X'X & X'Y \\ 0 & Y'X & Y'Y \end{pmatrix} \rightarrow \begin{pmatrix} 1 & O & C_1 \\ O & I & \underset{[(K-1)\times 1]}{C} \\ 0 & O & e'e \end{pmatrix}_{[(K+1)\times(K+1)]}
$$

## Finding $(X'X)^{-1}$ by Gaussian reduction

A final alteration to the reduction procedure is necessary if we eventually desire estimates of the variances and covariances of the least squares estimates in order to make tests of hypothesis and establish confidence or forecast intervals. For these purposes, $(X'X)^{-1}$ is essential. It can be easily obtained by performing on the identity matrix $I$, the same row transformations that we applied to the matrix $X'X$ in the reduction process. (See *Review* 12.2, item 3, and Exercise R.3.)

An easy way to do this is to augment the starting matrix by adding a $[(K - 1) \times (K - 1)]$ identity matrix on the right side with extra blank row vectors on the top and bottom to maintain the position only. Thus, the initial set up and transformation may be depicted as:

$$
\begin{pmatrix} 1 & \overline{X}' & \overline{Y} & — \\ O & X'X & X'Y & \underset{(K-1)\times(K-1)}{I} \\ 0 & Y'X & Y'Y & — \end{pmatrix}
$$

$$
\rightarrow \begin{pmatrix} 1 & O & C_1 & — \\ O & I & \underset{[(K-1)\times 1]}{C} & (X'X)^{-1} \\ 0 & O & e'e & — \end{pmatrix}_{[(K+1)\times 2K]}. \quad (12\text{–}1)
$$

The inverse matrix appears in the position shown.

## Other information given within the reduction process

As each column is transformed into a unit vector during the reduction process, one more variable is being included in the regression of $Y$ on $X_1$, $X_2, \ldots, X_K$. When the second column is reduced to $(0, 1, 0, 0, \ldots, 0)'$, then the $(K + 1)$ column contains the elements $(a_1, a_2, h_3, \ldots, h_K, e'e)'$, where the $h_i$ represents the number in the $i$th position and has no special meaning relative to the estimation. The $a_1, a_2$, and $e'e$ are the estimates and the unexplained variation for the estimating equation $\hat{Y}_t = a_1 + a_2 X_{t2}$. The columns

3, 4, ..., $K$, contain elements pertaining to the regression of each of the variables $X_3$, $X_4$, ..., $X_K$, on the variables $X_1$ and $X_2$. For example, column $i$, for some integer $3 \le i \le K$, has elements $(b_1, b_2, h_3, \ldots, h_{i-1}, v'v, h_{i+1}, \ldots, h_K, h_{K+1})'$ where $b_1$ and $b_2$ are least squares estimates and $v'v$ is the unexplained variation for the estimating equation $\hat{X}_{ti} = b_1 + b_2 X_{t2}$.

When the third column is reduced next to $(0, 0, 1, 0, \ldots, 0, 0)'$, then the $(K + 1)$ column contains the elements $(C_1, C_2, C_3, h_4, \ldots, h_K, e'e)$ for the estimating equation $\hat{Y}_t = C_1 + C_2 X_{t2} + C_3 X_{t3}$ with unexplained variation $e'e$. Each of the remaining columns, $i = 4, 5, \ldots, K$, contains elements $(d_1, d_2, d_3, h_4, \ldots, h_{i-1}, v'v, h_{i+1}, \ldots, h_K, h_{K+1})$ for the estimating equation $\hat{X}_{ti} = d_1 + d_2 X_{t2} + d_3 X_{t3}$ with unexplained variation $v'v$.

All these intermediate results do not demand any new theory or concepts. These various estimating equations can be visualized as estimations of submodels of the same type as the general model. The same concepts and procedures which apply to find the estimates of coefficients for $K$ exogenous variables can be used to find the solution for only three variables. Simply ignore rows and columns 4, 5, ..., $K$, and concentrate on 1, 2, 3, and $K + 1$. Alternately, the application for the submodels treating $X_i$ as the dependent variable and $X_1$, $X_2$, and $X_3$ as the independent variables ignores rows and columns 4, 5, ..., $i - 1$, $i + 1$, ..., $K$, $K + 1$, while concentrating on 1, 2, 3, and $i$.

|||||||||||||||||||||||||||||||||||||||||||||||||||||||||||||||||||||||||||||||||||||||||||||||||||||||||||||||||||||||||||||

***Discursive note.*** The ordering of the variables which are included need not be precisely the ordering in which the data for the variables is listed. Any variable may be the second, any variable the third, and so on. It is perfectly acceptable to include $X_1$ and $X_6$ in the first stage submodel. Then, bring in $X_K$, then $X_3$, or whatever is desired. The ordering of the variables, 2, 3, ..., $K$, whose associated columns are reduced to a unit vector, is arbitrary. In the forward and in-and-out stepwise procedures, this ordering is determined by statistical tests of significance.

|||||||||||||||||||||||||||||||||||||||||||||||||||||||||||||||||||||||||||||||||||||||||||||||||||||||||||||||||||||||||||||

Exercise 1 at the end of this chapter leads the reader through a detailed comparison of this method with the matrix inverse method and illustrates some of the interpretations discussed above.

## 12.5 DUMMY VARIABLES

### Category dummies for qualitative variables

Oftentimes in attempting to specify a model explaining some socioeconomic variable, the researcher believes some nonquantitative exogenous variables should be included. Such a variable may be sex with values male and female, or location with values, rural, suburban, urban, and ghetto. He believes the postulated model $Y = X\Gamma + \varepsilon$ is appropriate, where $X$ are quantitative, measured variables, but he also recognizes that sexual differences or locational differences may be significant in explaining $Y$. These differences may be examined by running separate regressions for each separate category and testing the difference by the Chow tests of Section 11.10. A simpler procedure is to use dummy variables to represent the different categories.

### Classification dummies for nonlinearly related variables

Sometimes a variable which theoretically should be included in a model is not measured continuously but is grouped into distinct classes. Moreover, the difference in effect on $Y$ among the classes is not well approximated by linear interpolations. Variables such as income class or age cohort often have such a nonlinear effect. By defining a set of dummy variables to represent the different classes, unbiased estimates can be obtained since the estimates of the coefficients for the dummy variables can conform to any curved relation that is implicit.[5]

|||||||||||||||||||||||||||||||||||||||||||||||||||||||||||||||||||||||||||||||||||||||||||||||||||||||||||||||||||||||||||||||||||||||||||||||||||||||||||||||||||

*Discursive note.* The use of dummy variables refers only to predetermined variables. If an endogenous variable is a qualitative or classified variable, then multiple regression is inappropriate. The technique known as multiple discriminant analysis might be used.[6] If the endogenous variable assumes only two values, zero and one, then Probit analysis is relevant.[7]

|||||||||||||||||||||||||||||||||||||||||||||||||||||||||||||||||||||||||||||||||||||||||||||||||||||||||||||||||||||||||||||||||||||||||||||||||||||||||||||||||||

### Formulating the model with dummy variables

Consider a model explaining the incidence of lung cancer among a certain age group of the population in terms of a vector of measurable variables, $X$, and the qualitative variable, sex. One might define two variables $S_1$ and $S_2$ where $S_1$ has value one if the subject is male and zero if female, and $S_2$ has value zero if the subject is male and one if female. Then a model, $Y = \gamma_1 + \gamma_2 X_2 + \cdots + \gamma_K X_K + \delta_1 S_1 + \delta_2 S_2 + \varepsilon$, might be specified. However, the least squares estimates for the coefficients of this model are indeterminate because the dummy variables $S_1$ and $S_2$ and the constant have a perfect linear correlation with each other. That is, the cross-product deviation matrix for the predetermined variables will be singular and $(X'X)^{-1}$ will not exist.

---

[5] In this and the following discussion, conclusions are used from Daniel B. Suits, "Use of Dummy Variables in Regression Equations," *JASA*, Vol. 52 (1957), pp. 548–51.

[6] See T. W. Anderson, *An Introduction to Multivariate Statistical Analysis* (New York: John Wiley & Sons, Inc., 1958).

[7] For an example, see A. S. Goldberger, *Econometric Theory* (New York: John Wiley & Sons, Inc., 1964), pp. 250–51.

To obtain a solution, it is convenient to set one of the coefficients for the dummy variable equal to zero, say $\delta_2 = 0$. There is no loss in information since the sex of any subject is still identified by the value of one (male) or zero (female) for the remaining dummy variable, $S_1$. The shift in the level of incidence of lung cancer between females and males will be given by the estimate of the coefficient $\delta_1$.

||||||||||||||||||||||||||||||||||||||||||||||||||||||||||||||||||||||||||||||||||||||||||||||||||||||||||||||||||||||||||||||||||||

*Explanatory note.*  The intercept of the equation, $\gamma_1$, represents the base for comparison corresponding to the female group of the population. Adding $\gamma_1$ and $\delta_1$ gives the intercept for the equation corresponding to the male group of the population.

||||||||||||||||||||||||||||||||||||||||||||||||||||||||||||||||||||||||||||||||||||||||||||||||||||||||||||||||||||||||||||||||||||

**The case of a multi-category dummy variable**

The above discussion can be extended for a treatment of a qualitative variable with more than two levels of distinct classes. Suppose a sociologist wishes to specify a model explaining literacy rates for a population group in different regions of countries throughout the world. (See Exercise 7 at the end of this chapter.) He may use a vector of measurable variables such as newspaper circulation, $X_2$, number of radios per thousand people, $X_3$, cinema attendance per capita per year, $X_4$, school enrollment as a percent of the population aged 5–19, $X_5$, lagged school enrollment a decade previous, $X_6$, etc. He may be unable to obtain accurate regional measures of the distribution of education level attained, government expenditures on education, or of personal income per capita. Instead he may simply categorize the state of economic development of the region into one of four classes, hopefully to represent different levels of some of these economic variables. The classification may be:

$D_1$ = rapidly developing with sustained growth;
$D_2$ = some sustained growth;
$D_3$ = relatively stagnant but with a reasonable prospect of soon experiencing growth; and
$D_4$ = not developing and little prospect of growth in the near future.

Such classes are somewhat arbitrary in definition, and the researcher may use subjective as well as objective criteria on economic, racial, and political conditions in making the assignments of regions to these classes. Such criteria and the classification should be clearly stated so they may be scrutinized by others.

Since there are four classes, three dummy variables must be used to represent them while still allowing a solution to exist. Denote the dummy variables, $S_1$, $S_2$, and $S_3$, with coefficients $\delta_1$, $\delta_2$, and $\delta_3$ and assign the following pattern of values.

| State of Development | Values of — | | |
|---|---|---|---|
| | $S_1$ | $S_2$ | $S_3$ |
| $D_1$ .................. 1 | | 0 | 0 |
| $D_2$ .................. 0 | | 1 | 0 |
| $D_3$ .................. 0 | | 0 | 1 |
| $D_4$ .................. 0 | | 0 | 0 |

The estimates of $\delta_1, \delta_2$, and $\delta_3$ in the regression model, $Y = \gamma_1 + \sum_{k=2}^{K} \gamma_k X_k$ $+ \delta_1 S_1 + \delta_2 S_2 + \delta_3 S_3 + \varepsilon$ measure the shifts in the intercept of the equation due to different developmental states as deviations from the intercept of the lowest state of development $D_4$, taken as the base.

||||||||||||||||||||||||||||||||||||||||||||||||||||||||||||||||||||||||||||||||||||||||||||||||||||||||||||||||||||||||||||||||||||||||||

*Explicative note.* The class used as the base is arbitrary, but it is usually easier to interpret the results if either the highest or lowest class is used as the base.

||||||||||||||||||||||||||||||||||||||||||||||||||||||||||||||||||||||||||||||||||||||||||||||||||||||||||||||||||||||||||||||||||||||||||

The difference between the estimates for $\delta_1$ and $\delta_3$ would represent the shift in literacy rates due to attainment of a rapidly growing regional economy as compared to regions with a relatively stagnant economy. Other differences between coefficients of dummy variable sets have similar interpretations.

### A digression on scaling of values for variables

Sometimes when a variable has multiple classes, say six classes, one is tempted to assign one dummy variable with levels 1, 2, 3, 4, 5, and 6 to represent these classes. The advantage seems to be that only one variable need be used rather than five; and so, the degrees of freedom $T - K$ is not reduced so much. However, such an ordering implies a linear weighting among the classes which is not implied when only the zero or one (inclusion levels) values for a dummy variable are used. If the researcher desires to weight class 6 three times as high as class 2 and to define an equal difference of one unit between each class, and so on, then and only then is the linear weighting appropriate.

By representing the classes on a scale with a single variable, the formulation does not strictly use a dummy variable. Rather, the specification is similar to using any ordinal measure as an index for a variable. Such measures must be used and interpreted with caution since arbitrary changes in the values, even though the same ordering is preserved, can change the least squares regression results considerably.

For an example, consider a simple model, $Y = \alpha_1 + \alpha_2 X_2 + \varepsilon$ where $X$ is an arbitrary assignment of values to an ordering of political systems among observations on three countries. Let the second be classed as least democratic and the third as most democratic with the first somewhere in between. Suppose variable $Y$ measures the number of new statutes passed by the corresponding government in a specific time interval. Let its values be 200, 100, and 300 for the three countries.

The values for $X$ may be set at 2, 1, and 3 representing the country's position in the political ordering. The correlation between $Y$ and $X$ would obviously be perfect. The same result is true for any linear scaling, say $X$ has values 5, 3, and 7. Then, we obtain by the least squares procedures of Chapters 3 and 4, $\hat{Y} = -50 + 50X$ with $r^2 = 1.0$ and $s_e = 0$. The explanation is perfect
       (0)     (0)
if we choose an ordering that corresponds to the differences in $Y$ values.

Alternately, suppose that country 1 is believed to be nearly as democratic as country 3, but still between country 2 and 3 in the ordering. Let the values for $X$ be 14, 1, and 15. The estimation results are,

$$\hat{Y} = 85.2 + 11.48X \text{ with } r^2 = 0.81 \text{ and } s_e = 35.78.$$
$$(38.5) \quad (3.24)$$

More extreme changes in the assignment of values would change the results even more.

The point to recognize is that specification of arbitrary orderings does represent an implicit weighting. It is generally improper to use such ordinal measures in computations such as least squares estimates which require use of the mean and variance of the variables.[8] When used in a large model, the arbitrary scaling values for one variable will interact with other explanatory variables also. Misrepresentation of the ordering can cause all the estimates to be biased in indeterminate directions and sizes. Consequently, any such scaling used must be widely accepted as a true and definite measure of the degree of difference among the ordered classes.

### Interaction between dummy and quantitative variables

In some specifications, allowances for different intercepts of the regression equation for different qualitative classes is not sufficient. The underlying theory may suggest that there are interaction effects between the distinct classes and the effect of another measured variable $X$ on the endogenous variable $Y$. Consequently, the use of dummy variables must allow for possible changes among classes in the slope $(\partial Y/\partial X)$ of the relation between $Y$ and $X$.

Consider a model to explain the level of earnings of males in their first full-time job after finishing their education. We posit that earnings $Y$ will depend on the level of education attained, $X$, and on the region of the country in which the education is taken, say North, West, or South. Let us designate

---

[8] See the discussion of this point in S. Siegel, *Nonparametric Statistics* (New York: McGraw-Hill Book Co., 1956), chap. 3.

the assignment of regions by dummy variables $R_1$ and $R_2$ with values as follows:

| Region | $R_1$ | $R_2$ |
|---|---|---|
| South ................. 0 | | 0 |
| West ................. 1 | | 0 |
| North ................. 0 | | 1 |

To whatever extent the quality of education and amount learned per school year may vary among the regions, then this interaction can affect earnings by creating differentials in job qualifications that are not accounted for otherwise. The model may be specified.

$$Y = \gamma_1 + (\gamma_2 + \gamma_3 R_1 + \gamma_4 R_2)X + \delta_1 R_1 + \delta_2 R_2 + \varepsilon.$$

‖‖‖‖‖‖‖‖‖‖‖‖‖‖‖‖‖‖‖‖‖‖‖‖‖‖‖‖‖‖‖‖‖‖‖‖‖‖‖‖‖‖‖‖‖‖‖‖‖‖‖‖‖‖‖‖‖‖‖‖‖‖‖‖‖‖‖‖‖‖‖‖‖‖‖‖‖‖‖‖‖‖‖‖‖‖‖‖‖‖‖‖‖‖‖‖

*Recursive note.*   Again, one less dummy variable is used than the number of classes being represented. This is also true in the inter-action terms. The same class should be used as the base (represented by zeros for all dummy variables in the set—in this example, region South) in both the direct and interaction terms for simplicity of interpretation.

‖‖‖‖‖‖‖‖‖‖‖‖‖‖‖‖‖‖‖‖‖‖‖‖‖‖‖‖‖‖‖‖‖‖‖‖‖‖‖‖‖‖‖‖‖‖‖‖‖‖‖‖‖‖‖‖‖‖‖‖‖‖‖‖‖‖‖‖‖‖‖‖‖‖‖‖‖‖‖‖‖‖‖‖‖‖‖‖‖‖‖‖‖‖‖‖‖‖‖‖

The estimates of $\gamma_1$ and $\gamma_2$ would provide the intercept and slope for the relation of earnings on education in the South. The marginal changes in the intercept and slope for the West region compared to the South are given by the estimates of $\delta_1$ and $\gamma_3$ respectively. Other coefficients are interpreted similarly.

## Several sets of dummy variables

The previous discussion has included only one qualitative or class vari-able in each model. There is no such logical or statistical rule, except that each dummy variable or each interaction term represents another coefficient to be estimated and we must be sure that the number of observations $T$ remains larger than this total number, $K$ (see Assumption 6 in Section 10.3). All the previous discussion on specifications with dummy variables applied to a single set of them for one particular qualitative variable. However, it does apply equally well to each of many sets of dummy variables for many qualitative variables. Suppose a model includes the variables sex (male, female), region (South, West, North), and age (18–25, 26–40, 41–50, 51–65) as well as measured education level attained for explaining the current earnings of a member of the labor force. Then six dummy variables would be used as follows: $S = (1, 0)$ for (male, female); $R_1$ and $R_2$ as in the previous paragraphs for regions; and $A_1$, $A_2$, and $A_3$ representing the four age cohorts with the group 18–25 taken as the base. In each set the number of dummy variables is one less than the number of classes. Additional terms would be included if interaction terms were specified.

## 12.6 DISTRIBUTED LAGS, AN INTRODUCTION

In some cases using time-series data, the specification of a model may seem to require the use of lagged values of some independent variables. Instead of merely relating $Y_t$ to a particular $X_t$ at the same time period, the econometrician may desire on theoretical grounds to relate current $Y_t$ to some previous value or values of $X$, say $X_{t-2}$, or $X_{t-1}$, $X_{t-2}, \ldots, X_{t-5}$. If only one of these previous period values is to be used, the specification of the model is not complicated and ordinary least squares estimation may be used. However, if the lagged effect on $Y$ of changes in $X$ is over several successive periods, then the model is more complicated as some specification of the distribution of this lagged effect over time must be considered. Such a specification is called a distributed lag model.[9]

### The need for a distributed lag model

For example, suppose a model is specified to explain $Y_t$ = thousands of dollars spent by tourists per quarter in a given state. One independent variable used to partially explain the variation in $Y$ over years may be $X_{t2}$, U.S. disposable personal income per capita, as a guide to overall affluency. Another explanatory variable may be $Z$, the amount of expenditure in the state on roads and highways, since this makes travel and access to scenic areas easier. One might suggest that $Y_t = f(Z_t)$, but the effect of new and improved roads on inducing more tourists is probably not immediate since it may take several quarters or even years for the effect of the expenditures to be realized. Therefore $Y_t = f(Z_{t-h})$ may be a more accurate representation, where $h$ is the number of quarters needed for completion. Even this relation may be too simple-minded since it implies that the effect on $Y$ of expenditures at period $(t - h)$ occurs only and wholly during period $t$. We would rather postulate that the total effect of $Z$ on $Y$ is *distributed* over several time periods with a partial effect relating to each lagged period. If we assume that the pattern of the distributive effect does not change, then the model might be specified as,

$$Y_t = \gamma_1 + \gamma_2 X_{t2} + (\beta_0 Z_t + \beta_1 Z_{t-1} + \beta_2 Z_{t-2} + \cdots + \beta_h Z_{t-h}) + \varepsilon_t \quad (12\text{–}2)$$

where $\beta_i Z_{t-i}$ is the partial effect on current tourism expenditures of previous expenditures on roads $i$ quarters earlier. The effect after $h$ periods is zero.

---

[9] For an overview of such mathematical specifications, see Z. Griliches, "Distributed Lags: A Survey," *Econometrica*, Vol. 35 (1967), pp. 16–49.

Obviously, it is a specification problem to know how large $h$ should be. If $h$ is only 1 or 2, the theoretical effect may not be satisfactorily distributed over time. If $h$ is large to allow a long pattern of lagged responses, then the number of parameters in the model may get excessive.

||||||||||||||||||||||||||||||||||||||||||||||||||||||||||||||||||||||||||||||||||||||||||||||||||||||||||||||||||||||||||||||||

**Recursive note.** The degrees of freedom for the tests on the coefficients in the general model is $T - K$. If $K$ is made very large by including many lagged variables, then the degrees of freedom may become very small unless the number of observations can be increased as well.

||||||||||||||||||||||||||||||||||||||||||||||||||||||||||||||||||||||||||||||||||||||||||||||||||||||||||||||||||||||||||||||||

## Some simple estimations using distributed lags

If the number of lagged periods, $h$, is reasonably small, the model (12–2) may be estimated directly using OLS, and individual coefficients could be tested to see if the associated lagged effect is significant. However, such an estimation often runs into difficulty since the lagged independent variables, $Z_t$, $Z_{t-1}$, $Z_{t-2}$, ..., $Z_{t-h}$, are usually highly correlated with each other. This multicorrelation effect violates assumption seven (Section 10.3) for the ideal general model. As a result of this *multicollinearity*, the estimates of the $\beta_i$, $i = 0, 1, ..., h$, coefficients are imprecise and the effects of the different lagged variables cannot be correctly separated and identified. (Refer to Section 8.4 and to Chapter 15.)

An alternative is to specify the lag structure completely as a single variable, say $X_{t3} = \sum_{i=0}^{h} \beta_i Z_{t-i}$, so that the model (12–2) is reduced to $Y_t = \gamma_1 + \gamma_2 X_{t2} + \gamma_3 X_{t3} + \varepsilon_t$. The variable $X_{t3}$ may be defined in light of whatever theoretical or empirical evidence is available. Several cases may be suggested:

*a)* The response is equal for all $h$ periods and then forever zero, so

$$X_{t3} = [1/(h + 1)](Z_t + Z_{t-1} + \cdots + Z_{t-h}).$$

*b)* The response is somewhat cyclical over $h$ periods. Suppose $h = 4$, then one might specify,

$$X_{t3} = 2/18\, Z_t + 7/18\, Z_{t-1} + 3/18\, Z_{t-2} + 1/18\, Z_{t-3} + 5/18\, Z_{t-4}.$$

*c)* The response may build up for half of the lagged periods and then decline symmetrically. Suppose $h = 4$, one might assume,

$$X_{t3} = 1/16\, Z_t + 4/16\, Z_{t-1} + 6/16\, Z_{t-2} + 4/16\, Z_{t-3} + 1/16\, Z_{t-4}.$$

*d)* The response may decline systematically over $h$ periods. Again, if $h = 4$ for a simple example, then one might use,

$$X_{t3} = 5/15\, Z_t + 4/15\, Z_{t-1} + 3/15\, Z_{t-2} + 2/15\, Z_{t-3} + 1/15\, Z_{t-4}.$$

The econometrician can use any pattern with any coefficients that he thinks are appropriate to describe the lagged effects, generally using a set of coefficients that sums to unity. However, the selection is arbitrary and he may have great difficulty in obtaining agreement among critics that he chose the most appropriate response pattern. Indeed, he may try many of these various types and then choose the one which provides the best explanation of $Y$ in the model based on a set of sample observations.

## The Koyck distributed lag

A particular response pattern of type $(d)$ above is quite popular and useful. The Koyck pattern uses a declining geometric sequence.[10] Consider only the part of the model (12–2) which involves the distributed lag and let that lag have an infinite number of periods.

$$Y_t = \beta_0 Z_t + \beta_1 Z_{t-1} + \beta_2 Z_{t-2} + \cdots + \varepsilon_t. \qquad (12\text{–}2a)$$

Using the notion of a lag operator $D^j$ such that $D^j Z_t = Z_{t-j}$, and if all the $\beta_i$'s are positive with a finite sum, this infinite lag can be rewritten as

$$Y_t = \beta(w_0 + w_1 D + w_2 D^2 + \cdots)Z_t + \varepsilon_t$$

where $\beta w_i = \beta_i$, $i = 0, 1, 2, \ldots$, each $w_i \geq 0$, and $\sum w_i = 1.0$. In particular, let $w_i = (1 - \delta)\delta^i$ with $0 < \delta < 1$ where $\delta$ is to be estimated. Under this geometrically declining pattern,

$$\sum w_i D^i = (1 - \delta)(1 + \delta D + \delta^2 D^2 + \delta^3 D^3 + \cdots).$$

This geometric sequence has a constant factor $\delta D$ so its sum is $1/(1 - \delta D)$. (See *Review* 13.2, item 4, for another application of this rule for summing a geometric progression.) Summarizing and collecting these results, $Y_t$ may be written as

$$Y_t = \beta(\sum w_i D^i)Z_t + \varepsilon_t = \frac{\beta(1 - \delta)}{(1 - \delta D)} Z_t + \varepsilon_t.$$

Solving this equation by multiplying both sides by $(1 - \delta D)$ gives,

$$Y_t - \delta Y_{t-1} = \beta(1 - \delta)Z_t + (\varepsilon_t - \delta\varepsilon_{t-1}),$$

or

$$Y_t = \beta(1 - \delta)Z_t + \delta Y_{t-1} + \varepsilon_t^*, \qquad (12\text{–}3)$$

where $\varepsilon_t^* = (\varepsilon_t - \delta\varepsilon_{t-1})$ is a new disturbance term assumed to satisfy the usual Assumptions 2–5 of Section 10.3.

The Koyck model (12–3) in this case involves a regression of $Y_t$ only on $Z_t$ and a lagged $Y_{t-1}$ instead of a large number of lagged independent variables,

---

[10] L. M. Koyck, *Distributed Lags and Investment Analysis*, (Amsterdam: North-Holland, 1954).

$Z_{t-i}$. Only two coefficients need to be estimated from which $\beta$ and $\delta$ can be determined algebraically; and hence, the weights $w_i$ and coefficients $\beta_i$, $i = 0, 1, 2, \ldots$, may be calculated. Using the lagged value of $Y$ as an explanatory variable usually helps provide a high degree of fit for the model so large $R^2$ for such a model is the general rule rather than a special result. The researcher must make other tests as in Chapter 11 to evaluate and interpret his model.

||||||||||||||||||||||||||||||||||||||||||||||||||||||||||||||||||||||||||||||||||||||||||||||||||||||||||||||||||||||||||||

*Interpretive note.* The Koyck lag structure assigns the largest weight to the most recent values and diminishing weights to each successive lag. If this is not deemed appropriate, another scheme would be better. Sometimes the first one or two lags may be left free and the Koyck pattern assumed for lags 3, 4, ..., etc. This allows the first lag coefficients to be estimated separately from the Koyck assumption.

||||||||||||||||||||||||||||||||||||||||||||||||||||||||||||||||||||||||||||||||||||||||||||||||||||||||||||||||||||||||||||

*A special problem of the Koyck method.* Using the Koyck weights, the model (12–2a) is simplified to the model (12–3) which involves a lagged endogenous variable. Throughout this book, the problems of estimation and testing involving this class of predetermined variable are not considered in detail. When a lagged endogenous variable appears in an explanatory role in conjunction with violations of some other assumptions, such as Assumption 5 of nonautocorrelation, the result is the loss of some desirable properties of the estimators including consistency. Also, the presence of a lagged endogenous variable in the model (*a*) implies some underlying dynamic model whose stability properties become an important concern; (*b*) introduces some problems in the testing methods of Chapter 11; and (*c*) requires more complex changes in the residual analysis and corresponding remedies for the econometric problems considered in the next three chapters.

The reader should be aware of these difficulties even if he does not try to understand them fully at this time. They are judged by the author to be topics of a more advanced level presentation or one in which the readers have very relaxed time constraints.

## The Almon distributed lag

A final method of handling the specification (12–2) is credited to Almon.[11] Instead of trying to estimate $h$ different lag coefficients $\beta_0, \beta_1, \ldots, \beta_h$, each is approximated by a polynomial approximation of a function $f(i) \simeq \beta_i$, $i = 0, 1, \ldots, h$.

---

[11] S. Almon, "The Distributed Lag between Capital Appropriations and Expenditures," *Econometrica*, Vol. 30 (1965), pp. 178–96. Only a simplified version of the Almon method is given here.

|||||||||||||||||||||||||||||||||||||||||||||||||||||||||||||||||||||||||||||||||||||||||||||||||||||||||||||||||

***Explicative note.*** There is a double approximation implied. The discrete values $\beta_i$ are approximated by values of a continuous function $f(i)$ which is approximated by an $n$th degree polynomial.

|||||||||||||||||||||||||||||||||||||||||||||||||||||||||||||||||||||||||||||||||||||||||||||||||||||||||||||||||

The polynomial approximation can be made arbitrarily close by using higher and higher degrees. Usually, a third or fourth degree polynomial is accurate enough, but in general $\beta_i \simeq f(i) \simeq \delta_0 + \delta_1 i + \delta_2 i^2 + \delta_3 i^3 + \cdots + \delta_n i^n$. Considering only that portion of (12–2) involving the lag structure, the following steps are itemized to use the Almon procedure to estimate the model,

$$Y_t = \delta_0 Z_t + \delta_1 Z_{t-1} + \cdots + \delta_h Z_{t-h} + \varepsilon_t. \qquad (12\text{–}2b)$$

1. Postulate a value for $h$, the number of lag effects.

|||||||||||||||||||||||||||||||||||||||||||||||||||||||||||||||||||||||||||||||||||||||||||||||||||||||||||||||||

***Discursive note.*** Actually a search may be made over various alternate values of $h$ in order to find the best-fitting one.

|||||||||||||||||||||||||||||||||||||||||||||||||||||||||||||||||||||||||||||||||||||||||||||||||||||||||||||||||

For example purposes, let us postulate that $h = 5$.
2. Write out the approximation polynomials of degree $n$ for each $\beta_i$.

|||||||||||||||||||||||||||||||||||||||||||||||||||||||||||||||||||||||||||||||||||||||||||||||||||||||||||||||||

***Discursive note.*** Some econometricians make a practice of specifying $n$ larger than they hope to actually use so as to be sure that the accuracy of this approximation is satisfactory.

|||||||||||||||||||||||||||||||||||||||||||||||||||||||||||||||||||||||||||||||||||||||||||||||||||||||||||||||||

Suppose a third degree polynomial is thought to be sufficient so to be safe, $n = 4$ is used. We obtain,

$$
\begin{aligned}
\beta_0 &= f(0) = \delta_0[+ \delta_1(0) + \delta_2(0)^2 + \delta_3(0)^3 + \delta_4(0)^4] \\
\beta_1 &= f(1) = \delta_0 + 1\delta_1 + 1^2\delta_2 + 1^3\delta_3 + 1^4\delta_4 \\
\beta_2 &= f(2) = \delta_0 + 2\delta_1 + 4\delta_2 + 8\delta_3 + 16\delta_4 \\
\beta_3 &= f(3) = \delta_0 + 3\delta_1 + 9\delta_2 + 27\delta_3 + 81\delta_4 \\
\beta_4 &= f(4) = \delta_0 + 4\delta_1 + 16\delta_2 + 64\delta_3 + 256\delta_4 \\
\beta_5 &= f(5) = \delta_0 + 5\delta_1 + 25\delta_2 + 125\delta_3 + 625\delta_4.
\end{aligned}
\qquad (12\text{–}4)
$$

3. Estimate the coefficients $\delta_j$, $j = 0, 1, \ldots, 4$, by applying OLS to the equation obtained by substituting (12–4) into the specified lagged model (12–2b). The new equation is,

$$
\begin{aligned}
Y_t = \ & \delta_0(Z_t + Z_{t-1} + Z_{t-2} + Z_{t-3} + Z_{t-4} + Z_{t-5}) \\
& + \delta_1(0 + Z_{t-1} + 2Z_{t-2} + 3Z_{t-3} + 4Z_{t-4} + 5Z_{t-5}) \\
& + \delta_2(0 + Z_{t-1} + 4Z_{t-2} + 9Z_{t-3} + 16Z_{t-4} + 25Z_{t-5}) \quad (12\text{–}5) \\
& + \delta_3(0 + Z_{t-1} + 8Z_{t-2} + 27Z_{t-3} + 64Z_{t-4} + 125Z_{t-5}) \\
& + \delta_4(0 + Z_{t-1} + 16Z_{t-2} + 81Z_{t-3} + 256Z_{t-4} + 625Z_{t-5}) + \varepsilon_t.
\end{aligned}
$$

4. Obtain the estimates of the coefficients of the lag variables by substituting the estimates of $\delta_j$ from (12–5) into the formulas (12–4) for $\beta_i$, $i = 0, 1, 2, \ldots, 5$.

The form of the equation (12–5) is especially convenient. Each coefficient $\delta_j$ is associated with the $j$th degree term in the approximating polynomial. Also, adding or deleting the term of degree $j$ does not affect the representation of the other independent variables corresponding to the coefficients $\delta_j$ in equation (12–5). Consequently, a simple test of the importance of the $j$th degree term in the polynomial can be made by testing the significance of the coefficient $\delta_j$.

|||||||||||||||||||||||||||||||||||||||||||||||||||||||||||||||||||||||||||||||||||||||||||||||||||||||||||||||||||||||||||||||||||||||||||||||||||||||

**Recursive note.** A stepwise regression procedure might be used on equation (12–5) adding in each variable corresponding to the next higher degree terms in the approximating polynomial one at a time. In this way, when a coefficient $\delta_j$ is not significant, the $j$th degree terms need not be used.

|||||||||||||||||||||||||||||||||||||||||||||||||||||||||||||||||||||||||||||||||||||||||||||||||||||||||||||||||||||||||||||||||||||||||||||||||||||||

The test on the coefficients can be made in the standard way (see Section 11.5) assuming that the assumptions of Section 10.3 hold for the model (12–5), including $V(\varepsilon_t) = \sigma_\varepsilon^2$. If the matrix $A$ is defined as the observation matrix of the explanatory variables in (12–5), then the $(h \times h)$ size variance-covariance matrix of the estimators of the $\delta_j$ is $V\text{-}Cov(\hat{\delta}) = \sigma_\varepsilon^2(A'A)^{-1}$. The square root of the elements on the diagonal of this matrix are the standard errors of the estimates.

|||||||||||||||||||||||||||||||||||||||||||||||||||||||||||||||||||||||||||||||||||||||||||||||||||||||||||||||||||||||||||||||||||||||||||||||||||||||

**Explicative note.** Since each estimate of a $\beta_i$ is a linear combination of these estimates, $\hat{\delta}_j$, the variance-covariance matrix of the estimates of $\beta_i$, $i = 0, 1, 2, \ldots, h$ can be obtained easily. From Table 6–1, in *Review* 6.2, $V(aX) = a^2 X$. In the present case, the random variable $X$ would represent $\hat{\delta}$ and the constant $a$ would represent a row vector of coefficients $a_i$ given by the coefficients of $\delta_j$ in the representation for $\beta_i$ in (12–4). That is,

$$V(\beta_0) = \sigma_\varepsilon^2 a_0(A'A)^{-1}a_0' \quad \text{with} \quad a_0 = (1 \quad 0 \quad 0 \quad 0 \quad 0),$$

$$V(\beta_1) = \sigma_\varepsilon^2 a_1(A'A)^{-1}a_1' \quad \text{with} \quad a_1 = (1 \quad 1 \quad 1 \quad 1 \quad 1),$$

$$V(\beta_2) = \sigma_\varepsilon^2 a_2(A'A)^{-1}a_2' \quad \text{with} \quad a_2 = (1 \quad 2 \quad 4 \quad 8 \quad 16),$$

$$\vdots \qquad\qquad\qquad \vdots$$

$$V(\beta_5) = \sigma_\varepsilon^2 a_5(A'A)^{-1}a_5' \quad \text{with} \quad a_5 = (1 \quad 5 \quad 25 \quad 125 \quad 625).$$

|||||||||||||||||||||||||||||||||||||||||||||||||||||||||||||||||||||||||||||||||||||||||||||||||||||||||||||||||||||||||||||||||||||||||||||||||||||||

## Extensions of the distributed lag structure

The methods discussed here of direct estimation, arbitrary assignment of a lag pattern, use of the Koyck pattern, and use of the Almon lag procedure referred to estimating a model of the form (12–2) where one independent variable was postulated to have a distributed lag effect on $Y_t$. Two common extensions should be briefly discussed to complete this presentation.

Returning to the example model (12–2) where

$Y_t$ = tourism expenditures in the state,

$X_{t2}$ = disposable personal income per capita, and

$Z_t$ = expenditures in the state on roads and highways,

let us first suppose that another variable with a distributed lag effect is also to be included, perhaps expenditures in the state on parks and recreational area development. This can be treated in the same way as $Z_t$ by specifying a separate lag structure for each such variable.[12] If these explanatory variables are denoted $Z_1$ and $Z_2$, then each could have a separate lag pattern with lags $h_1$ and $h_2$, with a Koyck weighting scheme giving $\delta_1$ and $\delta_2$, or with Almon approximating polynomials of degrees $n_1$ and $n_2$.

||||||||||||||||||||||||||||||||||||||||||||||||||||||||||||||||||||||||||||||||||||||||||||||||||||||||||||||||||||||||||||||||||||||||||

*Explicative note.* As more such variables are included the amount of computation and complexity increases. To whatever extent two or more such lagged structures are postulated to be of the same length ($h_1 = h_2$) or have the same weights ($\delta_1 = \delta_2$), or the same degree polynomial ($n_1 = n_2$), there is some corresponding lessening of the extra complexity.

||||||||||||||||||||||||||||||||||||||||||||||||||||||||||||||||||||||||||||||||||||||||||||||||||||||||||||||||||||||||||||||||||||||||||

A second type extension is required if the theoretical premises suggest that the effects in a single independent variable lag structure depend not only on the time elapsed, $i$ periods, but also on the level of some other variable. Suppose that in model (12–2), the coefficients $\beta_i$ of the lagged variables $Z_{t-i}$, $i = 0, 1, \ldots, h$, are postulated to be $\beta_i = \alpha_{1i} + \alpha_{2i} V_{t-i}$. The interpretation might be that the partial effect on tourism of expenditures on roads and highways $i$ periods earlier depends to some considerable extent on the level of the variable $V_{t-i}$, perhaps state expenditures on promotion and advertising of its scenic and recreational areas. In this case, a two-variable distributed lag pattern results just as in the first extension presented. However, the two variables are $(Z)$ and $(VZ)$. The reader who is interested in further study of such structures and associated estimating procedures is referred to footnotes 9–12 and their internal references.

---

[12] S. Almon, "Lags between Investment Decisions and Their Causes," *Review of Economics and Statistics*, Vol. 50 (1968), pp. 193–206.

## 12.7 SUMMARY

Specifying a model is often difficult because (*a*) the underlying theory is not developed, (*b*) there are too many second-best alternative measures of the desired theoretical variable, (*c*) there is postulated an unknown distributed lag structure, or (*d*) the theoretical variable is not quantifiable. In this chapter, the methods of stepwise regression are discussed as common devices for screening among variables to find a suitable set for use as predetermined variables in the econometric model. Also, the use of dummy variables is suggested for representing linear or nonlinear effects among class levels of variables for which only qualitative distinctions are available. Finally, some simplified alternatives for treating distributed lag specifications are suggested. All these topics are met frequently in discussions of model building in many applied areas. Some limitations and dangers of their use have also been discussed. These lie primarily in the area of interpretation and can be generalized in the following commandments: (*a*) do not become a fanatic in the use of any method;[13] (*b*) do not let a computer do your thinking for you; and (*c*) *do* use *theory* in formulating your model.

## NEW VOCABULARY

| | |
|---|---|
| Stepwise regression | Forward regression |
| Gaussian reduction method | In-and-out regression |
| Elementary row transformation | Dummy variables |
| Equivalent systems of equations | Interaction terms |
| Elementary matrix | Misspecification bias |
| Augmented matrix | Ordinal measured variables |
| Distributed lag | Circular reasoning |
| Koyck weighting scheme | Almon polynomial approximation |

## EXERCISES

1.  Consider the coded data of Tables 9–1 and 9–2 and the model of Section 9.6, $Y = \gamma_1 + \gamma_2 X_2 + \gamma_3 X_3 + \varepsilon$. Let us add another variable $X_4 =$ textile production in the country from which the largest amount of textiles are imported. The following new statistics are calculated:

$$\bar{X}_4 = 3.0387,$$
$$\sum x_4{}^2 = 4.8961,$$
$$\sum x_2 x_4 = 4.7748,$$
$$\sum x_3 x_4 = 1.4135,$$
$$\sum yx_4 = 5.2923.$$

a)  Set up the initial matrix for Gaussian reduction as given in the left-hand side of the transformation (12–1).

---

[13] A fanatic in this sense is a person who loses sight of his goal but redoubles his effort.

||||||||||||||||||||||||||||||||||||||||||||||||||||||||||||||||||||||||||||||||||||||||||||||||||||||||||||||||||||||||||||||||||

*Discursive note.* The square submatrix of rows and columns 2–5 inclusive is symmetric. Symmetry always is maintained among the dispersion matrix of rows and columns whose diagonal elements have not yet been normalized to unity.

||||||||||||||||||||||||||||||||||||||||||||||||||||||||||||||||||||||||||||||||||||||||||||||||||||||||||||||||||||||||||||||||||

b)   Reduce the second column to a unit vector, $(0, 1, 0, 0, 0)'$ by elementary row transformations applied across all rows. From elements of column 5, find the values of $a_1$, $a_2$, and $e'e$ for the simple model, $Y = \alpha_1 + \alpha_2 X_2 + \varepsilon$. Compare the results to those found in results (3–4) of Section 3.5 and (c) of Section 4.5.

   Also, give an interpretation of the elements in rows 1, 2, and 4 of column 4.

c)   Reduce the third column to a unit vector, $(0, 0, 1, 0, 0)'$.

   Find the results corresponding to the least squares estimation of the model $Y = \gamma_1 + \gamma_2 X_2 + \gamma_3 X_3 + \varepsilon$ as given in steps (d) and (f) of Section 9.6.

   Also, find the inverse matrix $(X'X)^{-1}$ for exogenous variables $X_2$ and $X_3$ only in rows 2 and 3 of columns 6 and 7. Compare to the inverse given by (9–8) in Section 9.6.

   Give an interpretation of the elements in rows 1–4 of column 4 and discuss the changes from the previous step.

d)   Reduce column 4 to the unit vector $(0, 0, 0, 1, 0)'$ by elementary row transformations.

   Find the inverse of $(X'X)$ relevant to the three exogenous variables $X_2$, $X_3$, and $X_4$.

   Interpret the effect on the model of adding variable $X_4$ and find $r_{Y4 \cdot 23}{}^2$.

   If this final step model is the true specification, discuss the sign of the bias in estimates of $C_2$ and $C_3$ if the model of the previous step (c) were used as the final specification.

   Test the significance at the 0.01 level of the inclusion of each new variable in steps (c) and (d).

2.  Examine other sources on stepwise regression to find another variant of the method. Compare and contrast this other method with the forward and the in-and-out stepwise procedures.

3.  Refer to the last subtopic in Section 12.5 on the use of several sets of dummy variables. Specify in equation form the suggested regression model using dummy variables for sex, region, and age, and interpret the meaning of the coefficients in the model.

4.  Consider a model, $Y$, for family size of households headed by 40-year-old males, for a particular country over time. One independent variable may be personal income, $X$. Others may be race and education level, and both these may interact with the variable $X$. Let race be classified by white and nonwhite, and education level attained be classified as primary, secondary, college, or

advanced graduate education. Define the appropriate dummy variable levels and formulate the model. Interpret the meaning of each type of coefficient in your model.

5. In the late 1960s, there was much discussion about the lack of growth in private housing construction. If the determinants of housing starts were known, then perhaps cycles in private construction could be modified or eliminated by appropriate counter balancing policy.

A study of annual housing starts in North Carolina in terms of variables reflecting various government expenditures, manufacturing employment, and personal savings uses a stepwise regression to find the three most important determinants. Data for years 1954 to 1966 are obtained from *Statistical Yearbooks* of the U.S. Department of Housing and Urban Development, *Statistical Abstracts of the U.S.* of the Commerce Department, and *Employment and Earnings Statistics for States and Areas* by the Department of Labor's Bureau of Labor Statistics.

The following selected results are obtained for the first three steps of a forward stepwise regression procedure using coded data.

Dependent variable, $Y$, $\bar{Y} = 1.0117$, $Y'Y = 0.20976$

*Correlation matrix*

|  | $Y$ | $X_2$ | $X_4$ | $X_7$ |
|---|---|---|---|---|
| $Y$ | 1.0 | −0.17228 | −0.36694 | −0.38691 |
| $X_2$ |  | 1.0 | −0.15958 | 0.17790 |
| $X_4$ |  |  | 1.0 | 0.25310 |
| $X_7$ | (symmetric) |  |  | 1.0 |

*Step 1:* Variable entered $X_7$.

Multiple $R$     0.38691     $r_{Y2 \cdot 7} = -0.11400$
Std. error     0.13355     $r_{Y4 \cdot 7} = -0.30155$
$Y = 1.17738 - 0.16488X_7$
        (0.12426)

*Step 2:* Multiple $R = 0.47647$     $r_{Y2 \cdot 74} = -0.19203$
Std. error $= 0.13422$
$Y = 2.76854 - 0.13388X_7 - 1.60758X_4$
        (0.12909)     (1.69432)

*Step 3:* Multiple $R = 0.50549$
Std. error $= 0.13972$
$Y = 3.28534 - 0.11642X_7 - 1.82238X_4 - 0.31235X_2$
        (0.13802)     (1.80585)     (0.56438)

Source: Class, 1970 (Eisenstadt).

*a)* Explain why variable $X_7$ entered first with a negative coefficient.

*b)* Explain the relation between the partial coefficients given in step 1 and the next variable to be entered.

*c)* Explain how both $R$ and $s_e$ can increase in each step.

*d)* Explain why the estimate of the standard errors of the estimate of the coefficient for $X_7$ increases at each step.

*e)* Give your interpretation of the merit of this selection of variables in explaining housing starts.

6. A forward stepwise regression is done on a model explaining real gross private domestic investment quarterly from 1948 through 1967. The results are given below:

*Step 1:*    Dependent variable $Y$    Real investment in time $t$.
Variable entered $X_4$    Real investment in time $(t-1)$.

|  | *Analysis of variance* | *d.f.* | *SS* | *F* |
|---|---|---|---|---|
| $R = 0.95787$ | Regression | 1 | 20,246.02 | 867.53 |
| $s_e = 4.83090$ | Residual | 78 | 1,820.33 | |

| *Variables in equation* | | | | *Variables not in equation* | |
|---|---|---|---|---|---|
| *Variable* | *C* | $s_c$ | *F* | *Variable* | *Partial* |
| $X_4$ | 0.97 | 0.033 | 867.53 | $X_2$ | 0.136 |
| Intercept | 2.79 | | | $X_3$ | 0.050 |
| | | | | $X_5$ | 0.372 |
| | | | | $X_6$ | 0.278 |

*Step 2:*    Variable entered $X_5$    Real GNP in time $t$

|  | *Analysis of variance* | *d.f.* | *SS* | *F* |
|---|---|---|---|---|
| $\dot{R} = 0.9638$ | Regression | 2 | 20,497.82 | 503.12 |
| $s_c = 4.5134$ | Residual | 77 | 1,568.54 | |

| *Variables in equation* | | | | *Variables not in equation* | |
|---|---|---|---|---|---|
| *Variable* | *C* | $s_c$ | *F* | *Variable* | *Partial* |
| $X_4$ | 0.72 | 0.078 | 86.34 | $X_2$ | −0.250 |
| $X_5$ | 0.04 | 0.012 | 12.36 | $X_3$ | −0.393 |
| Intercept | 1.56 | | | $X_6$ | −0.787 |

*Step 3:*    Variable entered $X_6$    Real GNP in time $(t-1)$

|  | *Analysis of variance* | *d.f.* | *SS* | *F* |
|---|---|---|---|---|
| $R = 0.9864$ | Regression | 3 | 21,469.66 | 911.51 |
| $s_c = 2.8020$ | Residual | 76 | 596.70 | |

| *Variables in equation* | | | | *Variables not in equation* | |
|---|---|---|---|---|---|
| *Variable* | *C* | $s_c$ | *F* | *Variable* | *Partial* |
| $X_4$ | 0.79 | 0.049 | 266.25 | $X_2$ | 0.031 |
| $X_5$ | 0.68 | 0.058 | 137.95 | $X_3$ | −0.064 |
| $X_6$ | −0.66 | 0.059 | 123.78 | | |
| Intercept | 2.36 | | | | |

*Step 4:*    Variable entered $X_3$    Interest rate in time $(t-1)$

$R = 0.9864$        $Y = 2.85 + 0.78X_4 + 0.67X_5 - 0.64X_6 - 0.59X_3$
$s_c = 2.8148$            $(0.053)$     $(0.061)$     $(0.067)$     $(1.06)$

*Step 5:*  Variable entered $X_2$   Interest rate in time $t$

| | Analysis of variance | d.f. | SS | F |
|---|---|---|---|---|
| $R = 0.9873$ | Regression | 5 | 21,509.09 | 571.24 |
| $s_c = 2.7442$ | Residual | 74 | 557.27 | |

| Variable | C | $s_c$ | F |
|---|---|---|---|
| $X_4$ | 0.76 | 0.052 | 214.74 |
| $X_5$ | 0.63 | 0.062 | 101.46 |
| $X_6$ | −0.60 | 0.067 | 79.67 |
| $X_2$ | −6.42 | 2.827 | 5.16 |
| $X_3$ | 5.95 | 2.684 | 4.91 |
| Intercept | 3.55 | | |

Source: Class, 1970 (Hughes).

*a)*  Trace through the steps to determine why the variables entered in this particular order.

*b)*  Note the exceptional increase in accuracy between steps 2 and 3 by citing as many statistics as relevant to demonstrate this. Can you explain this phenomenon? (Consider the sign of the partials in step 2.)

*c)*  Discuss which of the five steps might be the most appropriate specification in terms of statistics only.

*d)*  Explain the interpretation and relation (if any) between the $F$-values in the analysis of variance table and the $F$-values given for each coefficient of the variables in the equation.

7.  Refer to Section 12.5 and the subtopic on the multicategory dummy variables. Suppose the model suggested there for explaining literacy rates is estimated on the basis of data for 79 countries throughout the world obtained from the *Literacy Codebook* compiled by the Louis Harris Political Data Center at the University of North Carolina, Chapel Hill.

The model has five measured variables, $X_2$ to $X_6$, and three dummy variables $S_1$, $S_2$, and $S_3$, representing four states of economic development and growth.

An in-and-out stepwise regression is used to determine the order of importance and relative effects of these variables in the specified model. Some selected results are given below:

Stepwise regression            $F$-level for inclusion 0.01
                               $F$-level for deletion   0.005

Dependent variable $Y$, literacy rates, $\bar{Y} = 59.297$,

$$Y'Y = 73,875.877$$

*Step 1:*  Variable entered $X_5$   School enrollment
$$Y = -14.4119 + 1.548X_5$$
$$(0.0778)$$

| Variables not in equation | | Partial |
|---|---|---|
| Newspapers | $X_2$ | 0.393 |
| Radios | $X_3$ | 0.211 |
| Cinema | $X_4$ | 0.385 |
| Lagged enrollment | $X_6$ | 0.136 |
| Dummy | $S_1$ | 0.257 |
| Dummy | $S_2$ | 0.183 |
| Dummy | $S_3$ | −0.047 |

*Step 2:*   Variable entered $X_2$   Newspaper

$$Y = -6.4620 + 1.2196X_5 + 0.0592X_2$$
$$\phantom{Y = -6.4620 + } (0.1139) \phantom{X_5 + } (0.0159)$$

$\vdots$

*Step 8:*   Variable entered $X_3$   Radios

| Variable | C | $s_c$ | F to remove |
|---|---|---|---|
| Intercept | $-4.55$ | | |
| $X_2$ | 0.036 | 0.021 | 2.96 |
| $X_3$ | 0.022 | 0.023 | 0.87 |
| $X_4$ | 0.597 | 0.435 | 1.88 |
| $X_5$ | 1.017 | 0.125 | 64.36 |
| $X_6$ | $-0.012$ | 0.008 | 2.29 |
| $S_1$ | 21.220 | 8.235 | 6.64 |
| $S_2$ | 16.321 | 5.353 | 9.30 |
| $S_3$ | 9.417 | 3.985 | 5.59 |

**Summary table**

| Step | Variable Entered | | Removed | $R^2$ | $s_c$ | F-value* |
|---|---|---|---|---|---|---|
| 1 | enrollment | $X_5$ | — | 0.837 | 13.65 | 395.64 |
| 2 | newspaper | $X_2$ | — | 0.862 | 12.63 | 13.87 |
| 3 | cinema | $X_4$ | — | 0.875 | 12.12 | 7.57 |
| 4 | Dummy | $S_2$ | — | 0.880 | 11.95 | 3.14 |
| 5 | Dummy | $S_3$ | — | 0.884 | 11.84 | 2.37 |
| 6 | Dummy | $S_1$ | — | 0.892 | 11.52 | 5.17 |
| 7 | lagged enrollment | $X_6$ | — | 0.894 | 11.48 | 1.52 |
| 8 | radios | $X_3$ | — | 0.895 | 11.49 | 0.87 |

\* For added variable at step of inclusion.
Source: Class, 1970 (Duncan).

*a)*   Explain why variable $X_2$ entered in step 2.

*b)*   Explain why no variables dropped out at any step. (*Hint:* Compare the $F$ to remove values in step 8 with the present control for operation of the program.)

*c)*   Write the final model from step 8 and interpret the meaning of the coefficients estimated for the dummy variables. (See Section 12.5.)

*d)*   From the values of $T = 79$, $Y'Y$, and $R^2$, test the significance of the linear model at step 1. Then test the significance of adding variable $X_2$ on step 2. Finally, test the joint significance of the remaining six variables added between steps 2 and 8.

*e)*   Find the $t$-values for tests on each individual coefficient in step 8. Compare to the square root of the given $F$-values in step 8 and explain the obvious relation.

8.   Specify the equation analogous to (12–5) for a model with a twofold distributed lag where the Almon procedure is applied to $Z_1$ with $h = 5$ and $n = 4$ and to $Z_2$ with $h = 3$ and $n = 3$.

9.   Refer to equation (12–3) based on a Koyck pattern. Suppose the estimates of the coefficients of $Z_t$ and $Y_{t-1}$ in this model are determined to be 0.8

and 0.4 respectively. Find the estimates of the Koyck weights $w_i$ and of the lagged structure coefficients $\beta_i$ (in 12–2a) for $i = 0, 1, 2, 3$.

10. Apply the Almon procedure with $h = 3$ and $n = 3$ to the model and data of Exercise 4, Chapter 3, assuming that $X_2$ has a lagged effect on $Y$. Find and test the significance of the coefficients $\beta_0$, $\beta_1$, $\beta_2$, and $\beta_3$. Interpret the results.

11. Apply the Koyck scheme to the variables and data of Exercise 4, Chapter 3, and compare the resulting values of the coefficients $\beta_0$, $\beta_1$, $\beta_2$, and $\beta_3$ with those obtained in Exercise 10.

12. Apply the Koyck scheme to the variables and data of Exercise 10, Chapter 3, assuming a Koyck lag for $X_2$. Using the same information there about 1944 levels of $Y$ and $X_2$, use your estimated model in the form (12–3) to make the forecast requested in that exercise. Compare and interpret your results.

13. *a)* Apply an Almon lag with $h = 3$, $n = 2$, using the variables and data from Exercise 14, Chapter 3. Find and test the significance of the coefficients in your model of the form (12–2b).
    *b)* Repeat the estimation using $h = 2$, $n = 2$, and compare the results.

14. Apply an Almon lag with $h = 5$ to the variables and data in Exercise 15, Chapter 3. Use $n = 4$ and test to see if the third and fourth degree coefficients in the model form (12–5) are significant. Interpret your results.

15. Suggest your own model where a distributed lag specification seems appropriate. Collect the necessary data and determine a satisfactory lagged pattern by trial and error or by a search of alternate Almon lags.

*Chapter*

*13*

# SELECTED ECONOMETRIC PROBLEMS AND RESIDUAL ANALYSIS

## 13.1 PREVIEW

Throughout Chapters 8–12, the role of the Assumptions 1 to 7 listed in Chapter 10 has been emphasized in presenting the estimation and analysis of the general econometric model. The use of these assumptions imposes certain restrictions on the background conditions under which the model is presumed to operate. When these conditions are violated, the corresponding assumptions are no longer valid and the least squares estimators lose some of their desirable properties. In some cases, other methods of estimation can be used to remedy the ill effects of the assumption violation and to arrive at estimators with improved properties.

## The selected problems

Three special and common problems are considered in this chapter as violations of Assumptions 1, 4, and 5. The identification of these problems respectively are: *contemporaneous correlation between the independent variables and the disturbance term, heteroscedasticity,* and *autocorrelation.* All have been widely discussed in econometric literature. Continuing research seeks to find new and better statistical remedies for these problems as well as statistical techniques for detecting the occurrence of the violation of the assumptions.

Although the assumptions can be formulated clearly, each involves the properties of the random variables $\varepsilon_1, \varepsilon_2, \ldots, \varepsilon_T$ representing the disturbance terms in the model, $Y = X\Gamma + \varepsilon$. Therefore, the acceptability or violation of these assumptions is not so obvious since these disturbance terms are unknowns and unobservable. Instead, the validity of such assumptions relies on the empirical analysis of the best estimators available for $\varepsilon_t$, namely the least squares residuals $e_t$. The methods used in this process are included under the general term, *residual analysis.*

## The role of residual analysis

A separate group of methods has been developed for residual analysis because knowledge of the variances and covariances of the true disturbances $\varepsilon_t$ does not guarantee that the residuals, $e_t$, have the same variances and covariances. In particular if Assumptions 4 and 5 were true so that each $\varepsilon_t$ has the same variance $\sigma_\varepsilon^2$ and all covariances between different disturbance terms $\varepsilon_t$ and $\varepsilon_i$ were zero, it is still not necessarily true that the residuals $e_t$ would have constant variance and zero covariance. Therefore, test statistics involving the $e_t$ that may seem to have the $t$, chi-square, or $F$-distribution really do not. They would have different distributions because the $e_t$ may have different variances and be correlated with each other.

Thus, many special tests and techniques have been invented or derived involving the use of these residuals $e_t$. Not all such methods are included or mentioned in this chapter. Those which are presented are selected on the basis of being the most well-known, the most practical, and/or the most essential ones to know as a background and reference point for learning other more complex and theoretically more perfect methods.

## The plan of this chapter

Each of the three problems is discussed in turn in separate Sections 10.3 to 10.5 in this chapter. Four main aspects of each problem are considered:

1. Typical conditions under which the problem arises;
2. The effect on the properties of the least squares estimators $C$ of the coefficients $\Gamma$;
3. The methods of residual analysis used to detect the problem; and
4. Some suggested remedies for improving the estimation.

The final section presents a tabular array summarizing all these aspects of the three problems. Further discussion and examples of some remedies for the problems of heteroscedasticity and autocorrelation are given in Chapters 14 and 15.

## 13.2 REVIEW

The four review items presented below consist of two old familiar topics and two new ones. All are referred to later in this chapter.

### 1. Formulation of $\chi^2$ and $F$-distributed statistics

One chi-square distributed statistic which is commonly used is $\chi^2_{v \text{ d.f.}} = e'e/\sigma_\varepsilon^2$ where $v$ is degrees of freedom, $e$ is a least squares residuals vector, and $\sigma_\varepsilon^2$ is the variance of the disturbance term in the specified econometric model. Since the standard error of estimate is $s_e = \sqrt{(e'e)/v}$, the statistic can also be written $\chi^2 = s_e^2(v)/\sigma_\varepsilon^2$.

If two independent least squares residuals vectors were available for use in estimating $\sigma_\varepsilon^2$, say from different regressions using datasets denoted by $A$ and $B$, then both ratios $(e'e)_A/\sigma_\varepsilon^2$ and $(e'e)_B/\sigma_\varepsilon^2$ would be $\chi^2$ distributed. An $F$-distributed statistic could be formed as

$$F_{(v_A,\, v_B)} = \frac{(e'e)_A/\sigma_\varepsilon^2(v_A)}{(e'e)_B/\sigma_\varepsilon^2(v_B)},$$

or equivalently using the same substitution for standard error as above,

$$F = \frac{s_A^2(v_A)/(v_A)}{s_B^2(v_B)/(v_B)} = \frac{s_A^2}{s_B^2}.$$

### 2. Ordinary least squares estimators

In the simple model, the OLS estimate of the slope coefficient is always given as a ratio of the covariation between the endogenous and exogenous variables to the variation of the exogenous variable. [See (3–2*a*) in Section 3.4.]

For example in the simple regression of $Y$ on $X$, the slope estimate is $\sum xy / \sum x^2$ where lowercase symbols denote deviations from the sample mean. What would be the OLS estimate of the slope in a regression of residual $e_t$ on a lagged residual $e_{t-1}$? Presuming these symbols denote deviations from a mean residual of zero, then the slope estimate is $\sum e_t e_{t-1} / \sum e_{t-1}^2$ where the sums are over the appropriate indices.

As a reminder of previous results in the general model, the OLS estimates of the coefficients are given by $C = (X'X)^{-1} X'Y$, (9–3), and the variance-covariance matrix of these estimators is $V\text{-}Cov(C) = \sigma_\varepsilon^2 (X'X)^{-1}$ (10–4).

## 3. A first order autoregression

Consider a random variable $\varepsilon_t$, $t = 1, 2, \ldots, T$, which is regressed on preceding values of itself, such as in the model, $\varepsilon_t = \rho_1 \varepsilon_{t-1} + \rho_2 \varepsilon_{t-2} + \cdots + \rho_n \varepsilon_{t-n} + v$, where $v$ is a random error term and $\rho_i$ are the autoregressive coefficients. Such a relation is called an $n$th order autoregressive pattern because the variable is related to its own values for $n$ preceding periods.

A particular case of the $n$th order autoregression is the commonly used first order pattern when $n = 1$ and $\varepsilon_t$ represents the disturbances in an econometric model. The first order autoregressive scheme is written $\varepsilon_t = \rho \varepsilon_{t-1} + v$. The variable $\varepsilon_t$ is specified to be correlated with itself (in the preceding observation $\varepsilon_{t-1}$), and the slope of this relation is given by $\rho$. In addition, to avoid an explosive dynamic structure, the stability condition, $|\rho| < 1$, is always implied.

## 4. Moments of an autoregressive random variable under certain assumptions

Consider a random variable $\varepsilon_t$, $t = 1, 2, \ldots, T$, which is autoregressive according to the first order scheme $\varepsilon_t = \rho \varepsilon_{t-1} + v_t$ with $|\rho| < 1$ and $E(v_t) = 0$, $E(vv') = \sigma_v^2 I$, $t = 1, 2, \ldots, T$. The expected value, variance, and covariances between observations of this random variable can be determined from simple algebra and the algebra of expectations given in *Review* 6.2, Table 6–1.

The autoregressive structure can be compounded for each observation so that $\varepsilon_t$ can be written

$$\varepsilon_t = v_t + \rho v_{t-1} + \rho^2 v_{t-2} + \cdots = \sum_{h \neq 0}^{\infty} \rho^h v_{t-h}.$$

From this representation for $\varepsilon_t$, and using $E(v_t) = 0$ for any $t$, we determine

$$E(\varepsilon_t) = \sum_{h=0}^{\infty} \rho^h E(v_{t-h}) = 0.$$

By definition, then,

$$V(\varepsilon_t) = E[\varepsilon_t - E(\varepsilon_t)]^2 = E(\varepsilon_t^2) = \sigma_\varepsilon^2.$$

An expression for this variance can be found as follows:

$$E(\varepsilon_t^2) = E(v_t + \rho v_{t-1} + \rho^2 v_{t-2} + \cdots)^2$$

$$= E(v_t^2) + \rho^2 E(v_{t-1}^2) + \rho^4 E(v_{t-2}^2) + \cdots + 2 \sum_{i \neq j} \rho^i \rho^j E(v_{t-i} v_{t-j}).$$

Since all the cross-product terms contain

$$E(v_{t-i} v_{t-j}) = 0 \qquad \text{for} \quad i \neq j,$$

then

$$E(\varepsilon_t^2) = \sigma_v^2 + \rho^2 \sigma_v^2 + \rho^4 \sigma_v^2 + \cdots$$

$$= \sigma_v^2 (1 + \rho^2 + \rho^4 + \cdots).$$

According to rules for a geometric progression with a factor $r$, the sum is $[1/(1 - r)]$. In this case, the factor is $\rho^2$ and the sum of the progression is $[1/(1 - \rho^2)]$. Thus, $\sigma_\varepsilon^2 = E(\varepsilon_t^2) = \sigma_v^2 [1/(1 - \rho^2)]$ for all $t$.

Finally, the $Cov(\varepsilon_t \varepsilon_{t-i}) = E(\varepsilon_t \varepsilon_{t-i})$ can be determined in general for $i \neq 0$. This provides the lower triangular section of the complete variance-covariance matrix for $\varepsilon_t$. The upper triangular section can be filled in by symmetry. The covariance can be expressed in detail as

$$\underset{i \neq 0}{E}(\varepsilon_t \varepsilon_{t-i}) = E[(v_t + \rho v_{t-1} + \rho^2 v_{t-2} + \cdots)$$

$$\times (v_{t-i} + \rho v_{t-i-1} + \rho^2 v_{t-i-2} + \cdots)].$$

Separating the first expression into two parts where the first part contains terms unique to the first expression and the second part contains terms common to both expressions, one obtains,

$$E(\varepsilon_t \varepsilon_{t-i}) = E\{[v_t + \rho v_{t-1} + \rho^2 v_{t-2} + \cdots + \rho^i (v_{t-i} + \rho v_{t-i-1}$$

$$+ \rho^2 v_{t-i-2} + \cdots)] \times [v_{t-i} + \rho v_{t-i-1} + \rho^2 v_{t-i-2} + \cdots]\}.$$

Now, the product must be expanded and the expectation taken for each term.

$$E(\varepsilon_t \varepsilon_{t-i}) = E[v_t(v_{t-i} + \rho v_{t-i-1} + \cdots)]$$

$$+ E[\rho v_{t-i}(v_{t-1} + \rho v_{t-i-2} + \cdots)] + \cdots$$

$$+ E[\rho^{i-1} v_{t-i+1}(v_{t-i} + \rho v_{t-i-1} + \cdots)]$$

$$+ \rho^i E[(v_{t-i} + \rho v_{t-i-1} + \rho^2 v_{t-i-2} + \cdots)^2].$$

Again, since $E(v_i v_j) = 0$ for $i \neq j$, all but the last expression are zero. That is,

$$E(\varepsilon_t \varepsilon_{t-i}) = 0 + 0 + \cdots + 0 + \rho^i [E(v_{t-i}^2) + \rho^2 E(v_{t-i-1}^2)$$

$$+ \rho^4 E(v_{t-i-2}^2) + \cdots].$$

||||||||||||||||||||||||||||||||||||||||||||||||||||||||||||||||||||||||||||||||||||||||||||||||||||||||||||||||||||||||||||||||||||||||

**Explicative note.** The expectation operator has been applied to each term in the last expression, and the cross-product terms have been eliminated again.

||||||||||||||||||||||||||||||||||||||||||||||||||||||||||||||||||||||||||||||||||||||||||||||||||||||||||||||||||||||||||||||||||||||||

Thus, $E(\varepsilon_t \varepsilon_{t-i}) = \rho^i \sigma_v^2 (1 + \rho^2 + \rho^4 + \cdots) = \rho^i \sigma_v^2 [1/(1 - \rho^2)]$. Substituting from the expression for the variance, $\sigma_\varepsilon^2 = \sigma_v^2 [1/(1 - \rho^2)]$, this covariance can also be written, $E(\varepsilon_t \varepsilon_{t-i}) = \rho^i \sigma_\varepsilon^2$.

In summary, given the assumptions on the error $(v_t)$ of the autoregressive scheme, the autoregressive random variable $\varepsilon_t$ has expected value zero and a constant variance. In addition, the degree of correlation between disturbances at different observations, $t$ and $t - i$, declines geometrically with the size of the difference, $i$.

## 13.3 CONTEMPORANEOUS CORRELATION BETWEEN $X_t$ AND $\varepsilon_t$

One of the assumptions used in all the previous presentation on least squares estimation concerns the independence between the predetermined variables and the disturbance term in the same observation period. When this assumption is violated and $Cov(X_{tk}, \varepsilon_t) \neq 0$ for some $k = 2, 3, \ldots, K$, then many of our previous results are not true. The problem has been given the name, especially when the observations are over time, of *contemporaneous correlation* of $X$ and $\varepsilon$.

### Typical situations related to violations of Assumption 1

The problem of contemporaneous correlation between $X$ and $\varepsilon$ is most often linked with two specific econometric difficulties, error in measurement of $X$ and simultaneity of the relation between $Y$ and $X$. For a discussion of these and later problems, perhaps it is easiest to consider again the simple model which contains only one predetermined variable and this variable $X$ is exogenous. Special problems arise within the primary problems to be considered if the variable $X$ is a lagged endogenous variable. On the other hand, the discussion can generally be extended to the model with $K$ exogenous variables without any special modifications.

**Error in measurement of $X$.** The Assumption 1 of Section 10.3 or 5.4 is violated by errors in measurement of $X$ because the disturbance term absorbs such errors. Suppose the true value of the exogenous variable at observation $t$ is denoted by $\chi_t$, the measured value is $X_t$, and the error in measurement is $u_t = X_t - \chi_t$. The model formulated is $Y_t = \alpha_1 + \alpha_2 \chi_t + w_t$, but due to the error in measurement, the model estimated is $Y_t = \alpha_1 + \alpha_2 (X_t - u_t) + w_t$. The term, $w_t$, represents the usual disturbance term which is assumed to be independent of $X$. However, the size of the measurement error $u$ usually is correlated with the size of the variable $X$.

||||||||||||||||||||||||||||||||||||||||||||||||||||||||||||||||||||||||||||||||||||||||||||||||||||||||||||||||

*Discursive note.*   The measurement of $\chi$ by $X$ may be incorrect by a constant percentage, say 1 percent error in measurement. Then for larger values of $X_t$, the size of the error $u_t = 0.01X_t$ is also larger. To give another example, consider $\chi$ as an aggregate measure across consumers or across firms. When the values for each unit are quite small, care is taken to acquire accurate measures to the nearest cent. When the values for each unit are very large, they may be rounded off to the nearest thousand dollars. The size of the measurement error is probably larger in the latter case.

||||||||||||||||||||||||||||||||||||||||||||||||||||||||||||||||||||||||||||||||||||||||||||||||||||||||||||||||

When the composite disturbance term for the model is formulated as $\varepsilon_t = w_t - \alpha_2 u_t$, it is obvious that the correlation between $X$ and $\varepsilon_t$ will not be zero, especially if the error in measurement $u_t$ dominates the other disturbance factors represented by $w_t$. Then, $E(X_t, \varepsilon_t) \neq 0$ and Assumption 1 is violated.

*Simultaneity of the relation between Y and X.*   In the simple model, an implicit casual order is expressed from the exogenous variable $X$ to the endogenous variable $Y$. Suppose the underlying theory also suggests a rationale for a casual relation from $Y$ to $X$. Using the implication symbol ($\Rightarrow$) for direction of causality, the two-way relationship is denoted by $Y \Leftrightarrow X$ in contrast to the regression model relation $Y \Leftarrow X$. The single equation regression model is inadequate to reflect a two-way causality. Instead, a simultaneous equations regression model needs to be formulated in which $Y$ and $X$ are both endogenous variables to be jointly determined by other exogenous factors and one or more disturbance terms. A consideration of this simultaneous approach is delayed temporarily until Part IV, Chapters 16–19.

The problem of simultaneity for the ordinary least squares estimation of the simple model is the violation of Assumption 1. Consider $Y_t = \alpha_1 + \alpha_2 X_t + \varepsilon_t$ where both $X$ and $\varepsilon$ are used to determine $Y$, $(X_t, \varepsilon_t) \Rightarrow Y_t$. If $Y$ also is a cause of $X$ so that $Y_t \Rightarrow X_t$, then $\varepsilon_t \Rightarrow Y_t \Rightarrow X_t$ and a dependency is created between the disturbance term $\varepsilon_t$ and the explanatory variable $X$. It is no longer valid to assume that $Cov(X_t, \varepsilon_t) = 0$.

||||||||||||||||||||||||||||||||||||||||||||||||||||||||||||||||||||||||||||||||||||||||||||||||||||||||||||||||

*Interpretive note.*   All this is true in the general model when error in measurement or simultaneity problems involve any one or more of the exogenous variables in the set $\{X_k\}$, $k = 2, 3, \ldots, K$.

||||||||||||||||||||||||||||||||||||||||||||||||||||||||||||||||||||||||||||||||||||||||||||||||||||||||||||||||

## Effect on the estimators

To examine the effect of violations of the assumptions on the properties of the estimators, it is necessary to return to the derivation of the expected values, variances, and covariances of the estimators and consider what results are nullified or modified when the invalid assumption is not used. While some of these results have already been demonstrated by econometricians, many of the asymptotic properties involve more complex derivations than we wish to repeat here. In addition, some results, especially for combinations of violated assumptions and for finite sample approximating distributions of the estimators, are very much topics of continuing econometric research. At this beginning level, an awareness of some results is all that is necessary. For a discussion of the properties of estimates which are considered, return to Sections 6.4 and 10.4.

For a violation of the assumption, $Cov(X_t, \varepsilon_t) = 0$, it is shown that (*a*) the estimates of the coefficients in the regression model are biased; (*b*) the bias is not removed even for very large samples so the estimates are not consistent; (*c*) the estimate $s_e^2$ of the variance of the disturbance term is biased; and (*d*) the usual *t* and *F* tests of Chapter 11 are not exactly applicable. Each of these points can be considered briefly and then some discussion of their practical consequences follows.

*Bias of C.* Returning to Section 10.5, we find the equation $C - \Gamma = (X'X)^{-1}X'\varepsilon$ (10–3) which is useful for determining the expectation of the coefficients of the general model.[1] Taking expectations of both sides, we obtain $E(C) - \Gamma = E[(X'X)^{-1}X'\varepsilon]$. Since $E[X\varepsilon] \neq 0$ when Assumption 1 is violated, the right-hand term above is not zero. The expected value of the estimator $C$ is not the true value $\Gamma$. Rather, $C$ is a biased estimator.

*Inconsistency of C.* Even in large samples where the relevant sampling moment approaches the true covariance, this true covariance is still nonzero and the bias remains. The estimator $C$ does not have the property of consistency.

*Biased estimate of $\sigma_\varepsilon^2$.* One of the major problems of errors in measurement or simultaneity is that the disturbance term $\varepsilon$ becomes a composite of two or more different errors and the total error variance, $\sigma_\varepsilon^2$ cannot be decomposed unambiguously. It may be a random error associated with the specification plus an error of measurement, as seen before, $\varepsilon = w_t - \alpha_2 u_t$. In the case of simultaneity it may be a mixture of specification errors in two or more relations which interact with each other. When the estimate of $\sigma_\varepsilon^2$ is obtained by $s_e^2$, this is really a composite estimate, not the estimate of the single component desired. The true residual variance due only to the random error term associated with the specification of that particular equation is commonly overestimated by the measure of $s_e^2$ based on the observed data.

‖‖‖‖‖‖‖‖‖‖‖‖‖‖‖‖‖‖‖‖‖‖‖‖‖‖‖‖‖‖‖‖‖‖‖‖‖‖‖‖‖‖‖‖‖‖‖‖‖‖‖‖‖‖‖‖‖‖‖‖‖‖‖‖‖‖‖‖‖‖‖‖‖‖‖‖‖‖‖‖‖‖‖‖‖‖‖‖‖‖‖‖‖‖‖‖‖‖‖‖‖‖‖‖‖‖‖‖‖‖‖

*Discursive note.* With $s_e^2$ biased high, it follows that $R^2$ is a biased low estimate of the population multiple correlation coefficient in the true single equation regression. Presumably with better measurement or with better separation of the causal relations, the amount of unexplained variation could be reduced.

‖‖‖‖‖‖‖‖‖‖‖‖‖‖‖‖‖‖‖‖‖‖‖‖‖‖‖‖‖‖‖‖‖‖‖‖‖‖‖‖‖‖‖‖‖‖‖‖‖‖‖‖‖‖‖‖‖‖‖‖‖‖‖‖‖‖‖‖‖‖‖‖‖‖‖‖‖‖‖‖‖‖‖‖‖‖‖‖‖‖‖‖‖‖‖‖‖‖‖‖‖‖‖‖‖‖‖‖‖‖‖

---

[1] See Section 6.3, equation (6–2) for a similar expression in the simple model.

*Inappropriate use of t and F statistics.*   Finally, formulation in Chapters 7 and 11 of the $t$ and $F$ statistics used in testing the model required properly formed chi-square distributed random variables, normality of the disturbance term, and independence between the estimators and the residuals. Each of these requirements may be violated when $E(X, \varepsilon) \neq 0$.

If the estimator $s_e^2$ is biased to an unknown extent by these problems of error in measurement or simultaneity, then the random variable $(T - K)s_e^2/\sigma_\varepsilon^2$ is not a ratio of an unbiased estimate of variance to the true variance, and it does not have an exact chi-square distribution. If the errors in measurement are a relatively large component of the total error $\varepsilon$ and they are not normally distributed, then $\varepsilon$ may not be assumed to be normally distributed. If $X$ and $\varepsilon$ are not independent, then the frequently used condition of independence between $C$ and $s_e^2$ breaks down.[2] For these situations, the $t$ and $F$ distributed random variables used for testing the model (see Chapter 11) do not have exact $t$ and $F$ distributions. The tests of hypothesis using these random variables are not exactly valid.

*Practical consequences.*   In a practical sense, most socioeconomic aggregate and survey data have some error of measurement and many socioeconomic variable relations are indeed parts of more complex systems of interrelations. Consequently, the violation of Assumption 1 and all its consequences are almost always lurking behind our regression models. The hazards can be tempered to some extent by recognition of two further points. The extent of the bias in $C$ and $s_e^2$ may not be worth worrying about in relatively strong-fitting relations. That is, when the association between the exogenous and endogenous variables is strong, this bias is *relatively* small. The same reduction of concern over the bias occurs if the specification error component for the model is large relative to the measurement error component or the simultaneous feedback error component. On the other extreme, the practical import of the violation of $Cov(X_t, \varepsilon_t) = 0$ is heightened somewhat when the exogenous variables in the general model are highly multicollinear. (See the discussion following Assumption 7, Section 10.3.[3])

## Detection of contemporaneous correlation and some remedies

There is no set prescribed method of detecting excessive errors in measurement or simultaneity which cause the problems of contemporaneous correlation between $X_{tk}$ and $\varepsilon_t$. The econometrician must examine each model with a fresh view and try to determine theoretically if this problem may be a real danger to its analysis.

---

[2] This independence condition was first used in Section 7.4. It is a result of theorem 4.17 in F. A. Graybill, *An Introduction to Linear Statistical Models* (New York: McGraw-Hill, 1961), p. 87, which is dependent on the condition, $Cov(X, \varepsilon) = 0$.

[3] The special problem of multicollinearity is discussed in Chapter 15.

One simple statistical aid that is frequently informative is to plot the corresponding pairs of values $(X_{tk}, e_t)$ for some exogenous variable that is suspected to have a substantial error in measurement or a dual relation with the endogenous variable. Of course, the values of the residuals $e_t$ are not perfect estimates of the true disturbances $\varepsilon_t$ so the implications of the plot are not conclusive evidence for or against the validity of Assumption 1. Nevertheless, if the scatter diagram of $X_{tk}$ and $e_t$ gives evidence of a definite relation between these two, then the econometrician suspects that $X_{tk}$ and $\varepsilon_t$ may not be independent.

*The classical solution.* When $E(X_{tk}, \varepsilon_t) \neq 0$, the ordinary least squares (OLS) estimation method needs improvement. The basic problem arises in distinguishing the several components of the disturbance term, say $\varepsilon_t = w_t - \alpha_2 u_t$ in a simple case. The solution of classical statistics requires a restatement of the minimization of the sum of squares of residuals in which both type errors, $w_t$ and $u_t$, are represented as well as any interaction between them. Each of these components of the new sum of squares is then weighted inversely according to their importance as measured by the error variances, $V(w_t)$ and $V(u_t)$, and covariance $Cov(w_t u_t)$.

||||||||||||||||||||||||||||||||||||||||||||||||||||||||||||||||||||||||||||||||||||||||||||||||||||||||||||||||||||||||||||||

*Explicative note.* Such a procedure is called the method of weighted least squares. It requires additional assumptions or specific knowledge about the relative sizes of these variances and covariances of the errors.

||||||||||||||||||||||||||||||||||||||||||||||||||||||||||||||||||||||||||||||||||||||||||||||||||||||||||||||||||||||||||||||

The exact formulation for weighted regression is not presented here (see Chapter 14) since this is not a practical procedure. The reader can clearly see the impasse. Although the error of measurement and the specification error may be separate components of the disturbance term, both are unknown. Yet, to use this classical solution, we must be willing and able to specify the relative sizes of these error variances and covariances by stating the proportionality constants among them.

*The instrumental variable approach.* A more practical procedure for dealing with contemporaneous correlation between $X_{tk}$ and $\varepsilon_t$ is the *method of instrumental variables.*[4] In the case of ordinary least squares estimation on the model, $Y = X\Gamma + \varepsilon$, the solution is obtained by premultiplying all terms by $X'$. This gives $X'Y = X'X\Gamma + X'\varepsilon$, and if $E(X'\varepsilon) = O$ by assumption, then a second premultiplication by $(X'X)^{-1}$ (assuming this inverse exists by Assumption 7 of Section 10.3) gives the estimators of $\Gamma$ as $C = (X'X)^{-1}X'Y$.

With the instrumental variable method, the first premultiplication is by $Z'$ rather than $X'$ because $X$ is correlated with $\varepsilon$. This gives $Z'Y = Z'X\Gamma + Z'\varepsilon$,

---

[4] See J. D. Sargan, "The Estimation of Economic Relationships Using Instrumental Variables," *Econometrica*, 1958, pp. 393–415.

and a simple solution occurs if $(Z'X)^{-1}$ exists and if the instrumental variable $Z$ is selected so that it is not correlated with $\varepsilon$. That is, if $E(Z'\varepsilon) = O$, the solution for $\Gamma$ is

$$C^* = (Z'X)^{-1}Z'Y. \qquad (13\text{-}1)$$

A practical way of looking at this solution is as a two-step procedure in which ordinary least squares (OLS) is used twice and the separate variances of the error components are not needed (and are not estimated).

Consider a simple model $Y_t = \alpha_1 + \alpha_2 X_t + \varepsilon_t$ where $\varepsilon_t = w_t - \alpha_2 u_t$ due to a dependency between $X_t$ and $\varepsilon_t$ as represented by the term $(\alpha_2 u_t)$. Let the number of observations be $T$ so it is understood that all sums are over $t = 1, 2, \ldots, T$, and the subscript $t$ can be omitted for simplification. To circumvent the problem of $E(X, \varepsilon) \neq 0$, a roundabout procedure is used as follows:

1. Select an instrumental variable $Z$;
2. Use OLS to estimate the regression, $X = \delta_1 + \delta_2 Z + v$; and
3. Using $\hat{X}$, the estimated values from the previous regression, do OLS again for the regression, $Y = \alpha_1 + \alpha_2 \hat{X} + \varepsilon$.

||||||||||||||||||||||||||||||||||||||||||||||||||||||||||||||||||||||||||!|||||||||||||||||||||||||||||||||||||||||||||||||||||||||

***Explicative note.***   The estimates of $\alpha_1$ and $\alpha_2$ are still biased, but the estimates are now consistent if $Z$ was properly selected. However, the estimator obtained by the instrumental variable method is not efficient. Since the choice of $Z$ is arbitrary and different choices will result in different estimates of $\alpha_1$ and $\alpha_2$, the potential variance of these estimators is large.

||||||||||||||||||||||||||||||||||||||||||||||||||||||||||||||||||||||||||||||||||||||||||||||||||||||||||||||||||||||||||||||||||||||

***Computing the estimates using an instrumental variable.***   The computational steps 2 and 3 above are now repeated in more detail. In the first regression, $X = \delta_1 + \delta_2 Z + v$, the direction of causality is from $Z$ to $X$ and the OLS estimate of $\delta_2$ is $d_2 = \sum xz / \sum z^2$ where the lowercase indicates deviations from the respective sample means. (See *Review* 13.2, item 2.) If $Z$ has a large variance and is highly correlated with $X$, this model provides accurate predictions for $X$ denoted by $\hat{X} = d_1 + d_2 Z$. The second regression may be written in deviation form, using $\hat{x} = d_2 z$, as $y = \alpha_2 \hat{x} + (\varepsilon - \bar{\varepsilon})$.

||||||||||||||||||||||||||||||||||||||||||||||||||||||||||||||||||||||||||||||||||||||||||||||||||||||||||||||||||||||||||||||||||||||

***Recursive note.***   The disturbance term is $\varepsilon = w - \alpha_2 u$. We write the error term in deviation form as $\varepsilon - \bar{\varepsilon}$ because the mean $\bar{\varepsilon} \neq 0$ in this specification. The specification error component $w$ may have mean zero, but the measurement error component $u$ may not.

||||||||||||||||||||||||||||||||||||||||||||||||||||||||||||||||||||||||||||||||||||||||||||||||||||||||||||||||||||||||||||||||||||||

By substitution, $\hat{x} = d_2 z$, we obtain $y = \alpha_2(d_2 z) + \varepsilon - \bar{\varepsilon}$. Presuming that $Z$ is independent of $\varepsilon$, the OLS estimator in the second regression (step 3 above) is appropriately found by $a_2{}^* = \sum \hat{x}y/\sum \hat{x}^2 = \sum (d_2 z)y/\sum d_2{}^2 z^2$. Since $d_2$ is a constant estimate, not a variable, it can be brought out of the summations. Then by cancellation, and substitution for the remaining $d_2$, we mates obtain,

$$a_2{}^* = \frac{\sum zy}{d_2 \sum z^2} = \frac{\sum zy}{\left(\sum xz/\sum z^2\right) \sum z^2}$$

$$a_2{}^* = \frac{\sum zy}{\sum xz}. \tag{13–1a}$$

Using this estimate $a_2{}^*$, we can also find corresponding estimates $a_1{}^*$, $s_e{}^*$, and other statistics, in the usual manner. Tests on this model can be properly made when the number of observations is moderately large since these estimates are consistent.

**Choosing the instrumental variable.** All the properties of a well-selected instrumental variable can be listed. The variable $Z$ should (a) be independent of $\varepsilon$; (b) have a large variance; (c) be highly correlated with $X$; and (d) have a one-way causality relation with $X$. For interpretation purposes, it should also be theoretically related to both $X$ and $Y$.

If there are several exogenous variables in a general model, $Y = X\Gamma + \varepsilon$, which are not independent of the disturbance term, then more than one instrumental variable is required. In general, one instrumental variable is needed for each such exogenous variable, and the different instrumental variables should not be highly multicollinear with each other.

||||||||||||||||||||||||||||||||||||||||||||||||||||||||||||||||||||||||||||||||||||||||||||||||||||||||||||||||||||||||||||||||||||||||||||

*Discursive note.* The general case of several instrumental variables has a procedural form very similar to two-stage least squares (see Chapter 18). Both are remedies for the OLS procedure when $Cov(X_{tk}, \varepsilon_t) \neq 0$. The instrumental variable method is used when this violation of the Assumption 1 is due to errors in measurement of the exogenous variable. Two-stage least squares is used when the problem arises because of simultaneity.

||||||||||||||||||||||||||||||||||||||||||||||||||||||||||||||||||||||||||||||||||||||||||||||||||||||||||||||||||||||||||||||||||||||||||||

Finding the best instrumental variable(s) for a particular application of this method is difficult. Often, possible candidates will have some of the above properties but not another, and there is no definitive way to make trade-offs among the desired properties. Furthermore, determining if a particular $Z$ is independent of the unknown disturbance term $\varepsilon$ is certainly not a purely practical procedure.

Probably the best remedy for the problems caused by violation of the Assumption 1, $Cov(X_{tk}, \varepsilon_t) = 0$, is to avoid the problem. The econometrician should always attempt to use the most accurate measurements available for the variables in his model. He should express theoretical, two-way causal relations in a simultaneous equation model rather than a single equation model. Otherwise, he is bound to be restricted in his conclusions if his purpose is the empirical determination of theoretically crucial parameters. *Use of* OLS *for forecasting purposes.* On the other hand, if the purpose of the econometrician is to specify a good forecasting model for the endogenous variable *Y*, then he may ignore entirely the problems associated with contemporaneous correlation between *X* and $\varepsilon$. Particularly, if such a dependency is expected to continue among the observations in the forecasting period, and if the number of present observations is quite large, then using ordinary least squares is excusable.

This does not imply that it would be proper to use *t*-distributed test statistics for setting forecast intervals. Such test statistics are still not applicable. The forecaster would have to be satisfied with simple numerical comparisons between his forecasts for *Y* and the actual values of *Y* when and if they are available.

## 13.4 HETEROSCEDASTICITY

Referring to the disturbance terms $\varepsilon_t$ in the econometric model, heteroscedasticity defines the condition where the variance of $\varepsilon_t$ is not constant for all $\varepsilon_t$, $t = 1, 2, \ldots, T$. Thus, in this section we consider the violation of Assumption 4 of Sections 5.4 or 10.3 which states the condition of constant variance, $V(\varepsilon_t) = \sigma_\varepsilon^2$.

### Typical situations related to violations of Assumption 4

This violation occurs when some structural background condition changes so that the exactness of the specification of the model changes for different observations or sets of observations. The violation may be due to changes in the background conditions not included within the specification of the model. These are assumed to be constant in their effect on the model, but they may be changing if, for example, there are changes in laws, in interest ceilings, in reserve requirements, in quotas, in military expenditures, or in people's behavior in some way that affects the particular model.

Very frequently Assumption 4 is violated when cross-sectional data are used to estimate a model. The error of specification for one section may be quite different from the error for another section since different underlying and excluded factors are important for the two sections. The sections might be regions, age cohorts, or strata of firm sizes, etc. For example, a model may be concerned with explaining the investment level of a cross-section of manufacturing firms where one of the important independent variables is annual rate of change of sales. (See Exercise 9, Chapter 3.) Heteroscedasticity might be evident if firms with small rates of change of sales have very similar and rigid investment behavior (although on different absolute levels of magnitude, perhaps) while those firms with high rates of change in sales have very dissimilar and flexible investment behavior. Thereby, the distribution of errors about the linear regression would tend to have a larger variance associated with the observations on firms with high rates of change in sales relative to the others.

Another simple example illustrating a case of heteroscedasticity concerns estimation of a consumption function, relating consumption $C$ to income $Y$. For an individual consumer $i$ at time $t$, the model may be $C_{it} = \alpha_1 + \alpha_2 Y_{it} + \varepsilon_{it}$ where it is assumed that $E(\varepsilon_{it}) = 0$, $V(\varepsilon_{it}) = \sigma^2$, and $Cov(\varepsilon_{it}) = 0$. Now suppose that only aggregate data over all consumers is available at time $t$ and let $n_t$ denote the number of consumers at time $t$. By summing, we obtain

$$\sum_i C_{it} = n_t \alpha_1 + \alpha_2 \sum_i Y_{it} + \sum_i \varepsilon_{it}.$$

$$C_t = n_t \alpha_1 + \alpha_2 Y_t + \varepsilon_t$$

where $\varepsilon_t = \sum_i \varepsilon_{it}$; and so $V(\varepsilon_t) = V(\sum \varepsilon_{it}) = \sum_{i=1}^{n_t} V(\varepsilon_{it}) = n_t \sigma^2$. Therefore, if the number of consumers $n_t$ changes over time, then heteroscedasticity occurs.

Finally, the violation of Assumption 4 is not always independent of the violation of Assumption 1. Errors in measurement may exist, for example, as a large component of the disturbance term. If there are changes in measurement procedures over the observations so that some observations have significantly more accuracy than others, then the variance of the disturbance term can be smaller for the subset of observations which are measured with the greater accuracy.

## The effect of heteroscedasticity

When only Assumption 4 is violated, the distribution and expectations of the OLS estimators $C$ of the coefficients $\Gamma$ do not change. They are still linear and unbiased estimators with the property of consistency. The problem arises in the estimation of the variance of these coefficient estimates.

If we assume a constant variance of $\varepsilon_t$ when, in fact, the variance changes for different observations, then we are not making use of all the possible information. This is always an indication that the estimators are not efficient. That is, $V(a_2)$, or $V(C)$ in the general model, where the estimators are obtained by OLS, are greater than variances of $a_2$ or $C$ determined by some other estimating procedure which uses the additional information about the changing variance of the disturbance term.

In finding the OLS (or maximum likelihood) estimates of $\Gamma$ in the general model, $Y = X\Gamma + \varepsilon$, the function to be minimized is

$$(1/\sigma_\varepsilon^2)(Y - X\Gamma)'\Omega^{-1}(Y - X\Gamma) \tag{10-2}$$

where $\Omega\sigma_\varepsilon^2$ is the variance-covariance matrix of $\varepsilon_t$. When Assumptions 4 and 5 hold, $\Omega = \underset{(T \times T)}{I}$ and the estimator is

$$C = (X'X)^{-1}X'Y \tag{9-3}$$

with

$$V\text{-}Cov(C) = \sigma_\varepsilon^2 (X'X)^{-1}. \tag{10-4}$$

If Assumption 4 does not hold, then

$$\sigma_\varepsilon^2 \Omega = \sigma_\varepsilon^2 \begin{pmatrix} \omega_1 & 0 & \cdots & 0 \\ 0 & \omega_2 & \cdots & 0 \\ 0 & 0 & \cdots & \omega_T \end{pmatrix},$$

and the matrix $\Omega$ cannot be eliminated from the computations in the same way as the identity matrix. Pretending that it does cancel out gives less efficient estimates of $C$ than are otherwise possible. The $V\text{-}Cov(C)$ given by OLS is larger than say the $V\text{-}Cov(C) = \sigma_\varepsilon^2 (X'\Omega^{-1}X)^{-1}$ obtainable by using generalized least squares which utilizes the extra information about $\Omega$. (See Chapter 14.) The more the elements, $\omega_1, \omega_2, \ldots, \omega_T$, on the diagonal of $\Omega$ differ from each other the more inefficient are the OLS estimates based on the assumption that these are all the same.

Finally, the OLS estimate of $V\text{-}Cov(C)$ is often biased downward. That is, the estimated value of the standard error of an estimated coefficient $C_k$ is lower than it should be on the average.

||||||||||||||||||||||||||||||||||||||||||||||||||||||||||||||||||||||||||||||||||||||||||||||||||||||||||||||||||||

*Explicative note.* The reader may find these results paradoxical at first glance. The claim of inefficiency suggests that $V\text{-}Cov(C)$ using OLS is too large in the sense that it is not minimal among the class of linear unbiased estimators. There is some other estimator, say $\hat{C}$ such that its variance satisfies, $V(\hat{C}) < V(C)$. This is a comparative statement about the properties of two estimators, $C$ and $\hat{C}$, for the coefficients $\Gamma$.

The claim of biased low suggests that when the OLS estimates ($C$) are used, then [Est. $V\text{-}Cov(C)$] is too small. This is an absolute statement about the expectation of a particular estimator of variance. The two statements are not contradictory.[5]

||||||||||||||||||||||||||||||||||||||||||||||||||||||||||||||||||||||||||||||||||||||||||||||||||||||||||||||||||||

The effect of this low bias of estimates of $V(C)$ is that $t$ and $F$ distributed test statistics used for testing the significance of the coefficients will be overstated. The researcher will unwarily be rejecting the null hypothesis of no significance more often than he should.

## Detection of heteroscedasticity

Suppose in a simple model, $Y = \alpha_1 + \alpha_2 X + \varepsilon$, the econometrician suspects that there are three distinct groups of observations for which the variance

---

[5] The same two effects are illustrated in Figure 13–5 for a problem of positive autocorrelation of the residuals.

of the disturbance terms differs. Figure 13–1 illustrates the situation for the three groups $A$, $B$, and $C$. Detection of such differences in $V(\varepsilon_t)$ cannot be made using $\varepsilon_t$ directly since these are unknown. Instead, it is common to make plots of the residuals $\varepsilon_t$ to detect any signs of possible heteroscedasticity.

**FIGURE 13–1**
**Change in $V(\varepsilon_t)$ among three groups of observations**

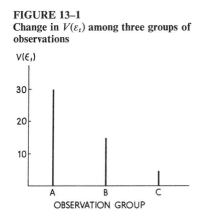

If the observation groups, $A$, $B$, $C$, run consecutively over time, then a useful plot shows the values of residuals with time as given in Figure 13–2. The distribution of errors seems to have an increasing variance over time, indicated by the $V$-slope of the bounding lines. A changing variance would also be indicated if the bounding lines approximated an inverted $V$, or if they widened and narrowed in the shape of an egg timer or a football, or had any systematic pattern other than parallel lines.

**FIGURE 13–2**
**Residual plot against time**

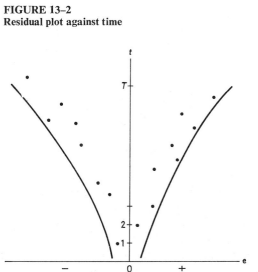

||||||||||||||||||||||||||||||||||||||||||||||||||||||||||||||||||||||||||||||||||||||||||||||||||||||||||||||||||||||||||||||||||

*Discursive note.* This plot may also reveal a linear or second degree relation between the residuals and time. This indicates that $t$ or $t^2$ or some excluded variable with a definite time trend should be included as an exogenous variable in the model.

||||||||||||||||||||||||||||||||||||||||||||||||||||||||||||||||||||||||||||||||||||||||||||||||||||||||||||||||||||||||||||||||||

If the observation groups are not consecutive, then similar information is obtained by plotting the residuals against the estimated values of the endogenous variable, $\hat{Y}_t$. Again, V-shaped, egg-timer shaped, football shaped distributions, etc., indicate that $V(\varepsilon_t)$ is not constant. If the residuals tend to be within approximately parallel lines, then Assumption 4 is presumed to be valid.

*An example plot for heteroscedasticity.* To illustrate the detection of heteroscedasticity by a plot of $e_t$ against $\hat{Y}_t$ consider again the model and data of Exercise 16 in Chapters 3 and 7. The simple regression model of GNP($Y$) on defense expenditures ($X$) gives the results of Table 13–1. A plot

**TABLE 13–1**

Results of GNP–defense expenditure model

$Y = \text{GNP}$           $r = 0.3849$
$X = \text{defense expenditures}$     $s_e = 50.4878$
$\hat{Y} = 165.516 + 0.63127X$
$\quad (26.513)\ (0.57208)$

| | | | | | | | Transformed data | |
| | | | | | | |---|---|
| Observation | Y | X | $\hat{Y}$ | e | Group | $s_e$ | Y* | X* |
|---|---|---|---|---|---|---|---|---|
| 1...... | 99.7 | 1.5 | 166.463 | −66.763 | | | 2.9926 | 0.0450 |
| 2...... | 124.5 | 6.1 | 169.366 | −44.867 | A | 33.315 | 3.7370 | 0.1831 |
| 9...... | 257.6 | 11.8 | 172.965 | 84.635 | | | 7.7322 | 0.3542 |
| 8...... | 231.3 | 14.4 | 174.606 | 56.694 | | | 6.9428 | 0.4322 |
| 3...... | 157.9 | 24.0 | 180.666 | −22.766 | | | 5.9866 | 0.9099 |
| 7...... | 208.5 | 43.2 | 192.787 | 15.713 | B | 26.375 | 7.9051 | 1.6379 |
| 4...... | 191.6 | 63.2 | 205.412 | −13.812 | | | 7.2643 | 2.3962 |
| 5...... | 210.1 | 76.8 | 213.997 | − 3.897 | C | 0.736 | 285.5017 | 104.362 |
| 6...... | 211.9 | 81.3 | 216.838 | − 4.938 | | | 287.9467 | 110.477 |

of the residuals with the estimated values is given in Figure 13–3. The plot indicates a decreasing variance of residuals about the estimating equation as the size of the estimated values increases.

To further detect this change in residual variance, the observations can be grouped according to the size of $X$. Table 13–1 presents a possible grouping of the four smallest values of $X$, the next three larger, and the two largest. A plot of the calculated variance of $e_t$ within each of these groups $A$, $B$, and $C$ would resemble Figure 13–1. If such obvious differences in the variance of $e_t$ reflect a change in the variance of the true disturbance terms $\varepsilon_t$, then Assumption 4 is violated. Another representation of the problem is shown in Figure 13–4.

**FIGURE 13–3**
**Residual plot against estimated $\hat{Y}$ for GNP-defense expend-iture model**

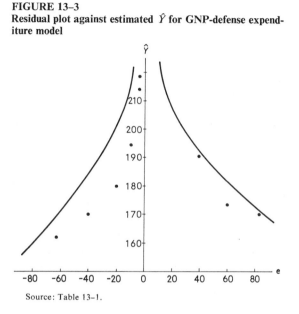

Source: Table 13–1.

**FIGURE 13–4**
**Example of heteroscedasticity**

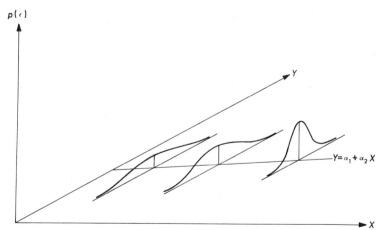

*As in the example problem with results in Table 13–1, heteroscedasticity occurs when the variance of the disturbance term changes. This case shows diminishing $V(\varepsilon)$ for larger values of X. The distribution of $\varepsilon$, assumed normal, becomes less dispersed for larger X.*

*Developing a test for homoscedasticity.* An $F$-distributed ratio of two chi-square distributed random variables could be used to test if the difference between variance of the separate groups of residuals is significant. Under the usual assumptions, the test on difference between variances uses a statistic

$$F_{(T_1-1, T_2-1)} = \frac{s_1^2}{s_2^2}$$

where $s_i^2$ is the unbiased sample estimate of variance. (See *Review* 13.2, item 1.) However, in this case the estimates being used are based on the sum of squares of subgroups of residuals from the same regression equation. These are not statistically independent since each residual depends on the estimate $C$ which depends on all the residuals. Thus, this statistic is not a ratio of two *independent* chi-square distributed variables as required for the $F$-distribution.

*The Goldfeld-Quandt test.* To satisfy the independence condition, we must find the variance of the subgroup of residuals from separate regressions based on the corresponding subgroups of observations.[6] The first regression is based on $T_A$ observations and the other on $T_B$ observations. Then, the sum of squares of residuals in each regression is a quadratic form, $(e'e)_A = Q_A$ and $(e'e)_B = Q_B$. Also each ratio of $Q/\sigma_\varepsilon^2$ has a chi-square distribution with $T_A - K$ and $T_B - K$ degrees of freedom respectively, and these two chi-square variables are independent if Assumption 4 holds so that $V\text{-}Cov(\varepsilon_t) = \sigma_\varepsilon^2 \underset{(T \times T)}{I}$.
Therefore, the ratio appropriate for an $F$-distributed test statistic when $V(\varepsilon_t)$ is constant for all $t$, is

$$F_{(T_A-K, T_B-K)} = \frac{(e'e)_A/(T_A - K)}{(e'e)_B/(T_B - K)}. \tag{13-2}$$

For a null hypothesis of homoscedasticity against a two-sided alternative, we reject the null and conclude that the variance of the disturbance term is larger (smaller) for the observation subgroup $A$ than for subgroup $B$ if the calculated $F$-value is in the upper (lower) rejection region. A one-sided alternate hypothesis is used with a similar interpretation when the observations have been ordered so that the subgroup with the larger residual variance is known a priori and designated as subgroup $A$ in the numerator.

*An example of the use of this test for homoscedasticity.* For an example, consider a model explaining a firm's level of employment based on four exogenous variables ($K = 5$) measuring particular firm characteristics. The model is estimated based on data from the annual *U.S. Census of Manufacturers*, Department of Commerce, Bureau of the Census, for 68 firms. The cross-sectional sample includes 44 firms in the food industry and 24 firms in the primary metals industry. It is suspected that the variance of the errors for the observations in the two separate industries may be different.

---

[6] See S. M. Goldfeld and R. E. Quandt, "Some Tests for Homoscedasticity," *Journal of the American Statistical Association*, 1965, pp. 539–47.

Denote the two industries by observation subgroup $A$ for the food industry with $T_A = 44$ and subgroup $B$ for the primary metals industry with $T_B = 24$. The null hypothesis is $H_0: V(\varepsilon_t)_A = V(\varepsilon_t)_B$ against a one-sided alternate, $V(\varepsilon_t)_A > V(\varepsilon_t)_B$. $H_0$ will be rejected if the calculated $F$-value exceeds $F_{(0.05; 39, 19)} = 2.02$. Two regressions are computed with the results, $(e'e)_A = 0.90888$ and $(e'e)_B = 0.25047$. The test statistic is determined to be $F = (0.9088/39)/(0.25047/19) = 0.0233/0.01318 = 1.77$. Assumption 4 of homoscedasticity is not rejected.

*Additional remarks concerning this test.* Sometimes, separate subgroups of the data are not so obvious and the test is to be applied in general to determine if $V(\varepsilon_t)$ is increasing or decreasing or constant over the complete set of observations (ordered by time or by size of $Y$, or by size of some $X_k$). In this situation, the data should be separated into three groups with number of observations $T_A$, $T_m$, and $T_B$, where the middle group includes about 20 percent of the observations. When $T_m$ observations in the middle are excluded, the test statistic (13–2) can be used in the same way as before. This disuse of some of the data gives a less powerful test, but comparing more widely separated observations has an opposite effect since it tends to make the difference between $(e'e)_A$ and $(e'e)_B$ larger. The combined net effect may be an increase in the power of the test.

## Correction for heteroscedasticity

Suppose the data are determined to have subgroups for which the variances of the corresponding disturbance terms are different. Then, if the variances of the disturbance terms within each subgroup can be assumed to be equal, the problem of heteroscedasticity can be avoided by determining separate estimations for the subgroups of data within which Assumption 4 is valid. Of course, the estimates of the coefficients based on the different subgroups of observations may then differ.

Or as an alternate, a separate dummy variable may be used for each subgroup. (See Section 12.5. The number of dummy variables required would be one less than the number of subgroups.) The dummy variables might serve as a proxy for some of the underlying causes of the heteroscedasticity, thereby partially decreasing the differences in variance of the disturbance terms among the subgroups. This use of dummy variables underlies the covariance method of estimation considered in Section 15.4.

*Weighted least squares.* If the variance of the disturbance term is continually changing for each different observation, then the classical procedure of weighted least squares is again appropriate. To obtain better estimates than the simple OLS estimates, the observations for which the disturbance variance is small should be given large weights in the least squares estimation and the observations for which the disturbance variance is large should be given smaller weights. Ordinary least squares without explicit weights presumes that each observation is equally important in estimating the "true" relation.

‖‖‖‖‖‖‖‖‖‖‖‖‖‖‖‖‖‖‖‖‖‖‖‖‖‖‖‖‖‖‖‖‖‖‖‖‖‖‖‖‖‖‖‖‖‖‖‖‖‖‖‖‖‖‖‖‖‖‖‖‖‖‖‖‖‖‖‖‖‖‖‖‖‖‖‖‖‖‖‖‖‖‖‖‖‖‖‖‖‖‖

*Interpretive note.* The "true" relation between the endogenous and exogenous variables is more easily determined when the level of disturbance noise or variation is small. Consequently, to obtain the most accurate estimation of this relation, more importance should be given to observations for which $V(\varepsilon_t)$ is small. The opposite type observations for which $V(\varepsilon_t)$ is large should be deemphasized.

‖‖‖‖‖‖‖‖‖‖‖‖‖‖‖‖‖‖‖‖‖‖‖‖‖‖‖‖‖‖‖‖‖‖‖‖‖‖‖‖‖‖‖‖‖‖‖‖‖‖‖‖‖‖‖‖‖‖‖‖‖‖‖‖‖‖‖‖‖‖‖‖‖‖‖‖‖‖‖‖‖‖‖‖‖‖‖‖‖‖‖

In weighted least squares this differential treatment is accomplished by dividing each observation for all variables, endogenous and exogenous, by some measure which hopefully corresponds to the size of the standard deviation of the disturbance random variable for that observation, $\sqrt{V(\varepsilon_t)}$.

*Typical weights for weighted least squares.* A very common weighting scheme in use by econometricians assumes that $V(\varepsilon_t)$ is proportional to the square of the observations on some exogenous variable. Thus, the standard error of $\varepsilon_t$ would be proportional to $X_{tk}$ for some $k$, perhaps because $X_{tk}$ is thought to have undergone a systematic change in its accuracy of measurement. The mathematical formulation of this weighting scheme is a special case of generalized least squares which is presented in the next chapter.

Another common procedure is to estimate the size of $V(\varepsilon_t)$ for separate subgroups of the observations based on $s_e^2$ for each subgroup. Then the original observations within each group can be weighted inversely according to the standard error of estimate for that group.

*The practical procedure.* Either of these weighting methods gives more efficient estimates than the use of OLS on the original data. They can be carried out by making a transformation of each observation for each variable and then repeating OLS on the transformed data. Finally, the new residuals from this second least squares estimation should be subjected to analysis such as the Goldfeld-Quandt test to check that heteroscedasticity has been significantly reduced.

### An example using subgroup weights to correct for heteroscedasticity

For example, reconsider the GNP–defense expenditure model and data with results given in Table 13–1. From the initial least squares estimation, the residuals are determined and divided into three groups $A$, $B$, and $C$ which seem to represent observations with different variances of the disturbances as indicated by Figure 13–1. The standard error of the residuals within each group are determined (and given in Table 13–1). The original observations are separated into corresponding groups $A$, $B$, and $C$, and the transformed variables (including the intercept variable) are obtained by dividing each observation by the estimated standard error of residuals for its respective group. A second estimation based on the transformed data is determined using the method of least squares again. The results give estimates of $\alpha_1$ and $\alpha_2$ in the model $Y = \alpha_1 + \alpha_2 X + \varepsilon$ which are more efficient than the initial OLS estimates on the original data.

Using the transformed data, $Y^*$ and $X^*$, in Table 13–1, the new regression equation is,

$$Y^* = 0.5005 + 171.5X^*$$
$$(0.2366) \quad (18.70)$$

with $s_e = 1.556$ and $r = 0.999$. The decrease in the size of the standard error of the coefficients and the increased fit of the model is remarkable. These are due to a large extent to the particular selection of observation groups in this particular example. If the reader would graph the original data of $Y$ and $X$, he observes a definite nonlinear relation. Trying to fit this with a linear model resulted in violations of both Assumptions 4 and 5. (See Section 13.5 for the detection of the violation of Assumption 5.) Ordering the observations by increasing size of $X$ and weighting them by $(1/s_e)$ has the effect of linearizing the nonlinear relation. In a general model with $K$ exogenous variables, such a simple method of improving the estimation is not likely to produce so remarkable a result.

## 13.5 AUTOCORRELATION

If disturbance terms at different observations are dependent on each other, then the dependency is reflected in the correlation of error terms with themselves in preceding or subsequent observations. This autocorrelation of disturbance terms violates Assumption 5 of Sections 5.4 and 10.3 which states $Cov(\varepsilon_t, \varepsilon_i) = 0$ for $t \neq i$.

### Situations tending to increase autocorrelation

The problem of autocorrelation arises very frequently when time-series data are used, especially if the time intervals between observations is small. Then, some of the same excluded factors which significantly affect the environment or background (in which the model operates) at observation $t$ are also likely to be important influences in the disturbance term at observations $t + 1$, $t + 2$, or $t - 1$, $t - 2$, etc.

A similar situation arises if the specification of the model *excludes* a cyclical variable which is an important determinant of the endogenous variable. In such a situation, the error term $\varepsilon_t$ will absorb this cyclical pattern and successive error terms will not be random. Indeed, knowing the size and sign of, say, three successive disturbances would be very useful information in predicting the next disturbance.

Autocorrelation can be related to some of the same causes as error in measurement or heteroscedasticity too. First, suppose that one exogenous variable is measured with error and is available only annually whereas the other variables are measured monthly. If the econometrician interpolates within the year to approximate a series of monthly values for his annually observed variable, then he is likely to be apportioning the error of measurement onto the monthly values also. This would introduce a stronger successive autocorrelation into the disturbances.

Second, cross-sectional data which leads to heteroscedasticity may also lead to *spatial autocorrelation*. Many of the same excluded factors may be influencing the error term in different observations from cross-sectional data. This is particularly true, for example, if the cross sections are regions such as states and the variables are aggregates of individual measures of economic activity. The state boundaries determine to which aggregate a certain individual measure belongs, but these boundaries are often politically or geographically determined. Economic activity on both sides of a particular state boundary may be affected to a significant extent by the same underlying factors, such as the weather, the productivity of the land, the culture of the laborers, etc. Since such common factors are absorbed by the error term, autocorrelation is likely to result between different regions.

These suggestions are not an exhaustive list of the situations likely to produce autocorrelation (which is probably the most frequently occurring problem in the use of ordinary least squares for estimating an econometric model). The reader might encounter others in his reading or in examining a model of his own.

### Effect of autocorrelation on the estimators

Since autocorrelation is concerned with the $Cov(\varepsilon_t, \varepsilon_i)$ for $t \neq i$, then the effects on OLS estimators in the general model are again a result of misrepresentation of the variance-covariance matrix of disturbances, $V\text{-}Cov(\varepsilon_t)$. Just as in the case of heteroscedasticity, it is wasteful of information to presume that $V\text{-}Cov(\varepsilon_t) = \sigma_\varepsilon^2 \underset{(T \times T)}{I}$ instead of $V\text{-}Cov(\varepsilon_t) = \sigma_\varepsilon^2 \Omega$. In the previous case, when $V(\varepsilon_t)$ was not constant, $\Omega$ was represented as a diagonal matrix. In the case of autocorrelation, the off-diagonal elements of $V\text{-}Cov(\varepsilon_t)$ should not be assumed to be zero. In this case

$$I \neq \Omega = \begin{pmatrix} \omega & \omega_{12} & \cdots & \omega_{1T} \\ \omega_{21} & \omega & \cdots & \omega_{2T} \\ \omega_{T1} & \omega_{T2} & \cdots & \omega \end{pmatrix},$$

where the off-diagonal elements, covariances of different error terms, are not zero and the diagonal elements can be assumed to be equal to each other.[7] (See *Review* 13.2, item 4, for particular values of $V\text{-}Cov(\varepsilon_t)$ in a first order autoregression under some usual assumptions.)

---

[7] Both Assumptions 4 and 5 may be violated in the same situation so that the diagonal elements may not all be the same. This extension is considered in detail in Chapter 15.

*Inefficiency.* The consequences of not including information about $\Omega$ in the use of OLS are the same as before. The OLS estimates $C$ of the coefficients $\Gamma$ in the general model $Y = X\Gamma + \varepsilon$ are still unbiased and consistent. However, the $V(C)$ as determined by OLS methods, $V\text{-}Cov(C) = \sigma_\varepsilon^2(X'X)^{-1}$, (10–4), is again not minimal. The estimates $C$ are inefficient.

**Bias in [Est. V-Cov(C)].**  Also, the least squares estimate, [Est. $V\text{-}Cov(C)$] $= s_e^2(X'X)^{-1}$, is biased due to its failure to include information on $\Omega$, such as $s_e^2(X'\Omega^{-1}X)^{-1}$ which is done in the method of generalized least squares (see Chapter 14).

|||||||||||||||||||||||||||||||||||||||||||||||||||||||||||||||||||||||||||||||||||||||||||||||||||||||||||||||||||||||||||||||||||||||||||||||||||||||||||||

*Discursive note.*  In the simple model, $Y = \alpha_1 + \alpha_2 X + \varepsilon$, the bias in the estimate of the standard error of $\alpha_2$ is downward in the most common case of positive autocorrelation of the disturbances, $Cov(\varepsilon_t \varepsilon_{t-1}) > 0$ and positive serial correlation in the time-series variable $X, r_{X_t, X_{t-1}} > 0$. If the autocorrelation is negative, $Cov(\varepsilon_t, \varepsilon_{t-1}) < 0$, then the bias in [Est. $V(\alpha_2)$] is upward. The calculated values of $t$ and $F$ statistics for testing significance of the coefficients will deviate from their proper value in a direction opposite from this bias.

|||||||||||||||||||||||||||||||||||||||||||||||||||||||||||||||||||||||||||||||||||||||||||||||||||||||||||||||||||||||||||||||||||||||||||||||||||||||||||||

**Bias in [Est. $V(\varepsilon_t)$].**  An additional effect of autocorrelation is that the standard error of estimate is a biased estimate of the true variance of the disturbance terms. Its expected value is too low in the case of positive autocorrelation, $E(s_e^2) = E[e'e/(T-K)] < \sigma_\varepsilon^2$.

|||||||||||||||||||||||||||||||||||||||||||||||||||||||||||||||||||||||||||||||||||||||||||||||||||||||||||||||||||||||||||||||||||||||||||||||||||||||||||||

*Discursive note.*  In the simple model with $K = 2$, the size of the bias depends on both the extent of autocorrelation measured by the autoregressive coefficient $\rho$ (see *Review* 13.2, item 3) and by the serial correlation of the explanatory variable measured by the correlation coefficient $r_{(X_t, X_{t-1})}$.[8] The bias can be reduced by substituting for $K$ the value of $[2/(1-\rho)] + 2\rho r_{(X_t, X_{t-1})}$. For example if $\rho = 0.7$ and $r = 0.4$, we obtain $2/0.3 + 2(0.3)(0.4) = 6.9$. An approximately unbiased estimate of $\sigma_\varepsilon^2$ would be $e'e/(T - 6.9)$, instead of $e'e/(T - 2)$.

|||||||||||||||||||||||||||||||||||||||||||||||||||||||||||||||||||||||||||||||||||||||||||||||||||||||||||||||||||||||||||||||||||||||||||||||||||||||||||||

---

[8] See Henri Theil, *Principles of Econometrics* (New York: John Wiley & Sons, 1971) pp. 256–57.

III

*Interpretive note.* If the first disturbance is positive and $Cov(\varepsilon_t, \varepsilon_{t-1}) > 0$, then the second disturbance has a high likelihood of being positive. If the values of $X_t$ also tend to be close to the preceding value, then the observed points tend to cluster above the "true" relation. (See Figure 13–5.) When the regression equation is fitted to the observed points, the size of the residuals measured from the regression equation tend to be smaller on the average than the size of the disturbances measured from the "true" relation. Hence, our usual estimate of $\sigma_\varepsilon^2$ is too small.

IIIIIIIIIIIIIIIIIIIIIIIIIIIIIIIIIIIIIIIIIIIIIIIIIIIIIIIIIIIIIIIIIIIIIIIIIIIIIIIIIIIIIIIIIIIIIIIIIIIIIIIIIIIIIIIIIIIIIIIIIIIIIIIII

**FIGURE 13–5**
**The effect of positively autocorrelated disturbances**

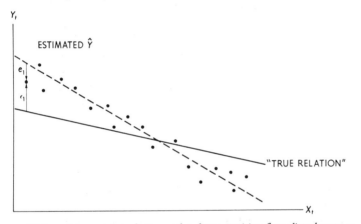

*With positive autocorrelation and a large positive first disturbance, $\varepsilon_1$, the successive residuals tend to systematically give an observation set that is "tilted" from the truth. If the first disturbance $\varepsilon_1$ were abnormally low, the tilt would be reversed; thus the amount and direction of the tilt in estimating the true relation is not always the same. Indeed, estimation of the slope and intercept are still unbiased but may range widely from the "truth." For this reason, least squares estimators are not efficient in this case. Also, the variance of the errors $\varepsilon_t$ about the true relation are underestimated by the variance of the residuals, $e_t$, measured about the estimated line. This means that $s_e^2$ is a biased low estimate of $\sigma_\varepsilon^2$.*

The combination of this bias of $s_e^2$ when it is incorporated into the bias of $V\text{-}Cov(C) = \sigma_\varepsilon^2(X'X)^{-1}$ results in a double bias of the same direction when we attempt to use the OLS estimate [Est. $V\text{-}Cov(C)] = s_e^2(X'X)^{-1}$.

## Detection of autocorrelation

The most common concern of econometricians with respect to autocorrelation is the possible presence of first order autoregressiveness among the disturbances so this receives primary emphasis in the remainder of this section. From *Review* 13.2, item 3, this pattern is written as $\varepsilon_t = \rho\varepsilon_{t-1} + v$

where $\rho$ is called the autoregressive coefficient. The detection of such a pattern necessarily involves the residuals $e_t$ as estimates of the disturbances $\varepsilon_t$.

*Plot of successive residuals.* Sometimes, a simple two-dimensional plot of the $T - 1$ ordered pairs $(e_t, e_{t-1})$ for $t = 2, 3, \ldots, T$, can reveal the existence of autocorrelation. The four quadrants of this plot can be labeled in the usual way. If the points are predominantly in quadrants I and III, then positive autocorrelation is indicated. Successive residuals tend to have the same sign. In the opposite case of alternating signs of successive residuals, then the points will lie in quadrants II and IV, indicating negative auto-correlation. If the points are randomly scattered among all four quadrants, then no autocorrelation is present. Successive disturbance terms are presumed to be independent, and the assumption, $Cov(\varepsilon_t, \varepsilon_i) = 0$, is considered valid.

For an example of such a plot, consider Figure 13–6 based on the data and model of Exercise 5 in Chapter 3. The results of the least squares estimation of this model are given in Table 13–2.

Of the nine points in Figure 13–6, seven are in quadrants I and III indicating positive autocorrelation.

*Autocorrelation coefficient.* Another quick indicator of autocorrelation is a correlation coefficient between $e_t$ and $e_{t-1}$. Positive values close to unity for this autocorrelation coefficient indicate positive autocorrelation. Similarly, values close to zero indicate independence, and values close to $-1.0$ indicate

**FIGURE 13–6**
**Plot of ordered pairs of successful residuals**

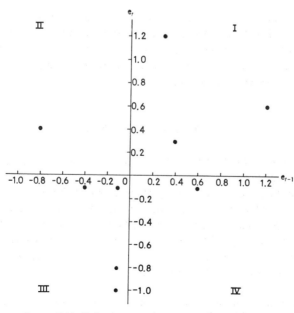

Source: Table 13–2.

TABLE 13-2

Results for the Thai consumption-income model

$$Y = 8.2 + 0.59X \qquad r = 0.997$$
$$s_e = 0.54$$

Residuals

| Year | $e_t$ | Year | $e_t$ |
|------|------|------|------|
| 1957 | −0.4 | 1962 | +0.3 |
| 1958 | −0.1 | 1963 | +1.2 |
| 1959 | −0.1 | 1964 | +0.6 |
| 1960 | −0.8 | 1965 | −0.1 |
| 1961 | +0.4 | 1966 | −1.0 |

Source: Exercise 5, Chapter 3.

negative autocorrelation. The coefficient can be calculated in the usual way allowing for the summation of terms,

$$r_{(e_t, e_{t-1})} = \sum_{t=2}^{T} e_t e_{t-1} \Big/ \left[ \left( \sum_{t=1}^{T} e_t^2 \right) \left( \sum_{t=2}^{T} e_{t-1}^2 \right) \right]^{1/2}.$$

In practice, this coefficient has only intuitive value since it cannot be tested for "closeness" to +1.0, zero, or −1.0. The test statistic for testing significance of a simple correlation coefficient does not apply to this autocorrelation coefficient. Its sampling distribution is more complex and has not been tabled.

*Durbin-Watson test.* A special distribution has been determined for a particular ratio involving residuals which does allow a statistical test of whether or not the disturbances are significantly autocorrelated. It is based on the Von-Neumann ratio of the mean square of successive differences to the variance of the least squares residuals.

The statistic is

$$d = \sum_{t=2}^{T} (e_t - e_{t-1})^2 \Big/ \sum_{t=1}^{T} e_t^2 \qquad (13-3)$$

and called the Durbin-Watson test statistic.[9] Its distribution is tabled for selected values of the number of observations $T$ and number of exogenous variables including the intercept $K$. (See Appendix Table E.)

By expansion of $d$, its typical value if no autocorrelation is present is found to be approximately two. Let us follow this reasoning. If the number of observations is large, the effect of the different summation indices is negligible. Thus, ignoring whether the sum is over terms 1 to $T - 2$ or terms 2 to $T$, etc., in the same series, we obtain,

---

[9] Developed by J. Durbin and G. S. Watson, "Testing for Serial Correlation in Least Squares Regression, I and II," *Biometrika*, 1950 and 1951.

$$d = \frac{\sum e_t^2 - 2\sum e_t e_{t-1} + \sum e_{t-1}^2}{\sum e_t^2} \doteq \frac{2\sum e_t^2 - 2\sum e_t e_{t-1}}{\sum e_t^2}.$$

If $\sum e_t e_{t-1}$ approaches $Cov(\varepsilon_t \varepsilon_{t-1}) = 0$ given Assumption 5, then $d \doteq 2\sum e_t^2 / \sum e_t^2 = 2$. Similarly, upper and lower limits on the range of $d$ can be determined to be four and zero respectively for cases of perfect negative and positive autocorrelation. (See Exercise 6 at the end of the chapter.)

The residuals from a least squares regression can be used to calculate $d$, and the calculated $d$-value can be compared to the upper $(d_U)$ and lower $(d_L)$ critical values for $d$ from the Durbin-Watson table. The results are interpreted with the aid of Table 13–3.

**TABLE 13–3**

**Conclusions for use of the Durbin-Watson $d$ statistic**

| *Value of the calculated d* | *Conclusion* |
|---|---|
| $d < d_L$ | Positive autocorrelation |
| $d > (4 - d_L)$ | Negative autocorrelation |
| $d_L < d < d_U$ <br> $(4 - d_U) < d < (4 - d_L)$ | Indeterminate |
| $d_U < d < (4 - d_U)$ | No autocorrelation |

Values of $d$ sufficiently close to zero or four indicate autocorrelation while values close to two indicate independence. A drawback to the use of the $d$-statistic is the existence of the inconclusive region. For $d$-values in this region, the econometrician must still be concerned with the possible presence of autocorrelation.

## An example of the use of the $d$-statistic

Using the results of Table 13–1, the $d$-statistic can be found for a test of the null hypothesis,

$H_0$: $Cov(\varepsilon_t \varepsilon_{t-1}) = 0$ for no autocorrelation against the alternate,
$H_0$: $Cov(\varepsilon_t \varepsilon_{t-1}) > 0$ for positive autocorrelation.
For this model and data, $K = 2$ and $T = 9$. The $d$-statistic is not tabled for $T < 15$ so if the critical values for $T = 15$ are used, the test has an unknown alpha-risk which is somewhat greater than 0.05. The size of the inconclusive region is larger for $T = 9$ than for $T = 15$.

Using $T = 15$, the critical values are $d_L = 1.08$ and $d_U = 1.36$. Based on the residuals from Table 13–1 arranged in order of the observations over time, 1, 2, ..., 9, the calculated $d$-value is 0.226. This is well below $d_L$ so we conclude that positive autocorrelation is present in the GNP–defense expenditure model.

Repeating the calculation of $d$ using the residuals in Table 13–1 as they appear arranged in order of increasing $X$, we find $d = 1.502$ which is greater than $d_U$. This indicates no autocorrelation among disturbances. The change in $d$ between observations ordered over time or according to the size of $X$ indicates again an underlying *nonlinear* relation between $Y$ and $X$ over time.

Finally, using the transformed data $Y^*$ and $X^*$ and the revised estimating line based on these, $Y^* = 0.5005 + 171.5X^*$, residuals $e_t^*$ can be determined. The $d$-statistic using these residuals is $d = 1.612$. In this case, also, the calculated $d$-value exceeds the upper critical value, 1.36. Autocorrelation does not seem to be a serious problem in the transformed model.

*Further remarks concerning the d-test.* The preceding discussion on the $d$-test statistic needs to be adjusted if the model includes lagged endogenous variables as explanatory variables $X$. In this case, the $d$-value is biased toward 2.0 and toward the acceptance of the null hypothesis of no autocorrelation. This greatly reduces the power of the Durbin-Watson $d$-test and makes the critical values in the table inappropriate for making the conclusions indicated in Table 13–3.[10]

Other methods of detection of autocorrelation have and are being developed which involve approximate distributions for $d$ which eliminate the inconclusive region of the test; or the exact distribution of $d$ based on revised residual vectors that are forced to have a scalar covariance matrix, or are forced to have an a priori fixed covariance matrix (not necessarily scalar) whose exact distribution depends on the particular exogenous observation matrix $X$ in the problem. All these involve computational complexities which are best treated only inside computers. They also have special problems when lagged endogenous variables are included in the model.

The reader continuing to study econometrics or doing empirical regression analysis should keep abreast of these new tests so he can use them when the appropriate statistics become part of the typical output of a regression computer program. Further reading in the references at the end of this chapter will serve this purpose and will also strengthen one's knowledge of the use of the Durbin-Watson test since it is the standard for comparison.

## Correction for autocorrelation

Sometimes the problem of autocorrelation can be corrected by improving the specification of the model. This is especially true if the cause of the autocorrelation is the significant role of an excluded variable which has a strong cyclical pattern. Inclusion of such a variable or a transformation of some included variables may often be effective. A commonly used transformation is suggested among the following statistical remedies.

The basic problem to be corrected is again inefficiency of the estimates because information about the variance-covariance matrix of the disturbances is misrepresented by $V\text{-}Cov(\varepsilon_t) = \sigma_\varepsilon^2 \underset{(T \times T)}{I}$ . The classical solution is to

---

[10] An improved test for use with *large samples* when lagged endogenous variables are used is given in J. Durbin, "Testing for Serial Correlation in Least Squares Regression When Some of the Regressors Are Lagged Dependent Variables," *Econometrica*, May 1970, pp. 410–21.

include information about $\Omega \neq I$ in the determination of the estimates $C$ and the [Est. $V$-$Cov(C)$]. If the proper information about $Cov(\varepsilon_t \varepsilon_{t-1})$ is known, or can be estimated by consistent estimation, and large sample sizes are being used, then the method of generalized least squares (Chapter 14) can be applied. More efficient estimators which are still unbiased and consistent can then be obtained.

*A practical remedy.* In the usual situation, the econometrician has no special information about $V$-$Cov(\varepsilon_t)$. He then proceeds according to the following steps, denoted as the Cochrane and Orcutt Iterative Least Squares method, C & O ILS.[11]

1. Estimate the underlying autoregressive scheme among the disturbances based on the residuals from the initial OLS estimation using the original data.
2. Transform all the original data (including the intercept) according to the same autoregressive pattern uncovered among the residuals.
3. Repeat the least squares estimation of the model using the transformed data and determine the residuals in this case.
4. Estimate the underlying autoregressive scheme among the disturbances based on the residuals of step 3.
5. Repeat steps 2–4 always using the most recently estimated autoregressive coefficients. Continue until successive estimates of these autoregressive coefficients are arbitrarily close to each other. Then the results of the model estimated on the basis of transformed data using these best estimates of the autoregressive coefficients give the final, efficient estimators of $\Gamma$ for which the testing procedures of Chapter 11 are applicable.

*The* C & O ILS *method.* The steps above are repeated now in more detail with an example and practical comments on their application.

*Step 1. Estimating the autoregressive coefficients*

The most frequently considered autoregressive scheme of disturbances is a first order pattern estimated by $e_t = \rho e_{t-1} + v$. Using OLS for this regression, the estimate of $\rho$ is approximately given by $p = \sum e_t e_{t-1} / \sum e_t^2$.

||||||||||||||||||||||||||||||||||||||||||||||||||||||||||||||||||||||||||||||||||||||||||||||||||||||||||||||||||||||||||||||||||||||||||||||||||||||||||||||

*Discursive note.* The value $p$ also approximates the autocorrelation coefficient between $e_t$ and $e_{t-1}$ given by

$$r_{(e_t e_{t-1})} = \sum e_t e_{t-1} / [(\sum e_t^2)(\sum e_{t-1}^2)]^{1/2}.$$

If $\sum_{t=1}^{T} e_t^2 \doteq \sum_{t=2}^{T} e_{t-1}^2$ for large $T$, then

$$[(\sum e_t^2)(\sum e_{t-1}^2)]^{1/2} \doteq [(\sum e_t^2)^2]^{1/2} = \sum e_t^2, \quad \text{and} \quad r_{(e_t e_{t-1})} \doteq p.$$

||||||||||||||||||||||||||||||||||||||||||||||||||||||||||||||||||||||||||||||||||||||||||||||||||||||||||||||||||||||||||||||||||||||||||||||||||||||||||||||

---

[11] D. Cochrane and G. H. Orcutt, "Application of Least Squares Regression to Relationships Containing Autocorrelated Error Terms," *Journal of the American Statistical Association*, 1949, pp. 32–61.

A quick method of obtaining $p$ is to approximate it from the reported values of the serial correlation coefficient $r_{(e_t e_{t-1})}$ or the Durbin-Watson $d$-statistic in the computer output of the initial OLS estimation of the model $Y = X\Gamma + \varepsilon$. The approximations are $p \doteq r_{(e_t e_{t-1})} \doteq 1/2(2 - d)$. (See Exercise 5 at the end of this chapter.)[12]

If a second or higher $n$th order autoregressive scheme is postulated, such as $e_t = \rho_1 e_{t-1} + \rho_2 e_{t-1} + \cdots + \rho_n e_{t-n} + v$, then the coefficients need to be estimated in a separate OLS regression. The disturbance term $v$ is always assumed to be distributed as $N(O, \sigma_v^2 I)$. (See *Review* 13.2, item 4.) Whether or not a higher order scheme is needed is sometimes indicated by examining the residuals $v_t = e_t - p e_{t-1}$ from the first order autoregression.

If these residuals are autocorrelated according to the $d$-test, then a second order autoregressive scheme may be indicated. Similarly, the residuals from a second order pattern could be examined to indicate if a third order scheme is suggested, and so forth.

|||||||||||||||||||||||||||||||||||||||||||||||||||||||||||||||||||||||||||||||||||||||||||||||||||||||||||||||||||||||||||||||||||||

*Explicative note.* Such $d$-statistics become less powerful for higher order schemes because autoregressive models include lagged endogenous variables by definition. The results of these tests merely give hints about higher order autoregressions which are sometimes useful. If $T$ is large, the improved Durbin test should be used in these cases. (See footnote 10.)

|||||||||||||||||||||||||||||||||||||||||||||||||||||||||||||||||||||||||||||||||||||||||||||||||||||||||||||||||||||||||||||||||||

*Example of step I.* Consider an example model, $Y = \alpha_1 + \alpha_2 X + \varepsilon$, which relates Japanese international reserves and GNP during the third cycle (26 quarterly observations) using data from *International Financial Statistics*. Both $Y =$ reserves and $X =$ GNP are measured in nominal terms in billions of yen. The original data and some transformed data used later are given in Table 13–4.

The OLS estimation of the model $Y = \alpha_1 + \alpha_2 X + \varepsilon$ is obtained using the data in the first two columns of Table 13–4. Analysis of the residuals $e_t = (Y_t - a_1 - a_2 X_t)$ provides a $d$-statistic of $d = 0.33 < d_L = 1.30$ for $K = 2$ and $T = 26$, indicating positive autocorrelation. (See Table 13–5.) An estimate of the first order autoregressive coefficient is obtained by $p \doteq 1/2(2 - d) = 0.835$ or by using OLS on the model, $e_t = \rho e_{t-1} + v$. The OLS estimate for $\rho$ is $p = 0.83441$. This is the value to be used in continuing the example in the next step.

---

[12] Another suggested approximation is $p \doteq [T^2(1 - 0.5d) + K^2]/(T^2 - K^2)$. See H. Theil and A. Nagar, "Testing the Independence of Regression Disturbances," *Journal of the American Statistical Association*, 1961, pp. 793–806.

**TABLE 13-4**

**Original and transformed data for the Japan reserves–GNP example model**

| $X =$ GNP | $Y = reserves$ | $X^*$ | $Y^*$ |
|---|---|---|---|
| 11,905 | 462 | — | — |
| 12,290 | 509 | 2356.40 | 123.505 |
| 13,292 | 550 | 3037.15 | 125.288 |
| 13,462 | 600 | 2371.08 | 141.077 |
| 14,334 | 613 | 3101.23 | 112.356 |
| 14,582 | 649 | 2621.63 | 137.509 |
| 15,364 | 729 | 3196.70 | 187.471 |
| 16,047 | 788 | 3227.19 | 179.718 |
| 17,311 | 851 | 3921.29 | 193.488 |
| 18,053 | 819 | 3608.60 | 108.921 |
| 18,711 | 728 | 3647.47 | 44.622 |
| 19,810 | 641 | 4197.43 | 33.553 |
| 20,320 | 629 | 3790.42 | 94.146 |
| 20,867 | 629 | 3911.87 | 104.159 |
| 20,582 | 595 | 3170.45 | 70.159 |
| 21,549 | 673 | 4375.26 | 176.529 |
| 21,616 | 730 | 3635.39 | 168.445 |
| 22,953 | 759 | 4916.48 | 149.884 |
| 24,586 | 763 | 5433.88 | 129.686 |
| 24,990 | 746 | 4475.30 | 109.348 |
| 26,128 | 727 | 5276.20 | 104.533 |
| 26,982 | 666 | 5180.64 | 59.387 |
| 28,340 | 662 | 5826.06 | 106.286 |
| 28,944 | 714 | 5296.94 | 161.623 |
| 29,264 | 732 | 5112.96 | 136.234 |
| 30,209 | 701 | 5790.95 | 90.215 |

## *Step 2. Transforming the data*

The estimation of the proper order autoregressive scheme provides estimates of the autoregressive coefficients, $p_1, p_2, \ldots, p_n$. The original measures of the variables $Y, X_1, X_2, \ldots, X_K$, are then transformed according to this same autoregressive pattern. For example, the general transformation for an $n$th order pattern would be

$$Y_t^* = Y_t - p_1 Y_{t-1} - p_2 Y_{t-2} - \cdots - p_n Y_{t-n}$$

and

$$X_{tk}^* = X_{tk} - p_1 X_{t-1, k} - p_2 X_{t-2, k} - \cdots - p_n X_{t-n, k}$$

for

$$k = 1, 2, \ldots, K.$$

To insure that least squares estimators based on the transformed data will have the property of efficiency, a transformation of the first $n$ observations is required also. We again consider only a first order autoregressive pattern for simplicity. From *Review* 13.2, item 4, the variance of the disturbance $\varepsilon_t$ is found to be $\sigma_v^2/(1 - \rho^2)$. The constant multiplier in this relation between $V(\varepsilon_t)$ and $V(v_t)$ can be estimated by $(1 - p^2)$. Thus, to obtain a regression model $Y^* = X^*\Gamma + \varepsilon^*$ for the transformed data in which the disturbance term $\varepsilon^*$ is homoscedastic, the observations on each variable could be weighted according to the relative sizes of the standard deviations of the disturbance terms in different observations. In this case, only a simple scalar multiple of the first observation is required. Namely, we transform,

$$Y_1^* = Y_1\sqrt{1 - p^2}, \quad X_{1k}^* = X_{1k}\sqrt{1 - p^2} \quad \text{for all} \quad k = 2, 3, \ldots, K, \quad \text{and}$$
$$\varepsilon_1^* = \varepsilon_1\sqrt{1 - p^2}.$$

||||||||||||||||||||||||||||||||||||||||||||||||||||||||||||||||||||||||||||||||||||||||||||||||||||||||||

*Interpretive note.* This adjustment for the first observation presumes that the complete and identical autogressive pattern has been in effect for a sufficiently long time prior to the first observation. If this is unlikely according to theoretical or historical judgment, then it may be better to drop the first observation and use only the final $T - 1$ observations in the next step.

||||||||||||||||||||||||||||||||||||||||||||||||||||||||||||||||||||||||||||||||||||||||||||||||||||||||||

*An example transformation.* To illustrate the transformation in a particular case, return to the example model relating Japanese international reserves to its GNP based on the data in Table 13–4. Using the previous result that the initial residuals indicate positive autocorrelation with $\rho$ estimated by $p = 0.83441$, the original data is transformed into $Y^*$ and $X^*$ given in columns 3 and 4. The transformation is

$$Y_t^* = Y_t - 0.83441 Y_{t-1} \quad \text{and} \quad X_t^* = X_t - 0.83441 X_{t-1}$$

creating new disturbance terms $\varepsilon_t^* = \varepsilon_t - 0.83441\varepsilon_{t-1}$. The new model to be estimated by OLS is

$$Y_t^* = \alpha_1(1 - 0.83441) + \alpha_2 X_t^* + \varepsilon_t^*.$$

||||||||||||||||||||||||||||||||||||||||||||||||||||||||||||||||||||||||||||||||||||||||||||||||||||||||||

*Recursive note.* One observation is lost by this procedure since the first available observation for the transformed variables is $X_2^* = 12{,}290 - (0.83441)(11{,}905) = 2356.35$, and $Y_2^* = 509 - (0.83441)(462) = 123.503$. (The deviation from the values in Table 13–4 is due to rounding since those were generated by a computer routine using seven significant decimals.)

||||||||||||||||||||||||||||||||||||||||||||||||||||||||||||||||||||||||||||||||||||||||||||||||||||||||||

The first observation could be used if the same autoregressive pattern estimated for this data from Japan's third cycle could be presumed to have been appropriate say for at least the previous eight quarters of the second cycle. The transformed first observations would be

$$Y_1{}^* = Y_1\sqrt{1 - p^2} = 462\sqrt{1 - (0.83441)^2} = 462(0.55114)$$

and

$$X_1{}^* = X_1\sqrt{1 - p^2} = 11{,}905(0.55114).$$

When the first observation is the first period of a new situation, then it may be best to exclude it. We do so in the following steps and use only $T - 1 = 25$ observations.

*Step 3. OLS on the transformed data*

Based on the $(T - n)$ transformed observations, a second least squares estimation is determined for the model, $Y^* = X^*\Gamma + \varepsilon^*$, where the sum of squares of residuals being minimized is $\sum_{t=n+1}^{T} e_t{}^{*2} = (Y^* - X^*C)'(Y^* - X^*C)$. New estimates of $\Gamma$ are obtained which are more efficient than those from the initial estimation of the model $Y = X\Gamma + \varepsilon$ based on the original observations. Tests of significance using $t$ and $F$ distributed statistics with $T - n - K$ degrees of freedom are now more appropriate.

||||||||||||||||||||||||||||||||||||||||||||||||||||||||||||||||||||||||||||||||||||||||||||||||||||||||||||||||||||||||||

*Explicative note.* Whereas the initial disturbances violated Assumption 5 of no autocorrelation, the disturbances in the model using transformed data are more independent.

||||||||||||||||||||||||||||||||||||||||||||||||||||||||||||||||||||||||||||||||||||||||||||||||||||||||||||||||||||||||||

The Durbin–Watson test should be repeated on the new residuals to check if the autocorrelation has been satisfactorily eliminated.

*Example of step 3.* For the example data of Table 13–4, the estimation of the model using data transformed according to a first order autoregressive scheme is based on $(T-1) = 25$ observations. The typical residual is

$$e_t{}^* = e_t - pe_{t-1} = Y_t{}^* - a_1(1 - p) - a_2 X_t{}^*$$
$$= (Y_t - pY_{t-1}) - a_1(1 - p) - a_2(X_t - pX_{t-1}).$$

||||||||||||||||||||||||||||||||||||||||||||||||||||||||||||||||||||||||||||||||||||||||||||||||||||||||||||||||||||||||||

*Discursive note.* Another common transformation is a simple first difference of successive observations which is the special case for $p = 1$. If this is used, the econometrician is expressing an intuitive feeling that the true $\rho$ is very close to one. It cannot actually be one since then the $V(\varepsilon_t) = V(v_t)/(1 - \rho^2)$ would be mathematically undefined due to division by zero.

||||||||||||||||||||||||||||||||||||||||||||||||||||||||||||||||||||||||||||||||||||||||||||||||||||||||||||||||||||||||||

The results of the estimation of the model based on the original data and on the transformed data are given in Table 13–5.

**TABLE 13–5**

**Results for the Japan reserves model using original and transformed observations**

| Description | Based on original data $(Y, X)$ | | Based on transformed data $(Y^*, X^*)$ | |
|---|---|---|---|---|
| Estimated equation | $Y = 538.5 + 0.00688X$ | | $Y^* = 887.7 - 0.00618X^*$ | |
| Std. error | (63.58) | (0.0030) | (211.6) | (0.00836) |
| $t$-value | 8.47 | 2.30 | 4.20 | $-0.739$ |
| Corr. coeff. | 0.4245 | | $-0.1522$ | |
| $d$-statistic | 0.3309 | | 1.037 | |
| Residuals | $e_1$ | $-158.416$ | | $-$ |
| | | $-114.065$ | $e_2^*$ | $-8.938$ |
| | | $-79.9597$ | | $-2.950$ |
| | | $-31.1294$ | | 8.725 |
| | $e_5$ | $-24.1297$ | $e_5^*$ | $-15.49$ |
| | | 10.1639 | | 6.705 |
| | | 84.7829 | | 60.22 |
| | | 139.083 | | 52.65 |
| | | 193.386 | | 70.71 |
| | $e_{10}$ | 156.28 | $e_{10}^*$ | $-15.79$ |
| | | 60.7523 | | $-79.85$ |
| | | $-33.8099$ | | $-87.52$ |
| | | $-49.3192$ | | $-29.44$ |
| | | $-53.0831$ | | $-18.68$ |
| | $e_{15}$ | $-85.122$ | $e_{15}^*$ | $-57.26$ |
| | | $-13.7759$ | | 56.56 |
| | | 42.763 | | 43.90 |
| | | 62.5632 | | 33.25 |
| | | 55.3265 | | 16.25 |
| | $e_{20}$ | 35.5466 | $e_{20}^*$ | $-10.01$ |
| | | 8.71605 | | $-9.876$ |
| | | $-58.1603$ | | $-55.61$ |
| | | $-71.5047$ | | $-4.727$ |
| | | $-23.6608$ | | 47.34 |
| | | $-7.8627$ | | 20.82 |
| | $e_{26}$ | $-45.3652$ | $e_{26}^*$ | $-21.01$ |

|||||||||||||||||||||||||||||||||||||||||||||||||||||||||||||||||||||||||||||||||||||||||||||||||||||||||||||||||||||||||||||||||||||||||||||||||||||||||||||||||||||||||||||||||||||||||||||||

*Explicative note.* In estimating the revised equation with the transformed variables, the correct variable $X_{t1}$ associated with the intercept is no longer $X_{t1} = 1$ for all $t$, but rather $X_{t1}^* = (1 - p)$ for all $t$. Therefore, if a regular intercept is used, the estimate of $\alpha_1$ and of $\sqrt{V(\alpha_1)}$ need to be multiplied by the factor $1/(1-p)$ to obtain the correct values. The other coefficients and residuals are not affected by this misspecification of $X_{t1}$ by a constant factor.

||||||||||||||||||||||||||||||||||||||||||||||||||||||||||||||||||||||||||||||||||||||||||||||||||||||||||||||||||||||||||||||||||||||||||||||||||||||||

The residuals $e_t$ of the original least squares estimation show strong positive autocorrelation. This is reduced somewhat in the least squares estimation based on the transformed data as shown by analysis of the residuals $e_t$*. The new $d$-statistic is 1.037 which is still less than $d_L = 1.29$ for $K = 2$ and 25 observations. This value can be used to reestimate $\rho$ and iterate the entire transformation process again.

Before continuing to this next iteration in step 4, some other comparisons from Table 13–5 are interesting. The estimate $s_e^2$ is biased low using the original data resulting in an overstated value of the correlation coefficient. The degree of fit is much smaller and even insignificant when the transformed data are used. Also, the [Est. $V(a_1)$] and [Est. $V(a_2)$] are biased low when original data are used so that the values of the $t$-statistic for testing significance are too large. The econometrician finds that the coefficient $\alpha_2$ is not significant (remember the degrees of freedom are $T - 1 - K$) based on the transformed data with some autocorrelation removed.[13]

*Step 4. Another iteration*

Based on the residuals $e_t$* from the estimation using the transformed data, the autoregressive coefficients $\rho_1, \rho_2, \ldots, \rho_n$, can be estimated again. If the revised estimates are sufficiently close to the previous estimates, say $|p_i{}^* - p_i| < \delta$ where $\delta$ is an arbitrarily selected positive number, then the process is terminated. The best estimates of $\rho_i$ have been obtained and the least squares estimation using data transformed according to these best estimates is the one desired.

On the other hand, if the revised estimates $p_i{}^*$ are not close to the previous estimates $p_i$, then the transformation is repeated using $p_i{}^*$. The process may go through several iterations before the termination condition holds.

In the autocorrelation example with data in Table 13–4 and results in Table 13–5, a second iteration seems desirable. The second estimate of $\rho$ would be obtained from a first order autoregression on the revised residuals where each residual is calculated by $e_t{}^* = Y_t{}^* - a_1{}^*(1-p) - a_2{}^*X_t{}^*$ using the transformed data and estimates based on the transformed data. A new

---

[13] As a rule of thumb, it is worthwhile in terms of increased efficiency to use the two-step transformation process in cases when the estimated autoregressive coefficient $\rho > 0.3$. See P. Rao and Z. Griliches, "Small Sample Properties of Several Two-Stage Regression Methods in the Context of Auto-Correlated Errors," *Journal of the American Statistical Association*, 1969, pp. 253–69.

estimate of $\rho$ can be obtained as $p^* = 1/2(2 - d^*) = 1/2(2 - 1.037) = 0.4815$ compared to the original estimate $p = 0.83441$. The reader may wish to continue the procedure another iteration using this second estimate to transform the original data, reestimating the model, determining the residuals, and then finding a third estimate of $\rho$ to compare with $p^*$.

## Use of the C & O ILS method for forecasting purposes

If the purpose of the econometrician in specifying the model is to generate reliable forecasts of the endogenous variable, then it is very useful for him to use the Cochrane and Orcutt Iterative Least Squares procedure. It provides more efficient forecasts than the simple least squares procedure for two reasons. First, it makes use of the information about the autoregressive structure. Second, it takes into account the level of the estimate of the most recent disturbance.

Consider the model $Y = X\Gamma + \varepsilon$ and let $Y_t$ and $\varepsilon_t$ represent the $t$th observations on the endogenous and disturbance variables respectively. Suppose a first order autoregressive pattern holds for $\varepsilon_t$. Also let $X_t$ represent a $(1 \times K)$ row vector of the $t$th observation of all $K$ exogenous variables (including the intercept). Using the OLS estimator $C$ of $\Gamma$ the linear predictor of $Y_{T+1}$ is obtained as $Y_{T+1} = X_{T+1}\Gamma$ and estimated by $\hat{Y}_{T+1} = X_{T+1}C$.

Using the transformed data in the C & O ILS method and obtaining the estimates $C^*$ of $\Gamma$, a forecast is made of $(Y_{T+1} - \rho Y_T) = (X_{T+1} - \rho X_T)\Gamma$. From this, the best linear predictor of $Y_{T+1}$ can be found to be,

$$Y_{T+1} = (X_{T+1} - \rho X_T)\Gamma + \rho Y_T.$$

By collecting terms, we rewrite,

$$Y_{T+1} = X_{T+1}\Gamma + \rho(Y_T - X_T\Gamma).$$

||||||||||||||||||||||||||||||||||||||||||||||||||||||||||||||||||||||||||||||||||||||||||||||||||||||||||||||||||||||||||||||||||||||||||||

*Recursive note.*  This linear predictor of $Y_{T+1}$ uses the autoregressive coefficient and the estimate of the most recent disturbance, $e_T = (Y_T - X_T\Gamma)$. Recall the two reasons above that make this the "best" (efficient) linear predictor.

||||||||||||||||||||||||||||||||||||||||||||||||||||||||||||||||||||||||||||||||||||||||||||||||||||||||||||||||||||||||||||||||||||||||||

The forecast of $Y_{T+1}$ is then obtained by substituting the estimate $p$ for $\rho$ and the estimates and residual based on the transformed data, denoted by $C^*$ and $e_T^*$, into the same form as this best linear prediction. We obtain, $Y_{T+1} = X_{T+1}C^* + pe_T^*$. These results could be extended for representation of a higher order autoregressive scheme. Also, confidence intervals can be set on the forecast by adapting the usual methods for least squares forecasts (see Section 11.8) to this revised model.

## 13.6 SUMMARY

Violation of Assumptions 1, 4, and 5 frequently occur for the specification of an econometric model and are termed contemporaneous correlation between $X$ and $\varepsilon$, heteroscedasticity, and autocorrelation respectively. The primary effect of the first of these is biased and inconsistent estimation of the coefficients. For the latter two, the property of efficiency is lost for the least squares estimates of the coefficients, although they are still unbiased and consistent. In addition, violations of Assumptions 1 or 5 result in biased estimates of $\sigma_\varepsilon^2$.

Special plots and tests involving the residuals from the OLS estimation are used to detect these violations. Corrective procedures are possible by improving the specification of the model so that the disturbance terms in the new specification more closely satisfy Assumptions 1, 4, and 5. Some particular transformations using estimates of $X$ based on instrumental variables, or using weighted least squares, or using estimates of an underlying autoregressive structure among the disturbances are suggested as practical remedies.

Examples and further interpretive remarks are given as an aid to understanding the problem, its effects, when it typically occurs, how to detect it, how to correct for it, and its implications for testing the model or making forecasts.

The principal points are summarized in Table 13–6 for quick reference presuming throughout that none of the variables $X_k$ is a lagged endogenous variable.


### NEW VOCABULARY

Contemporaneous correlation of $X$ with $\varepsilon$
Heteroscedasticity
Autocorrelation
Residual analysis
Error in measurement
Simultaneity
Method of weighted least squares
Method of instrumental variables

Goldfeld–Quandt test
Transformation of variables
First order autoregressive pattern
Durbin–Watson $d$-test
Autoregressive coefficient
Autocorrelation coefficient
Best linear predictor
Cochrane & Orcutt iterative least squares method


### REFERENCES

For some statistics associated with the suggested plots of residuals, see Anscombe, F. J., and Tukey, J. W.   "The Examination and Analysis of Residuals." *Technometrics*, 1963, pp. 141–60.

More on the heteroscedasticity problem is in Rutzmiller, H. C., and Bowers, D. A.   "Estimation in a Heteroscedastic Regression Model." *Journal of the American Statistical Association*, 1968, pp. 552–57.

**TABLE 13-6**

**Summary of selected problems and associated residual analysis**

| Assumption violated | Name of problem | Typical situations for which the problem arises | Effect on OLS estimation (most common situations)* |
|---|---|---|---|
| 1. $Cov(X_{tk}, \varepsilon_t) = 0$ | Contemporaneous correlation of $X$ and $\varepsilon$ | 1. Error in measurement<br>2. Simultaneity | 1. Estimates $C$ of $\Gamma$ are biased and inconsistent<br>2. Estimate $s_e^2$ of $\sigma_\varepsilon^2$ is biased (high)<br>3. $t$ and $F$ tests are not applicable |
| 4. $V(\varepsilon_t) = \sigma_\varepsilon^2$ | Heteroscedasticity | 1. Cross-sectional data<br>2. Structural change in background<br>3. Change in accuracy of measurement | 1. Estimates $C$ of $\Gamma$ remain unbiased and consistent<br>2. $V(C)$ is not minimal among linear unbiased estimators, so estimator $C$ is inefficient<br>3. [Est. $V(C)$] is biased<br>4. Sample $t$ and $F$ values are wrong |
| 5. $Cov(\varepsilon_t, \varepsilon_t) = 0$ | Autocorrelation | 1. Time-series analysis<br>2. Specification excludes a significant serially correlated variable<br>3. Interpolation of incorrectly measured raw data for $X$<br>4. Spatial similarities among noneconomically defined regions | 1. Estimates $C$ of $\Gamma$ remain unbiased and consistent<br>2. $V(C)$ is not minimal so $C$ is inefficient<br>3. †[Est. $V(C)$] is biased (low)<br>4. †Sample $t$ and $F$ values are wrong (too large)<br>5. †Estimate $s_e^2$ of $V(\varepsilon_t)$ is biased (low) so $R^2$ is biased (high) |

\* Additional problems occur if any $X_k$ is a lagged endogenous variable. These complications are not reflected in any part of Table 13-6.
† The direction of error given presumes positive autocorrelation. It would be reversed in the case of negative autocorrelation.

**TABLE 13–6** (Continued)

| Assumption violated | Method of detection | Possible remedies |
|---|---|---|
| 1. $Cov(X_{tk}\,\varepsilon_t) = 0$ | Plot of $e_t$ with $X_{tk}$ | 1. Acquire better data and/or improve specification<br>2. Use weighted least squares if independent estimates are available for constants of proportionality among variances and covariances of error components<br>3. Use method of instrumental variables to get consistent, but inefficient estimates $C$ of $\Gamma$<br>4. Use OLS for forecasting purposes |
| 4. $V(\varepsilon_t) = \sigma_\varepsilon^2$ | 1. Plot of $e_t$ with time or with $\hat{Y}_t$<br>2. Goldfeld–Quandt test<br>3. Other tests using special residual vectors (see references) | 1. Improve specification, perhaps using dummy shift variables among cross-sections<br>2. Use weighted least squares<br>3. Divide data into subgroups with equal variances and estimate separately |
| 5. $Cov(\varepsilon_t\,\varepsilon_i) = 0$ | 1. Plot of ordered pairs $(e_t,\,e_{t-1})$<br>2. Plot of $e_t$ and $\hat{Y}_t$<br>3. Durbin–Watson $d$-test | 1. Improve specification, perhaps by including cyclical exogenous variables<br>2. Use generalized least squares (see Chapter 14)<br>3. Use Cochrane and Orcutt Iterative Least Squares method with autoregressive transformation of data. This is especially recommended to obtain more efficient forecasts. |

For an alternate test of heteroscedasticity which uses the absolute value of the residuals, see Glejser, H. "A New Test for Heteroscedasticity." *Journal of the American Statistical Association*, 1969, pp. 316–23.

A more extensive discussion of the rules for selecting a good instrumental variable is Valavanis, S. *Econometrics*, chap. 7. New York: McGraw-Hill Book Co., 1959.

For further discussion on alternate tests for autocorrelation and special residual vectors (BLUS and *v* in particular), see the following papers and their own list of references of preceding papers:

Theil, H. "The Analysis of Disturbances in Regression Analysis." *Journal of the American Statistical Association*, 1965, pp. 1067–79.

Abrahamse, A. P. J., and Koerts, J. "New Estimators of Disturbances in Regression Analysis." *Journal of the American Statistical Association*, 1971, pp. 71–74.

Hannan, E. J., and Terrill, R. D. "Testing for Serial Correlation after Least Squares Regression." *Econometrica*, 1968, pp. 133–50.

Henshaw, Jr., R. C. "Testing Single-equation Least Squares Regression Models for Autocorrelated Disturbances." *Econometrica*, 1966, pp. 646–60.

For a discussion of effects and remedies concerning first order autoregressive patterns, see Orcutt, G. H., and Winokur, Jr., H. S. "First Order Autoregression: Inference, Estimation, and Prediction." *Econometrica*, 1969, pp. 1–14; and Kadiyala, K. R. "A Transformation Used to Circumvent the Problem of Autocorrelation." *Econometrica*, 1968, pp. 93–96.

A recommended alternate two-stage procedure whose estimators compare favorably with those of the C & O ILS estimates and which is applicable for higher order auto-regressive schemes is given by Durbin, J. "Estimation of Parameters in Time-Series Regression Models." *Journal of the Royal Statistical Society*, 1960, Series B, pp. 139–53.

## EXERCISES

1. Make an argument why one or more of the three assumptions (1, 4, 5) considered in this chapter might be violated in each of the following cases:

   *a)* A revolution occurs in the data collecting country, and the data is much less accurate for a period of three years.

   *b)* There is a break in the time-series data for an exogenous variable with a different indexing method used in aggregating the measures after the break point.

   *c)* A model is estimated on the basis of daily quotations of stock market values.

   *d)* Data is used on average earnings and educational level composition of the civilian labor force across states.

   *e)* In a model of trade analysis, quotas become effective for seven consecutive quarters for several important import commodities, and quotas are not explicitly included in the model.

   *f)* A supply relation specified by the model is subject to the Cobweb phenomenon.

2. If negative autocorrelation exists, explain why a null hypothesis $H_0: \gamma_i = 0$ would be rejected (too often, not often enough) on the average using the usual OLS estimates and a $t$-test.

3. Suppose the disturbance term $\varepsilon_t$ follows a second order autoregression given by $\varepsilon_t = \rho_1 \varepsilon_{t-1} + \rho_2 \varepsilon_{t-2} + \nu$. Following Section 13.5, write the best linear predictor for $Y_{t+1}$.

4. Examine the effects on the OLS estimates of a model, $Y = X\Gamma + \varepsilon$, if there is substantial error in the measurement of the endogenous variable $Y$.

5. Show under what conditions the approximation $p = 1/2(2 - d)$ is valid where $p$ is an estimate of the first order autoregressive coefficient and $d$ is the Durbin–Watson statistic.

6. Demonstrate that the upper limit on the Durbin–Watson $d$ is 4 when perfect negative autocorrelation exists. (*Hint*: $r_{(e_t e_{t-1})} = -1.0$.) Show when the value for $d$ is zero and argue why this is its lower limit.

⎮⎮⎮⎮⎮⎮⎮⎮⎮⎮⎮⎮⎮⎮⎮⎮⎮⎮⎮⎮⎮⎮⎮⎮⎮⎮⎮⎮⎮⎮⎮⎮⎮⎮⎮⎮⎮⎮⎮⎮⎮⎮⎮⎮⎮⎮⎮⎮⎮⎮⎮⎮⎮⎮⎮⎮⎮⎮⎮⎮⎮⎮⎮⎮⎮⎮⎮⎮⎮⎮⎮⎮⎮⎮⎮⎮⎮⎮⎮⎮⎮⎮⎮⎮⎮⎮⎮⎮⎮⎮

***Discursive note.*** Problems involving the detection and correction methods of this chapter can be based on the models, data, and results of previously given examples or exercises from Chapters 3, 7, or 11 or the example model and data from Chapter 9. A typical general exercise is stated as Exercise 7. Following it are some particular exercises based on data from examples used within this chapter.

⎮⎮⎮⎮⎮⎮⎮⎮⎮⎮⎮⎮⎮⎮⎮⎮⎮⎮⎮⎮⎮⎮⎮⎮⎮⎮⎮⎮⎮⎮⎮⎮⎮⎮⎮⎮⎮⎮⎮⎮⎮⎮⎮⎮⎮⎮⎮⎮⎮⎮⎮⎮⎮⎮⎮⎮⎮⎮⎮⎮⎮⎮⎮⎮⎮⎮⎮⎮⎮⎮⎮⎮⎮⎮⎮⎮⎮⎮⎮⎮⎮⎮⎮⎮⎮⎮⎮⎮⎮⎮

7. Determine the residuals from the least squares estimation using the model and data of (to be specified, perhaps Exercise 4, Chapter 3, or perhaps using data you personally collected to estimate and test your own model in Exercise 21, Chapter 11.) Analyze these residuals for possible violations of assumptions 1, 4, and/or 5. If a violation occurs, specify its effects on your first estimating results and use some corrective remedy to get better estimates.

8. Make a plot of the residuals in Table 13–2 against time and interpret the results.

9. Make a plot of the residuals in Table 13–2 against the estimated values of consumption, $\hat{Y}_t$, and interpret the results.

10. For the residuals in Table 13–2, find the value of $d$ and interpret the results of the $d$-test for autocorrelation.

11. Using the residuals in Table 13–1, show that autocorrelation is likely and follow the C & O ILS procedure to get efficient estimates of the coefficients.

12. Given the model and results in Table 13–1, find the forecast of $Y_{10}$ given $X_{10} = 12$. Compare this to the forecast of $Y_{10}$ obtained from the best linear predictor based on the revised estimation in Exercise 11 (again using $X_{10} = 12$).

13. The data for the example model relating GNP and defense expenditures is given in Table 13–1. Arrange the data in order of increasing size of $X$. Determine and interpret the results of a Goldfeld–Quandt test for homoscedasticity by subdividing the data into three groups including the four observations with the smallest values of $X$ in the first group $A$, the four observations with the

largest values of $X$ in the third group $B$, and leaving one observation for the median $X$ in the middle group.

The resulting sum of squares of residuals for least squares estimation on data subgroups $A$ and $B$ are $(e'e)_A = 2522.54$ and $(e'e)_B = 248.45$.

14. Using the same subgroups of observations as in Exercise 13, determine and interpret the results of a Goldfeld–Quandt test for homoscedasticity based on the transformed data, $Y^*$ and $X^*$ in Table 13–1. Compare the results of Exercises 13 and 14 to determine if the transformation helped to significantly reduce heteroscedasticity.

15. Suppose a consumption function is to be estimated as $C_t = \alpha_1 + \alpha_2 Y_t + \varepsilon_t$. However, it is realized that consumption is also a component which determines $Y = \text{GNP} = C + I + G$. Due to this simultaneity, $C \Leftrightarrow Y$, Assumption 1 may be violated.

   *a)* Using the data below, follow the two-step instrumental variable method to obtain consistent estimates of $\alpha_1$ and $\alpha_2$. Use the pooled variable $(I + G)$, an autonomous expenditure component, for the instrumental variable.

   *b)* Discuss the suitability of $(I + G)$ for this purpose by examining it in view of the desired properties for instrumental variables.

**Data for Exercise 15**

| Year | $C$ | $Y$ | $I + G$ |
|------|------|------|------|
| 1929 | 79.0 | 214.1 | 24.7 |
| 1930 | 71.0 | 194.6 | 19.5 |
| 1931 | 61.3 | 180.3 | 14.7 |
| 1932 | 49.3 | 153.8 | 9.0 |
| 1933 | 46.4 | 150.0 | 9.4 |
| 1934 | 51.9 | 164.3 | 12.7 |
| 1935 | 56.3 | 179.9 | 16.3 |
| 1936 | 62.6 | 205.0 | 20.2 |
| 1937 | 67.3 | 215.7 | 23.4 |
| 1938 | 64.6 | 206.3 | 19.5 |

16. Examine the least squares residuals, based on the model and data of Exercise 9, Chapter 3, for homoscedasticity.

17. Suppose the variable $X_2 =$ unemployment rate used in Exercise 23, Chapter 7, has a serious error of measurement. Reestimate the slope coefficient in that exercise using the instrumental variable method where $Z =$ rate of increase in consumer expenditures given below:

| Year | 1956 | 1957 | 1958 | 1959 | 1960 | 1961 | 1962 | 1963 | 1964 | 1965 |
|------|------|------|------|------|------|------|------|------|------|------|
| $Z$ | 5.06 | 5.56 | 2.81 | 7.17 | 4.78 | 3.04 | 4.72 | 5.35 | 6.95 | 6.25 |

Briefly comment on the advantages and disadvantages of using this method and on the selection of the instrumental variable used.

18. Estimation of a slope in the relationship between $Y$ and $X$ can be obtained from two observations $(Y_1, X_1)$ and $(Y_2, X_2)$ as $\hat{\alpha} = (Y_2 - Y_1)/(X_2 - X_1)$. If one point is the mean point, $(\bar{Y}, \bar{X})$, then using deviation notation, $\hat{\alpha} = (Y_2 - \bar{Y})/(X_2 - \bar{X}) = y/x$. If more observations are available, then a weighted average of all such ratios of deviations may be used, and $\hat{\alpha} = \sum_{i=1}^{T} w_i(y_i/x_i)$ where $\sum_{i=1}^{T} w_i = 1.0$. Indeed all estimation procedures are based on this concept, but some use different sets of weights from the others.

a) Show that for the OLS estimate of $\alpha$, the weights are $w_i = \left( x_i^2 \middle/ \sum_{i=1}^{T} x_i^2 \right)$.

b) Show that for the instrumental variable method, the weights used are $w_i = \left( x_i z_i \middle/ \sum_{i=1}^{T} x_i z_i \right)$.

Chapter
14

# CLASSICAL LINEAR ESTIMATION AND GENERALIZED LEAST SQUARES

## 14.1 PREVIEW

This chapter is a continuation of the previous chapter to the extent that it formalizes some of the methods of estimation considered there. In particular, the estimation procedure known as *generalized least squares* is in the spotlight throughout this chapter.

To set the stage, the classical presentation and solution for linear estimation is presented in Sections 14.3 and 14.4. By considering its historical development, the reader will recognize this as the original version of the method of least squares. Classical linear estimation principles are then extended to allow for violation of Assumptions 4 or 5 as considered in Chapter 13. The formal derivation of the generalized least squares estimators and their relation to weighted least squares estimates and to Cochrane and Orcutt Iterative Least Squares estimates are given in Section 14.5.

Then, in Sections 14.6–14.8, some particular uses of the generalized least squares method are detailed. Again, the formal solutions are presented here for the practical procedures of Chapter 13 concerning the problems of heteroscedasticity and autocorrelation. Thus, much of this chapter is a theoretical completion to the coverage of methods presented previously. For those readers who are more interested in "doing" than in "knowing why," this chapter does contain some additional tips for setting up consistent estimates of variance-covariance matrices of residuals that are heteroscedastic or autocorrelated. In addition a special case which partially concerns both these problems is given in Section 14.8. This new problem of estimating coefficients in two seemingly unrelated regression equations is interesting from both a theoretical and a practical viewpoint.

## 14.2 REVIEW

The reader will recognize the use in Sections 14.3 to 14.8 of many mathematical and statistical topics or equations from previous chapters. These and the simple review items below in matrix algebra should be reviewed as necessary.

### 1 Inverse of a diagonal matrix

A diagonal matrix $D$ with elements $d_{ij}$ has nonzero elements only on the major diagonal with $d_{ij} = 0$ if $i \neq j$. The diagonal elements of the inverse of such a matrix are given by the reciprocal of each diagonal element. The off-diagonal elements of the inverse matrix are zero. If $d^{ij}$ denotes the elements of the inverse matrix $D^{-1}$, then $d^{ij} = d_{ij} = 0$ if $i \neq j$ and $d^{ij} = 1/d_{ij}$ if $i = j$.

For example, define

$$D = \begin{pmatrix} 2 & 0 & 0 \\ 0 & 3 & 0 \\ 0 & 0 & -5 \end{pmatrix}, \quad \text{then } D^{-1} = \begin{pmatrix} 1/2 & 0 & 0 \\ 0 & 1/3 & 0 \\ 0 & 0 & -1/5 \end{pmatrix}.$$

## 2 A block diagonal matrix and its inverse

Suppose a matrix $W$ can be partitioned into $m$ blocks including the diagonal elements so that all other blocks (submatrices) not containing a diagonal element are null matrices. The matrix $W$ is then called a block diagonal matrix and may be represented as

$$W = \begin{pmatrix} w_1 & O & \cdots & O \\ O & w_2 & \cdots & O \\ \vdots & \vdots & \ddots & \vdots \\ O & O & \cdots & w_m \end{pmatrix}.$$

The inverse of such a matrix is given by a similarly blocked matrix $W^{-1}$ where the corresponding diagonal blocks are the inverse matrices of $w_1, w_2, \ldots, w_m$. That is, each block can be treated independently when determining the inverse.

For example, consider the matrix

$$W = \begin{pmatrix} 3 & 2 & 0 & 0 & 0 \\ 1 & 4 & 0 & 0 & 0 \\ 0 & 0 & 5 & 0 & 0 \\ 0 & 0 & 0 & -2 & 1 \\ 0 & 0 & 0 & 6 & 1 \end{pmatrix}$$

with diagonal blocks

$$w_1 = \begin{pmatrix} 3 & 2 \\ 1 & 4 \end{pmatrix}, \quad w_2 = (5), \quad \text{and} \quad w_3 = \begin{pmatrix} -2 & 1 \\ 6 & 1 \end{pmatrix}.$$

The inverse matrix is given by

$$W^{-1} = \begin{pmatrix} w_1^{-1} & O & O \\ O & w_2^{-1} & O \\ O & O & w_3^{-1} \end{pmatrix}$$

where

$$w_1^{-1} = \begin{pmatrix} 0.4 & -0.2 \\ -0.1 & 0.3 \end{pmatrix}, \quad w_2^{-1} = 1/5, \quad \text{and} \quad w_3^{-1} = \begin{pmatrix} -0.125 & 0.125 \\ 0.75 & 0.25 \end{pmatrix}.$$

## 3 Positive definite matrix

A matrix $A$ is a positive definite matrix if its associated quadratic form $u'Au$ is positive definite. (See *Review* 10.2, item 1.) Some characteristics about a positive definite matrix are: (a) it is nonsingular; and (b) its inverse is also positive definite.

In addition, for any matrix $A$ of size $T \times K$ with rank $K < T$, then $AA'$ is
$$\underset{(T \times T)}{}$$
positive semidefinite ($u'Au \geq 0$ for any $u$), but not positive definite and $A'A$
$$\underset{(K \times K)}{}$$

is positive definite. This result is frequently applied to illustrate that variance–covariance or moment matrices are positive semidefinite or definite.

## 4 Property of a symmetric positive definite matrix

For a symmetric positive definite matrix $A$ of size $(T \times T)$, there always exists a nonsingular matrix $H$ of size $(T \times T)$ such that $H'H = A$. This result is commonly used in applying linear transformations to observation matrices (see Section 14.5).

## REVIEW EXERCISES

R.1.  Find the inverse of

$$D = \begin{pmatrix} a & 0 & 0 \\ 0 & b & 0 \\ 0 & 0 & c \end{pmatrix}$$

and demonstrate that $DD^{-1} = \underset{(3 \times 3)}{I}$ .

R.2.  Find the inverse of

$$W = \begin{pmatrix} a_{11} & a_{12} & 0 & 0 \\ a_{21} & a_{22} & 0 & 0 \\ 0 & 0 & b_{11} & b_{12} \\ 0 & 0 & b_{21} & b_{22} \end{pmatrix}$$

and demonstrate that $WW^{-1} = \underset{(4 \times 4)}{I}$ .

R.3.  Show that the matrix

$$A = \begin{pmatrix} a_1 & a_2 \\ a_2 & a_1 \end{pmatrix}$$

is positive definite if $a_1 > |a_2|$.

R.4.  Prove that any positive definite matrix is nonsingular. (*Hint*: If it were singular, $Au = O$ for some $u = O$. What does this imply about $u'Au$?)

R.5.  *a*)  Suppose

$$A = \begin{pmatrix} 3 & 0 \\ 0 & 5 \end{pmatrix}.$$

Find a nonsingular matrix $H$ such that $H'H = A$.

*b*)  Suppose

$$\Omega = \begin{pmatrix} \sigma_1 & 0 & 0 \\ 0 & \sigma_2 & 0 \\ 0 & 0 & \sigma_3 \end{pmatrix},$$

generalize from your first result to write down a nonsingular matrix $H$ such that $H'H = \Omega$.

R.6.   *a)*   If a residual vector $e$ has size $(T \times 1)$, discuss if the variance-covariance matrix $ee'$ is positive semidefinite or definite, or neither.

   *b)*   If an observation matrix $X$ has size $T \times K$ and rank $K$, discuss if the moment matrix $X'X$ is positive semidefinite or definite, or neither.

## 14.3 THE CRITERIA OF CLASSICAL LINEAR ESTIMATION

Finding the estimators of the parameters in a linear model, $Y = X\Gamma + \varepsilon$ is not a recent problem. It was considered by Gauss (1807, 1821), Laplace (1811), and Legendre (1806) independently. (See the references at the end of this chapter.) The assumptions used and the criteria for estimators specified in these early treatments is the basis for what we now call *classical linear estimation*.

### Classical assumptions

Two particular assumptions are often termed the classical assumptions about the disturbances, $\varepsilon_t$, in the linear model. The first states that $\varepsilon_t$ is symmetrically distributed with a single mode. For example, $\varepsilon_t$ could be normally distributed, although this is not required. The second assumption states that the $\varepsilon_t$ are identically and independently distributed for all $t = 1, 2, \ldots, T$. This assumption implies a constant mean, say zero, and constant variance $\sigma_\varepsilon^2$ for all $\varepsilon_t$ and no autocorrelation among them. They were adopted as essential assumptions so that the resulting estimator $\hat{\gamma}_k$ would be symmetrically distributed with a single mode at the value $\gamma_k$. They are also important if the mean and variance are to be effective measures of the statistical precision of the estimators. In particular, if only linear estimators are considered, and these all have the same form for their probability density functions, then selecting unbiased estimators is appealing. Also, selecting from among these the one with minimum variance as the "best" one also makes sense. Without some basic assumptions which restrict the type of estimator, there would be no way of making tradeoffs among estimators with different PDF's, different bias, and different variances to decide on the "best" one.

Two other assumptions needed in the classical presentation are that the observation matrix $X$ of exogenous variables has rank $K < T$ and that either $X$ is fixed or the number of observations is very large, $T \to \infty$.

### Classical criteria of linear, unbiased, and minimal variance

Using these assumptions, three criteria allow for the determination of the classical estimates $\hat{\Gamma}$ of $\Gamma$. The first requirement for ease of calculation is that the estimates must be linear functions of the endogenous variable, say each $\hat{\gamma}_k = \sum_{t=1}^{T} u_{tk} Y_t$ where $u_{tk}$ are constants. In matrix notation we require,

$$\hat{\Gamma}_{(K \times 1)} = U'_{(K \times T)} \, Y_{(T \times 1)}.$$

The second criterion is the condition of unbiasedness. Since $E(\hat{\Gamma}) = E(U'Y)$ $= E(U'X\Gamma) + E(U'\varepsilon)$, and if $E(\varepsilon_t)$ is zero for all $t$, then $\hat{\Gamma}$ can be unbiased only if $U'X = \underset{(K \times K)}{I}$. Then, $E(\hat{\Gamma}) = E(U'X\Gamma) = E(I\Gamma) = \Gamma$. There are still many vectors $\hat{\Gamma}$ which would satisfy both these criteria, so the problem is to choose one that is best in some sense.

Laplace examined the problem for large size samples using the criterion that for any two unbiased, estimators of the same form, the one with the smaller variance is to be preferred. Consider a case of two alternate unbiased estimators for a particular coefficient $\gamma_k$. The use of the estimator with the smaller variance would result in a greater probability of the event $(a < \gamma_k < b)$ for a given interval $(a, b)$. Using the estimator with the smaller variance would give higher power to tests of significance based on the same size sample.

Gauss arrived at the same result considering a finite sample with $X$ fixed. Using the inequality,

$$\Pr\{|\hat{\gamma}_k - \gamma_k| \le \delta\} > 1 - \frac{4}{9}\frac{V(\hat{\gamma}_k)}{\delta^2},$$

Gauss argues that the upper bound of probability on the event $[\hat{\gamma}_k - \gamma_k| > \delta]$, where $\delta$ is a given small positive number, is minimized if $V(\hat{\gamma}_k)$ is minimized.[1]

Applying these results for all $k = 1, 2, \ldots, K$, the best estimator is obtained as the one such that $V(\hat{\Gamma})$ is minimal. An expression for $V(\hat{\Gamma})$ is easily obtained given the model $Y = X\Gamma + \varepsilon$ and the conditions required for $\hat{\Gamma}$ to be linear and unbiased, namely $\hat{\Gamma} = U'Y$, and $U'X = I$ respectively. Beginning with $\hat{\Gamma} = U'Y$ and substituting for $Y$, we obtain $\hat{\Gamma} = U'X\Gamma + U'\varepsilon$. Since $U'X = I$, then $\hat{\Gamma} - \Gamma = U'\varepsilon$. Finally, $V\text{-}Cov(\hat{\Gamma}) = E[(\hat{\Gamma} - \Gamma)(\hat{\Gamma} - \Gamma)'] = E[U'\varepsilon\varepsilon'U] = U'UE(\varepsilon\varepsilon')$. The latter simplification is possible since the elements $u_{tk}$ are constants. Given the classical assumptions, $E(\varepsilon\varepsilon') = \sigma_\varepsilon^2 I$; and so, $V\text{-}Cov(\hat{\Gamma}) = \sigma_\varepsilon^2 U'U$.

The diagonal elements of $\sigma_\varepsilon^2 U'U$ represent the variances of the estimators $\hat{\Gamma} = (\hat{\gamma}_1, \hat{\gamma}_2, \ldots, \hat{\gamma}_K)'$. Consequently, to find the estimates with minimal variances, the estimator $\hat{\gamma}_k$ should be chosen so that $\sum_{t=1}^{T} u_{tk}^2$ is a minimum for each $k = 1, 2, \ldots, K$ subject to the unbiased condition $U'X = I_K$. The classical solution to this minimization problem is given in the next section.

## 14.4 THE SOLUTION OF CLASSICAL LINEAR ESTIMATION

To find a solution to the problem, "Minimize $\sum u_{tk}^2$ subject to $U'X = I_K$," we first select any arbitrary form for $U$ which satisfies the condition and then discover what restrictions are necessary to insure that the minimization occurs.

---

[1] This result of Gauss is in Article 10, pp. 10 and 11 of his 1821 work. See the references at the end of this chapter. It is known as the Gauss inequality. See H. Cramér, *Mathematical Methods of Statistics* (Princeton: Princeton University Press, 1945), p. 183.

**The solution of Gauss**

If $U'X = I_K$ is required, then $U$ must have the form $U = X(X'X)^{-1} + \underset{(T \times K)}{D}$ where $D$ is any matrix such that $D'X = O$. The term, $\sum u_{tk}^2$ is given by the $k$th diagonal element of $U'U = [(X'X)^{-1}X' + D'][X(X'X)^{-1} + D]$ which simplifies to $U'U = (X'X)^{-1} + D'D$. (The reader can demonstrate this in Exercise 2 at the end of this chapter.) For any $k = 1, 2, \ldots, K$, we obtain $\sum u_{tk}^2 = (1/\sum x_{tk}^2) + \sum d_{kt}^2$. For a given observation matrix $X$, $\sum u_{kt}^2$ is minimized if each $d_{tk} = 0$.[2] Since this condition holds for all diagonal elements $k$, then $D = O$ gives the desired minimum at $U'U = (X'X)^{-1}$. Thus, $U = X(X'X)^{-1}$ is the solution which gives the linear, unbiased estimate which has minimal variance.

In modern terminology, the solution for the BLUE is $C = U'Y = (X'X)^{-1} X'Y$ with $V\text{-}Cov(C) = \sigma_\varepsilon^2 U'U = \sigma_\varepsilon^2 (X'X)^{-1}$. These are identical to the least squares results and to the corresponding maximum likelihood results in Chapters 9 and 10 which minimize a quadratic form in the residuals, $Q(e) = e'I^{-1}e$. The above derivation constitutes a proof of the minimal variance (efficiency) property of this least squares estimator among the class of all linear unbiased estimates. This conclusion is known as the Gauss-Markov theorem.[3]

Throughout Sections 14.3 and 14.4, the variance-covariance matrix of the disturbances has been assumed to be $V\text{-}Cov(\varepsilon) = \sigma_\varepsilon^2 \underset{(T \times T)}{I}$. In the next section, the results are extended to consider the less ideal but frequently occurring case of $V\text{-}Cov(\varepsilon) = \sigma_\varepsilon^2 \underset{(T \times T)}{\Omega}$ where $\Omega \neq I$.

## 14.5 GENERALIZED CLASSICAL LINEAR ESTIMATION

If the classical assumption, $V\text{-}Cov(\varepsilon) = \sigma_\varepsilon^2 I$ is violated and heteroscedasticity and/or autocorrelation is allowed, then a more general result occurs. Indeed, the ideal case solved above is a special case of the more general result. Gauss considered the possibility that $V\text{-}Cov(\varepsilon)$ may be a diagonal matrix (allowing heteroscedasticity) rather than a scalar matrix.[4] However, the extension to any positive definite matrix, $V\text{-}Cov(\varepsilon) = \sigma_\varepsilon^2\Omega$, is credited to Aitken and his solution of this generalized classical linear estimation problem is called Aitken least squares, or more commonly, generalized least squares, GLS.[5]

The GLS estimates are obtained using the same classical criteria of linear, unbiased, and minimum variance estimators. The difference in the underlying assumption, however, requires that we minimize a quadratic form $Q(e) = e'\Omega^{-1}e$ rather than $e'I^{-1}e = e'e$ as in ordinary least squares.

---

[2] This solution was found by Gauss (1821), Article 20, pp. 22–24.

[3] At a later date than Gauss, A. A. Markov independently arrived at the same results. Being more recent, his results attracted more attention and stirred modern interest in linear processes. See the reference at the end of the chapter.

[4] Gauss (1921), Article 22, pp. 25–26.

[5] See the reference for A. C. Aitken (1935) at the end of this chapter.

||||||||||||||||||||||||||||||||||||||||||||||||||||||||||||||||||||||||||||||||||||||||||||||||||||||||||||||||||||||||||||

*Explicative note.* It makes no difference in the solution of a minimization problem if a constant multiplier is included or factored out of the objective function. Thus, the form to be minimized could also be written $Q(e) = e'(\sigma_\varepsilon^2 \Omega)^{-1} e$. This inclusion of the constant $\sigma_\varepsilon^2$ is sometimes convenient for exposition purposes and for practical calculational procedures.

||||||||||||||||||||||||||||||||||||||||||||||||||||||||||||||||||||||||||||||||||||||||||||||||||||||||||||||||||||||||||||

## Generalized least squares solution

Consider the general model, $\underset{(T \times 1)}{Y} = \underset{(T \times K)}{X} \underset{(K \times 1)}{\Gamma} + \underset{(T \times 1)}{\varepsilon}$ for which the variance-covariance matrix of the disturbances is given by $V\text{-}Cov(\varepsilon) = \sigma_\varepsilon^2 \Omega$.

||||||||||||||||||||||||||||||||||||||||||||||||||||||||||||||||||||||||||||||||||||||||||||||||||||||||||||||||||||||||||||

*Recursive note.* The diagonal elements of $(\sigma_\varepsilon^2 \Omega)$ are variances, $V(\varepsilon_t)$, $t = 1, 2, \ldots, T$. If these are not all equal, then Assumption 4 of constant variance is violated. The off-diagonal elements are covariances $V(\varepsilon_t \varepsilon_i)$, $t \neq i$. If these are not all zero, then Assumption 5 of independence is violated. Thus, this general formulation allows heteroscedasticity and autocorrelation.

||||||||||||||||||||||||||||||||||||||||||||||||||||||||||||||||||||||||||||||||||||||||||||||||||||||||||||||||||||||||||||

The quadratic form to be minimized is $\hat{Q}(e) = e'(\sigma_\varepsilon^2 \Omega)^{-1} e$ where $e$ is the residual $e = Y - X\hat{C}$ and $\hat{C}$ is the GLS estimator vector desired.

||||||||||||||||||||||||||||||||||||||||||||||||||||||||||||||||||||||||||||||||||||||||||||||||||||||||||||||||||||||||||||

*Interpretive note.* The GLS estimator of $\Gamma$ is denoted with a "hat" on top, $\hat{C}$, to distinguish it from the OLS estimator $C$. Later in this chapter, the so-called modified GLS estimators are denoted with a "tilda" on top, $\tilde{C}$, and the OLS estimators based on transformed data are denoted with an "asterisk" by $C^*$. Associated symbols are denoted similarly for each type estimation.

||||||||||||||||||||||||||||||||||||||||||||||||||||||||||||||||||||||||||||||||||||||||||||||||||||||||||||||||||||||||||||

The derivation of the GLS estimator $\hat{C}$ is given in the following four steps:

1. Substitute $e = Y - X\hat{C}$ in the quadratic form $\hat{Q}(e) = e'(\sigma_\varepsilon^2 \Omega)^{-1} e$ and factor out the constant to obtain $\sigma_\varepsilon^2 \hat{Q}(e) = (Y - X\hat{C})'\Omega^{-1}(Y - X\hat{C})$.
2. Expand the right-hand side to obtain

$$\sigma_\varepsilon^2 \hat{Q}(e) = Y'\Omega^{-1}Y + \hat{C}'X'\Omega^{-1}X\hat{C} - \hat{C}'X'\Omega^{-1}Y - Y'\Omega^{-1}X\hat{C}.$$

||||||||||||||||||||||||||||||||||||||||||||||||||||||||||||||||||||||||||||||||||||||||||||||||||||||||||||||||

*Explicative note.* The dimensions of the matrices in the third term on the right side of this equation are $(1 \times K)(K \times T)(T \times T)$ $\times (T \times 1)$, which is defined to be a $(1 \times 1)$ scalar. The transpose of a scalar is itself; and since $\Omega$ is a symmetric matrix, $\Omega^{-1}$ is also. Thus, $\hat{C}'X'\Omega^{-1}Y = Y'\Omega^{-1}X\hat{C}$.

|||||||||||||||||||||||||||||||||||||||||||||||| |||||||||||||||||||||||||||||||||||||||| |||||||||||||||||||||||||||||

3. Add together the final two similar terms and take the vector differentiation of $\sigma_\varepsilon^2 \hat{Q}(e)$ with respect to the unknown estimates $\hat{C}$. (See *Review 9.2*, item 3.) We obtain,

$$\frac{\partial(Y'\Omega^{-1}Y + \hat{C}'X'\Omega^{-1}X\hat{C} - 2\hat{C}'X'\Omega^{-1}Y)}{\partial\hat{C}} = 2X'\Omega^{-1}X\hat{C} - 2X'\Omega^{-1}Y.$$

4. Set this expression equal to zero and solve for $\hat{C}$ by premultiplying both sides by the $(K \times K)$ inverse matrix $(X'\Omega^{-1}X)^{-1}$. The GLS estimator vector is $\hat{C} = (X'\Omega^{-1}X)^{-1}(X'\Omega^{-1}Y)$.                  (14–1)

|||||||| ||||||||||||||||||||||||||||||||||||||||||||||||||||||||||||||||||||||||||||||||| ||||||||||||||||||||||||||||||||

*Recursive note.* If the term $\sigma_\varepsilon^2$ had not been factored out and the differentiation of step 3 were taken of $\hat{Q}(e)$, then the result is

$$\hat{C} = [X'(\sigma_\varepsilon^2\Omega)^{-1}X]^{-1}[X'(\sigma_\varepsilon^2\Omega)^{-1}Y].$$

Now factoring out the scalar multiple $\sigma_\varepsilon^2$, one obtains $\hat{C} = \sigma_\varepsilon^2$ $(X'\Omega^{-1}X)^{-1}(X'\Omega^{-1}Y)(1/\sigma_\varepsilon^2)$ and the $\sigma_\varepsilon^2$ term in both numerator and denominator cancel each other. The result for the GLS estimator $\hat{C}$ is the same as (14–1).

||||||||||||||||||||||||||||||||||||||||||||||||||||||||||||||||||||||||||||||||||||||||||||||||||||||||||||||||

The estimate of the variance-covariance matrix of the GLS estimator is obtained by a procedure identical to that for the OLS estimator in Section 10.5. The result is

$$V\text{-}Cov(\hat{C}) = [X'(\sigma_\varepsilon^2\Omega)^{-1}X]^{-1} = \sigma_\varepsilon^2(X'\Omega^{-1}X)^{-1}.  \quad (14–2)$$

The estimates $\hat{C}$ are linear and unbiased. Also, if the disturbance variance-covariance matrix, $\sigma_\varepsilon^2\Omega$, is assumed to be positive definite, then by a direct extension of the Gauss-Markov theorem, they are "best" in the minimal variance sense.

An unbiased estimate of the variance $\sigma_\varepsilon^2$ is obtained by a derivation similar to that using the OLS estimates. The OLS estimate of $\sigma_\varepsilon^2$ is $s_e^2 = e'e/(T - K)$. However, when $Cov(\varepsilon_t \varepsilon_i) \neq 0$ for $t \neq i$, as is possible when $\Omega \neq I$, this estimate is no longer unbiased. (See Section 13.5.) The corrected unbiased estimate making use of the matrix $\Omega$ is

$$[\text{Est. } \sigma_\varepsilon^2] = \hat{s}_e^2 = \hat{e}'\hat{e} = e'\Omega^{-1}e/(T - K)  \quad (14–3)$$

where the residual vector $\hat{e}$ is $\hat{e} = Y - X\hat{C}$.

## Modified GLS

The generalized least squares method is often impractical since the true matrix $\Omega$ is generally unknown. Modified GLS is here defined as the estimating procedure using a consistent estimator of $\Omega$, say $\tilde{\Omega}$, in the formulas for the generalized least squares estimators. With this substitution, one obtains the modified GLS estimator

$$\tilde{C} = (X'\tilde{\Omega}^{-1}X)^{-1}(X'\tilde{\Omega}^{-1}Y). \tag{14-4}$$

Similarly,

$$V\text{-}Cov(\tilde{C}) = \sigma_\varepsilon^2(X'\tilde{\Omega}^{-1}X)^{-1} \tag{14-5}$$

and

$$[\text{Est. } \sigma_\varepsilon^2] = \tilde{s}_e^2 = \tilde{e}'\tilde{e} = e'\tilde{\Omega}^{-1}e/(T - K) \tag{14-6}$$

where the residual vector $\tilde{e}$ is $\tilde{e} = Y - X\tilde{C}$.

Determining a consistent estimator for $\Omega$ is not always possible and is often a tedious and complex problem. One temptation to avoid is the use of the residuals from ordinary least squares to obtain an estimate of $V\text{-}Cov(\varepsilon)$. If the residual variance-covariance matrix is set up as

$$ee' = \begin{pmatrix} e_1e_1 & e_1e_2 & \cdots & e_1e_T \\ e_2e_1 & e_2e_2 & \cdots & e_2e_T \\ e_Te_1 & e_Te_2 & \cdots & e_Te_T \end{pmatrix},$$

it is clear that the inverse $(ee')^{-1}$ does not exist.

‖‖‖‖‖‖‖‖‖‖‖‖‖‖‖‖‖‖‖‖‖‖‖‖‖‖‖‖‖‖‖‖‖‖‖‖‖‖‖‖‖‖‖‖‖‖‖‖‖‖‖‖‖‖‖‖‖‖‖‖‖‖‖‖‖‖‖‖‖‖‖‖‖‖‖‖‖‖‖‖‖‖‖‖

***Recursive note.*** If $e_i$ is factored out of row $i$, $i = 1, 2, \ldots, T$, then we find that the determinant of $(ee')$ is zero,

$$|ee'| = (e_1 \cdot e_2 \cdot \ldots \cdot e_T) \begin{vmatrix} e_1 & e_2 & \cdots & e_T \\ e_1 & e_2 & \cdots & e_T \\ e_1 & e_2 & \cdots & e_T \end{vmatrix}$$

$$= (e_1 \cdot e_2 \cdot \ldots \cdot e_T)(0),$$

because each row in the remaining matrix is identical.

‖‖‖‖‖‖‖‖‖‖‖‖‖‖‖‖‖‖‖‖‖‖‖‖‖‖‖‖‖‖‖‖‖‖‖‖‖‖‖‖‖‖‖‖‖‖‖‖‖‖‖‖‖‖‖‖‖‖‖‖‖‖‖‖‖‖‖‖‖‖‖‖‖‖‖‖‖‖‖‖‖‖‖‖

Thus $(ee')$ is not a feasible approximation of $\tilde{\Omega}$. To solve for the modified GLS estimator $\tilde{C}$ in 14-4, the inverse, $\tilde{\Omega}^{-1}$, must exist.

## OLS on transformed observations

As seen in the previous chapter, an alternate method of estimation which gives estimates $C^*$ with the same properties as $\tilde{C}$ can sometimes be used. The basic principle of this method is to replace the observations of the regression model involving a nonscalar matrix, $V\text{-}Cov(\varepsilon) = \sigma_\varepsilon^2\Omega$, with transformed observations giving a regression model involving a scalar variance-covariance matrix of disturbances, $V\text{-}Cov(\varepsilon^*) = \sigma_\varepsilon^2 I$. The basic procedure requires some determination of the relations among the disturbance variances and covariances. Then, the original variables are transformed according to these same relationships; and, finally, ordinary least squares estimators can be used on the transformed observations. The OLS method is then appropriate because $V\text{-}Cov(\varepsilon^*)$ is a scalar matrix satisfying assumptions 4 and 5 of Section 10.3.

The linear transformation required can be represented by a nonsingular transformation matrix $H$ determined such that $H'H = \Omega^{-1}$. Since $\Omega$ is symmetric and assumed to be positive definite, then $\Omega^{-1}$ also has these properties. Therefore, such a matrix $\underset{(T \times T)}{H}$ always exists. (See *Review* 14.2, items 3 and 4.)

If the original model $Y = X\Gamma + \varepsilon$ is premultiplied by $H$, we obtain the transformed model $Y^* = X^*\Gamma^* + \varepsilon^*$ defined as $HY = HX\Gamma + H\varepsilon$. With some luck and determination, the reader can now show that the variance-covariance matrix of $\varepsilon^*$ is scalar as follows:

*a)*   $V\text{-}Cov(\varepsilon^*) = V\text{-}Cov(H\varepsilon) = E[(H\varepsilon)(H\varepsilon')]$    by definition since $E(\varepsilon) = O$;

*b)*           $= HE(\varepsilon\varepsilon')H' = H(\sigma_\varepsilon^2\Omega)H'$    by taking expectations;

*c)*           $= \sigma_\varepsilon^2 H\Omega H'(HH^{-1})$ using the nonsingularity of $H$;

*d)*           $= \sigma_\varepsilon^2 H\Omega(H'H)H^{-1} = \sigma_\varepsilon^2 H\Omega\Omega^{-1}H^{-1}$ if $H'H = \Omega^{-1}$;

and

*e)*   $V\text{-}Cov(\varepsilon^*) = \sigma_\varepsilon^2 HIH^{-1} = \sigma_\varepsilon^2 \underset{(T \times T)}{I}$    by definition of an inverse matrix.

Since $V\text{-}Cov(\varepsilon^*)$ is a scalar matrix, ordinary least squares can be applied to the model $Y^* = X^*\Gamma^* + \varepsilon^*$ to obtain estimates $C^*$. We use the transformed observation matrix,

$$\underset{[T \times (K+1)]}{(Y^* \quad X^*)} = (HY, HX),$$

and the OLS formulas (9–3), and (10–4), to obtain

$$C^* = (X^{*\prime}X^*)^{-1}(X^{*\prime}Y^*) = (X'H'HX)^{-1}X'H'HY$$

or

$$C^* = (X'\Omega^{-1}X)^{-1}(X'\Omega^{-1}Y) \quad \text{[same as (14–1) for GLS].}$$

Also,

$$V\text{-}Cov(C^*) = \sigma_\varepsilon^2(X^{*\prime}X^*)^{-1} = \sigma_\varepsilon^2(X'H'HX)^{-1}$$

or

$$V\text{-}Cov(C^*) = \sigma_\varepsilon^2(X'\Omega^{-1}X)^{-1}; \quad \text{[same as (14–2)]}$$

and

$$[\text{Est. } \sigma_\varepsilon^2] = e^{*\prime}e^*/(T - K) = e'H'He/(T - K)$$

or

$$(s_e*)^2 = e'\Omega^{-1}e/(T - K) \qquad \text{[same as (14-3)].}$$

Thus, the use of OLS on the transformed observations is comparable to GLS on the original variables. The estimators $\hat{C}$ and $C^*$ have the same properties if $H'H = \Omega^{-1}$ identically.

If $\Omega$ is unknown but a consistent estimate $\tilde{\Omega}$ is available, then the same method is applied using a transformation matrix $\tilde{H}$ such that $\tilde{H}'\tilde{H} = \tilde{\Omega}^{-1}$. Under these circumstances, the use of OLS based on the transformed observation matrix $(\tilde{Y} \quad \tilde{X}) = (\tilde{H} Y \quad \tilde{H}X)$ gives the same results as modified GLS. The appropriate formulas are (14–4), (14–5), and (14–6).

One use of this procedure already mentioned in Section 13.4 is weighted least squares where an approximation to a diagonal matrix $\Omega$ was used. Another application of this transformation method to achieve the efficiency property of GLS estimates is the C & O ILS method used in Section 13.5. In the following sections, the formal details of these and other practical procedures are presented.

## 14.6 USE OF GLS IN CASES OF HETEROSCEDASTICITY

Consider a model $Y = X\Gamma + \varepsilon$ to be estimated on the basis of $N$ cross-sectional observations so that the variances of the disturbance term $\varepsilon_j, j = 1, 2, \ldots, N$ are not constant.

|||||||||||||||||||||||||||||||||||||||||||||||||||||||||||||||||||||||||||||||||||||||||||||||||||||||||||||||||||||||||||||||||

*Discursive note.* The observation subscripts in this section are $j = 1, 2, \ldots, N$ instead of $t = 1, 2, \ldots, T$ merely to acquaint the reader with the notation that is necessary in Chapter 15 where both cross-sectional and time-series observations are used.

|||||||||||||||||||||||||||||||||||||||||||||||||||||||||||||||||||||||||||||||||||||||||||||||||||||||||||||||||||||||||||||||||

We assume that $Cov(\varepsilon_i \varepsilon_j) = 0$ for $i \neq j$ so that $(\varepsilon_\varepsilon^2 \Omega) = V\text{-}Cov(\varepsilon)$ is a *diagonal* matrix. From Section 13.4, the more these diagonal elements differ from each other, the less efficient are the OLS estimators. In this case, we denote

$$V\text{-}Cov(\varepsilon) = \begin{pmatrix} \sigma_1^2 & 0 & \cdots & 0 \\ 0 & \sigma_2^2 & \cdots & 0 \\ 0 & 0 & \cdots & \sigma_N^2 \end{pmatrix}.$$

|||||||||||||||||||||||||||||||||||||||||||||||||||||||||||||||||||||||||||||||||||||||||||||||||||||||||||||||||||||||||||||||||

*Interpretive note.* Actually, not all the diagonal elements need to be different. More frequently, there may be several subgroups of observations with common variance within the subgroup, but different variances between the subgroups. The matrix above is applicable for the most general case.

|||||||||||||||||||||||||||||||||||||||||||||||||||||||||||||||||||||||||||||||||||||||||||||||||||||||||||||||||||||||||||||||||

If the elements of $V$-$Cov(\varepsilon)$ were known, the GLS estimates using (14–1), (14–2), and (14–3) would be appropriate. Usually, it is only possible to obtain some estimate of the proportionality constants among the variances. If a matrix $W$ is a diagonal matrix whose elements are consistent estimates of $\sigma_j^2$, $j = 1, 2, \ldots, N$, then $W^{-1}$ can be used as a consistent estimate of $(\sigma_\varepsilon^2 \Omega)^{-1}$. For example, if

$$W = \begin{pmatrix} s_1^2 & 0 & \cdots & 0 \\ 0 & s_2^2 & \cdots & 0 \\ \vdots & \vdots & \ddots & \vdots \\ 0 & 0 & \cdots & s_N^2 \end{pmatrix}$$

where $s_j^2$ is a sample variance estimating $\sigma_j^2$, then

$$W^{-1} = \begin{pmatrix} 1/s_1^2 & 0 & \cdots & 0 \\ 0 & 1/s_2^2 & \cdots & 0 \\ \vdots & \vdots & \ddots & \vdots \\ 0 & 0 & \cdots & 1/s_N^2 \end{pmatrix}$$

provides an estimate of $(\sigma_\varepsilon^2 \Omega)^{-1}$. Substitution of $(\sigma_\varepsilon^2 W^{-1})$ for $\tilde{\Omega}^{-1}$ in formulas (14–4) and (14–5) would give the modified GLS results for $\tilde{C}$ and for $V$-$Cov(\tilde{C})$. The sum of squares of residuals $\tilde{e}'\tilde{e}$ from this modified GLS estimation can be substituted for $e'\tilde{\Omega}^{-1}e$ in formula (14–6) to get an estimate of $\sigma_\varepsilon^2$. (See Exercise 7.) The usual $t$ and $F$ tests can be used to analyze the results of this estimation.

In Section 13.4, this method is used in a particular example where three separate subgroups of observations are used to get three estimates of the different variances of the disturbances presumed to be different among the observational subgroups but constant within each subgroup.

### Special case of weighted least squares

When the estimate used for $V$-$Cov(\varepsilon)$ is a diagonal matrix, the method is called weighted least squares. It is a special case of generalized least squares. It is the same as using ordinary least squares on transformed data, $(Y^* \quad X^*)_{[T \times (K+1)]}$ obtained by dividing row $j$ of the observation matrix $(Y \quad X)$ by $\sigma_j$ for $j = 1, 2, \ldots, N$. Each observation is weighted inversely proportional to the standard deviation of the disturbance $\varepsilon_j$.

‖‖‖‖‖‖‖‖‖‖‖‖‖‖‖‖‖‖‖‖‖‖‖‖‖‖‖‖‖‖‖‖‖‖‖‖‖‖‖‖‖‖‖‖‖‖‖‖‖‖‖‖‖‖‖‖‖‖‖‖‖‖‖‖‖‖‖‖‖‖‖‖‖‖‖‖‖‖‖‖‖‖‖‖‖‖‖‖‖

*Explicative note.*    In terms of the transformation matrix, one uses

$$H = \begin{pmatrix} 1/\sigma_1 & 0 & \cdots & 0 \\ 0 & 1/\sigma_2 & \cdots & 0 \\ \vdots & \vdots & \ddots & \vdots \\ 0 & 0 & \cdots & 1/\sigma_N \end{pmatrix}$$

so that $\sigma_\varepsilon^2 H'H = \Omega^{-1}$. In practice, using estimates of $\sigma_j$, the transformation is $\tilde{H}'\tilde{H} = W^{-1} = (\sigma_\varepsilon^2 \tilde{\Omega})^{-1}$. In the case of weighted least squares, it is more convenient not to factor out $\sigma_\varepsilon^2$ in the GLS derivation. (Refer to the two *Notes* concerning this alternative in Section 14.5).

## An application when the endogenous variable is a dummy variable

An interesting application of this same procedure occurs when the endogenous variable $Y$ in the model $Y = X\Gamma + \varepsilon$ is a dummy variable with two values, zero and one. Such a model is useful to characterize different levels of importance among various factors between two population groups; for example driving attitudes of married versus nonmarried teenagers, consumption patterns of high and low income families, determinants of injuries among football backs versus linemen, etc. The disturbance $\varepsilon_j$ is given by $\varepsilon_j = Y_j - X_j'\Gamma$ where $\underset{(1 \times K)}{X_j'} = (X_{j1}, X_{j2}, \ldots, X_{jK})$ represents observation $j$ on all exogenous variables.

If $Y_j = 1$, then $\varepsilon_j = 1 - X_j'\Gamma$, and if $Y_j = 0$, then $\varepsilon_j = X_j'\Gamma$. Consequently, assuming that $E(\varepsilon_j)$ may be zero, $V(\varepsilon_j)$ is certainly not constant. Although this result should not be obvious to the reader, it can be determined that

$$V\text{-}Cov(\varepsilon) = \begin{pmatrix} X_1'\Gamma(1 - X_1'\Gamma) & 0 & \cdots & 0 \\ 0 & X_2'\Gamma(1 - X_2'\Gamma) & \cdots & 0 \\ \vdots & \vdots & \ddots & \vdots \\ 0 & 0 & \cdots & X_N'\Gamma(1 - X_N'\Gamma) \end{pmatrix},$$

a diagonal matrix in terms of the $N$ row observation vectors $X_j'$ and the unknown coefficients $\Gamma$.[6] The estimates $C$ of $\Gamma$ using OLS are not efficient in this case. However, they are unbiased and consistent and can be substituted for $\Gamma$ in the above matrix, $V\text{-}Cov(\varepsilon)$, to obtain a matrix

$$W = \begin{pmatrix} X_1'C(1 - X_1'C) & 0 & \cdots & 0 \\ 0 & X_2'C(1 - X_2'C) & \cdots & 0 \\ \vdots & \vdots & \ddots & \vdots \\ 0 & 0 & \cdots & X_N'C(1 - X_N'C) \end{pmatrix}$$

which is a consistent estimate of $V\text{-}Cov(\varepsilon)$. Substitution of $(\sigma_\varepsilon^2 W^{-1})$ for $\tilde{\Omega}^{-1}$ in formulas (14–4) and (14–5) gives the modified generalized least squares estimates. The term, $\sigma_\varepsilon^2$, cancels out.

---

[6] For more details of this derivation, see A. S. Goldberger, *Econometric Theory* (New York: John Wiley & Sons, Inc., 1964), pp. 248–51.

## 14.7 USE OF GLS IN CASES OF NONZERO COVARIANCES OF DISTURBANCES

Another set of problems can be characterized by a reversal of the assumptions in the previous section. Consider now a model

$$\underset{(T \times 1)}{Y} = \underset{(T \times K)}{X} \underset{(K \times 1)}{\Gamma} + \underset{(T \times 1)}{\varepsilon}$$

for which the variances of the disturbance terms are constant but the covariances, $Cov(\varepsilon_i \varepsilon_j) \neq 0$ for $i \neq j$. If the observations are cross-sectional, this is termed *mutual* (or *spatial* when the cross sections are geographical) *correlation*. If the observations are over time, this is called *autocorrelation*.

Let $V\text{-}Cov(\varepsilon) = \sigma_\varepsilon^2 \Omega$ where the diagonal terms of the matrix $\Omega$ are unity and the off-diagonal terms represent proportionality constants relating the size of the covariance to the constant variance $\sigma_\varepsilon^2$. If these elements of $\Omega$ are known, then the GLS estimates can be obtained using (14–1). If a consistent estimate of $\Omega$ is available, then modified GLS estimates can be determined using (14–4). The related estimates for the disturbance variance and the variance-covariance matrix of estimates of the coefficients are also found using the some formulas as before (given in Section 14.5).

### Special case of first order autocorrelation

The most common problem situation which arises is first order autocorrelation among the disturbances as presented in Section 13.5. This situation is described by the autoregression, $\varepsilon_t = \rho \varepsilon_{t-1} + v_t$, where the autoregressive disturbance term $v$ is assumed to be distributed as $N(O, \sigma_v^2 I)$ and the coefficient is restricted such that $|\rho| < 1$.

In *Review* 13.2, item 4, it is shown that under these conditions, $V(\varepsilon_t) = \sigma_\varepsilon^2 = \sigma_v^2/(1 - \rho^2)$ and $Cov(\varepsilon_t \varepsilon_{t-i}) = \rho^i \sigma_v^2$. Consequently, the variance-covariance matrix of disturbances in this situation is

$$V\text{-}Cov(\varepsilon) = \sigma_\varepsilon^2 \Omega = \sigma_\varepsilon^2 \begin{pmatrix} 1 & \rho & \rho^2 & \cdots & \rho^{T-1} \\ \rho & 1 & \rho & \cdots & \rho^{T-2} \\ \rho^2 & \rho & 1 & \cdots & \rho^{T-3} \\ \vdots & \vdots & \vdots & \ddots & \vdots \\ \rho^{T-1} & \rho^{T-2} & \rho^{T-3} & \cdots & 1 \end{pmatrix}.$$

If $\sigma_\varepsilon^2$ and $\rho$ could be determined exactly, then the GLS formulas could be applied. Instead, it is usually necessary to make an imperfect guess of the true $\rho$ and use an estimate $\tilde{\Omega}$ for $\Omega$. Methods of obtaining consistent estimates of $\rho$ using an autoregression of OLS residuals or the Durbin-Watson $d$-value based on an OLS estimation are suggested and used in Section 13.5. Substituting $p$ for $\rho$ in the matrix $\Omega$ above, the consistent estimate $\tilde{\Omega}$ is obtained.

Since $\tilde{\Omega}$ is nonsingular, its inverse can be found to be

$$
\tilde{\Omega}^{-1} = \frac{1}{1-p^2}
\begin{pmatrix}
1 & -p & 0 & \cdots & 0 & 0 \\
-p & 1+p^2 & -p & \cdots & 0 & 0 \\
0 & -p & 1+p^2 & \cdots & 0 & 0 \\
\vdots & \vdots & \vdots & \ddots & \vdots & \vdots \\
0 & 0 & 0 & \cdots & 1+p^2 & -p \\
0 & 0 & 0 & \cdots & -p & 1
\end{pmatrix}
$$

The modified GLS estimates can then be obtained by the use of formulas (14–4), (14–5), and (14–6).

## The alternate C & O Iterative Least Squares approach

The same results are achieved with less complex calculations by using OLS estimation on the transformed observations $(\tilde{H}\,Y \quad \tilde{H}X)$. In terms of a transformation matrix, $\tilde{H}$, the inverse matrix $\tilde{\Omega}^{-1}$ of the previous subtopic can be written as $\tilde{\Omega}^{-1} = \tilde{H}'\tilde{H}$ where

$$
\tilde{H} = \frac{1}{\sqrt{1-p^2}}
\begin{pmatrix}
\sqrt{1-p^2} & 0 & 0 & \cdots & 0 & 0 \\
-p & 1 & 0 & \cdots & 0 & 0 \\
0 & -p & 1 & \cdots & 0 & 0 \\
\vdots & \vdots & \vdots & \ddots & \vdots \\
0 & 0 & 0 & \cdots & 1 & 0 \\
0 & 0 & 0 & \cdots & -p & 1
\end{pmatrix}.
$$

Ignoring the constant multiplier in $\tilde{H}$ of $1/\sqrt{1-p^2}$ since it cancels out in the derivation of OLS estimates, the transformation implied by $\tilde{H}$ is identical to the one presented in Section 13.5. The first observation of each variable is multiplied by $\sqrt{1-p^2}$, and all other observations are transformed according to the estimated autoregressive scheme to obtain the values,

$$
Y_1^* = \sqrt{1-p^2}\,Y_1 \quad \text{and} \quad X_{1k}^* = \sqrt{1-p^2}\,X_{1k}; \qquad (14\text{–}7)
$$

and $Y_t^* = Y_t - pY_{t-1}$ and $X_t^* = X_{tk} - pX_{t-1,k}$ for $t = 2, 3, \ldots, T$

and all $k$. This transformation might be denoted by $H^* = \sqrt{1-p^2}\,\tilde{H}$. Based on the transformed observations, we obtain unbiased, consistent, and efficient estimates using the OLS formulas (9–3).

$$
C^* = (X^{*\prime}X^*)^{-1}(X^{*\prime}Y^*).
$$

||||||||||||||||||||||||||||||||||||||||||||||||||||||||||||||||||||||||||||||||||||||||||||||||||||||||||||||||||||||||||||||||||||||||||

*Discursive note.* This estimate $C^*$ is easily shown to be identical to the modified GLS estimate $\tilde{C}$. By substitution,

$$
C^* = (X'H^{*\prime}H^*X)^{-1}(X'H^{*\prime}H^*Y).
$$

Since

$$H^* = \sqrt{1 - p^2}\,\tilde{H}, \quad \text{then} \quad H^{*\prime} H^* = (1 - p^2)\tilde{H}'\tilde{H} = (1 - p^2)\tilde{\Omega}^{-1}.$$

Thus,

$$C^* = (1 - p^2)^{-1}(X'\tilde{\Omega}^{-1}X)^{-1}(X'\tilde{\Omega}^{-1}Y)(1 - p^2) = \tilde{C} \qquad (14\text{--}4)$$

since the first and last factors cancel each other.

‖‖‖‖‖‖‖‖‖‖‖‖‖‖‖‖‖‖‖‖‖‖‖‖‖‖‖‖‖‖‖‖‖‖‖‖‖‖‖‖‖‖‖‖‖‖‖‖‖‖‖‖‖‖‖‖‖‖‖‖‖‖‖‖‖‖‖‖‖‖‖‖‖‖‖‖‖‖‖‖‖‖‖‖‖‖‖‖‖‖‖‖‖‖‖‖‖‖‖‖

Equivalent results to the modified GLS formulas (14–5) and (14–6) can also be obtained from this OLS regression on transformed data, $(Y^* \quad X^*) = (H^*Y \quad H^*X)$ from (14–7), if proper consideration is given to the constant multiplier in $\tilde{H}$ of $1/\sqrt{1 - p^2}$. (See Exercises 8 and 9 at the end of this chapter.) Using this transformed data, the OLS estimates of the coefficients and their standard errors are appropriate for the usual $t$ and $F$ tests of significance.

This first order autoregressive transformation defined in (14–7) is commonly used, although it may not always be appropriate. When a higher order autoregressive scheme is suspected, the methods of finding a consistent estimate of $\Omega$ and of obtaining efficient estimates of $\Gamma$ are more complex. Such procedures for higher order autoregression problems are still topics of research in econometric theory and methods. Some references are given at the end of the chapter.

## 14.8  USE OF GLS IN ESTIMATING SEEMINGLY UNRELATED REGRESSIONS

The application of generalized classical linear estimation is not limited to estimations of single equations. This concept can be extended to systems of regression equations and to simultaneous equations models. This latter extension is deferred to Chapter 18, but a special situation of the former is considered now. In a system of equations that are seemingly independent and are estimated separately, the problems of heteroscedasticity and nonzero covariances of disturbances may occur in an unsuspected way. The use of *joint GLS* estimation helps to correct for such problems and allows the determination of efficient estimates of the coefficients in each equation.[7]

### Contemporaneous covariance of disturbances

The unsuspected problems occur because the disturbances in the seemingly unrelated regressions are in fact correlated. Consider for example a system of regressions dealing with gross corporate investment as determined by expected profits, retained earnings, capital stock, and an interest rate for several

---

[7] See the following paper and its references to earlier research for development of this method, A. Zellner, "Estimators for Seemingly Unrelated Regression Equations: Some Exact Finite Results," *Journal of the American Statistical Association*, 1963, pp. 977–92.

different corporations.[8] If the data for each corporation is obtained over the same time period, it is likely that the same underlying factors in the economy, not specified in the equation, are affecting the disturbance terms in each regression. Consequently, the disturbance terms are related to each other in the same time period. This situation may be called *contemporaneous covariance of disturbances*. It has the effect of making the OLS estimates of the coefficients in each equation inefficient.

Some other situations where this problem arises are also common. An analyst may wish to estimate demand functions for different commodities in the same region over the same time period. Also, models explaining earnings, incomes, migration patterns, etc., for subgroups of the population such as different age cohorts, or different races, or different sexes would be likely to have contemporaneous covariance of the disturbances if the cross-sectional data is measured at the same point in time for each equation. The reader can add his own arguments (hints: discrimination, family characteristics, welfare programs) why unspecified factors may produce similar effects on disturbances in such seemingly unrelated regressions.

||||||||||||||||||||||||||||||||||||||||||||||||||||||||||||||||||||||||||||||||||||||||||||||||||||||||||||||||||||||||||||||||||

*Interpretive note.* The term seemingly unrelated is misleading. Theoretical consideration of such pairs or systems of regression equations usually indicates that they are related even if they have no simultaneous cause-effect relations between the variables. They are seemingly unrelated only in the sense that this condition is implicitly assumed when the econometrician uses ordinary least squares as the estimation method.

||||||||||||||||||||||||||||||||||||||||||||||||||||||||||||||||||||||||||||||||||||||||||||||||||||||||||||||||||||||||||||||||||

## Formulation of the problem

The problem setup is considered for a pair of seemingly unrelated regressions. We denote the equations,

$$Y_A = \underset{(T \times 1)}{X_A} \underset{(T \times K)(K \times 1)}{\Gamma_A} + \underset{(T \times 1)}{\varepsilon_A} \quad \text{and} \quad Y_B = \underset{(T \times 1)}{X_B} \underset{(T \times K)(K \times 1)}{\Gamma_B} + \underset{(T \times 1)}{\varepsilon_B}$$

where $X_A$ and $X_B$ are different observation matrices, although each may contain measures of the same variables.

||||||||||||||||||||||||||||||||||||||||||||||||||||||||||||||||||||||||||||||||||||||||||||||||||||||||||||||||||||||||||||||||||

*Interpretive note.* The exogenous variables in both equations may be "years of education" and "years of job experience." Yet the measures of each would differ because one might concern males and the other, females.

||||||||||||||||||||||||||||||||||||||||||||||||||||||||||||||||||||||||||||||||||||||||||||||||||||||||||||||||||||||||||||||||||

---

[8] Such a relation is part of a simultaneous equation model described in J. L. Murphy, "An Appraisal of Repeated Predictive Tests on an Econometric Model," *The Southern Economic Journal*, April 1969, pp. 293–307.

*Assumptions.* The usual assumptions are specified for the disturbances, $\varepsilon_A \sim N(0, \sigma_A^2 I)$ and $\varepsilon_B \sim N(0, \sigma_B^2 I)$. In addition, the disturbances at different observations for different equations are assumed independent, $Cov(\varepsilon_{At}, \varepsilon_{Bi}) = 0$ for $t \neq i$. However, contemporaneous covariance exists so that $Cov(\varepsilon_{At} \varepsilon_{Bt}) \neq 0$. The two equations have related disturbances so they should not be estimated independently.

If the observations on both are combined, the interpretation of the separate groups would be lost. Also, the disturbances of the combined regression would clearly be heteroscedastic since those from observation set $A$ have variance, $V(\varepsilon_A) = \sigma_A^2$, and those from observation set $B$ have a different variance, $V(\varepsilon_A) = \sigma_B^2$.

*Transforming the model.* A solution can be obtained if the data is pooled by alternately ordering corresponding observations from each regression. In this combined set of $2T$ observations, the odd numbered observations come from the original matrix, $(Y_A, X_A)$ and the even numbered observations are rows of $(Y_B \ X_B)$. The coefficient vector is extended to $2K$ components with the first $K$ corresponding to $\Gamma_A$ and the last $K$ corresponding to $\Gamma_B$. The new model to be estimated is denoted by

$$\underset{(2T \times 1)}{Y} = \underset{(2T \times 2K)}{X} \ \underset{(2K \times 1)}{\Gamma} + \underset{(2T \times 1)}{\varepsilon}$$

and defined in detail by the following matrices:

$$
\begin{pmatrix} Y_{A1} \\ Y_{B1} \\ Y_{A2} \\ Y_{B2} \\ \vdots \\ Y_{AT} \\ Y_{BT} \end{pmatrix} = \begin{pmatrix} X_{A1} & O \\ O & X_{B1} \\ X_{A2} & O \\ O & X_{B2} \\ \vdots & \vdots \\ X_{AT} & O \\ O & X_{BT} \end{pmatrix} \underset{(2K \times 1)}{\begin{pmatrix} \Gamma_A \\ \Gamma_B \end{pmatrix}} + \begin{pmatrix} \varepsilon_{A1} \\ \varepsilon_{B1} \\ \varepsilon_{A2} \\ \varepsilon_{B2} \\ \vdots \\ \varepsilon_{AT} \\ \varepsilon_{BT} \end{pmatrix}. \tag{14-8}
$$

$$\underset{(2T \times 1)}{\phantom{X}} \qquad \underset{(2T \times 2K)}{\phantom{X}} \qquad \underset{(2T \times 1)}{\phantom{X}}$$

*Determination of $\Omega$.* The variance-covariance matrix of disturbances $\varepsilon$ in this model has dimension $(2T \times 2T)$. Based on the assumptions concerning $V\text{-}Cov(\varepsilon_A)$ and $V\text{-}Cov(\varepsilon_B)$ for the two separate regressions and the condition of contemporaneous covariance, the new $V\text{-}Cov(\varepsilon)$ can be described. It is a block diagonal matrix where the block for a given observation $t$ is size $(2 \times 2)$ and composed of

$$V\text{-}Cov(\varepsilon_{At} \varepsilon_{Bt}) = \begin{pmatrix} V(\varepsilon_A) & Cov(\varepsilon_A \varepsilon_B) \\ Cov(\varepsilon_B \varepsilon_A) & V(\varepsilon_B) \end{pmatrix}.$$

The other off-diagonal elements are all zero.

Implicit in this formulation are the assumptions stated previously. The zero off-diagonal elements correspond to $Cov(\varepsilon_{At} \varepsilon_{Bi}) = 0$ for $t \neq i$. The different variances $V(\varepsilon_A)$ and $V(\varepsilon_B)$ without observation subscripts indicate constant variance of $\varepsilon_{At}$ and $\varepsilon_{Bt}$ for all $t = 1, 2, \ldots, T$, although these constants may be different from each other, say $\sigma_A{}^2 \neq \sigma_B{}^2$. In addition, contemporaneous covariation is included within each block as $Cov(\varepsilon_A \varepsilon_B) \neq 0$. Finally, this contemporaneous covariance between the disturbances in two different regressions is assumed to be the same for all observations. That is, there is homoscedasticity of the (2 × 2) blocks describing $V\text{-}Cov(\varepsilon_{At} \varepsilon_{Bt})$.

If the (2 × 2) constant matrix is denoted by

$$\underset{(2 \times 2)}{\omega} = V\text{-}Cov(\varepsilon_{At} \varepsilon_{Bt}) = \begin{pmatrix} \sigma_A{}^2 & \sigma_{AB} \\ \sigma_{BA} & \sigma_B{}^2 \end{pmatrix},$$

then the complete block diagonal variance-covariance matrix is represented by,

$$V\text{-}Cov(\varepsilon) = \sigma^2 \Omega = \begin{pmatrix} \omega & O & \cdots & O \\ O & \omega & \cdots & O \\ \vdots & \vdots & \ddots & \vdots \\ O & O & \cdots & \omega \end{pmatrix}$$
$$\scriptstyle (2T \times 2T)$$

where $\omega$ has size (2 × 2).

*The inverse of* $\Omega$. The inverse of a block diagonal matrix is another block diagonal matrix whose blocks are the inverse of the original blocks. (See *Review* 14.2, item 2.) If $\omega^{-1}$ denotes the inverse of $\omega$, then $(\sigma^2 \Omega)^{-1}$ is depicted in the same way as $\sigma^2 \Omega$ with the substitution of $\omega^{-1}$ for each $\omega$.

## The procedure of joint GLS

If the elements of $\omega$ were known, $\omega^{-1}$ and $\Omega^{-1}$ would also be known and the coefficient $\Gamma = (\Gamma_A \ \Gamma_B)'$ in (14–8) could be estimated using GLS formula (14–1). Unfortunately, $\omega$ is unknown. If it can be estimated by a consistent estimator $\tilde{\omega}$, then modified GLS can be used on (14–8). Efficient estimates for the coefficients $\Gamma_A$ and $\Gamma_B$ in the separate equations are then obtained by a single GLS estimation based on the combined observation matrix shown in (14–8). This procedure of joint GLS is described in the following steps:

1.  Obtain a consistent estimate of $\omega$. The residuals from ordinary least squares estimation of each equation separately can be used to obtain the estimate of $\omega$. Let the usual symbol, $e_A$. denote the residual vector from OLS estimation of the single equation, $Y_A = X_A \Gamma_A + \varepsilon_A$. Let $e_B$ have a similar interpretation for the second seemingly unrelated regression. Then, consistent estimates of the elements of $\omega$ are obtained in the same way an estimate of $\sigma_\varepsilon{}^2$ is obtained in the usual OLS regression on a single equation. The appropriate statistics are:

$$[\text{Est. } \omega] = \tilde{\omega} = \frac{1}{T-K} \begin{pmatrix} s_A{}^2 & s_{AB} \\ s_{BA} & s_B{}^2 \end{pmatrix} = \frac{1}{T-K} \begin{pmatrix} e_A'e_A & e_A'e_B \\ e_B'e_A & e_B'e_B \end{pmatrix}$$

or

$$\tilde{\omega} = \frac{1}{T-K} \begin{pmatrix} \sum e_A{}^2 & \sum e_A e_B \\ \sum e_B e_A & \sum e_B{}^2 \end{pmatrix}$$  (14–9)

where all sums are over $t = 1, 2, \ldots, T$.

2. Determine the estimate of $(\sigma_\varepsilon{}^2 \Omega)^{-1}$.

||||||||||||||||||||||||||||||||||||||||||||||||||||||||||||||||||||||||||||||||||||||||||||||||||||||||||||||||||||||||||||||||||||||||

***Explicative note.*** Separate estimates of $\sigma_\varepsilon{}^2$ and $\Omega$ need not be determined to apply the modified GLS formulas. Recall that a scalar multiplier may or may not be included without affecting the minimization solution of classical linear estimation.

||||||||||||||||||||||||||||||||||||||||||||||||||||||||||||||||||||||||||||||||||||||||||||||||||||||||||||||||||||||||||||||||||||||||

The inverse matrix $\omega^{-1}$ can be estimated by $\tilde{\omega}^{-1}$ using $\tilde{\omega}$ from (14–9). Let us denote the estimate of $(\sigma_\varepsilon{}^2 \Omega)^{-1}$ by

$$W^{-1} = \begin{pmatrix} \tilde{\omega}^{-1} & O & \cdots & O \\ O & \tilde{\omega}^{-1} & \cdots & O \\ O & O & \cdots & \tilde{\omega}^{-1} \end{pmatrix}.$$

3. Use modified GLS to estimate the joint model

$$\underset{(2T \times 1)}{Y} = \underset{(2T \times 2K)}{X} \underset{(2K \times 1)}{\Gamma} + \underset{(2T \times 1)}{\varepsilon}$$

described by (14–8). Substituting $W^{-1}$ for $(\sigma_\varepsilon{}^2 \Omega)^{-1}$ in formulas (14–4) and (14–5), the joint GLS estimates of $(\Gamma_A, \Gamma_B)'$ are

$$\underset{(2K \times 1)}{\begin{pmatrix} \tilde{C}_A \\ \tilde{C}_B \end{pmatrix}} = \underset{(2K \times 2K)}{(X'W^{-1}X)^{-1}} \underset{(2K \times 1)}{(X'W^{-1}Y)},$$  (14–10)

with

$$\left[ \text{Est. } V\text{-}Cov\begin{pmatrix} \tilde{C}_A \\ \tilde{C}_B \end{pmatrix} \right] = (X'W^{-1}X)^{-1}.$$  (14–11)

The difference in improved efficiency for the estimates of $\Gamma_A$ and $\Gamma_B$ will be evident in the smaller size of the standard errors of the estimates as given by (14–11) compared to those obtained by the use of OLS on each separate equation in step 1. (See Exercise 11 at the end of this chapter.)

## 14.9 SUMMARY

The formal derivation of the generalized least squares estimators is presented as the theoretical solution to linear estimation of econometric models with a nonscalar variance-covariance matrix of disturbances. The historical development of this procedure lies in the method known as classical linear estimation. In its simplest form, this is equivalent to the least squares solution obtained by minimizing the quadratic form in the residuals, $Q(e) = e'Ie$. When $V\text{-}Cov(\varepsilon) = \sigma_\varepsilon{}^2 \Omega$ is not scalar so that heteroscedasticity or autocorrelation occurs, then classical linear estimation is generalized to minimizing $\hat{Q}(e) = e'\Omega^{-1}e$.

In practice, the matrix $\Omega$ is unknown. But if a consistent estimate of $\Omega$ is available, then estimates with the same asymptotic properties can be obtained by substituting this estimate $\tilde{\Omega}$ into the form and minimizing $\tilde{Q}(e) = e'\tilde{\Omega}^{-1}e$. This procedure is here termed modified generalized least squares. It is shown that transformation of the observations by a nonsingular matrix $\tilde{H}$, where $\tilde{H}'\tilde{H} = \tilde{\Omega}$, offers an alternate procedure which involves less complex computations. The use of OLS on the transformed observation matrix $(\tilde{H}Y \quad \tilde{H}X)$
$$[T \times (K + 1)]$$
results in equivalent results to using modified GLS on the original observations. Indeed, this is the procedure applied in the special cases of weighted least squares and Cochrane and Orcutt Iterative Least Squares.

A further generalization of classical least squares is reached when the residual vector in the quadratic form to be minimized is a combination of residuals from several different equations. The case of two seemingly unrelated regression equations is illustrated as a simple generalization of this type.

## What comes next?

A more complex example of generalized classical linear estimation is considered in Chapter 18. It is a method of estimating overidentified equations in simultaneous equations econometric models known as two-stage least squares. Before proceeding directly with this related estimation procedure, the concepts and notation for simultaneous equations models is presented and the new problem of identifiability is considered. All this and more discussion of the extension of the econometric model to more than one equation is in Chapters 16–19.

The reader should conserve some time and energy for studying these topics of Part IV as these will undoubtedly be a primary concern in a subsequent course. Also, for the development of the reader's personal ability to read research papers using econometric methods and to specify, estimate, and test his own models, a lack of attention to the topics of Part IV could become a serious bottleneck.

Prior to Part IV on the simultaneous equations model, we present one more practical chapter on special problems of the single equation model. In particular, the use of both time-series and cross-sectional data in a single estimation and the frequently mentioned problem of multicollinearity are discussed.

## NEW VOCABULARY

| | |
|---|---|
| Classical linear estimation | Seemingly unrelated regressions |
| Generalized least squares | Contemporaneous covariance of disturbances |
| Block diagonal matrix | Aitken least squares |
| Positive definite matrix | Modified GLS |
| Gauss-Markov theorem | Dummy endogenous variable |
| Joint GLS | Nonscalar variance-covariance matrix of disturbances |

## REFERENCES

The early works involving linear estimation in part are:

Gauss, K. F.    *Theorie Combinationis Observationum Erroribus Minimus Obnaxiae.*
1821.

Laplace, P. S.    *Theorie analytique des probabilities.* 1812.

Legendre, A. M.    *Nouvelles méthodes pour la determination des orbites des cométes.*
1806.

Markov, A. A.    *Wahrscheinlichkeitsrechnung.* 1912.

The extension of classical linear estimation for a nonscalar variance-covariance
matrix of disturbances is made by:

Aitken, A. C.    "On Least Squares and Linear Combination of Observations."
*Proceedings of the Royal Society of Edinburgh,* 1935, pp. 42–48.

A further extension to generalized classical linear estimation which includes
two-stage least squares is in:

Basmann, R. L.    "A Generalized Classical Method of Linear Estimation of Coefficients in a Structural Equation." *Econometrics,* 1957, pp. 77–83.

For further insights into obtaining a consistent estimate of the variance-covariance matrix of disturbances involving an $n$th order autoregression, see:

Cassidy, Henry.    "Consistent Estimation in an $n$th Order Autoregressive Disturbance Model." *The Southern Economic Journal,* 1969, pp. 263–64.

Dhrymes, P.    "On the Treatment of Certain Recurrent Non-Linearities in Regression Analysis." *The Southern Economic Journal,* 1966, pp. 187–96.

The particular paper outlining the procedure for joint GLS on seemingly unrelated regressions is:

Zellner, A.    "An Efficient Method of Estimating Seemingly Unrelated Regressions
and Tests for Aggregation Bias." *Journal of the American Statistical Association,*
1962, pp. 348–68.

## EXERCISES

1.  Show that equations (14–1) and (14–2) reduce to formulas (9–3) and (10–4) if
    $\Omega = I$.

2.  If $\underset{(T \times K)}{U} = [X(X'X)^{-1} + D]$, show that $U'U = (X'X)^{-1} + D'D$.

3.  Following the pattern given in Section 10.5, derive formula (14–2).

4.  Compare and contrast the classical assumptions in Section 14.3 with the
    assumption list for the general model in Section 10.3.

5.  Write in complete sentences the interpretation of each symbol in formula
    (14–4).

6.  *a)* Using the definition of $\Omega$ in Section 14.7 for a first order autoregressive
    pattern, find $\det(\Omega)$ in general for $T = 4$ and show it is nonzero for any
    $|\rho| < 1$.

    *b)* For $p = 0.6$ and $T = 4$, show that $\tilde{H}'\tilde{H} = \tilde{\Omega}^{-1}$ using the definitions of $\tilde{H}$
    and $\tilde{\Omega}^{-1}$ in Section 14.7.

7.  Referring to the symbols as used in Section 14.6, show that $\tilde{e}'\tilde{e} = e'\tilde{\Omega}^{-1}e$.
    (*Hint*: Use $\tilde{e} = \tilde{H}e$ and $\tilde{\Omega}^{-1} = \tilde{H}'\tilde{H}$.) Rewrite formula (14–6) using this sub-
    stitution and write a sentence explaining each symbol in your formula.

8.  Using the definition of the symbols as in Section 14.7, show that $e^{*\prime}e^{*} =$

$(1 - p^2)e'\tilde{\Omega}^{-1}e$. Also, show that $V\text{-}Cov(C^*) = V\text{-}Cov(\tilde{C})/(1 - p^2)$ referring to formula (14–5).

9. Use the results stated in Exercise 8 to show that

$$[\text{Est. } V\text{-}Cov(C^*)] = [\text{Est. } V\text{-}Cov(\tilde{C})].$$

[*Hint*: The estimate of $V\text{-}Cov(C)$ for any estimator $C$ is found by substituting the estimate of $\sigma_\varepsilon^2$ into the formula for $V\text{-}Cov(C)$.]

10. Suppose you wish to estimate a system of three seemingly unrelated regressions. Explain how to set up the combined equation to be estimated similar to (14–8), and explain how you would obtain an estimate for $\bar{\omega}$ similar to (14–9).

11. Refer to Exercise 18 in Chapter 3. Suppose two regressions of the form

$$\ln \frac{W_i}{W_j} = \alpha_1 + \alpha_2 \ln \frac{L_i}{L_j} + \varepsilon_t$$

are to be estimated. Let $i, j = 1, 2, 3$, where 1 refers to high school dropout, 2 to high school graduate, and 3 to college graduate. The symbol $L_i$ denotes the number of people in the labor force with education level $i$. The median income of these laborers is $W_i$. In the first regression, $i = 1$ and $j = 2$. In the second regression $i = 2$ and $j = 3$. Let $Y_{ij}$ denote the endogenous variable, $\ln(W_i/W_j)$ and let $X_{ij}$ denote the exogenous variable, $\ln(L_i/L_j)$. Suppose the equations are estimated on the basis of cross-sectional data for 50 states and the District of Columbia from the 1960 Census. The estimation results using OLS are:

*Estimated equation with standard errors*

| | | | |
|---|---|---|---|
| OLS 1 | $Y_{12} = -0.1614 - 0.1152 X_{12}$ | $R^2 = 0.129,$ | $d = 2.102,$ |
| | $(0.01117)(0.04280)$ | $e_1'e_1 = 0.1586$ | |
| OLS 2 | $Y_{23} = -0.4631 + 0.1572 X_{23}$ | $R^2 = 0.287,$ | $d = 2.068,$ |
| | $(0.03080)\,(0.03539)$ | $e_2'e_2 = 0.1794$ | |

$$e_1'e_2 = -0.07726$$

a) Considering the Durbin–Watson $d$ values, do you think there is any problem of autocorrelation in either regression?

b) Suggest some economic reasons why there may be contemporaneous covariance of the disturbances in these two regressions.

c) If contemporaneous covariance exists, discuss the effect on the OLS results above and set up a model formulation which permits improved estimates.

d) Find $(\bar{\omega})^{-1}$ based on (14–9) for this problem and explain its purpose.

e) Given the joint GLS estimation of the same two equations below, what can you conclude about the seriousness of the problem of contemporaneous covariance in this case?

*Estimated equation with standard errors*

| | |
|---|---|
| Joint GLS 1 | $Y_{12} = -0.1609 - 0.1124 X_{12}$ |
| | $(0.01115)(0.04267)$ |
| Joint GLS 2 | $Y_{23} = -0.4686 + 0.1637 X_{23}$ |
| | $(0.03072)(0.03528)$ |

f) Using the joint GLS results for the second equation, find and interpret the meaning of the elasticity of substitution between laborers of education levels 2 and 3.

Chapter
15

# CORRECTIVE PROCEDURES FOR SELECTED ECONOMETRIC PROBLEMS

354

## 15.1 PREVIEW

In this final chapter dealing with the single equation econometric model, two special problems are considered.

### Pooling cross-sectional and time-series data

The first is the combination of the problems of heteroscedasticity and autocorrelation which often occur when the model is estimated on the basis of pooled time-series and cross-sectional data. Sections 15.3, 15.4, and 15.5 present practical procedures for estimating the model in this situation.

The procedure in 15.3 is a direct extension of the use of ordinary least squares on transformed data as described for the separate problems of heteroscedasticity and autocorrelation in Chapter 13. The covariance method in Section 15.4 makes use of dummy variables similar to those considered in Chapter 12. The third procedure is a generalization of the method of Section 15.3 in which some simplifying restrictions are removed. Although the method seems complex, it is really quite a reasonable development based on the methods of modified generalized least squares given in Chapter 14.

These procedures should be mastered quite easily since the basic routine has been repeated several times. Only the fringe elements are more intricate as more of the underlying assumptions about the variance-covariance matrix of the disturbances are relaxed. The reader could probably impose a slightly different set of assumptions and carry through a similar routine to derive his own best estimates for his particular situation.

### Multicollinearity

The second problem considered in this chapter is the lack of independence among the predetermined variables. This condition, known as multicollinearity, is a near violation of Assumption 7 in Section 10.3 which requires that the matrix $(X'X)$ be nonsingular so that the inverse matrix $(X'X)^{-1}$ exists and the OLS estimates can be found.

Using sample data, it is very improbable in a well-specified model that a perfect linear dependency will exist among the column vectors of observations on the exogenous variables. However, using economic and related variables, it is also very unusual to obtain column vectors of observations on the exogenous variables which are uncorrelated. The problem of multicollinearity is more or less severe depending on the degree of intracorrelation among these presumably independent variables. The problems of a high degree of multicollinearity are discussed in Section 15.6. A suggested set of procedures for detecting if the multicollinearity is of high or low degree and some possible remedies for multicollinearity are presented in Sections 15.7 and 15.8. Since the question of multicollinearity may be raised in reference to the estimation of any econometric model (for which the predetermined variables are not designed to be orthogonal), the reader will undoubtedly encounter this issue again. An example of the detection procedures is included in Section 15.7 to aid in your understanding and interpretation of this frequently encountered problem.

## 15.2 REVIEW

In this chapter, some previous mathematical and statistical review items are brought off the disabled list and reinserted on the regular roster. There are really no new draftees which must be absorbed into your existing team of background knowledge. However, the use of some topics becomes more subtle so that a profound conceptual understanding of these items is recommended rather than simply a memorization of some terms and definitions.

A list is given here of the names of particular concepts used in this chapter along with a reference to the previous section where these concepts are introduced.

1. *Determinant of a matrix.* See *Review* 3.2, item 4.
2. *Matrix inverse.* See *Review* 9.2, item 2.
3. *Linear independence and rank of a matrix.* See *Review* 10.2, item 6.

The reader may wish to supplement these brief presentations by studying some matrix algebra text, perhaps, G. Hadley, *Linear Algebra* (Reading, Mass.: Addison-Wesley Publishing Co., Inc., 1961), selected topics in chaps. 3 and 4.

4. *Multiple and partial correlation coefficients.* It is suggested that the reader look over Sections 3–5 of Chapter 8.
5. *Autoregression and modified generalized least squares estimation.* The extensions in this chapter relating to these previous topics will be simpler after a quick cram session on all of *Review* 13.2 and the subsections on generalized least squares (GLS) and modified GLS in Section 14.5. Much of this material is probably still fresh in your mind and will require less review than items 3 and 4.

References to these and to other previous results are given in the chapter as they are used.

## 15.3 MODIFIED GLS ESTIMATION BASED ON $NT$ POOLED CROSS-SECTIONAL AND TIME-SERIES OBSERVATIONS

Frequently, an econometrician may wish to estimate a particular relation but he is limited because he only has data available at three different points in time which are relevant for his analysis. Perhaps, these data come from census reports in 1950, 1960, and 1970. He cannot estimate the model using only three observations so he may use cross-sectional observations at each point in time to supplement the data. For another simplified example, data may be available only for six regions rather than by state, county, or city. Rather than base an estimation on 6 observations, the researcher may use annual data for 10 years for each of the 6 regions, thereby using 60 observations. Many times, the nature of the economic mechanism being studied requires the use of both $T$ time-series and $N$ cross-sectional observations for a total of $NT$ observations. For these situations, both periodic autocorrelation and cross-sectional heteroscedasticity may be present.

## A model with heteroscedasticity and autocorrelation

The statement of the model may be given by,

$$\underset{(NT \times 1)}{Y} = \underset{(NT \times K)}{X} \underset{(K \times 1)}{\Gamma} + \underset{(NT \times 1)}{\varepsilon}$$

where the usual assumptions are satisfied except for,

*a*)  $\underset{(1 \times 1)}{V(\varepsilon_{jt})} = \sigma_j^2$  for all $t = 1, 2, \ldots, T$, and

*b*)  $\underset{(1 \times 1)}{\varepsilon_{jt}} = \rho\varepsilon_{j, t-1} + v_{jt}$  for each $j = 1, 2, \ldots, N$,  where

$\underset{(T \times T)}{v_j} \sim \text{normal } (O, \phi_j^2 I).$

Condition (*a*) indicates cross-sectional heteroscedasticity and condition (*b*) indicates a first order autoregressive pattern which we assume is appropriate even at the first observation and is the same for all cross-sectional units.

||||||||||||||||||||||||||||||||||||||||||||||||||||||||||||||||||||||||||||||||||||||||||||||||||||||||||||||||||||||||||||||||||||||||||||||||||||||

*Explicative note.* Throughout this section, the variance of the disturbance term $\varepsilon_{jt}$ in the original model is denoted by $\sigma_j^2$ and estimated by $s_j^2$ for a cross-sectional unit $j$. The variance of the autoregressive disturbance term $v_{jt}$ is denoted by $\phi_j^2$ and estimated by $f_j^2$ for a cross-sectional unit $j$.

||||||||||||||||||||||||||||||||||||||||||||||||||||||||||||||||||||||||||||||||||||||||||||||||||||||||||||||||||||||||||||||||||||||||||||||||||||||

## Obtaining efficient estimates of $\Gamma$

The same type estimation procedures as given in Chapters 13 and 14 can be used in this situation. The autoregressive coefficient can be estimated, and the original data transformed according to this scheme. The differences in variance can be estimated, and weighted least squares can be applied to correct for the heteroscedasticity. In this section, these two separate procedures are combined to correct for the combined problem.

The variance-covariance matrix of disturbances is now size $(NT \times NT)$ and is still assumed to be positive definite. It is a block diagonal matrix in

$$
\underset{(NT \times NT)}{V\text{-}Cov(\varepsilon)} =
\begin{pmatrix}
\begin{pmatrix}
\sigma_1^2 & \rho\sigma_1^2 & \cdots & \rho^{T-1}\sigma_1^2 \\
\rho\sigma_1^2 & \sigma_1^2 & \cdots & \rho^{T-2}\sigma_1^2 \\
\vdots & \vdots & \ddots & \vdots \\
\rho^{T-1}\sigma_1^2 & \rho^{T-2}\sigma_1^2 & \cdots & \sigma_1^2
\end{pmatrix}
& \underset{(T \times T)}{\begin{pmatrix} O \end{pmatrix}} & \cdots & \underset{(T \times T)}{\begin{pmatrix} O \end{pmatrix}} \\
\underset{(T \times T)}{\begin{pmatrix} O \end{pmatrix}} & \cdots & \cdots & \vdots \\
\vdots & & & \underset{(T \times T)}{\begin{pmatrix} O \end{pmatrix}} \\
\underset{(T \times T)}{\begin{pmatrix} O \end{pmatrix}} & \cdots & \cdots &
\begin{pmatrix}
\sigma_N^2 & \rho\sigma_N^2 & \cdots & \rho^{T-1}\sigma_N^2 \\
\rho\sigma_N^2 & \sigma_N^2 & \cdots & \rho^{T-2}\sigma_N^2 \\
\vdots & \vdots & \ddots & \vdots \\
\rho^{T-1}\sigma_N^2 & \rho^{T-2}\sigma_N^2 & \cdots & \sigma_N^2
\end{pmatrix}
\end{pmatrix}
\qquad (15\text{-}1)
$$

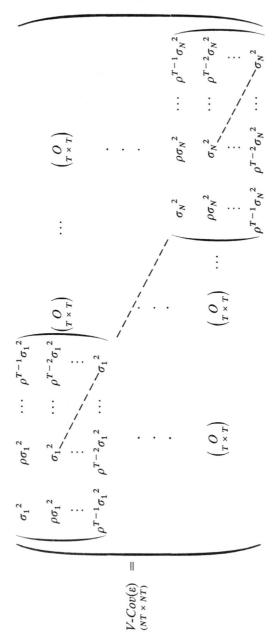

which each block is similar to $V\text{-}Cov(\varepsilon_j)$ of size $(T \times T)$ for the case of auto-correlation alone using $T$ time-series observations. However, there are now $N$ such diagonal blocks, one for each cross section. The matrix $V\text{-}Cov(\varepsilon)$ is shown in detail in (15–1).

## Summary procedure

By using four applications of ordinary least squares, consistent and efficient estimates of the coefficients $\Gamma$ in the specified model can be obtained.

1. The first OLS regression is on the original model, $Y = X\Gamma + \varepsilon$ based on all $(NT)$ observations. From this regression, the $NT$ residuals, $e_{jt}$ are calculated.

2. The second OLS regression is on the autoregressive model, $e_{jt} = \rho e_{j, t-1} + v_{jt}$ based on $N(T - 1)$ observations. The autoregressive coefficient is estimated by

$$p = \frac{\displaystyle\sum_j \sum_t e_{jt} e_{j, t-1}}{\displaystyle\sum_j \sum_t e_{j, t-1}^{\,2}} \qquad \text{for} \quad j = 1, 2, \ldots, N, \quad t = 2, 3, \ldots, T. \quad (15\text{–}2)$$

3. The third OLS regression is on the transformed data, $(HY, HX)$ in the model $HY = HX\Gamma + H\varepsilon$ where $H$ is a transformation matrix to remove the autoregressive scheme as in Section 13.5 or 14.7. The details of the transformation for all observations except the first, are

$$\begin{aligned} \breve{Y}_{jt} &= Y_{jt} - pY_{j, t-1} \\ \breve{X}_{jt, k} &= X_{jt, k} - pX_{j, t-1, k} \\ \breve{\varepsilon}_{jt} &= \varepsilon_{jt} - p\varepsilon_{j, t-1} \end{aligned} \qquad \text{for} \quad \begin{cases} k = 1, 2, \ldots, K \\ t = 2, 3, \ldots, T \\ j = 1, 2, \ldots, N. \end{cases}$$

Thus, the residuals, $\breve{e}_{jt}$, from this regression are defined similarly to the autoregressive residuals $v_{jt} = e_{jt} - pe_{j, t-1}$ from the second OLS regression in step 2 above. Thus, these OLS residuals, $\breve{e}_{jt}$, can be used to obtain consistent estimates of the variances of the autoregressive disturbances, $v$. That is, $\breve{e}_{jt}$ can be used to find $f_j^{\,2}$ which are estimates of $\phi_j^{\,2}$. The usual formula applies,

$$f_j^{\,2} = \frac{\breve{e}'\breve{e}}{T - K} \tag{15–3}$$

based on the residuals from the third OLS regression.

4. The fourth and final OLS regression is on the twice transformed data, $(Y^* \quad X^*)$ in the model, $Y^* = X^*\Gamma^* + \varepsilon^*$. Heteroscedasticity has been removed according to a transformation similar to that of Section 14.6,

$$Y_{jt}^* = (\breve{Y}_{jt}/f_j), \quad X_{jt, k}^* = (\breve{X}_{jt, k}/f_j), \quad \text{and} \quad \varepsilon_{jt}^* = (\breve{\varepsilon}_{jt}/f_j),$$

using $f_j$ as defined in (15–3) and $\breve{Y}_{jt}, \breve{X}_{jt, k}$, and $\breve{\varepsilon}_{jt}$ as defined by the first transformation in step 3.

The disturbance term, $\varepsilon^*$, in this regression after two transformations is asymptotically devoid of any autoregressiveness or heteroscedasticity. Thus, the final equation can be estimated using OLS based on $N(T-1)$ pooled observations giving estimates with the same asymptotic properties as obtained by using modified generalized least squares. The usual OLS formulas (9–3) and (10–4) are appropriate.

### The use of modified GLS

If no computer procedure is available to perform the tedious calculations of GLS, then the modified GLS procedure would be a more direct estimation procedure. Following the same first three steps above using OLS estimates, the elements of the variance-covariance matrix of disturbances in the original model can be estimated. From the estimates $f_j^2$ of $\phi_j^2 = V(v_{jt})$, and $p$ of $\rho$, consistent estimates of the variances, $V(\varepsilon_{jt}) = \sigma_j^2$, can be calculated by

$$s_j^2 = \frac{f_j^2}{1 - p^2} \tag{15-4}$$

according to the results of *Review* 13.2, item 4.

The estimate of $V\text{-}Cov(\varepsilon)$ described in (15–1) is then given by

$$\underset{(NT \times NT)}{W} = \begin{pmatrix} s_1^2 P & O & \cdots & O \\ O & s_2^2 P & \cdots & O \\ \vdots & \vdots & \ddots & \vdots \\ O & O & \cdots & s_N^2 P \end{pmatrix}$$

with

$$\underset{(T \times T)}{P} = \begin{pmatrix} 1 & p & \cdots & p^{T-1} \\ p & 1 & \cdots & p^{T-2} \\ \vdots & \vdots & \ddots & \vdots \\ p^{T-1} & p^{T-2} & \cdots & 1 \end{pmatrix}$$

where each $O$ represents a $(T \times T)$ null matrix.

This estimate $W$ can be substituted for $(\sigma_\varepsilon^2 \tilde{\Omega})$ in (14–4) and (14–5) to obtain the estimates of the regression coefficients $\Gamma$ and estimates of their variance-covariance matrix based on $NT$ pooled observations.

## 15.4 USE OF DUMMY VARIABLES IN OLS ESTIMATION BASED ON $NT$ POOLED CROSS-SECTIONAL AND TIME-SERIES DATA

Another method of applying OLS is sometimes used when the combined problems of heteroscedasticity and autocorrelation occur due to the pooling of cross-sectional and time-series observations. This so-called *covariance method* uses dummy variables to absorb these problems and allow more efficient estimation of the coefficients of the original exogenous variables specified in the model.

Suppose the model to be estimated is $Y = X\Gamma + \varepsilon$ based on $T = 20$ time-wise observations on each of $N = 50$ cross-sectional units. The disturbance terms $\varepsilon_{jt}$ probably do not have a constant variance for each $j = 1, 2, \ldots, N$ and may also be correlated with the previous disturbance terms $\varepsilon_{j,\,t-1}$ for $t = 2, 3, \ldots, T$.

## Adding the dummy variables

A new model may be defined in which each cross-sectional unit $j$ and each time period $t$ has its own intercept. This new model is obtained by introducing $(N + T - 2)$ dummy variables defined as:

$$Z_{jt} = \begin{cases} 1 & \text{for cross-sectional unit } j = 2, 3, \ldots, N \\ 0 & \text{otherwise} \end{cases}$$

and

$$Q_{jt} = \begin{cases} 1 & \text{for time period } t = 2, 3, \ldots, T \\ 0 & \text{otherwise.} \end{cases}$$

||||||||||||||||||||||||||||||||||||||||||||||||||||||||||||||||||||||||||||||||||||||||||||||||||||||||||||||||||||||||||||||||||

***Interpretive note.*** Since the original model includes an intercept denoted by $\gamma_1$, no dummy variables $Z_{1t}$ or $Q_{j1}$ are included in the definition. One dummy variable in each set is omitted so that the sample moment matrix is not singular. (See Section 12.5.) Consequently, the new specification involves $(K + N - 1 + T - 1)$ coefficients to be estimated on the basis of $NT$ pooled observations.

||||||||||||||||||||||||||||||||||||||||||||||||||||||||||||||||||||||||||||||||||||||||||||||||||||||||||||||||||||||||||||||||||

The revised econometric model is,

$$\begin{aligned} Y_{jt} = {} & \gamma_1 + \gamma_2 X_{jt,\,2} + \cdots + \gamma_K X_{jt,\,K} \\ & + \alpha_2 Z_{2t} + \alpha_3 Z_{3t} + \cdots + \alpha_N Z_{Nt} \\ & + \delta_2 Q_{j2} + \delta_3 Q_{j3} + \cdots + \delta_T Q_{jT} + \varepsilon_{jt}. \end{aligned}$$

The disturbance terms in this model are considered to have a scalar variance-covariance matrix so that ordinary least squares is appropriate. The $NT$ different intercepts implied by this new model are obvious from a more detailed writing of the equation. Let $A_{jt}$ represent the linear combination,

$A_{jt} = \gamma_2 X_{jt, 2} + \cdots + \gamma_K X_{jt, K}$, to obtain the following equations corresponding to the rows of the observation matrix,

$$Y_{11} = \gamma_1 + A_{11} + \varepsilon_{11}$$
$$Y_{12} = (\gamma_1 + \delta_2) + A_{12} + \varepsilon_{12}$$
$$\vdots$$
$$Y_{1T} = (\gamma_1 + \delta_T) + A_{1T} + \varepsilon_{1T}$$
$$Y_{21} = (\gamma_1 + \alpha_2) + A_{21} + \varepsilon_{21}$$
$$Y_{22} = (\gamma_1 + \alpha_2 + \delta_2) + A_{22} + \varepsilon_{22}$$
$$\vdots$$
$$Y_{2T} = (\gamma_1 + \alpha_2 + \delta_T) + A_{2T} + \varepsilon_{2T}$$
$$Y_{31} = (\gamma_1 + \alpha_3) + A_{31} + \varepsilon_{31}$$
$$\vdots$$
$$Y_{3T} = (\gamma_1 + \alpha_3 + \delta_T) + A_{3T} + \varepsilon_{3T}$$
$$\vdots$$
$$Y_{NT} = (\gamma_1 + \alpha_N + \delta_T) + A_{NT} + \varepsilon_{NT}.$$

### Further modifications of the covariance method

All $NT$ observations are used to estimate $\Gamma$ in this formulation. If some $\gamma_k$ is thought to be different for different cross sections, it is possible to use the dummy variables $Z_{jt}$ in interaction with the variable $X_k$ to allow for this. The model becomes,

$$Y_{jt} = \gamma_1 + \gamma_2 X_{jt, 2} + \cdots + \left(\gamma_k + \sum_{j=2}^{N} \alpha_j Z_{jt}\right) X_{jt, k} + \cdots + \gamma_K X_{jt, K}$$
$$+ \alpha_2 Z_{2t} + \cdots + \alpha_N Z_{NT} + \delta_2 Q_{j2} + \cdots + \delta_T Q_{jT} + \varepsilon_{jt},$$

and the above list of $NT$ equations remains the same if $A_{jt}$ is redefined as

$$A_{jt} = \gamma_2 X_{jt, 2} + \cdots + \left(\gamma_k + \sum_{j=2}^{N} \alpha_j Z_{jt}\right) X_{jt, k} + \cdots + \gamma_K X_{jt, K}.$$

A similar condition could be imposed if some coefficients were thought to differ between time periods. Of course, each such modification adds $N - 1$ or $T - 1$ more coefficients to be estimated. The total number should remain well below $NT$ in order to retain a sufficient number of degrees of freedom to obtain meaningful estimators.

### 15.5 EXTENSIONS OF THE COMBINED PROBLEMS USING POOLED TIME-SERIES AND CROSS-SECTIONAL DATA

The model of Section 15.3 allowing for both heteroscedasticity and autocorrelation used two assumptions which may often be violated. First, it was assumed in that model that the coefficient $\rho$ of the autoregressive scheme over time is constant for all cross-sectional units. However, in some circumstances, this may be a poor assumption. Suppose the regression model intends to explain the level of excess reserves in commercial banks over time and across different Federal Reserve districts. Due to the predominance of big city banks in some districts serving primarily industrial and financial sector customers as opposed to the importance of agricultural sector customers in another district with many conservative rural banks, the reaction time and lags in effecting monetary policy may vary. If these characteristics are not explicit in the model, different patterns of autocorrelation could result between different districts.

Second, it was assumed that the disturbances in the same time period over different cross sections are mutually independent. However, $Cov(\varepsilon_{it}\varepsilon_{jt}) = 0$ for $i \neq j$ may be violated in some situations for which cross-sectional mutual or spatial correlation prevails. Concerning an explanatory model for excess reserves as suggested above, it may be that excluded variables reflecting national or international financial, economic, and political conditions in any given time period may affect the disturbance terms for different Federal Reserve districts in a similar way. If these responses are strong enough relative to the other components of the disturbance terms, then these error terms may become quite highly correlated with each other.

## A model with heteroscedasticity, mutual cross-sectional correlation, and different autoregressive schemes among different cross sections

Each of these assumptions can be relaxed in turn to develop a general procedure for estimating the coefficients of the model characterized as follows:

$$\underset{(NT \times 1)}{Y} = \underset{(NT \times K)}{X} \underset{(K \times 1)}{\Gamma} + \underset{(NT \times 1)}{\varepsilon}$$

where the usual assumptions are satisfied except for:

a)  $\underset{(1 \times 1)}{V(\varepsilon_{jt})} = \sigma_j^2$ for all $t = 1, 2, \ldots, T$,

b)  $\underset{(1 \times 1)}{\varepsilon_{jt}} = \rho_j \varepsilon_{j, t-1} + v_{jt}$ for each $j = 1, 2, \ldots, N$ where

   $\underset{(t \times 1)}{v_j} \sim$ normal $(O, \underset{(T \times T)}{\phi_j^2 I})$,

   but $Cov(v_{it}v_{jt}) = \underset{(1 \times 1)}{\phi_{ij}}$ for $i, j = 1, 2, \ldots, N$, to be consistent with the final condition,

c)  $Cov(\varepsilon_{it}\varepsilon_{jt}) = \underset{(1 \times 1)}{\sigma_{ij}}$ for $i \neq j$.

Condition (*a*) allows cross-sectional heteroscedasticity and condition (*c*) allows cross-sectional mutual correlation of disturbances. Condition (*b*) allows a different first order autoregression of disturbances for each cross section.

||||||||||||||||||||||||||||||||||||||||||||||||||||||||||||||||||||||||||||||||||||||||||||||||||||||||||||||||||||||||||||||||||||||||

**Interpretive note.** Compared to condition (*b*) for the model in Section 15.3, the only difference in notation is the inclusion of a subscript *j* for the autoregressive coefficient. Although the values of $\rho_j$ may be the same for some sets of cross-sectional units with common characteristics, the extension is needed if there are at least two distinct $\rho_j$. In this general presentation, it is no more difficult to allow for *N* distinct autoregressive coefficients.

||||||||||||||||||||||||||||||||||||||||||||||||||||||||||||||||||||||||||||||||||||||||||||||||||||||||||||||||||||||||||||||||||||||||

The autoregressive schemes are assumed to be appropriate even at the initial observation. That is, the first observation is not the first period in a strikingly novel environment but rather a continuation of the same type periods in which the autoregressive scheme has been operating. Observation one should not be the first year following the end of World War II, for example.

The autoregressive disturbances are assumed to be normally distributed with constant variance and zero covariance between time periods for the same cross-sectional unit. Thus, each first order autoregressive model satisfies the usual assumptions of Section 10.3 required for ordinary least squares estimates to be BLUE and maximum likelihood. Also, the relation between $V\text{-}Cov(\varepsilon_j)$ $(T \times 1)$ and $V\text{-}Cov(v_j)$ $(T \times 1)$ is the same as given in *Review* 13.2, item 4. We have

$$\sigma_j^{\,2} = \frac{\phi_j^{\,2}}{1 - \rho_j^{\,2}} \quad \text{and} \quad \sigma_{ij} = \frac{\phi_{ij}}{1 - \rho_i \rho_j}. \tag{15-5}$$

In condition (*b*) we allow the autoregressive disturbances at the same time period in different cross sections to be correlated and denote this associated covariance by $\phi_{ij}$. Independence is still assumed between $v_{it}$ and $v_{jh}$ for $i \neq j$ and $t \neq h$, and between $\varepsilon_{j,\,t-1}$ and $v_{it}$ for all $i, j = 1, 2, \ldots, N$.

### Obtaining efficient estimates of $\Gamma$

To find efficient estimates of $\Gamma$, the modified GLS procedure can be used if a consistent estimator for $V\text{-}Cov(\varepsilon)$ can be determined. This matrix is $(NT \times NT)$ displayed in detail in (15-6) for comparison with (15-1) in Section 15.3. The diagonal blocks now differ from each other in that the variance $\sigma_j^{\,2}$ is different and the autoregressive coefficient $\rho_j$ is different in each block. The off-diagonal blocks are no longer zero because we now allow mutual correlations between cross sections.

To obtain consistent estimates of the elements of (15-6), a procedure is followed in which the beginning steps are similar to steps 1–3 in Section 15.3. The complete process is repeated for the present case.

$$V\text{-}Cov(\varepsilon) \atop (NT \times NT) =$$

$$
\begin{pmatrix}
\begin{pmatrix} \sigma_1^2 & \rho_1\sigma_1^2 & \cdots & \rho_1^{T-1}\sigma_1^2 \\ \rho_1\sigma_1^2 & \sigma_1^2 & \cdots & \rho_1^{T-2}\sigma_1^2 \\ \vdots & \vdots & \vdots & \vdots \\ \rho_1^{T-1}\sigma_1^2 & \rho_1^{T-2}\sigma_1^2 & \cdots & \sigma_1^2 \end{pmatrix}
&
\begin{pmatrix} \sigma_{12} & \sigma_{12}\rho_2 & \cdots & \sigma_{12}\rho_2^{T-1} \\ \sigma_{12}\rho_1 & \sigma_{12} & \cdots & \sigma_{12}\rho_2^{T-2} \\ \vdots & \vdots & \vdots & \vdots \\ \sigma_{12}\rho_1^{T-1} & \sigma_{12}\rho_1^{T-2} & \cdots & \sigma_{12} \end{pmatrix}
& \cdots &
\begin{pmatrix} \sigma_{1N} & \sigma_{1N}\rho_N & \cdots & \sigma_{1N}\rho_N^{T-1} \\ \sigma_{1N}\rho_1 & \sigma_{1N} & \cdots & \sigma_{1N}\rho_N^{T-2} \\ \vdots & \vdots & \vdots & \vdots \\ \sigma_{1N}\rho_1^{T-1} & \sigma_{1N}\rho_1^{T-2} & \cdots & \sigma_{1N} \end{pmatrix}
\\[6pt]
\begin{pmatrix} \sigma_{21} & \sigma_{21}\rho_1 & \cdots & \sigma_{21}\rho_1^{T-1} \\ \sigma_{21}\rho_2 & \sigma_{21} & \cdots & \sigma_{21}\rho_1^{T-2} \\ \vdots & \vdots & \vdots & \vdots \\ \sigma_{21}\rho_2^{T-1} & \sigma_{21}\rho_2^{T-2} & \cdots & \sigma_{21} \end{pmatrix}
&
\begin{pmatrix} \sigma_2^2 & \rho_2\sigma_2^2 & \cdots & \rho_2^{T-1}\sigma_2^2 \\ \rho_2\sigma_2^2 & \sigma_2^2 & \cdots & \rho_2^{T-2}\sigma_2^2 \\ \vdots & \vdots & \vdots & \vdots \\ \rho_2^{T-1}\sigma_2^2 & \rho_2^{T-2}\sigma_2^2 & \cdots & \sigma_2^2 \end{pmatrix}
& \cdots &
\begin{pmatrix} \sigma_{2N} & \sigma_{2N}\rho_N & \cdots & \sigma_{2N}\rho_N^{T-1} \\ \sigma_{2N}\rho_2 & \sigma_{2N} & \cdots & \sigma_{2N}\rho_N^{T-2} \\ \vdots & \vdots & \vdots & \vdots \\ \sigma_{2N}\rho_2^{T-1} & \sigma_{2N}\rho_2^{T-2} & \cdots & \sigma_{2N} \end{pmatrix}
\\[6pt]
\cdots & \cdots & \cdots & \cdots
\\[6pt]
\begin{pmatrix} \sigma_{N1} & \sigma_{N1}\rho_1 & \cdots & \sigma_{N1}\rho_1^{T-1} \\ \sigma_{N1}\rho_N & \sigma_{N1} & \cdots & \sigma_{N1}\rho_1^{T-2} \\ \vdots & \vdots & \vdots & \vdots \\ \sigma_{N1}\rho_N^{T-1} & \sigma_{N1}\rho_N^{T-2} & \cdots & \sigma_{N1} \end{pmatrix}
&
\begin{pmatrix} \sigma_{N2} & \sigma_{N2}\rho_2 & \cdots & \sigma_{N2}\rho_2^{T-1} \\ \sigma_{N2}\rho_N & \sigma_{N2} & \cdots & \sigma_{N2}\rho_2^{T-2} \\ \vdots & \vdots & \vdots & \vdots \\ \sigma_{N2}\rho_N^{T-1} & \sigma_{N2}\rho_N^{T-2} & \cdots & \sigma_{N2} \end{pmatrix}
& \cdots &
\begin{pmatrix} \sigma_N^2 & \rho_N\sigma_N^2 & \cdots & \rho_N^{T-1}\sigma_N^2 \\ \rho_N\sigma_N^2 & \sigma_N^2 & \cdots & \rho_N^{T-2}\sigma_N^2 \\ \vdots & \vdots & \vdots & \vdots \\ \rho_N^{T-1}\sigma_N^2 & \rho_N^{T-2}\sigma_N^2 & \cdots & \sigma_N^2 \end{pmatrix}
\end{pmatrix}
$$

(15-6)

**Summary procedure**

1. Find OLS estimates for the original model $Y = X\Gamma + \varepsilon$ based on all $(NT)$ pooled observations. From this regression, calculate the $NT$ residuals, $e_{jt}$.

2. Find OLS estimates of the $N$ different autoregressive models, $e_{jt} = \rho_j e_{j,t-1} + v_{jt}$ for $j = 1, 2, \ldots, N$. This involves $N$ regressions, each based on $(T - 1)$ observations to obtain the estimates $(p_1, p_2, \ldots, p_j, \ldots, p_N)$ of the autoregressive coefficients. Each $p_j$ is determined by

$$p_j = \left( \sum_{t=2}^{T} e_{jt} e_{j,t-1} \right) \bigg/ \sum_{t=2}^{T} e_{j,t-1}^{2} \qquad (15\text{-}7)$$

for each $j = 1, 2, \ldots, N$.

||||||||||||||||||||||||||||||||||||||||||||||||||||||||||||||||||||||||||||||||||||||||||||||||||||||||||||||||||||||||||||||||||||||||||||||

***Recursive note.***   Compare this to (15–2) in which all $N(T - 1)$ residuals were used to estimate a single autoregressive coefficient $\rho$.

||||||||||||||||||||||||||||||||||||||||||||||||||||||||||||||||||||||||||||||||||||||||||||||||||||||||||||||||||||||||||||||||||||||||||||||

3. Find OLS estimates for the model using transformed data $HY = HX\Gamma + H\varepsilon$ where $H$ is a transformation matrix of size $(NT \times NT)$ to remove the autoregressive schemes as in Section 14.7. In this case $H$ is block diagonal with $N$ blocks of size $(T \times T)$, denoted by $H_j$, $j = 1, 2, \ldots, N$ so that

$$H = \begin{pmatrix} H_1 & O & \ldots & O \\ O & H_2 & \ldots & O \\ \vdots & \vdots & \ddots & \vdots \\ O & O & \ldots & H_N \end{pmatrix}$$

where

$$\underset{(T \times T)}{H_j} = \frac{1}{\sqrt{1 - p_j^2}} \begin{pmatrix} \sqrt{1 - p_j^2} & 0 & 0 & \ldots & 0 & 0 \\ -p_j & 1 & 0 & \ldots & 0 & 0 \\ 0 & -p_j & 1 & \ldots & 0 & 0 \\ \vdots & \vdots & \vdots & & \vdots & \vdots \\ 0 & 0 & 0 & \ldots & 1 & 0 \\ 0 & 0 & 0 & \ldots & -p_j & 1 \end{pmatrix}.$$

From this regression, determine the residuals $\check{e}_{jt}$ which can be used as estimates of the autoregressive disturbances, $v_{jt}$.

4. Find consistent estimates for $\sigma_j^2$ and $\sigma_{ij}$ from estimates of $\phi_j^2$ and $\phi_{ij}$

based on the sample variance and covariance of the residuals, $\breve{e}_{jt}$, from step 3. The appropriate formulas are familiar,

$$[\text{Est. } \phi_j^2] = f_j^2 = \sum_t \breve{e}_{jt}^2/(T - K) \qquad \text{for} \quad j = 1, 2, \ldots, N;$$

$$[\text{Est. } \phi_{ij}] = f_{ij} = \sum_t \breve{e}_{jt}\breve{e}_{it}/(T - K) \qquad \text{for} \quad i \neq j$$

$$[\text{Est. } \sigma_j^2] = s_j^2 = f_j^2/(1 - p_j^2) \qquad \text{for} \quad j = 1, 2, \ldots, N; \qquad (15\text{-}8)$$

and

$$[\text{Est. } \sigma_{ij}] = s_{ij} = f_{ij}/(1 - p_ip_j) \qquad \text{for} \quad i \neq j.$$

***Recursive note.*** Compare these formulas to (15–4) in which the same estimate $p$ was used in obtaining the estimate of $\sigma_j^2$ for all $j$. Also, in that case, the estimate of $\sigma_{ij}$ was not needed since this covariance was assumed to be zero (no mutual correlation between cross sections was allowed).

5. Substitute the consistent estimates $p_j$, $s_j^2$, and $s_{ij}$ into the elements of $V\text{-}Cov(\varepsilon)$ given by (15–6) to obtain the matrix,

$$\underset{(NT \times NT)}{W} = \begin{pmatrix} s_1^2 P_{11} & s_{12} P_{12} & \cdots & s_{1N} P_{1N} \\ s_{21} P_{21} & s_2^2 P_{22} & \cdots & s_{2N} P_{2N} \\ \vdots & \vdots & \ddots & \vdots \\ s_{N1} P_{N1} & s_{N2} P_{N2} & \cdots & s_N^2 P_{NN} \end{pmatrix}$$

with

$$P_{ij} = \begin{pmatrix} 1 & p_j & p_j^2 & \cdots & p_j^{T-1} \\ p_i & 1 & p_j & \cdots & p_j^{T-2} \\ p_i^2 & p_i & 1 & \cdots & p_j^{T-3} \\ \vdots & \vdots & \vdots & \ddots & \vdots \\ p_i^{T-1} & p_i^{T-2} & p_i^{T-3} & \cdots & 1 \end{pmatrix}.$$

This matrix $W$ can be substituted for $(\sigma_\varepsilon^2 \tilde{\Omega})$ in (14–4) and (14–5) to obtain the modified GLS estimates of the coefficients $\Gamma$ and estimates of their variance-covariance matrix based on the original $NT$ observations. The usual $t$ and $F$ tests can be applied to test the results of this regression.

## 15.6 MULTICOLLINEARITY, THE PROBLEM AND ITS EFFECTS

One of the assumptions in Section 10.3 specified for the use of least squares estimation on a general model is Assumption 7 that the inverse matrix, $(X'X)^{-1}$, exists. This implies that the column vectors of observations on the predetermined variables are not a linearly dependent set so that the matrix

$(X'X)$ has full rank. The meaning of this assumption is that no column vector of observations can be written as a multiple of any other column or as a linear combination of any of the other observation vectors. It is assumed that the predetermined variables are independent of each other so that each has a separate, measurable effect on the endogenous variable. Then, according to the now familiar formulas, the estimates obtained by least squares are

$$C = (X'X)^{-1}X'Y \qquad (9\text{-}3),$$

with

$$V\text{-}Cov(C) = \sigma_\varepsilon^2 (X'X)^{-1} \qquad (10\text{-}4).$$

### Recognition of the problems

An obvious problem occurs if two or more of the columns of observations are exactly linearly related. Then, the inverse, $(X'X)^{-1}$, cannot be found. It is undefined since the determinant of $(X'X)$ would be zero. (See *Review* 10.2, item 4) This is the most drastic case of multiple dependency among the predetermined variables. In such a case, the dependency can be eliminated by removal of one or more predetermined variables from the specification without any loss of explanatory power for the estimated relation. However, this perfect dependency is not the problem of multicollinearity.

*Sensitivity of the estimates to particular data.* Multicollinearity is the more difficult and subtle problem of *high* correlation among the observation vectors of the predetermined variables which results in a near perfect dependency. In such a case, a nonzero value, but a small value, for the determinant of $(X'X)$ is calculated and the inverse matrix, $(X'X)^{-1}$, is determinable. However, its values are very sensitive to even slight changes in the observations.

|||||||||||||||||||||||||||||||||||||||||||||||||||||||||||||||||||||||||||||||||||||||||||||||||||||||||||||||||||||||||||||||||||||||||||||||

*Interpretive note.*    Consider a simple arithmetic example of a division, $q = 100/d$. Suppose $d$ is large, say $500 \pm 1$. Then the quotient $q$ is not greatly affected by the slight inaccuracy in $d$ of one unit; $q = 0.200$ whether $d$ is 499 or 501. But suppose the denominator $d$ is quite small, say $d = 0.02$. Then even a slight absolute inaccuracy in $d$ of 0.01 is crucial since $q = 100/0.01 = 10,000$, whereas $q = 100/0.03 = 3333.33$.

|||||||||||||||||||||||||||||||||||||||||||||||||||||||||||||||||||||||||||||||||||||||||||||||||||||||||||||||||||||||||||||||||||||||||||||||

Since an inverse matrix is determined by the rule, *inverse = adjoint/determinant*, small changes in the adjoint may be negligible whereas small changes in the value of $\det(X'X)$ in the case of multicollinearity can induce significant changes in the inverse $(X'X)^{-1}$ and hence in the values of the least squares estimates. Any change in the data can be crucial if it induces large percentage changes in the determinant of $(X'X)$.

*Sensitivity of the estimates to the specification of the model.*    A further sensitivity due to multicollinearity arises from changes in the specification of the model. The inclusion or exclusion of any variable which is highly collinear with some other predetermined variables can greatly affect the estimates. As we discussed in Chapter 12 in terms of stepwise regression, adding a new variable which is correlated with the previously included variables tends to change the size of both the coefficient estimated and the estimate of its standard error. Similarly, dropping a collinear variable from the model may result in a specification error that causes the estimators of the coefficients of the remaining variables to be biased.

|||||||||||||||||||||||||||||||||||||||||||||||||||||||||||||||||||||||||||||||||||||||||||||||||||||||||||||||||||||||||||||||||||||||||||||

*Discursive note.* Some rules can be stated which indicate the direction of the bias or the change in the estimates of the standard errors of the coefficients depending on the signs of the estimates and the sign and size of the simple and partial correlation coefficients among the predetermined variables. However, these are tedious and not always unambiguous. In any particular case, experience and trial and error are the best teachers of the effects of including or excluding certain highly correlated variables.

|||||||||||||||||||||||||||||||||||||||||||||||||||||||||||||||||||||||||||||||||||||||||||||||||||||||||||||||||||||||||||||||||||||||||||||

To summarize thus far, multicollinearity is a problem in the sense that it causes the estimates in the model to be highly sensitive to the particular observation set and to the specification of the model. Added to this difficulty is also a problem of interpretation.

*Interpretation difficulties with the estimates.* In a multiple regression, the partial regression coefficient is supposed to provide the partial effect on the endogenous variable due to a unit change in the corresponding predetermined variable holding the linear effect of all other included variables constant. (See Section 8.4.) However, when multicollinearity occurs, each variable in the collinear set may be sharing in the explanatory role of any and all variables in the set. Consequently, it is very misleading to interpret the partial regression coefficient as the distinct effect of a separate, individual variable.

Consider a model with $K$ exogenous variables of which only $m < K$ are linearly independent. Then, it is theoretically impossible to estimate $K$ separate parameters because the data only gives an $m$ dimensional scatter of observation points. Only $m$ parameters can be determined in terms of the other $K - m$ if these can be known from additional, independent information. The separate estimate of each parameter depends on the separate estimates of the other parameters. If one coefficient is changed, all those associated with collinear variables also must change.

The problem is illustrated in Figure 15–1 for a model $Y = \gamma_1 + \gamma_2 X_2 + \gamma_3 X_3 + \varepsilon$ with two exogenous variables with coefficients being estimated by $C_2$ and $C_3$. In part ($a$) of the figure, we see that the observations have very little scatter in the $(X_2, X_3)$ plane because of the high degree of collinearity between $X_2$ and $X_3$. The slope of the regression plane for the endogenous

**FIGURE 15-1**

**A case of multicollinearity**

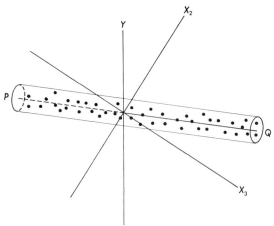

a) *Minimal scatter occurs in the* $(X_2, X_3)$ *plane.*

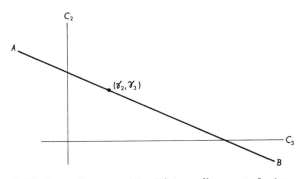

b) *The locus of estimates* $(C_2, C_3)$ *is a collinear set of points.*

variable $Y$ can be easily determined by the line $PQ$. However, finding the best plane passing through this line is somewhat arbitrary because the locus of estimates $C_2$ and $C_3$ is, for all practical purposes, a collinear set of points as in part (*b*) of the figure.

The fit of the plane to the scatter of points in part (*a*) is equally good whether we select a large value for $C_2$ and small value of $C_3$ or vice versa. The cylinder in part (*a*) may have either vertical wings or horizontal wings or wings rotated somewhere in between. From part (*b*) of Figure 15-1, any pair of values $(C_2, C_3)$ on the line $AB$ may be used with no loss in the total explanatory power of the estimated model. Whether this explanatory role is delegated to variable $X_2$ or to $X_3$ or split between them is arbitrary since they seem to measure the same thing. The separate explanatory roles of the two variables cannot be isolated. If the multicollinearity could be reduced, then the locus of points $(C_2, C_3)$ collapses to the neighborhood of the true point $(\gamma_2, \gamma_3)$, and the distinct effects of the variables $X_2$ and $X_3$ could be meaningfully interpreted. The scatter of points in the $(X_2, X_3)$ plane becomes definitive as the cylinder in part (*a*) changes from circular to very elliptic, and the best location of its wings is clear.

## The effect on the estimators

The effect of multicollinearity on the properties of the estimates does not seem too damaging at first glance. The estimates $C$ of the coefficients $\Gamma$ are unbiased and efficient theoretically. Also, the estimate of $\sigma_\varepsilon^2$ is unbiased and the estimate of the $V\text{-}Cov(C)$ is unbiased.

||||||||||||||||||||||||||||||||||||||||||||||||||||||||||||||||||||||||||||||||||||||||||||||||||||||||||||||||||||||||||||||||||||||||||||||||||||||||||||

*Recursive note.* Recall that unbiasedness refers to the value of estimation on the average but does not imply that a particular estimate is the true value. Also, efficiency refers to minimal variance among alternate estimators in the same class (linear and unbiased in this case) but does not imply that the variance of this estimator is necessarily small.

||||||||||||||||||||||||||||||||||||||||||||||||||||||||||||||||||||||||||||||||||||||||||||||||||||||||||||||||||||||||||||||||||||||||||||||||||||||||||

*Variance of the estimates $C_k$ are increased.* Nevertheless, the problems of multicollinearity are serious due to the increased size of the $V\text{-}Cov(C)$ compared to a situation without multicollinearity. Because the estimates are very sensitive to changes in data or in the specification, and since high multicollinearity results in the parameters forming a collinear set of points, there is a great variety and range of potential estimates. Although these may on the average give the true value and although the least squares estimators have as small a variance as any other linear unbiased estimator in the presence of multicollinearity, the size of this variance about the expected or "true" value of the estimator is significantly greater than in the absence of multicollinearity.

One way of representing the potential effect on the variance of an estimate $C_k$ of a coefficient $\gamma_k$ is by the relation,[1]

$$V(C_k) = \frac{1}{T - K} \frac{\sigma_y^2}{\sigma_k^2} \frac{1 - R^2}{1 - R_k^2}. \tag{15-9}$$

where $\sigma_k^2$ is the variance of $X_k$, $R$ is the multiple correlation coefficient between the endogenous variable $Y$ and all the predetermined variables, and $R_k$ is the multiple correlation coefficient between variable $X_k$ and the other predetermined variables.

---

[1] This formula is given by R. Stone, "The Analysis of Market Demand," *Journal of the Royal Statistical Society*, 1945, p. 297.

Two extreme cases are evident, one of orthogonality and the other of perfect collinearity. If variable $X_k$ is orthogonal relative to the other $X_j$, $j \neq k$, so it is linearly independent of the others, then $R_k^2 = 0$ and the denominator of the last term in (15–9) is unity. The $V(C_k)$ is small, and the estimate $C_k$ is not as sensitive to changes in the observations or in the specification concerning the other predetermined variables. The singular partial effect of $X_k$ on $Y$ is measurable.

At the other extreme, suppose there is a near perfect linear dependency of $X_k$ on the other predetermined variables. Then, $R_k^2$ becomes very close to unity, and the denominator of the last term in (15–9) becomes very close to zero. The $V(C)$ becomes very large approaching infinity, since the value of the estimate $C_k$ could vary $\pm 10$ units or $\pm 5000$ units or $\pm 10^{20}$ units if compensating changes are made in the estimates of the coefficients $C_j$ for the other collinear $X_j$, $j \neq k$. Only a joint or total effect of the collinear variables can be measured, but not the separate effect of individual variables.

||||||||||||||||||||||||||||||||||||||||||||||||||||||||||||||||||||||||||||||||||||||||||||||||||||||||||||||||||||||||||||||||||||||||

*Interpretive note.* Some value for $C_k$ will be calculated unless the calculational procedure includes a stopping rule for situations of near perfect dependency. The temptation to interpret this point value as a separate, partial effect must be avoided if multicollinearity is severe. Moreover in models with more than two predetermined variables, there are no clear simple rules that will always indicate whether the value of $C_k$ is too high or too low.

||||||||||||||||||||||||||||||||||||||||||||||||||||||||||||||||||||||||||||||||||||||||||||||||||||||||||||||||||||||||||||||||||||||||

In the case between the two extremes, high values of $R_k^2$, relative to the value of the overall $R^2$, present the difficulty known as multicollinearity. As $R_k^2$ becomes larger, the $V(C_k)$ becomes larger [assuming that $V(X_k) = \sigma_k^2$ is not changing]. When $R_k^2$ is a large value, then slight changes in the data for the other $X_j$, $j \neq k$, or exclusion or inclusion of another variable $X_i$, $i \neq k$, may greatly affect the estimate even though it is precipitated by only a small change in $R_k$.

*A numerical illustration.* As a numerical example, let $T = 25$, $K = 5$, $\sigma_y^2 = 800$, $\sigma_k^2 = 40$, and $R^2 = 0.8$. Then

$$V(C_k) = \left(\frac{1}{20}\right)\left(\frac{800}{40}\right)\left(\frac{1 - 0.8}{1 - R_k^2}\right) = \frac{1 - 0.8}{1 - R_k^2},$$

and the effect on $V(C_k)$ of a change in $R_k^2$ can be easily calculated. Further suppose the estimate $C_k = 3$. If $R_k^2 = 0.2$ in a case of low multicollinearity, then $V(C_k) = (0.2/0.8) = 0.25$. The coefficient $C_k$ would be significant according to a $t$ or $F$ test as in Section 11.5. However, suppose $R_k^2 = 0.96$ in a case of severe multicollinearity and the other postulated values are as before. Then, $V(C_k) = (0.2/0.04) = 5.0$ and the $t$-value for significance of the coefficient $C_k$ is now $(3/\sqrt{5}) = 1.342$. The effect of increased multicollinearity among the predetermined variables is an increase in $V(C_k)$ which leads to lower values for test statistics examining the significance of $C_k$ even though the observations of $Y$ and $X_k$ and the effect of $X_k$ on $Y$ were not directly changed. When multicollinearity occurs, coefficients are often found to be insignificant merely because of the inflated values of the estimates of their standard errors.

As a final step in the numerical illustration to demonstrate the sensitivity of a coefficient to changes in the data or in the specification, consider as probable values for the estimate $C_k$ any values within a range of two standard errors of the estimate about the hypothesized true value $\gamma_k$. With $R_k^2 = 0.96$ and keeping the other postulated values the same, then probable values of $C_k$ may lie within the interval $\gamma_k \pm 2\sqrt{5}$ or $\gamma_k \pm 4.472$.

For comparison, suppose one additional observation is included and an additional variable is included so $T = 26$ and $K = 6$ and $T - K = 20$ as before. We assume a situation in which the value of $\sigma_y^2(1 - R^2)/\sigma_k^2$ remains unchanged but the multicollinearity is slightly increased from 0.96 to $R_k^2 = 0.98$. This is a 2.1 percent change in $R_k^2$. Under these conditions, $V(C_k)$ is $(0.2/0.02) = 10$. Then probable values of $C_k$ may lie in the interval $\gamma_k \pm 2\sqrt{10}$ or $\gamma_k \pm 6.324$. The width of the interval for $C_k$ increases from 8.944 to 12.648, an increase of 41.4 percent in the range of probable values for a single estimate $C_k$. When multicollinearity is severe, the calculated variance of an estimate can change significantly due to seemingly insignificant changes in the data or specification.

## 15.7 DETECTION OF MULTICOLLINEARITY

Methods of detection of multicollinearity follow from a knowledge of the problem and its effects. Basically, two schemes prevail as the most commonly used. The first method involves detecting severe or at least worrisome multicollinearity by examining the values of various regression estimates, their variances, and multiple correlation coefficients to see if they are sensitive to changes in the estimation or the specification. The second method involves detection of multicollinearity by examining the potential existence of linear dependencies among the explanatory variables.

### Looking for evidence of the effects of multicollinearity

Perhaps, the first attempt to detect and deal with multicollinearity problems is reflected in the methods of confluence analysis and bunch map analysis.[2] The suggested detection method is to calculate the least squares estimates of the coefficients in the model by minimizing the sum of squares of residuals in various directions, not only in the vertical or $Y$-axis direction. This involves rotating the axis along which the residuals are measured. A

---

[2] These applications are attributed to Ragnar Frisch, *Statistical Confluence Analysis by Means of Complete Regression Systems* (Oslo: University Economics Institute, 1934).

comparison of the various estimates obtained for any coefficient then gives insights into whether or not the corresponding variable is useful in the regression, or superfluous due to multicollinearity or perhaps detrimental in the sense of introducing spurious correlations which severely hamper the interpretation.

*Examining correlation coefficients.* Much of the same type analysis is more conveniently considered and interpreted in terms of simple, partial, and multiple correlation coefficients. If the model only contains two explanatory variables, $X_2$ and $X_3$, then the simple correlation coefficient between them, $r_{23}$, is an indication of their linear dependence. When this correlation is high, or $1 - r_{23}$ is not significantly different from zero, then the multicollinearity problem is severe.

||||||||||||||||||||||||||||||||||||||||||||||||||||||||||||||||||||||||||||||||||||||||||||||||||||||||||||||||||||||||||||||||||||||||||||

*Recursive note.* The regression coefficients in this case are given by formulas (8–5) which have denominator $(1 - r_{23}^2)$. As this denominator approaches zero, the value of $C_2$ or $C_3$ becomes undefined and the variance of the estimates explodes.

||||||||||||||||||||||||||||||||||||||||||||||||||||||||||||||||||||||||||||||||||||||||||||||||||||||||||||||||||||||||||||||||||||||||||||

*Use of stepwise regression results.* As seen in Chapter 12, a stepwise regression provides the essential information for evaluating the collinearity between two exogenous variables. If the two variables are relatively independent, then the addition of the variable $X_3$ will not greatly change the coefficient of $X_2$, nor its standard error, nor its significance. Also, the combined effect of the two variables in explaining the variation of $Y$ would be about equal to the sum of the individual effects of each variable alone in explaining the variation of $Y$.

On the other hand, if $X_3$ is highly correlated with $X_2$, then its addition to the regression would change $C_2$ significantly; and the combined explanatory effect of the two variables would be much smaller than the sum of their simple, individual explanatory effects. The example model in Chapter 9 illustrates these characteristics of multicollinearity.

*Examining different regression models.* If the model contains more than two predetermined variables, then the detection of multicollinearity becomes more complex. A large simple correlation coefficient between a pair of variables is evidence of multicollinearity as before. However, all variables may be pairwise independent and yet jointly dependent if one is a linear combination of two or more of the others.

Ideally, all combinations of subgroups of variables need to be considered in separate regression models in order to detect possible collinearities. Since this is a very tedious procedure, the econometrician may simply select the variable which seems a priori to be involved most in the collinearity and drop it from the model to see how the results change. Depending on the judgment of the econometrician concerning the relative merits of low $V(C_k)$, high $R^2$, and low specification bias, he may conclude that the multicollinearity effect related to that particular variable is or is not serious.[3]

## Measures of the multicollinearity effect

One fairly simple way to obtain some measure of the extent of multi-collinearity is to calculate the incremental contribution of each predetermined variable in explaining the variation of $Y$, given the inclusion of all other variables, to sum these, and to compare the sum to the collective or joint contribution of all the variables simultaneously.

The incremental sum of squares of variation explained by a single variable may be determined by an analysis of variance table as in Section 11.7. The total sum of squares explained by all variables is obtained from the analysis of variance table for the complete regression. In order to always obtain the same interpretation not affected by the scale of measurement, it is convenient to determine the *proportions* of variation explained incrementally and totally, rather than the absolute amounts. These can be determined by ratios of the amounts explained to the amount of the total variation of $Y$ in each case.

*A multicollinearity measure.* A simple way of obtaining these proportional measures is to use $R^2$ for the total contribution of all variables and to obtain the incremental contribution of any variable, $X_k$, by

$$\theta_k = (1 - R^2)F_k/(T - K), \tag{15-10}$$

where $F_k$ is the usual $F$-value for significance of the variable $X_k$.

|||||||||||||||||||||||||||||||||||||||||||||||||||||||||||||||||||||||||||||||||||||||||||||||||||||||||||||||||||||||||||||||||

*Recursive note.* Both $R^2$ and the $F$-values are commonly given in computer outputs for regression analysis. Instead of $F$-values, sometimes the Student's $t$-value for significance of the coefficient $C_k$ is given. Remember that the value $F_k = t_k^2$ in this case.

|||||||||||||||||||||||||||||||||||||||||||||||||||||||||||||||||||||||||||||||||||||||||||||||||||||||||||||||||||||||||||||||||

The multicollinearity effect is denoted by $\overline{M}$ and is given by

$$\left[\sum_{k=2}^{K} \theta_k - R^2\right] = \overline{M}. \tag{15-11}$$

If all the predetermined variables form an orthogonal set, then the sum of the incremental contributions will equal the total contribution and $\overline{M} = 0$. If the explanatory variables overlap in their explanatory roles, then $\overline{M} \neq 0$ indicating some multicollinearity. The sign of $\overline{M}$ may be either positive or negative

---

[3] One such test can be based on the comparison of the $V(C_k)$ in the presence of the collinear variable, say $X_j, j \neq k$, to the $V(C_k)$ plus the squared bias due to misspecification when the collinear variable $X_j$ is removed. See C. Toro-Vizcarrondo and T. D. Wallace, "A Test of the Mean Square Error Criterion for Restrictions in Linear Regression," *Journal of the American Statistical Association*, June 1968, pp. 558–72.

with a larger absolute value indicating more severe multicollinearity. Unfortunately, experience and intuition are the only guides for determining if $\overline{M}$ is significantly large or not relative to the value of $R^2$. However, simple comparisons of $\overline{M}$ between models can often be made using common sense, such as a value of $\overline{M} = 0.20$ with $R^2 = 0.95$ is less severe than a value of $\overline{M} = 0.20$ with $R^2 = 0.40$, or than a value of $\overline{M} = 0.60$ with $R^2 = 0.95$.

*Multiple-partial coefficients of determination among the predetermined variables.* Another measure of the extent of collinearity between a variable $X_k$ and the other explanatory variables $X_j$, $j \neq k$, is $R_k^2$ which is defined as before to measure the proportion of variation in $X_k$ which is explained in a linear regression of $X_k$ on all the other explanatory variables. If $R_k^2$ is near zero, then $X_k$ is relatively independent of the other $X_j$. If $R_k^2$ is near one, then $X_k$ is highly collinear with the other $X_j$.

Finally, the partial coefficient of determination, $r_{Yk \cdot H}^2$ is frequently useful in measuring the degree of overlapping or independent explanation among the set of predetermined variables and providing hints about the pattern of multicollinearity. The symbol $H$ represents the set of all predetermined variables excluding $X_k$. The measure, $r_{Yk \cdot H}^2$ gives the proportion of extra variation in $Y$ explained by adding the variable $X_k$ relative to the amount of residual variation in $Y$ after removing all explanatory contribution of the variables $X_j$ in the set $H$. (See the numerical illustration of this meaning in Section 8.5.) If variable $X_k$ is perfectly collinear with the variables $X_j$ in $H$, then its added explanatory contribution would be zero. The residual variation left unexplained by the set $H$ is not reduced by the addition of variable $X_k$ because it is merely a combination of the variables already considered. It would make no independent or extra contribution.

The best of these measures for indicating multicollinearity is probably the multicollinearity effect measure $\overline{M}$ since each of its additive terms $\theta_k$ involves the partial coefficient of determination $r_{Yk \cdot H}^2$ as well as the total measure of proportion of variation in $Y$ explained by all other predetermined variables, $R_{Y \cdot H}^2$. That is, equation (15–10) can be rewritten as

$$\theta_k = r_{Yk \cdot H}^2 (1 - R_{Y \cdot H}^2).$$

## 'Testing' for linear dependencies

Although these measures, $R_k^2$, $r_{Yk \cdot H}^2$, $R_{k \cdot H}^2$, $\theta_k$, and $\overline{M}$, are helpful in detecting multicollinearity, it is desirable to develop and utilize test statistics to determine if the degree of multicollinearity is significant or not. If the set of predetermined variables had a joint multinormal distribution, then some exact tests in multivariate statistical analysis could be applied.[4] In the case of most econometric models, the distribution of the predetermined variables is not specified and is not presumed to be normal. Hence, when these tests

---

[4] See D. F. Morrison, *Multivariate Statistical Methods* (New York: McGraw-Hill, 1967), sec. 3.7 for a simple example.

are applied to the set $\{X_k\}$ in an econometric model, they are approximations and the calculated values of the test statistic and the associated resulting significance levels must not be interpreted as exact cardinal measures. For most models, however, such tests of multicollinearity do provide a reliable index of the severity of the problem.

||||||||||||||||||||||||||||||||||||||||||||||||||||||||||||||||||||||||||||||||||||||||||||||||||||||||||||||||||||||||

**Explicative note.** "Tests" is used here to indicate the familiar statistical procedure, not the theoretical structure of testing a population parameter. If the variables $\{X_k\}$ are fixed, not random, no test of *population* collinearity is being suggested, but only a testing of the *degree* of multicollinearity in the *sample*.

||||||||||||||||||||||||||||||||||||||||||||||||||||||||||||||||||||||||||||||||||||||||||||||||||||||||||||||||||||||||

Three tests of this type are helpful in detecting the degree and pattern of collinearity among the predetermined variables. Their presentation is given in conjunction with an example of their use to check for multicollinearity in a model with nine predetermined variables.

*An example of multicollinearity.* A model is specified to explain the number of mobile homes produced quarterly. The growth in mobile home shipments from 118,000 units in 1962 to 413,000 units in 1969 represents a change in the market share from 7.9 percent to 21.6 percent of conventional housing starts. Due to this structural change in the housing market, a city planner can no longer avoid consideration of zoning and public facilities for mobile homes. Overall, the level of mobile home shipments may be explained in terms of purchaser characteristics and demand and supply factors for both mobile homes and conventional housing.

*Specification of the model.* The model is denoted $Y = X\Gamma + \varepsilon$ where the variables are defined as shown in Table 15–1. Data are obtained for 32 quarters from 1962 through 1969 for the United States.

*Results for the example model.* The least squares estimation of the model provides the results in Table 15–2. As always, there is a potential problem of multicollinearity which should be considered.

*Rationale of a test for dependency.* Dependencies among the predetermined variables are reflected in the matrix of simple correlation coefficients between all pairs of these variables since this matrix is calculated from the sample moment matrix. (See Section 9.6, step *h.*) Let this matrix be denoted by

$$R^* = \begin{pmatrix} 1.0 & r_{23} & r_{24} & \cdots & r_{2K} \\ r_{32} & 1.0 & r_{34} & \cdots & r_{3K} \\ \vdots & \vdots & \vdots & \ddots & \vdots \\ r_{K2} & r_{K3} & r_{K4} & \cdots & 1.0 \end{pmatrix}.$$

If the set of variables $\{X_k\}$, $k = 2, 3, \ldots, 10$ is a linearly dependent set, the sample observation matrix $X$ would not have full rank (rank $X < K - 1$).

$$[T \times (K-1)]$$

**TABLE 15–1**

Definition of variables and symbols for example model of mobile home production

| Variable symbol | Variable name | Variable description | Statistical source |
|---|---|---|---|
| $Y$ | MHS | Mobile home shipments (000) | Mobile Homes Manufacturers Association (MHMA) |
| $X_2$ | HHF | Household formations (000) | *Public Health Service Vital Statistics* (PHS) |
| $X_3$ | DPI | Disposable personal income ($10^9$) | *Survey of Current Business* (SCB) |
| $X_4$ | MHP | Mobile home price index ($/ft^2$) | MHMA |
| $X_5$ | HP | Conventional housing price index | SCB |
| $X_6$ | CC | Net consumer credit extensions ($10^6$) | *Federal Reserve Bulletin* (FRB) |
| $X_7$ | M | Net acquisitions of mortgages ($10^6$) | FRB |
| $X_8$ | MHI | Inventory of mobile homes (000) | MHS lagged one quarter |
| $X_9$ | HI | Inventory of conventional housing (000) represented by conventional housing starts lagged three quarters | SCB |
| $X_{10}$ | V | Vacancy rate (percent unoccupied) | *Census Bureau Housing Series* |

**TABLE 15–2**

Results for mobile home shipments model

Dependent variable MHS    $R^2 = 0.9805$,    $s_e = 0.0417$
$T = 32$,    $K = 10$

| Variable Name | Coefficient | Std. error | F-value | Incremental contribution $\theta_k$ |
|---|---|---|---|---|
| HHF | 0.07846 | 0.01255 | 39.0979 | 0.03480 |
| DPI | −0.01141 | 0.08788 | 0.0169 | 0.00002 |
| MHP | 1.26119 | 0.64754 | 3.7934 | 0.00338 |
| HP | 3.29966 | 0.78792 | 17.5377 | 0.01561 |
| CC | −0.03709 | 0.02516 | 2.1737 | 0.00193 |
| M | 0.02164 | 0.00904 | 5.7299 | 0.00510 |
| MHI | −0.06475 | 0.16342 | 0.1570 | 0.00014 |
| HI | 0.06232 | 0.01496 | 17.3543 | 0.01545 |
| V | 0.05570 | 0.03137 | 3.1528 | 0.00281 |
| Constant | −5.41610 | | | |

Source: Class, 1971 (Lynn).

Then, $(X'X)$ also has rank less than $K - 1$. Finally, the matrix $R^*$ of simple
$$[(K-1)\times(K-1)]$$
$$[(K-1)\times(K-1)]$$
correlation coefficients would also have rank less than $K - 1$. Therefore, a dependency among the set $\{X_k\}$ would imply that the determinant of $R^*$ is zero.

At the other extreme, if the set of variables $\{X_k\}$ is orthogonal, then $X$ would have full rank and $R^*$ would be an identity matrix with determinant of one.

‖‖‖‖‖‖‖‖‖‖‖‖‖‖‖‖‖‖‖‖‖‖‖‖‖‖‖‖‖‖‖‖‖‖‖‖‖‖‖‖‖‖‖‖‖‖‖‖‖‖‖‖‖‖‖‖‖‖‖‖‖‖‖‖‖‖‖‖‖‖‖‖‖‖‖‖‖‖‖‖‖‖‖

**Recursive note.** The diagonal elements of a matrix of simple correlation coefficients are always unity since each variable is perfectly correlated with itself. If the variables are orthogonal, then the correlations between pairs of variables are all zero. These zeros would fill all the off-diagonal elements of the matrix $R^*$.

‖‖‖‖‖‖‖‖‖‖‖‖‖‖‖‖‖‖‖‖‖‖‖‖‖‖‖‖‖‖‖‖‖‖‖‖‖‖‖‖‖‖‖‖‖‖‖‖‖‖‖‖‖‖‖‖‖‖‖‖‖‖‖‖‖‖‖‖‖‖‖‖‖‖‖‖‖‖‖‖‖‖‖

The null hypothesis to be tested as an indication of severe multicollinearity is $[H_0: |R^*| = 0]$, against the alternate, $[H_a: |R^*| > 0]$. A test statistic which is approximately applicable has a chi-square distribution and is given by

$$\chi^2 = -[T - 1 - (1/6)(2K + 5)] \ln(1 - |R^*|) \qquad (15\text{–}12)$$

with $K(K - 1)/2$ degrees of freedom.[5]

**Application of the test for dependency.** For the model and results considered in Tables 15–1 and 15–2, the determinant of the simple correlation matrix is $|R^*| = 0.0005$, $T = 32$ observations, and $K = 10$ coefficients being estimated. The null hypothesis of multicollinearity would be rejected at the 0.05 significance level if the calculated value exceeds $\chi^2 \doteq 61.4$ for $10(9)/2 = 45$ degrees of freedom. The calculated value of the test statistic using (15–12) is,

$$\chi^2 = -[32 - 1 - (1/6)(20 + 5)] \ln(1 - 0.0005)$$
$$= (-26.833)(-0.001) = 0.0268.$$

‖‖‖‖‖‖‖‖‖‖‖‖‖‖‖‖‖‖‖‖‖‖‖‖‖‖‖‖‖‖‖‖‖‖‖‖‖‖‖‖‖‖‖‖‖‖‖‖‖‖‖‖‖‖‖‖‖‖‖‖‖‖‖‖‖‖‖‖‖‖‖‖‖‖‖‖‖‖‖‖‖‖‖

**Discursive note.** Using the approximation

$$\ln(1 - |R^*|) = 1 - \sum_{i<j}\sum r_{ij}$$

in note 5, one obtains $(1 - \sum\sum r_{ij}) = (-0.003)$ and $\chi^2 = 0.08$. The test conclusion is unchanged.

‖‖‖‖‖‖‖‖‖‖‖‖‖‖‖‖‖‖‖‖‖‖‖‖‖‖‖‖‖‖‖‖‖‖‖‖‖‖‖‖‖‖‖‖‖‖‖‖‖‖‖‖‖‖‖‖‖‖‖‖‖‖‖‖‖‖‖‖‖‖‖‖‖‖‖‖‖‖‖‖‖‖‖

---

[5] See Yoel Haitovsky, "Multicollinearity in Regression Analysis, Comment," *Review of Economics and Statistics* 1969, pp. 486–89. It is possible to approximate $\ln(1 - |R^*|)$ in (15–12) by $(1 - \sum\sum_{i<j} r_{ij}{}^2)$ using the sum of squares of the upper triangular elements of $R^*$. See D. N. Lawley, "The Estimation of Factor Loadings by the Method of Maximum Likelihood," *Proceedings of the Royal Society of Edinburgh*, 1940, pp. 64–82.

In this case, $\det(R^*)$ is very small and the chi-square test indicates that the problem of multicollinearity is severe. Referring to Table 15–2, the measure of the multicollinearity effect can be determined using (15–11) and the incremental contributions $\theta_k$ calculated according to (15–10). We obtain,

$$\overline{M} = \left[ \sum_{k=2}^{K} \theta_k - R^2 \right] = 0.07924 - 0.9805 = -0.90126,$$

which is very large relative to $R^2 = 0.9805$ and indicative of severe multicollinearity.

**A test to identify which variables are involved in the dependency**

To test which individual variables are most affected by the multicollinearity, a test is used for the null hypothesis, [$H_0$: $X_k$ is not affected) against the alternate ($H_0$: $X_k$ is affected). The null hypothesis is rejected if the calculated value of the following $F$-distributed statistic exceeds $F_{(\alpha; T-K, K-1)}$:[6]

$$F_{(T-K, K-1)} = (r^{*k} - 1) \frac{(T - K)}{(K - 1)} \tag{15-13}$$

where $r^{*k}$ denotes the $k$th diagonal element of the inverse matrix of simple correlation coefficients, $(R^*)^{-1}$.

||||||||||||||||||||||||||||||||||||||||||||||||||||||||||||||||||||||||||||||||||||||||||||||||||||||||||||||||||||||||||||||||||||||||||||

*Recursive note.* This test statistic in (15–13) is exactly $F$-distributed only in the case where all predetermined variables have a joint normal distribution. For most econometric models, this condition is not met so the calculated value of $F$ in (15–13) should be interpreted only as an index, an ordinal measure of the degree to which variable $X_k$ is affected by the multicollinearity.

||||||||||||||||||||||||||||||||||||||||||||||||||||||||||||||||||||||||||||||||||||||||||||||||||||||||||||||||||||||||||||||||||||||||||||

For the example model and the results described in Tables 15–1 and 15–2, this test gives the results shown in Table 15–3.

*Interpreting the results.* The results in Table 15–3 indicate that household formations (HHF), supply of mortgage funds (M), and the inventory of conventional housing (HI) are not significantly affected by the multicollinearity among the set of predetermined variables. The supply of consumer credit (CC) is weakly affected, and all other variables are strongly collinear.

**A test to detect patterns of collinearity**

As a final step in the detection of multicollinearity, it is important for correction purposes to know more about the patterns of correlation among the predetermined variables. The partial correlation coefficients help provide

---

[6] See D. E. Farrar and D. R. Glauber, "Multicollinearity in Regression Analysis, the Problem Revisited," *Review of Economics and Statistics*, 1967, pp. 92–107.

TABLE 15–3

**Test results for the extent of multicollinearity affecting each predetermined variable**

| Variable | $r^{*k}$ | F-value (15–13) | Significance* |
|----------|----------|-----------------|---------------|
| HHF | 1.854 | 2.09 | Not at 0.05 |
| DPI | 108.787 | 263.48 | Yes at 0.001 |
| MHP | 25.199 | 59.15 | Yes at 0.001 |
| HP | 153.184 | 372.00 | Yes at 0.001 |
| CC | 2.720 | 4.20 | Yes at 0.05 |
| M | 1.842 | 2.06 | Not at 0.05 |
| MHI | 24.296 | 56.95 | Yes at 0.001 |
| HI | 1.854 | 2.09 | Not at 0.05 |
| V | 18.571 | 42.95 | Yes at 0.001 |

* Critical values for $F$ with 22 and 9 degrees of freedom are 2.92 for $\alpha = 0.05$, 4.78 for $\alpha = 0.01$, and 8.86 for $\alpha = 0.001$.

this information. Using a $t$-distributed test statistic as in note 5, Section 7.3, for a simple correlation coefficient, each partial correlation coefficient, $r_{kj \cdot G}$, can be tested to determine if it is significantly different from zero. The symbol $G$ denotes the set of all predetermined variables excluding variables $X_k$ and $X_j$, $j \neq k$. The test statistic is

$$t_{(T-K-1)} = r_{kj \cdot G}\sqrt{T - K - 1}\Big/\sqrt{1 - r_{kj \cdot G}^2} \qquad (15\text{–}14)$$

with $(T - K - 1)$ degrees of freedom.

The paths by which the variables are related can be traced by careful examination of the matrix of all these partial correlation coefficients. Table 15–4 provides the values of the partial correlation coefficients in the first matrix and the values of both the calculated $t$-statistics and their significance level below and above the diagonal in the second matrix. If the test result is not significant, it means that $r_{kj \cdot G}$ is not significantly different from zero so that the variables $X_k$ and $X_j$ are not dependent after removing the linear effect on each of all the other predetermined variables. If the $t$-value is large, then the corresponding variables $X_k$ and $X_j$ are linked as collinear variables.

*Interpreting the results.*   Table 15–4 shows quite clearly the interrelations among the predetermined variables. The price of mobile homes (MHP) and the price of conventional housing (HP) are strongly interrelated with disposable personal income (DPI). Through the price of conventional housing, this whole set of variables is interdependent with the inventory of mobile homes (MHI) and the vacancy rate (V). Also, a weaker dependency occurs in the relationship of consumer credit (CC) with the supply of mortgage funds (M) and the inventory of conventional homes (HI). Corrections for the severe multicollinearity of the complete model should concentrate on reducing these dependency relations.

TABLE 15–4

Partial correlation coefficients and associated *t*-values and significance levels

|      | HHF   | DPI   | MHP   | HP    | CC    | M     | MHI   | HI    | V   |
|------|-------|-------|-------|-------|-------|-------|-------|-------|-----|
| HHF  | 1.0   |       |       |       |       |       |       |       |     |
| DPI  | −0.28 | 1.0   |       |       | (symmetric) |  |       |       |     |
| MHP  | −0.11 | 0.77  | 1.0   |       |       |       |       |       |     |
| HP   | 0.27  | −0.69 | −0.21 | 1.0   |       |       |       |       |     |
| CC   | 0.02  | −0.34 | −0.37 | 0.13  | 1.0   |       |       |       |     |
| M    | −0.35 | 0.32  | 0.25  | −0.06 | −0.45 | 1.0   |       |       |     |
| MHI  | −0.17 | 0.06  | −0.30 | −0.68 | −0.10 | −0.15 | 1.0   |       |     |
| HI   | 0.23  | 0.30  | 0.20  | −0.31 | −0.52 | 0.09  | 0.26  | 1.0   |     |
| V    | 0.20  | −0.54 | −0.29 | 0.82  | 0.13  | −0.04 | −0.47 | −0.25 | 1.0 |

Values of $r_{kJ \cdot G'}$ the partial correlation coefficient between each pair of variables as indicated by position holding the effect of all the other variables constant.

|      | HHF  | DPI  | MHP  | HP   | CC   | M    | MHI   | HI   | V     |
|------|------|------|------|------|------|------|-------|------|-------|
| HHF  | —    | n.s. | n.s. | n.s. | n.s. | n.s. | n.s.  | n.s. | n.s.  |
| DPI  | 1.37 | —    | 0.001| 0.001| n.s. | n.s. | n.s.  | n.s. | 0.01  |
| MHP  | 0.52 | 5.63 | —    | n.s. | 0.10 | n.s. | n.s.  | n.s. | n.s.  |
| HP   | 1.27 | 4.47 | 1.00 | —    | n.s. | n.s. | 0.001 | n.s. | 0.001 |
| CC   | 0.09 | 1.70 | 1.87 | 0.62 | —    | 0.05 | n.s.  | 0.02 | n.s.  |
| M    | 1.76 | 1.58 | 1.22 | 0.28 | 2.35 | —    | n.s.  | n.s. | n.s.  |
| MHI  | 0.81 | 0.28 | 1.55 | 4.35 | 0.46 | 0.71 | —     | n.s. | 0.05  |
| HI   | 1.11 | 1.55 | 0.95 | 1.54 | 2.85 | 0.42 | 1.26  | —    | n.s.  |
| V    | 0.95 | 3.01 | 1.42 | 6.66 | 0.60 | 0.19 | 2.50  | 1.21 | —     |

Elements in the lower triangular matrix are *t*-values from (15–14). Values in the upper triangular matrix are significance levels for a two-sided test based on a *t*-distribution with 21 degrees of freedom. The symbols n.s. mean "not significant".

## 15.8 CORRECTIONS FOR MULTICOLLINEARITY

When the presence of multicollinearity in a model is quite severe, the econometrician has less confidence in the estimates of the coefficients because they are prone to have excessively large variances and are not precise in distinguishing the separate effects on the endogenous variable of the individual predetermined variables.

### Forecasting not severely affected

If the purpose for the model is forecasting values for the endogenous variable based on new observations of the predetermined variables, then the multicollinearity problem may not need any drastic correction. If the multicollinearity can be expected to continue, then forecasts are not seriously disturbed since the individual estimates of the coefficients are unbiased. Further, the forecasts are not severely upset by minor changes in the specification among sets of collinear variables. For example, if some excluded variable should be in the true specification but it is highly correlated with the set of included variables, then its omission is not serious in terms of forecasting. Although its absence introduces a specification bias in the estimated coefficients, the combined effect would be relatively neutral so that forecasts would not be significantly affected. (See Exercise 4 at the end of this chapter.)

To repeat this point in a slightly different way, the effect of severe multicollinearity may be to increase $V(C_k)$ so much that no coefficient $C_k$ is significantly different from zero, and yet, the joint effect of all the predetermined variables in the model is highly significant. The model may have a high value of $R^2$ based on the sample observations. Due to this high degree of fit, the estimated values will be very close to the observed values within the sample experience. If this multicollinearity continues for new observations and the specification is not changed, then the model will also give a close fit for these new sample values. Forecasts based on them will be close to the actual values.

## Types of remedies

The primary problem of multicollinearity is that the values of $C_k$ are quite imprecise. Thus, if the purpose of the model is to aid the econometrician in establishing accurate numerical values for economic parameters or testing implications of economic theory in terms of these values based on economic experience, then some correction is required. Unfortunately, there is no one best remedy for multicollinearity in all cases nor even a consistent ranking of possible remedies that should be attempted. The econometrician must use his best judgment and skill and not exclude a little luck in changing the specification, or redefining the measures of the variables, or acquiring new data, or improving the accuracy of the calculation. Some frequently used alternatives belonging to these classes of modifications are considered briefly in the following list.

*Changing the specification.* One common notion for reducing multicollinearity is to select the variable most seriously involved in the collinearity and to remove it from the model. As discussed before, this does reduce the multicollinearity, but it also introduces a specification error if this variable is one which is significant and is an important variable in the unknown "true" specification.

In the example of the last section, the two variables most affected by collinearity according to the test statistic (15–13) are disposable personal income (DPI) and the conventional housing price index (HP) as shown by the *F*-values in Table 15–3. These would be likely candidates for removal from the model. However, from Table 15–2, the results of tests of significance on the individual variables indicate that DPI is the least significant variable while HP is the second most significant variable. Consequently, removal of DPI would introduce much less specification bias based on this sample evidence.

The specification bias may be minimized if the variable dropped is replaced by some other variable serving to measure the same economic influence, but perhaps from a slightly different point of view. Of course, the change in variables is only useful if the new variable is less collinear with the other predetermined variables.

A second way to change the specification is to express all the important interrelations among the predetermined variables as separate equations in the specification. The econometrician then has to specify a number of the variables (equal to the number of equations in his model) as jointly endogenous as he reconsiders and reestimates the coefficients in the context of a simultaneous equations econometric model. The formulation, interpretation, and estimation of such models and their unique problems are introduced in the final part of this book, Chapters 16–19.

For the example model of the last section, the interrelations might be expressed in several ways. Based on the tracing of multicollinearity given in Table 15–4 and the definitions of the variables in Table 15–1, a simultaneous set of linear relationships may be,

$$
\left.
\begin{aligned}
\text{MHS} &= f(\text{HHF, MHP, HP, CC, M, HI}) \\
\text{MHP} &= f(\text{MHS, M, DPI, CC}) \\
\text{HP} &= f(\text{MHP, HHF, DPI, MHI, V}) \\
\text{M} &= f(\text{MHS, HHF, CC, V})
\end{aligned}
\right\}
\qquad (15\text{–}15)
$$

where the endogenous variables to be jointly determined are mobile home shipments (MHS) and price (MHP), conventional housing price (HP), and net mortgages acquired (M) in terms of the other variables as identified in the above relations.

*Redefining the variables.*    Sometimes the problem of multicollinearity is resolved by making suitable changes in the definitions of the variables in the model. Two popular suggestions are transformations and aggregations of variables. These are only appropriate in a specific case if the resulting model and its parameters still reflect the intended economic mechanisms and still support the purpose of the econometrician in specifying some testable economic propositions.

Transformations that are commonly used are ordinary first differences or logarithmic first differences. For a variable $X$, these are represented by the transformation rules, $X_t^* = X_t - X_{t-1}$, and $X_t^* = \ln(X_t/X_{t-1})$ respectively.

||||||||||||||||||||||||||||||||||||||||||||||||||||||||||||||||||||||||||||||||||||||||||||||||||||||||||||||||||||||||||||||||||||||||||

*Recursive note.*    The error terms in the model must also be transformed accordingly. The assumptions for least squares estimation from Section 10.3 must apply to the transformed variables and error terms. These do not automatically hold true even if they were true for the model before the transformation.

||||||||||||||||||||||||||||||||||||||||||||||||||||||||||||||||||||||||||||||||||||||||||||||||||||||||||||||||||||||||||||||||||||||||||

The logarithmic first difference is often used to eliminate the effect of trends and cycles in a time series. To the extent that the predetermined variables have common trends and cyclical components, this transformation helps to reduce multicollinearity.

||||||||||||||||||||||||||||||||||||||||||||||||||||||||||||||||||||||||||||||||||||||||||||||||||||||||||||||||||||||||||||||||||

*Discursive note.* Such transformations are also useful when forecasts are to be made based on new observations of the predetermined variables. If a growth trend occurs, new values would tend to be larger than any previously observed values and forecast intervals would be excessively large due to the large deviation from the sample mean. (Recall Section 7.7.) However, the size of the first difference or of the logarithmic first difference is probably within the range of previous experience of such differences. Thus the confidence interval for the forecast of the difference would not have an exaggerated standard error.

||||||||||||||||||||||||||||||||||||||||||||||||||||||||||||||||||||||||||||||||||||||||||||||||||||||||||||||||||||||||||||||||||

The type of aggregation of variables that is most common is a grouping of collinear variables into a composite index which allows a similar economic interpretation. For example, a model including four separate interest rate variables which are highly correlated with each other may be replaced by some single weighted composite of these variables. The total effect of the interest rate variables on the endogenous variable may still be reflected by the coefficient of this single variable, and the multicollinearity in the model may be eliminated.

||||||||||||||||||||||||||||||||||||||||||||||||||||||||||||||||||||||||||||||||||||||||||||||||||||||||||||||||||||||||||||||||||

*Interpretive note.* Forming a composite in this way is fruitful only if the variables included in the composite have some useful combined economic interpretation. For example, combining disposable personal income, mobile home inventory, and the housing vacancy rate into a single composite may help to reduce multicollinearity in the example model of Section 15.7. However, the meaning of the composite is unclear because too many diverse economic factors are involved.

||||||||||||||||||||||||||||||||||||||||||||||||||||||||||||||||||||||||||||||||||||||||||||||||||||||||||||||||||||||||||||||||||

*Explicative note.* Statistically, the formation of a composite is most useful if the included variables are highly correlated with each other and each has a low correlation with the remaining predetermined variables not included within the composite.

||||||||||||||||||||||||||||||||||||||||||||||||||||||||||||||||||||||||||||||||||||||||||||||||||||||||||||||||||||||||||||||||||

*Acquiring additional data.* Very frequently multicollinearity may occur as a result of censored data which is limited in its coverage of the economic experience being sampled. If additional data could be acquired, it is possible that more independent variation among the variables would be observed and the multicollinearity thereby reduced. The new data may be simply obtained by increasing the sample size. If this is not possible within the restraints of the variable definitions, model specification, and purpose of the analysis, then an independent study may be done on a suitable submodel for which other data can be used. On the basis of this submodel, one or more of the coefficients of some collinear variables in the original model may be approximated by these so-called extraneous estimates. Using these extraneous estimates, the other coefficients in the original model may be estimated from the original data under conditions of reduced multicollinearity from that which previously occurred.

Suppose the model $Y = \gamma_1 + \gamma_2 X_2 + \gamma_3 X_3 + \gamma_4 X_4 + \varepsilon$ is to be estimated but $X_3$ and $X_4$ are highly correlated. If independent data is available which provides evidence on the relation between $X_4$ and the endogenous variable $Y$, then an extraneous estimate of $\gamma_4$ may be obtained, say $\hat{\gamma}_4$. Finally, the model can be rewritten as

$$(Y - \hat{\gamma}_4 X_4) = \gamma_1 + \gamma_2 X_2 + \gamma_3 X_3 + \varepsilon$$

with the remaining coefficients being estimated on the basis of the original data.

The use of extraneous estimates arouses some other questions of interpretation and validity. If the reader should desire to use this approach, he is advised to read more of the literature on extraneous estimates. (A few references are given at the end of this chapter.)

*Using more accurate calculations.* When multicollinearity is a problem, the calculation of the inverse matrix $(X'X)^{-1}$ and of the inverse matrix $(R^*)^{-1}$ are subject to serious roundoff error. These errors affect the calculations of the estimates $C$, the estimates of the standard errors of these estimates, the statistics for testing significance, and even the statistics from (15–13) for testing the extent of collinearity for each predetermined variable. Consequently, when a particular estimation of a model seems to involve multicollinearity, the econometrician should try to make the calculations of these inverses as precise as possible. In using a computer for the calculations, double precision should be used.

## 15.9 SUMMARY

In this chapter, two rather typical applied problems are considered, namely the merging of time-series and cross-sectional data to estimate a regression model and multicollinearity among the predetermined variables in the model. Some reasonably practical suggestions are described for coping with these problems.

Reiterating these procedures would be too lengthy and redundant for this summary. Instead, two dangers lurking between the lines must be emphasized again. Concerning the combined problems of autocorrelation and hetero-scedasticity, the analysis given here has presumed that all the predetermined variables are exogenous; none of them are lagged values of the endogenous variable. When the specification includes such lagged endogenous variables, theoretical complications arise and their dismissal is seldom perfunctory.

Concerning the multicollinearity discussion, it is presumed that this problem occurs singularly. If multicollinearity occurs along with heteroscedasticity and/or autocorrelation, then interest centers on the dependencies of the matrix $(X'\Omega^{-1}X)$ rather than $(X'X)$, where $\Omega = V\text{-}Cov(\varepsilon)$.

If multicollinearity occurs along with errors in the variables, a very dangerous situation develops. Although the true values of the variables may be highly collinear, it is less likely for their errors to be multicollinear. Consequently, the least squares estimators may become primarily functions of the errors of measurement scattered about the collinear set of observations. Referring to Figure 15–1(*a*), the scatter of true points $(X_2, X_3)$ may lie within the cylinder, but the scatter of the observed points with errors in the variables may be in the $(X_2, X_3)$ plane outside the cylinder. The resulting estimates of the coefficients of these variables may test out significantly even though they provide no real information on the true relation.

Techniques of analysis in the presence of one or more of these problems of estimation of the single equation model are still topics of research. The interested reader should continue to study more advanced and rigorous discussions of these topics and to keep aware of new discoveries in the current econometric literature.

## NEW VOCABULARY

Covariance method
Multicollinearity
Perfect linear dependency
Cross-sectional and time-series data
Confluence analysis

Incremental effect $\theta_k$
Multicollinearity measure $\overline{M}$
Extraneous estimates
Logarithmic first differences

## REFERENCES

Some other situations involving the use of both time-series and cross-sectional data in the estimation of an econometric model as well as some other estimating procedures are described in the following papers. The first four are also relevant to the topic of extraneous estimation.

Balestra, P., and Nerlove, M. "Pooling Cross Section and Time Series Data in the Estimation of a Dynamic Model: The Demand for Natural Gas." *Econometrica*, 1966, pp. 585–612.

Chetty, V. K. "Pooling of Time Series and Cross Section Data." *Econometrica*, 1968, pp. 279–90.

Hoch, I. "Estimation of Production Function Parameters Combining Time-series and Cross-section Data." *Econometrica*, 1962, pp. 34–53.

Kuh, E.  "The Validity of Cross-sectionally Estimated Behavior Equations in Time Series Applications." *Econometrica*, 1959, pp. 197–214.

Wallace, T. D., and Hussain, A.  "The Use of Error Components Models in Combining Cross Section with Time Series Data." *Econometrica*, 1969, pp. 55–72.

A good way to begin learning more about the use and validity of extraneous information in finding independent estimates for some coefficients in a regression model would include reading the following discussions:

Goldberger, A. S.  *Econometric Theory*, pp. 255–61. New York: John Wiley & Sons, Inc., 1964.

Klein, L.  *A Textbook of Econometrics*, chap. 5. Evanston: Row, Peterson, & Co., 1953.

Meyer, J. R., and Kuh, E.  "How Extraneous Are Extraneous Estimates." *Review of Economics and Statistics*, November 1957, pp. 380–93.

Two early presentations relating to dependencies among the set of economic variables in an econometric model are good beginning points for study about the problem of multicollinearity.

Haavelmo, T.  "Remarks on Frisch's Confluence Analysis and Its Use in Econometrics." chap. 5. In *Statistical Inference in Dynamic Economic Models*, edited by T. Koopmans. New York: John Wiley & Sons, Inc., 1950.

Klein, L. R., and Nakamura, M.  "Singularity in the Equation Systems of Econometrics: Some Aspects of the Problem of Multicollinearity." *International Economic Review*, 1962, pp. 274–99.

## EXERCISES

1.  Write a summary procedure (as in Section 15.5) for obtaining efficient estimates in a model with no timewise autocorrelation but with heteroscedasticity and mutual correlation among cross sections based on $NT$ pooled time-series and cross-sectional observations.

2.  Carefully examine the matrix representations for the matrix $W$ at the end of Sections 15.3 and 15.5. State precisely the meaning of each type element of $W$ and explain the underlying causes of the differences between elements in the two matrices.

3.  Explain what would be the value of the multicollinearity effect $\overline{M}$ in a situation where all the predetermined variables are a multiple of each other.

4.  Use the results from Table 15–2 to obtain a forecast for mobile home shipments (MHS) if the values of the predetermined variables are:

| Variable | HHF | DPI | MHP | HP | CC | M | MHI | HI | V |
|---|---|---|---|---|---|---|---|---|---|
| New value | 3.4 | 5.0 | 1.0 | 1.2 | 1.6 | 5.2 | 0.56 | 3.54 | 6.7 |

Compare the forecast to the actual value of MHS = 0.61.

Find the forecast for MHS based on the following equation in which the two variables DPI and MHI are omitted. These are two of the variables most highly involved in the multicollinearity according to Tables 15–3 and 15–4.

Compare this forecast to the previous one and to the true value. What generalizations might you make about the effect of multicollinearity on forecasts?

| Variable | HHF | MHP | HP | CC | M | HI | V | Constant |
|---|---|---|---|---|---|---|---|---|
| Coefficient | 0.0790 | 1.2397 | 3.0236 | −0.0392 | 0.021 | 0.0649 | 0.0479 | −5.1095 |

5. Suggest some econometric model of your own which in order to be estimated may require use of both time-series and cross-sectional data, and explain why such pooling of data may be useful.

6. Consider a model with seven predetermined variables plus an intercept $(\gamma_1 X_1)$ to be estimated on the basis of 486 observations. The determinant of the matrix of simple correlation coefficients is $|R^*| = 0.00862$. The diagonal elements of the inverse of $R^*$ are:

| Diagonal element | $r^{*2}$ | $r^{*3}$ | $r^{*4}$ | $r^{*5}$ | $r^{*6}$ | $r^{*7}$ | $r^{*8}$ |
|---|---|---|---|---|---|---|---|
| Value | 3.04690 | 1.52973 | 1.28813 | 1.43609 | 7.5224 | 5.60770 | 3.41533 |

Finally, the matrix of partial correlation coefficients and their level of significance in a two-sided test are given as:

| | $X_2$ | $X_3$ | $X_4$ | $X_5$ | $X_6$ | $X_7$ | $X_8$ |
|---|---|---|---|---|---|---|---|
| $X_2$ | — | n.s. | n.s. | n.s. | 0.001 | n.s. | 0.001 |
| $X_3$ | −0.0025 | — | n.s. | 0.001 | 0.001 | n.s. | n.s. |
| $X_4$ | 0.1156 | −0.0138 | — | 0.001 | 0.001 | n.s. | n.s. |
| $X_5$ | 0.0139 | 0.3552 | 0.1495 | — | n.s. | n.s. | n.s. |
| $X_6$ | 0.4350 | 0.1589 | 0.1543 | −0.0166 | — | 0.001 | 0.001 |
| $X_7$ | −0.0676 | 0.0393 | −0.0899 | 0.0994 | 0.6161 | — | 0.001 |
| $X_8$ | 0.1985 | −0.0479 | 0.0194 | 0.0142 | 0.1987 | 0.3259 | — |

Use the testing procedures suggested in Section 15.7 to determine if this model gives evidence of multicollinearity, which variables are most affected, and by what apparent linkages.

7. A model to determine the effects on wage rates in the United States of some factors representing demand for labor and the cost of living is suggested to be:

$$Y = \gamma_1 + \gamma_2 X_2 + \gamma_3 X_3 + \gamma_4 X_4 + \varepsilon$$

where

$Y$ = wage rates for manufacturing in the United States,
$X_2$ = consumer price index,
$X_3$ = GNP less gross private investment for the previous year,
$X_4$ = gross private investment for the previous year.

Data for 22 annual periods is obtained from the *Survey of Current Business*, U.S. Department of Commerce, and the *Monthly Review of Labor*, U.S. Department of Labor. The matrix of simple correlation coefficients is

$$R^* = \begin{pmatrix} 1.0 & 0.9062 & 0.9890 \\ & 1.0 & 0.8811 \\ & & 1.0 \end{pmatrix}$$

for the predetermined variables $X_2$, $X_3$, and $X_4$. The diagonal elements of the inverse of $R^*$ are $r^{*2} = 26.22$, $r^{*3} = 30.88$, and $r^{*4} = 5.59$.

Source: Class, 1971 (Guilkey).

*a)* Use the methods of Section 15.7 to detect the extent of multicollinearity in this model.

*b)* Given that $R^2 = 0.9929$ and the $t$-values for significance of the coefficients are $t_2 = 5.862$, $t_3 = 4.336$, and $t_4 = -1.782$, find the incremental contributions of each predetermined variable and the measure $\overline{M}$ of the multicollinearity effect for this estimation.

8. The determinants of labor force participation have been examined and reported by W. G. Bowen and T. A. Finegan, *The Economics of Labor Force Participation* (Princeton: Princeton University Press, 1969). A model based on these results may be specified to apply separately for whites and nonwhites and estimated based on 1960 Census data for 20 Standard Metropolitan Statistical Areas (SMSA's) found in *U.S. Census, 1960, Population,* Vol. 3, selected area reports, Part 1D, and *U.S. Census, 1960, Detailed Characteristics of the States,* Part D. The model is

$$\underset{(20 \times 1)}{Y} = \underset{(20 \times 7)}{X} \quad \underset{(7 \times 1)}{\Gamma} + \underset{(20 \times 1)}{\varepsilon}$$

for each group where

$Y =$ Civilian labor force participation rate for males aged 18 to 45. It is the ratio of men employed or seeking employment to the total number of men in the age group.

$X_2 =$ Unemployment rate for the group; the ratio of unemployment to the labor force.

$X_3 =$ median income of males not in school aged 14 and over.

$X_4 =$ the percentage of high school graduates in the population 18 years and over.

$X_5 =$ the ratio of nonwhite unemployment to white unemployment.

$X_6 =$ the ratio of white median income to nonwhite median income.

$X_7 =$ the percentage of nonwhites in the population; the number of nonwhites divided by total SMSA population.

The estimation results for the white and nonwhite data are given below:

*White data*

| $R^2 = 0.7976$ | $T = 20$ |
|---|---|
| $s_e = 0.9216$ | $K = 7$ |
| SS due to regression | 43.52 |
| SS due to residual | 11.04 |
| $F$-value | 8.539 |

| Variable | Coefficient | $t$-value | Diagonal element of $(R^*)^{-1}$ |
|---|---|---|---|
| Constant | 47.26 | | |
| $X_2$ | 0.070 | 0.32 | 1.893 |
| $X_3$ | 3.856 | 4.00 | 2.030 |
| $X_4$ | 0.210 | 0.25 | 1.201 |
| $X_5$ | 0.326 | 0.70 | 1.559 |
| $X_6$ | 7.053 | 4.00 | 2.491 |
| $X_7$ | 0.007 | 0.15 | 1.852 |

Nonwhite data

| | |
|---|---|
| $R^2 = 0.6190$ | $T = 20$ |
| $s_e = 2.2309$ | $K = 7$ |
| SS due to regression | 105.11 |
| SS due to residual | 64.70 |
| F-value | 3.52 |

| Variable | Coefficient | t-value | Diagonal element of $(R^*)^{-1}$ |
|---|---|---|---|
| Constant | 13.19 | | |
| $X_2$ | −0.340 | −1.68 | 1.786 |
| $X_3$ | 10.302 | 3.01 | 9.061 |
| $X_4$ | 1.115 | 0.63 | 1.926 |
| $X_5$ | −1.104 | −0.87 | 1.963 |
| $X_6$ | 20.243 | 2.40 | 9.719 |
| $X_7$ | −0.119 | −1.13 | 1.628 |

Source: Class, 1971 (Schmitz).

a) Determine if $C_2$ is significantly negative in each group (interpreted as the discouraged worker hypothesis).

b) Determine if $C_3$ is significantly positive in each group (interpreted as the income incentive hypothesis).

c) Examine the two estimations and discuss the significance of the three ratio variables ($X_5$, $X_6$, $X_7$) in each model. Specify what other information you would need to make a test of this joint significance (see Chapter 11).

d) Compare and interpret the economic meaning of the differences in results between the two estimations.

e) Explain why your answer to Exercise 1 above may be partially appropriate for estimating this model.

f) Determine and compare the measure $\overline{M}$ of the multicollinearity effect for these two models.

g) Use the F-test of (15–13) to find which variables in each model seem to be affected by multicollinearity. Explain any apparent collinearity using economic reasoning.

h) Suggest which correction procedure for multicollinearity from Section 15.8 might be worthwhile in the model based on the nonwhite data.

# PART IV

# Simultaneous Equations Econometric Models

In Parts II and III of this text, the presentation focused on the single equation econometric model with one endogenous variable being explained in terms of one or more predetermined variables and a disturbance term. The understanding of the assumptions and estimation of the single equation model and the interpretation of tests concerning it are probably the most essential statistical requirements for economists due to the very common and widespread use of single equation models and regression analysis in social science research. Furthermore, proper procedures for corrections in the estimating procedure based on residual analysis are also very important even though they are often considered as advanced topics. Recognition and remedy of commonly occurring problems in the estimation of single equation models have been considered in relatively great detail (considering the desired attempt to avoid mathematical complexity) in the previous chapters.

One potential problem for the use of ordinary least squares estimation of the single equation model has not been emphasized so far. If this single equation is theoretically and conceptually a part of a larger model representing a system of economic relations, then the problem of simultaneity is likely to occur. Estimation of the single equation may be quite misleading in this case because it is really only a component of a simultaneous equations econometric model.

Just as in the analysis of an electronic (say, a stereo) system, conclusions based on analysis of only a single component in the system are dangerous when interactions and feedbacks among the components exist.

In Part IV, the simultaneous equations econometric model is discussed using a notational development first introduced in Part I. A much less comprehensive treatment is given to the simultaneous equations model compared to that already presented for the single equation model because of the increased complexity. Many relevant topics in the estimation of such models and the properties of the estimators cannot be adequately treated within the scope of this text. Rather than resort to a superficial survey or introduction of many theoretically interesting topics, the discussion is instead intended to familiarize the reader with the most commonly mentioned topics and the most frequently and easily used estimating procedures.

In Chapter 16, the problem of simultaneity is discussed in relation first to the violation of an independence assumption (see Assumption 1 in Section 10.3) required for the use of ordinary least squares to obtain unbiased estimates; and, second, in relation to the identifiability concept of recognizing which economic relation is being estimated on the basis of the data generated from the operation of the system of economic relations. The standard formal counting rules for identifiability and the method of indirect least squares (ILS) estimation are the subjects of Chapter 17. The most frequently used procedure for estimating parameters in individual equations of simultaneous equations models is two-stage least squares (2SLS). This method is described with the aid of an example calculation in Chapter 18. The final chapter poses some methodological difficulties in testing the simultaneous equations econometric model.

# Chapter 16

# THE PROBLEMS OF
# SIMULTANEITY

## 16.1 PREVIEW

Simultaneity occurs in an econometric model within which more than one causal relationship among the variables is specified. When interrelations exist among the variables, the single equation specification with its one-way implied causality from predetermined to one endogenous variable is not an accurate nor sufficient representation.

A model might be specified in which the quantity of a commodity demanded depends on its price, but it is also possible to specify that the price depends on the quantity supplied. In an equilibrium with market clearance, the quantity demanded equals the quantity supplied so the relation between price and quantity is a two-way interaction that should be specified as a simultaneous demand and supply equations model.

As another example, a consumption function may specify that consumption depends on the level of income. However, one of the components of aggregate income is the expenditure on consumption according to the familiar and simplified accounting identity, income = consumption + government + investment expenditures. Again a single equation estimation can be misleading since consumption and income have a simultaneous two-way relationship.

The simultaneity problem occurs whenever at least one explanatory variable in one specified relation is conceptually an endogenous variable in another theoretical relation involving some of the same variables as those present in the first relation. The simultaneous equations model has two or more equations, say $G$ equations, in which $G$ endogenous variables are jointly determined from a set of variables which are always predetermined variables wherever they appear in the specification and from $G$ or less stochastic (disturbance) terms depending on the number of nonestimated identities in the simultaneous system.

## Some examples of simultaneous equations models

For example, assuming that quantity demanded equals quantity supplied at the observed market price, then a simultaneous demand and supply equation model could have two equations with two endogenous variables, with a number $K_1$ of predetermined factors of demand, with a number $K_2$ of predetermined factors of supply, and with two disturbance terms. The simultaneous model might be written.[1]

$$
\begin{array}{llll}
\text{Demand:} & \underset{(T\times 1)}{Q} = \underset{(\text{scalar})}{\beta_1} \underset{(T\times 1)}{P} + \underset{(T\times K_1)}{X_1} \underset{(K_1\times 1)}{\Gamma_1} + \underset{(T\times 1)}{\varepsilon_1} \\
\text{Supply:} & \underset{(T\times 1)}{P} = \underset{(\text{scalar})}{\beta_2} \underset{(T\times 1)}{Q} + \underset{(T\times K_2)}{X_2} \underset{(K_2\times 1)}{\Gamma_2} + \underset{(T\times 1)}{\varepsilon_2}
\end{array}
\tag{16-1}
$$

where $Q$ and $P$ represent quantity and price jointly determined by both demand factors $X_1$ and supply factors $X_2$ and by disturbance terms $\varepsilon_1$ and $\varepsilon_2$. Parameters $\beta_1$, $\beta_2$, and $\Gamma_1$ and $\Gamma_2$ need to be estimated in both equations on the basis of $T$ observations.

---

[1] Coefficients of endogenous variables are denoted by betas and coefficients of predetermined variables are denoted by gammas.

Using the other example, a consumption function and an income identity may be represented as

Consumption: $\underset{(T \times 1)}{C} = \beta_1 \underset{(T \times 1)}{Y} + \underset{(T \times K)}{X} \underset{(K \times 1)}{\Gamma} + \underset{(T \times 1)}{\varepsilon}$

Income: $\underset{(T \times 1)}{Y} = \underset{(T \times 1)}{C} + \underset{(T \times 1)}{Z}$

$$(16\text{--}2)$$

where $C$ and $Y$ represent consumption and income jointly determined by other factors of consumption $X$ and other autonomous expenditures $Z$ and by a single disturbance term $\varepsilon$.

In this case there are two equations with two joint endogenous variables but only one disturbance term and one equation to be estimated. There are no parameters to be estimated in the identity relation. Nevertheless, its theoretical presence in the economic specification poses a simultaneity problem for the estimation of the consumption equation.

In this chapter, such simple models are considered in order to illustrate the added difficulty of estimation for a simultaneous equations econometric model. The two problems encountered are nonindependence conditions between the predetermined variable and the disturbance term, and identifiability of the specific parameters being estimated. To prepare for this discussion some common terminology for the simultaneous model should be reviewed and the assumptions concerning the disturbance terms must be extended. New notational devices will be defined as they are introduced.

## 16.2 REVIEW

In studying the econometric methods associated with a simultaneous equations model, linear and matrix algebra is very important. The reader is advised to review matrix operations and the concept of rank of a matrix in preparation for the next two chapters. For this chapter, the following items may be useful.

### 1 Independence assumption between predetermined and disturbance variables

An important assumption for least squares estimation and regression analysis is the independence Assumption 1 of Sections 5.4 and 10.3. The assumption states that the predetermined variable $X_{tk}$ is independent of the disturbance variable $\varepsilon_t$ in the same equation for any predetermined variable $k = 1, 2, \ldots, K$, and any observation $t = 1, 2, \ldots, T$. This condition is necessary for the ordinary least squares estimate of the coefficient $\gamma_k$ to be unbiased in the single equation estimation.

### 2 Structural form and reduced form

The structural form of a simultaneous equations econometric model is the theoretically conceived representation of the economic relations. In the structural form, the econometrician specifies the number and form of the simultaneous relations being considered, indicates the variables to be included, and identifies which variables are considered to be endogenous.

In specifying the structural form of the model, one endogenous variable in each equation is usually normalized and represented in terms of other endogenous and predetermined variables and a disturbance variable.

|||||||||||||||||||||||||||||||||||||||||||||||||||||||||||||||||||||||||||||||||||||||||||||||||||||||||||||||||||||||||||||||||||

***Explicative note.*** A normalized variable has a coefficient of unity and usually is set alone on the left side of the equation. In this way, the causality implied within the model and the label given to each variable as endogenous or predetermined is quite clearly indicated.

|||||||||||||||||||||||||||||||||||||||||||||||||||||||||||||||||||||||||||||||||||||||||||||||||||||||||||||||||||||||||||||||||||

This specified structure symbolically represents the economic mechanism as viewed by the econometrician and it depends on his understanding of the underlying economic theory, the availability to him of measures of the included variables, and the purpose of his model. There is no one set of perfect relations which are involved in all simultaneous equations econometric models. In fact, a variable may be endogenous in one model and exogenous in another model involving the same total set of variables due to a change in the point of view or a change in the hypothesis to be tested.[2]

The reduced form of the model is a mathematically derived solution of the structural form. To obtain the reduced form, the structural form set of $G$ equations with $G$ endogenous variables is solved for each of the endogenous variables in terms of only predetermined and disturbance variables. Consequently, the reduced form also has $G$ equations, but each equation includes only one endogenous variable set equal to its derived representation in terms of all the predetermined variables in the structural form and the appropriate disturbance terms.

For example, consider the structural form (16–2) of the consumption function and income identity. For simplicity, suppose the only component of $X$ is the constant $X_1 = 1$ with coefficient $\gamma_1$ representing the intercept. The endogenous variables, $C$ and $Y$, and the implied causality are clear by the normalization of each equation.

$$C = \beta Y + \gamma_1 + \varepsilon,$$
$$Y = C + Z. \tag{16–2a}$$

$C$ and $Y$ are represented in this structure as codetermined by the two equations in terms of the exogenous variable $Z$ and the disturbance term $\varepsilon$.

The reduced form can be obtained by the substitution method of solving simultaneous equations. Solving for $Y$, we have

$$Y = (\beta Y + \gamma_1 + \varepsilon) + Z$$

---

[2] For a summary view of different structural forms of macroeconomic models, see M. Nerlove, "A Tabular Survey of Macro-econometric Models," *International Economic Review*, 1966, pp. 127–75.

or

$$Y = \frac{\gamma_1}{1 - \beta} + \frac{1}{1 - \beta}Z + \frac{1}{1 - \beta}\varepsilon.$$

Then solving for $C$ by substitution and writing $Z = \frac{1 - \beta}{1 - \beta}Z$, we obtain

$$C = Y - Z = \left(\frac{\gamma_1}{1 - \beta} + \frac{1}{1 - \beta}Z + \frac{1}{1 - \beta}\varepsilon\right) - \frac{1 - \beta}{1 - \beta}Z,$$

$$C = \frac{\gamma_1}{1 - \beta} + \frac{\beta}{1 - \beta}Z + \frac{1}{1 - \beta}\varepsilon.$$

In each of these two reduced form equations, one endogenous variable is represented in terms of only predetermined and disturbance variables. Each reduced form equation contains only one endogenous variable.

### 3 Jacobian of a transformation

The Jacobian of a transformation is defined in *Review* 6.2, item 3. It is relevant to the identifiability problem of the simultaneous equations econometric model in two ways. It can serve as an indicator of the existence of the inverse transformation between structural form and reduced form parameters. It is essential in formal determination of the joint probability density function for the endogenous variables from the assumed joint probability density functions for the disturbance terms. These complexities are not detailed in this book, but the use of the Jacobian is indicated so that it will not someday appear unannounced to the reader continuing in further study of these topics.

### REVIEW EXERCISES

R.1.  Given a structural form of a demand and supply equation as follows, mathematically solve for the reduced form considering $P$ and $Q$ as joint endogenous variables.

Demand:  $Q = \beta_1 P + \gamma_1 + \gamma_2 Y + \varepsilon_1,$

Supply:   $Q = \beta_2 P + \gamma_3 + \varepsilon_2.$

R.2.  Given the structural form,

Demand:  $Q = \beta_1 P + \gamma_1 + \gamma_2 Y + \varepsilon_1,$

Supply:   $Q = \beta_2 P + \gamma_3 + \gamma_4 Z + \varepsilon_2,$

*a*)  Find the reduced form coefficients in terms of the structural form coefficients where the reduced form is written,

$$Q = \pi_{11} + \pi_{12} Y + \pi_{13} Z + v_1,$$

$$P = \pi_{21} + \pi_{22} Y + \pi_{23} Z + v_2,$$

*b)* Find the Jacobian of the transformation obtained in part (*a*) from the structural form coefficients into the reduced form coefficients and show that it is nonzero so that an inverse transformation exists.

*c)* Find the inverse transformation from the reduced form coefficients back to the structural form coefficients.

*d)* Find the Jacobian of the inverse transformation, $J^{-1}$, and show that $JJ^{-1} = 1.0$.

## 16.3 ADDITIONAL ASSUMPTIONS FOR THE SIMULTANEOUS EQUATIONS MODEL

The simultaneous equations econometric model involves an extension of the single equation model of Parts II and III in the form of additional equations and additional disturbance terms. Usually accompanying such an extension are new assumptions required to specify simplifying restraints on the background or environment in which the economic mechanism, represented by the model, is intended to operate. These further assumptions are in addition to the seven assumptions specified in Section 10.3 for the general single equation model.

For a simultaneous equations model, the assumptions of Section 10.3 are presumed to hold for *each* structural equation that includes a stochastic disturbance term. The new assumptions are concerned with the properties of interaction among the disturbance terms from different equations and with mathematical simplification to reduce the complexity in the analysis of the simultaneous equations model.

### Changes in the previous assumptions

The assumptions that remain in effect can be restated with proper modifications to extend to all disturbance terms in the several equations. The only change required is inclusion of a subscript on the disturbance symbol so that $\varepsilon_i$, $i = 1, 2, \ldots, G$, represents the disturbance term in the $i$th equation.

*Interpretive note.* The structural form is presumed to be written with identities ordered last. For identities, the disturbance term is always zero and the following assumptions are not needed.

The modified assumptions from Section 10.3 which hold for each equation, $i = 1, 2, \ldots, G$, and each observation, $t = 1, 2, \ldots, T$, are:

ASSUMPTION 2.  $\varepsilon_{it}$ is a normally distributed random variable so $\varepsilon_{.t} = (\varepsilon_{1t}, \varepsilon_{2t}, \ldots, \varepsilon_{Gt})$ has a joint normal probability density function.

ASSUMPTION 3.  $E(\varepsilon_{it}) = 0$.

Assumption 4. $V(\varepsilon_{it}) = \sigma_i^2$ is finite and constant for all $t$.

Assumption 5. $Cov(\varepsilon_{it}\,\varepsilon_{ij}) = 0$ for $t \neq j$.

‖‖‖‖‖‖‖‖‖‖‖‖‖‖‖‖‖‖‖‖‖‖‖‖‖‖‖‖‖‖‖‖‖‖‖‖‖‖‖‖‖‖‖‖‖‖‖‖‖‖‖‖‖‖‖‖‖‖‖‖‖‖‖‖‖‖‖‖‖‖‖‖‖‖‖‖‖‖‖‖‖‖‖‖‖‖‖‖‖‖‖‖‖‖‖‖‖‖‖‖‖‖‖

**Recursive note.** The Assumptions 4 and 5 could again be generalized as in Chapters 13–15. The more general combined assumption would be that the variance covariance matrix of size $(T \times T)$, $V\text{-}Cov(\varepsilon_{it}\,\varepsilon_{ij}) = \Omega$ is symmetric and positive definite.

‖‖‖‖‖‖‖‖‖‖‖‖‖‖‖‖‖‖‖‖‖‖‖‖‖‖‖‖‖‖‖‖‖‖‖‖‖‖‖‖‖‖‖‖‖‖‖‖‖‖‖‖‖‖‖‖‖‖ ‖‖‖‖‖‖‖‖‖‖‖‖‖‖‖‖‖‖‖‖‖‖‖‖‖‖‖‖‖‖‖‖‖‖‖‖‖‖‖‖‖‖‖‖‖

Assumption 6, which states that the number of observations must exceed the number of parameters to be estimated, and Assumption 7 on the existence of the inverse matrix, $(X'X)^{-1}$, also apply in principle for the equations of the simultaneous equations model. Their purpose is to guarantee a meaningful solution to the least squares estimation procedure. Their particular form and meaning in reference to the simultaneous equations model is deferred until the discussion of the estimation procedures in Chapters 17 and 18.

## New assumptions

Since there may exist more than one disturbance term $\varepsilon_i$ in the simultaneous equations model, a new dimension of covariances between these random terms in different equations arises. The usual assumptions about these interequation relationships are that these different disturbance terms have a constant relation to each other in each time period and that all their noncontemporaneous covariances are zero. Such assumptions imply that the disturbance term in one relation may be correlated with the disturbance term in any other relation since they may result to a considerable extent from the same underlying and excluded factors that affect the sector or economy represented by the model. However, this dependency is assumed to be unchanging over the observations. Also, the dependency is assumed to exist only between disturbances drawn in the same observation period. Disturbances in different equations and from different observations are assumed to be independent.

The assumptions can be formally written as follows:

Assumption 8. $Cov(\varepsilon_{it}\,\varepsilon_{gt}) = \sigma_{ig}$ for $i, g = 1, 2, \ldots, G$, but $i \neq g$, which indicates a constant covariance between contemporaneous disturbance terms in different equations; and

Assumption 9. $Cov(\varepsilon_{it}\,\varepsilon_{gj}) = 0$ for $i \neq g$ and $t \neq j$, which indicates that noncontemporaneous disturbances in different equations are independent.

In a more general approach, these simplifying Assumptions 8 and 9 could also be relaxed to allow changing covariances and noncontemporaneous dependencies. However, this extension is not considered in this text.

## The troublesome assumption

A final assumption which has been ignored so far, but which is crucial for ordinary least squares estimators to be unbiased, is Assumption 1. For the simultaneous equations model, this assumption can be modified to include all combinations of explanatory and disturbance variables as follows:

*Assumption 1.* All exogenous variables are fixed; and the covariance between any explanatory variable and the disturbance term in any equation, past, present, or future (or between any cross sections if the observations are not from time series) is zero.

In the next section, it is shown that the use of an *endogenous* variable in an *explanatory* role in an equation of a simultaneous equations model (determining two or more endogenous variables jointly in a simultaneous equations model in which at least one endogenous variable is used as an explanatory variable in at least one equation) always results in the violation of assumption one.

## 16.4 THE BIAS OF OLS ESTIMATORS IN A SIMULTANEOUS EQUATIONS MODEL

Whenever an explanatory variable in an equation is not independent of the disturbance term, then estimating the parameters in the equation by ordinary least squares results in biased and inconsistent estimates. In particular, this presents a problem of estimation in a simultaneous equations model because an endogenous variable used in an explanatory role in one equation is likely to be correlated with the disturbance term in that equation.

### An intuitive approach

The general problem can be seen from an intuitive argument. Suppose in one equation, a variable $Y_1$ depends on variables $Y_2$, $X$, and $Z$, whatever these may represent, and a disturbance term $\varepsilon_1$. Also, in a second equation, $Y_2$ depends on variables $Z$ and $W$ and a disturbance term $\varepsilon_2$. That is, $Y_1 = f(Y_2, X, Z, \varepsilon_1)$ and $Y_2 = g(Z, W, \varepsilon_2)$. Suppose all the Assumptions 2–5, 8, and 9 hold as given in Section 16.3 and variables $X$, $Z$, and $W$ are fixed exogenous variables which are independent of $\varepsilon_1$ and $\varepsilon_2$ across all observations.

Then, the distribution of $Y_2$ depends on that for $\varepsilon_2$. By Assumption 8, $\varepsilon_2$ may be correlated with $\varepsilon_1$. In such a case, $Y_2$ is similarly correlated with $\varepsilon_1$. But in the estimation of $Y_1$, the variable $Y_2$ is used as an explanatory variable and should be independent of $\varepsilon_1$ if ordinary least squares estimates of the parameters in the first relation are to be unbiased. The result is, of course, that such estimates will not be unbiased due to the simultaneity or codetermination of $Y_1$ and $Y_2$ in terms of both $\varepsilon_1$ and $\varepsilon_2$.

## An algebraic example

The algebra of such a situation can be derived easily for the simple structural form (16–2) in which the only component of $X$ is $X_1 = 1$ with coefficient $\gamma_1$ representing the intercept in a simple consumption function. The model is,

$$C_t = \gamma_1 + \beta Y_t + \varepsilon_t$$
$$Y_t = C_t + Z_t \qquad\qquad (16\text{–}2a)$$

for which all the assumptions mentioned above hold. The variables $Z_t$ and $\varepsilon_t$ are independent in the same observation or with lags; $\gamma_1$ and $\beta$ are constants; $Z$ is fixed and exogenous; and $\varepsilon$ is random satisfying Assumptions 2–5 so that by the two equations, $\gamma_1$, $\beta$, $Z$, and $\varepsilon$ necessarily codetermine $Y$ and $C$.

To examine the condition of independence between $Y_t$ and $\varepsilon_t$, the respective expected values and then the covariance must be determined. By Assumption 3, $E(\varepsilon_t) = 0$. Also, solving for $Y_t$ (see *Review* 16.2, item 2), we obtain

$$Y_t = (\gamma_1 + Z_t + \varepsilon_t)/(1 - \beta) \qquad \text{so} \quad E(Y_t) = (\gamma_1 + Z_t)/(1 - \beta) + 0.$$

Thus,

$$
\begin{aligned}
Cov(\varepsilon_t, Y_t) &= E[(\varepsilon_t - 0)(Y_t - E(Y_t))] && \text{(by definition)} \\
&= E[\varepsilon_t(\gamma_1 + Z_t + \varepsilon_t - (\gamma_1 + Z_t))/(1 - \beta)] && \text{(by substitution)} \\
&= E[\varepsilon_t(\varepsilon_t/(1 - \beta))] . && \text{(by simplification)}
\end{aligned}
$$

$Cov(\varepsilon_t, Y_t) = E(\varepsilon_t^2)/(1 - \beta) \neq 0$, since the variance of $\varepsilon_t$ is necessarily positive and $\beta$ is presumed to be different from one and finite.

Therefore, in the consumption function, the explanatory variable $Y$ is related to the disturbance term $\varepsilon_t$. If OLS is applied, the estimates of $\gamma_1$ and $\beta$ in the consumption function will be biased and inconsistent. This result occurred using the simplest possible structural form for a simultaneous equations model, namely only one stochastic relation and one identity. In more complex structures, the same result occurs, often due to more than one dependency relation.

## Digression showing the bias of the estimates

Given the consumption function, $C = \gamma_1 + \beta Y + \varepsilon$, OLS might be applied to obtain the estimates, $b = m_{CY}/m_{YY}$ and $C_1 = \bar{C} - b\,\bar{Y}$ for $\beta$ and $\gamma_1$ respectively.

||||||||||||||||||||||||||||||||||||||||||||||||||||||||||||||||||||||||||||||||||||||||||||||||||||||||||||||||||||||||||||||||||||||||

***Explicative note.*** The notation $m_{CY}$ refers to the sample moment based on the observations of variables $C$ and $Y$. It is defined as

$$m_{CY} = \frac{1}{T} \sum_t (C - \bar{C})(Y - \bar{Y}).$$

Refer to *Review* 10.2, item 2. $m_{YY}$ denotes the sample second moment about the mean of the variable $Y$. Other uses of the moment notation should be interpreted similarly.

The formula for $b = m_{CY}/m_{YY}$ is identical to the least squares formula (3–2) in the simple model but applied in the present context.

||||||||||||||||||||||||||||||||||||||||||||||||||||||||||||||||||||||||||||||||||||||||||||||||||||||||||||||||||||||||||||||||||

Using the substitution, $C = \gamma_1 + \beta Y + \varepsilon$, the definition of sample moments and the rules for summations, the estimate can be written,

$$b = \frac{m_{(\gamma_1 + \beta Y + \varepsilon)Y}}{m_{YY}} = \frac{(m_{\gamma_1 Y} + m_{\beta Y, Y} + m_{\varepsilon Y})}{m_{YY}}.$$

A further simplification using $m_{\gamma_1 Y} = 0$ and $m_{\beta Y, Y} = \beta m_{YY}$ gives (see Exercise 2 at the end of this chapter):

$$b = 0 + \beta(1) + \frac{m_{\varepsilon Y}}{m_{YY}}.$$

To be unbiased $E(b) = B$, but in this case $E(b) = \beta + E(m_{\varepsilon Y}/m_{YY})$ which indicates a bias. Even in the limit as $T \to \infty$ and the sample moments approach the true covariances and variances, it is shown above that $Cov(\varepsilon Y)$ is not zero. Thus, under the assumption that the variance of $Y$ is finite, then the bias persists so that the estimate, $b$, is inconsistent.[3]

## A geometrical analysis of the bias

The problem of estimating the consumption function when it is viewed as part of a simultaneous system can be illustrated as in Figure 16–1. The result of an upward bias in the estimate of $\beta$, the marginal propensity to consume (MPC), is known as Haavelmo's proposition.[4]

In the two-dimensional $(C, Y)$ diagram, equilibrium is represented by points lying on the family of 45-degree lines with intercept on the $Y$-axis of $Z_t$, the amount of autonomous investment so that $Y = C + Z$. The slope of such a line in the $(C, Y)$ plane is $+1.0$. Every unit change in $C$ is identically a unit change in $Y$ holding $Z$ constant. On the other hand, the true consumption function relating $C$ and $Y$ is presumed to have a slope (MPC), $0 < \beta < 1.0$.

In Figure 16–1, a true relation for $C = \gamma_1 + \beta Y$ is drawn and bordered by two parallel lines allowing for disturbance terms $\varepsilon_t$ of size $+\theta$ and $-\theta$. Also, for simplicity, only two of the family of 45-degree lines is drawn representing

---

[3] See J. Johnston, *Econometric Methods* (2d ed.; New York: McGraw-Hill Book Co., 1972), pp. 342–44, for a more complete discussion. This result shows that an asymptotic bias exists which precludes consistency for this estimator.

[4] T. Haavelmo uncovers this and discusses other problems in the equivalent of the first econometrics text, "The Probability Approach in Econometrics," *Econometrica*, Vol. 12, Supplement (July 1944), 118 pages.

**FIGURE 16–1**
**Haavelmo's proposition indicating bias in OLS estimates of the MPC in a simple model**

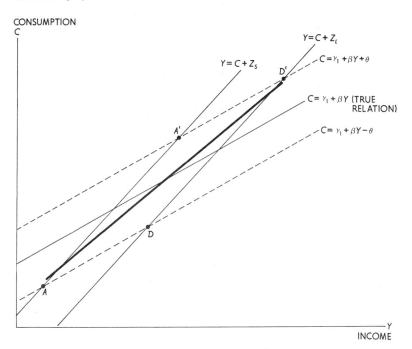

*An observed scatter of points within AA'D'D would result in an OLS regression line as shown by the heavy line with a greater slope than the true relation.*

only two levels of investment, say the largest $(Z_L)$ and smallest $(Z_S)$ values observed during the period under consideration. These lines are then, $Y = C + Z_S$ and $Y = C + Z_L$.

Suppose that investment level, $Z_S$, occurs twice and the error $\varepsilon$ is equal to $+\theta$ in one case and $-\theta$ in the other. Then, points $A'$ and $A$ could be observed. Similarly, if $Z_L$ occurs twice, once with each extreme error, then points $D'$ and $D$ would be observed. In general, the errors occurring at investment levels $Z_S$ or $Z_L$ may not be the most extreme levels but somewhere in between. Then, points on the lines $AA'$ and $DD'$ would be observed. Further, levels between the extreme values of investment would also occur so that all points observed would lie within the parallelogram $AA'D'D$.

If a scatter of points were observed within this region $AA'D'D$ and ordinary least squares were applied to estimate $\beta$ by minimizing the sum of squares of vertical deviations, the resulting estimating line is bound to be tilted upward from the true regression line because of the influence of the extreme points in the scatter diagram lying near the corners $A$ and $D'$. Consequently, the estimate of the slope, $b$, is biased upwards and the intercept $\gamma_1$ is most likely underestimated. The heavy line in Figure 16–1 indicates the tendency of the resulting estimating line. The bias can be shown to be greater, the smaller is the observed range in $Z$ and the larger are the values, $|\theta|$, of the disturbances. (See Exercise 3 at the end of this chapter.)

The result points to the need for a different method of estimation in the simultaneous equations case. In this case, the consumption function has slope, $dC/dY = \beta$, while the income identity has slope, $dC/dY = 1.0$. The joint effect gives OLS estimates of the slope of the single consumption function somewhere in between; and so, $\beta < b < 1.0$, is biased high. The MPC is over-estimated regardless of the number of observations within the region $AA'D'D$. For policy implications, the multiplier $[1/(1 - \text{MPC})]$ is overstated and counter cyclical policy measures would undershoot the full-employment level or act too slowly against inflation. The expected effect of public policy based on the biased estimate of the MPC would be overestimated, and the actual effect realized would be too weak.[5]

## 16.5 THE IDENTIFIABILITY OF PARAMETERS IN A SIMULTANEOUS EQUATIONS MODEL

When the same two endogenous variables appear in at least two different stochastic equations in a simultaneous equations model, a problem exists of identifying which relationship can be estimated on the basis of the data. An early discussion of the problem arose in the estimation of demand functions for various commodities.[6] The *observed* market price and quantity at a given period are determined by both demand and supply factors. Moreover, the demand relationship (abstracted from other factors of demand) may be written with quantity demanded as a function of the demand price, $Q = f(P)$, or vice versa as $P = g(Q)$.

||||||||||||||||||||||||||||||||||||||||||||||||||||||||||||||||||||||||||||||||||||||||||||||||||||||||||||||||

*Discursive note.* Mathematically, there is no difference between the equations, $Q = \gamma_1 + \beta P$ and $P = (-\gamma_1/\beta) + (1/\beta)Q$. However, statistically, based on time series of $P$ and $Q$, the least squares estimate of $\beta$ in the first equation will not equal the reciprocal of the least squares estimate of $(1/\beta)$ in the second equation. (See Exercise 4 at the end of this chapter.)

||||||||||||||||||||||||||||||||||||||||||||||||||||||||||||||||||||||||||||||||||||||||||||||||||||||||||||||||

The supply relation can similarly be written with the cause and effect between $P$ and $Q$ stated either way. The determination of a demand equation or a supply equation must allow for the two-way relation and is, therefore, a simultaneous equations estimation problem.

---

[5] An example of the bias in the estimation of the MPC by least squares is given by T. Haavelmo, "Methods of Measuring the MPC," *Journal of the American Statistical Association*, March 1947, pp. 105–22.

[6] See E. J. Working, "What Do Statistical 'Demand Curves' Show?" *Quarterly Journal of Economics*, 1927, pp. 212–35.

## The meaning of identifiability

The problem is examined with the aid of Figure 16–2. In part (*a*) of the figure, a simplified demand curve is shown as $DD'$ representing the equation, $Q = \gamma_1 + \beta_1 P$. This linear relation could be determined by two points such as $(P_1, Q_1)$ and $(P_2, Q_2)$. However, there is also a supply curve, say $P = \gamma_2 + \beta_2 Q$, shown as $SS'$ for which $\beta_2 \neq (1/\beta_1)$. Any observations available are actually all the same, namely at the intersection point $E$ of demand and supply. It is impossible to distinguish the true demand curve from the true supply curve or any other line which passes through the intersection point $E$. No estimating technique can help to determine the estimates of the parameters $\gamma_1$ and $\beta_2$ of the demand curve. They are said to be *unidentifiable*, and the demand function is *not identified*.

**FIGURE 16–2**
**The identifiability problems for a demand curve**

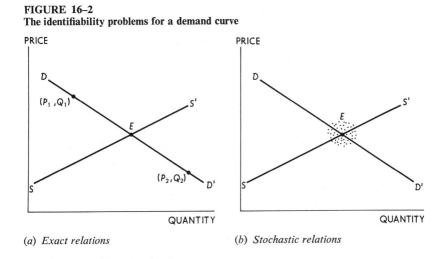

(*a*) *Exact relations*          (*b*) *Stochastic relations*

IIIIIIIIIIIIIIIIIIIIIIIIIIIIIIIIIIIIIIIIIIIIIIIIIIIIIIIIIIIIIIIIIIIIIIIIIIIIIIIIIIIIIIIIIIIIIIIIIIIIIIIIIIIIIIIIIIIIIIIIIIIIIIIIIIIIIIIIIIIIIIIIIIIIIIIIIIIIIIIIIIIIIIIIII

*Discursive note.* The supply function is not identified either. In various models, it is possible that none, all, or some of the equations may be identified. Each must be examined separately to determine its identifiability. If an equation is identified, all its parameters are identifiable; and if it is not, none of its parameters are identifiable. It is *never* the case that one parameter of an equation is identifiable and the others in the same equation are not, given the type of a priori restrictions considered in this text.

IIIIIIIIIIIIIIIIIIIIIIIIIIIIIIIIIIIIIIIIIIIIIIIIIIIIIIIIIIIIIIIIIIIIIIIIIIIIIIIIIIIIIIIIIIIIIIIIIIIIIIIIIIIIIIIIIIIIIIIIIIIIIIIIIIIIIIIIIIIIIIIIIIIIIIIIIIIIIIIIIIIIIIIIII

The situation is unaltered if either or both of the demand and supply equations are allowed to contain a disturbance term. If both are stochastic, there will be a scatter of observations about the true intersection point as in Figure 16–2, part (*b*). The equations might be,

Demand:   $Q = \gamma_1 + \beta_1 P + \varepsilon_1$

and

Supply:   $P = \gamma_2 + \beta_2 Q + \varepsilon_2$ .

It remains impossible to distinguish $DD'$ from any other line whose non-stochastic part passes through $E$ and which has an additive disturbance. Without further information or assumptions, no estimation of the demand curve can be made.

|||||||||||||||||||||||||||||||||||||||||||||||||||||||||||||||||||||||||||||||||||||||||||||||||||||||||||||||||||||||||||||||||||

*Recursive note.*   Also in this case, the explanatory variable, $P$, in the demand relation cannot be assumed to be independent of the disturbance term $\varepsilon_1$. In the demand relation, $\varepsilon_1$ affects $Q$. Then, in the supply relation, $Q$ affects $P$, so the linkage between $\varepsilon_1$ and $P$ is logically quite clear. Even if the demand curve were identifiable, OLS estimates would be biased and inconsistent.

|||||||||||||||||||||||||||||||||||||||||||||||||||||||||||||||||||||||||||||||||||||||||||||||||||||||||||||||||||||||||||||||||||

## Information necessary for identifiability of demand or supply

One type of extra information that would be very useful is knowledge of actual shifts in demand or supply due to changes in some factor which affects only one of the curves. For example, a supply factor such as climate or labor strikes may create shifts in the supply function but not in demand. Also, demand factors such as changes in tastes due to advertising or retail store promotions on complementary or substitute goods may create shifts in the demand function, but not in supply.

When one curve is shifting relative to the other due to exogenous factors, then a series of observations scattered about the changing intersection points of $DD$ and $SS'$ will trace out the locus of the curve which *is not shifting*. In Figure 16–3, part (*a*), shifts in supply trace out the shape of the demand function. In part (*b*), shifts in demand help to identify the supply function.

|||||||||||||||||||||||||||||||||||||||||||||||||||||||||||||||||||||||||||||||||||||||||||||||||||||||||||||||||||||||||||||||||||

*Interpretive note.*   The reader should satisfy himself that there is no increase in identification of either curve if both shift at the same time due to changes in the same factor. The resulting scatter of observations about a grid of intersection points does not distinguish either the demand or supply curves.

|||||||||||||||||||||||||||||||||||||||||||||||||||||||||||||||||||||||||||||||||||||||||||||||||||||||||||||||||||||||||||||||||||

Depending on the size of the relative shifts and the number of observations, the parameters of the relatively stable relation can be estimated to a high degree of approximation.

**FIGURE 16-3**
**Shifting demand or supply functions**

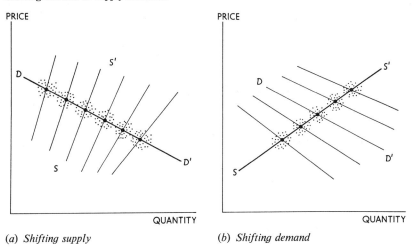

(a) *Shifting supply*                 (b) *Shifting demand*

## An algebraic example of the identifiability problem

The notion of identifiability of a function due to shifts in another function involving the same endogenous variables but a different exogenous factor can also be demonstrated algebraically. Consider the same two relations as before, written now with $P$ normalized in both equations,

$$\text{Demand:} \quad P = \gamma_1 + \beta_1 Q + \varepsilon_1{}^*.$$
$$\text{Supply:} \quad P = \gamma_2 + \beta_2 Q + \varepsilon_2{}^*.$$

The equations look identical except for different parameters and different interpretations according to the labels, demand and supply.

Converting to deviation form for simplicity, the equations are, $p - \beta_1 q = \varepsilon_1$ and $p - \beta_2 q = \varepsilon_2$ where lowercase symbols denote deviations of price and quantity based on $T$ observations, and $\varepsilon_1$ and $\varepsilon_2$ represent deviations of $\varepsilon_1{}^*$ and $\varepsilon_2{}^*$. Using Cramer's rule, we solve for $p$ and $q$ in the reduced form of this system of two equations. The results are shown to be,

$$p = \begin{vmatrix} \varepsilon_1 & -\beta_1 \\ \varepsilon_2 & -\beta_2 \end{vmatrix} \Big/ \begin{vmatrix} 1 & -\beta_1 \\ 1 & -\beta_2 \end{vmatrix} = (\beta_1 \varepsilon_2 - \beta_2 \varepsilon_1)/(\beta_1 - \beta_2)$$

and

$$q = \begin{vmatrix} 1 & \varepsilon_1 \\ 1 & \varepsilon_2 \end{vmatrix} \Big/ \begin{vmatrix} 1 & -\beta_1 \\ 1 & -\beta_2 \end{vmatrix} = (\varepsilon_2 - \varepsilon_1)/(\beta_1 - \beta_2).$$

If ordinary least squares were used to regress $p$ on $q$, the resulting estimator, say $b$, would be $b = \sum pq / \sum q^2$. Making substitutions for $p$ and $q$ from the reduced form solutions, this estimator can be written,[7]

$$b = \sum \frac{(\beta_1 \varepsilon_2 - \beta_2 \varepsilon_1)(\varepsilon_2 - \varepsilon_1)}{(\beta_1 - \beta_2)^2} \Big/ \sum \frac{\varepsilon_2 - \varepsilon_1{}^2}{(\beta_1 - \beta_2)^2} \quad \text{(by substitution)}$$

$$b = \frac{\sum (\beta_1 \varepsilon_2{}^2 - \beta_1 \varepsilon_1 \varepsilon_2 - \beta_2 \varepsilon_1 \varepsilon_2 + \beta_2 \varepsilon_1{}^2)}{\sum (\varepsilon_2{}^2 - 2\varepsilon_1 \varepsilon_2 + \varepsilon_1{}^2)}. \quad \text{(by simplification)}$$

Now we recognize that

$$\frac{\sum \varepsilon_1{}^2}{T-1} = V(\varepsilon_1{}^*) = \sigma_1{}^2, \qquad \frac{\sum \varepsilon_2{}^2}{T-1} = V(\varepsilon_2{}^*) = \sigma_2{}^2,$$

and

$$\frac{\sum (\varepsilon_1 \varepsilon_2)}{T-1} = Cov(\varepsilon_1{}^* \varepsilon_2{}^*) = \sigma_{12}.$$

Also $\rho_{12} = \sigma_{12}/\sigma_1 \sigma_2$, so $\sigma_{12}$ can be expressed as $\sigma_{12} = \rho_{12} \sigma_1 \sigma_2$ where $\rho_{12}$ is the correlation coefficient between $\varepsilon_1{}^*$ and $\varepsilon_2{}^*$. By dividing numerator and denominator by $(T-1)$ and making these substitutions, the resulting expression for the least squares estimator can be written,

$$b = [\beta_1 \sigma_2{}^2 - (\beta_1 + \beta_2)\rho_{12} \sigma_1 \sigma_2 + \beta_2 \sigma_1{}^2]/(\sigma_2{}^2 - 2\rho_{12}\sigma_1\sigma_2 + \sigma_1{}^2). \quad (16\text{–}3)$$

In this situation $\sigma_1{}^2$ is a measure of the variability of disturbances about the true average demand curve. The case of $\sigma_1 = 0$ could be interpreted as a situation in which demand does not shift. Similarly, if the supply curve does not shift, then $\sigma_2 = 0$.

Applying this interpretation to equation (16–3), then a case where demand is not shifting gives $\sigma_1 = 0$ and thus, $b = \beta_1 \sigma_2{}^2 / \sigma_2{}^2 = \beta_1$. The regression of $p$ with $q$ gives the slope of the nonshifting demand function. If demand is shifting and supply is stable, then $\sigma_2 = 0$ and by (16–3), $b = \beta_2 \sigma_1{}^2 / \sigma_1{}^2 = \beta_2$. In this case, the regression of $p$ with $q$ gives the slope of the nonshifting supply function.

In reality, neither case usually applies as both demand and supply are shifting over the observation period so that estimation of a simple single equation model will provide estimates of neither the slope of the demand curve nor the slope of the supply curve, but rather, the slope of some irrelevant line in between.

---

[7] The observation subscripts on $\varepsilon_1$ and $\varepsilon_2$ are omitted for simplicity, but the sums are over all $t = 1, 2, \ldots, T$ disturbance observations.

## 16.6 A MORE FORMAL SUMMARY PRESENTATION OF THESE SIMULTANEITY PROBLEMS

Two problems associated with estimation of parameters in simultaneous equations models are given in this chapter. One is the loss of the properties of unbiasedness and consistency for ordinary least squares estimation of parameters in a single equation of a simultaneous equations model. The second is the inability to distinguish between parameters relating variables that are involved in more than one equation in opposite cause and effect positions.

The approach in the explanation has been intuitive with some simple geometrical and algebraic examples. To summarize the simultaneity problem, it is worthwhile to use a somewhat more formal, but not rigorous, explanation.

### The maximum likelihood approach

In a simple model, an appealing approach to estimation is to assume that the most probable sample is observed and that the usual simplifying assumptions apply. Then, the distribution of the endogenous variable can be inferred from,

$$q(Y_t) = J\left(\frac{\varepsilon_t}{Y_t}\right) p(\varepsilon_t)$$

(see *Review* 6.2, item 3), and the likelihood function for the parameters can be formed and maximized. In the simple model, $J\left(\frac{\varepsilon_t}{Y_t}\right) = \left|\frac{d\varepsilon}{dY}\right| = 1$, and the maximum likelihood estimators were the same as the ordinary least squares estimators.

In the simultaneous equations model, the same approach could be used to obtain a joint probability function for the endogenous variables ($Y_{1t}$, $Y_{2t}$, ..., $Y_{Gt}$)$' = Y'_{.t}$ based on the Jacobian, $J\left(\frac{\varepsilon_{it}}{Y_{it}}\right)$, $i = 1, 2, \ldots, G$ and a given $t$, and on the joint PDF for the disturbance terms, $\varepsilon'_{.t} = (\varepsilon_{1t}, \varepsilon_{2t}', \ldots, \varepsilon_{Gt})'$. From the joint PDF for the observations $Y$,

$$q(Y_{.1}, Y_{.2}, \ldots, Y_{.T} | X) = \left[J\left(\frac{\varepsilon_{it}}{Y_{it}}\right)\right]^T p(\varepsilon_{.1}) p(\varepsilon_2) \cdot \ldots \cdot p(\varepsilon_T) \quad (16\text{--}4)$$

the likelihood function can be formed and maximized. The right-hand side involves only parameters being estimated, observable values of variables in the Jacobian, and the probability distribution of the disturbances which is specified in the assumptions as part of the background conditions for the model.

If ordinary least squares is applied to one equation separately drawn from the simultaneous equations model, the immediate problem is that the Jacobian is being ignored, but $J(\varepsilon_i/Y_i)$ is not unity in this case as it is in the single equation model.[8] For example, compare $J(\varepsilon/Y_1)$ for the single equation

---

[8] The observation subscript $t$ has been dropped for simplicity in this paragraph.

demand function, $Y_1 = \gamma_1 + \gamma_2 X_2 + \gamma_3 P + \varepsilon$ where $Y_1$ is the endogenous quantity with $J(\varepsilon_i/Y_i)$ for the simultaneous equation demand and supply functions,

$$Y_1 = \beta_1 Y_2 + \gamma_1 + \gamma_2 X_2 + \varepsilon_1,$$
$$Y_2 = \beta_2 Y_1 + \gamma_3 X_3 + \gamma_4 + \varepsilon_2,$$

where $Y_2$ is the jointly endogenous price. In the single equation case,

$$J\left(\frac{\varepsilon}{Y_1}\right) = \left|\frac{d\varepsilon}{dY_1}\right| = |1| = 1.0.$$

In the two-equation case,

$$J\left(\frac{\varepsilon_i}{Y_i}\right) = \begin{vmatrix} \dfrac{\partial \varepsilon_1}{\partial Y_1} & \dfrac{\partial \varepsilon_1}{\partial Y_2} \\ \dfrac{\partial \varepsilon_2}{\partial Y_1} & \dfrac{\partial \varepsilon_2}{\partial Y_2} \end{vmatrix} = \begin{vmatrix} 1 & -\beta_1 \\ -\beta_2 & 1 \end{vmatrix} = (1 - \beta_1\beta_2).$$

## The oversights of ordinary least squares

The procedure of using OLS separately on each equation in a simultaneous equations model is deficient because it—

1.  Does not allow parameters of one equation to influence the estimation of parameters in another equation;
2.  Does not allow the covariances $Cov(\varepsilon_{it}, \varepsilon_{gt})$ to influence the estimation of the parameters; and
3.  Estimates the variances, $V(\varepsilon_i)$, one at a time without involving the other disturbances.

Consequently, ordinary least squares estimates are no longer the same as maximum likelihood estimators of parameters in a simultaneous equations model. They are biased, and they do *not* have the desirable property of consistency.

## A general statement on identifiability

Turning now to the problem of identification of a single equation in a simultaneous equations model, let the general $i$th equation of the structural form be represented as

$$\beta_{i1} Y_{1t} + \beta_{i2} Y_{2t} + \cdots + (1) Y_{it} + \cdots + \beta_{iG} Y_{Gt}$$
$$+ \gamma_{i1}(1) + \gamma_{i2} X_{2t} + \cdots + \gamma_{iK} X_{Kt} = \varepsilon_{it}$$

where the joint endogenous variables are denoted with $Y$'s, the predetermined variables by $X$'s, the disturbance term by $\varepsilon$, and the parameters by $\beta$'s and $\gamma$'s.

This notation is convenient since the $i$th row of the Jacobian for the general simultaneous equation system is then

$$\left(\frac{\partial \varepsilon_{it}}{\partial Y_{1t}} \quad \frac{\partial \varepsilon_{it}}{\partial Y_{2t}} \quad \cdots \quad \frac{\partial \varepsilon_{it}}{\partial Y_{Gt}}\right)$$

which is the same as the row vector of coefficients of the endogenous variables, $(\beta_{i1} \quad \beta_{i2} \quad \cdots \quad \beta_{iG})$.

In the case where all the structural equations are linear (the only case considered in this book) and each is normalized so that the coefficient $\beta_{ii}$ is always 1.0, the total Jacobian is easily obtained. Using the above result for each row, then

$$J\left(\frac{\varepsilon_{it}}{Y_{it}}\right) = \begin{vmatrix} 1 & \beta_{12} & \beta_{13} & \cdots & \beta_{1G} \\ \beta_{21} & 1 & \beta_{23} & \cdots & \beta_{2G} \\ \cdot & \cdot & & \cdot \\ \cdot & \cdot & & \cdot \\ \cdot & \cdot & & \cdot \\ \beta_{G1} & \beta_{G2} & \beta_{G3} & \cdots & 1 \end{vmatrix} = \underset{(G \times G)}{|\beta|},$$

where $\beta$ is the matrix of coefficients of the $G$ endogenous variables in all $G$ equations.

The relevance of all this becomes apparent upon encountering the following result which is not proven here. Any structural equation is identifiable if and only if knowledge of its coefficients is implied by knowledge of the parameters of the joint distribution function (16–4) of the observations. For this, one necessary condition is that the Jacobian $J(\varepsilon_{it}/Y_{it}) \neq 0$, so that equation (16–4) is not trivial. Further, this complete set of parameters of the likelihood function is equivalent to the parameters of the reduced form derived from the structural form,[9] namely the reduced form coefficients of predetermined variables (to be denoted by $\pi_{ik}$) and the variance-covariances of reduced form disturbances [to be denoted by $V\text{-}Cov(v)$]. The result can be more simply stated in the following way: a structural equation is identifiable if knowledge of its parameters can be deduced from knowledge of the reduced form parameters. The Jacobian of the transformation from the structural to the reduced form parameters is very useful in recognizing this condition. (See *Review* 16.2, item 3, and Exercise R.2.)

## The next step

Some other conditions for identifiability are examined in the next chapter as we return to less formal and more practical aspects of the question of identification of structural form equations. Here, only the meaning of the

---

[9] See T. C. Koopmans and W. C. Hood, "The Estimation of Simultaneous Linear Economic Relationships," *Studies in Econometric Method* (New York: John Wiley & Sons, Inc., 1953), chap. 6.

term and its consequences for estimation of parameters in a simultaneous equations system have been considered. The next step is to examine some rules for determining if an equation is identified. Then, some estimating procedures must be developed to substitute for ordinary least squares so that consistent estimators may be determined of the parameters in these equations when they are identified.

## NEW VOCABULARY

| | |
|---|---|
| Reduced form | Structural form |
| Simultaneity | Independent noncontemporaneous disturbances |
| Joint endogenous variables | Haavelmo's proposition |
| Stochastic equation | Two-way causal relation |
| Identity equation | Identifiability |

## REFERENCES

For examination of the Haavelmo bias in simultaneous equations models, see: Bronfenbrenner, J. "Sources and Size of Least-Squares Bias in a Two-Equation Model," chap. 9. Edited by Wm. C. Hood and T. C. Koopmans. *Studies in Econometric Method.* New York: John Wiley & Sons, Inc., 1953.

For the classic explanation of identifiability, see T. C. Koopmans, "Identification Problems in Economic Model Construction," chap. 2 in *Studies in Econometric Method* (see above reference). This paper is recommended reading for all students and is applicable to both Chapters 16 and 17.

## EXERCISES

1. Draw a diagram of a supply and demand function in the price-quantity co-ordinates. Let each curve shift to four different positions. Suppose observations of price and quantity are obtained throughout all these shifts. Indicate what your scatter diagram might look like and explain the problem in estimating either the demand or the supply curve.

2. Given a constant $k$ and a random variable $Y$ with mean $\bar{Y}$, show:
   *a)* $m_{kY} = 0$.
   *b)* $m_{kY, Y} = km_{YY}$.

3. Draw your own diagram similar to Figure 16–1 illustrating Haavelmo's proposition for *each* of the following situations and comment on the size of the bias in estimating the slope and the intercept.
   *a)* The size of the disturbances is much larger, say $\pm 3\theta$.
   *b)* The range in values of autonomous $Z$ observed is very small.
   *c)* The range observed in values of $Z$ is very large, *and* the size of the disturbances is very small.

4. Use the data of Exercise 22, Chapter 7, and ordinary least squares to estimate the slope in the relation,

$$Q_t = \gamma_1 + \beta P_t + \varepsilon_t.$$

Then, find the OLS estimate of $(1/\beta)$ as the slope of the relation,

$$P_t = (-\gamma_1/\beta) + (1/\beta)Q_t + \varepsilon_t.$$

Explain why $1/(\text{Est. } \beta) \neq \text{Est. } (1/\beta)$.

5. For the consumption-income model, (16–2) in Section 16.1, rewrite Assumptions 1, 2–5, 8, and 9 in detail and explain their meaning in this model.

6. Explain the underlying economic meaning of Assumptions 1, 4, 5, 7, 8, and 9 in terms of the demand-supply model (16–1).

7. Present an argument why Assumptions 8 and 9 of Section 16.3 logically imply that Assumption 5 holds.

8. For the simple model, $C = \gamma_1 + \beta Y$ and $Y = C + Z$, suppose $Y = 500$ and $Z = 100$, and let there be an increased government expenditure of 20 represented by a change in $Z$. Find the difference in the resulting change in income $Y$ due to this government action based on an estimated MPC of 0.9 compared to the actual MPC of 0.75.

   Give one carefully explained reason why a MPC might be overestimated.

9. Review the models in the exercises at the end of Chapter 3 and suggest which ones may have a simultaneity problem. Discuss the nature of the problem and its effects on the meaning of the estimates for the parameters. Also, present an alternate simultaneous equations model which you think better represents the economic relations under analysis.

*Chapter*
*17*

# IDENTIFIABILITY RULES AND INDIRECT LEAST SQUARES ESTIMATION

## 17.1 PREVIEW

Many different structural forms could be specified for a simultaneous equations model. In order to estimate and analyze any specification though, the econometrician may disregard many structural forms in which the key parameters in the crucial equations are not identifiable. Much effort can be wasted in estimating and analyzing the results of a simultaneous equations model if the important relations are not identified because the conclusions based on the numerical results are ambiguous. Therefore, it is usually good practice in specifying a simultaneous equations model to follow some guidelines that are necessary for identifiability.

As indicated in the previous chapter, these conditions are those that guarantee the existence of a solution for the structural form parameters in terms of the reduced form parameters. For completeness, the parameter set of the structural form (SF) includes all its coefficients ($\beta$'s and $\gamma$'s) and the elements of the variance-covariance matrix of structural form disturbances. The parameters of the reduced form (RF) are all its coefficients ($\pi$'s) and the elements of the variance-covariance matrix of reduced form disturbances. For any structural form, with a nonsingular coefficient matrix $\underset{(G \times G)}{\beta}$, there exists a derived solution for the RF parameters in terms of the original SF parameters. However, several structural forms may be transformed into the same reduced form. The model is identified only if its particular SF parameters can be derived from the RF parameters. if two or more values of the same parameters can be derived, then the model is over identified.

Mathematically, several types of restrictions on the structural form parameters help to establish identifiability.[1] Occasionally, a priori values for a parameter or equalities between parameters may be specified as restrictions, such as $\beta_{23} = 1.6$ or $\beta_{12} = \beta_{13}$. Also, linear relations among parameters from different equations may be specified, such as $\beta_{12} + \beta_{24} - 3\gamma_{21} = 4$.

||||||||||||||||||||||||||||||||||||||||||||||||||||||||||||||||||||||||||||||||||||||||||||||||||||||||||||||||||

*Explicative note.* In a general notation, the coefficients in SF equations have two subscripts. The first indicates the equation number. The second identifies the number of the associated endogenous (for $\beta$'s) or predetermined (for $\gamma$'s) variable.

||||||||||||||||||||||||||||||||||||||||||||||||||||||||||||||||||||||||||||||||||||||||||||||||||||||||||||||||||

Finally, special assumptions concerning the elements of the variance-covariance matrix of SF disturbance terms can serve as restrictions on the set of parameters so that the system is identifiable.

---

[1] See F. M. Fisher, *The Identification Problem in Econometrics* (New York: McGraw-Hill Book Co., 1966), for a thorough treatment of these restrictions.

|||||||||||||||||||||||||||||||||||||||||||||||||||||||||||||||||||||||||||||||||||||||||||||||||||||||||||||||||||||||||||||||||||||||||||

***Discursive note.*** Nonlinear relations among parameters can also help to remove unidentifiability, although these may be too difficult to manipulate. Inequalities of the type, $\beta_{12} > 0$ or $\beta_{23} \leq 0$, or even $\gamma_{12} \geq \gamma_{13}$, are usually not restrictive enough to help in the unambiguous solution of a SF in terms of the RF parameters.

|||||||||||||||||||||||||||||||||||||||||||||||||||||||||||||||||||||||||||||||||||||||||||||||||||||||||||||||||||||||||||||||||||||||||||

However, in the simplest case, and throughout the presentation in this chapter of the so-called *rank* and *order conditions* of identifiability, the only type of restriction allowed is the zero-type—(exclusion) restriction. This type restriction imposes a condition on a given equation in the model such that a variable is excluded from that equation. The restriction is formulated by specifying a zero value for the coefficient of that variable in the particular equation.

Using only zero-type restrictions, certain counting rules and guidelines for the specification of the model are determinable so that the equations in the model may be identifiable. Such rules are derived in Sections 17.3 and 17.4 of this chapter with examples of their use on two simple models.

In the remaining sections of the chapter, the question of how to estimate the identifiable parameters in a model is confronted. The applicability of OLS in a special situation of a recursive model is the topic of Section 17.5.

In the case of exact identifiability, a new method called *indirect least squares* (ILS) is shown to be effective. In Section 17.6, the theoretical formulation of ILS is given. An algebraic example of its use is presented in Section 17.7 with a numerical solution for the example model based on a given set of data. Throughout the entire chapter, the emphasis is on the practical use of both the rules for identifiability and the estimation method of indirect least squares.

However, some mathematical considerations cannot be bypassed in seeking an understanding of these topics and in preparing for any further study and use of them.

### 17.2 REVIEW

The presentation in this chapter requires some new notation with the use of double subscripts as well as the repeated use of topics of matrix algebra. In particular, the reader should review the following concepts, definitions, or operations.

### 1 Necessary and sufficient conditions

Let $A_1$ and $A_2$ represent two propositions. Then the mathematical statement, "$A_1$ holds if and only if $A_2$ holds," is composed of two statements. First, the statement "$A_1$ holds only if $A_2$ holds," reflects the *necessary* condition for $A_1$. It can be shortened for simplicity in the form, "If $A_1$, then $A_2$," and represented by $A_1 \Rightarrow A_2$. The proposition that $A_1$ holds necessarily implies that $A_2$ holds as a precondition.

||||||||||||||||||||||||||||||||||||||||||||||||||||||||||||||||||||||||||||||||||||||||||||||||||||||||||||||||||||||||||||||||||||||||||||||||

*Interpretive note.* Let $A_1$ be the proposition that "Tom is Judy's brother" and let $A_2$ be the proposition that "Judy is Tom's sister." If $A_1$ holds, then $A_2$ is necessarily true also.

||||||||||||||||||||||||||||||||||||||||||||||||||||||||||||||||||||||||||||||||||||||||||||||||||||||||||||||||||||||||||||||||||||||||||||||||

The second part of the statement reflects the *sufficient* condition for $A_1$; namely, "$A_1$ holds if $A_2$ holds." Symbolically, this is represented as the reverse implication of the former statement, $A_1 \Leftarrow A_2$ and is given in short form by, "If $A_2$, then $A_1$."
The fact that $A_2$ holds is sufficient evidence that $A_1$ holds also.

||||||||||||||||||||||||||||||||||||||||||||||||||||||||||||||||||||||||||||||||||||||||||||||||||||||||||||||||||||||||||||||||||||||||||||||||

*Recursive note.* As in the previous example, the implication is obvious. The truth of the statement that "Judy is Tom's sister" is sufficient to guarantee that "Tom is Judy's brother."

||||||||||||||||||||||||||||||||||||||||||||||||||||||||||||||||||||||||||||||||||||||||||||||||||||||||||||||||||||||||||||||||||||||||||||||||

To illustrate a necessary but not sufficient relation, let proposition $D_1$ be "The man jumped off a bridge," and let proposition $D_2$ be, "A bridge exists." Then it is *incorrect* to state that, "$D_1$ holds if and only if $D_2$ holds." $D_2$ is a necessary condition for $D_1$ but not sufficient. That is, if a man jumped off a bridge, then it is necessary that a bridge existed from which he jumped. However, the fact that a bridge existed is not sufficient evidence to know that a man jumped off a bridge.

## 2 Echelon form of a matrix

A matrix may be reduced to echelon form by applying row and column transformations. (See *Review* 12.2, item 1.) A matrix in echelon form has all zero elements except for some unit elements in the diagonal $(i\,i)$ positions. The number of these unit elements on the diagonal indicates the number of linearly independent columns which is the rank of the original, equivalent matrix.

For example consider a matrix,

$$A = \begin{pmatrix} 1 & B_3 & 0 & \gamma_2 & 0 \\ B_5 & 0 & 1 & 0 & 0 \\ 0 & 0 & 1 & 0 & \gamma_4 \\ 1 & 0 & 0 & 0 & 0 \end{pmatrix}.$$

Applying the following sequence of transformations:

$R_{14}$, interchange rows 1 and 4;

$(-B_5)$ $R_{12}$, multiply row 1 by $(-B_5)$ and add it to row 2; and

$(-1)$ $R_{14}$, multiply row 1 by $(-1)$ and add it to row 4,

we obtain,

$$A^I = \begin{pmatrix} 1 & 0 & 0 & 0 & 0 \\ 0 & 0 & 1 & 0 & 0 \\ 0 & 0 & 1 & 0 & \gamma_4 \\ 0 & B_3 & 0 & \gamma_2 & 0 \end{pmatrix}.$$

Then, apply the transformations:

$(-1)$ $R_{23}$, multiply row 2 by $(-1)$ and add it to row 3;

$(-1/\gamma_4)$ $R_3$, multiply row 3 by $(1/\gamma_4)$; and

$R_{23}$, interchange rows 2 and 3 to obtain

$$A^{II} = \begin{pmatrix} 1 & 0 & 0 & 0 & 0 \\ 0 & 0 & 0 & 0 & 1 \\ 0 & 0 & 1 & 0 & 0 \\ 0 & B_3 & 0 & \gamma_2 & 0 \end{pmatrix}$$

Finally, apply the transformations:

$(1/B_3)R_4$, multiply row 4 by $(1/B_3)$;

$(-1)C_{24}$, multiply column 2 by $(-1)$ and add it to column 4;

and column and row interchanges $C_{45}$, $R_{24}$, to obtain

$$A^{III} = \begin{pmatrix} 1 & 0 & 0 & 0 & 0 \\ 0 & 1 & 0 & 0 & 0 \\ 0 & 0 & 1 & 0 & 0 \\ 0 & 0 & 0 & 1 & 0 \end{pmatrix}.$$

Clearly, $A^{III}$ has four linearly independent columns and has rank equal to four.

### 3 Solutions for linear homogeneous equation systems

A set of equations of the form

$$\underset{(n \times g)}{A} \underset{(g \times 1)}{Z} = \underset{(n \times 1)}{O}$$

with $g$ unknowns in $n$ equations is called a set of linear homogeneous equations.

III

**Discursive note.** If the unknowns appear in terms of order two or greater, the equations are nonlinear. If the right-hand side vector has nonzero elements, the equations are nonhomogeneous.

IIIIIIIIIIIIIIIIIIIIIIIIIIIIIIIIIIIIIIIIIIIIIIIIIIIIIIIIIIIIIIIIIIIIIIIIIIIIIIIIIIIIIIIIIIIIIIIIIIIIIIIIIIIIIIIIIIIIIIIIIIIIIIIIIIIIIIIIIIIIIIIIIIIIIIIIIII

A nontrivial solution for $Z$ exists ($Z \neq 0$) only if the number of linearly independent columns of $A$ is less than $g$ by the definition of linear independence (see *Review* 10.2, item 4). If the rank of $A$ is $g$, then there is no nonzero vector $Z$ which will satisfy the equations.

If the rank of $A$ is less than $g$, say $g - q$, then a solution exists whereby some $g - q$ of the unknown elements of $Z$ may be solved in terms of the other $q$ elements.

For example, consider these simple two equation systems.

*Example (a)*:

$$\begin{pmatrix} 1 & 2 \\ 3 & 4 \end{pmatrix} \begin{pmatrix} Z_1 \\ Z_2 \end{pmatrix} = \begin{pmatrix} 0 \\ 0 \end{pmatrix} \quad \text{with} \quad n = 2, q = 2$$

In this example, the rank of $A$ is equal to $q = 2$. From the first equation, $Z_1 = -2Z_2$, and from the second equation, $3Z_1 = -4Z_2$. Both these equations hold only if $Z_1 = Z_2 = 0$, a trivial solution.

*Example (b)*:

$$\begin{pmatrix} 1 & 2 & 2 \\ 3 & 4 & 8 \end{pmatrix} \begin{pmatrix} Z_1 \\ Z_2 \\ Z_3 \end{pmatrix} = \begin{pmatrix} 0 \\ 0 \end{pmatrix} \quad \text{with} \quad n = 2, g = 3.$$

In this example, the rank of $A$ is still equal to two $= g - 1$ since the matrix $A = \begin{pmatrix} 1 & 2 & 2 \\ 3 & 4 & 8 \end{pmatrix}$ is equivalent to the echelon form of this matrix, $\begin{pmatrix} 1 & 0 & 0 \\ 0 & 1 & 0 \end{pmatrix}$. (The reader can show this in Exercise R.1 following this section.)

A solution exists for $Z_1$ and $Z_2$ in terms of $Z_3$. For example if $Z_3 = 1$, then $Z_1 = -4$ and $Z_2 = 1$ gives the equations $1(-4) + 2(1) + 2(1) = 0$ and $3(-4) + 4(1) + 8(1) = 0$.

## 4 A characteristic of matrix multiplication

Suppose a matrix multiplication is defined as

$$\underset{(m \times h)}{A} \underset{(h \times n)}{B} = \underset{(m \times n)}{E}.$$

(See *Review* 9.2, item 2e.) If the rows of $A$ and $E$ are denoted by $A_i$. and $E_i$. respectively, $i = 1, 2, \ldots, m$, then the multiplication $(A_i.)B$ results in the row, $E_i.$. If the columns of $B$ and $E$ are denoted by $B_{.j}$ and $E_{.j}$, then the multiplication $A(B_{.j})$ results in the column $E_{.j}$.

## REVIEW EXERCISES

R.1.    Reduce the matrix $A = \begin{pmatrix} 1 & 2 & 2 \\ 3 & 4 & 8 \end{pmatrix}$ to echelon form.

R.2.    Reduce the matrix $A = \begin{pmatrix} B_1 & 1 & \gamma_1 & 0 & \gamma_2 \\ 1 & B_2 & \gamma_3 & \gamma_4 & 0 \\ 1 & 1 & 0 & 0 & 0 \end{pmatrix}$ to echelon form.

R.3.    Give a sufficient condition for a value of $X$ to satisfy each of the following equations. Also state if this is a necessary condition and explain.

*a)*    $X + 2 = 5$ (when $X = ?$)
        (if $X = ?$, does "only if" statement apply?)

*b)*    $X^2 + 2 = 11$.

*c)*    $\sin X = 1.0$.

*d)*    $X \times 2 = X \times 5$.

R.4.    Given the set of $n$ linear homogeneous equations in $g$ unknowns defined by $AZ = O$ where

$$A = \begin{pmatrix} 1 & 2 & 2 & 2 \\ 3 & 4 & 8 & 6 \end{pmatrix}, \quad Z' = (Z_1, Z_2, Z_3, Z_4), \quad \text{and} \quad O' = (0, 0),$$

*a)*    Show that the rank of $A$ is $2 = g - 2$.

*b)*    Find a general solution for $Z_1$ and $Z_2$ in terms of $Z_3$ and $Z_4$.

*c)*    Find a specific solution for $Z_1$ and $Z_2$ if $Z_3 = 1$ and $Z_4 = -2$.

## 17.3 FORMULATION OF THE RANK AND ORDER CONDITIONS OF IDENTIFIABILITY

In many activities, it is very useful to know the set of rules which apply. For example, driving a car would be a very chaotic experience if there were no rules or guidelines for all the drivers. Also, playing a game of cards, checkers, or chess would be a frustrating and mostly useless exercise if there were no rules governing the play. Even when there are driving regulations and even when the rules of a game are known, the experience may still be chaotic and frustrating. Merely having the rules does not guarantee "success," but without any rules, the activity is almost hopeless.

Similarly, in building an econometric model with two or more simultaneous relations, some rules or guidelines for specifying an identifiable model are useful to avoid a meaningless or frustrating experience. Although following the rules does not guarantee that the model will be a "success," ignoring the rules can only lead to difficulties.

The common rules that are applicable when only zero-type (exclusion) restrictions are specified for the model are the common rank and order conditions.[2] The names refer to the key measures of a matrix involved in the rule where rank refers to the number of linearly independent rows or columns and order refers to simply the number of rows or columns of the matrix.

---

[2] These are derived in T. C. Koopmans, H. Rubin, and R. B. Leipnik, "Measuring the Equation Systems of Dynamic Economics," in T. C. Koopmans (ed.), *Statistical Inference in Dynamic Economic Models* (New York: John Wiley & Sons, Inc., 1950), chap. 2.

## New notation for the SF and RF coefficients

Consider the general form of the $i$th equation in a simultaneous equations model of $G$ equations with $G$ endogenous variables and $K$ predetermined variables. Further, consider that some endogenous variables and some predetermined variables which appear in the system of equations are not included in equation $i$.

||||||||||||||||||||||||||||||||||||||||||||||||||||||||||||||||||||||||||||||||||||||||||||||||||||||||||||||||||||||||||||||||||||||||||||||||||||||||||||||||||||||||||||||||

*Discursive note.* Indeed, no one equation in the system can contain all the variables in the model or the model would not be identified. Identification of a model requires that no equation in the model could be written as a linear combination of any of the other equations.

||||||||||||||||||||||||||||||||||||||||||||||||||||||||||||||||||||||||||||||||||||||||||||||||||||||||||||||||||||||||||||||||||||||||||||||||||||||||||||||||||||||||||||||||

The number of each type variable that is included or excluded from equation $i$ is denoted by symbols $g$, $h$, $m$, and $n$ as illustrated in Table 17–1.

**TABLE 17–1**

**Symbols denoting the number of separate variable types in equation $i$**

|  | Endogenous variables | Predetermined variables |
|---|---|---|
| Number included......... $g$ | | $m$ |
| Number excluded......... $h$ | | $n$ |
| Total number ......... $G$ | | $K$ |

Using this notation of Table 17–1, and assuming that equation $i$ is normalized so the coefficient for the $i$th endogenous variable is unity, ($\beta_{ii} = 1.0$), and setting $X_{it} = 1$ for all $t$ so that $\gamma_{i1}$ represents the intercept, and reordering the two types of variables so that within each type those with nonzero coefficients are listed first, the $i$th equation is denoted as

$$\beta_{i1} Y_{1t} + \beta_{i2} Y_{2t} + \cdots + (1) Y_{it} + \cdots + \beta_{ig} Y_{gt}$$
$$+ (0) Y_{g+1, t} + \cdots + (0) Y_{Gt} + \gamma_{i1}(1) + \gamma_{i2} X_{2t}$$
$$+ \cdots + \gamma_{im} X_{mt} + (0) X_{m+1, t} + \cdots + (0) X_{Kt} = \varepsilon_{it}. \qquad (17-1)$$

This equation includes $g$ endogenous variables including the normalized one and excludes $h = G - g$ endogenous variables by specifying their coefficients to be zero. Similarly, it includes $m$ and excludes $n = K - m$ predetermined variables.

Equation (17–1) can be conveniently written in matrix form for all $t$ observations by partitioning the vectors and matrices into two parts corresponding to the elements relevant to the variables included (IN) and to the elements relevant to the variables that are excluded (EX). The complete description of the *i*th equation is then given by,

$$
\left.
\begin{array}{ll}
\underset{(1 \times G)}{\beta_i'} = [\ \underset{(1 \times g)}{\beta_{IN}'} \quad \underset{(1 \times h)}{\beta_{EX}'}\ ] & \underset{(1 \times K)}{\Gamma_i'} = [\ \underset{(1 \times m)}{\Gamma_{IN}'} \quad \underset{(1 \times n)}{\Gamma_{EX}'}\ ] \\[2em]
\underset{(G \times T)}{Y'} = \begin{bmatrix} \underset{(g \times T)}{Y_{IN}'} \\[1em] \underset{(h \times T)}{Y_{EX}'} \end{bmatrix} & \underset{(K \times T)}{X'} = \begin{bmatrix} \underset{(m \times T)}{X_{IN}'} \\[1em] \underset{(n \times T)}{X_{EX}'} \end{bmatrix} \\[3em]
\multicolumn{2}{c}{\beta_i'\,Y' + \Gamma_i'\,X' = \underset{(1 \times T)}{\varepsilon_i'}}
\end{array}
\right\}
\qquad (17\text{-}2.
$$

This *i*th equation (17-2) represents any one of *G* equations in the model)

$$
\underset{(G \times G)}{\beta'} \ \underset{(G \times T)}{Y'} + \underset{(G \times K)}{\Gamma'} \ \underset{(K \times T)}{X'} = \underset{(G \times T)}{\varepsilon'} \ . \qquad (17\text{-}3)
$$

||||||||||||||||||||||||||||||||||||||||||||||||||||||||||||||||||||||||||||||||||||||||||||||||||||||||||||||||||||||||||

***Interpretive note.*** The order of the subscripts here differs from that for the single equation model. In representing and interpreting the simultaneous equations model, it is convenient to use the second subscript for the observation index. In this way, the coefficients in any equation *i* are simply read as those in the row *i* of the coefficient matrices. This simplicity is achieved at the cost of transposing each matrix from those commonly used in representing a single equation model. See Section 2.5 for the first mention of this difference.

||||||||||||||||||||||||||||||||||||||||||||||||||||||||||||||||||||||||||||||||||||||||||||||||||||||||||||||||||||||||||

Given the structural form of a model as in (17-3), the solution for the reduced form can be found (if the inverse of $\beta'$ exists) by premultiplying both sides of the equation by $(\beta')^{-1}$.

||||||||||||||||||||||||||||||||||||||||||||||||||||||||||||||||||||||||||||||||||||||||||||||||||||||||||||||||||||||||||

***Recursive note.*** The inverse cannot exist if the determinant of $\beta'$ is zero. Since $|\beta| = J(\varepsilon_{it}/Y_{it})$, as given in Section 16.6, it is important that this Jacobian is not zero.

||||||||||||||||||||||||||||||||||||||||||||||||||||||||||||||||||||||||||||||||||||||||||||||||||||||||||||||||||||||||||

The result is,

$$
(\beta')^{-1}\beta'\,Y' + (\beta')^{-1}\Gamma'X' = (\beta')^{-1}\varepsilon'
$$

or

$$
IY = -(\beta')^{-1}\Gamma'X' + (\beta')^{-1}\varepsilon'.
$$

Defining $\underset{(G \times K)}{\Pi'} = -(\beta')^{-1}\Gamma'$ as the matrix of coefficients in the reduced form and $\underset{(G \times T)}{v'} = (\beta')^{-1}\varepsilon'$ as the matrix of disturbance terms in the reduced form, the reduced form is denoted by,

$$\underset{(G \times T)}{Y'} = \underset{(G \times K)}{\Pi'} \underset{(K \times T)}{X'} + \underset{(G \times T)}{v'} \tag{17-4}$$

In this representation, the coefficients of the $i$th reduced form equation are the elements of the $i$th row of $\Pi'$.

It is possible to obtain the specification of the $i$th row of the structural form from the reduced form simply by premultiplying the reduced form by the row vector $\beta'_i$. The details of the matrix algebra are as follows:

*a*)   Premultiply (17–4) by $\beta'_i$ to obtain

$$\beta'_i Y' = \beta'_i \Pi' X' + \beta'_i v'.$$

*b*)   Substitute for $\Pi'$ and $v'$ to obtain

$$\beta'_i Y' + \beta'_i(\beta')^{-1}\Gamma'X' = \beta_i(\beta')^{-1}\varepsilon'.$$

*c*)   Simplify (see *Review* 17.2, item 4) to get (17–2),

$$\beta'_i Y' + \Gamma'_i X' = \varepsilon'_i.$$

Thus, considering only the coefficients in the SF and the RF, it is necessarily true that

$$-\beta'_i \Pi' = \Gamma'_i. \tag{17-5}$$

From this equation relating the coefficients in structural form equation $i$ with all the coefficients in the reduced form, the rank and order conditions for identifiability can be derived.

**Rewriting the identifiability relations.** The identifiability relation (17–5), $-\beta'_i \Pi' = \Gamma'_i$, can be expressed in more detail by partitioning the matrices corresponding to the variables included and excluded. Let $\Pi'$ be partitioned as

$$\underset{(G \times K)}{\Pi'} = \begin{pmatrix} \Pi'_{gm} & \Pi'_{gn} \\ \Pi'_{hm} & \Pi'_{hn} \end{pmatrix} \tag{17-6}$$

where the subscripts serve to indicate both the number and type of variables associated with each submatrix of coefficients. Table 17–2 illustrates this notational device.

Using the partitioning of (17–2) and (17–6), the identifiability relations for coefficients in the $i$th equation of the structural form can be written,

$$-[\beta_{IN}\,\beta_{EX}]' \begin{pmatrix} \Pi'_{gm} & \Pi'_{gn} \\ \Pi'_{hm} & \Pi'_{hn} \end{pmatrix} = [\Gamma_{IN}\,\Gamma_{EX}]' \tag{17-5a}$$

Now in the $i$th equation,

$$\underset{(1 \times h)}{\beta'_{EX} = O} \qquad \text{and} \qquad \underset{(1 \times n)}{\Gamma'_{EX} = O}$$

**TABLE 17–2**

**Partitions of the reduced form coefficient matrix**

|  |  | Contains elements of the— | |
|---|---|---|---|
| Submatrix | | Rows of coefficients of the endogenous | Columns of coefficients of the predetermined |
| Symbol | Dimension | variables | variables |
| $\Pi'_{gm}$ | $g \times m$ | Included | Included |
| $\Pi'_{gn}$ | $g \times n$ | Included | Excluded |
| $\Pi'_{hm}$ | $h \times m$ | Excluded | Included |
| $\Pi'_{hn}$ | $h \times n$ | Excluded | Excluded |

(where $O$ represents a null vector of appropriate dimension) since these are coefficients of excluded variables. For the identifiability equations (17–5a) to hold, it is necessary and sufficient that the first $m$ terms on each side be identical and the last $n$ terms on each side be identical. The condition of vector equality gives the two equations,

$$-\beta'_{IN}\Pi'_{gm} + (-O\Pi'_{hm}) = \Gamma'_{IN} \quad \text{and} \quad -\beta'_{IN}\Pi'_{gn} + (-O\Pi'_{hn}) = O,$$

or simplifying,

$$-\beta'_{IN}\Pi'_{gm} = \Gamma'_{IN} \quad \text{and} \quad -\beta'_{IN}\Pi'_{gn} = \underset{(1 \times n)}{O} . \quad (17\text{–}7a, b)$$

Based on this derivation, the parameters in the $i$th equation are identified if and only if the equations (17–7b) can be solved for $\beta'_{IN}$. Once a solution is obtained for $\beta'_{IN}$, then a solution $\Gamma'_{IN}$ will follow by substitution in equation (17–7a).

### Solving the identifiability relations

The $n$ equations, $\beta'_{IN}\Pi'_{gn} = \underset{(1 \times n)}{O}$ , must be examined to determine the conditions under which solutions for the $g$ components of $\beta'_{IN}$ can be obtained given the elements of $\Pi'_{gn}$. Since the right-hand side is all zeros (a set of $n$ linear homogeneous equations in $g$ unknowns), the existence of a solution depends on the rank of the matrix $\Pi'_{gn}$. (See *Review* 17.2, item 3.)

This rank cannot be greater than $g$ since the number of linearly independent rows cannot exceed the number of rows. Three possibilities for the rank of $\Pi'_{gn}$ can be distinguished.

1. If the rank of $\Pi'_{gn}$ is $g$, then the only solution to $\beta'_{IN}\Pi'_{gn} = O$ (17–7b) is the trivial solution where all $\beta'_{IN} = O$. However, not all the coefficients of endogenous variables in equation $i$ can be zero because equation $i$ must contain at least one endogenous variable, the normalized one

with $\beta_{ii} = 1.0$. Therefore, this case is ruled out by contradiction and the rank of $\Pi'_{gn}$ must be less than $g$.

2.  If the rank of $\Pi'_{gn}$ is $g - 1$, then there are only $g - 1$ linear *independent* equations in $g$ unknowns. The equations (17–7*b*) could be solved uniquely for $g - 1$ of the unknowns in terms of the remaining one. Since one unknown is normalized, $\beta_{ii} = 1.0$, it is a " known " unknown and solving for each other unknown in terms of $\beta_{ii}$ is completely satisfactory. That is, solutions of the type, $\beta_{1i}/\beta_{ii}, \ldots, \beta_{gi}/\beta_{ii}$, are fully as informative as solution values for each unknown since $\beta_{ii} = 1.0$.

3.  If the rank of $\Pi'_{gn}$ is less than $g - 1$, then an infinite number of solutions for the set of unknowns $\beta'_{\text{IN}}$ is possible depending on the arbitrary value given to at least one of them besides the value of 1.0 assigned to $\beta_{ii}$.

## The rank and order conditions

Based on the three results above, a unique solution exists for $\beta'_{\text{IN}}$, and hence for $\Gamma'_{\text{IN}}$ too, in the $i$th equation of a structural form based on know-ledge of the reduced form coefficients only in case (2). Therefore, assuming only zero-type (exclusion) restrictions, we state:

*Rank condition of identifiability.* For the exact identification of structural equation $i$, it is a *necessary and sufficient* condition mathematically that the rank of $\Pi'_{gn} = g - 1$, where $\Pi'_{gn}$ is the submatrix of reduced form coefficients of the $n$ predetermined variables (excluded from structural equation $i$) selected from $g$ reduced form equations (corresponding to the $g$ endogenous variables included in structural equation $i$).

Since $\Pi'_{gn}$ has size $g \times n$, it can only have rank $g - 1$ if it has at least $g - 1$ rows and at least $g - 1$ columns. Obviously, the number of rows $g$ exceeds $g - 1$, but the condition concerning the columns can be stated as a secondary order rule.

*Order condition for identifiability.* For the identification of structural equation $i$ including $g$ endogenous variables and excluding $n$ predetermined variables, it is a *necessary* condition that $n \geq g - 1$ so that the number of columns of $\Pi'_{gn}$ is at least as large as the required number of linearly inde-pendent columns.[3]

|||||||||||||||||||||||||||||||||||||||||||||||||||||||||||||||||||||||||||||||||||||||||||||||||||||||||||||||||||||||||||||||||||||||||||||

*Explicative note.* The order condition is not sufficient to insure that a solution for $\beta'_{\text{IN}}$ exists since the coefficient matrix could have many dependencies. It is possible, mathematically, that a matrix might have 5 rows and 10 columns, but only have rank 3. Usually though, in practical applications, if the order condition is fulfilled, the rank condition will be also. The only exceptions would include cases where some apparently different variables were really the

---

[3] The condition can be generalized in cases allowing other than zero-type restrictions by defining $n$ as the number of independent linear restrictions on the coefficients of the $i$th equation.

same, or one or more of the variables did not in fact vary based on the sample data. A statistical test of identifiability is therefore necessary as well as this mathematical condition. (See Chapter 19.)

||||||||||||||||||||||||||||||||||||||||||||||||||||||||||||||||||||||||||||||||||||||||||||||||||||||||||||||||||||||||||||||||||||||

*Interpretive note.* The order condition can be easily examined by simply counting the number ($G$ and $K$) of each type (endogenous and exogenous respectively) variable in the specified model, as well as the number ($g$ and $m$) of each type variable included in the $i$th structural equation. The counting rule requires that the number of predetermined variables *excluded* ($n = K - m$) from equation $i$ must be at least one more than the number ($g$) of endogenous variables *included.*

||||||||||||||||||||||||||||||||||||||||||||||||||||||||||||||||||||||||||||||||||||||||||||||||||||||||||||||||||||||||||||||||||||||

The comparison of $g - 1$ with $n$ according to the order condition allows three logical outcomes, each of which has a special meaning. It is common to classify the property of identifiability according to these three possibilities. If $n = g - 1$, the level of identifiability is termed *exactly identified*, and usually, the parameters of the equation are uniquely determined. If $n < g - 1$, the equation is *unidentified* or *underidentified*. There exists *no* way to obtain any meaningful estimates of the parameters. If $n > g - 1$, then there is more than one set of consistent estimates for the parameters which are, in practice, different values. The parameters in this situation are termed *overidentified*. The difficulty of estimating in this case resides in choosing how to use the excess information available and how to choose among the different possible consistent estimates. Two-stage least squares (see Chapter 18) is a method which specifies a particular way of using the extra information in the overidentified case.

*A problem in applying these rules.* Before turning to some examples of the determination of rank and order conditions in specific models, it is probably worthwhile to call the reader's attention to an asymmetry in the application of these identifiability conditions. The order condition can be checked quite readily by examination of the specified structural form. However, checking for the rank condition is often neither simple nor immediate.

In order to determine the rank of a matrix, the dimension of the largest submatrix with a nonzero determinant could be sought, or the number of linearly independent rows of the matrix could be determined by a systematic use of elementary row and column transformations to reduce the matrix to echelon form (see *Review* 17.2, item 2). Either procedure could be tedious. In addition to struggling with the mathematics of determining the rank of a matrix, the econometrician must first find the matrix, $\Pi'_{gn}$ by deriving the reduced form of the model. In a relatively small model, this is not difficult as shown in the next section and in Chapter 16. However, the solution of the reduced form in a large model can be a long-term project.

## A rank condition using coefficients of the structural form

It is useful on occasion to be able to examine the rank condition of identifiability in terms of the structural form coefficients. The complete derivation of this rule will not be presented here since it holds no special interest in its own right. In order to state the result, some additional notation must be digested, even if the reader already feels stuffed in this regard.

Let the matrix of all coefficients in the structural form of the model be given by $\begin{bmatrix} \beta' & \Gamma' \\ (G \times G) & (G \times K) \end{bmatrix}$ with dimension $[G \times (G + K)]$. Partition this matrix into the coefficients in the $i$th structural equation under consideration and the coefficients in all the remaining $G - 1$ equations. Also, order the $i$th equation first with no loss of generality. The partitioned matrix is denoted as follows:

$$[\beta' \quad \Gamma'] = \begin{pmatrix} \beta'_{IN} & \beta'_{EX} & \Gamma'_{IN} & \Gamma'_{EX} \\ (1 \times g) & (1 \times h) & (1 \times m) & (1 \times n) \\ \beta'_g & \beta'_h & \Gamma'_m & \Gamma'_n \\ (G-1) \times g & (G-1) \times h & (G-1) \times m & (G-1) \times n \end{pmatrix}. \quad (17\text{-}8)$$

Using this notation, the condition for identifiability can be written in terms of the coefficients of the structural form.

**Rank condition using** $(\beta' \quad \Gamma')$. For structural equation $i$ to be exactly identified, it is necessary and sufficient that the rank of the submatrix, $[\beta'_h \quad \Gamma'_n]$, be $G - 1$ where this matrix of dimensions $[(G - 1) \times (h + n)]$ is defined by the partitioning in (17-8).

||||||||||||||||||||||||||||||||||||||||||||||||||||||||||||||||||||||||||||||||||||||||||||||||||||||||||||||||||||||||||||||||||||||||

*Interpretive note.* The matrix $[\beta'_h \quad \Gamma'_n]$ contains only coefficients from the $G - 1$ equations in the model excluding the equation $i$ that is being examined for identifiability. In addition, the only entries selected in these $G - 1$ rows are the coefficients of the variables that are excluded from equation $i$.

||||||||||||||||||||||||||||||||||||||||||||||||||||||||||||||||||||||||||||||||||||||||||||||||||||||||||||||||||||||||||||||||||||||||

The rank condition guarantees a mathematical solution for $\beta'_{IN}$ and $\Gamma'_{IN}$ in terms of the elements of $\Pi'$. The condition can be restated without symbols: the matrix of coefficients from the other $G - 1$ equations in the structural form associated with the endogenous and predetermined variables excluded from the $i$th equation must have rank equal to the total number of endogenous variables in the model less one. Some examples of the application of these conditions are given in the next section.

## 17.4 APPLICATION OF THE RANK AND ORDER CONDITIONS

Consider a two-equation model of demand and supply where $Y_1 =$ quantity, $Y_2 =$ price, $X_1 = 1$, and $X_2 =$ income. Let the model be written as

$$\text{Demand:} \quad Y_1 = \beta_1 Y_2 + \gamma_1(1) + \gamma_2 X_2 + \varepsilon_1$$
$$\text{Supply:} \quad Y_2 = \beta_2 Y_1 + \gamma_3 + \varepsilon_2 \quad (17\text{-}9)$$

||||||||||||||||||||||||||||||||||||||||||||||||||||||||||||||||||||||||||||||||||||||||||||||||||||||||||||||||||||||||||||||||||||||||||||||||||||||||||||||||

*Explicative note.* For a small model such as (17–9), the coefficients are assigned a single subscript sequentially as they appear. There is no need to resort to double subscripting by equation and variable number.

||||||||||||||||||||||||||||||||||||||||||||||||||||||||||||||||||||||||||||||||||||||||||||||||||||||||||||||||||||||||||||||||||||||||||||||||||||||||||||||||

In the structural form (17–3), $\beta'Y' + \Gamma'X' = \varepsilon'$, the model is

$$\begin{pmatrix} 1 & -\beta_1 \\ -\beta_2 & 1 \end{pmatrix}\begin{pmatrix} Y_1 \\ Y_2 \end{pmatrix} + \begin{pmatrix} -\gamma_1 & -\gamma_2 \\ -\gamma_3 & 0 \end{pmatrix}\begin{pmatrix} X_1 \\ X_2 \end{pmatrix} = \begin{pmatrix} \varepsilon_1 \\ \varepsilon_2 \end{pmatrix}.$$

The determinant of $\beta'$ is not zero, so the reduced form can be written using

$$(\beta')^{-1} = [1/(1 - \beta_1\beta_2)]\begin{pmatrix} 1 & \beta_1 \\ \beta_2 & 1 \end{pmatrix}$$

and the form (17–4), $Y' = \Pi'X' + v'$, as follows (see Exercise 2 at the end of this chapter):

$$\begin{pmatrix} Y_1 \\ Y_2 \end{pmatrix} = \frac{1}{1 - \beta_1\beta_2}\begin{pmatrix} \gamma_1 + \beta_1\gamma_3 & \gamma_2 \\ \beta_2\gamma_1 + \gamma_3 & \beta_2\gamma_2 \end{pmatrix}\begin{pmatrix} X_1 \\ X_2 \end{pmatrix} + \begin{pmatrix} v_1 \\ v_2 \end{pmatrix} \qquad (17\text{--}10)$$

*Demand is underidentified.* The identifiability of the structural equations can now be examined. Consider the first (demand) equation which includes both endogenous variables in the model ($g = G = 2$, $h = 0$) and includes both of the predetermined variables in the model ($m = K = 2$, $n = 0$). Using the order condition it is found that $n < g - 1$ $(0 < 2 - 1)$ so that the demand equation is underidentified. There is no way to solve for $\beta_1$ and $\gamma_1$ and $\gamma_2$ given the values for the coefficients in $\Pi'$. It is unnecessary to examine the rank condition since it cannot hold if the order condition is not satisfied.

*Supply is exactly identified.* Next, consider the supply equation of (17–9). It now becomes the $i$th equation under consideration in terms of the formal notation of Section 17.3. It has a different set of variables included and excluded. For this equation, both endogenous variables are included so, again, $g = G = 2$ and $h = 0$. However, it includes only one predetermined variable and excludes $X_2$ giving $m = n = 1$ and $K = 2$. The order condition is satisfied with $n = g - 1$ $(1 = 2 - 1)$ so that the supply equation may be exactly identified.

Since the order condition is satisfied, the rank condition should be examined next. Using the reduced form (17–10), it is found that the submatrix $\Pi'_{gn}$, including the coefficients from the two rows corresponding to the $g = 2$ endogenous variables in this supply equation and from the one column corresponding to the $n = 1$ predetermined variable ($X_2$) excluded from the supply equation, is given by

$$\Pi'_{gn} = \begin{pmatrix} \gamma_2 \\ \beta_2\gamma_2 \end{pmatrix}\bigg/(1 - \beta_1\beta_2).$$

If neither the determinant $(1 - \beta_1\beta_2)$ nor the coefficient $\gamma_2$ is zero, then the rank of $\Pi'_{gn}$ equals one. The second element is a multiple of the first, and the rank condition, rank $\Pi'_{gn} = g - 1$ is satisfied. Consequently, the parameters of the supply equation can be uniquely determined from the reduced form coefficients if income $(X_2)$ does significantly contribute to the explanation of the quantity demanded as specified.

||||||||||||||||||||||||||||||||||||||||||||||||||||||||||||||||||||||||||||||||||||||||||||||||||||||||||||||||||||||||||||||||

*Recursive note.*    The mathematical conditions for identifiability of the structural supply equation are satisfied. However, in an application, it is also necessary that the statistical results based on sample observations do indeed show that $\gamma_2$ is significantly different from zero. In addition, an identifiability test showing that the determinant of $\beta'$ is significantly different from zero is also recommended.

||||||||||||||||||||||||||||||||||||||||||||||||||||||||||||||||||||||||||||||||||||||||||||||||||||||||||||||||||||||||||||||||

In this model, the demand equation is subject to shifts due to changes in income $X_2$ while the supply equation is relatively stable in the $(P, Q)$ plane. Thus, the observations of intersections of supply and demand in the market enable the econometrician to identify the parameters in the nonshifting supply equation.

||||||||||||||||||||||||||||||||||||||||||||||||||||||||||||||||||||||||||||||||||||||||||||||||||||||||||||||||||||||||||||||||

*Interpretive note.*    The mathematical identification of an equation is necessary for its statistical estimation to be meaningful, but the reader should recognize that identification in itself does not imply that the specified model or equation is true.

||||||||||||||||||||||||||||||||||||||||||||||||||||||||||||||||||||||||||||||||||||||||||||||||||||||||||||||||||||||||||||||||

*Solving for the parameters in the supply equation.*    Under the limitations of this discussion (only zero-type restrictions and linear equations), identifiability implies that a transformation exists from the coefficients of the RF to the coefficients of the structural equation. It should be possible to get unique solutions for $\beta_2$ and $\gamma_3$ of the supply equation in terms of coefficients $\pi_{ij}$ of the reduced form (17–10).

The obvious solution is, $\beta_2 = \pi_{22}/\pi_{12} = (\beta_2\gamma_2/\gamma_2)$ and

$$\gamma_3 = \pi_{21} - \beta_2\pi_{11} = (\beta_2\gamma_1 + \gamma_3 - \beta_2\gamma_1 - \beta_2\beta_1\gamma_3)/(1 - \beta_1\beta_2)$$
$$= \gamma_3(1 - \beta_1\beta_2)/(1 - \beta_1\beta_2).$$

*Identifying the demand curve.*    The reader can see by examination that there is no such solution for $\beta_1$, $\gamma_1$, or $\gamma_2$. These cannot be recovered from the coefficients of the reduced form equations. In order to identify the demand curve, some variable is needed in the model (in the supply equation) which is excluded from the demand equation.

||||||||||||||||||||||||||||||||||||||||||||||||||||||||||||||||||||||||||||||||||||||||||||||||||||||||||||||||||||||||||||||||||||||||||

*Discursive note.*    More information in terms of a priori restrictions are necessary in order to identify the demand equation. These must be different from those (coefficient of $X_2$ equals zero) which enabled us to identify the supply equation. It is not useful to restrict $\gamma_2 = 0$ also. Neither is it useful to know a great many variables, say $Z_1, Z_2, \ldots, Z_{99}$, which we excluded from the demand equation if these variables are also excluded from the supply equation.

||||||||||||||||||||||||||||||||||||||||||||||||||||||||||||||||||||||||||||||||||||||||||||||||||||||||||||||||||||||||||||||||||||||||||

A variable representing some cost of production such as a wage level, or a condition of production such as amount of rainfall or absence of strikes might be included in the supply equation (denoted by $X_3$ perhaps) with the restriction that its coefficient in the demand equation is zero. Then, the demand equation could be identified also. (See Exercise 3 at the end of the chapter.) Restrictions other than the zero type or assumptions on the variance-covariance matrix of disturbances could also be used to help identify the demand curve. These are not discussed within this book but the interested reader is referred to note one of this chapter.

## A change in the structure creating an overidentified supply equation

Before going to a more complex example of a larger model, the condition of overidentified parameters can be explained in terms of the simple demand and supply model. Suppose the specification of only the demand equation in (17–9) is changed to $Y_1 = \beta_1 Y_2 + \gamma_1(1) + \gamma_2 X_2 + \gamma_4 X_3 + \varepsilon_1$ where $X_3$ represents the price in the previous period, $X_{t3} = P_{t-1}$. Then (as the reader can demonstrate in Exercise 4 at the end of this chapter), the order condition for identifiability of the supply equation becomes $n > g - 1$ $(2 > 2 - 1)$. Furthermore, the coefficient $\beta_2$ in the supply equation can be obtained from the coefficients of the reduced form in two ways. The two zero restrictions on coefficients of $X_2$ and $X_3$ in the supply equation give an excess amount of information pertaining to the one parameter $\beta_2$. The RF coefficient matrix $\Pi'$ now has size $(2 \times 3)$ and $\beta_2$ can be obtained either by the solution $\beta_2 = \pi_{22}/\pi_{12}$ as before, or also by $\beta_2 = \pi_{23}/\pi_{13} = (\beta_2 \gamma_4/\gamma_4)$. Although in the true relations both values for $\beta_2$ would be the same, it is found that in the estimated relations based on sample data, the two estimated values for $\beta_2$ would differ. (See Section 17.7.)

## Rank conditions on equations in a larger model

In small models it is not too difficult to apply the rank test using the reduced form of the model. However, it is convenient in larger models to be able to apply the rank condition for identifiability directly on the structural form. For an example of this application, the following four-equation Keynesian type model is suggested.[4]

| | |
|---|---|
| Consumption: | $Y_1 = \beta_1 Y_2 + \gamma_1 + \varepsilon_1$ |
| Investment: | $Y_3 = \beta_2 Y_2 + \beta_3 Y_4 + \gamma_2 X_2 + \varepsilon_2$ |
| Liquidity preference: | $Y_5 = \beta_4 Y_2 + \beta_5 Y_3 + \varepsilon_3$     (17–11) |
| Liquidity supply: | $Y_5 = \gamma_3 + \gamma_4 X_3 + \varepsilon_4$ |
| Income identity: | $Y_2 = Y_1 + Y_3$ |

where the variables are defined to be:

| Endogenous $(G = 5)$ | Exogenous $(K = 3)$ |
|---|---|
| $Y_1$   Consumption | $X_1$   Constant $= 1$ |
| $Y_2$   GNP | $X_2$   Shift parameter |
| $Y_3$   Private investment | $X_3$   Currency base |
| $Y_4$   Long-term rate of interest | |
| $Y_5$   Quantity of money | |

Writing the model in the structural form (17–3), $\beta' Y' + \Gamma' X' = \varepsilon'$, we obtain

$$
\begin{pmatrix}
1 & -\beta_1 & 0 & 0 & 0 \\
0 & -\beta_2 & 1 & -\beta_3 & 0 \\
0 & -\beta_4 & -\beta_5 & 0 & 1 \\
0 & 0 & 0 & 0 & 1 \\
-1 & 1 & -1 & 0 & 0
\end{pmatrix}
\begin{pmatrix} Y_1 \\ Y_2 \\ Y_3 \\ Y_4 \\ Y_5 \end{pmatrix}
+
\begin{pmatrix}
-\gamma_1 & 0 & 0 \\
0 & -\gamma_2 & 0 \\
0 & 0 & 0 \\
-\gamma_3 & 0 & -\gamma_4 \\
0 & 0 & 0
\end{pmatrix}
\begin{pmatrix} X_1 \\ X_2 \\ X_3 \end{pmatrix}
=
\begin{pmatrix} \varepsilon_1 \\ \varepsilon_2 \\ \varepsilon_3 \\ \varepsilon_4 \\ 0 \end{pmatrix}.
$$

The identifiability of an equation in this model can be checked by using the order and rank correlations on this structural form. For the first (consumption) equation, inspection indicates that the number of endogenous variables included is $g = 2$ and the number of predetermined variables excluded is $n = 2$. Using the order condition, $n \geq g - 1$, we conclude that the consumption equation may be overidentified $(2 > 2 - 1)$.

To apply the rank condition to the consumption equation we consider only the coefficients in the other four equations that we associated with variables excluded from the consumption equation. Accordingly, we obtain,

For consumption
equation:

$$
\begin{array}{ccccc}
\;\;\;Y_3 & Y_4 & Y_5 & X_2 & X_3
\end{array}
$$

$$
(\beta_h' \;\; \Gamma_n') = \\
{\scriptstyle (4 \times 5)}
\begin{pmatrix}
1 & -\beta_3 & 0 & -\gamma_2 & 0 \\
-\beta_5 & 0 & 1 & 0 & 0 \\
0 & 0 & 1 & 0 & -\gamma_4 \\
-1 & 0 & 0 & 0 & 0
\end{pmatrix}
\begin{array}{l}
\text{Investment} \\
\text{Liquidity preference} \\
\text{Liquidity supply} \\
\text{Income identity}
\end{array}
$$

---

[4] The model is adapted from R. L. Basmann, "Remarks concerning the Application of Exact Finite Sample Distribution Functions of GCL Estimators in Econometric Statistical Inference," *Journal of the American Statistical Association*, 1963, pp. 943–76.

For the consumption equation to be identified, the rank of this matrix should equal $G - 1 = 4$. The determinant of a $4 \times 4$ submatrix of $(\beta'_h \, \Gamma'_n)$ may be shown to be nonzero. (The reader may use columns 1, 2, 3, and 5 and show that the determinant is equal to $\beta_3 \gamma_4$. Alternately, the matrix can be reduced to echelon form by column and row transformation to determine that the number of linearly independent columns is four See *Review* 17.2, item 2.)

Now consider the identifiability of the second (investment) equation. For this equation, $Y_2$, $Y_3$, and $Y_4$ are included as well as $X_2$. Therefore, $n = g - 1$ $(2 = 3 - 1)$ as two predetermined variables ($X_1$ and $X_3$) are excluded. The rank condition is examined by obtaining $(\beta'_h \, \Gamma'_n)$ associated with the investment equation as,

For investment equation:

$$
\underset{(4 \times 4)}{(\beta'_h \, \Gamma'_n)} =
\begin{array}{cccc}
Y_1 & Y_5 & X_1 & X_3
\end{array}
\begin{pmatrix}
1 & 0 & -\gamma_1 & 0 \\
0 & 1 & 0 & 0 \\
0 & 1 & -\gamma_3 & -\gamma_4 \\
-1 & 0 & 0 & 0
\end{pmatrix}
\begin{array}{l}
\text{Consumption} \\
\text{Liquidity preference} \\
\text{Liquidity supply} \\
\text{Income identity}
\end{array}
$$

The investment equation is identified because the rank of $(\beta'_h \, \Gamma'_n) = 4$. This is easily seen by calculating its determinant (by expansion of cofactors using first row four and then row two) to be

$$
|\beta'_h \, \Gamma'_n| = 1 \begin{pmatrix} 0 & -\gamma_1 & 0 \\ 1 & 0 & 0 \\ 1 & -\gamma_3 & -\gamma_4 \end{pmatrix} = -\begin{pmatrix} -\gamma_1 & 0 \\ -\gamma_3 & -\gamma_4 \end{pmatrix} = -\gamma_1 \gamma_4 .
$$

|||||||||||||||||||||||||||||||||||||||||||||||||||||||||||||||||||||||||||||||||||||||||||||||||||||||||||||||||

***Recursive note.*** Since the determinant is not zero, the $(4 \times 4)$ matrix is known to have full rank equal to 4.

|||||||||||||||||||||||||||||||||||||||||||||||||||||||||||||||||||||||||||||||||||||||||||||||||||||||||||||||||

In Exercises 5 and 8 at the end of this chapter, the reader can check the identifiability of the liquidity preference and liquidity supply functions of this model. Also in Exercise 9, the reader is asked to reduce the size of the model to a revised structure by eliminating the identity and setting the liquidity preference function equal to the liquidity supply function.[5] Such an elimination is sometimes advisable for estimation purposes since the number of reduced form equations is reduced. In doing this, the econometrician must not allow any change in the roles of endogenous and predetermined variables between the original and revised structures. The revision merely reduces the number of endogenous variables being jointly determined. The

[5] For the use and meaning of this reduced structural model with two equations, see Basmann, " Remarks concerning the application of Finite Sample Distribution Functions "; and R. L. Basmann, " On the Application of the Identifiability Test Statistic in Predictive Testing of Explanatory Economic Models," *Econometric Annual of the Indian Economic Journal*, Vol. 13 (1965), pp. 387–423, and Vol. 14, (1966), pp. 233–52.

remaining endogenous variables can still be determined and the other SF coefficients can still be estimated by substitution into the identities.

## 17.5 ESTIMATION OF A RECURSIVE MODEL BY OLS

In general, parameters in a simultaneous equation should not be estimated by ordinary least squares (OLS) if the econometrician desires consistent estimators. However, in a special type of simultaneous equations model, known as a *recursive* model, the use of OLS is appropriate.

### Defining a recursive model

A recursive model is one in which there may be a simultaneous dependency of some endogenous variables on others, but in which this cause and effect role is only in one direction. The causal chain within the model must be from predetermined variables to the first endogenous variable, then from this first endogenous variable and perhaps, other predetermined variables to the second endogenous variable, and so forth, to the last endogenous variable. There must not be any feedback from any endogenous variable to one of a lower order in the causal chain.

|||||||||||||||||||||||||||||||||||||||||||||||||||||||||||||||||||||||||||||||||||||||||||||||||||||||||||||||||||||||||||||

*Explicative note.* The causal relation from $\{X_i\} \to Y_1$ is called the first order relation. Then, the next link in the causal chain from $\{X_j, Y_1\} \to Y_2$ is called the second order, and so forth to the final link called order $G$ determining the last of the $G$ endogenous variables.

|||||||||||||||||||||||||||||||||||||||||||||||||||||||||||||||||||||||||||||||||||||||||||||||||||||||||||||||||||||||||||||

A recursive model can be characterized as having a triangular matrix $\beta'$ of coefficients of the endogenous variables, in the structural form,
$(G \times G)$

$$\beta' Y' + \Gamma' X' = \varepsilon', \tag{17-3}$$

and a diagonal variance-covariance matrix of contemporaneous disturbance terms. Assumption 8 of Section 16.3 must be made stronger in a recursive model so that $Cov(\varepsilon_{it}\varepsilon_{jt}) = 0$, $i \neq j$. If the $\beta'$ matrix is not triangular, then the model represents an interdependent system.

### The appropriateness of OLS

The special characteristics of a recursive model can be seen by a simple example. Consider the interdependent simultaneous equations model of demand and supply given by

$$\begin{aligned}
\text{Demand:} \quad & P_t = \beta_1 Q_t + \gamma_1 + \gamma_2 X_2 + \varepsilon_1 \\
\text{Supply:} \quad & Q_t = \beta_2 P_t + \gamma_3 + \gamma_4 X_3 + \varepsilon_2
\end{aligned} \tag{17-12}$$

where $P$ = price and $Q$ = quantity are endogenous and $X_1 = 1$, $X_2 =$ disposable income, and $X_3 =$ cost of materials are predetermined. Ordinary least squares gives biased estimates when applied to such a model because the explanatory endogenous variables are not independent of the error terms. As suggested in Section 16.4, $\varepsilon_1$ affects $P$ in the demand equation and $P$ affects $Q$ in the supply equation. Thus, a linkage is developed between $Q$ and $\varepsilon_1$, an explanatory variable and the disturbance in the same demand equation.

However, suppose price is not a significant variable in the supply equation. Perhaps current supply depends on the previous period price and not on the current price. (This is a common situation in agriculture where some production planning for a current crop year depends on the price of crops at the previous harvest season, as an expectation of this season's price.) Then, the model is changed so that the endogenous variable, $P_t$, in the supply equation is replaced by a predetermined variable, $P_{t-1}$. The matrix of coefficients of the endogenous variables changes from

$$\begin{pmatrix} 1 & -\beta_1 \\ -\beta_2 & 1 \end{pmatrix} \quad \text{to} \quad \begin{pmatrix} 1 & -\beta_1 \\ 0 & 1 \end{pmatrix}.$$

The system is no longer interdependent but recursive.

|||||||||||||||||||||||||||||||||||||||||||||||||||||||||||||||||||||||||||||||||||||||||||||||||||||||||||||||||||||||||||||||||||||||||||

*Interpretive note.*    The matrix $\beta'$ is now triangular. The first order of the causal chain is from ($X_1$, $X_3$, and $X_4 = P_{t-1}$) to $Q$ and the second order is from ($Q$, $X_1$, and $X_2$) to $P$.

|||||||||||||||||||||||||||||||||||||||||||||||||||||||||||||||||||||||||||||||||||||||||||||||||||||||||||||||||||||||||||||||||||||||||||

There is no longer a direct link between $Q$ and $\varepsilon_1$, although it is still possible for them to be correlated. As suggested in Section 16.4, if $\varepsilon_1$ and $\varepsilon_2$ are correlated, then $\varepsilon_1$ and $Q$ may be correlated since $Q$ depends directly on $\varepsilon_2$. Therefore, the condition of nonindependence between an explanatory variable and the error term which plagues OLS estimates is only controlled in a simultaneous equations model if the model is recursive meaning that (*a*) the matrix $\beta$ is triangular and (*b*) the disturbance terms are not correlated.

In this special circumstance, the use of OLS is appropriate in a simultaneous equations model. For estimation purposes and in the examination of the required assumptions, each equation of such a simultaneous equations model is considered similar to a single equation model containing only one endogenous variable. The estimates of the coefficients will have the usual desirable properties unless some other assumption is violated. Therefore, nothing more complex than a repeated, sequential use of OLS is needed to estimate the coefficients in a recursive model.

## An example of a recursive model

For example, consider an agricultural commodity such as cherries where the amount usually produced in much less than the potential demand, or consider tobacco or a grain for which a stabilization board will act to purchase any excess production. The production of the commodity may depend on exogenous factors, so that the quantity supplied, $Y_1$ is a function of $X_1 = 1$, $X_2 = $ climatic variables, and $X_3 = $ last season's price.

The retail price $Y_2$ for the commodity may depend on the production level $Y_1$, and $X_1 = 1$, and $X_4 = $ disposable income. Finally, the price for the producer $Y_3$ can be expressed in terms of the retail price $Y_2$, a constant $X_1 = 1$, and $X_5 = $ the cost of marketing the product. The structural form of the model just described is given by:

$$\begin{pmatrix} 1 & 0 & 0 \\ -\beta_1 & 1 & 0 \\ 0 & -\beta_2 & 1 \end{pmatrix}\begin{pmatrix} Y_1 \\ Y_2 \\ Y_3 \end{pmatrix} + \begin{pmatrix} -\gamma_1 & -\gamma_2 & -\gamma_3 & 0 & 0 \\ -\gamma_4 & 0 & 0 & -\gamma_5 & 0 \\ -\gamma_6 & 0 & 0 & 0 & -\gamma_7 \end{pmatrix}\begin{pmatrix} X_1 \\ X_2 \\ X_3 \\ X_4 \\ X_5 \end{pmatrix} = \begin{pmatrix} \varepsilon_1 \\ \varepsilon_2 \\ \varepsilon_3 \end{pmatrix}.$$

The matrix $\beta'$ is triangular; and assuming that $Cov(\varepsilon_{it}\,\varepsilon_{jt}) = 0$, $i \neq j$, for both $i, j = 1, 2, 3$, then ordinary least squares can be applied.

The first equation estimated is $Y_1 = \gamma_1 + \gamma_2 X_2 + \gamma_3 X_3 + \varepsilon_1$. All explanatory variables are predetermined and assumed to be independent of $\varepsilon_1$. The next equation to be estimated is $Y_2 = \beta_1 Y_1 + \gamma_4 + \gamma_5 X_4 + \varepsilon_2$. Since $Y_2$ never acts as an explanatory variable for $Y_1$, the causal relation between $Y_2$ and $Y_1$ is in one direction only, yet the theoretical interdependency among the equations is preserved by the linkage between factors of production and retail price. Also, $Y_1$ is independent of $\varepsilon_2$ and can be treated just like a predetermined variable. Similarly, since $Y_2$ is independent of $\varepsilon_3$, ordinary least squares can then be applied to the third equation,

$$Y_3 = \beta_2 Y_2 + \gamma_6 + \gamma_7 X_5 + \varepsilon_3.$$

||||||||||||||||||||||||||||||||||||||||||||||||||||||||||||||||||||||||||||||||||||||||||||||||||||||||||||||||||||||||||||||||||||||

***Discursive note.*** If any of the problems of single equation estimation occur, then the remedies as suggested in Chapters 13–15, instead of the direct application of OLS, might be proper to obtain the best possible estimates. For example, if the stabilization policy changed over the period and affected the retail price equation such that its disturbance did not have a constant variance, then weighted least squares might be used to estimate that equation. The important concept in a recursive model is that each equation may be treated individually rather than interdependently.

||||||||||||||||||||||||||||||||||||||||||||||||||||||||||||||||||||||||||||||||||||||||||||||||||||||||||||||||||||||||||||||||||||||

## 17.6 INDIRECT LEAST SQUARES ESTIMATION

In the general nonrecursive simultaneous equations model, estimating procedures different from ordinary least squares must be used in order to get consistent estimates. One method suggested is called *indirect least squares* (ILS) because it uses the method of least squares but not directly on the structural form equations.[6] Instead, an indirect method of estimation of the parameters of a structural equation is used. The process has three steps. First, the reduced form (RF) of the model is derived from the structural form (SF). Second, the coefficients in the equations of the RF are estimated by the method of least squares. Third, the estimates of the coefficients in the SF are determined from these estimates of the RF by using the inverse transformation from the RF to the SF. Each step deserves some discussion.

### Deriving the RF

If the SF is written as $\beta'Y' + \Gamma'X' = \varepsilon'$, (17–3), then the reduced form may be derived by premultiplying (17–3) by $(\beta')^{-1}$ to obtain

$$Y' = -(\beta')^{-1}\Gamma'X' + (\beta')^{-1}\varepsilon'$$

which may be written as $Y' = \Pi'X' + v'$, (17–4). We wish to obtain estimates of $\beta'$ and $\Gamma'$, the coefficients in the SF; however, the estimates will be biased and inconsistent if OLS is applied directly (see Section 16.4). If $(\beta')$ has full rank, the RF can be derived as in (17–4) with a coefficient matrix, $\Pi'$ that can be estimated directly.

### Using OLS in estimating the equations of the RF

In the RF each equation contains only one endogenous variable. Also, if all the predetermined variables are assumed fixed and independent of the disturbance terms in the SF, then they are also fixed and independent of the disturbance terms in the RF. Further, if the disturbances $\varepsilon'$ in the structural form satisfy the Assumptions 5–8 of Section 16.3, then so do the disturbances $v'$ in the RF.

|||||||||||||||||||||||||||||||||||||||||||||||||||||||||||||||||||||||||||||||||||||||||||||||||||||||||||||||||||||||||||||||||||||||||||||||||||||||||||||||||

*Explicative note.* The reader may wish to carry through the derivations required to prove these statements. For example, the proof relevant to Assumption 3 might be: given that $E(\varepsilon) = O$, and $v' = (\beta')^{-1}\varepsilon'$, then $E(v') = E[(\beta')^{-1}\varepsilon'] = (\beta')^{-1}E(\varepsilon') = O$. Since the disturbances in the RF are merely linear combinations of the disturbances in the SF, the derivations are not difficult.

|||||||||||||||||||||||||||||||||||||||||||||||||||||||||||||||||||||||||||||||||||||||||||||||||||||||||||||||||||||||||||||||||||||||||||||||||||||||||||||||||

Since the Gauss-Markov assumptions do hold for the RF, then estimates of its coefficients using OLS will be BLUE and consistent. Rewriting the reduced form as

$$\underset{(T \times G)}{Y} = \underset{(T \times K)}{X} \underset{(K \times G)}{\Pi} + \underset{(T \times G)}{v}$$

---

[6] The method of ILS was apparently suggested by M. A. Girshick. See W. C. Hood and T. C. Koopmans (eds.), *Studies in Econometric Method*, (New York: John Wiley and Sons, 1953), pp. 139–43.

[taking the transpose of both sides of (17–4), then the matrix representation of the OLS estimates $P$ of $\Pi$ is given by [see (9–3)],

$$\underset{(K \times G)}{P} = (X'X)^{-1}(X'Y).$$

For any particular equation $i$ of the RF, the estimates of the coefficients are given by,

$$\underset{(K \times 1)}{P_i} = (X'X)^{-1}(X'Y_i). \tag{17–13}$$

||||||||||||||||||||||||||||||||||||||||||||||||||||||||||||||||||||||||||||||||||||||||||||||||||||||||||||||||

*Recursive note.*   Assumptions 6 and 7 must apply to each RF equation. Thus, $T > K$ and the existence of $(X'X)^{-1}$ are assumed.

||||||||||||||||||||||||||||||||||||||||||||||||||||||||||||||||||||||||||||||||||||||||||||||||||||||||||||||||

The estimates of the $i$th endogenous variable based on the regression equation for the $i$th equation in the RF are given for each $i = 1, 2, \ldots, G$, by

$$\underset{(T \times 1)}{\hat{Y}_i} = \underset{(T \times K)}{X} \; \underset{(K \times 1)}{P_i} = X(X'X)^{-1}(X'Y_i). \tag{17–14}$$

All the properties of estimators and test statistics and other related discussions concerning single equation econometric models in Chapters 8–15 apply to each single equation of the reduced form. For example, the estimates $P_i$ of the $K$ coefficients in the $i$th equation of the RF are approximately joint normally distributed with $E(P_i) = \Pi_i$ and $V\text{-}Cov(P_i) = \underset{(K \times K)}{\sigma_{v_i}^2(X'X)^{-1}}$.

## Indirectly finding the estimates of coefficients in the SF

The reduced form is always derivable from the structural form when $(\beta')^{-1}$ has full rank. Thus, there is always a transformation from $(\beta' \quad \Gamma')$ into $\Pi'$ whereby the coefficients $\pi_{ik}$ of the RF can be expressed in terms of the coefficients of the SF. If the $i$th equation of the SF is identified, then there is also an inverse transformation from $\Pi'$ into $(\beta'_i \quad \Gamma'_i)$ whereby the coefficients $\beta'_i$ and $\Gamma'_i$ can be expressed in terms of $\Pi'$.

||||||||||||||||||||||||||||||||||||||||||||||||||||||||||||||||||||||||||||||||||||||||||||||||||||||||||||||||

*Recursive note.*   The solution for $(\beta'_i \quad \Gamma'_i)$ is unique if the $i$th equation is exactly identified. There is more than one solution if equation $i$ is overidentified. There is no solution at all if equation $i$ is underidentified.

||||||||||||||||||||||||||||||||||||||||||||||||||||||||||||||||||||||||||||||||||||||||||||||||||||||||||||||||

If the identification of equation $i$ is *exact* and an inverse transformation exists, then a single solution for *estimates* of $\beta'_i$ and $\Gamma'_i$ may be obtained by using this same inverse transformation on the *estimates* of $\Pi'$. This calculation of estimates $(b'_i \quad C'_i)$ of $(\beta'_i \quad \Gamma'_i)$ from ordinary least squares estimates $P'$ of $\Pi'$ is called the method of indirect least squares (ILS).

The ILS estimates of the coefficients of the structural form are an improvement over simple least squares direct estimates since the ILS estimates take into account the simultaneity of the model in solving the inverse transformation from $P'$ to $(b_i'\ \ C_i')$. The ILS estimates are maximum likelihood estimates so they are *consistent*. Also, the ILS method does make use of the sample information about all the predetermined variables in the model whereas OLS on a single structural equation only considers the predetermined variables included in that equation. However, the ILS estimates are still *biased* when based on small samples. To illustrate these properties and the use of ILS, the simple consumption-income model is again used.

**Estimating the MPC in a structural equation**

Consider again the two-equation model of Section 16.1,

$$C_t = \beta Y_t + \gamma + \varepsilon$$
$$Y = C + Z \qquad (16\text{-}2a)$$

in which $\beta$ represents a marginal propensity to consume (MPC). A direct estimate of $\beta$ using OLS on the consumption function involves the use of a biased and inconsistent estimator.

The RF of this model is given by (see *Review* 16.2, item 2),

$$C_t = \gamma/(1 - \beta) + \beta Z_t/(1 - \beta) + \varepsilon_t/(1 - \beta) = \pi_{11} + \pi_{12} Z_t + v_{1t}$$
$$Y_t = \gamma/(1 - \beta) + Z_t/(1 - \beta) + \varepsilon_t/(1 - \beta) = \pi_{21} + \pi_{22} Z_t + v_{2t}$$

for which the usual assumptions are satisfied. The OLS estimates of the coefficients $\pi_{11}$ and $\pi_{22}$ in the RF are given by [(see (3–2)] $p_{12} = \sum cz/\sum z^2$ and $p_{22} = \sum yz/\sum z^2$, where the lowercase letters $c$, $y$, and $z$ represent deviations from the respective sample means and the sums are over $T$ observed values. These estimates of slopes in the equations of the RF are BLUE (best, linear unbiased estimators), of the theoretical coefficients $\pi_{12} = \beta/(1 - \beta)$ and $\pi_{22} = 1/(1 - \beta)$ respectively.

The object of the estimation though is to estimate $\beta$, not $\pi_{12}$ or $\pi_{22}$. Since the consumption function includes two endogenous variables, $C$ and $Y$, and excludes one predetermined variable, $Z$, it is exactly identified $(n = g - 1 = 1)$. Therefore, a unique solution for $\beta$ (and $\gamma$) exists in terms of the elements of $\Pi$. The solution is obviously,

$$\beta = \pi_{12}/\pi_{22} = \beta(1 - \beta)/(1 - \beta).$$

Similarly, an estimate of $\beta$ can be written in terms of estimates of $\pi_{12}$ and $\pi_{22}$ as, $b = p_{12}/p_{22}$.

Using the least squares estimates $p_{12}$ and $p_{22}$, the ILS estimate of $b$ is given by,

$$b = p_{12}/p_{22} = \frac{\sum cz/\sum z^2}{\sum yz/\sum z^2} = \sum cz/\sum yz. \qquad (17\text{-}15)$$

The properties of $b$ can be seen more clearly by shifting to moment notation and substituting for $c$ and $y$ the expressions, $c = (\beta_1 z + \varepsilon)/(1 - \beta)$ and $y = (z + \varepsilon)/(1 - \beta)$, obtained from the equations of the reduced form.

The representation of the ILS estimate $b$ is then,

$$b = (\beta_1 m_{zz} + m_{z\varepsilon})/(m_{zz} + m_{z\varepsilon}).$$

The expected value of the estimate, $E(b) \neq \beta$, is not the true value of the MPC since the other terms cannot be dropped. Therefore, the ILS estimate $b$ is biased.

However, in the limit as the sample size approaches infinity, the sample moments $m_{zz}$ and $m_{z\varepsilon}$ approach the true variance, $V(Z)$, and covariance, $Cov(Z, \varepsilon)$ respectively. Since $Cov(Z, \varepsilon) = O$ by the assumption cf independence (Assumption 1 of Section 16.3), then for large samples $b \simeq [\beta V(Z) + O]/[V(Z) + O] = \beta$. In this way, the ILS estimate can be shown to be consistent.

In summary, the ILS estimate of the MPC in this simple model is obtained by mathematical deduction from the values of the OLS estimates of the reduced form coefficients [(see (17–15)]. This ILS estimate is biased but consistent.

## 17.7 ILS ESTIMATES IN A DEMAND–SUPPLY MODEL

The method of indirect least squares can be applied in any model for which all the equations are exactly identified. The reader is asked to determine such estimates for some simple models in Exercises 10, 13, 14 and 15 at the end of this chapter. In this section, an overidentified model is used as an example to demonstrate the procedure and the limitations of the indirect least squares estimation procedure.

### Specification of the model

Consider a model including a demand and a supply equation for fresh fruits as follows,

Demand: $\quad Y_1 = \beta_1 Y_2 + \gamma_1 + \gamma_2 X_2 + \varepsilon_1$

Supply: $\quad Y_2 = \beta_2 Y_1 + \gamma_3 + \gamma_4 X_3 + \gamma_5 X_4 + \varepsilon_2$

where all variables are defined as index numbers with the same base period. Since all variables are measured in the same period, the observation subscript is omitted for simplicity.

The measures are:

$Y_1$ = retail price of fresh fruits deflated by the consumer price index (CPI),
$Y_2$ = fresh fruit consumption per capita,
$X_1 = 1$,
$X_2$ = disposable income per capita deflated by the CPI,

$X_3$ = a climate scale reflecting the value of potential crops destroyed due to weather conditions, and

$X_4$ = net investment by fresh fruit producers per capita deflated by the CPI reflecting a production cost.

## Matrix representation of the SF and the RF

The model can be rewritten in the matrix form (17–3) as

$$\beta' Y' + \Gamma' X' = \varepsilon',$$

or

$$\begin{pmatrix} 1 & -\beta_1 \\ -\beta_2 & 1 \end{pmatrix} \begin{pmatrix} Y_1 \\ Y_2 \end{pmatrix} + \begin{pmatrix} -\gamma_1 & -\gamma_2 & 0 & 0 \\ -\gamma_3 & 0 & -\gamma_4 & -\gamma_5 \end{pmatrix} \begin{pmatrix} X_1 \\ X_2 \\ X_3 \\ X_4 \end{pmatrix} = \begin{pmatrix} \varepsilon_1 \\ \varepsilon_2 \end{pmatrix}.$$

Since the matrix $\beta'$ is not triangular, this SF represents an interdependent (nonrecursive) system. Also, since the matrix $\beta'$ is nonsingular, its inverse can be found to be

$$(\beta')^{-1} = \begin{pmatrix} 1 & \beta_1 \\ \beta_2 & 1 \end{pmatrix} / (1 - \beta_1\beta_2).$$

Consequently, the reduced form of the model can be written, $Y' = \Pi' X' + v'$ (17–4), or as

$$\begin{pmatrix} Y_1 \\ Y_2 \end{pmatrix} = \begin{pmatrix} \pi_{11} & \pi_{12} & \pi_{13} & \pi_{14} \\ \pi_{21} & \pi_{22} & \pi_{23} & \pi_{24} \end{pmatrix} \begin{pmatrix} X_1 \\ X_2 \\ X_3 \\ X_4 \end{pmatrix} = \begin{pmatrix} v_1 \\ v_2 \end{pmatrix}$$

where

$$\begin{pmatrix} \pi_{11} & \pi_{12} & \pi_{13} & \pi_{14} \\ \pi_{21} & \pi_{22} & \pi_{23} & \pi_{24} \end{pmatrix}$$

$$= -(\beta')^{-1}\Gamma' = \frac{1}{1 - \beta_1\beta_2} \begin{pmatrix} \gamma_1 + \beta_1\gamma_3 & \gamma_2 & \beta_1\gamma_4 & \beta_1\gamma_5 \\ \beta_2\gamma_1 + \gamma_3 & \beta_2\gamma_2 & \gamma_4 & \gamma_5 \end{pmatrix}. \qquad (17\text{–}16)$$

The equation (17–16) defines the RF coefficients in terms of the SF coefficients. A similar relationship holds between the *estimates* of the RF coefficients and the *estimates* of the SF coefficients since (17–16) is a mathematical derivation and not dependent on any set values of these parameters. If the SF coefficients could be estimated, then the RF coefficients could be estimated using the equation (17–16).

However, the problem is exactly the reverse. It is the RF equations which more accurately satisfy the assumptions (of Section 16.3) and which can appropriately be estimated using ordinary least squares. Thus, the question is whether the desired estimates of the SF coefficients can be determined given the estimates of the RF coefficients.

## Identifiability of the model

The existence of the unique transformation from the RF coefficients into the SF coefficients can in general be determined by the Jacobian of the transformation (see Exercise R.2, *Review* 16.2). It exists if the structural equations are exactly identified. In this model, the supply equation is exactly identified and the demand equation is overidentified.

|||||||||||||||||||||||||||||||||||||||||||||||||||||||||||||||||||||||||||||||||||||||||||||||||||||||||||||||||||||||||||||||||||||||||||||||||||

> *Recursive note.*   Using the previous notation of Section 17.3, the reader can quickly examine the rank and order conditions of this model. Besides these, the necessary condition for identifiability of the model is that the determinant of $\beta'$ is nonzero. Therefore, $1 - \beta_1\beta_2 \neq 0$ requires that the estimates $b_1$ and $b_2$ of $\beta_1$ and $\beta_2$ based on the sample data must satisfy, $b_1 b_2 \neq 1$.

|||||||||||||||||||||||||||||||||||||||||||||||||||||||||||||||||||||||||||||||||||||||||||||||||||||||||||||||||||||||||||||||||||||||||||||||||||

Thus, there is a solution for all the SF parameters in terms of the RF parameters, but this solution is not unique for the SF parameters. Indeed, only the coefficients of the supply equation can be determined uniquely due to the exact identification of the supply equation. Based on equation (17–16), the representations of the coefficients associated with the endogenous variables in the SF are

$$\beta_2 = \frac{\pi_{22}}{\pi_{12}} = \frac{\beta_2 \gamma_2}{\gamma_2},$$

and

$$\beta_1 = \frac{\pi_{13}}{\pi_{21}} = \frac{\beta_1 \gamma_4}{\gamma_4},$$

or

$$\beta_1 = \frac{\pi_{14}}{\pi_{24}} = \frac{\beta_1 \gamma_5}{\gamma_5};$$

and based on sample data, these two alternate estimates of $\beta_1$ would be different. The solutions for the other coefficients in the demand equation depend on which estimate of $\beta_1$ is used. The formulas derived from (17–16) are:

$$\gamma_1 = \pi_{11} - \beta_1 \pi_{21}$$
$$= (\gamma_1 + \beta_1 \gamma_3 - \beta_1 \beta_2 \gamma_1 - \beta_1 \gamma_3)/(1 - \beta_1 \beta_2) = \gamma_1;$$

and

$$\gamma_2 = \pi_{12}(1 - \beta_1 \beta_2) = \gamma_2(1 - \beta_1 \beta_2)/(1 - \beta_1 \beta_2).$$

The other coefficients in the supply equation are determinable according to the formulas,

$$\gamma_3 = \pi_{21} - \beta_2 \pi_{11}; \quad \gamma_4 = \pi_{23} - \beta_2 \pi_{13}; \quad \text{and} \quad \gamma_5 = \pi_{24} - \beta_2 \pi_{14}$$

$$(17\text{–}17)$$

using the unique estimate of $\beta_2$ and the estimates of the RF coefficients.

## A numerical solution

To illustrate more specifically the process of indirect least squares estimation and its limitations in overidentified models, the data of Table 17–3 can be used to find estimates of the coefficients in the demand and supply equations model. The reduced form has been derived and includes two equations, each of which has one endogenous variable expressed in terms of an intercept and three predetermined variables. For estimation purposes, each

**TABLE 17–3**

**Sample data for the estimation of the demand-supply model**

| Variable: | $Y_1$ | $Y_2$ | $X_2$ | $X_3$ | $X_4$ |
|---|---|---|---|---|---|
| Index description: | Price | Quantity | Income | Weather | Cost |
| Observations: | 101.6 | 101.2 | 97.6 | 99.1 | 142.9 |
| ($T = 10$) | 106.0 | 100.9 | 98.2 | 98.9 | 123.8 |
| | 108.7 | 102.3 | 99.8 | 110.8 | 111.9 |
| | 106.7 | 101.5 | 100.5 | 108.2 | 121.4 |
| | 105.5 | 99.8 | 96.6 | 108.7 | 92.9 |
| | 95.6 | 100.3 | 88.9 | 100.6 | 97.6 |
| | 97.9 | 97.3 | 84.6 | 70.9 | 64.3 |
| | 97.0 | 100.3 | 96.4 | 110.5 | 78.6 |
| | 95.8 | 104.1 | 104.4 | 92.5 | 109.5 |
| | 96.4 | 105.3 | 110.7 | 89.3 | 128.6 |
| Mean | 101.12 | 101.30 | 97.77 | 98.95 | 107.15 |
| Std. deviation | 5.1663 | 2.2435 | 7.29 | 12.377 | 24.019 |

of these RF equations is exactly similar to the general single equation model discussed throughout Part III of this book. Each RF equation can be estimated using OLS to obtain the results given in Table 17–4.

The properties of these estimators of the RF coefficients and the test statistics discussed in Chapters 10 and 11 are applicable to these results. However, in the method of ILS, these estimates are merely intermediate results that are used to obtain the estimates of the SF coefficients.

**TABLE 17–4**

**Results of OLS estimation of the reduced form of the demand-supply model**

Price $= Y_1 = 92.46 - 0.2104X_2 + 0.2069X_3 + 0.0817X_4$
$s_b$     (26.68)    (0.3147)     (0.1433)      (0.0955)      $R^2 = 0.35$
$t$       3.46    $-0.67$        1.44        0.86

Quantity $= Y_2 = 74.98 + 0.2765X_2 - 0.0160X_3 + 0.0081X_4$
$s_b$     (4.951)    (0.0584)     (0.0266)      (0.0177)      $R^2 = 0.88$
$t$  =   15.14      4.74      $-0.60$       0.46

Using the formulas derived above from equation (17–16), we can find the estimates of $\beta_2$, $\gamma_3$, $\gamma_4$, and $\gamma_5$ uniquely. In particular, $\beta_2 = \pi_{22}/\pi_{12}$ so $b_2 = p_{22}/p_{12}$ where the estimates $p_{ij}$ are obtained from Table 17–4 to be,

$$
(\text{Est. } \Pi) = P = \begin{array}{cccc|c}
 & 1 & 2 & 3 & 4 & \diagup\; i \\
\hline
92.46 & -0.2104 & 0.2069 & 0.0817 & 1 \\
74.98 & 0.2765 & -0.0160 & 0.0081 & 2
\end{array}
\qquad (17\text{–}18)
$$

Using the values $p_{22} = 0.2765$ and $p_{12} = -0.2104$ from (17–18), the estimate of $\beta_2$ is calculated to be

$$b_2 = -1.314. \qquad (17\text{–}19)$$

||||||||||||||||||||||||||||||||||||||||||||||||||||||||||||||||||||||||||||||||||||||||||||||||||||||||||||||||||||||||||||||||||||||||||||||||

*Discursive note.* The reader can show similarly that estimates of $\gamma_3$, $\gamma_4$, and $\gamma_5$ may be obtained using (17–17) as

$$C_3 = 74.98 - (-1.314)92.46 = 196.48;$$
$$C_4 = -0.0160 - (-1.314)(0.2069) = 0.256;$$

and

$$C_5 = 0.0081 - (-1.314)(0.0817) = 0.115.$$

||||||||||||||||||||||||||||||||||||||||||||||||||||||||||||||||||||||||||||||||||||||||||||||||||||||||||||||||||||||||||||||||||||||||||||||||

The coefficients in the demand equation are overidentified so it is not clear which of the alternate consistent estimators to use. For example, the estimate of $\beta_1$ may be determined based on either of the formulas, $\beta_1 = \pi_{13}/\pi_{23}$ or $\beta_1 = \pi_{14}/\pi_{24}$. The alternate results would be $b_1 = p_{13}/p_{23} = 0.2069/(-0.0160) = -12.931$ or $b_1 = p_{14}/p_{24} = 0.0817/(0.0081) = +10.086$.

||||||||||||||||||||||||||||||||||||||||||||||||||||||||||||||||||||||||||||||||||||||||||||||||||||||||||||||||||||||||||||||||||||||||||||||||

*Interpretive note.* The first estimate is based on shifts in the supply equation due to changes in the weather. The second is based on shifts in the supply equation due to changes in costs. Either type of exogenous shift would help to trace out the demand curve and determine its slope in the price-quantity plane.

||||||||||||||||||||||||||||||||||||||||||||||||||||||||||||||||||||||||||||||||||||||||||||||||||||||||||||||||||||||||||||||||||||||||||||||||

Since the estimates of the other SF coefficients $\gamma_1$ and $\gamma_2$ depend on this estimate of $\beta_1$, they can vary significantly depending on whether the econometrician chooses to use the value $-12.931$ or $+10.086$ or some value in between.[7] It is even possible that $b_1 = 0$ might be the best choice, in which

---

[7] The reader should substitute the two alternate values for $b_1$ into the formulas derived from (17–16) for $\gamma_1$ and $\gamma_2$ to see how much difference it makes in the estimates $C_1$ and $C_2$ of these coefficients.

case the quantity consumed may not be a significant variable in the specified demand equation. In that situation, the matrix $\beta'$ may in fact be triangular, and the relations may be represented by a recursive model.

The econometrician might attempt to use some weighted average of the two alternate estimates of $\beta_1$ in calculating the other estimates of the SF coefficients.

||||||||||||||||||||||||||||||||||||||||||||||||||||||||||||||||||||||||||||||||||||||||||||||||||||||||||||||||||||||||||||||||

> *Interpretive note.* In this way, both exogenous factors of supply (weather and costs) would be recognized as jointly shifting the supply function and, thereby, tracing out and identifying the demand curve with a slope $\beta_1$.

||||||||||||||||||||||||||||||||||||||||||||||||||||||||||||||||||||||||||||||||||||||||||||||||||||||||||||||||||||||||||||||||

A simple average with each alternate estimate weighted equally would give the estimate $b_1 = (-12.931 + 10.086)/2 = -1.4225$. Use of this estimate would imply that the extra information about shifts in the supply curve due to either changes in $X_3 =$ weather or $X_4 =$ costs is equally important in identifying the demand curve with its slope $\beta_1 = \partial \text{ price}/\partial \text{ quantity}$. However, these two variables obviously do not exert equal influence in explaining either price or quantity. In Table 17–4, the estimates for the coefficients of $X_3$ and $X_4$ in either reduced form equation as well as their significance levels in each equation are different. Indeed, a proper weighting of the extra information should consider these significance levels as well as the relation of these exogenous variables to each other in determining their mixed effect on demand and supply.

The reader should understand that the choice between these alternate estimates or some complex combination of them is the primary difficulty in using ILS in an overidentified model. Only in the special case of exact identification, as in estimating the coefficients in this supply equation, is the method of indirect least squares useful. (See Exercise 10 at the end of this chapter.)

## 17.8 SUMMARY

In this chapter, some guidelines for recognizing the identifiability of an equation in a simultaneous equations model are developed. The only situation considered is one in which zero-type restrictions are imposed. The specific identifiability rules in this case are known as the rank and order conditions. In nontechnical terms, these conditions require that equation $i$, in order to be identified, must exclude some variables that are included elsewhere in the model. Also, whenever any of the variables included in equation $i$ also appear in another equation, that other equation must also include at least one of the variables excluded from equation $i$. The whole model is identified if each equation is identified. That is, all the equations in the model must be different in the sense that no combination of a subset of two or more equations would result in an equation identical in form, involving exactly the same variables, as any one other equation in the model.

Throughout the discussion, only identification of the coefficients in the model was considered. Further study in the identification problem would involve the identification of the elements in the variance-covariance matrix of the disturbances in the model and the use of other type restrictions on the parameters.

Estimation of the coefficients in the SF equations of a simultaneous equations model is also considered in this chapter. Two special results deserve to be repeated. In the case of a recursive model, the use of ordinary least squares is suggested. In the case of an interdependent system that is exactly identified, the use of indirect least squares is feasible. Examples of some simple models of each type are given. Finally, the new procedure of indirect least squares is shown to be inadequate to estimate the coefficients in an overidentified equation. The next chapter discusses an estimation procedure, two-stage least squares, which is appropriate in the overidentified case.

## NEW VOCABULARY

| | |
|---|---|
| Echelon form | Identifiability equations |
| Necessary and sufficient conditions | Indirect least squares |
| SF parameter set | Normalized endogenous variable |
| Zero-type restrictions | Causal chain |
| Rank and order conditions | Recursive model |
| Underidentified | Exact identifiability |
| Overidentified | |

## EXERCISES

1.  Consider a three-equation (simultaneous) model with $G = 3$ and $K = 4$. Using the rank and order conditions for identifiability,
    *a)* Show that if one equation includes all seven variables, then the model is not identified.
    *b)* Show that if two of the equations contain the same variables, then the model is not identified.

2.  Derive the reduced form (17–10) from the structural form (17–9).

3.  Change the supply equation of (17–9) to

$$Y_2 = \beta_2 Y_1 + \gamma_3 + \gamma_4 X_3 + \varepsilon_2,$$

where $X_3 = $ production cost index.
    *a)* Using the order condition of identifiability, show that both demand and supply are exactly identified.
    *b)* Derive the reduced form of this model.

    *c)*   Derive formulas for the solution of the SF coefficients in terms of the RF coefficients.

4.  Beginning with model (17–9), change the demand equation to,

$$Y_1 = \beta_1 Y_2 + \gamma_1 + \gamma_2 X_2 + \gamma_4 X_4 + \varepsilon_1$$

where $X_4 =$ lagged price.

    *a)*   Show that the supply equation is then overidentified.

    *b)*   Derive the reduced form of this model.

    *c)*   Derive alternate formulas for the solution of the coefficients in the supply equation in terms of the RF coefficients.

5.  Examine equations three and four of the five-equation model (17–11) for identifiability using the rank and order conditions.

6.  Show that the determinant is nonzero for the coefficient matrix, $\beta'$, of the endogenous variables in the model (17–11).

7.  Demonstrate the use of the rank condition for identifiability using only the *structural* form of model (17–9). Examine the identifiability of both equations.

8.  Find the reduced form of the model (17–11). Using this RF, check the rank condition for identifiability of the consumption and liquidity preference functions.

9.  Beginning with model (17–11), reduce the form of the model to a two-equation model with endogenous variables $Y_2 = $ GNP and $Y_4 = $ long-term interest rate by using the following two identities, $Y_2 = Y_1 + Y_3$ and liquidity preference = liquidity supply in equilibrium.

    *a)*   Specify the revised two-equation structural form.

    *b)*   Check the identifiability of these two equations.

    *c)*   Derive the two-equation reduced form for this revised model.

    *d)*   Try to derive formulas for determining each structural form coefficient (in the two-equation revised structure) in terms of the RF coefficients.

    *e)*   Try to derive formulas for determining each structural form coefficient in the original model (17–11) from the results of steps (*c*) and (*d*) above.

10.  Use the data for $Y_1 = $ price index, $Y_2 = $ quantity index, $X_2 = $ income index, and $X_4 = $ production costs index from Table 17–3 to find indirect least squares estimates of the coefficients in the following model,

$$Y_1 = \beta_1 Y_2 + \gamma_1 + \gamma_2 X_2 + \varepsilon_1,$$
$$Y_2 = \beta_2 Y_1 + \gamma_3 + \gamma_4 X_4 + \varepsilon_2.$$

The steps are:

    *a)*   Derive the reduced form of the model.

    *b)*   Estimate the RF equations using OLS.

    *c)*   Solve for the estimates of the SF coefficients based on the estimates of the RF coefficients.

11.  Check the identifiability of the consumption and investment equations in the model specified at the beginning of Section 2.5.

12.  A commonly referred to model is the Klein Model I representing the U.S. economy in simplified form for the period, 1921–41. Write the model in the form (17–3) and use the rank and order conditions to examine the identifi-

ability of the three stochastic equations in this model. Also, explain why the model is, or is not, a recursive model.

**Klein Model I, L. R. Klein, U.S. Economic Fluctuations, 1921–1941**

| *Endogenous variables* | | *Predetermined variables* | |
|---|---|---|---|
| $Y_1$ | Consumption expenditures | $X_1$ | Constant $= 1$ |
| $Y_2$ | Net investment | $X_2$ | Labor income originating in government |
| $Y_3$ | Labor income originating in private employment | $X_3$ | Indirect taxes |
| $Y_4$ | Profit | $X_4$ | Exogenous investment |
| $Y_5$ | Net national income | $X_5$ | Time in years, $t = 0$ in 1931 |
| $Y_6$ | End of year stock of capital | $X_6$ | Previous year's profit |
| $Y_7$ | Total wage bill | $X_7$ | Beginning of year stock of capital |
| $Y_8$ | Private product | $X_8$ | Previous year's private product |

Stochastic equations:

$$Y_1 = \beta_{14} Y_4 + \beta_{17} Y_7 + \gamma_{11} + \gamma_{16} X_6 + \varepsilon_1$$
$$Y_2 = \beta_{24} Y_4 + \gamma_{21} + \gamma_{26} X_6 + \gamma_{27} X_7 + \varepsilon_2$$
$$Y_3 = \beta_{38} Y_8 + \gamma_{31} + \gamma_{35} X_5 + \gamma_{38} X_8$$

Identities:

$$Y_5 + X_3 = Y_1 + Y_2 + X_4$$
$$Y_5 = Y_4 + Y_7$$
$$Y_6 = X_7 + Y_2$$
$$Y_7 = Y_3 + X_2$$
$$Y_8 = Y_5 + X_3 - X_2$$

13. Form your own two- or three-equation simultaneous model representing some interrelated economic mechanism of your own interest. Check your equations for identifiability. Modify your model if necessary so all its equations are exactly identified. For this final model,
   a) Specify clearly the meaning of the relations and the definition of the variables.
   b) Demonstrate that this model is exactly identified.
   c) Based on some data which you can find to represent measures of the variables in your model, find ordinary least squares estimates of the coefficients in each equation.
   d) Derive the reduced form of your model and find mathematical representations of the coefficients in the SF in terms of the coefficients of the RF.
   e) Using the same data as in step (c), and the formulas from step (d), find indirect least squares estimates of the coefficients in the SF.
   f) Compare the results of steps (c) and (e) and discuss the reason for the differences.

14. *a)* Using the data below, estimate the coefficients in the consumption function of model (16–2*a*) by the method of indirect least squares.

$$C_t = \beta Y_t + \gamma + \varepsilon \qquad (16\text{–}2a)$$
$$Y_t = C_t + Z_t$$

**Data**

| $C_t$ | $Y_t$ | $Z_t$ |
|------|------|------|
| 34.9 | 45.2 | 9.2 |
| 35.9 | 47.0 | 10.5 |
| 37.9 | 50.3 | 12.1 |
| 41.1 | 55.7 | 14.4 |
| 43.5 | 59.9 | 16.1 |
| 46.7 | 65.2 | 16.4 |
| 48.9 | 68.9 | 17.3 |
| 52.0 | 74.3 | 18.0 |
| 56.1 | 81.2 | 19.3 |
| 62.6 | 92.2 | 21.0 |

*b)* Compare these ILS estimates to the OLS estimates of the consumption function as obtained in Exercise 5 of Chapter 3.

15. Using the same model (16–2*a*) as in Exercise 14 above and using the data from Exercise 15 of Chapter 13 (where $Z$ is defined to be $Z = I + G$), find indirect least squares estimates of $\beta$ and $\gamma$. Compare these results to the estimates obtained in Exercise 15 of Chapter 13 using the method of instrumental variables. Can you generalize and explain why the methods of instrumental variables and indirect least squares yield the same results when applied to an exactly identified model?

16. Suggest why an econometrician might use the logs of the variables in the estimation of the demand-supply example model of Section 17.7. Rewrite the structural form using $\ln Y_1, \ln Y_2, \ldots, \ln X_3$ as variables. Estimate the demand and supply equations using ILS in this case and interpret the meaning of the results. (A logarithmic transformation of the data in Table 17–3 should be applied before calculating the estimates.)

*Chapter*

*18*

# TWO-STAGE LEAST SQUARES ESTIMATION

## 18.1 PREVIEW

Throughout this book, the method of least squares has received special attention since it is a relatively simple estimation method and is so widely applied. Also, in Chapters 13–15, some two-stage estimation procedures are presented in the list of remedies for certain econometric problems. In these procedures, more than one estimation is performed and some result from the first stage is used as an input in the second stage.

In this chapter the two concepts of least squares and two-stage procedures are combined in the method of two-stage least squares (2SLS). For estimating

451

coefficients in a structural equation of a simultaneous equations model, 2SLS is the most commonly used procedure. The method of 2SLS is appropriate if the equation being estimated is exactly identified or overidentified. Thus, it can be used in cases of overidentification in which indirect least squares is unsatisfactory. It is of no help in cases of underidentification.

Other methods of estimating coefficients in the overidentified structural equation are known, and comparisons of the properties of the various estimators are the subjects of econometric research. In this book, the method of 2SLS receives primary emphasis not only because it has been most commonly used in simultaneous equations econometric studies and is the most readily available procedure in terms of computer programs, but also because it has become the reference point for comparison with more recent advances in estimation theory. For example, more efficient procedures such as three-stage least squares cannot be fully understood or appreciated without knowing 2SLS.

The procedure of 2SLS is outlined in Section 3 of this chapter. An alternate form of the development is given in Section 4 to relate 2SLS to the maximum likelihood estimators and the generalized classical linear estimator seen earlier in Chapters 10 and 14 respectively. In Section 5, a numerical illustration of the use of 2SLS is given. Finally, some remarks are made on the comparison of 2SLS with ordinary least squares, indirect least squares, and the method of instrumental variables.

## 18.2 REVIEW

In working through this chapter, the reader should be familiar with the earlier topics on the assumptions and maximum likelihood estimators for the general single equation model. In particular, a review of Chapter 10 and Sections 13.3 and 16.3 is recommended. In addition, two easy results from linear algebra will be useful in following the discussion of Section 18.3.

### 1 Rank of a product matrix

Since a matrix multiplication is merely a repetition of forming linear combinations of the rows (or columns) of the individual matrices, the number of linearly independent rows (or columns) of the product matrix cannot exceed the number of linearly independent rows (or columns) in either of the individual matrices. The statement may be expressed in terms of ranks.

If $A$ and $B$ are two matrices, then the rank of $AB$ can be no larger than either the rank of $A$ or the rank of $B$.

### 2 A matrix factor

It is quite common in algebra to factor expressions into their multiplicative parts, such as $X^2 - Y^2$ is factored into $(X - Y)(X + Y)$. Also, numbers may be factored into primes, such as $12 = 2 \cdot 2 \cdot 3$. Often, a single term is "factored out" of a more complex expression, such as $X^2 + 2X = X(X + 2)$ or

$50 = 2(5^2)$. The purpose of such factoring is usually simplification of the expression for interpretation or for combination with other terms. The same sort of factoring can be performed in matrix multiplications. For example, $(X'Y + 2X'X)$ could be factored into $X'(Y + 2X)$ where $X$ and $Y$ are $n \times n$ size matrices.

It is also possible to factor out a term which does not appear in the original expression. In algebraic factoring, for example, the term $4y$ may be factored out of $(2X + 12)$ by writing $4y(X/2y + 3/y) = 2X + 12$.

||||||||||||||||||||||||||||||||||||||||||||||||||||||||||||||||||||||||||||||||||||||||||||||||||||||||||||||||||||||||||||||||||

*Interpretive note.*   In such cases, it appears that a simple expression is made more complex by factoring. This is true, but it is only useful to do so if the end result is a real simplification in the context of the problem involved.

||||||||||||||||||||||||||||||||||||||||||||||||||||||||||||||||||||||||||||||||||||||||||||||||||||||||||||||||||||||||||||||||||

In matrix algebra, it is also sometimes useful to factor in this way. A given matrix $(C'X + I)$ of dimension $(m \times m)$ may be factored into $(C' + X^{-1})X$. The matrix $X$ is factored out of an identity matrix leaving the term, $X^{-1}$. Since $X^{-1}X = I$, this factoring is correct. It is even possible to factor out a different sized matrix. Let a matrix $C$ be size $(G \times K)$, a matrix $X'$ be $(K \times T)$, and let $C$ be a matrix product defined by

$$C_{(G \times K)} = A_{(G \times h)} \ B_{(h \times K)},$$

then the factor $A$ could be removed from the expression $(CX')$ of size $(G \times T)$ to obtain

$$CX' = A_{(G \times h)} \ [BX']_{(h \times T)}.$$

## REVIEW EXERCISES

R.1.   Show that the product matrix, $C = A_{(m \times h)} \ B_{(h \times n)}$ must have rank $\leq \min(m, h, n)$.

R.2.   Demonstrate the proposition stated in R.1 using the product matrix $C = AB$ where,

a)   $A = \begin{pmatrix} 1 & 0 \\ 0 & 1 \\ 1 & 1 \end{pmatrix}$   and   $B = \begin{pmatrix} 1 & 0 & -1 & 1 \\ 0 & 1 & 1 & 1 \end{pmatrix}$,

b)   $A = (2 \quad 3)$   and   $B = \begin{pmatrix} 2 & 0 & 1 \\ -1 & 1 & 0 \end{pmatrix}$,

c)   $A = \begin{pmatrix} 1 & 0 & 0 \\ 0 & 3 & 0 \\ 2 & 1 & -1 \end{pmatrix}$   and   $B = \begin{pmatrix} 1 & -1 \\ 2 & 0 \\ 0 & 3 \end{pmatrix}$.

R.3.   Given matrices $A$ and $B$ from part (c) of Exercise R.2 above, and given the
matrix $X = (3 \quad -2)$,
 a)  Find $C = AB$.
 b)  Find $CX'$.
 c)  Factor the matrix $A$ out of the product $CX'$.
 d)  Form the augmented matrix $(CX' \quad A^*)$ where

$$A^* = \begin{pmatrix} 1 & 0 \\ 0 & 3 \\ 2 & 1 \end{pmatrix}.$$

 e)  Factor the matrix $A$ out of the augmented matrix in part (d).

Ans.: $A \left\{ BX' \quad \begin{pmatrix} I \\ {\scriptstyle 2 \times 2} \\ O \\ {\scriptstyle 1 \times 2} \end{pmatrix} \right\}.$

## 18.3 THE 2SLS PROCEDURE

The structural form of a simultaneous equations model may be written,
$\beta' Y' + \Gamma' X' = \varepsilon'$ (17–3) with the reduced form given by $Y' = \Pi' X' + v'$
(17–4). A particular equation, say the $i$th, in the structural form may be written,

$$\beta_{i1} Y_{1t} + \beta_{i2} Y_{2t} + \cdots + Y_{it} + \cdots + \beta_{iG} Y_{Gt}$$
$$+ \gamma_{i1} + \gamma_{i2} X_{2t} + \cdots + \gamma_{iK} X_{Kt} = \varepsilon_{it} \qquad (17\text{–}1)$$

where some of the coefficients may be zero.

### A notational convenience

It is more convenient to eliminate these excluded variables in the equation
(17–1) and to be concerned only with the included variables. Also, it is convenient to write the equation with the normalized variable on the left and the
others on the right-hand side of the equation. In doing this the sign of the
coefficient may be implicitly changed so that the terms can be represented as
positive for simplicity in later manipulations. The observation subscript is also
dropped for simplicity. The single $i$th equation in the structural form can then
be written as

$$\underset{(T \times 1)}{Y_i} \; = \; \underset{[T \times (g-1)][g-1) \times 1]}{Y^* \qquad \beta} \qquad + \; \underset{(T \times h)\ (h \times 1)}{Y_{EX} \quad O} \; + \; \underset{(T \times m)\ (m \times 1)}{X_{IN} \quad \Gamma_{IN}} \; + \; \underset{(T \times n)\ (n \times 1)}{X_{EX} \quad O} \; + \; \underset{(T \times 1)}{\varepsilon_i}$$
$$(18\text{–}1)$$

where $Y_{IN}$, the endogenous variables included in the equation, has been
partitioned into $Y_i$, the normalized endogenous variable, and $Y^*$, the other
$(g - 1)$ endogenous variables included in the $i$th equation as explanatory
variables.

## The rationale of 2SLS

The problem of estimating a structural equation such as (18–1) directly is that the variables $Y^*$ and $\varepsilon_i$ are probably not independent due to the simultaneity of the model. (See Section 13.3 and Chapter 16.) The method of two-stage least squares seeks to remove the influence of $\varepsilon$ on the explanatory variables $Y^*$ in the first stage and then to use the adjusted values for $Y^*$ in a second stage estimation of the equation (18–1). These adjusted values, denoted by $\hat{Y}^*$, are then independent of $\varepsilon$ so that least squares estimation becomes appropriate.

## The procedure of 2SLS

The actual method of removing the influence of $\varepsilon$ on $Y^*$ is to represent $Y^*$ in terms of all the predetermined variables in the model, $X = (X_{\text{IN}} \quad X_{\text{EX}})$. These variables should be independent of $\varepsilon$ so that if $\hat{Y}^*$ is a function of these variables only, then $\hat{Y}^*$ should be independent of $\varepsilon$. All the predetermined variables are used since these all interact within the simultaneous equations model to affect each of the endogenous variables.

|||||||||||||||||||||||||||||||||||||||||||||||||||||||||||||||||||||||||||||||||||||||||||||||||||||||||||||||||||||||||||||||||||||||||||

*Discursive note.* Sometimes to avoid severe multicollinearity in the first stage, the variables $Y^*$ may each be represented in terms of their principal components or by a selected subset of instruments which gives the best forecasts of $Y^*$. However, the econometrician must be careful in making such a selection for two reasons. The simultaneity or interpretation of the model may be severely compromised, or the adjusted variables $\hat{Y}^*$ may not be linearly independent of $X_{\text{IN}}$ in the sample so that the moment matrix of explanatory variables is singular. Then, no least squares solution can be obtained for estimates of the coefficients $\beta$ and $\Gamma_{\text{IN}}$.

|||||||||||||||||||||||||||||||||||||||||||||||||||||||||||||||||||||||||||||||||||||||||||||||||||||||||||||||||||||||||||||||||||||||||||

The representation of a variable $Y_j$, included in the set $Y^*$ of endogenous variables in the $i$th equation, in terms of all the predetermined variables in the model is exactly the same as the reduced form (RF) equation for $Y_j$. Consequently, the first stage of 2SLS is simply the least squares estimation of the reduced form equations for $Y^*$. In regressing $Y^*$ on all $X$, we have $(g - 1)$ different equations, which all have the same variables on the right-hand side. These RF equations are not estimated simultaneously since each includes only one endogenous variable.

The form of each RF equation is,

$$\underset{(T \times 1)}{Y_j} = \underset{(T \times K)}{X} \underset{(K \times 1)}{\Pi_j} + \underset{(T \times 1)}{v_j} .$$

The OLS estimates of $\Pi_j$ are given by $P_j = (X'X)^{-1}X'Y_j$ (17–13) so that estimates of $Y_j$ based on the RF equations are given by

$$\hat{Y}_j = XP_j = X(X'X)^{-1}X'Y_j. \qquad (17\text{–}14)$$

These estimated values for $Y_j$ obtained from the reduced form are substituted into the structural equation being estimated. The revised structural equation (18–1) is then

$$Y_i = \hat{Y}^*\beta + X_{\text{IN}}\Gamma_{\text{IN}} + \varepsilon_i. \qquad (18\text{–}2)$$

The coefficients $\beta$ and $\Gamma_{\text{IN}}$ are estimated using ordinary least squares since the problem of interdependence between $Y^*$ and $\varepsilon_i$ has been removed by replacing $Y^*$ with $\hat{Y}^*$.

## Formulation of the 2SLS estimators

Let the explanatory variables in (18–2) be denoted by

$$\underset{[T \times (g-1+m)]}{Z} = (\hat{Y}^* \quad X_{\text{IN}})$$

with coefficient vector $\underset{[(g-1+m) \times 1]}{(\beta \quad \Gamma_{\text{IN}})'}$ . The OLS estimators of $(\beta \quad \Gamma_{\text{IN}})'$ in equation $i$ are obtained in the second-stage estimation by

$$[\text{Est. }(\beta \quad \Gamma_{\text{IN}})'] = (Z'Z)^{-1}Z'Y_i$$

where $Z = (\hat{Y}^* \quad X_{\text{IN}})$.

Expanding this formula gives the result for 2SLS estimates of $\beta$ and $\Gamma_{\text{IN}}$,

$$\underset{[(g-1+m) \times 1]}{\begin{pmatrix} b \\ C_{\text{IN}} \end{pmatrix}_i} = \underset{[(g-1+m) \times (g-1+m)]}{\begin{bmatrix} \hat{Y}^{*\prime}\,\hat{Y}^* & \hat{Y}^{*\prime}\,X_{\text{IN}} \\ X'_{\text{IN}}\,\hat{Y}^* & X'_{\text{IN}}\,X_{\text{IN}} \end{bmatrix}^{-1}} \underset{[(g-1+m) \times T]}{\begin{pmatrix} \hat{Y}^{*\prime} \\ X'_{\text{IN}} \end{pmatrix}} \underset{(T \times 1)}{Y_i} \qquad (18\text{–}3)$$

## A necessary condition for 2SLS estimation

The 2SLS solution for estimates of the coefficients in structural equation $i$ as given by (18–3) can only exist if the inverse matrix on the right-hand side exists. This inverse exists for the square matrix of size $(g-1+m)$ if and only if it is nonsingular (has rank equal to $g-1+m$).

Using a result on ranks from *Review* 18.2, item 1, the rank of this matrix, $(Z'Z)$, can be no larger than the rank of

$$Z = (\hat{Y}^* \quad X_{\text{IN}}) = [X(X'X)^{-1}X'Y^* \quad X_{\text{IN}}].$$

[The latter equality uses the substitution for $\hat{Y}^*$ from (17–14) above.]

The latter matrix can be written as a product of two matrices by factoring $X$ out of both partitions (see *Review* 18.2, item 2) to obtain,

$$Z = \underset{(T \times K)}{X} \left[ \begin{array}{c|c} (X'X)^{-1}X'Y^* & \underset{(m \times m)}{I} \\ \hline \underset{[K \times (g-1)]}{} & \underset{(n \times m)}{O} \end{array} \right],_{\;[(m+n) \times m]}$$

since

$$X_{(T \times K)} \begin{pmatrix} I \\ O \end{pmatrix}_{(K \times m)} = (X_{\text{IN}})_{(T \times m)}$$

||||||||||||||||||||||||||||||||||||||||||||||||||||||||||||||||||||||||||||||||||||||||||||||||||||||||||||||||||||||||||||||||||||||||||||||||||

**Explicative note.**   Careful analysis of the dimensions and meaning of each of these matrices helps to make the result clearer. $X$ is a $(T \times K)$ matrix of $T$ observations on $K$ predetermined variables. $(X'X)^{-1}X'Y^*$ is a $[K \times (g - 1)]$ matrix, the transform of the reduced form coefficient matrix $\Pi'$ excluding row $i$. The partitioned matrix $\begin{pmatrix} I \\ O \end{pmatrix}$ has $m$ columns and $m + n = K$ rows. Thus, the matrix $Z$ is still size $[T \times (g - 1 + m)]$ since it is the product of a well-defined matrix multiplication of two matrices of sizes $(T \times K)$ and $[K \times (g - 1 + m)]$.

||||||||||||||||||||||||||||||||||||||||||||||||||||||||||||||||||||||||||||||||||||||||||||||||||||||||||||||||||||||||||||||||||||||||||||||||||

In the above form, it is clear that the rank of $Z$ cannot be larger than the rank of $X$ which is at most $K$ since $T > K$ by Assumption 6. (See Section 10.3.)

||||||||||||||||||||||||||||||||||||||||||||||||||||||||||||||||||||||||||||||||||||||||||||||||||||||||||||||||||||||||||||||||||||||||||||||||||

**Recursive note.**   The number of observations must exceed the number of predetermined variables or the degrees of freedom in the RF estimation would be zero or negative.

||||||||||||||||||||||||||||||||||||||||||||||||||||||||||||||||||||||||||||||||||||||||||||||||||||||||||||||||||||||||||||||||||||||||||||||||||

Since the rank of $(Z'Z)^{-1}$ in 18.3 must be $(g - 1 + m)$ in order to obtain a solution, and since it has been shown that rank $(Z'Z) \leq$ rank $(Z) \leq$ rank $X \leq K$, then a necessary condition for 2SLS estimation is that $K$ must be at least as large as $g - 1 + m$. Since $K = m + n$, this condition reduces from $K \geq g - 1 + m$ to $m + n \geq g - 1 + m$, or $n \geq g - 1$.

||||||||||||||||||||||||||||||||||||||||||||||||||||||||||||||||||||||||||||||||||||||||||||||||||||||||||||||||||||||||||||||||||||||||||||||||||

**Interpretive note.**   The necessary condition for the application of 2SLS estimation of structural form equation $i$ is that the number of predetermined variables excluded from equation $i$, $(X_{\text{EX}})$, must be at least as large as the number of endogenous variables included in the equation as explanatory variables, $(Y^*)$.

||||||||||||||||||||||||||||||||||||||||||||||||||||||||||||||||||||||||||||||||||||||||||||||||||||||||||||||||||||||||||||||||||||||||||||||||||

The condition is *identical* to the necessary (order) condition for the identifiability of equation $i$. Thus, 2SLS can be used on any identified structural equation, whether it is exactly or overidentified. In forming the first-stage estimate of $Y^*$, the method of 2SLS uses the identifying information from all other predetermined variables in the model, whether or not this is overidentifying information. The excess information is weighted, in a sense, by the importance of these predetermined variables in the respective reduced form equations.

## 18.4 ALTERNATE ESTIMATORS OF THE STRUCTURAL COEFFICIENTS

This section is somewhat of a digression, but it is often helpful in understanding a single concept such as 2SLS to have some awareness of related concepts. Two such related formulations of estimators are briefly and nonrigorously examined in this section for symmetry with the similar concepts earlier in the book. In Chapters 6 and 10 in particular, a comparison of the least squares and maximum likelihood concepts was given; and in Chapter 14, the formulation of least squares estimators as generalized classical linear estimators was presented. The method of 2SLS can also be compared conceptually with a maximum likelihood method, and the formulation of both can be presented in a generalized classical linear estimation framework.

Needless to say, a complete comparison in the case of a simultaneous equations model is quite a bit more complex than for the single equation model. Only the bare essentials are referred to here, and proofs of the results are not given. If the reader finds this section much simpler than the prior buildup would indicate, perhaps he should not be too surprised. The true purpose of this introduction is to warn the reader that the simple material given here is not "all there is to know." Further study in econometrics would expand greatly on this material since current research in econometrics is expanding the knowledge on these and other simultaneous estimating techniques.

### A maximum likelihood approach

The method of maximum likelihood estimation involves maximizing a likelihood function in the unknown parameters based on the given information of the model and the probability density functions of the sample observations which are treated as random variables. In the simultaneous equations model, several levels of information can be used. Certainly, the knowledge of the variables included and excluded from the equation being estimated is crucial. If the excluded variables are merely recognized as appearing in the model elsewhere than in equation $i$, then the maximum likelihood estimation of equation $i$ is said to use limited information. If the formulation of the likelihood functions makes use of the complete model specification including which excluded variables in equation $i$ appear in what other equations and in what combinations, etc., then the procedure is called full information maximum likelihood. This is a very complex method requiring much calculation and is seldom applied in practice.

***The effect of simultaneity.***    The limited information maximum likelihood (LIML) method is more frequently applied. Consider a structural equation such as

$$Y_i = Y^*\beta + X_{IN}\Gamma_{IN} + \varepsilon_i. \tag{18-1}$$

Figure 18–1 illustrates the complex causal relations involved in the estimation of $\beta$ and $\Gamma_{IN}$. Finding an estimate of $\beta$ involves an assessment of the importance of the relation in equation $i$ between $Y_i$ and $Y^*$. Intuitively, this is done by measuring the amount of variability in $Y_i$ that is explained by its association with $Y^*$. In so doing, it must be recognized that the variability of $Y^*$ is

**FIGURE 18–1**
**Causal relations underlying a structural form equation**

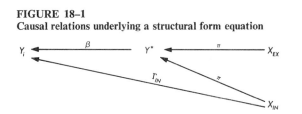

dependent on all the $X$ in the model and that some of the variability in $Y_i$ is explained by $X_{IN}$, which is a subset of all the $X$. Returning to the simple intuitive representation of a regression coefficient as a covariation over a variation, the interpretation of the estimate of $\beta$ in the causal pattern shown in Figure 18–1 is given by the ratio,

$$\frac{\text{(variation in } Y_i \text{ not explained by } X_{IN} \text{ that is explained by } Y^*)}{\text{(variation in } Y^* \text{ not explained by } X_{IN} \text{ that is explained by } X_{EX})}.$$

||||||||||||||||||||||||||||||||||||||||||||||||||||||||||||||||||||||||||||||||||||||||||||||||||||||||||||||||||||||||||||||||||||||||||||

***Recursive note.***    The estimate $\beta$ in the simultaneous case is more complex than if (18–1) were a single equation model. In the latter case, the usual multiple regression interpretation of the estimator $\beta$ is given by the following ratio with a simpler denominator,

$$\frac{\text{(variation in } Y_i \text{ not explained by } X_{IN} \text{ that is explained by } Y^*)}{\text{(variation in } Y^* \text{ not explained by } X_{IN})}.$$

||||||||||||||||||||||||||||||||||||||||||||||||||||||||||||||||||||||||||||||||||||||||||||||||||||||||||||||||||||||||||||||||||||||||||||

***Forming the likelihood function.***    For a given $\beta$, the structural equation (18–1) can be rewritten as

$$(Y_i - Y^*\beta) = X_{IN}\Gamma_{IN} + \varepsilon_i, \tag{18-4}$$

in which a composite variable $(Y_i - Y^*\beta)$ is regressed on the $X_{IN}$.

For this type regression, the maximum likelihood function for $\Gamma_{IN}$ could be set up as in Chapter 10 and estimates obtained for $\Gamma_{IN}$ in terms of $X_{IN}$ and $(Y_i - Y^*\beta)$.

The maximization of the likelihood function, $L(\beta, \Gamma_{IN}; Y_i, Y^*, X_{IN}, X_{EX})$ involves finding estimates of $\beta$ and $\Gamma_{IN}$ such that the excluded variables, $X_{EX}$, really do not occur in this $i$th equation but do interact within the model in some unspecified way.

||||||||||||||||||||||||||||||||||||||||||||||||||||||||||||||||||||||||||||||||||||||||||||||||||||||||||||||||||||||||||||||

*Recursive note.*  A full information maximum likelihood procedure would involve the exact way in which these excluded variables are specified in the entire model.

||||||||||||||||||||||||||||||||||||||||||||||||||||||||||||||||||||||||||||||||||||||||||||||||||||||||||||||||||||||||||||||

In terms of the simpler likelihood function associated with the single equation model (18–4) with the composite endogenous variable $(Y_i - Y^*\beta)$, this means that the sampling variance from a regression of this composite on $X_{IN}$ is made as small as possible relative to the sampling variance from the regression of the composite on all $X$. The likelihood function is maximized by attributing as much of the explained variation in $Y_i$ as possible to the variables included in equation $i$.

*The least variance ratio.*  If two regression equations explaining the composite variable are written as

$$a)\quad (Y_i - Y^*\hat{\beta}) = X_{IN}\hat{\Gamma}_{IN} + e_i$$

and

$$b)\quad (Y_i - Y^*\hat{\beta}) = X_{IN}\tilde{\Gamma}_{IN} + X_{EX}\tilde{\Gamma}_{EX} + w_i$$

where $e_i$ and $w_i$ are the vectors of $T$ residuals for the two regressions, then the maximum likelihood estimates $\hat{\beta}$ and $\hat{\Gamma}_{IN}$ are chosen so that $e_i'e_i$ is as close as possible to $w_i'w_i$.

||||||||||||||||||||||||||||||||||||||||||||||||||||||||||||||||||||||||||||||||||||||||||||||||||||||||||||||||||||||||||||||

*Recursive note.*  The sum of squares of residuals can be obtained from the sample moment matrix for each regression according to the pattern in Section 10.6, formula (10–9). See Exercise 1 at the end of this chapter.

||||||||||||||||||||||||||||||||||||||||||||||||||||||||||||||||||||||||||||||||||||||||||||||||||||||||||||||||||||||||||||||

*Explicative note.*  The so-called variance ratio, $l = (e_i'e_i)/(w_i'w_i)$ is minimized. The denominator $w_i'w_i$ is a sum of squares of residuals using the equation with all $X$, whereas the numerator is a sum of squares of residuals using the equation involving only $X_{IN}$. Thus, the denominator is necessarily no larger than the numerator. In symbols $e_i'e_i \geq w_i'w_i$, so $l \geq 1$.

||||||||||||||||||||||||||||||||||||||||||||||||||||||||||||||||||||||||||||||||||||||||||||||||||||||||||||||||||||||||||||||

The smallest possible value for the least variance ratio, $l$, is unity. This occurs when the explanation of $Y_i$ in equation ($a$) above is equally as good as the explanation of $Y_i$ in equation (*b*). That is, the addition of the extra variables $X_{EX}$ contributes nothing to the explanation of $Y_i$ so $w_i'w_i = e_i'e_i$. In this case, the variables $X_{EX}$ really should be excluded from equation *i* and the over-identifiability restrictions are exactly correct.

*Some comparisons of estimators.* In the case of perfect identification when $l = 1$, the LIML estimates are identical to the indirect least squares estimates.

|||||||||||||||||||||||||||||||||||||||||||||||||||||||||||||||||||||||||||||||||||||||||||||||||||||||||||||||||||||||||||||||||||||||||||||||||||||||||

> *Recursive note.* Since maximum likelihood estimators are consistent, this equivalence helps to explain why the ILS estimates are consistent.

|||||||||||||||||||||||||||||||||||||||||||||||||||||||||||||||||||||||||||||||||||||||||||||||||||||||||||||||||||||||||||||||||||||||||||||||||||||||||

Also in the case of exact identification, ILS and 2SLS give identical estimates as illustrated in the subsequent numerical example. Therefore, the appropriate least squares estimation and these maximum likelihood estimators for the coefficients in a simultaneous equations model are identical under certain conditions just as they were in the single equation model. The conditions are the assumptions of 10.3 and exact identification of the structural equations.

|||||||||||||||||||||||||||||||||||||||||||||||||||||||||||||||||||||||||||||||||||||||||||||||||||||||||||||||||||||||||||||||||||||||||||||||||||||||||

> *Discursive note.* In this book, the estimation of the variance-covariance matrix of the structural *disturbances* is not considered. Although the estimates of the structural form *coefficients* are identical by ILS, 2SLS, or LIML under exact identification, the estimates of $V\text{-}Cov(\varepsilon)$ will be different.

|||||||||||||||||||||||||||||||||||||||||||||||||||||||||||||||||||||||||||||||||||||||||||||||||||||||||||||||||||||||||||||||||||||||||||||||||||||||||

When the structural equation is overidentified and the value of $l > 1$, then ILS is not applicable and estimates obtained by LIML and 2SLS will be different. Since 2SLS estimators are easier to understand and to calculate, they are more commonly used in the overidentified case than the LIML estimators.

## The generalized classical linear estimator approach

As discussed in Chapter 14, a general classical linear estimation of a coefficient may be determined from the minimization of a quadratic form in the disturbances of an equation in an econometric model. A typical matrix in this quadratic form is the inverse of the variance-covariance matrix of the disturbances. Consequently the quadratic form to be minimized in the case of the single equation model was given as $Q(e) = e'\Omega^{-1}e$ where $V\text{-}Cov(\varepsilon) = \sigma_\varepsilon^2\Omega$, and $\Omega$ may have to be estimated ($\tilde{\Omega}$) or replaced by a product of non-singular matrices $\tilde{H}'\tilde{H}$. All this need not be reviewed in detail here. However, the crucial point for estimation in the simultaneous equations model is that the disturbances in this quadratic form *need not* be disturbances in a single equation. They may represent linear combinations of disturbances from several equations without violating the previous theoretical results.

**The use of reduced form residuals.**   In particular, if the SF and RF of a simultaneous equations model are represented in our usual notation by (17–3) and (17–4), the residuals in the RF equations might be denoted by

$$\underset{(G \times T)}{v'} = (v_1, v_2, \ldots, v_G)'.$$

Each $\underset{(T \times 1)}{v_j}$ is obtained by $v_j = Y_j - \hat{Y}_j$ where $\hat{Y}_j$ is obtained from the OLS estimation of the reduced form equation for $Y_j$. Considering the 2SLS structural equation estimates,

$$\begin{pmatrix} b \\ C_{IN} \end{pmatrix}_i = \begin{bmatrix} \hat{Y}^{*\prime} \hat{Y}^* & \hat{Y}^{*\prime} X_{IN} \\ X'_{IN} \hat{Y}^* & X'_{IN} X_{IN} \end{bmatrix}^{-1} \begin{pmatrix} \hat{Y}^{*\prime} \\ X'_{IN} \end{pmatrix} Y_i \qquad (18\text{–}3)$$

the estimates $\underset{[T \times (g-1)]}{\hat{Y}^*}$ could be written as $\hat{Y}^* = Y^* - v^*$ where the asterisk designates the respective set of variables corresponding in the index ordering to the $g - 1$ endogenous variables appearing in equation $i$ as explanatory variables.

**Some simplifying manipulations.**   The substitution of $Y^* - v^*$ for $\hat{Y}^*$ in (18–3) is made simpler by prior consideration of the following two terms:

1.  $X'v^* = O$ since the independent variables are uncorrelated with the reduced form disturbances by assumption; and
2.  $Y^{*\prime}v^* = (v^* + \hat{Y}^*)'v^* = v^{*\prime}v^* + \hat{Y}^{*\prime}v^* = v^{*\prime}v^* + O$ since the residuals are not correlated with the regression estimates in least squares regression analysis and $\hat{Y}^*$ depends on these regression estimates and the independent variables $X$.

Using results (1) and (2), the following simplification is routine:

$$\begin{aligned}
\hat{Y}^{*\prime} \hat{Y}^* &= (Y^* - v^*)'(Y^* - v^*) \\
&= Y^{*\prime} Y^* - v^{*\prime} Y^* - Y^{*\prime} v^* + v^{*\prime} v^* \\
&= Y^{*\prime} Y^* + (-1 - 1 + 1) v^{*\prime} v^* \\
&= Y^{*\prime} Y^* - v^{*\prime} v^*.
\end{aligned}$$

**Rewriting the 2SLS estimators.**   The substitution for $\hat{Y}^*$ in (18–3) now gives,

$$\begin{pmatrix} b \\ C_{IN} \end{pmatrix}_i = \begin{bmatrix} Y^{*\prime} Y^* - v^{*\prime} v^* & Y^{*\prime} X_{IN} \\ X'_{IN} Y^* & X'_{IN} X_{IN} \end{bmatrix}^{-1} \begin{pmatrix} Y^{*\prime} - v^{*\prime} \\ X'_{IN} \end{pmatrix} Y_i.$$

Such a least squares estimate results from the minimization of the sum of squares of residuals in the estimation of the equation,

$$Y_i = \hat{Y}^* \beta + X_{IN} \Gamma_{IN} + \varepsilon_i$$

or by substitution,

$$Y_i = \underset{(T \times (g-1))}{(Y^* - v^*)} \quad \underset{[(g-1) \times 1]}{\beta} \quad + \quad \underset{(T \times m)(m \times 1)}{X_{IN} \Gamma_{IN}} \quad + \quad \underset{(T \times 1)}{\varepsilon_i} \quad .$$

Using $b$ as the estimate of $\beta$, $C_{IN}$ as the estimate of $\Gamma_{IN}$, and $e_i$ as the residual vector in structural equation $i$, then the form being minimized is $Q(e_i) = e_i' \Omega^{-1} e_i$. Taking the simplest case of $\Omega$ equal to an identity matrix, then

$$Q(e_i) = \underset{(1 \times T)}{[Y_i - (Y^* - v^*)b - X_{IN} C_{IN}]'} \quad \underset{(T \times 1)}{[Y_i - (Y^* - v^*)b - X_{IN} C_{IN}]}.$$

Each of the terms in this quadratic form is a linear combination, $\sum_{j=1}^{g-1} (Y_j - v_j)b_j$ of the reduced form residuals $v_j$ from $g - 1$ different equations. In this formulation, 2SLS is seen as a special case of generalized classical linear estimation applied to the simultaneous equations model.

## A family of estimators

An even more general formulation of the estimator can be obtained by weighting the linear combination of the residuals $v_j$. If the weight is given by a constant $k$, then the form being minimized could be written as,

$$[Y_i - (Y^* - kv^*)b - X_{IN} C_{IN}]'[Y_i - (Y^* - kv^*)b - X_{IN} C_{IN}].$$

Depending on different values of $k$, a family of so-called $k$-class estimators is obtained. Some of these deserve special mention.

(i) If $k = 1$, then $Y^* - kv^* = (Y^* - v^*) = \hat{Y}^*$ which is the case described above for 2SLS.

(ii) If $k = 0$, then $Y^* - kv^* = Y^*$ and the reduced form disturbances are not considered at all. The original values of $Y^*$ are used in the least squares estimation. This is identical to using ordinary least squares directly on the structural equation, and this results in inconsistent estimates.

(iii) If $k = l =$ the least variance ratio, then the estimates are the same as limited information maximum likelihood estimates.

Since all these estimators involve a quadratic form of residuals or linear combinations of residuals, they all are special cases of generalized classical linear estimation. More complex estimators for which $\Omega \neq I$ could also be formulated and are sometimes necessary in special situations where some other problems of econometric analysis (such as error in measurement, heteroscedasticity, or autocorrelation) occur in the presence of simultaneity. No set rules can be given for the best estimator in each instance since the interaction effects on these estimators of multiple or joint problems are still an unresolved topic of econometric research.

## 18.5 AN EXAMPLE CALCULATION OF 2SLS ESTIMATES

To illustrate the procedure of two-stage least squares, the same example model used in Section 17.7 is presented. The model includes an overidentified demand equation and an exactly identified supply equation, given by

$$\left. \begin{array}{ll} \text{Demand:} & Y_1 = \beta_1 Y_2 + \gamma_1 + \gamma_2 X_2 + \varepsilon_1 \\ \text{Supply:} & Y_2 = \beta_2 Y_1 + \gamma_3 + \gamma_4 X_3 + \gamma_5 X_4 + \varepsilon_2 . \end{array} \right\} \qquad (18\text{--}5a)$$

The data for the estimation of the model are given in Table 17–3.

### The two-stage procedure

The first stage of 2SLS is the estimation of the reduced form equations by ordinary least squares. These results are given in Table 17–4. Next, the adjusted or estimated values, $\hat{Y}_1$ and $\hat{Y}_2$, must be determined from these RF equations according to the usual method (17–14). These values are given in Table 18–1. Substituting $\hat{Y}_2$ for $Y_2$ in the demand equation and substituting $\hat{Y}_1$ for $Y_1$ in the supply equation, each structural equation then has one normalized endogenous variable expressed solely in terms of exogenous variables and previously estimated endogenous variables, all of which can be considered as predetermined and independent of the disturbance term. If the other usual assumptions for a single equation appear to be satisfied (see Section 10.3), then ordinary least squares can be applied to these revised structural equations,

$$\left. \begin{array}{ll} \text{Demand:} & Y_1 = \beta_1 \hat{Y}_2 + \gamma_1 + \gamma_2 X_2 + \varepsilon_1 \\ \text{Supply:} & Y_2 = \beta_2 \hat{Y}_1 + \gamma_3 + \gamma_4 X_3 + \gamma_5 X_4 + \varepsilon_2 \end{array} \right\} \qquad (18\text{--}5b)$$

to obtain the 2SLS estimates, $(b_1 \quad C_{\text{IN}})'_{\text{demand}}$ and $(b_2 \quad C_{\text{IN}})'_{\text{supply}}$.

TABLE 18–1

Estimated values of price and quantity based on the reduced form equations

| Observation | Price $= \hat{Y}_1$ | Quantity $= \hat{Y}_2$ |
|---|---|---|
| 1 . . . . . . . . | 104.10 | 101.54 |
| 2 . . . . . . . . | 102.37 | 101.56 |
| 3 . . . . . . . . | 103.53 | 101.71 |
| 4 . . . . . . . . | 103.62 | 102.02 |
| 5 . . . . . . . . | 102.21 | 100.71 |
| 6 . . . . . . . . | 102.54 | 98.74 |
| 7 . . . . . . . . | 94.58 | 97.76 |
| 8 . . . . . . . . | 101.46 | 100.51 |
| 9 . . . . . . . . | 98.58 | 103.26 |
| 10 . . . . . . . . | 98.15 | 105.20 |
| Mean . . . . . . . . | 101.14 | 101.30 |
| Std. dev. . . . . . . | 3.053 | 2.106 |

## The example solution

Following the formula (18–3), the 2SLS estimates of the coefficients in the supply equation can be obtained by,

$$
\begin{pmatrix} b_2 \\ C_3 \\ C_4 \\ C_5 \end{pmatrix} = \begin{bmatrix} \sum \hat{Y}_1^2 & \sum \hat{Y}_1(1) & \sum \hat{Y}_1 X_3 & \sum \hat{Y}_1 X_4 \\ & T & \sum (1)X_3 & \sum (1)X_4 \\ & \text{(symmetric)} & \sum X_3^2 & \sum X_3 X_4 \\ & & & \sum X_4^2 \end{bmatrix}^{-1} \begin{pmatrix} \sum \hat{Y}_1 Y_2 \\ \sum (1) Y_2 \\ \sum X_3 Y_2 \\ \sum X_4 Y_2 \end{pmatrix}. \quad (18\text{–}6)
$$

Considering the explanatory variables in the revised supply equation to be $Z = (\hat{Y}_1, 1, X_3, X_4)$, then the solution (18–6) is identical to the ordinary least squares formulation, $(b_2 \quad C_{IN})' = (Z'Z)^{-1} Z' Y_2$. Thus, no new computational formulas need be derived to calculate the 2SLS estimates. Using the matrix solution method of Chapter 9, the 2SLS estimates of the demand and supply equations shown in Table 18–2 are obtained.

TABLE 18–2

**Results of 2SLS estimation of the structural demand and supply equations**

| | |
|---|---|
| Demand: | $Y_1 = -4.9104 \hat{Y}_2 + 454.88 + 1.4695 X_2$ |
| | $\quad\quad\quad (8.42) \quad\quad (564) \quad\quad (2.43)$ |
| Supply: | $Y_2 = -1.3141 \hat{Y}_1 + 196.48 + 0.2559 X_3 + 0.1154 X_4$ |
| | $\quad\quad\quad (0.278) \quad\quad (142) \quad\quad (0.060) \quad\quad (0.018)$ |

||||||||||||||||||||||||||||||||||||||||||||||||||||||||||||||||||||||||||||||||||||||||||||||||||||||||||

***Discursive note.*** No $t$-values for the significance of the estimates of the coefficients are given in Table 18–2 because the distribution of structural form estimators based on a small finite sample is not known to be a normal distribution. Indeed the exact distribution of such estimators has been derived for small models such as this one, and it is not a normal distribution. However, it is still conjectured that significance tests based on the use of a $t$-statistic may give approximately accurate results in special cases.[1]

||||||||||||||||||||||||||||||||||||||||||||||||||||||||||||||||||||||||||||||||||||||||||||||||||||||||||

---

[1] Research on the properties of the structural estimators based on finite samples continues. It has been shown that a $t$ statistic is approximately correct in a small sample case. See D. H. Richardson and R. J. Rohr, "Distribution of a Structural $t$-Statistic for the Case of Two Included Endogenous Variables," *Journal of the American Statistical Association*, June 1971, pp. 375–82, and its references.

## The difference between 2SLS and OLS estimates

These 2SLS coefficient estimates are consistent whereas the direct application of OLS on the original structural form equations gives inconsistent estimates. For comparison, the OLS estimates of the SF equations directly are:

Demand:   $Y_1 = -3.293Y_2 + 336.49 + 1.005X_2$

Supply:   $Y_2 = -0.192Y_1 + 109.64 + 0.0367X_3 + 0.0697X_4$.   (18–7)

The essential difference between the estimation of the structural form by OLS or by 2SLS is in the amount of information used. Ordinary least squares allows only for the direct effects on the endogenous variables by variables within its explanatory equation. Estimation by 2SLS also allows for an indirect effect on the endogenous variable of all predetermined variables in the model via their influence on explanatory endogenous variables.

## 18.6 SOME EQUIVALENCES OF ESTIMATORS OF STRUCTURAL COEFFICIENTS

Some interesting derivations, which need not be repeated in order to understand the conclusions, concern the relation of 2SLS estimates of structural coefficients with those obtained using other estimators. In Section 18.4 it was mentioned that 2SLS and a special case of maximum likelihood estimators are identical for models that are exactly identified.

### Comparison of the 2SLS and ILS estimates

Another case of exact equivalence when the model is exactly identified concerns the 2SLS and ILS estimators. Considering the example model with a demand and a supply equation, Section 17.7 presented the unique indirect least squares estimate of $\beta_2$ to be $b_2 = -1.314$ (17–19). This is exactly the same as the 2SLS estimate as given in Table 18–2. Similar comparisons are possible for the estimates of coefficients $\gamma_3$, $\gamma_4$, and $\gamma_5$. The coefficients in the demand equation were not uniquely determined by the ILS method since the overidentifying restrictions on the demand equation permitted two alternate consistent estimates of $\beta_1$, namely $b_1 = -12.931$ or $+10.086$. The 2SLS estimate of $\beta_1$ is found to be (see Table 18–2) $b_1 = -4.9104$, somewhere in between these two. Since the 2SLS provides a single consistent estimate, it is obviously preferable to ILS in the overidentified case. Since they are the same in the exactly identified case, many econometricians find it most convenient to use 2SLS in either case. It does not involve mathematical solution of the inverse transformation between the structural form and the reduced form coefficients. However, for testing purposes, knowledge and use of this reduced form and this transformation is often necessary anyway. Some more comments on the testing of simultaneous equations models are given in Chapter 19.

## Comparison of the 2SLS and instrumental variable methods of estimation

Finally, the reader may have recognized the similarity between two-stage least squares and the instrumental variable method. Both methods are developed to remedy a situation where Assumption 1 of independence between an explanatory variable and the disturbance term is violated. When this violation arises due to the problem of simultaneity, 2SLS is appropriate. When it arises due to errors in measurement, the method of instrumental variables is appropriate (see Section 13.3). In both cases, the explanatory variable involved in the correlation with $\varepsilon_t$ is expressed in terms of exogenous instrumental variables which are not correlated with $\varepsilon$. In this way, the effect of $\varepsilon$ on that explanatory variable is removed; and so, OLS may be applied to the revised equation. In the case of a simultaneous equations model, the explanatory variable involved is a jointly endogenous variable. The instrumental variables used to estimate the adjusted variables $Y^*$ are the predetermined variables in the model.[2] This specification of the instruments is done in the first stage and is usually the reduced form representation for $Y^*$. The final application of OLS is on the revised equation in which the values substituted for $Y^*$ are $\hat{Y}^*$ estimated in the first stage.

### 18.7 SUMMARY

A method for estimating coefficients of structural form equations in a simultaneous, overidentified model is two-stage least squares (2SLS). In this method, the endogenous variables used in an explanatory role are first estimated by an OLS regression on all the predetermined variables in the model. Then, these estimated variables are substituted into the original structural equations wherever the endogenous variable has an explanatory (independent) role. Finally, OLS is used in the second stage to estimate these revised structural form equations. The resulting estimators are consistent; and in the case of exact identification, they correspond to indirect least squares estimators and to limited information maximum likelihood estimators.

Other more efficient estimators can be derived, but the computational effort is substantially increased. Two-stage least squares has been the most commonly used estimation method in econometric studies involving the estimation of simultaneous equations models. It belongs to the class of generalized classical linear estimators which involve the minimization of a quadratic form in the residuals of least squares estimations. Two-stage least squares can also be likened to the instrumental variable method if one selects the instruments for the explanatory endogenous variables in terms of their reduced form representation.

---

[2] For details of this interpretation of 2SLS estimates in terms of instrumental variables, see L. R. Klein, "On the Interpretation of Theil's Method of Estimating Economic Relationships," *Metroeconomica*, 1955, pp. 147–53.

The reader should carry out a 2SLS estimation using a two-stage computer program if it is available, or if not, by using a simple multiple regression (OLS) program in two stages. In the first stage, the reduced form equations are estimated. Then new variables are defined for $\hat{Y}_i$ according to the RF estimation as needed for substitution into the SF equations. Then, the OLS program is used a second time to estimate the coefficients of the revised structural form. However, the reader should not believe the ancillary output of test statistic values for $t$-tests or analysis of variance applied to the structural equations. These are appropriate in the simple least squares application on a single equation model (as in the reduced form), but not for the second stage regression of a structural form equation involving more than one endogenous variable.

||||||||||||||||||||||||||||||||||||||||||||||||||||||||||||||||||||||||||||||||||||||||||||||||||||||||||||||||||||||||||||||||||||||||||

***Recursive note.*** In performing the calculations of the RF or SF estimation, the deviation form of the equation may be used. Indeed, the complete discussion could be considered as referring to the deviation form model estimating $K - 1$ coefficients in each RF equation and $(g - 1 + m - 1)$ coefficients in a SF equation with no loss of theoretical relevance.

||||||||||||||||||||||||||||||||||||||||||||||||||||||||||||||||||||||||||||||||||||||||||||||||||||||||||||||||||||||||||||||||||||||||||

## NEW VOCABULARY

| | |
|---|---|
| 2SLS | $k$-class estimators |
| LIML | First-stage instruments |
| Least variance ratio | Explanatory endogenous variables |

## REFERENCES

The development of two-stage least squares estimates is credited to H. Theil in papers for The Hague: Central Planning Bureau, 1953 and 1955. See:

Theil, H. *Economic Forecasts and Policy.* Amsterdam: North Holland Publishing Co., 1961.

———. *Principles of Econometrics.* New York: John Wiley & Sons, Inc., 1971.

The method was also constructed independently in the framework of generalized classical linear estimation (GCLE) by:

Basmann, R. L. "GCLE of Coefficients in a Structural Equation," *Econometrica*, 1957, pp. 77–83.

Also, see:

Basmann, R. L. "The Computation of GCLE of Coefficients in a Structural Equation." *Econometrica*, 1959, pp. 72–81.

The primary starting point for a study of the maximum likelihood estimates in structural equations is:

Hood, W. C., and Koopmans, T. C. *Studies in Econometric Method*, especially chaps. 6, 7, and 10. New York: John Wiley & Sons, Inc., 1953.

The reference above to H. Theil, *Economic Forecasts and Policy*, also serves as a source for the notion of $k$-class estimators; see Chapter 6.

## EXERCISES

1. Referring to Section 10.6 and the subsection on the general form for residual sum of squares, write the least variance ratio, $e'e/w'w$, in more detail in terms of the sample moments of the appropriate variables. (Treat the left-hand side composite variable as a single variable, say $V = Y_i - Y*\hat{\beta}$.)

2. Consider a single equation model, $Y = X\Gamma + \varepsilon$ where the residual $e$ can be written $e = A\varepsilon$ with $A = [I - X(X'X)^{-1}X']$. The estimator of $\Gamma$ can be written $\hat{\Gamma} = (X'AX)^{-1}X'AY$ by minimizing $e'e = \varepsilon'A\varepsilon$ with respect to $\Gamma$. A particular coefficient $\gamma_i$ might be represented by

$$\hat{\gamma}_i = \underset{(1 \times 1)}{(X_i'AX_i)^{-1}} \underset{(1 \times 1)}{X_i'AY} = (X_i'AY)/(X_i'AX_i).$$

   a) For a structural equation, $Y_1 = \beta_1 Y_2 + X_{1N}\Gamma_{1N} = \varepsilon_1$, show that the OLS estimate of $\beta_1$ can be written $b_1 = (Y_1 A Y_2)/(Y_2 A Y_2)$ where

$$A = [I_t - X_{1N}(X_{1N}' X_{1N})^{-1} X_{1N}'].$$

   b) For comparison with part (a), show that the 2SLS estimator of $\beta_1$ in the same structural equation can be written in the same way, $b_1 = (Y_1 A^* Y_2)/(Y_2 A^* Y_2)$ where $A^* = [X(X'X)^{-1}X' - X_{1N}(X_{1N}' X_{1N})^{-1} X_{1N}']$.

3. Using the consumption-income model (16–2a) and the data from Exercise 14, Chapter 17, find the 2SLS estimate of the marginal propensity to consume, $\beta$. Compare this answer with the indirect least squares estimate in that Exercise 14.

4. Give an argument for the proposition that if the $i$th structural equation contains no endogenous variable other than the normalized one $(g - 1 = 0)$, then 2SLS estimates of its coefficients are the same as OLS estimates of the $i$th equation directly.

5. Using the model (16–2a) involving the consumption-income relations and the data from Exercise 15 of Chapter 13 with $Z = I + G$, find 2SLS estimates of the coefficients in the consumption function. Compare these results with those for that Exercise 15 using the instrumental variable method.

6. In the second-stage regression of Exercises 3 and 5, let the explanatory variable be denoted by $\hat{Y}$ and the disturbance by $\varepsilon$. Find the variance of the estimator $b$ of the MPC according to the usual single equation method. [(Est. $\sigma_\varepsilon^2) = s_e^2 = \sum e^2/(T - K)$, and $V(b) = s_e^2/\sum \hat{y}^2$.] Explain if $b/\sqrt{V(b)}$ can be interpreted as a $t$-value.

7. As in equation (18–6), write in detail the expression for the 2SLS estimates of the coefficients in the demand equation of model (18–5b) as found in Section 18.5.

8. In Chapter 9, the OLS estimates of the coefficients in the single equation model,

$$\text{imports} = \gamma_1 + \gamma_2(\text{price}) + \gamma_3(\text{income}) + \varepsilon,$$

were obtained. Now suppose this equation is viewed as part of a two-equation simultaneous model in which imports and price are jointly determined. The new model is,

$$Y_1 = \beta_1 Y_2 + \gamma_1 + \gamma_2 X_2 + \varepsilon_1$$
$$Y_2 = \beta_2 Y_1 + \gamma_3 + \gamma_4 X_3 + \varepsilon_2$$

where the association between the new symbols and the old is defined by $Y_1 =$ imports (previously $Y$), $Y_2 =$ price (previously $X_2$), $X_2 =$ income (previously $X_3$), and $X_3 =$ a new exogenous variable.

Using the coded data of Table 9–1 and the following coded observations for the new variable,

a) Check the identifiability of each equation;
b) Find the estimates of the reduced form equations for $Y_1$ and $Y_2$;
c) Determine the ILS estimates of the import equation using the mathematical relations between RF and SF coefficients;
d) Find the 2SLS estimates of the import equation; and
e) Compare and discuss the OLS results in (9–9) and (9–10) with your ILS and with your 2SLS results. Explain the similarities or differences.

| New variable $X_3$ | 5.8 | 6.92 | 7.47 | 8.32 | 9.63 | 10.00 | 11.31 | 13.48 |
|---|---|---|---|---|---|---|---|---|
| Observation | 1 | 2 | 3 | 4 | 5 | 6 | 7 | 8 |

2SLS Ans.: $Y_1 = -0.017 \hat{Y}_2 - 0.48 + 3.82X_2$.

9.  Estimate your own model of Exercise 13, Chapter 17, using 2SLS and discuss the advantages or disadvantages if any for you between using 2SLS rather than ILS.

# Chapter 19

# TESTING THE SIMULTANEOUS EQUATIONS MODEL

## 19.1 PREVIEW

Ideally, this chapter would parallel Chapters 7 and 11. Just as they described tests, the associated statistics and their interpretation for the simple and general single equation models, this chapter should give corresponding tests for the simulaneous equations model. However, some special theoretical problems exist for testing in the latter type model. Also, since this is the final chapter, it is preferable to present a more general discussion that may help to relate back to the introductory chapters of this book.

### Some common problems of all testing of econometric models

Referring back to the earlier chapters on testing, it is apparent that one handicap in testing any econometric model is the inability of the researcher to obtain a complete and perfect specification. In a broad sense, every econometric model must be quite large in order to be realistic. It is impossible to totally exclude all other economic, socio-demographic, political, and cultural interrelations of variables while concentrating on a simple mechanism in one subsector of an economy. Abstractly, these influences are implicitly included in the assertions and assumptions of initial and background conditions (see Section 2.3) that are a part of every model. It is unlikely that these assertions and assumptions ever perfectly depict reality.

On the other hand, the econometrician must also make every econometric model quite simple and narrow in scope in order to be pragmatic. For reasons of interpretation (and to some lesser extent, of computation) the model must be small in order to fully understand its implications, to distinguish separate theoretical formulations that need to be tested, and to collect the required observations and derive meaningful tests. Consequently in specifying an econometric model, there always exists a conflict between the relative extent of the explicit specification of the theory ($\Theta$) and the implicit specification of the initial and background conditions ($I$).

The conjunction of both $\Theta$ and $I$ in the specification of a model which is to be tested has implications for this testing which are often overlooked by the beginning student of econometrics. Tests of the model are made on the basis of empirical results by comparing these results based on a sample with some set of predictive statements ($S$). If the results conform to $S$, then the theory $\Theta$ is often thought to be right. If the results falsify $S$, then revision of the theory is usually suggested.

However, it is not simply the specified relations and restrictions of the model which imply the set of predictive statements, but the *conjunction* of these theoretical specifications with the initial and background conditions that imply $S$. Thus, regardless of whether the statements are confirmed or falsified by statistical analysis of the empirical results, no clear, unambiguous implication follows concerning the theory of the model. The implication can only be that the conjunction of $\Theta$ *and* $I$ appears to be true or false.

For example, consider the following truth table:[1]

**Truth table for implications** $[(\Theta \cdot I) \Rightarrow S]$

|  | Column | | | | | | |
|---|---|---|---|---|---|---|---|
|  | 1 | 2 | 3 | 4 | 5 | 6 | 7 |
| Conditions $I$ ............. | t | t | t | f | f | f | f |
| Theory $\Theta$ ................. | t | f | f | t | f | f | t |
| Predictive statements $S$ ...... | t | t | f | f | t | f | t |

False predictions can result even if the theory is true as in column 4. Also, a true prediction can result from a true theory as in column 1, or in spite of a true theory when $I$ is false as in column 7, or by coincidence from a false theory regardless of the conditions $I$, as in columns 2 and 5.

These latter possibilities are easily demonstrated by dreaming up false theories. (With some practice in econometrics, this is easy.) Suppose I propose to throw a baseball straight up into the air. I claim that because the air becomes more dense at increasing heights, the momentum of the ball eventually becomes too low to push up farther into the heavier air. Thus, the upward velocity of the ball becomes zero. Then, the heavy air pushing down on the ball causes it to return to the ground at ever increasing velocity. Or once again, consider the same proposal. This time, I claim that the ball slows down and eventually stops its upward movement because friction with the air uses up the energy imparted to it in throwing. Moreover, at each instant of its upward flight, a partial vacuum was created immediately below the ball. The ball now moves to fill in this partial vacuum in space and descends back to the ground. In both of these cases, corresponding to columns 5 and 2 respectively, the theory is wrong. In the first, even the initial condition concerning the density of air was wrong. However, from observation, I find that their predictions are true.

In the analysis of econometric models, much the same thing can occur. Therefore, conclusions about the theory can never be made with certainty. Knowledge of $\Theta$ depends on the truth of $I$, but these conditions are often assumptions about measurements, behavior, and history. In order to make claims about $\Theta$, even in terms of probability, the researcher must guarantee the truth of $I$ as well as the accuracy of the predictive statements.

## Additional problems of testing a simultaneous equations model

Keeping these general complications of testing in mind, we can proceed with the special difficulties of testing in the context of a simultaneous equations model. Presuming that the researcher has confirmed, or at least clearly

---

[1] The reader interested in symbolic logic and development of truth tables might consult K. R. Popper, *The Logic of Scientific Discovery* (London: Hutchinson, 1959).

stated the required underlying conditions so that others may scrutinize them, the first step in testing the simultaneous equations model is to test its identifiability. Section 3 considers a practical suggestion for this test. Next, if the model contains lagged endogenous variables, the solution of the model in terms of a linear difference equation system must be determined in order to find and test the stability conditions for the model.[2] Since this solution involves more complex mathematical techniques and since the special problems of lagged endogenous variables have generally been deferred in this book, the special questions of stability are not examined in this chapter.

If the simultaneous equations model is identified and dynamically stable, then it is meaningful to test it for further information. However, there is a theoretical gap still to be overcome in developing test statistics appropriate in the simultaneous equations case. The distributions of some of the statistics commonly used in the analogous testing of the single equation model are either unknown or relatively complex in the simultaneous equations model.

## Alternative methodologies of testing

Faced with this difficulty, econometricians have advocated several alternative methodologies for testing the results of estimations of a simultaneous equations model.

In this chapter, Sections 4, 5, and 6 discuss these alternatives of direct tests on the estimates, indirect predictive tests, and forecasting tests respectively.

As often occurs, no one of these alternatives is always best. Each of them has special advantages depending on the different purposes of the econometric model.

||||||||||||||||||||||||||||||||||||||||||||||||||||||||||||||||||||||||||||||||||||||||||||||||||||||||||||||||||||||||||||||||||||||||||||||||

*Recursive note.*   From the first chapter, the general applications of an econometric model are:

1.  To establish numerical values for parameters;
2.  To test economic relations;
3.  To forecast levels of economic variables; and
4.  To provide guidelines for policy.

Any of the first three may lead to the fourth application.

||||||||||||||||||||||||||||||||||||||||||||||||||||||||||||||||||||||||||||||||||||||||||||||||||||||||||||||||||||||||||||||||||||||||||||||||

Each of the testing alternatives has disadvantages in their use which makes them inappropriate for different types and sizes of models. This chapter does

---

[2] Stability conditions in a single equation model are also important but involve only the usual type tests about coefficients in the same equation.

not attempt to give a comprehensive listing of these advantages or disadvantages since this would require much more depth in the technical aspects of their use than we can honestly present in a single summary chapter (and would surely reveal the author's biases too openly). However, some brief comments are included in the presentation since tests of a model must be made. After all is said and done, the reader must begin to form his own mind on how to judge if a model is " good," if it is " useful," if it is " believable."

## 19.2 REVIEW

In the sense that this chapter is a concluding chapter, the reader is advised to review the introduction section of the book, Chapters 1 and 2. In the sense that this chapter is about testing of econometric models, the topics of Chapters 7 and 11 are relevant. Finally, the following specific items are useful within the presentation.

### 1  Residual sums of squares in the least variance ratio

In Section 18.4 the least variance ratio was defined as the minimum value of $l$ where $l = e_i' e_i / w_i' w_i$. These sums of squares of residuals are useful in discussing the identifiability tests in Section 3 of this chapter. The residuals come from OLS estimations of two different representations of the composite endogenous variables in structural equation $i$ of a simultaneous equations model. The first equation includes only the predetermined variables included in equation $i$. The second includes all the predetermined variables in the model. Thus,

$$e_i = (Y_i - Y^* b_i) - X_{\text{IN}} C_{\text{IN}}$$

and

$$w_i = (Y_i - Y^* b_i) - X_{\text{IN}} \tilde{\Gamma}_{\text{IN}} - X_{\text{EX}} \tilde{\Gamma}_{\text{EX}}$$

where $b_i$ is a $[(g - 1) \times 1]$ vector of 2SLS estimates.

### 2  OLS estimates in a single equation

Given a single equation estimation involving one dependent variable $Y_i$ and a set of explanatory variables $Z$ (in a structural equation, these may include other endogenous variables $Y_j$ with $j \neq i$, lagged endogenous variables, and exogenous variables), and given the appropriate assumptions (1–7 of Section 10.3 or 1–9 of Section 16.3), ordinary least squares estimates have been previously derived. The estimates of the coefficients would be given by (9–3), Est. $(\widehat{\text{coef.}}) = (Z'Z)^{-1} Z' Y_i$. The estimate of the variance of disturbances in that equation is given by $e'e / \text{d.f.} = s_e^2$ where d.f. is the appropriate degrees of freedom. Finally, the estimates of the variance-covariance matrix of estimates of the coefficients are given by (10–4), [Est. $V\text{-}Cov(\widehat{\text{coef}})] = s_e^2 (Z'Z)^{-1}$. These formulas can be applied to the second stage estimation of a structural equation by OLS when the explanatory variables $Z$ are defined as $Z = (\hat{Y}^* \quad X_{IN})$ where $\hat{Y}^*$ are the first-stage (reduced form) estimates of included jointly endogenous variables, excluding the normalized one.

## 19.3 TESTS FOR IDENTIFIABILITY

The three states of identifiability are called under, exact, and overidentified (see Section 17.3). If the equation is underidentified according to the rank and order conditions, then its coefficients cannot be estimated. There is no need for statistical tests of identifiability based on the particular sample observations if the mathematical conditions based on the structure of the model are not satisfied.

If the equation is exactly identified according to the mathematical conditions, it is still possible that it may be underidentified in terms of the sample observations. An equation that appears to be exactly identified may not be if the excluded variables are statistically dependent based on the data. A test for this dependency among the excluded variables would be similar to tests of multicollinearity among a set of predetermined variables. In such tests (see Sections 15.6 and 15.7), the matrix of observations of the variables, $X_{EX}$, could be examined for dependencies. Although the variables are specified in the model as independent variables, they may be highly correlated among themselves, or one may be nearly a constant in the observed sample. If so, then the presumed $n = g - 1$ linear restrictions (exclusions of $n$ variables from equation $i$) may really only be $n - 1$ linear restrictions since not all these excluded variables are independent. Then, the equation is underidentified in terms of the statistical tests.

Finally in the third classification, the equation may be overidentified in terms of the mathematical structure of the model. In this case, a test of the identifiability restrictions must be made in terms of the sample data to determine if these overidentifying conditions are correct. Since the two-stage least squares estimation method makes special use of the presence in the model of variables that are excluded from equation $i$, a test must be made to confirm or falsify (so far as possible in the probabilistic test of hypothesis sense) that these variables are correctly excluded. Thus, if the order condition indicates overidentifiability, a statistical test is necessary to judge if these extra exclusions are correctly specified in terms of the data. If not, then the 2SLS (or other simultaneous) estimates suffer from the consequences of this misspecification and are not satisfactory.

### An asymptotic chi-square distribution test on overidentifying restrictions

A test of the null hypothesis, [$H_0$: the overidentifying restrictions are correct and the estimates based on the 2SLS procedure are appropriate], must be made against the alternate hypothesis, [$H_a$: the overidentifying restrictions are incorrect and the model should be respecified before interpreting the 2SLS results]. Insight into this test can be achieved by examining whether or not the variables, $X_{EX}$, excluded from the overidentified equation should really be excluded. If they are excluded, the unexplained variation in $Y_i$ is given by the residual sum of squares, $e_i'e_i$, based on the OLS regression equation, $(Y_i - Y^*b_i) = X_{IN}C_{IN} + e_i$. (See *Review* 19.2, item 1.) If they were included, the unexplained variation in $Y_i$ would be given by the residual sum of squares $w_i'w_i$ from the OLS regression equation, $(Y_i - Y^*b_i) = X_{IN}\tilde{\Gamma}_{IN} + X_{EX}\tilde{\Gamma}_{EX} + w_i$. Both these regressions are based on the same $T$ sample observations.

*Formulating a test.* If the variables, $X_{EX}$, should really be excluded from this equation in the model specification, then the estimates of the coefficients $\tilde{\Gamma}_{EX}$ should not be significantly different from zero. How to make a statistical test of this significance of coefficients in a structural equation is not perfectly understood. This problem is discussed in the next two sections.

Fortunately, another effect of the exclusion of $X_{EX}$ is testable. If the variables $X_{EX}$ should really be excluded since they account for no additional explanation of the variation in $Y_i$, then the measures of unexplained variation in the two equations should be the same. If $e_i'e_i = w_i'w_i$, then the least variance ratio is $l = 1$.

||||||||||||||||||||||||||||||||||||||||||||||||||||||||||||||||||||||||||||||||||||||||||||||||||||||||||||||||||||||||||||||||||||||||||||||||||||||||||||||||||

*Recursive note.* The condition $l = 1$ is indicative of exact identification (see Section 18.4). In terms of the actual data, the variable $X_{EX}$ will contribute some explanation for $Y_i$ unless they are orthogonal to $Y_i$ and to $X_{IN}$. Consequently $e_i'e_i > w_i'w_i$ and $l > 1$. The question is whether or not $l$ is significantly greater than one.

||||||||||||||||||||||||||||||||||||||||||||||||||||||||||||||||||||||||||||||||||||||||||||||||||||||||||||||||||||||||||||||||||||||||||||||||||||||||||||||||||

If $e_i'e_i$ is significantly greater than $w_i'w_i$, then more of the variation in $Y_i$ can be explained by adding at least one of the variables in the set $X_{EX}$ to the $i$th equation. Thus, the specified model is incorrect in terms of the data. At least one of the excluded variables should be respecified as an included variable. The overidentifying (exclusion) restrictions are incorrect.

*The test statistic.* A test of the null hypothesis, $[H_0: l = 1]$, against the alternate, $[H_a: l > 1]$, would serve to test the desired null hypothesis as written in full earlier.

Such a test is derived by Anderson and Rubin using a test statistic which has an asymptotic chi-square distribution.[3] It is given as $\chi^2 \sim T \ln l$ with $n - g + 1$ degrees of freedom, where $l$ is the least variance ratio, $n$ is the

---

[3] T. W. Anderson and H. Rubin, " Estimation of the Parameters of a Single Equation in a Complete System of Stochastic Equations," *Annals of Mathematical Statistics*, 1949, pp. 46–63.

number of variables in the set $X_{EX}$, and $g$ is the number of endogenous variables in equation $i$ excluding the normalized variable $Y_i$.[4]

||||||||||||||||||||||||||||||||||||||||||||||||||||||||||||||||||||||||||||||||||||||||||||||||||||||||||||||||||||||||||||||||||||||||||||||||||||

*Discursive note.* The test is only appropriate in overidentified cases. If $n \leq g - 1$, as in exact or underidentified equations, the degrees of freedom would be zero or negative respectively.

||||||||||||||||||||||||||||||||||||||||||||||||||||||||||||||||||||||||||||||||||||||||||||||||||||||||||||||||||||||||||||||||||||||||||||||||||||

*Explicative note.* The use of the chi-square statistic $T \ln l$ is only appropriate for large samples. Monte Carlo studies indicate that for small samples, use of the statistic tends toward excessive rejection of valid overidentifying restrictions. It indicates that the equation needs to be revised when, in fact, the variables $X_{EX}$ are correctly excluded.[5]

||||||||||||||||||||||||||||||||||||||||||||||||||||||||||||||||||||||||||||||||||||||||||||||||||||||||||||||||||||||||||||||||||||||||||||||||||||

The test procedure requires the determination of $l$ by the LIML estimation method; calculation of the test statistic, $T \ln l$; comparison of $T \ln l$ with a critical value from a chi-square distribution table; and rejection of the null hypothesis, $H_0$ of correct identifying restrictions if $(T \ln l)$ exceeds the critical value.

## A finite sample, approximately $F$-distribution test on overidentifying restrictions

If the sums of squares of residuals, $e_i'e_i$ and $w_i'w_i$, are based on the use of a generalized classical linear estimation (in particular, if 2SLS is to be used for its computational ease), then Basmann has offered a preferred test statistic for examining the validity of overidentifying restrictions.[6]

Instead of the ratio of $e_i'e_i$ to $w_i'w_i$, consider the difference, $e_i'e_i - w_i'w_i$. If this difference is "small," then adding $X_{EX}$ to equation $i$ does not significantly reduce the unexplained variation in $Y_i$. The interpretation of this result is that equation $i$ is identified by a correct inclusion in the *model* of other predetermined variables not included in this *equation*.

---

[4] Technically, $l$ is the smallest root of a polynomial in $l$ of degree $g$ obtained in the solution for the limited information maximum likelihood estimators (LIML) of the coefficients in structural equation $i$. For a full discussion, see W. C. Hood and T. C. Koopmans, *Studies in Econometric Method* (New York: John Wiley and Sons, 1953), chap. 6, secs. 8.1 to 8.3.

[5] See Section 10.4 for the meaning of Monte Carlo studies. The particular result is in R. L. Basmann, "On Finite Sample Distributions of GCLE Identifiability Test Statistics," *Journal of the American Statistical Association*, December 1960, pp. 650–59.

[6] Ibid.

|||||||||||||||||||||||||||||||||||||||||||||||||||||||||||||||||||||||||||||||||||||||||||||||||||||||||||||||||||||||||||||||||||||||||||||||||||

**Interpretive note.** How small is "small"? The difference is judged to be small by comparison with the amount of variation in the endogenous composite variable not explained by all the $X$; that is, small relative to $w_i'w_i$.

|||||||||||||||||||||||||||||||||||||||||||||||||||||||||||||||||||||||||||||||||||||||||||||||||||||||||||||||||||||||||||||||||||||||||||||||||||

**The identifiability test statistic.** The statistic developed is based on the ratio $(e_i'e_i - w_i'w_i)/w_i'w_i = \phi$.

|||||||||||||||||||||||||||||||||||||||||||||||||||||||||||||||||||||||||||||||||||||||||||||||||||||||||||||||||||||||||||||||||||||||||||||||||||

**Explicative note.** There is a relation between $l$ and $\phi$ given by

$$\phi = \frac{e_i'e_i}{w_i'w_i} - \frac{w_i'w_i}{w_i'w_i} = l - 1.$$

|||||||||||||||||||||||||||||||||||||||||||||||||||||||||||||||||||||||||||||||||||||||||||||||||||||||||||||||||||||||||||||||||||||||||||||||||||

When the numerator and denominator of $\phi$ are each divided by the appropriate degrees of freedom, a test statistic with approximately an $F$-distribution is obtained. It is denoted by $\bar{F}$ and given by,

$$\bar{F} = \phi(T - K)/(n - g + 1),$$

or

$$\bar{F} = \frac{(e_i'e_i - w_i'w_i)/(n - g + 1)}{(w_i'w_i)/(T - K)}, \tag{19-1}$$

with $(n - g + 1)$ and $(T - K)$ degrees of freedom.

The usual procedure of a test of hypothesis is used where the null hypothesis, [$H_0$: equation $i$ is correctly identified], is accepted over the alternate [$H_a$: the overidentifying restrictions on equation $i$ are not valid], whenever $\bar{F}$ is not greater than the critical value $F_\alpha$ for the upper tail of an $F$-distribution at the $\alpha$ significance level. In the case of such an acceptance, then the econometrician may go on to make further tests and interpretations of the 2SLS estimates. If the identifiability test statistic, $\bar{F}$, exceeds the critical value, then the econometrician should not trust the 2SLS estimates and need not continue his analysis of the results of the estimation. Instead, he must reconsider the formulation of the model with the possibility in mind of adding to equation $i$ at least one of the predetermined variables previously excluded from it.

**A check for respecification.** To help identify which member of the set $X_{EX}$ might be transferred to the set $X_{IN}$, the researcher might do another OLS regression of the 2SLS residuals, $e_i$, on the $n$ excluded variables, $X_{EX}$. The estimates of the coefficients in this regression can be denoted

$$\underset{(n \times 1)}{\hat{C}} = (X_{EX}'X_{EX})^{-1}X_{EX}'e_i.$$

For any variable in the set $X_{EX}$ which should actually be absent from equation $i$, the corresponding estimate $\hat{C}_j$ should be zero. If some variable from $X_{EX}$ does explain a significant amount of the residual variation, $e_i'e_i$, then that variable could be included in equation $i$. The tests of Chapter 11 are appropriate for this single equation estimation.

**An example of the identifiability test procedure.**    Consider the model,

$$
\begin{aligned}
\text{Demand:} \quad & Y_1 = \beta_1 Y_2 + \gamma_1 + \gamma_2 X_2 + \varepsilon_1 \\
\text{Supply:} \quad & Y_2 = \beta_2 Y_1 + \gamma_3 + \gamma_4 X_3 + \gamma_5 X_4 + \varepsilon_2
\end{aligned} \Bigg\}
\quad (18\text{--}5a)
$$

in which the demand equation is seemingly overidentified. Let the 2SLS estimation of the demand equation be given by

$$
\underset{(T \times 1)}{Y_1} = b_1 \hat{Y}_2 + C_1 + C_2 X_2
$$

and determine the residuals, $e_1 = Y_1 - b_2 Y_2 - C_1 - C_2 X_2$. Define the equation $(Y_1 - b_1 Y_2) = \tilde{\gamma}_1 + \tilde{\gamma}_2 X_2 + \tilde{\gamma}_3 X_3 + \tilde{\gamma}_4 X_4 + w_1$, estimate the coefficients $\tilde{\gamma}_j$ by ordinary least squares, and define the residuals to be $w_1$. Then, if

$$
\bar{F} = \frac{(e_1'e_1 - w_1'w_1)/(2 - 2 + 1)}{(w_1'w_1)/(T - 4)}
$$

exceeds $F_{(\alpha;\, 1,\, T-4)}$, the conclusion is obtained that the overidentifying restrictions on the demand equation are not valid and the 2SLS estimates $(b_1, C_1, C_2)$ should not be trusted.

The regression equation of $e_1$ on $X_3$ and $X_4$ may be obtained by OLS to give, $e_1 = \hat{C}_3 X_3 + \hat{C}_4 X_4$. If the coefficients $\hat{C}_3$ or $\hat{C}_4$ are significant, then the variables $X_3$ or $X_4$ should be considered for inclusion in the demand equation. Other variables which were previously excluded from the entire model may, of course, also be reconsidered for inclusion in either the demand or supply equation as dictated by a renewed examination of the underlying economic theory. Any revised specification must also satisfy the identifiability conditions before proceeding to tests on the estimates of the structural form parameters and equations.

## 19.4 DIRECT TESTS ON STRUCTURAL PARAMETERS

If the structural form equation passes the identifiability test, then consideration of its parameters becomes the next focal point for analysis. In many applications of model building and estimation, it is the coefficients in the structural equation which are of principal interest.

For example, in a Keynesian model, the coefficient representing the marginal propensity to consume is of special interest. In general, the slopes of particular theoretical functions, the elasticities of particular demand or supply schedules, elasticities of substitution in production functions, and other parameters may be involved in testable theoretical propositions.

These are often stated as linear restrictions which postulate certain signs or relative or absolute comparisons among the coefficients in the specified equation according to a priori expectations. Further testable propositions about these coefficients may result from necessary and sufficient conditions for identifiability or for stability of the model. In particular, the determinant of the coefficient matrix of endogenous variables ($\beta$) must always be nonzero in order for a reduced form solution to exist. Using the example demand-supply model (18–5a), this condition requires that $(1 - \beta_1\beta_2) \neq 0$.

## Large sample testing methods

Two different types of tests have been suggested for testing propositions about structural coefficients. The first involves courageous assumptions that the asymptotic (large sample) properties of the estimation hold reasonably well even for smaller sized samples. In this case, the usual test procedures associated with the general single equation model (see Chapter 11) are commonly used.

The matrix of explanatory variables in equation $i$ is given by

$$\underset{[T \times (g-1+m)]}{Z_i} = (\hat{Y}^* \quad X_{\text{IN}})$$

where the notation follows that of the previous two chapters. Referring to *Review* 19.2, item 2, the estimates of the coefficients and of the variance of the disturbance term can be obtained by the usual OLS formulas. The appropriate degrees of freedom is $[T - (g - 1 + m)]$ since $g + m$ coefficients of the variables $\hat{Y}^*$ and $X_{\text{IN}}$ are estimated on the basis of $T$ observations. An approximation to the asymptotic covariance matrix of the coefficients is also found by the adaptation of formula (10–4) to be a square, symmetrical matrix of size $(g - 1 + m)$,[7]

$$[\text{Est. } V\text{-}Cov(\hat{\text{coef.}})] = E\left[\binom{b}{C_{\text{IN}}}(b \quad C_{\text{IN}})\right]$$

$$= \frac{(e_i'e_i)}{T - g + 1 - m}(Z_i'Z_i)^{-1}.$$

|||||||||||||||||||||||||||||||||||||||||||||||||||||||||||||||||||||||||||||||||||||||||||||||||||||||||||||||||||||||||||||||

*Recursive note.*   The square roots of the diagonal elements of this matrix are the estimates of the standard errors of the 2SLS estimates of the structural coefficients.

|||||||||||||||||||||||||||||||||||||||||||||||||||||||||||||||||||||||||||||||||||||||||||||||||||||||||||||||||||||||||||||||

The distribution function of the estimate of the variance of the disturbance term is often treated as if it could be approximated by a chi-square random

---

[7] See H. Theil, *Economic Forecasts and Policy* (Amsterdam: North-Holland Publishing Co., 1961), p. 232.

variable, and the distributions of the estimators of the coefficients are approximated by a standardized normal. Under these useful but misleading assumptions, $t$-statistics can be used just as in the single equation case. However, the resulting confidence intervals or test conclusions based on a preset significance level $\alpha$ are not accurate. The econometrician may use such procedures as relative guidelines for making comparisons about the importance of different variables, but he is fooling himself if he really believes the particular numbers. He cannot meaningfully conclude that a certain proposition is accepted or rejected at the $\alpha$ significance level because the true distributions are not known to be chi-square, normal, and $t$-distributions, even approximately, when the sample size is finite as it most certainly is (and usually quite small, say $T < 60$) in actual econometric practice.

## Finite sample testing methods

A second method of testing propositions about the coefficients in a structural equation involves some heroic mathematical statistics involving special functions that enables the econometrician to derive the exact distribution of the structural estimate based on a finite sample. With a known exact distribution of the estimator, tests of hypothesis and confidence intervals concerning the corresponding parameter can be made exactly.

Some derivations of exact distributions have been made for special two- or three-equation overidentified models without any lagged endogenous variables. (See the references at the end of this chapter.) The statistical derivations are much too complex to repeat here. The studies each present some new insights in both possibilities and problems for making direct tests on structural coefficients. A favorable possibility under certain assumptions of the knowledge of the variance of the disturbance terms in the structural equations is that the approximate $t$-distributions commonly used may be appropriate. An unfavorable problem is that for large models of say five or more equations, or models including lagged endogenous variables, the exact distributions of structural estimators are too complex or do not have finite variances.

Consequently, in order to test a proposition about a structural parameter, the econometrician must either assume the asymptotic distributions, not knowing how misleading or inaccurate they may be, or he must concern himself only with very small and simple models for which the exact distribution is known (and may be applied directly or approximated by the asymptotic distributions with a known error of approximation). In general practice, the first alternative has been applied awaiting further developments and research about the use of the exact distributions.

In some cases, a different approach altogether has been used. Instead of making tests on propositions about structural parameters directly, it is sometimes feasible to test the implications of these propositions and thereby conclude if they appear to be confirmed or falsified.

## 19.5 INDIRECT TESTS ON STRUCTURAL PARAMETERS

Since a direct statistical test of hypothesis on the structural parameter has serious drawbacks, it has been suggested by Basmann that theoretical postulates on these parameters may be tested in terms of their implications on the reduced form parameters.[8] If the model is identified, perhaps tests of hypothesis using estimates of the reduced form coefficients can indirectly provide evidence for confirming or falsifying the original postulates in the structural coefficients.

### The method of predictive testing

This approach, called *predictive testing*, is appealing since the reduced form equations are estimated exactly as if they were single equations with one endogenous variable. Thus, the assumptions of Section 10.3 and the tests of Chapter 11 for the single equation model can be applied directly to the reduced form (RF). The estimates, $\Pi_i$, of the coefficients in RF equation $i$, are multivariate normal. The estimate $s_v^2$ of the variance of the RF disturbance term, $v_i$, may be used in a chi-square distributed random variable. However, to make such tests, the researcher must propose quite definite postulates (precise statements of the theory $\Theta$), so that he has something to test. Also, the need for serious historical study to demonstrate the appropriateness of the background conditions $I$ is not avoided.

The method of predictive testing can be described in the following seven steps:

*a)*   Specify the structural form and postulates about its parameters.

*b)*   Derive the reduced form parameters as functions of the structural form parameters.

*c)*   Derive the acceptance region for reduced form parameters to satisfy the identifiability hypothesis.

*d)*   If the model contains lagged endogenous variables, derive a linear difference equation system from the reduced form parameters to satisfy the stability hypothesis.

*e)*   From the structural postulates and identifiability conditions, derive the acceptance region for the reduced form parameters to satisfy $\Theta$.

*f)*   Make the appropriate tests, first checking the identifiability, then stability, and then $\Theta$ in terms of the reduced form estimates of $\Pi$.

*g)*   Assuming that the conjoining conditions $I$ have been accepted to hold true by serious and intensive historical (or perhaps, psychological or sociological) study, make the proper conclusions about $\Theta$.

If the estimates of $\Pi$ lie in the acceptance region, then $\Theta$ has been confirmed and should be tested further for continued confirmations and refinement

---

[8] R. L. Basmann, "Remarks concerning the Application of Exact Finite Sample Distribution Functions of GCL Estimators in Econometric Statistical Inference," *Journal of the American Statistical Association*, 1963, pp. 943–76.

which would lead to its acceptance. If the estimates of $\Pi$ lie in the rejection region, then $\Theta$ is rejected. More likely, some of the derived restrictions on $\Pi$ will be satisfied and others will be violated. Then, tracing back through the mathematical derivations, the one or more postulates of $\Theta$ which lead to the violations can be rejected while the remainder of $\Theta$ is not rejected. Again, further testing is encouraged to adjust and reformulate $\Theta$, the theoretical specification of the model.

### Some problems of predictive testing

One practical problem associated with this method of predictive testing is that the mathematical derivations and algebraic manipulations required are painful exercises. There is no general procedure for deriving all possible and relevant predictive statements $S$ that help to define and restrict the acceptance region for $\Pi$ based on the postulated theory $\Theta$ (and assuming the background conditions $I$). Each new model with its own $\Theta$ represents a new specific problem. It is likely that some statements predicted (implied) by $\Theta$ which are important within economic theory would be overlooked. Also, many statements might be derived mathematically whose economic interpretation has not been formalized before in economic theory.

‖‖‖‖‖‖‖‖‖‖‖‖‖‖‖‖‖‖‖‖‖‖‖‖‖‖‖‖‖‖‖‖‖‖‖‖‖‖‖‖‖‖‖‖‖‖‖‖‖‖‖‖‖‖‖‖‖‖‖‖‖‖‖‖‖‖‖‖‖‖‖‖‖‖‖‖‖‖‖‖‖‖‖‖‖‖‖‖‖‖‖‖‖‖‖‖‖‖‖

*Interpretive note.* In this sense, the analysis may lead to some "strange economics" purely for or from mathematical considerations. While some economic theory is being tested, the tests themselves are introducing further untested theory.

‖‖‖‖‖‖‖‖‖‖‖‖‖‖‖‖‖‖‖‖‖‖‖‖‖‖‖‖‖‖‖‖‖‖‖‖‖‖‖‖‖‖‖‖‖‖‖‖‖‖‖‖‖‖‖‖‖‖‖‖‖‖‖‖‖‖‖‖‖‖‖‖‖‖‖‖‖‖‖‖‖‖‖‖‖‖‖‖‖‖‖‖‖‖‖‖‖‖‖

Finally, although the statistical concept of predictive testing is rigorous and attractive, the procedure becomes practically inapplicable on models of five or more equations or models with more than three endogenous variables in any single equation.[9] The jungle of possible predictive statements and the mountain of tedious derivations become too large for the normal sized explorer to chart.

### An example of predictive testing

The studies in the econometric literature which deal with predictive testing are necessarily quite involved and difficult. The basic procedure, however, can be illustrated in a simple way. The reader would find additional complications quite readily in any such study (see footnote 9, for example) or when he attempts to use the procedure himself.

---

[9] See James L. Murphy, "An Appraisal of Repeated Predictive Tests on an Econometric Model," *The Southern Economic Journal*, April 1969, pp. 293–307, on which this discussion is based.

Consider the following two-equation model in our usual notation,

$$Y_1 = \beta_1 Y_2 + \gamma_1 + \gamma_2 X_2 + \varepsilon_1,$$
$$Y_2 = \gamma_3 + \gamma_4 X_3 + \varepsilon_2. \qquad (19\text{--}2)$$

The reduced form of this model is given by,

$$\begin{pmatrix} Y_1 \\ Y_2 \end{pmatrix} = \begin{pmatrix} \gamma_1 + \beta_1\gamma_3 & \gamma_2 & \beta_1\gamma_4 \\ \gamma_3 & 0 & \gamma_4 \end{pmatrix} \begin{pmatrix} 1 \\ X_2 \\ X_3 \end{pmatrix} + \begin{pmatrix} \varepsilon_1 + \beta_1\varepsilon_2 \\ \varepsilon_2 \end{pmatrix}. \qquad (19\text{--}3)$$

This detailed writing of the reduced form serves as a definition of the reduced form parameters,

$$\Pi = \begin{pmatrix} \pi_{11} & \pi_{12} & \pi_{13} \\ \pi_{21} & \pi_{22} & \pi_{23} \end{pmatrix},$$

according to a position by position comparison with the coefficient matrix.

For simplicity, assume that the relations and the variables (none of which are lagged endogenous variables) have been defined, the background conditions $I$ have been studied and accepted, and sample data have been gathered.

Suppose the following postulates are added: $0.7 \le \beta_1 \le 0.8$, $\gamma_1 = 90$, $\gamma_2 \le 0$, $3.3 \le \gamma_4 \le 5$, and $50 \le \gamma_3 \le 100$. Now, these postulates and (19–2) are the null hypothesis. The alternate hypothesis is any other $\Theta$ which can be represented as the same reduced form (19–3).

From the specifications, predictive statements about the reduced form can be derived. Many other theorems could also be derived, but consider only the direct deductions on the reduced form coefficients represented as functions of the structural parameters.

$\pi_{11} = \gamma_1 + \beta_1\gamma_3$    so    $[90 + 0.7(50)] \le \pi_{11} \le [90 + 0.8(100)]$    or

$$125 \le \pi_{11} \le 170$$

$\pi_{12} = \gamma_2$    so                    $\pi_{12} \le 0$

$\pi_{13} = \beta_1\gamma_4$    so    $0.7(3.3) \le \pi_{13} \le 0.8(5)$           or

$$2.31 \le \pi_{13} \le 4.0$$

$\pi_{21} = \gamma_3$    so            $50 \le \pi_{21} \le 100$

$\pi_{22} = 0$    so                   $\pi_{22} = 0$

$\pi_{23} = \gamma_4$    so           $3.3 \le \pi_{23} \le 5.0$.

Suppose the reduced form estimates $p_{ij}$ of $\pi_{ij}$ are obtained and the identifiability conditions are tested. If the identifiability test statistic [see formula (19–1)] is accepted, then it is meaningful to test, say at the 0.05 level of significance, the above set of restrictions on $\Pi$.

||||||||||||||||||||||||||||||||||||||||||||||||||||||||||||||||||||||||||||||||||||||||||||||||||||||||||||||||||||||||

***Explicative note.*** It is not always a simple matter to obtain a testable model. The theoretical postulates which are made a priori must be restrictive enough to limit the acceptable parameter subspace. The smaller the acceptance region, the greater the power of the tests.

||||||||||||||||||||||||||||||||||||||||||||||||||||||||||||||||||||||||||||||||||||||||||||||||||||||||||||||||||||||||||||||||||||||||||||||||||||||||||||||||||||||

Using a confidence interval for $\pi_{21}$ based on the OLS estimate $p_{21}$ and its standard error, suppose $p_{21}$ lies outside the acceptance region for $\pi_{21}$. Obviously, using (19–3), the postulate concerning $\gamma_3$ is rejected. On the basis of the sample observations, we reject that $50 \leq \gamma_3 \leq 100$ with a risk of 0.05 that this postulate is true. The interpretation or use of $\gamma_3$ in the model, the hypothesized intercept for $Y_2$ is in need of revision.

Sometimes the analysis is not so direct. Suppose *all* the reduced form restrictions were satisfied *except* $125 \leq \pi_{11} \leq 170$. Is the entire model bad? $\pi_{11}$ involves $\gamma_{11}, \beta_1$, and $\gamma_3$. Analysis indicates that the postulate concerning $\gamma_3$ is not rejected since $\pi_{21}$ was acceptable. The postulate concerning $\beta_1$ is not rejected since $\pi_{23}$ and $\pi_{13}$ were both acceptable. Consequently, the error involves $\gamma_1$, and so the postulate $\gamma_1 = 90$ is rejected. The only part of $\theta$ which is rejected is the stated intercept for $Y_1$. This postulate may be revised; other variables which have been shown to be important from testing by forecasting might be included; additional tests might be made; and a refined, more satisfactory model may be developed.

||||||||||||||||||||||||||||||||||||||||||||||||||||||||||||||||||||||||||||||||||||||||||||||||||||||||||||||||||||||||||||||||||||||||||||||||||||||||||||||||||||||

***Discursive note.*** For small models, both indirect predictive testing and direct testing based on exact distributions may be possible. Both involve more tedious mathematics than the more commonly used tests based on asymptotic distributions or on the accuracy of forecasts. These forecasting tests are discussed in the next section, 19.6. For large models, they serve as the most convenient testing mechanism, but they do not provide statistically rigorous confidence statements as conclusions in the way that predictive testing and tests using exact distributions may do.

||||||||||||||||||||||||||||||||||||||||||||||||||||||||||||||||||||||||||||||||||||||||||||||||||||||||||||||||||||||||||||||||||||||||||||||||||||||||||||||||||||||

## An indirect test using ILS results

One final possibility exists for transferring information and conclusions from statistical analysis of the testable reduced form parameters to the "nontestable" structural form (SF) parameters. If the model is exactly identified, the method of indirect least squares could be used to obtain estimates of the SF parameters, and confidence intervals on the RF estimates may be useful in deriving confidence intervals on SF parameters.

Consider the simple consumption-income model

$$C = \beta Y + \gamma + \varepsilon,$$
$$Y = C + Z. \tag{16–2a}$$

In the reduced form for the model (16–2a), the coefficient for $Z$ in the equation explaining $Y$ is $\pi_{22} = 1/(1 - \beta)$. (See *Review* 16.2, item 2 and Section 17.6, p. 440.) The OLS estimate of this coefficient in the reduced form may be denoted by $p_{22}$ and its estimated standard error may be denoted by $s_{p_{22}}$. Given some significance level $\alpha$, the upper and lower confidence limits on the reduced form coefficient $\pi_{22}$ are given by, $p_{22} \pm t_{\alpha/2} s_{p_{22}}$. Call these limits $U$ and $L$ respectively. The inequalities, $L < [1/(1 - \beta)] < U$, can be solved for upper and lower limits on $\beta$ implied by the RF estimation. These values, $\beta_U = (U - 1)/U$ and $\beta_L = (L - 1)/L$, may be used to obtain an estimate of the standard error of the structural estimate $b$ which is needed for making tests of hypothesis about a priori propositions of the marginal propensity to consume, $\beta$. Since the length of the confidence interval is given by a specific multiple $(2t_{\alpha/2})$ of standard errors of the estimator, the estimation of this standard error can be inversely deduced from the expression $2t_{\alpha/2} s_b = (\beta_U - \beta_L)$. The solution is $s_b = (\beta_U - \beta_L)/2t_{\alpha/2}$.

||||||||||||||||||||||||||||||||||||||||||||||||||||||||||||||||||||||||||||||||||||||||||||||||||||||||||||||||||||||||||||||||||||||||

***Interpretive note.*** In more complex models, even if they are exactly identified, the inverse deductions from the RF confidence intervals to SF confidence intervals may be quite difficult. Therefore, this more exacting method is similarly inapplicable for testing large-scale simultaneous equations econometric models.

||||||||||||||||||||||||||||||||||||||||||||||||||||||||||||||||||||||||||||||||||||||||||||||||||||||||||||||||||||||||||||||||||||||||

## 19.6 TESTING BY FORECASTING

Suppose a simultaneous equations model has more than three equations, is overidentified, and includes little specified theory other than the description of the equations and variables. (It includes only a few a priori postulates about signs or absolute sizes of individual coefficients and perhaps no linear restrictions on combinations of the coefficients.) Can such a model be tested?

The previous sections have already answered part of the question. Probably, any exact tests with accurate confidence statements about the few a priori postulates cannot be found. The indirect methods will not work because the acceptance region in the reduced form parameters subspace will not be sufficiently limited to obtain unambiguous test results. Since the equations are overidentified, the indirect least squares method is unusable. If a very large sample, say $T > 300$, is to be used, the econometrician would probably use the direct asymptotic distribution tests for some hints about his model, but these will only be hints, not conclusions from statistical inference. The exact distributions necessary for conclusive test results are unknown.

A second aspect of the question still needs to be discussed. Since few theoretical propositions were postulated, the econometrician is probably not primarily concerned with testing economic theory or establishing numerical values for certain theoretical parameters. The purpose of his model is probably to describe one possible system that corresponds to economic experience as observed in a set of data with the hope and intention that such a model may then be useful for forecasting or simulating. If he does not intend to give a theoretical interpretation of the parameters or use their estimated values in policy recommendations or evaluations, then the most sensible test to apply is a forecasting test.

|||||||||||||||||||||||||||||||||||||||||||||||||||||||||||||||||||||||||||||||||||||||||||||||||||||||||||||||||||||||||||||||||||||||||||||||||||||||||||||||||||||||||||||||||||

**Discursive note.** In generating the forecasts of an endogenous variable, the OLS estimates of the parameters may be used. Indeed, forecasts based on OLS estimates are unbiased even though the estimates themselves are biased. Forecasts based on 2SLS estimates of the parameters and these *2SLS* estimates are both biased.[10]

|||||||||||||||||||||||||||||||||||||||||||||||||||||||||||||||||||||||||||||||||||||||||||||||||||||||||||||||||||||||||||||||||||||||||||||||||||||||||||||||||||||||||||||||||

## The procedure of testing by forecasting

The crucial aspect of testing by forecasting is a comparison of forecasts for the endogenous variables generated by the model with observed values of these variables. Such a test would provide valuable evidence about the model if the forecasts were generated strictly from the a priori theoretical specification of the model and its parameters. Usually, the model specifies only the form of the relations, but not their parameters. These parameters are usually estimated on the basis of some data before forecasts can be made on the basis of some *other* data. Two difficulties are apparent. First, two sets of data relevant to the model are needed. Second, the process of forecasting cannot be separated from the difficulties of estimation of the parameters. In this sense, the forecasting test is based on only an estimated structure treated as if it were the true structure.

## Summary of the method

Before detailing the consequences of these problems for application and interpretation, a summary outline of the basic method of testing by forecasting is given in the following five steps.[11]

a) Collect data and make estimates of the parameters (often in the reduced form).

b) Assume the theory $\Theta$ is correct, assume the background conditions $I$ are true, and assume the estimates are the actual parameter values.

---

[10] For a much fuller treatment of forecasting tests, see Carl Christ, *Econometric Models and Methods* (New York: John Wiley & Sons, Inc., 1966), pp. 543–71.

[11] The method is illustrated by L. Klein, *Textbook of Econometrics* (Evanston; Row, Peterson and Co., 1953), pp. 259–61.

c) Use more data for the exogenous variables and generate samples of endogenous variables.

d) Compare these forecasted samples with actual sample observations.

e) Make conclusions about the validity of $\Theta$ on the basis of this comparison.

|||||||||||||||||||||||||||||||||||||||||||||||||||||||||||||||||||||||||||||||||||||||||||||||||||||||||||||||||||||||||||||||||||||||||||||||||

*Discursive note.* Not every estimation and forecasting procedure of an econometric model is necessarily a test of $\Theta$. Readers must not mistake successful reports on estimation techniques or forecasts as evidence for or against the theory of the econometric model used as the subject for such experiments. Sometimes a Monte Carlo procedure (see Section 10.4) is used to examine different estimators in terms of their performance in generating accurate forecasts.[12] This is not a test of the theory, and any conclusions about the theory are presumptuous. Such a procedure assumes that the theory is correctly formulated. The econometrician is discovering which estimating procedure is best on the basis of this presumedly correct theory. This procedure is analogous to tests of various antibiotics on white mice to see which is most effective. The antibiotics are analogous to the different estimators, and the white mice are analogous to the specified theory in the model being used to study the estimators and their (forecasting) effects. A conclusion that antibiotic type A is the most effective does not imply that white mice are " better " than brown mice or field mice or gray squirrels.

|||||||||||||||||||||||||||||||||||||||||||||||||||||||||||||||||||||||||||||||||||||||||||||||||||||||||||||||||||||||||||||||||||||||||||||||||

## Some problems of the forecasting test

Several problems associated with testing by forecasting might be discussed. To avoid too much confusion or excess technical considerations, only two are presented now, one tactical and one logical. The tactical problem involves the choice of the structural form or reduced form for generating the forecasts. The reduced form is often used since it expresses each endogenous variable in terms of only predetermined variables. There is no confusion about which endogenous variable is to be generated first and which second (based partially on the first) and so on.

|||||||||||||||||||||||||||||||||||||||||||||||||||||||||||||||||||||||||||||||||||||||||||||||||||||||||||||||||||||||||||||||||||||||||||||||||

*Explicative note.* If the model is recursive, then this " chicken and the egg " problem is nonexistent and the structural form equations can be used beginning with the one of lowest causal order. (See Section 17.5.)

|||||||||||||||||||||||||||||||||||||||||||||||||||||||||||||||||||||||||||||||||||||||||||||||||||||||||||||||||||||||||||||||||||||||||||||||||

---

[12] For example, see Joel Cord, "A Small Model of Semi-Annual Employment in the U.S.," *Review of Economics and Statistics*, February 1962.

However, the reduced form may be compatible with a multitude of different structural forms so that the forecasting test really does not provide evidence about the specific structural form under investigation.

If the structural form is used for forecasting, there is the problem of not knowing (at any given confidence level) which coefficients are significant and which are not. Thus, if a researcher uses the 2SLS estimates for the parameters of the SF and solves the system of simultaneous equations for the endogenous variables to make his forecasts, he may be using misleading and insignificant values for certain parameters that can greatly affect his forecasts.

The logical problem follows from this tactical problem since some estimates of the parameters of the theory are needed before forecasts can be made. Thus, if the forecasts are based on *estimates* of the true theoretical values, how can the accuracy of the forecasts be valid evidence for or against the unknown true theory? It seems circular to argue that the theory $\Theta$ can be tested by this process which assumes that the estimates from a single set of sample observations are the true values of the parameters in this same economic theory $\Theta$. By coincidence of the particular sample observations, the best forecasting results may be obtained from the worst theory. This should not be true over many repeated tests by forecasting. However, there is no available test statistic nor probability distribution which can be applied to determine how many correct forecasts must be made before the evidence is significant in favor of one specified theory $\Theta$ against any or all alternative specifications.

## Some practical points on the design and interpretation of forecasting tests

In addition to this circularity of reasoning problem, it is sometimes not clear how the forecasting test is to be applied when the researcher has all past data on hand and no future data. Suppose a model is expected to represent some economic relations over time. Observations are available for the variables in these relations from 1950 to 1973. No data are available for years beyond 1973. The researcher must somehow estimate the model and also generate forecasts for comparison with the data.

||||||||||||||||||||||||||||||||||||||||||||||||||||||||||||||||||||||||||||||||||||||||||||||||||||||||||||||||||||||||||||||||||||||||

*Discursive note.*   Obviously, if he uses all the data in obtaining the estimates, he has no independent data left to use in making forecasts. Forecasts based on the same data would certainly be biased toward accuracy since the observations were used in determining the parameter values of the best-fitting relation. It is a game-losing error to make inferences about the model based upon data with which the model was designed to agree.

||||||||||||||||||||||||||||||||||||||||||||||||||||||||||||||||||||||||||||||||||||||||||||||||||||||||||||||||||||||||||||||||||||||||

The usual practice is to withhold some of the available data from the estimating stage to use in the forecasting test. In so doing, the estimates obtained are somewhat poorer than those possible by using the larger size. Also, the model builder must testify that the model was built without consideration of this withheld data.

Suppose the data from 1950 to 1971 are used to estimate the parameters of the model, and suppose the observations of 1972 and 1973 are used to test the forecasting ability of the model. If the forecasts are quite accurate, all that is implied is that the data of 1972 and 1973 follow the same pattern as the data of 1950–71. The model is found to agree with the data of the overall period 1950–73. Since some (or many) other models may also agree with this data, there can be no implication that this model is the most correct without some comparisons of all these other potential models. Furthermore, there is no assurance that this model will agree with the data of 1974, or 1975, or any post-analysis period.

||||||||||||||||||||||||||||||||||||||||||||||||||||||||||||||||||||||||||||||||||||||||||||||||||||||||||||||||||||||||||||||||||||||||||||

*Discursive note.*   The opposite conclusions follow from inaccurate forecasts. The implication is only that the data of 1972–73 do not agree with the data 1950–71. It is not known whether all other theories would illustrate a similar disagreement. It is not known whether this model would agree or disagree with the data of 1974.

||||||||||||||||||||||||||||||||||||||||||||||||||||||||||||||||||||||||||||||||||||||||||||||||||||||||||||||||||||||||||||||||||||||||||||

*Explicative note.*   The forecasting test of the model is a very weak statistical test. It has no set significance level for testing the null hypothesis, [$H_0$: the model is good because the forecasts are "accurate"]. It has no clearly stated alternate hypothesis of which model is accepted if the null hypothesis is rejected.

||||||||||||||||||||||||||||||||||||||||||||||||||||||||||||||||||||||||||||||||||||||||||||||||||||||||||||||||||||||||||||||||||||||||||||

Most econometricians agree that the results of a single forecast are not sufficient to help confirm or falsify the model being tested as a good representation of the economic relationships. The researcher can *have more confidence* in the test results if they are consistent over several or many forecasting tests.[13] However, the statistical question remains unanswered as to how much more confidence is attributable to a second and to a third successful forecast. Moreover, what is the total level of confidence in the model after five

---

[13] See Christ, *Econometric Models*, p. 548.

successful forecasts? How can I compare the confidence level in my model with the confidence level in another model which also has five "accurate" forecasts? How much greater confidence can I have if the forecasts are within 1 percent of the observed values rather than within 2 percent? How many times must the model agree with new data in order to reach a 90 percent confidence level in the forecasts; or in the estimates of the parameters; or in the theory $\Theta$ specified in the model?

Such questions are not answerable since there is no known test statistic that is appropriate to set confidence levels on the forecasts generated in this process of testing by forecasting. Nevertheless, the procedure is an interesting one and very widely used. After all, if you cannot accept (at least partially) a model that gives successful forecasts for all available data, what can you accept? The econometrician must believe that if a model repeatedly represents the observed experience, its underlying theory must be relevant, useful, and worthy of continuing analysis.

## Measures of forecasting accuracy

The forecasts generated by the model must be compared to the observed values in order to judge the accuracy of the forecasts. Several simple statistics have been employed to make such a judgment. Sometimes the absolute size of the forecasting error or the percentage of the average difference between the forecast value and the observed value to the average of the actual values is used. The researcher makes his own judgments about the "significance" of this error. The estimating equation itself may be checked for its goodness of fit by calculating the usual measures (see Chapters 4 and 8). In particular, the coefficient of determination, $R^2$, is frequently given as a summary statistic only. It is not useful for making specific confidence statements since its sampling characteristics are unknown in the simultaneous equations case.

Other alternatives can be used if several forecasts are to be made and compared to the corresponding actual values. Let $T^*$ be the number of new observations to be compared to forecasts for making tests of the forecasting ability of the model. Let the $T^*$ actual values be $A_j$ and the $T^*$ forecasted values be $F_j$, $j = 1, 2, \ldots, T^*$. The goodness of fit of the model for these $T^*$ additional observations may be measured as a guide to the forecasting accuracy.

Two suggested statistics are the Theil inequality coefficient and the Janus quotient.[14] The first is generally included in any forecasting study to measure

---

[14] For the former see H. Theil, *Economic Forecasts*, sec. 2.5. For the latter see A. Gadd and H. Wold, "The Janus Quotient: A Measure for the Accuracy of Prediction," in H. Wold (ed.), *Econometric Model Building* (Amsterdam: North-Holland Publishing Co., 1964), pp. 229–34.

the predictive ability of a model. It is measured by,

$$U = \frac{\left[(1/T^*) \sum (F_j - A_j)^2\right]^{1/2}}{\left[(1/T^*) \sum F_j^2\right]^{1/2} + \left[(1/T^*) \sum A_j^2\right]^{1/2}}. \tag{19-4}$$

It compares a standard size of the forecast error with the sum of variability measures of the forecasted and actual values. The smaller the value of $U$, the more accurate the forecasts.

The second quotient is similar but measures a somewhat different concept. The Janus quotient compares the errors in forecasts using the $T^*$ new observations with the similar errors generated by using the $T$ original observations on which the estimation of the model is based. The coefficient is obtained by,

$$J^2 = \frac{(1/T^*) \sum_{j=1}^{T^*} (F_j - A_j)^2}{(1/T) \sum_{t=1}^{T} (F_t - A_t)^2}. \tag{19-5}$$

It is a measure of the agreement of the model to the entire set of $(T + T^*)$ observations. The numerator is calculated using the forecasting data. The denominator is calculated using the estimating data. The more that the numerator and denominator differ, the less the model agrees with both sets of data. The value of $J^2$ may be used as an indicator of the stability of the model structure over the two sets of data.

## 19.7 SUMMARY

The tests available for examining a simultaneous equations model are varied, somewhat complex, and not completely satisfactory. An identifiability test statistic (19–1) is available to check whether the overidentifying restrictions on a particular equation are correct. If so, then interpretation and testing of the significance of the parameters in the equation based on the sample estimates can be meaningful. However, except for quite small and simple models under certain conditions (such as no lagged endogenous variables), the exact distributions of the structural estimates are unknown. Often, the asymptotic distributions are presumed to hold, at least approximately, and the common $t$-tests of significance of regression coefficients are used. These should be recognized as possibly erroneous and misleading.

Two other approaches for testing simultaneous equations models are considered, predictive testing and testing by forecasting. The former is very useful for testing specific theoretical postulates in small, well-defined models; and the latter is very useful for providing insights into the best fitting and most accurate forecasting relationships. However, there are some dangers and limitations in both methods.

## Some Precautionary Remarks

Before using the method of predictive testing, the econometrician must thoroughly examine his theory and specify signs, values, or relative sizes of the parameters so that a very specific null hypothesis exists. This intensive theoretical work is certainly worthwhile; however, there is no clear line of separation between postulates based on theory and those based only on supposition or intuition or mathematical convenience. The entire procedure is always relatively tedious and is totally overwhelming if applied to a medium or large sized model.

Testing by forecasting does not allow any confidence statements in the usual sense of statistical inference. It is an "eyeball" type test for all practical purposes, although some statistics are suggested for measuring forecasting accuracy. The danger in using this method is that the econometrician is tempted to revise the specification and include or exclude variables strictly on the basis of their contribution to reducing the residual variation in the equation. Although this helps to develop "good fitting" relations, they may be difficult to interpret because the basic economic theory has been compromised. The good fit of a forecasting model containing ambiguous or irrelevant concepts of economic theory are viewed by some as analogous to the fabled discovery of a fabulous wonder cure for an unknown or nonexistent disease.

Finally, it must be recognized that a model which gives accurate predictions may have parameter values that disagree with the postulates of economic theory. Also, a small model that is acceptable in terms of an a priori set of theoretical postulates may be a very poor forecasting model. Thus, persons interested primarily in developing a good forecasting model would prefer to use testing by forecasting for its ease and directness to this purpose. Researchers interested only indirectly in good forecasting rules, but chiefly in testing statements of theory or in establishing numerical values for some theoretical parameters, would prefer predictive testing.

Much econometric research involves the discovery of models describing certain economic relations which provide good forecasts and which also have parameter values consistent with economic theory. Throughout such studies, the role of the initial and background conditions must also be emphasized. Conclusions about the goodness of the model, about the theory specified, and about the forecasts generated can only be seriously considered if the important underlying assumptions have been acknowledged and some attempt has been made to analyze and justify them. By repeated model building, estimation, and testing of single equation or simultaneous equations models, econometricians hope to eventually arrive at accurate descriptions of economic phenomena that are consistent with a refined theory having standardized regions of acceptance for all its parameters. Such models could become decision tools of economic policy-makers to help in meeting target values for specific endogenous variables and in making the "best" decisions to maximize social utility.

## NEW VOCABULARY

Predictive statements

Truth table

Overidentifying restrictions

Identifiability test statistic $\bar{F}$

Exact finite sample distributions

Approximate asymptotic distributions

Predictive testing

Testing by forecasting

Theil inequality coefficient

Janus quotient

## REFERENCES

A readable discussion on testing a model may be found in:

Malinvaud, E. *Statistical Methods of Econometrics*. Chicago: Rand McNally & Co., 1966.

Many papers deal with the derivation of exact finite sample distributions of various structural parameters. Some of them which also give references to prior papers on the same topics are:

Basmann, R. L. "A Note on the Exact Finite Sample Frequency Functions of GCL Estimators in a Leading Three Equation Case." *Journal of the American Statistical Association*, 1963, pp. 161–71;

Bergstrom, A. R. "The Exact Sampling Distributions of Least Squares and Maximum Likelihood Estimators of the Marginal Propensity to Consume." *Econometrica*, 1962, pp. 480–90.

Kmenta, J., and Gilbert, R. F. "Small Sample Properties of Alternative Estimators of Seemingly Unrelated Regressions." *Journal of the American Statistical Association*, 1968, pp. 1180–1200.

Richardson, D. H. "The Exact Distribution of a Structural Coefficient Estimator." *Journal of the American Statistical Association*, 1968, pp. 1214–26.

Sawa, T. "The Exact Sampling Distribution of Ordinary Least Squares and TSLS Estimators." *Journal of the American Statistical Association*, 1969, pp. 923–37.

## EXERCISES

1.  Make a list of the advantages and disadvantages of the method (*a*) of predictive testing and (*b*) of testing by forecasting.
2.  Discuss the different possibilities and problems in testing based on—
    *a*)  Very large samples compared to quite small samples.
    *b*)  Very restricted small models compared to very large models.
3.  Use the identifiability test statistic in (19–1) to check the identifiability of the equations for the model and data of—
    *a*)  Exercise 3, Chapter 18.
    *b*)  Exercise 5, Chapter 18.
    *c*)  Exercise 8, Chapter 18.
    *d*)  Exercise 9, Chapter 18.
4.  Suppose a simultaneous equations model is used for forecasting. The actual and forecasted values for the first 14 observations used in the estimation and for the next 8 observations used for forecasting are given below.

| Observation | Actual value A | Estimated value F | Observation | Actual value A | Forecast value F |
|---|---|---|---|---|---|
| 1 | 1.38381 | 1.37545 | 1 | 1.54033 | 1.52864 |
| 2 | 1.37658 | 1.41684 | 2 | 1.52892 | 1.52824 |
| 3 | 1.38202 | 1.44446 | 3 | 1.54158 | 1.53437 |
| 4 | 1.44871 | 1.45571 | 4 | 1.54777 | 1.54554 |
| 5 | 1.45332 | 1.46930 | 5 | 1.57403 | 1.55419 |
| 6 | 1.46687 | 1.48522 | 6 | 1.56110 | 1.56093 |
| 7 | 1.47567 | 1.48791 | 7 | 1.53403 | 1.61526 |
| 8 | 1.49136 | 1.50360 | 8 | 1.62118 | 1.62042 |
| 9 | 1.53403 | 1.49194 | | | |
| 10 | 1.54303 | 1.50996 | | | |
| 11 | 1.62325 | 1.50378 | | | |
| 12 | 1.50378 | 1.50261 | | | |
| 13 | 1.50106 | 1.49937 | | | |
| 14 | 1.52634 | 1.51590 | | | |

Source: Suvaphorn, Class (1971).

Determine the following statistics and discuss their meaning relative to the forecasting ability of this model:

a)  The ratio of the average absolute value of the forecasting error $(i = 1, \ldots, 8)$ to the mean of the actual values $Y_i$;

b)  The Theil inequality coefficient;

c)  The Janus quotient.

5.  A model estimated on the basis of 20 observations is to be tested by forecasting based on 10 new observations.

a)  Using the data below, determine the same statistics as in Exercise 4 and discuss their meaning relative to the forecasting ability of this model.

b)  Compare the results of the forecasts between Exercises 4 and 5(a) and argue which one is the " best " forecasting model.

| Observation | Actual value A | Forecast value F | Observation | Actual value A | Forecast value F |
|---|---|---|---|---|---|
| 1 | 1.5260 | 1.5963 | 16 | 2.0669 | 1.8985 |
| 2 | 1.8903 | 1.8726 | 17 | 1.8007 | 1.7614 |
| 3 | 1.5307 | 1.4105 | 18 | 2.3472 | 2.0211 |
| 4 | 1.6348 | 1.8501 | 19 | 1.9383 | 1.7268 |
| 5 | 1.2692 | 1.6538 | 20 | 1.9788 | 2.0281 |
| 6 | 1.6119 | 1.7019 | 1 | 2.0968 | 1.9995 |
| 7 | 1.3416 | 1.5037 | 2 | 2.5788 | 2.2360 |
| 8 | 1.6332 | 1.7438 | 3 | 2.1988 | 1.8538 |
| 9 | 1.5711 | 1.7117 | 4 | 2.4484 | 2.2898 |
| 10 | 1.8803 | 1.8951 | 5 | 2.2070 | 2.3106 |
| 11 | 1.5277 | 1.5590 | 6 | 2.3523 | 2.4373 |
| 12 | 1.9496 | 1.9274 | 7 | 2.1501 | 2.1063 |
| 13 | 1.6761 | 1.7223 | 8 | 2.3070 | 2.3865 |
| 14 | 2.1651 | 1.8909 | 9 | 1.8258 | 2.2492 |
| 15 | 1.6625 | 1.5759 | 10 | 2.4132 | 2.4165 |

Source: McRae, Class (1971).

*Appendixes of Tables*

APPENDIX A. Values of chi-square ($\chi_P^2$) for specified probability levels ($P$) and degrees of freedom ($v$).

$\chi_P^2$ is the value of the chi-square random variable such that the probability of obtaining a sample $\chi^2$ value at least as large as $\chi_P^2$ is $P$. For very large degrees of freedom, the chi-square value may be approximated by $\chi^2 \doteq \frac{1}{2}(z_P \pm \sqrt{2v-1})^2$ where $z_P$ is the standardized normal deviate (as given in Appendix B).

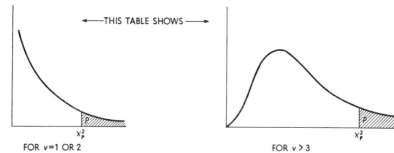

<----THIS TABLE SHOWS---->

FOR v=1 OR 2          FOR v > 3

| Degrees of freedom $v$ | Level of significance $P$ for one-sided statements | | | | | | | |
|---|---|---|---|---|---|---|---|---|
| | 0.995 | 0.990 | 0.975 | 0.950 | 0.900 | 0.80 | 0.70 | 0.50 |
| 1 | 0.0⁴393 | 0.0³157 | 0.0³982 | 0.00393 | 0.0158 | 0.0642 | 0.148 | 0.455 |
| 2 | 0.0100 | 0.0201 | 0.0506 | 0.103 | 0.211 | 0.446 | 0.713 | 1.39 |
| 3 | 0.0717 | 0.115 | 0.216 | 0.352 | 0.584 | 1.01 | 1.42 | 2.37 |
| 4 | 0.207 | 0.297 | 0.484 | 0.711 | 1.06 | 1.65 | 2.20 | 3.36 |
| 5 | 0.412 | 0.554 | 0.831 | 1.15 | 1.61 | 2.34 | 3.00 | 4.35 |
| 6 | 0.676 | 0.872 | 1.24 | 1.64 | 2.20 | 3.07 | 3.83 | 5.35 |
| 7 | 0.989 | 1.24 | 1.69 | 2.17 | 2.83 | 3.82 | 4.67 | 6.35 |
| 8 | 1.34 | 1.65 | 2.18 | 2.73 | 3.49 | 4.59 | 5.53 | 7.34 |
| 9 | 1.73 | 2.09 | 2.70 | 3.33 | 4.17 | 5.38 | 6.39 | 8.34 |
| 10 | 2.16 | 2.56 | 3.25 | 3.94 | 4.87 | 6.18 | 7.27 | 9.34 |
| 11 | 2.60 | 3.05 | 3.82 | 4.57 | 5.58 | 6.99 | 8.15 | 10.3 |
| 12 | 3.07 | 3.57 | 4.40 | 5.23 | 6.30 | 7.81 | 9.03 | 11.3 |
| 13 | 3.57 | 4.11 | 5.01 | 5.89 | 7.04 | 8.63 | 9.93 | 12.3 |
| 14 | 4.07 | 4.66 | 5.63 | 6.57 | 7.79 | 9.47 | 10.8 | 13.3 |
| 15 | 4.60 | 5.23 | 6.26 | 7.26 | 8.55 | 10.3 | 11.7 | 14.3 |
| 16 | 5.14 | 5.81 | 6.91 | 7.96 | 9.31 | 11.2 | 12.6 | 15.3 |
| 17 | 5.70 | 6.41 | 7.56 | 8.67 | 10.1 | 12.0 | 13.5 | 16.3 |
| 18 | 6.26 | 7.01 | 8.23 | 9.39 | 10.9 | 12.9 | 14.4 | 17.3 |
| 19 | 6.84 | 7.63 | 8.91 | 10.1 | 11.7 | 13.7 | 15.4 | 18.3 |
| 20 | 7.43 | 8.26 | 9.59 | 10.9 | 12.4 | 14.6 | 16.3 | 19.3 |
| 21 | 8.03 | 8.90 | 10.3 | 11.6 | 13.2 | 15.4 | 17.2 | 20.3 |
| 22 | 8.64 | 9.54 | 11.0 | 12.3 | 14.0 | 16.3 | 18.1 | 21.3 |
| 23 | 9.26 | 10.2 | 11.7 | 13.1 | 14.8 | 17.2 | 19.0 | 22.3 |
| 24 | 9.89 | 10.9 | 12.4 | 13.8 | 15.7 | 18.1 | 19.9 | 23.3 |
| 25 | 10.5 | 11.5 | 13.1 | 14.6 | 16.5 | 18.9 | 20.9 | 24.3 |
| 26 | 11.2 | 12.2 | 13.8 | 15.4 | 17.3 | 19.8 | 21.8 | 25.3 |
| 27 | 11.8 | 12.9 | 14.6 | 16.2 | 18.1 | 20.7 | 22.7 | 26.3 |
| 28 | 12.5 | 13.6 | 15.3 | 16.9 | 18.9 | 21.6 | 23.6 | 27.3 |
| 29 | 13.1 | 14.3 | 16.0 | 17.7 | 19.8 | 22.5 | 24.6 | 28.3 |
| 30 | 13.8 | 15.0 | 16.8 | 18.5 | 20.6 | 23.4 | 25.5 | 29.3 |

APPENDIX A—*Continued*

| Degrees of freedom $\nu$ | Level of significance P for one-sided statements | | | | | | | |
|---|---|---|---|---|---|---|---|---|
| | 0.30 | 0.20 | 0.10 | 0.05 | 0.025 | 0.010 | 0.005 | 0.001 |
| 1 | 1.07 | 1.64 | 2.71 | 3.84 | 5.02 | 6.63 | 7.88 | 10.8 |
| 2 | 2.41 | 3.22 | 4.61 | 5.99 | 7.38 | 9.21 | 10.6 | 13.8 |
| 3 | 3.67 | 4.64 | 6.25 | 7.82 | 9.35 | 11.3 | 12.8 | 16.3 |
| 4 | 4.88 | 5.99 | 7.78 | 9.49 | 11.1 | 13.3 | 14.9 | 18.5 |
| 5 | 6.06 | 7.29 | 9.24 | 11.1 | 12.8 | 15.1 | 16.7 | 20.5 |
| 6 | 7.23 | 8.56 | 10.6 | 12.6 | 14.4 | 16.8 | 18.5 | 22.5 |
| 7 | 8.38 | 9.80 | 12.0 | 14.1 | 16.0 | 18.5 | 20.3 | 24.3 |
| 8 | 9.52 | 11.0 | 13.4 | 15.5 | 17.5 | 20.1 | 22.0 | 26.1 |
| 9 | 10.7 | 12.2 | 14.7 | 16.9 | 19.0 | 21.7 | 23.6 | 27.9 |
| 10 | 11.8 | 13.4 | 16.0 | 18.3 | 20.5 | 23.2 | 25.2 | 29.6 |
| 11 | 12.9 | 14.6 | 17.3 | 19.7 | 21.9 | 24.7 | 26.8 | 31.3 |
| 12 | 14.0 | 15.8 | 18.5 | 21.0 | 23.3 | 26.2 | 28.3 | 32.9 |
| 13 | 15.1 | 17.0 | 19.8 | 22.4 | 24.7 | 27.7 | 29.8 | 34.5 |
| 14 | 16.2 | 18.2 | 21.1 | 23.7 | 26.1 | 29.1 | 31.3 | 36.1 |
| 15 | 17.3 | 19.3 | 22.3 | 25.0 | 27.5 | 30.6 | 32.8 | 37.7 |
| 16 | 18.4 | 20.5 | 23.5 | 26.3 | 28.8 | 32.0 | 34.3 | 39.3 |
| 17 | 19.5 | 21.6 | 24.8 | 27.6 | 30.2 | 33.4 | 35.7 | 40.8 |
| 18 | 20.6 | 22.8 | 26.0 | 28.9 | 31.5 | 34.8 | 37.2 | 42.3 |
| 19 | 21.7 | 23.9 | 27.2 | 30.1 | 32.9 | 36.2 | 38.6 | 43.8 |
| 20 | 22.8 | 25.0 | 28.4 | 31.4 | 34.2 | 37.6 | 40.0 | 45.3 |
| 21 | 23.9 | 26.2 | 29.6 | 32.7 | 35.5 | 38.9 | 41.4 | 46.8 |
| 22 | 24.9 | 27.3 | 30.8 | 33.9 | 36.8 | 40.3 | 42.8 | 48.3 |
| 23 | 26.0 | 28.4 | 32.0 | 35.2 | 38.1 | 41.6 | 44.2 | 49.7 |
| 24 | 27.1 | 29.6 | 33.2 | 36.4 | 39.4 | 43.0 | 45.6 | 51.2 |
| 25 | 28.2 | 30.7 | 34.4 | 37.7 | 40.6 | 44.3 | 46.9 | 52.6 |
| 26 | 29.2 | 31.8 | 35.6 | 38.9 | 41.9 | 45.6 | 48.3 | 54.1 |
| 27 | 30.3 | 32.9 | 36.7 | 40.1 | 43.2 | 47.0 | 49.6 | 55.5 |
| 28 | 31.4 | 34.0 | 37.9 | 41.3 | 44.5 | 48.3 | 51.0 | 56.9 |
| 29 | 32.5 | 35.1 | 39.1 | 42.6 | 45.7 | 49.6 | 52.3 | 58.3 |
| 30 | 33.5 | 36.3 | 40.3 | 43.8 | 47.0 | 50.9 | 53.7 | 59.7 |

Source: Catherine M. Thompson, "Tables of the Percentage Points of the $\chi^2$-Distribution," *Biometrika*, Vol. 32 (1941), pp. 188–89. The remainder of the table is taken from Table IV of R. A. Fisher and F. Yates, *Statistical Tables for Biological, Agricultural and Medical Research*, published by Oliver and Boyd, (Edinburgh: and by permission of the authors and publishers.

## APPENDIX B.    Values of $z_P$ for specified probabilities $P$

$z_P$ is the value of the standardized normal (mean $= 0$, standard deviation $= 1$) random variable $z$ such that the probability of obtaining a sample $z$ value at least as large as $z_P$ is $P$. The value of $P$ must be doubled if two sided statements are made using the same $z_P$ value.

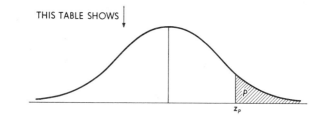

THIS TABLE SHOWS

| $P$ | $z_P$ | $P$ | $z_P$ | $P$ | $z_P$ |
|---|---|---|---|---|---|
| 0.0005 | 3.29053 | 0.005 | 2.57583 | 0.11 | 1.22653 |
| 0.0010 | 3.09023 | 0.010 | 2.32635 | 0.12 | 1.17499 |
| 0.0015 | 2.96774 | 0.015 | 2.17009 | 0.13 | 1.12639 |
| 0.0020 | 2.87816 | 0.020 | 2.05375 | 0.14 | 1.08032 |
| 0.0025 | 2.80703 | 0.025 | 1.95996 | 0.15 | 1.03643 |
| 0.0030 | 2.74778 | 0.030 | 1.88079 | 0.16 | 0.99446 |
| 0.0035 | 2.69684 | 0.035 | 1.81191 | 0.17 | 0.95417 |
| 0.0040 | 2.65207 | 0.040 | 1.75069 | 0.18 | 0.91537 |
| 0.0045 | 2.61205 | 0.045 | 1.69540 | 0.19 | 0.87790 |
| 0.0050 | 2.57583 | 0.050 | 1.64485 | 0.20 | 0.84162 |
| 0.006 | 2.51214 | 0.06 | 1.55477 | 0.25 | 0.67449 |
| 0.007 | 2.45726 | 0.07 | 1.47579 | 0.30 | 0.52440 |
| 0.008 | 2.40892 | 0.08 | 1.40507 | 0.35 | 0.38532 |
| 0.009 | 2.36562 | 0.09 | 1.34076 | 0.40 | 0.25335 |
| 0.010 | 2.32635 | 0.10 | 1.28155 | 0.45 | 0.12566 |

Source: Frederick E. Croxton, Dudley J. Cowden, and Ben W. Bolch, *Practical Business Statistics*, 4th ed., © 1969, Prentice-Hall, Inc., Englewood Cliffs, N.J.

# APPENDIX C.  Values of $t_P$ for specified probabilities P and degrees of freedom v

$t_P$ is the value of the Student's t random variable such that the probability of obtaining a sample t value at least as large as $t_P$ is P. The value of P must be doubled if two-sided statements are made using the same $t_P$ value.

THIS TABLE SHOWS

| Degrees of freedom v | 0.45 | 0.40 | 0.35 | 0.30 | 0.25 | 0.20 | 0.15 | 0.10 | 0.05 | 0.025 | 0.01 | 0.005 | 0.0005 |
|---|---|---|---|---|---|---|---|---|---|---|---|---|---|
| | | | | | Level of significance P for one-sided statements | | | | | | | | |
| 1 | 0.158 | 0.325 | 0.510 | 0.727 | 1.000 | 1.376 | 1.963 | 3.078 | 6.314 | 12.706 | 31.821 | 63.657 | 636.692 |
| 2 | 0.142 | 0.289 | 0.445 | 0.617 | 0.816 | 1.061 | 1.386 | 1.886 | 2.920 | 4.303 | 6.965 | 9.925 | 31.598 |
| 3 | 0.137 | 0.277 | 0.424 | 0.584 | 0.765 | 0.978 | 1.250 | 1.638 | 2.353 | 3.182 | 4.541 | 5.841 | 12.924 |
| 4 | 0.134 | 0.271 | 0.414 | 0.569 | 0.741 | 0.941 | 1.190 | 1.533 | 2.132 | 2.776 | 3.747 | 4.604 | 8.610 |
| 5 | 0.132 | 0.267 | 0.408 | 0.559 | 0.727 | 0.920 | 1.156 | 1.476 | 2.015 | 2.571 | 3.365 | 4.032 | 6.869 |
| 6 | 0.131 | 0.265 | 0.404 | 0.553 | 0.718 | 0.906 | 1.134 | 1.440 | 1.943 | 2.447 | 3.143 | 3.707 | 5.959 |
| 7 | 0.130 | 0.263 | 0.402 | 0.549 | 0.711 | 0.896 | 1.119 | 1.415 | 1.895 | 2.365 | 2.998 | 3.499 | 5.408 |
| 8 | 0.130 | 0.262 | 0.399 | 0.546 | 0.706 | 0.889 | 1.108 | 1.397 | 1.860 | 2.306 | 2.896 | 3.355 | 5.041 |
| 9 | 0.129 | 0.261 | 0.398 | 0.543 | 0.703 | 0.883 | 1.100 | 1.383 | 1.833 | 2.262 | 2.821 | 3.250 | 4.781 |
| 10 | 0.129 | 0.260 | 0.397 | 0.542 | 0.700 | 0.879 | 1.093 | 1.372 | 1.812 | 2.228 | 2.764 | 3.169 | 4.587 |
| 11 | 0.129 | 0.260 | 0.396 | 0.540 | 0.697 | 0.876 | 1.088 | 1.363 | 1.796 | 2.201 | 2.718 | 3.106 | 4.437 |
| 12 | 0.128 | 0.259 | 0.395 | 0.539 | 0.695 | 0.873 | 1.083 | 1.356 | 1.782 | 2.179 | 2.681 | 3.055 | 4.318 |
| 13 | 0.128 | 0.259 | 0.394 | 0.538 | 0.694 | 0.870 | 1.079 | 1.350 | 1.771 | 2.160 | 2.650 | 3.012 | 4.221 |
| 14 | 0.128 | 0.258 | 0.393 | 0.537 | 0.692 | 0.868 | 1.076 | 1.345 | 1.761 | 2.145 | 2.624 | 2.977 | 4.140 |
| 15 | 0.128 | 0.258 | 0.393 | 0.536 | 0.691 | 0.866 | 1.074 | 1.341 | 1.753 | 2.131 | 2.602 | 2.947 | 4.073 |
| 16 | 0.128 | 0.258 | 0.392 | 0.535 | 0.690 | 0.865 | 1.071 | 1.337 | 1.746 | 2.120 | 2.583 | 2.921 | 4.015 |
| 17 | 0.128 | 0.257 | 0.392 | 0.534 | 0.689 | 0.863 | 1.069 | 1.333 | 1.740 | 2.110 | 2.567 | 2.898 | 3.965 |
| 18 | 0.127 | 0.257 | 0.392 | 0.534 | 0.688 | 0.862 | 1.067 | 1.330 | 1.734 | 2.101 | 2.552 | 2.878 | 3.922 |
| 19 | 0.127 | 0.257 | 0.391 | 0.533 | 0.688 | 0.861 | 1.066 | 1.328 | 1.729 | 2.093 | 2.539 | 2.861 | 3.883 |
| 20 | 0.127 | 0.257 | 0.391 | 0.533 | 0.687 | 0.860 | 1.064 | 1.325 | 1.725 | 2.086 | 2.528 | 2.845 | 3.850 |
| 21 | 0.127 | 0.257 | 0.391 | 0.532 | 0.686 | 0.859 | 1.063 | 1.323 | 1.721 | 2.080 | 2.518 | 2.831 | 3.819 |
| 22 | 0.127 | 0.256 | 0.390 | 0.532 | 0.686 | 0.858 | 1.061 | 1.321 | 1.717 | 2.074 | 2.508 | 2.819 | 3.792 |
| 23 | 0.127 | 0.256 | 0.390 | 0.532 | 0.685 | 0.858 | 1.060 | 1.319 | 1.714 | 2.069 | 2.500 | 2.807 | 3.767 |
| 24 | 0.127 | 0.256 | 0.390 | 0.531 | 0.685 | 0.857 | 1.059 | 1.318 | 1.711 | 2.064 | 2.492 | 2.797 | 3.745 |
| 25 | 0.127 | 0.256 | 0.390 | 0.531 | 0.684 | 0.856 | 1.058 | 1.316 | 1.708 | 2.060 | 2.485 | 2.787 | 3.725 |
| 26 | 0.127 | 0.256 | 0.390 | 0.531 | 0.684 | 0.856 | 1.058 | 1.315 | 1.706 | 2.056 | 2.479 | 2.779 | 3.707 |
| 27 | 0.127 | 0.256 | 0.389 | 0.531 | 0.684 | 0.855 | 1.057 | 1.314 | 1.703 | 2.052 | 2.473 | 2.771 | 3.690 |
| 28 | 0.127 | 0.256 | 0.389 | 0.530 | 0.683 | 0.855 | 1.056 | 1.313 | 1.701 | 2.048 | 2.467 | 2.763 | 3.674 |
| 29 | 0.127 | 0.256 | 0.389 | 0.530 | 0.683 | 0.854 | 1.055 | 1.311 | 1.699 | 2.045 | 2.462 | 2.756 | 3.659 |
| 30 | 0.127 | 0.256 | 0.389 | 0.530 | 0.683 | 0.854 | 1.055 | 1.310 | 1.697 | 2.042 | 2.457 | 2.750 | 3.646 |
| 40 | 0.126 | 0.255 | 0.388 | 0.529 | 0.681 | 0.851 | 1.050 | 1.303 | 1.684 | 2.021 | 2.423 | 2.704 | 3.551 |
| 60 | 0.126 | 0.254 | 0.387 | 0.527 | 0.679 | 0.848 | 1.046 | 1.296 | 1.671 | 2.000 | 2.390 | 2.660 | 3.460 |
| 120 | 0.126 | 0.254 | 0.386 | 0.526 | 0.677 | 0.845 | 1.041 | 1.289 | 1.658 | 1.980 | 2.358 | 2.617 | 3.373 |
| ∞ | 0.126 | 0.253 | 0.385 | 0.524 | 0.674 | 0.842 | 1.036 | 1.282 | 1.645 | 1.960 | 2.326 | 2.576 | 3.291 |

Source: This table is taken from Table III of Fisher and Yates, *Statistical Tables for Biological, Agricultural and Medical Research*, published by Oliver and Boyd, Edinburgh, and by permission of the authors and publishers.

APPENDIX  D.    Values of $F_P$ for specified probabilities $P$ and degrees of freedom in the numerator $v_1$ and degrees of freedom in the denominator $v_2$.

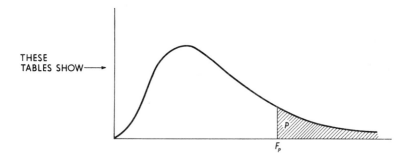

THESE
TABLES SHOW→

$F_P$ is the value of the Snedecor $F$ random variable such that the probability of obtaining a sample $F$ value at least as large as $F_P$ is $P$. In the first comprehensive table, the level of significance $P$ is 0.05 *for all lightface entries* and 0.01 *for all boldface entries.* This table continues on four pages with the degrees of freedom in the numerator specified across the top and the degrees of freedom in the denominator specified along the side. The areas are shown in the illustration above. For example, given $n_1 = 4$ and $n_2 = 9$, the value of $F$ is 3.63 when 5 % of the total area is in the right tail of the distribution.

This table is reproduced by permission from *Statistical Methods*, 5th edition, by George W. Snedecor, © 1956 by the Iowa State University Press, Ames, Iowa.

Two additional short tables are given for levels of significance $P = 0.025$ and $P = 0.001$. These tables are abridged from Table V of Fisher and Yates, *Statistical Tables for Biological, Agricultural and Medical Research*, published by Oliver and Boyd, Edinburgh, and by permission of the authors and publishers.

## APPENDIX D—*Continued*

$n_1$ = degrees of freedom for numerator

|  | 1 | 2 | 3 | 4 | 5 | 6 | 7 | 8 | 9 | 10 | 11 | 12 |
|---|---|---|---|---|---|---|---|---|---|---|---|---|
| 1 | 161<br>**4,052** | 200<br>**4,999** | 216<br>**5,403** | 225<br>**5,625** | 230<br>**5,764** | 234<br>**5,859** | 237<br>**5,928** | 239<br>**5,981** | 241<br>**6,022** | 242<br>**6,056** | 243<br>**6,082** | 244<br>**6,106** |
| 2 | 18.51<br>**98.49** | 19.00<br>**99.01** | 19.16<br>**99.17** | 19.25<br>**99.25** | 19.30<br>**99.30** | 19.33<br>**99.33** | 19.36<br>**99.34** | 19.37<br>**99.36** | 19.38<br>**99.38** | 19.39<br>**99.40** | 19.40<br>**99.41** | 19.41<br>**99.42** |
| 3 | 10.13<br>**34.12** | 9.55<br>**30.81** | 9.28<br>**29.46** | 9.12<br>**28.71** | 9.01<br>**28.24** | 8.94<br>**27.91** | 8.88<br>**27.67** | 8.84<br>**27.49** | 8.81<br>**27.34** | 8.78<br>**27.23** | 8.76<br>**27.13** | 8.74<br>**27.05** |
| 4 | 7.71<br>**21.20** | 6.94<br>**18.00** | 6.59<br>**16.69** | 6.39<br>**15.98** | 6.26<br>**15.52** | 6.16<br>**15.21** | 6.09<br>**14.98** | 6.04<br>**14.80** | 6.00<br>**14.66** | 5.96<br>**14.54** | 5.93<br>**14.45** | 5.91<br>**14.37** |
| 5 | 6.61<br>**16.26** | 5.79<br>**13.27** | 5.41<br>**12.06** | 5.19<br>**11.39** | 5.05<br>**10.97** | 4.95<br>**10.67** | 4.88<br>**10.45** | 4.82<br>**10.27** | 4.78<br>**10.15** | 4.74<br>**10.05** | 4.70<br>**9.96** | 4.68<br>**9.89** |
| 6 | 5.99<br>**13.74** | 5.14<br>**10.92** | 4.76<br>**9.78** | 4.53<br>**9.15** | 4.39<br>**8.75** | 4.28<br>**8.47** | 4.21<br>**8.26** | 4.15<br>**8.10** | 4.10<br>**7.98** | 4.06<br>**7.87** | 4.03<br>**7.79** | 4.00<br>**7.72** |
| 7 | 5.59<br>**12.25** | 4.74<br>**9.55** | 4.35<br>**8.45** | 4.12<br>**7.85** | 3.97<br>**7.46** | 3.87<br>**7.19** | 3.79<br>**7.00** | 3.73<br>**6.84** | 3.68<br>**6.71** | 3.63<br>**6.62** | 3.60<br>**6.54** | 3.57<br>**6.47** |
| 8 | 5.32<br>**11.26** | 4.46<br>**8.65** | 4.07<br>**7.59** | 3.84<br>**7.01** | 3.69<br>**6.63** | 3.58<br>**6.37** | 3.50<br>**6.19** | 3.44<br>**6.03** | 3.39<br>**5.91** | 3.34<br>**5.82** | 3.31<br>**5.74** | 3.28<br>**5.67** |
| 9 | 5.12<br>**10.56** | 4.26<br>**8.02** | 3.86<br>**6.99** | 3.63<br>**6.42** | 3.48<br>**6.06** | 3.37<br>**5.80** | 3.29<br>**5.62** | 3.23<br>**5.47** | 3.18<br>**5.35** | 3.13<br>**5.26** | 3.10<br>**5.18** | 3.07<br>**5.11** |
| 10 | 4.96<br>**10.04** | 4.10<br>**7.56** | 3.71<br>**6.55** | 3.48<br>**5.99** | 3.33<br>**5.64** | 3.22<br>**5.39** | 3.14<br>**5.21** | 3.07<br>**5.06** | 3.02<br>**4.95** | 2.97<br>**4.85** | 2.94<br>**4.78** | 2.91<br>**4.71** |
| 11 | 4.84<br>**9.65** | 3.98<br>**7.20** | 3.59<br>**6.22** | 3.36<br>**5.67** | 3.20<br>**5.32** | 3.09<br>**5.07** | 3.01<br>**4.88** | 2.95<br>**4.74** | 2.90<br>**4.63** | 2.86<br>**4.54** | 2.82<br>**4.46** | 2.79<br>**4.40** |
| 12 | 4.75<br>**9.33** | 3.88<br>**6.93** | 3.49<br>**5.95** | 3.26<br>**5.41** | 3.11<br>**5.06** | 3.00<br>**4.82** | 2.92<br>**4.65** | 2.85<br>**4.50** | 2.80<br>**4.39** | 2.76<br>**4.30** | 2.72<br>**4.22** | 2.69<br>**4.16** |
| 13 | 4.67<br>**9.07** | 3.80<br>**6.70** | 3.41<br>**5.74** | 3.18<br>**5.20** | 3.02<br>**4.86** | 2.92<br>**4.62** | 2.84<br>**4.44** | 2.77<br>**4.30** | 2.72<br>**4.19** | 2.67<br>**4.10** | 2.63<br>**4.02** | 2.60<br>**3.96** |
| 14 | 4.60<br>**8.86** | 3.74<br>**6.51** | 3.34<br>**5.56** | 3.11<br>**5.03** | 2.96<br>**4.69** | 2.85<br>**4.46** | 2.77<br>**4.28** | 2.70<br>**4.14** | 2.65<br>**4.03** | 2.60<br>**3.94** | 2.56<br>**3.86** | 2.53<br>**3.80** |
| 15 | 4.54<br>**8.68** | 3.68<br>**6.36** | 3.29<br>**5.42** | 3.06<br>**4.89** | 2.90<br>**4.56** | 2.79<br>**4.32** | 2.70<br>**4.14** | 2.64<br>**4.00** | 2.59<br>**3.89** | 2.55<br>**3.80** | 2.51<br>**3.73** | 2.48<br>**3.67** |
| 16 | 4.49<br>**8.53** | 3.63<br>**6.23** | 3.24<br>**5.29** | 3.01<br>**4.77** | 2.85<br>**4.44** | 2.74<br>**4.20** | 2.66<br>**4.03** | 2.59<br>**3.89** | 2.54<br>**3.78** | 2.49<br>**3.69** | 2.45<br>**3.61** | 2.42<br>**3.55** |
| 17 | 4.45<br>**8.40** | 3.59<br>**6.11** | 3.20<br>**5.18** | 2.96<br>**4.67** | 2.81<br>**4.34** | 2.70<br>**4.10** | 2.62<br>**3.93** | 2.55<br>**3.79** | 2.50<br>**3.68** | 2.45<br>**3.59** | 2.41<br>**3.52** | 2.38<br>**3.45** |
| 18 | 4.41<br>**8.28** | 3.55<br>**6.01** | 3.16<br>**5.09** | 2.93<br>**4.58** | 2.77<br>**4.25** | 2.66<br>**4.01** | 2.58<br>**3.85** | 2.51<br>**3.71** | 2.46<br>**3.60** | 2.41<br>**3.51** | 2.37<br>**3.44** | 2.34<br>**3.37** |
| 19 | 4.38<br>**8.18** | 3.52<br>**5.93** | 3.13<br>**5.01** | 2.90<br>**4.50** | 2.74<br>**4.17** | 2.63<br>**3.94** | 2.55<br>**3.77** | 2.48<br>**3.63** | 2.43<br>**3.52** | 2.38<br>**3.43** | 2.34<br>**3.36** | 2.31<br>**3.30** |
| 20 | 4.35<br>**8.10** | 3.49<br>**5.85** | 3.10<br>**4.94** | 2.87<br>**4.43** | 2.71<br>**4.10** | 2.60<br>**3.87** | 2.52<br>**3.71** | 2.45<br>**3.56** | 2.40<br>**3.45** | 2.35<br>**3.37** | 2.31<br>**3.30** | 2.28<br>**3.23** |
| 21 | 4.32<br>**8.02** | 3.47<br>**5.78** | 3.07<br>**4.87** | 2.84<br>**4.37** | 2.68<br>**4.04** | 2.57<br>**3.81** | 2.49<br>**3.65** | 2.42<br>**3.51** | 2.37<br>**3.40** | 2.32<br>**3.31** | 2.28<br>**3.24** | 2.25<br>**3.17** |
| 22 | 4.30<br>**7.94** | 3.44<br>**5.72** | 3.05<br>**4.82** | 2.82<br>**4.31** | 2.66<br>**3.99** | 2.55<br>**3.76** | 2.47<br>**3.59** | 2.40<br>**3.45** | 2.35<br>**3.35** | 2.30<br>**3.26** | 2.26<br>**3.18** | 2.23<br>**3.12** |
| 23 | 4.28<br>**7.88** | 3.42<br>**5.66** | 3.03<br>**4.76** | 2.80<br>**4.26** | 2.64<br>**3.94** | 2.53<br>**3.71** | 2.45<br>**3.54** | 2.38<br>**3.41** | 2.32<br>**3.30** | 2.28<br>**3.21** | 2.24<br>**3.14** | 2.20<br>**3.07** |
| 24 | 4.26<br>**7.82** | 3.40<br>**5.61** | 3.01<br>**4.72** | 2.78<br>**4.22** | 2.62<br>**3.90** | 2.51<br>**3.67** | 2.43<br>**3.50** | 2.36<br>**3.36** | 2.30<br>**3.25** | 2.26<br>**3.17** | 2.22<br>**3.09** | 2.18<br>**3.03** |
| 25 | 4.24<br>**7.77** | 3.38<br>**5.57** | 2.99<br>**4.68** | 2.76<br>**4.18** | 2.60<br>**3.86** | 2.49<br>**3.63** | 2.41<br>**3.46** | 2.34<br>**3.32** | 2.28<br>**3.21** | 2.24<br>**3.13** | 2.20<br>**3.05** | 2.16<br>**2.99** |
| 26 | 4.22<br>**7.72** | 3.37<br>**5.53** | 2.98<br>**4.64** | 2.74<br>**4.14** | 2.59<br>**3.82** | 2.47<br>**3.59** | 2.39<br>**3.42** | 2.32<br>**3.29** | 2.27<br>**3.17** | 2.22<br>**3.09** | 2.18<br>**3.02** | 2.15<br>**2.96** |

$n_2$ = degrees of freedom for denominator

## APPENDIX D—*Continued*

$n_1$ = degrees of freedom for numerator

$n_2$ = degrees of freedom for denominator

| | 14 | 16 | 20 | 24 | 30 | 40 | 50 | 75 | 100 | 200 | 500 | ∞ |
|---|---|---|---|---|---|---|---|---|---|---|---|---|
| 1 | 245 | 246 | 248 | 249 | 250 | 251 | 252 | 253 | 253 | 254 | 254 | 254 |
| | 6,142 | 6,169 | 6,208 | 6,234 | 6,258 | 6,286 | 6,302 | 6,323 | 6,334 | 6,352 | 6,361 | 6,366 |
| 2 | 19.42 | 19.43 | 19.44 | 19.45 | 19.46 | 19.47 | 19.47 | 19.48 | 19.49 | 19.49 | 19.50 | 19.50 |
| | 99.43 | 99.44 | 99.45 | 99.46 | 99.47 | 99.48 | 99.48 | 99.49 | 99.49 | 99.49 | 99.50 | 99.50 |
| 3 | 8.71 | 8.69 | 8.66 | 8.64 | 8.62 | 8.60 | 8.58 | 8.57 | 8.56 | 8.54 | 8.54 | 8.53 |
| | 26.92 | 26.83 | 26.69 | 26.60 | 26.50 | 26.41 | 26.35 | 26.27 | 26.23 | 26.18 | 26.14 | 26.12 |
| 4 | 5.87 | 5.84 | 5.80 | 5.77 | 5.74 | 5.71 | 5.70 | 5.68 | 5.66 | 5.65 | 5.64 | 5.63 |
| | 14.24 | 14.15 | 14.02 | 13.93 | 13.83 | 13.74 | 13.69 | 13.61 | 13.57 | 13.52 | 13.48 | 13.46 |
| 5 | 4.64 | 4.60 | 4.56 | 4.53 | 4.50 | 4.46 | 4.44 | 4.42 | 4.40 | 4.38 | 4.37 | 4.36 |
| | 9.77 | 9.68 | 9.55 | 9.47 | 9.38 | 9.29 | 9.24 | 9.17 | 9.13 | 9.07 | 9.04 | 9.02 |
| 6 | 3.96 | 3.92 | 3.87 | 3.84 | 3.81 | 3.77 | 3.75 | 3.72 | 3.71 | 3.69 | 3.68 | 3.67 |
| | 7.60 | 7.52 | 7.39 | 7.31 | 7.23 | 7.14 | 7.09 | 7.02 | 6.99 | 6.94 | 6.90 | 6.88 |
| 7 | 3.52 | 3.49 | 3.44 | 3.41 | 3.38 | 3.34 | 3.32 | 3.29 | 3.28 | 3.25 | 3.24 | 3.23 |
| | 6.35 | 6.27 | 6.15 | 6.07 | 5.98 | 5.90 | 5.85 | 5.78 | 5.75 | 5.70 | 5.67 | 5.65 |
| 8 | 3.23 | 3.20 | 3.15 | 3.12 | 3.08 | 3.05 | 3.03 | 3.00 | 2.98 | 2.96 | 2.94 | 2.93 |
| | 5.56 | 5.48 | 5.36 | 5.28 | 5.20 | 5.11 | 5.06 | 5.00 | 4.96 | 4.91 | 4.88 | 4.86 |
| 9 | 3.02 | 2.98 | 2.93 | 2.90 | 2.86 | 2.82 | 2.80 | 2.77 | 2.76 | 2.73 | 2.72 | 2.71 |
| | 5.00 | 4.92 | 4.80 | 4.73 | 4.64 | 4.56 | 4.51 | 4.45 | 4.41 | 4.36 | 4.33 | 4.31 |
| 10 | 2.86 | 2.82 | 2.77 | 2.74 | 2.70 | 2.67 | 2.64 | 2.61 | 2.59 | 2.56 | 2.55 | 2.54 |
| | 4.60 | 4.52 | 4.41 | 4.33 | 4.25 | 4.17 | 4.12 | 4.05 | 4.01 | 3.96 | 3.93 | 3.91 |
| 11 | 2.74 | 2.70 | 2.65 | 2.61 | 2.57 | 2.53 | 2.50 | 2.47 | 2.45 | 2.42 | 2.41 | 2.40 |
| | 4.29 | 4.21 | 4.10 | 4.02 | 3.94 | 3.86 | 3.80 | 3.74 | 3.70 | 3.66 | 3.62 | 3.60 |
| 12 | 2.64 | 2.60 | 2.54 | 2.50 | 2.46 | 2.42 | 2.40 | 2.36 | 2.35 | 2.32 | 2.31 | 2.30 |
| | 4.05 | 3.98 | 3.86 | 3.78 | 3.70 | 3.61 | 3.56 | 3.49 | 3.46 | 3.41 | 3.38 | 3.36 |
| 13 | 2.55 | 2.51 | 2.46 | 2.42 | 2.38 | 2.34 | 2.32 | 2.28 | 2.26 | 2.24 | 2.22 | 2.21 |
| | 3.85 | 3.78 | 3.67 | 3.59 | 3.51 | 3.42 | 3.37 | 3.30 | 3.27 | 3.21 | 3.18 | 3.16 |
| 14 | 2.48 | 2.44 | 2.39 | 2.35 | 2.31 | 2.27 | 2.24 | 2.21 | 2.19 | 2.16 | 2.14 | 2.13 |
| | 3.70 | 3.62 | 3.51 | 3.43 | 3.34 | 3.26 | 3.21 | 3.14 | 3.11 | 3.06 | 3.02 | 3.00 |
| 15 | 2.43 | 2.39 | 2.33 | 2.29 | 2.25 | 2.21 | 2.18 | 2.15 | 2.12 | 2.10 | 2.08 | 2.07 |
| | 3.56 | 3.48 | 3.36 | 3.29 | 3.20 | 3.12 | 3.07 | 3.00 | 2.97 | 2.92 | 2.89 | 2.87 |
| 16 | 2.37 | 2.33 | 2.28 | 2.24 | 2.20 | 2.16 | 2.13 | 2.09 | 2.07 | 2.04 | 2.02 | 2.01 |
| | 3.45 | 3.37 | 3.25 | 3.18 | 3.10 | 3.01 | 2.96 | 2.89 | 2.86 | 2.80 | 2.77 | 2.75 |
| 17 | 2.33 | 2.29 | 2.23 | 2.19 | 2.15 | 2.11 | 2.08 | 2.04 | 2.02 | 1.99 | 1.97 | 1.96 |
| | 3.35 | 3.27 | 3.16 | 3.08 | 3.00 | 2.92 | 2.86 | 2.79 | 2.76 | 2.70 | 2.67 | 2.65 |
| 18 | 2.29 | 2.25 | 2.19 | 2.15 | 2.11 | 2.07 | 2.04 | 2.00 | 1.98 | 1.95 | 1.93 | 1.92 |
| | 3.27 | 3.19 | 3.07 | 3.00 | 2.91 | 2.83 | 2.78 | 2.71 | 2.68 | 2.62 | 2.59 | 2.57 |
| 19 | 2.26 | 2.21 | 2.15 | 2.11 | 2.07 | 2.02 | 2.00 | 1.96 | 1.94 | 1.91 | 1.90 | 1.88 |
| | 3.19 | 3.12 | 3.00 | 2.92 | 2.84 | 2.76 | 2.70 | 2.63 | 2.60 | 2.54 | 2.51 | 2.49 |
| 20 | 2.23 | 2.18 | 2.12 | 2.08 | 2.04 | 1.99 | 1.96 | 1.92 | 1.90 | 1.87 | 1.85 | 1.84 |
| | 3.13 | 3.05 | 2.94 | 2.86 | 2.77 | 2.69 | 2.63 | 2.56 | 2.53 | 2.47 | 2.44 | 2.42 |
| 21 | 2.20 | 2.15 | 2.09 | 2.05 | 2.00 | 1.96 | 1.93 | 1.89 | 1.87 | 1.84 | 1.82 | 1.81 |
| | 3.07 | 2.99 | 2.88 | 2.80 | 2.72 | 2.63 | 2.58 | 2.51 | 2.47 | 2.42 | 2.38 | 2.36 |
| 22 | 2.18 | 2.13 | 2.07 | 2.03 | 1.98 | 1.93 | 1.91 | 1.87 | 1.84 | 1.81 | 1.80 | 1.78 |
| | 3.02 | 2.94 | 2.83 | 2.75 | 2.67 | 2.58 | 2.53 | 2.46 | 2.42 | 2.37 | 2.33 | 2.31 |
| 23 | 2.14 | 2.10 | 2.04 | 2.00 | 1.96 | 1.91 | 1.88 | 1.84 | 1.82 | 1.79 | 1.77 | 1.76 |
| | 2.97 | 2.89 | 2.78 | 2.70 | 2.62 | 2.53 | 2.48 | 2.41 | 2.37 | 2.32 | 2.28 | 2.26 |
| 24 | 2.13 | 2.09 | 2.02 | 1.98 | 1.94 | 1.89 | 1.86 | 1.82 | 1.80 | 1.76 | 1.74 | 1.73 |
| | 2.93 | 2.85 | 2.74 | 2.66 | 2.58 | 2.49 | 2.44 | 2.36 | 2.33 | 2.27 | 2.23 | 2.21 |
| 25 | 2.11 | 2.06 | 2.00 | 1.96 | 1.92 | 1.87 | 1.84 | 1.80 | 1.77 | 1.74 | 1.72 | 1.71 |
| | 2.89 | 2.81 | 2.70 | 2.62 | 2.54 | 2.45 | 2.40 | 2.32 | 2.29 | 2.23 | 2.19 | 2.17 |
| 26 | 2.10 | 2.05 | 1.99 | 1.95 | 1.90 | 1.85 | 1.82 | 1.78 | 1.76 | 1.72 | 1.70 | 1.69 |
| | 2.86 | 2.77 | 2.66 | 2.58 | 2.50 | 2.41 | 2.36 | 2.28 | 2.25 | 2.19 | 2.15 | 2.13 |

# APPENDIX D—*Continued*

$n_1 =$ degrees of freedom for numerator

$n_2 =$ degrees of freedom for denominator

| | 1 | 2 | 3 | 4 | 5 | 6 | 7 | 8 | 9 | 10 | 11 | 12 |
|---|---|---|---|---|---|---|---|---|---|---|---|---|
| 27 | 4.21 | 3.35 | 2.96 | 2.73 | 2.57 | 2.46 | 2.37 | 2.30 | 2.25 | 2.20 | 2.16 | 2.13 |
| | **7.68** | **5.49** | **4.60** | **4.11** | **3.79** | **3.56** | **3.39** | **3.26** | **3.14** | **3.06** | **2.98** | **2.93** |
| 28 | 4.20 | 3.34 | 2.95 | 2.71 | 2.56 | 2.44 | 2.36 | 2.29 | 2.24 | 2.19 | 2.15 | 2.12 |
| | **7.64** | **5.45** | **4.57** | **4.07** | **3.76** | **3.53** | **3.36** | **3.23** | **3.11** | **3.03** | **2.95** | **2.90** |
| 29 | 4.18 | 3.33 | 2.93 | 2.70 | 2.54 | 2.43 | 2.35 | 2.28 | 2.22 | 2.18 | 2.14 | 2.10 |
| | **7.60** | **5.42** | **4.54** | **4.04** | **3.73** | **3.50** | **3.33** | **3.20** | **3.08** | **3.00** | **2.92** | **2.87** |
| 30 | 4.17 | 3.32 | 2.92 | 2.69 | 2.53 | 2.42 | 2.34 | 2.27 | 2.21 | 2.16 | 2.12 | 2.09 |
| | **7.56** | **5.39** | **4.51** | **4.02** | **3.70** | **3.47** | **3.30** | **3.17** | **3.06** | **2.98** | **2.90** | **2.84** |
| 32 | 4.15 | 3.30 | 2.90 | 2.67 | 2.51 | 2.40 | 2.32 | 2.25 | 2.19 | 2.14 | 2.10 | 2.07 |
| | **7.50** | **5.34** | **4.46** | **3.97** | **3.66** | **3.42** | **3.25** | **3.12** | **3.01** | **2.94** | **2.86** | **2.80** |
| 34 | 4.13 | 3.28 | 2.88 | 2.65 | 2.49 | 2.38 | 2.30 | 2.23 | 2.17 | 2.12 | 2.08 | 2.05 |
| | **7.44** | **5.29** | **4.42** | **3.93** | **3.61** | **3.38** | **3.21** | **3.08** | **2.97** | **2.89** | **2.82** | **2.76** |
| 36 | 4.11 | 3.26 | 2.86 | 2.63 | 2.48 | 2.36 | 2.28 | 2.21 | 2.15 | 2.10 | 2.06 | 2.03 |
| | **7.39** | **5.25** | **4.38** | **3.89** | **3.58** | **3.35** | **3.18** | **3.04** | **2.94** | **2.86** | **2.78** | **2.72** |
| 38 | 4.10 | 3.25 | 2.85 | 2.62 | 2.46 | 2.35 | 2.26 | 2.19 | 2.14 | 2.09 | 2.05 | 2.02 |
| | **7.35** | **5.21** | **4.34** | **3.86** | **3.54** | **3.32** | **3.15** | **3.02** | **2.91** | **2.82** | **2.75** | **2.69** |
| 40 | 4.08 | 3.23 | 2.84 | 2.61 | 2.45 | 2.34 | 2.25 | 2.18 | 2.12 | 2.07 | 2.04 | 2.00 |
| | **7.31** | **5.18** | **4.31** | **3.83** | **3.51** | **3.29** | **3.12** | **2.99** | **2.88** | **2.80** | **2.73** | **2.66** |
| 42 | 4.07 | 3.22 | 2.83 | 2.59 | 2.44 | 2.32 | 2.24 | 2.17 | 2.11 | 2.06 | 2.02 | 1.99 |
| | **7.27** | **5.15** | **4.29** | **3.80** | **3.49** | **3.26** | **3.10** | **2.96** | **2.86** | **2.77** | **2.70** | **2.64** |
| 44 | 4.06 | 3.21 | 2.82 | 2.58 | 2.43 | 2.31 | 2.23 | 2.16 | 2.10 | 2.05 | 2.01 | 1.98 |
| | **7.24** | **5.12** | **4.26** | **3.78** | **3.46** | **3.24** | **3.07** | **2.94** | **2.84** | **2.75** | **2.68** | **2.62** |
| 46 | 4.05 | 3.20 | 2.81 | 2.57 | 2.42 | 2.30 | 2.22 | 2.14 | 2.09 | 2.04 | 2.00 | 1.97 |
| | **7.21** | **5.10** | **4.24** | **3.76** | **3.44** | **3.22** | **3.05** | **2.92** | **2.82** | **2.73** | **2.66** | **2.60** |
| 48 | 4.04 | 3.19 | 2.80 | 2.56 | 2.41 | 2.30 | 2.21 | 2.14 | 2.08 | 2.03 | 1.99 | 1.96 |
| | **7.19** | **5.08** | **4.22** | **3.74** | **3.42** | **3.20** | **3.04** | **2.90** | **2.80** | **2.71** | **2.64** | **2.58** |
| 50 | 4.03 | 3.18 | 2.79 | 2.56 | 2.40 | 2.29 | 2.20 | 2.13 | 2.07 | 2.02 | 1.98 | 1.95 |
| | **7.17** | **5.06** | **4.20** | **3.72** | **3.41** | **3.18** | **3.02** | **2.88** | **2.78** | **2.70** | **2.62** | **2.56** |
| 55 | 4.02 | 3.17 | 2.78 | 2.54 | 2.38 | 2.27 | 2.18 | 2.11 | 2.05 | 2.00 | 1.97 | 1.93 |
| | **7.12** | **5.01** | **4.16** | **3.68** | **3.37** | **3.15** | **2.98** | **2.85** | **2.75** | **2.66** | **2.59** | **2.53** |
| 60 | 4.00 | 3.15 | 2.76 | 2.52 | 2.37 | 2.25 | 2.17 | 2.10 | 2.04 | 1.99 | 1.95 | 1.92 |
| | **7.08** | **4.98** | **4.13** | **3.65** | **3.34** | **3.12** | **2.95** | **2.82** | **2.72** | **2.63** | **2.56** | **2.50** |
| 65 | 3.99 | 3.14 | 2.75 | 2.51 | 2.36 | 2.24 | 2.15 | 2.08 | 2.02 | 1.98 | 1.94 | 1.90 |
| | **7.04** | **4.95** | **4.10** | **3.62** | **3.31** | **3.09** | **2.93** | **2.79** | **2.70** | **2.61** | **2.54** | **2.47** |
| 70 | 3.98 | 3.13 | 2.74 | 2.50 | 2.35 | 2.23 | 2.14 | 2.07 | 2.01 | 1.97 | 1.93 | 1.89 |
| | **7.01** | **4.92** | **4.08** | **3.60** | **3.29** | **3.07** | **2.91** | **2.77** | **2.67** | **2.59** | **2.51** | **2.45** |
| 80 | 3.96 | 3.11 | 2.72 | 2.48 | 2.33 | 2.21 | 2.12 | 2.05 | 1.99 | 1.95 | 1.91 | 1.88 |
| | **6.96** | **4.88** | **4.04** | **3.56** | **3.25** | **3.04** | **2.87** | **2.74** | **2.64** | **2.55** | **2.48** | **2.41** |
| 100 | 3.94 | 3.09 | 2.70 | 2.46 | 2.30 | 2.19 | 2.10 | 2.03 | 1.97 | 1.92 | 1.88 | 1.85 |
| | **6.90** | **4.82** | **3.98** | **3.51** | **3.20** | **2.99** | **2.82** | **2.69** | **2.59** | **2.51** | **2.43** | **2.36** |
| 125 | 3.92 | 3.07 | 2.68 | 2.44 | 2.29 | 2.17 | 2.08 | 2.01 | 1.95 | 1.90 | 1.86 | 1.83 |
| | **6.84** | **4.78** | **3.94** | **3.47** | **3.17** | **2.95** | **2.79** | **2.65** | **2.56** | **2.47** | **2.40** | **2.33** |
| 150 | 3.91 | 3.06 | 2.67 | 2.43 | 2.27 | 2.16 | 2.07 | 2.00 | 1.94 | 1.89 | 1.85 | 1.82 |
| | **6.81** | **4.75** | **3.91** | **3.44** | **3.14** | **2.92** | **2.76** | **2.62** | **2.53** | **2.44** | **2.37** | **2.30** |
| 200 | 3.89 | 3.04 | 2.65 | 2.41 | 2.26 | 2.14 | 2.05 | 1.98 | 1.92 | 1.87 | 1.83 | 1.80 |
| | **6.76** | **4.71** | **3.88** | **3.41** | **3.11** | **2.90** | **2.73** | **2.60** | **2.50** | **2.41** | **2.34** | **2.28** |
| 400 | 3.86 | 3.02 | 2.62 | 2.39 | 2.23 | 2.12 | 2.03 | 1.96 | 1.90 | 1.85 | 1.81 | 1.78 |
| | **6.70** | **4.66** | **3.83** | **3.36** | **3.06** | **2.85** | **2.69** | **2.55** | **2.46** | **2.37** | **2.29** | **2.23** |
| 1,000 | 3.85 | 3.00 | 2.61 | 2.38 | 2.22 | 2.10 | 2.02 | 1.95 | 1.89 | 1.84 | 1.80 | 1.76 |
| | **6.66** | **4.62** | **3.80** | **3.34** | **3.04** | **2.82** | **2.66** | **2.53** | **2.43** | **2.34** | **2.26** | **2.20** |
| ∞ | 3.84 | 2.99 | 2.60 | 2.37 | 2.21 | 2.09 | 2.01 | 1.94 | 1.88 | 1.83 | 1.79 | 1.75 |
| | **6.64** | **4.60** | **3.78** | **3.32** | **3.02** | **2.80** | **2.64** | **2.51** | **2.41** | **2.32** | **2.24** | **2.18** |

## APPENDIX D—*Continued*

$n_1$ = degrees of freedom for numerator

| $n_2$ | 14 | 16 | 20 | 24 | 30 | 40 | 50 | 75 | 100 | 200 | 500 | ∞ |
|---|---|---|---|---|---|---|---|---|---|---|---|---|
| 27 | 2.08 | 2.03 | 1.97 | 1.93 | 1.88 | 1.84 | 1.80 | 1.76 | 1.74 | 1.71 | 1.68 | 1.67 |
|    | **2.83** | **2.74** | **2.63** | **2.55** | **2.47** | **2.38** | **2.33** | **2.25** | **2.21** | **2.16** | **2.12** | **2.10** |
| 28 | 2.06 | 2.02 | 1.96 | 1.91 | 1.87 | 1.81 | 1.78 | 1.75 | 1.72 | 1.69 | 1.67 | 1.65 |
|    | **2.80** | **2.71** | **2.60** | **2.52** | **2.44** | **2.35** | **2.30** | **2.22** | **2.18** | **2.13** | **2.09** | **2.06** |
| 29 | 2.05 | 2.00 | 1.94 | 1.90 | 1.85 | 1.80 | 1.77 | 1.73 | 1.71 | 1.68 | 1.65 | 1.64 |
|    | **2.77** | **2.68** | **2.57** | **2.49** | **2.41** | **2.32** | **2.27** | **2.19** | **2.15** | **2.10** | **2.06** | **2.03** |
| 30 | 2.04 | 1.99 | 1.93 | 1.89 | 1.84 | 1.79 | 1.76 | 1.72 | 1.69 | 1.66 | 1.64 | 1.62 |
|    | **2.74** | **2.66** | **2.55** | **2.47** | **2.38** | **2.29** | **2.24** | **2.16** | **2.13** | **2.07** | **2.03** | **2.01** |
| 32 | 2.02 | 1.97 | 1.91 | 1.86 | 1.82 | 1.76 | 1.74 | 1.69 | 1.67 | 1.64 | 1.61 | 1.59 |
|    | **2.70** | **2.62** | **2.51** | **2.42** | **2.34** | **2.25** | **2.20** | **2.12** | **2.08** | **2.02** | **1.98** | **1.96** |
| 34 | 2.00 | 1.95 | 1.89 | 1.84 | 1.80 | 1.74 | 1.71 | 1.67 | 1.64 | 1.61 | 1.59 | 1.57 |
|    | **2.66** | **2.58** | **2.47** | **2.38** | **2.30** | **2.21** | **2.15** | **2.08** | **2.04** | **1.98** | **1.94** | **1.91** |
| 36 | 1.98 | 1.93 | 1.87 | 1.82 | 1.78 | 1.72 | 1.69 | 1.65 | 1.62 | 1.59 | 1.56 | 1.55 |
|    | **2.62** | **2.54** | **2.43** | **2.35** | **2.26** | **2.17** | **2.12** | **2.04** | **2.00** | **1.94** | **1.90** | **1.87** |
| 38 | 1.96 | 1.92 | 1.85 | 1.80 | 1.76 | 1.71 | 1.67 | 1.63 | 1.60 | 1.57 | 1.54 | 1.53 |
|    | **2.59** | **2.51** | **2.40** | **2.32** | **2.22** | **2.14** | **2.08** | **2.00** | **1.97** | **1.90** | **1.86** | **1.84** |
| 40 | 1.95 | 1.90 | 1.84 | 1.79 | 1.74 | 1.69 | 1.66 | 1.61 | 1.59 | 1.55 | 1.53 | 1.51 |
|    | **2.56** | **2.49** | **2.37** | **2.29** | **2.20** | **2.11** | **2.05** | **1.97** | **1.94** | **1.88** | **1.84** | **1.81** |
| 42 | 1.94 | 1.89 | 1.82 | 1.78 | 1.73 | 1.68 | 1.64 | 1.60 | 1.57 | 1.54 | 1.51 | 1.49 |
|    | **2.54** | **2.46** | **2.35** | **2.26** | **2.17** | **2.08** | **2.02** | **1.94** | **1.91** | **1.85** | **1.80** | **1.78** |
| 44 | 1.92 | 1.88 | 1.81 | 1.76 | 1.72 | 1.66 | 1.63 | 1.58 | 1.56 | 1.52 | 1.50 | 1.48 |
|    | **2.52** | **2.44** | **2.32** | **2.24** | **2.15** | **2.06** | **2.00** | **1.92** | **1.88** | **1.82** | **1.78** | **1.75** |
| 46 | 1.91 | 1.87 | 1.80 | 1.75 | 1.71 | 1.65 | 1.62 | 1.57 | 1.54 | 1.51 | 1.48 | 1.46 |
|    | **2.50** | **2.42** | **2.30** | **2.22** | **2.13** | **2.04** | **1.98** | **1.90** | **1.86** | **1.80** | **1.76** | **1.72** |
| 48 | 1.90 | 1.86 | 1.79 | 1.74 | 1.70 | 1.64 | 1.61 | 1.56 | 1.53 | 1.50 | 1.47 | 1.45 |
|    | **2.48** | **2.40** | **2.28** | **2.20** | **2.11** | **2.02** | **1.96** | **1.88** | **1.84** | **1.78** | **1.73** | **1.70** |
| 50 | 1.90 | 1.85 | 1.78 | 1.74 | 1.69 | 1.63 | 1.60 | 1.55 | 1.52 | 1.48 | 1.46 | 1.44 |
|    | **2.46** | **2.39** | **2.26** | **2.18** | **2.10** | **2.00** | **1.94** | **1.86** | **1.82** | **1.76** | **1.71** | **1.68** |
| 55 | 1.88 | 1.83 | 1.76 | 1.72 | 1.67 | 1.61 | 1.58 | 1.52 | 1.50 | 1.46 | 1.43 | 1.41 |
|    | **2.43** | **2.35** | **2.23** | **2.15** | **2.06** | **1.96** | **1.90** | **1.82** | **1.78** | **1.71** | **1.66** | **1.64** |
| 60 | 1.86 | 1.81 | 1.75 | 1.70 | 1.65 | 1.59 | 1.56 | 1.50 | 1.48 | 1.44 | 1.41 | 1.39 |
|    | **2.40** | **2.32** | **2.20** | **2.12** | **2.03** | **1.93** | **1.87** | **1.79** | **1.74** | **1.68** | **1.63** | **1.60** |
| 65 | 1.85 | 1.80 | 1.73 | 1.68 | 1.63 | 1.57 | 1.54 | 1.49 | 1.46 | 1.42 | 1.39 | 1.37 |
|    | **2.37** | **2.30** | **2.18** | **2.09** | **2.00** | **1.90** | **1.84** | **1.76** | **1.71** | **1.64** | **1.60** | **1.56** |
| 70 | 1.84 | 1.79 | 1.72 | 1.67 | 1.62 | 1.56 | 1.53 | 1.47 | 1.45 | 1.40 | 1.37 | 1.35 |
|    | **2.35** | **2.28** | **2.15** | **2.07** | **1.98** | **1.88** | **1.82** | **1.74** | **1.69** | **1.62** | **1.56** | **1.53** |
| 80 | 1.82 | 1.77 | 1.70 | 1.65 | 1.60 | 1.54 | 1.51 | 1.45 | 1.42 | 1.38 | 1.35 | 1.32 |
|    | **2.32** | **2.24** | **2.11** | **2.03** | **1.94** | **1.84** | **1.78** | **1.70** | **1.65** | **1.57** | **1.52** | **1.49** |
| 100 | 1.79 | 1.75 | 1.68 | 1.63 | 1.57 | 1.51 | 1.48 | 1.42 | 1.39 | 1.34 | 1.30 | 1.28 |
|     | **2.26** | **2.19** | **2.06** | **1.98** | **1.89** | **1.79** | **1.73** | **1.64** | **1.59** | **1.51** | **1.46** | **1.43** |
| 125 | 1.77 | 1.72 | 1.65 | 1.60 | 1.55 | 1.49 | 1.45 | 1.39 | 1.36 | 1.31 | 1.27 | 1.25 |
|     | **2.23** | **2.15** | **2.03** | **1.94** | **1.85** | **1.75** | **1.68** | **1.59** | **1.54** | **1.46** | **1.40** | **1.37** |
| 150 | 1.76 | 1.71 | 1.64 | 1.59 | 1.54 | 1.47 | 1.44 | 1.37 | 1.34 | 1.29 | 1.25 | 1.22 |
|     | **2.20** | **2.12** | **2.00** | **1.91** | **1.83** | **1.72** | **1.66** | **1.56** | **1.51** | **1.43** | **1.37** | **1.33** |
| 200 | 1.74 | 1.69 | 1.62 | 1.57 | 1.52 | 1.45 | 1.42 | 1.35 | 1.32 | 1.26 | 1.22 | 1.19 |
|     | **2.17** | **2.09** | **1.97** | **1.88** | **1.79** | **1.69** | **1.62** | **1.53** | **1.48** | **1.39** | **1.33** | **1.28** |
| 400 | 1.72 | 1.67 | 1.60 | 1.54 | 1.49 | 1.42 | 1.38 | 1.32 | 1.28 | 1.22 | 1.16 | 1.13 |
|     | **2.12** | **2.04** | **1.92** | **1.84** | **1.74** | **1.64** | **1.57** | **1.47** | **1.42** | **1.32** | **1.24** | **1.19** |
| 1,000 | 1.70 | 1.65 | 1.58 | 1.53 | 1.47 | 1.41 | 1.36 | 1.30 | 1.26 | 1.19 | 1.13 | 1.08 |
|       | **2.09** | **2.01** | **1.89** | **1.81** | **1.71** | **1.61** | **1.54** | **1.44** | **1.38** | **1.28** | **1.19** | **1.11** |
| ∞ | 1.69 | 1.64 | 1.57 | 1.52 | 1.46 | 1.40 | 1.35 | 1.28 | 1.24 | 1.17 | 1.11 | 1.00 |
|   | **2.07** | **1.99** | **1.87** | **1.79** | **1.69** | **1.59** | **1.52** | **1.41** | **1.36** | **1.25** | **1.15** | **1.00** |

*$n_2$ = degrees of freedom for denominator*

# APPENDIX D—Concluded

## Values of $F_p$ for $P = 0.025$

| $\nu_2$ \\ $\nu_1$ | 1 | 2 | 3 | 4 | 5 | 6 | 8 | 10 | 12 | 20 | 24 | 30 | 40 | 60 | 120 | ∞ |
|---|---|---|---|---|---|---|---|---|---|---|---|---|---|---|---|---|
| 1 | 647.8 | 799.5 | 864.2 | 899.6 | 921.8 | 937.1 | 956.7 | 968.6 | 976.7 | 993.1 | 997.2 | 1001 | 1006 | 1010 | 1014 | 1018 |
| 2 | 38.51 | 39.00 | 39.17 | 39.25 | 39.30 | 39.33 | 39.37 | 39.40 | 39.41 | 39.45 | 39.46 | 39.46 | 39.47 | 39.48 | 39.49 | 39.50 |
| 3 | 17.44 | 16.04 | 15.44 | 15.10 | 14.88 | 14.73 | 14.54 | 14.42 | 14.34 | 14.17 | 14.12 | 14.08 | 14.04 | 13.99 | 13.95 | 13.90 |
| 4 | 12.22 | 10.65 | 9.98 | 9.60 | 9.36 | 9.20 | 8.98 | 8.84 | 8.75 | 8.56 | 8.51 | 8.46 | 8.41 | 8.36 | 8.31 | 8.26 |
| 5 | 10.01 | 8.43 | 7.76 | 7.39 | 7.15 | 6.98 | 6.76 | 6.62 | 6.52 | 6.33 | 6.28 | 6.23 | 6.18 | 6.12 | 6.07 | 6.02 |
| 6 | 8.81 | 7.26 | 6.60 | 6.23 | 5.99 | 5.82 | 5.60 | 5.46 | 5.37 | 5.17 | 5.12 | 5.07 | 5.01 | 4.96 | 4.90 | 4.85 |
| 8 | 7.57 | 6.06 | 5.42 | 5.05 | 4.82 | 4.65 | 4.43 | 4.30 | 4.20 | 4.00 | 3.95 | 3.89 | 3.84 | 3.78 | 3.73 | 3.67 |
| 10 | 6.94 | 5.46 | 4.83 | 4.47 | 4.24 | 4.07 | 3.85 | 3.72 | 3.62 | 3.42 | 3.37 | 3.31 | 3.26 | 3.20 | 3.14 | 3.08 |
| 12 | 6.55 | 5.10 | 4.47 | 4.12 | 3.89 | 3.73 | 3.51 | 3.37 | 3.28 | 3.07 | 3.02 | 2.96 | 2.91 | 2.85 | 2.79 | 2.72 |
| 20 | 5.87 | 4.46 | 3.86 | 3.51 | 3.29 | 3.13 | 2.91 | 2.77 | 2.68 | 2.46 | 2.41 | 2.35 | 2.29 | 2.22 | 2.16 | 2.09 |
| 24 | 5.72 | 4.32 | 3.72 | 3.38 | 3.15 | 2.99 | 2.78 | 2.64 | 2.54 | 2.33 | 2.27 | 2.21 | 2.15 | 2.08 | 2.01 | 1.94 |
| 30 | 5.57 | 4.18 | 3.59 | 3.25 | 3.03 | 2.87 | 2.65 | 2.51 | 2.41 | 2.20 | 2.14 | 2.07 | 2.01 | 1.94 | 1.87 | 1.79 |
| 40 | 5.42 | 4.05 | 3.46 | 3.13 | 2.90 | 2.74 | 2.53 | 2.39 | 2.29 | 2.07 | 2.01 | 1.94 | 1.88 | 1.80 | 1.72 | 1.64 |
| 60 | 5.29 | 3.93 | 3.34 | 3.01 | 2.79 | 2.63 | 2.41 | 2.27 | 2.17 | 1.94 | 1.88 | 1.82 | 1.74 | 1.67 | 1.58 | 1.48 |
| 120 | 5.15 | 3.80 | 3.23 | 2.89 | 2.67 | 2.52 | 2.30 | 2.16 | 2.05 | 1.82 | 1.76 | 1.69 | 1.61 | 1.53 | 1.43 | 1.31 |
| ∞ | 5.02 | 3.69 | 3.12 | 2.79 | 2.57 | 2.41 | 2.19 | 2.05 | 1.94 | 1.71 | 1.64 | 1.57 | 1.48 | 1.39 | 1.27 | 1.00 |

## Values of $F_p$ for $P = 0.001$

| $\nu_2$ \\ $\nu_1$ | 1 | 2 | 3 | 4 | 5 | 6 | 8 | 10 | 12 | 20 | 24 | 30 | 40 | 60 | 120 | ∞ |
|---|---|---|---|---|---|---|---|---|---|---|---|---|---|---|---|---|
| 1* | 405.3 | 500.0 | 540.4 | 562.5 | 576.4 | 585.9 | 598.1 | 605.6 | 610.7 | 620.9 | 623.5 | 626.1 | 628.7 | 631.3 | 634.0 | 636.6 |
| 2 | 998.5 | 999.0 | 999.2 | 999.2 | 999.3 | 999.3 | 999.4 | 999.4 | 999.4 | 999.4 | 999.5 | 999.5 | 999.5 | 999.5 | 999.5 | 999.5 |
| 3 | 167.0 | 148.5 | 141.1 | 137.1 | 134.6 | 132.8 | 130.6 | 129.2 | 128.3 | 126.4 | 125.9 | 125.4 | 125.0 | 124.5 | 124.0 | 123.5 |
| 4 | 74.14 | 61.25 | 56.18 | 53.44 | 51.71 | 50.53 | 49.00 | 48.05 | 47.41 | 46.10 | 45.77 | 45.43 | 45.09 | 44.75 | 44.40 | 44.05 |
| 5 | 47.18 | 37.12 | 33.20 | 31.09 | 29.75 | 28.84 | 27.64 | 26.92 | 26.42 | 25.39 | 25.14 | 24.87 | 24.60 | 24.33 | 24.06 | 23.79 |
| 6 | 35.51 | 27.00 | 23.70 | 21.92 | 20.81 | 20.03 | 19.03 | 18.41 | 17.99 | 17.12 | 16.89 | 16.67 | 16.44 | 16.21 | 15.99 | 15.75 |
| 8 | 25.42 | 18.49 | 15.83 | 14.39 | 13.49 | 12.86 | 12.04 | 11.54 | 11.19 | 10.48 | 10.30 | 10.11 | 9.92 | 9.73 | 9.53 | 9.33 |
| 10 | 21.04 | 14.91 | 12.55 | 11.28 | 10.48 | 9.92 | 9.20 | 8.75 | 8.45 | 7.80 | 7.64 | 7.47 | 7.30 | 7.12 | 6.94 | 6.76 |
| 12 | 18.64 | 12.97 | 10.80 | 9.63 | 8.89 | 8.38 | 7.71 | 7.29 | 7.00 | 6.40 | 6.25 | 6.09 | 5.93 | 5.76 | 5.59 | 5.42 |
| 20 | 14.82 | 9.95 | 8.10 | 7.10 | 6.46 | 6.02 | 5.44 | 5.08 | 4.82 | 4.29 | 4.15 | 4.00 | 3.86 | 3.70 | 3.54 | 3.38 |
| 24 | 14.03 | 9.34 | 7.55 | 6.59 | 5.98 | 5.55 | 4.99 | 4.64 | 4.39 | 3.87 | 3.74 | 3.59 | 3.45 | 3.29 | 3.14 | 2.97 |
| 30 | 13.29 | 8.77 | 7.05 | 6.12 | 5.53 | 5.12 | 4.58 | 4.24 | 4.00 | 3.49 | 3.36 | 3.22 | 3.07 | 2.92 | 2.76 | 2.59 |
| 40 | 12.61 | 8.25 | 6.60 | 5.70 | 5.13 | 4.73 | 4.21 | 3.87 | 3.64 | 3.15 | 3.01 | 2.87 | 2.73 | 2.57 | 2.41 | 2.23 |
| 60 | 11.97 | 7.76 | 6.17 | 5.31 | 4.76 | 4.37 | 3.87 | 3.54 | 3.31 | 2.83 | 2.69 | 2.55 | 2.41 | 2.25 | 2.08 | 1.89 |
| 120 | 11.38 | 7.32 | 5.79 | 4.95 | 4.42 | 4.04 | 3.55 | 3.24 | 3.02 | 2.53 | 2.40 | 2.26 | 2.11 | 1.95 | 1.76 | 1.54 |
| ∞ | 10.83 | 6.91 | 5.42 | 4.62 | 4.10 | 3.74 | 3.27 | 2.96 | 2.74 | 2.27 | 2.13 | 1.99 | 1.84 | 1.66 | 1.45 | 1.00 |

* Multiply all entries on this line by 1000.

APPENDIX E.    Values of the Durbin-Watson $d$ for specified sample sizes ($T$) and explanatory variables ($K' = K - 1$)

This table gives the significance points for $d_L$ and $d_U$ for tests on the autocorrelation of residuals (when no explanatory variable is a lagged endogenous variable) using the Durbin-Watson test statistic at the 0.05 significance level. The number of explanatory variables, $K'$, *excludes* the constant term. The next page of the table gives corresponding values for the 0.01 significance level.

Significance level $= 0.01$

| Number of residuals | $K = 1$ | | $K = 2$ | | $K = 3$ | | $K = 4$ | | $K = 5$ | |
|---|---|---|---|---|---|---|---|---|---|---|
| $T$ | $d_L$ | $d_U$ | $d_L$ | $d_U$ | $d_L$ | $d_U$ | $d_L$ | $d_U$ | $d_L$ | $d_U$ |
| 15 | 1.08 | 1.36 | 0.95 | 1.54 | 0.82 | 1.75 | 0.69 | 1.97 | 0.56 | 2.21 |
| 16 | 1.10 | 1.37 | 0.98 | 1.54 | 0.86 | 1.73 | 0.74 | 1.93 | 0.62 | 2.15 |
| 17 | 1.13 | 1.38 | 1.02 | 1.54 | 0.90 | 1.71 | 0.78 | 1.90 | 0.67 | 2.10 |
| 18 | 1.16 | 1.39 | 1.05 | 1.53 | 0.93 | 1.69 | 0.82 | 1.87 | 0.71 | 2.06 |
| 19 | 1.18 | 1.40 | 1.08 | 1.53 | 0.97 | 1.68 | 0.86 | 1.85 | 0.75 | 2.02 |
| 20 | 1.20 | 1.41 | 1.10 | 1.54 | 1.00 | 1.68 | 0.90 | 1.83 | 0.79 | 1.99 |
| 21 | 1.22 | 1.42 | 1.13 | 1.54 | 1.03 | 1.67 | 0.93 | 1.81 | 0.83 | 1.96 |
| 22 | 1.24 | 1.43 | 1.15 | 1.54 | 1.05 | 1.66 | 0.96 | 1.80 | 0.86 | 1.94 |
| 23 | 1.26 | 1.44 | 1.17 | 1.54 | 1.08 | 1.66 | 0.99 | 1.79 | 0.90 | 1.92 |
| 24 | 1.27 | 1.45 | 1.19 | 1.55 | 1.10 | 1.66 | 1.01 | 1.78 | 0.93 | 1.90 |
| 25 | 1.29 | 1.45 | 1.21 | 1.55 | 1.12 | 1.66 | 1.04 | 1.77 | 0.95 | 1.89 |
| 26 | 1.30 | 1.46 | 1.22 | 1.55 | 1.14 | 1.65 | 1.06 | 1.76 | 0.98 | 1.88 |
| 27 | 1.32 | 1.47 | 1.24 | 1.56 | 1.16 | 1.65 | 1.08 | 1.76 | 1.01 | 1.86 |
| 28 | 1.33 | 1.48 | 1.26 | 1.56 | 1.18 | 1.65 | 1.10 | 1.75 | 1.03 | 1.85 |
| 29 | 1.34 | 1.48 | 1.27 | 1.56 | 1.20 | 1.65 | 1.12 | 1.74 | 1.05 | 1.84 |
| 30 | 1.35 | 1.49 | 1.28 | 1.57 | 1.21 | 1.65 | 1.14 | 1.74 | 1.07 | 1.83 |
| 31 | 1.36 | 1.50 | 1.30 | 1.57 | 1.23 | 1.65 | 1.16 | 1.74 | 1.09 | 1.83 |
| 32 | 1.37 | 1.50 | 1.31 | 1.57 | 1.24 | 1.65 | 1.18 | 1.73 | 1.11 | 1.82 |
| 33 | 1.38 | 1.51 | 1.32 | 1.58 | 1.26 | 1.65 | 1.19 | 1.73 | 1.13 | 1.81 |
| 34 | 1.39 | 1.51 | 1.33 | 1.58 | 1.27 | 1.65 | 1.21 | 1.73 | 1.15 | 1.81 |
| 35 | 1.40 | 1.52 | 1.34 | 1.58 | 1.28 | 1.65 | 1.22 | 1.73 | 1.16 | 1.80 |
| 36 | 1.41 | 1.52 | 1.35 | 1.59 | 1.29 | 1.65 | 1.24 | 1.73 | 1.18 | 1.80 |
| 37 | 1.42 | 1.53 | 1.36 | 1.59 | 1.31 | 1.66 | 1.25 | 1.72 | 1.19 | 1.80 |
| 38 | 1.43 | 1.54 | 1.37 | 1.59 | 1.32 | 1.66 | 1.26 | 1.72 | 1.21 | 1.79 |
| 39 | 1.43 | 1.54 | 1.38 | 1.60 | 1.33 | 1.66 | 1.27 | 1.72 | 1.22 | 1.79 |
| 40 | 1.44 | 1.54 | 1.39 | 1.60 | 1.34 | 1.66 | 1.29 | 1.72 | 1.23 | 1.79 |
| 45 | 1.48 | 1.57 | 1.43 | 1.62 | 1.38 | 1.67 | 1.34 | 1.72 | 1.29 | 1.78 |
| 50 | 1.50 | 1.59 | 1.46 | 1.63 | 1.42 | 1.67 | 1.38 | 1.72 | 1.34 | 1.77 |
| 55 | 1.53 | 1.60 | 1.49 | 1.64 | 1.45 | 1.68 | 1.41 | 1.72 | 1.38 | 1.77 |
| 60 | 1.55 | 1.62 | 1.51 | 1.65 | 1.48 | 1.69 | 1.44 | 1.73 | 1.41 | 1.77 |
| 65 | 1.57 | 1.63 | 1.54 | 1.66 | 1.50 | 1.70 | 1.47 | 1.73 | 1.44 | 1.77 |
| 70 | 1.58 | 1.64 | 1.55 | 1.67 | 1.52 | 1.70 | 1.49 | 1.74 | 1.46 | 1.77 |
| 75 | 1.60 | 1.65 | 1.57 | 1.68 | 1.54 | 1.71 | 1.51 | 1.74 | 1.49 | 1.77 |
| 80 | 1.61 | 1.66 | 1.59 | 1.69 | 1.56 | 1.72 | 1.53 | 1.74 | 1.51 | 1.77 |
| 85 | 1.62 | 1.67 | 1.60 | 1.70 | 1.57 | 1.72 | 1.55 | 1.75 | 1.52 | 1.77 |
| 90 | 1.63 | 1.68 | 1.61 | 1.70 | 1.59 | 1.73 | 1.57 | 1.75 | 1.54 | 1.78 |
| 95 | 1.64 | 1.69 | 1.62 | 1.71 | 1.60 | 1.73 | 1.58 | 1.75 | 1.56 | 1.78 |
| 100 | 1.65 | 1.69 | 1.63 | 1.72 | 1.61 | 1.74 | 1.59 | 1.76 | 1.57 | 1.78 |

## APPENDIX E—*Continued*

Significance level $= 0.05$

| Number of residuals T | $K = 1$ | | $K = 2$ | | $K = 3$ | | $K = 4$ | | $K = 5$ | |
|---|---|---|---|---|---|---|---|---|---|---|
| | $d_L$ | $d_U$ | $d_L$ | $d_U$ | $d_L$ | $d_U$ | $d_L$ | $d_U$ | $d_L$ | $d_U$ |
| 15 | 0.81 | 1.07 | 0.70 | 1.25 | 0.59 | 1.46 | 0.49 | 1.70 | 0.39 | 1.96 |
| 16 | 0.84 | 1.09 | 0.74 | 1.25 | 0.63 | 1.44 | 0.53 | 1.66 | 0.44 | 1.90 |
| 17 | 0.87 | 1.10 | 0.77 | 1.25 | 0.67 | 1.43 | 0.57 | 1.63 | 0.48 | 1.85 |
| 18 | 0.90 | 1.12 | 0.80 | 1.26 | 0.71 | 1.42 | 0.61 | 1.60 | 0.52 | 1.80 |
| 19 | 0.93 | 1.13 | 0.83 | 1.26 | 0.74 | 1.41 | 0.65 | 1.58 | 0.56 | 1.77 |
| 20 | 0.95 | 1.15 | 0.86 | 1.27 | 0.77 | 1.41 | 0.68 | 1.57 | 0.60 | 1.74 |
| 21 | 0.97 | 1.16 | 0.89 | 1.27 | 0.80 | 1.41 | 0.72 | 1.55 | 0.63 | 1.71 |
| 22 | 1.00 | 1.17 | 0.91 | 1.28 | 0.83 | 1.40 | 0.75 | 1.54 | 0.66 | 1.69 |
| 23 | 1.02 | 1.19 | 0.94 | 1.29 | 0.86 | 1.40 | 0.77 | 1.53 | 0.70 | 1.67 |
| 24 | 1.04 | 1.20 | 0.96 | 1.30 | 0.88 | 1.41 | 0.80 | 1.53 | 0.72 | 1.66 |
| 25 | 1.05 | 1.21 | 0.98 | 1.30 | 0.90 | 1.41 | 0.83 | 1.52 | 0.75 | 1.65 |
| 26 | 1.07 | 1.22 | 1.00 | 1.31 | 0.93 | 1.41 | 0.85 | 1.52 | 0.78 | 1.64 |
| 27 | 1.09 | 1.23 | 1.02 | 1.32 | 0.95 | 1.41 | 0.88 | 1.51 | 0.81 | 1.63 |
| 28 | 1.10 | 1.24 | 1.04 | 1.32 | 0.97 | 1.41 | 0.90 | 1.51 | 0.83 | 1.62 |
| 29 | 1.12 | 1.25 | 1.05 | 1.33 | 0.99 | 1.42 | 0.92 | 1.51 | 0.85 | 1.61 |
| 30 | 1.13 | 1.26 | 1.07 | 1.34 | 1.01 | 1.42 | 0.94 | 1.51 | 0.88 | 1.61 |
| 31 | 1.15 | 1.27 | 1.08 | 1.34 | 1.02 | 1.42 | 0.96 | 1.51 | 0.90 | 1.60 |
| 32 | 1.16 | 1.28 | 1.10 | 1.35 | 1.04 | 1.43 | 0.98 | 1.51 | 0.92 | 1.60 |
| 33 | 1.17 | 1.29 | 1.11 | 1.36 | 1.05 | 1.43 | 1.00 | 1.51 | 0.94 | 1.59 |
| 34 | 1.18 | 1.30 | 1.13 | 1.36 | 1.07 | 1.43 | 1.01 | 1.51 | 0.95 | 1.59 |
| 35 | 1.19 | 1.31 | 1.14 | 1.37 | 1.08 | 1.44 | 1.03 | 1.51 | 0.97 | 1.59 |
| 36 | 1.21 | 1.32 | 1.15 | 1.38 | 1.10 | 1.44 | 1.04 | 1.51 | 0.99 | 1.59 |
| 37 | 1.22 | 1.32 | 1.16 | 1.38 | 1.11 | 1.45 | 1.06 | 1.51 | 1.00 | 1.59 |
| 38 | 1.23 | 1.33 | 1.18 | 1.39 | 1.12 | 1.45 | 1.07 | 1.52 | 1.02 | 1.58 |
| 39 | 1.24 | 1.34 | 1.19 | 1.39 | 1.14 | 1.45 | 1.09 | 1.52 | 1.03 | 1.58 |
| 40 | 1.25 | 1.34 | 1.20 | 1.40 | 1.15 | 1.46 | 1.10 | 1.52 | 1.05 | 1.58 |
| 45 | 1.29 | 1.38 | 1.24 | 1.42 | 1.20 | 1.48 | 1.16 | 1.53 | 1.11 | 1.58 |
| 50 | 1.32 | 1.40 | 1.28 | 1.45 | 1.24 | 1.49 | 1.20 | 1.54 | 1.16 | 1.59 |
| 55 | 1.36 | 1.43 | 1.32 | 1.47 | 1.28 | 1.51 | 1.25 | 1.55 | 1.21 | 1.59 |
| 60 | 1.38 | 1.45 | 1.35 | 1.48 | 1.32 | 1.52 | 1.28 | 1.56 | 1.25 | 1.60 |
| 65 | 1.41 | 1.47 | 1.38 | 1.50 | 1.35 | 1.53 | 1.31 | 1.57 | 1.28 | 1.61 |
| 70 | 1.43 | 1.49 | 1.40 | 1.52 | 1.37 | 1.55 | 1.34 | 1.58 | 1.31 | 1.61 |
| 75 | 1.45 | 1.50 | 1.42 | 1.53 | 1.39 | 1.56 | 1.37 | 1.59 | 1.34 | 1.62 |
| 80 | 1.47 | 1.52 | 1.44 | 1.54 | 1.42 | 1.57 | 1.39 | 1.60 | 1.36 | 1.62 |
| 85 | 1.48 | 1.53 | 1.46 | 1.55 | 1.43 | 1.58 | 1.41 | 1.60 | 1.39 | 1.63 |
| 90 | 1.50 | 1.54 | 1.47 | 1.56 | 1.45 | 1.59 | 1.43 | 1.61 | 1.41 | 1.64 |
| 95 | 1.51 | 1.55 | 1.49 | 1.57 | 1.47 | 1.60 | 1.45 | 1.62 | 1.42 | 1.64 |
| 100 | 1.52 | 1.56 | 1.50 | 1.58 | 1.48 | 1.60 | 1.46 | 1.63 | 1.44 | 1.65 |

Note: $K'$ = number of explanatory variables excluding the constant term.
Source: J. Durbin and G. S. Watson, " Testing for Serial Correlation in Least Squares Regression," *Biometrika*, Vol. 38, 1951, pp. 159–77. Reprinted with the permission of the authors and the *Biometrika* trustees.

510     *Introductory econometrics*

## APPENDIX F.   A list of uses of common symbols

*Greek symbols*

| | |
|---|---|
| $\alpha$ (alpha) | A coefficient in a simple econometric model |
| $\beta$ (beta) | Coefficient of an endogenous variable in a simultaneous equations model; also a lag coefficient for lagged endogenous variables |
| $\gamma_k$ (gamma) | Coefficient of the $k$th exogenous variable in the general model |
| $\Gamma$ (cap. gamma) | Vector or matrix of coefficients of exogenous variables in a model |
| $\delta$ (delta) | Coefficient of an explanatory variable in a special discussion |
| $\varepsilon$ (epsilon) | Disturbance term in the econometric model |
| $\eta$ (eta) | An elasticity |
| $\theta_k$ (theta) | Incremental explanatory contribution of a variable $X_k$ |
| $\Theta$ (cap. theta) | The theory embodied in the model specification; also an estimator in a special discussion |
| $\nu$ (nu) | Disturbance term in a special discussion |
| $\pi$ (pi) | Coefficients in a reduced form of a simultaneous equations model |
| $\Pi$ (cap. pi) | The product of terms as indicated; also the matrix of reduced form coefficients |
| $\rho$ (rho) | Population correlation coefficient; also an autoregressive coefficient |
| $\sigma$ (sigma) | Population standard deviation |
| $\sum$ (cap. sigma) | The summation of terms as indicated |
| $\phi_j^2$ (phi) | Variance of a particular disturbance $\nu_j$ |
| $\chi^2$ (chi) | Chi-square distributed random variable |
| $\omega_{ij}$ (omega) | Elements of an unknown variance-covariance matrix |
| $\Omega$ (cap. omega) | Variance-covariance matrix of disturbances, $V\text{-}Cov(\varepsilon)$ |

*Roman symbols*

| | |
|---|---|
| $a_k$ | Estimator of the coefficient $\alpha_k$ in a simple model |
| $C_k$ | Estimator of the coefficient $\gamma_k$ in the general model |
| $d$ | Estimator of a particular coefficient $\delta$; also the Durbin-Watson statistic for testing autocorrelation |
| $D$ | A lag operator; also a diagonal matrix |
| $e$ | Residual term, $(Y - \hat{Y})$; also the base of the natural logarithm |
| $E(\ )$ | The expectation of $\ldots$; also an elementary matrix |
| $\hat{f}$ | Expected forecast |
| $f_j^2$ | Estimator of the variance $\phi_j^2$ of a disturbance term |
| $F$ | An $F$-distributed random variable |
| $\bar{F}$ | Identifiability test statistic |
| $G$ | Number of endogenous variables in the econometric model |
| $h$ | Specified constant in a given discussion |
| $I$ | Identity matrix; also the set of initial and background conditions for any model |
| $J$ | Jacobian of a transformation |
| $J^2$ | Janus quotient |
| $k$ | Index for the exogenous variables |
| $K$ | Number of exogenous variables in the econometric model |
| $L$ | Likelihood function |
| $m_{ij}$ | Sample moment |

| $\overline{M}$ | Measure of the multicollinearity effect |
|---|---|
| $p$ | A probability function; also an estimate of an autoregressive coefficient $\rho$, or of a reduced form coefficient $\pi$ |
| $Q$ | Quadratic form; also an orthogonal matrix |
| $r$ | Sample correlation coefficient |
| $R$ | Sample multiple correlation coefficient |
| $\bar{R}^2$ | Adjusted multiple coefficient of determination |
| $s$ | Sample standard deviation |
| $t$ | Index for the observation subscript; also used for the $t$-distributed random variable |
| $T$ | Number of observations |
| $v$ | Degrees of freedom in a given discussion |
| $V(\ )$ | The variance of ... |
| $x$ | Deviation of exogenous variable from its mean |
| $X$ | Exogenous variable |
| $y$ | Deviation of endogenous variable from its mean |
| $Y$ | Endogenous variable |
| $\hat{Y}$ | Estimated value of the endogenous variable |
| $z$ | Standard normal deviate |
| $Z$ | One or more explanatory variables in a special discussion |

*Other symbols*

| $O$ | Null vector or matrix |
|---|---|
| $\partial$ | Partial derivative |

*Other abbreviations*

| 2SLS | Two stage least squares |
|---|---|
| ANOVA | Analysis of variance |
| BLUE | Best linear unbiased estimate |
| C & O ILS | Cochrane and Orcutt iterative least squares |
| GCLE | Generalized classical linear estimation |
| GLS | Generalized least squares |
| ILS | Indirect least squares |
| LIML | Limited information maximum likelihood |
| LSE | Least squares estimate |
| MLE | Maximum likelihood estimate |
| MPC | Marginal propensity to consume |
| OLS | Ordinary least squares |
| PDF | Probability density function |
| RF | Reduced form |
| SF | Structural form |
| SS | Sum of squares |

*Index*

# Index

*This book has been set in 10 and 9 point Times New Roman, leaded 2 points. Part numbers and titles and chapter numbers are 16 point Univers Medium italic; chapter titles are 16 point Univers Medium. The size of the type page is 27 by 46½ picas.*